Contents

Women and Alcohol

A National Conference arranged jointly
by the Department of Health and
the Royal College of General Practitioners

Exeter

21 Day

London. HMSO

Editorial Note

The information presented in this volume reflects papers 'as presented' at the conference 'Women and Alcohol', which, sponsored jointly by the Department of Health and Royal College of General Practitioners, was held at the Queen Elizabeth II Conference Centre, London on 2 December 1991.

Special thanks are due to all the busy contributors and HMSO design/publishing whose cooperation and expertise made both the meeting and publication possible. Readers should note that references and titles under further reading have been printed 'as presented'. Authors will welcome inquiries directed to the appropriate address for contact.

Robyn Young, Editor
Formerly, Senior Medical Officer, Department of Health

Cover illustration
Taken from a photograph by Robert Aberman.

Introduction

BARONESS HOOPER, Parliamentary Under Secretary of State,
Department of Health

Welcome, and thank you all for coming to this National Conference on Women and Alcohol, arranged jointly by the Department of Health and the Royal College of General Practitioners. The conference is not an isolated event, but part of a much larger campaign which the Government is encouraging to tackle the problems surrounding the misuse of alcohol, and to reduce alcohol-related harm.

The format of the conference is in large measure the result of thinking that went on in a small steering group which we called together to consider the question of women and alcohol, and everybody whose name appears in today's programme (with the exception of the Lord President) is a member of that steering group. I should like to thank them all both for the contribution that they made during the steering group meetings, and also for agreeing to make today's presentations and chair today's sessions.

I should also like to thank the Royal College of General Practitioners for cosponsoring the conference, and the Queen Elizabeth the Second Conference Centre for enabling us to hold it here.

And now I should like to thank John MacGregor, Lord President of the Council and Leader of the House of Commons, for agreeing to make the keynote speech. Alcohol is an intrinsic part of our society, and it provides a great many people with a great deal of enjoyment. But when it is misused, it can lead to a great deal of misery and cause a great deal of harm. There are no less than twelve different Government Departments with an interest in the use or the misuse of alcohol, and Ministers from all these Departments meet regularly, under John MacGregor's chairmanship, to coordinate policies, to develop strategies, and to initiate action like arranging today's conference. So there is no better person to deliver today's keynote address than John MacGregor, Lord President of the Council.

WOMEN AND ALCOHOL

Keynote Address

THE RT HON JOHN MACGREGOR OBE, MP, Lord President of the
Council and Leader of the House of Commons [1]

One of the messages you will hear today is that the misuse of alcohol can cause
a great deal of damage to individuals, to families, and to society generally, and
that the costs of alcohol misuse, personal, social and economic, are very high.

Another is that the misuse of alcohol is overwhelmingly a *male* problem. We
estimate that men drink on average about three times as much as women. And
we also estimate that about one man in four drinks more than is recommended
by the medical profession, compared with about one woman in 12, even taking
into account the fact that the medical profession recommends that women
drink only two thirds the amount it recommends for men.

Why 'Women and Alcohol'?

So why was it decided to arrange a national conference on *Women and Alcohol*
when a conference on *Men and Alcohol* would have seemed a more obvious
course? There are three reasons:

The most important reason is that the Government, and society generally, have
a strong interest in reducing alcohol misuse and the incidence of alcohol-
related harm in all its forms. Medical harm such as deaths from liver cirrhosis;
social harm such as domestic violence and family breakdown; and the sort of
harm which can happen unexpectedly, such as accidents resulting from
drunken driving. It is clear that women play a key role in moderating people's
drinking habits, and in encouraging people to drink sensibly. They do this by
their example and by expressing concern, both in their families and also in all
the various communities of which they are a part: where they live and also
where they work. I would not want to lay this as a *responsibility* on women (no
Government Minister should be allowed to get away with that), it is just
something that women actually do. We value this and we are grateful for it,
and we want to help women do it. The clearer women are about the *sensible
drinking* message, and the better informed they are, the more good they will be
able to do. This is an important area where *women take the lead*.

The second reason is that women drink a great deal more sensibly than men,
and we want to do what we can to ensure that this sensible drinking continues.

---

[1]. The Lord President is responsible for co-ordinating the Government's
alcohol policies and is Chairman of the group of Ministers from all the
Departments with an interest in the use or misuse of alcohol.

There is no doubt that the pressures on women to drink more can be expected to increase. As the differences in lifestyle between men and women erode, so will the differences in their drinking patterns. We want to help women resist the pressures to drink more in order to 'keep up with the boys'. And we want to make it clear to women who are under very heavy social and domestic pressures, that heavy drinking makes those pressures worse rather than better.

The third reason is that society makes it very difficult for women who have an alcohol problem, particularly when they need help. Much of our society is remarkably tolerant of men who drink heavily; heavy drinking is still seen in some quarters as a sign of some sort of virility—despite the dangers that this sort of approval brings. But society as a whole has a much less tolerant attitude towards *women*.

We still seem to attach a special stigma to women who drink heavily, and this makes it hard for them to admit, either publicly or to themselves, that they need help. It makes it harder for them to ask for help once they have made this important admission. Because most helping agencies are more geared to meeting the needs of men than of women, the help provided may be somewhat insensitively offered to women when they arrive: it might not take account of this special stigma, and it might not take account of women's special needs such as the possibility that they may have children to look after. I know that most helping agencies are aware of these problems, and I appreciate that introducing the necessary changes may be difficult. I hope that this conference will help to move things forward.

Madam Chairman, the theme of this conference is *Women take the Lead*. I congratulate you and your steering group for bringing everyone together with such an interesting and important agenda, and I hope that in the course of today's deliberations you will bear in mind three things:

Women take the Lead in encouraging sensible drinking in their families and in their communities. We want to do what we can to strengthen their hand.

Women take the Lead in drinking sensibly themselves. We want to support them, and do what we can to ensure that this common sense approach is not eroded by external pressures.

Women take the Lead in asking that the sort of help provided be more sensitive, not just to their own needs, but also to the needs of each individual, male or female. It is crucially important, when encouraging women who want help, not to fall victim to society's attitudes, because guilt and shame can stand in the way of a person's benefiting from help.

Madam Chairman, I know that most of the delegates are representing organisations which are concerned either with women's interests, or with interests in which women have a particular concern. I hope that, as a result of the conference, delegates will return to their organisations and encourage *them* to take the lead in encouraging and helping *women to take the lead* in this important area.

A WOMEN AND ALCOHOL

1 Women and Alcohol: Social and epidemiological aspects

MOIRA PLANT, Alcohol Research Group, Department of Psychiatry, Edinburgh University

SUMMARY

The post war rise in per capita alcohol consumption reached a peak in 1979. In association with this rise, alcohol-related problems proliferated. These changes led to increased concern about the misuse of alcohol by women. This review considers evidence related to trends in alcohol consumption and alcohol misuse, licensing law changes, alcohol and young people, alcohol and risky sex, drinking and pregnancy, alcohol and breast cancer, alcohol education and alcohol use and misuse amongst female nurses.

Background

Between the end of the Second World War and 1979, per capita alcohol consumption in the United Kingdom virtually doubled. In association with this rise there was a proliferation of alcohol-related crimes, illnesses, accidents, deaths and many other problems. Changing national drinking habits prompted increased concern about the use and misuse of alcohol amongst women[1] and a burgeoning body of research into various aspects of their drinking habits.

Trends in alcohol consumption and alcohol-related problems

As noted above, per capita alcohol consumption in the United Kingdom (UK) increased markedly between 1945–1979. Figure 1.1 shows the overall pattern of per capita alcohol consumption between 1900 and 1989. The post war peak in 1979 was followed by a slight fall, then an upward trend. Consumption has remained rather lower since then although Goddard[2] has noted that between 1978 and 1987, alcohol consumption in females in England and Wales rose very slightly amongst all but the youngest group.

A review of general trends in alcohol-related mortality in the UK from 1970–1985[3] indicated that fluctuations in per capita alcohol consumption were accompanied by simultaneous changes in rates of alcohol-related mortality. Even the rates of 'chronic' conditions such as liver cirrhosis change rapidly in line with fluctuations in alcohol consumption. This is consistent with the view of Bruun et al[4] that general rates of alcohol-related problems are strongly influenced by changes in the level of per capita alcohol consumption. Even so, two points need to be emphasised:

3

i. As noted recently by Duffy[5], different subgroups of drinkers are influenced differently by changes in national per capita alcohol consumption. All people do not respond uniformly to such changes.

ii. Individual alcohol-related problems have varied relationships with per capita alcohol consumption. For example, there has recently been a marked decrease in the proportion of motor vehicle drivers killed in road traffic accidents who were over the legal blood alcohol level at the time of death[6,7]. This fall has been far greater than the decline in alcohol consumption and must be due to other factors such as hardening public attitudes towards drinking and driving.

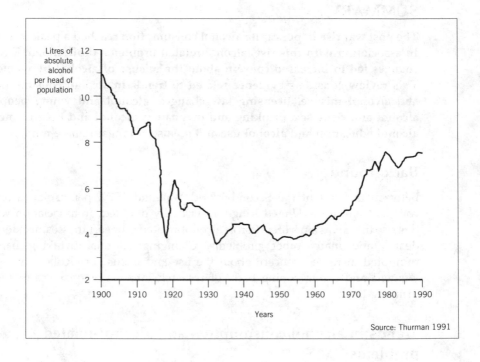

Figure 1.1: *Per capita alcohol consumption in the United Kingdom (1900–1989)* (Source: Thurman 1991)

Differences between male and female drinking patterns

Females are more likely to be abstainers than are males. Goddard[2] reported earlier this year that 12 per cent of women and 8 per cent of men in England and Wales never consume alcohol. However, 58 per cent of women and 76 per cent of men had drunk alcohol in the previous week. Females who drink also consume markedly lower quantities than do males[8,9,10,11]. Goddard concluded that the mean alcohol consumption amongst females aged 16 and above who had drunk in the past week was only 4.5 units, compared with 14.3 units amongst males.

Liquor licensing and consumption

Liquor licensing arrangements in Britain were reviewed by two departmental committees: the Erroll Committee for England and Wales (1971)[12]; and the Clayson Committee for Scotland (1972)[13]. Both recommended liberalisation of existing laws. Changes in Scotland were introduced in December 1976: those for England and Wales not until 1988. The Scottish changes allowed:

> public bars to open after 10pm;
> public houses to open on Sundays; and
> some all-day licenses—regular extensions of permitted hours—have been issued since 1977.

Duffy and Plant examined the impact of these Scottish changes[14] and compared trends in alcohol-related crimes, morbidity and mortality in Scotland (where the changes had been introduced) with England and Wales (no such changes yet introduced) between 1970–1983. They found that the overall impact of the changes had been neutral. The authors concluded:

> 'This evidence suggests that in relation to health, the new Scottish licensing arrangements may be viewed as neither a cause of harm nor as a source of benefit . . .

> The reduction in the Scottish level of public order offences related to alcohol is encouraging. Even so this may be due to a multiplicity of factors'. (p39).

Their data also indicated that, Scotland had a generally higher rate of alcohol-related problems than did England and Wales. Trends in alcohol-related morbidity and mortality amongst women throughout Britain closely resembled those amongst men. There was no evidence of a convergence of the levels of such problems amongst males and females. Males consistently had markedly higher rates of alcohol problems than females.

The question of national and regional variations in alcohol-related problems was examined by Crawford and Plant[15] who confirmed the existence of local differences in levels of alcohol consumption and rates of officially-recorded alcohol problems. Even so, it was concluded that such rates did not differ markedly as had previously been assumed.

Alcohol and young people

Several recent studies of alcohol use amongst young people indicate that the drinking habits of adolescents and young adults have remained generally stable during the past decade[2,16,17]. Most young females and males have at least tasted alcohol by the ages of 14 and 15 and approximately a third of girls are drinking regularly by the ages of 15 and 16. Intoxication is a commonplace experience for teenage drinkers. Recent national surveys amongst 14 to 16-year-olds in England and Scotland indicated that heavy drinking is more commonplace in Scotland than in England[18,19]. The survey of English teenagers[18] involved 6,236 boys and girls aged 14–16. Only 4 per cent of either gender had not consumed alcohol. Both sexes were similar in relation to where and with whom they had last drunk: mainly at home; in licensed premises (under age); and with relatives or friends. Teenage girls consumed markedly smaller quantities of alcohol than did boys. Even so, 5.1% of the girls who were drinkers had consumed 11 units or more on their last drinking occasion.

Available evidence indicates that a minority of teenage girls, and a larger minority of teenage boys, drink heavily. This is, however, a chronic problem— not an escalating epidemic. Youthful heavy drinking is associated with the use of tobacco and illicit drugs and with accidents. Heavy drinking amongst young people does not appear to predict the development of later alcohol misuse or chronic heavy drinking[20,21].

Alcohol and risky sex

The spread of HIV/AIDS has increased concern about the disinhibiting effects of alcohol. Several studies have indicated that the combination of alcohol with sexual activity is associated with 'high risk' sexual behaviours, notably failure to use condoms[22,23]. Others have emphasised the complexity of the connection between alcohol and 'risky sex'. These include studies of females and males in the sex industry[24], sex industry clients[25], and young adults[26].

Alcohol is linked with sexuality for many reasons; including myths and assumptions about its aphrodisiac or disinhibiting effects and social and cultural links between alcohol, bar-rooms and dating. No clear cause-or-effect relationship has been delineated. Even so, available evidence supports the conclusion that the use of alcohol and of less-widely-used drugs, such as cannabis, amphetamines and cocaine, are associated with risky sex.

The consumption of alcohol immediately prior to, or in combination with, sexual activity is associated with high levels of high-risk activity. A survey of young women who had married while only teenagers revealed large differences in contraceptive use between those who had been drinking at the time of their first experience of sexual intercourse and those who had not. Only 13 per cent of those who had consumed alcohol used contraception, compared to 57 per cent of those who had not[22].

A prospective study of the drinking habits of young people aged 15 and 16 was commenced in 1979[26]. Ten years later, 75 per cent of the original participants (then aged 25 and 26) were again interviewed. The results revealed that, *males and females who regularly combined drinking and sex were seven times less likely than others to use condoms.*

Ongoing research into the alcohol-sex connection suggests that

i. some people are more likely than others to engage in 'risky behaviours', regardless of whether or not they have been drinking; and

ii. at least a minority of young women and men are more likely to have unprotected sex after drinking than they would be otherwise.

Drinking and pregnancy

Modern interest in a possible relationship between maternal alcohol consumption and fetal damage was provoked by the description of the 'Fetal Alcohol Syndrome' by Jones and Smith in 1973[27]. Figure 1.2 depicts the facial characteristics of that syndrome.

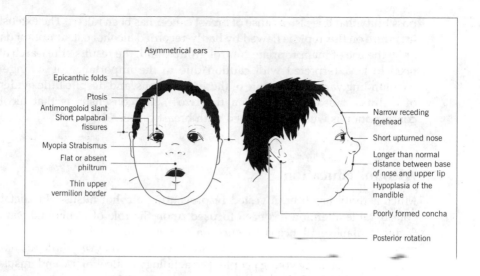

Figure 1.2: *Features of the Fetal Alcohol Syndrome*

The growing body of evidence, which has been reviewed by several authors[28,29], confirms that *heavy* maternal drinking during pregnancy is associated with birth defects. But alcohol per se is only one of a constellation of factors associated with such harm. This finding was supported by the results of a prospective study, conducted in Scotland, which involved monitoring a cohort of 1,008 pregnant women from the third month of pregnancy until their surviving offspring were three months old[29]. Self reports elicited from the respondents related to a wide range of variables and indicated that fetal harm was associated with several factors; eg, the mother's previous obstetric history, socio-economic status, tobacco smoking, height, diet, use of prescribed and illicit drugs, age and marital status.

Maternal alcohol consumption was *associated* with birth abnormalities, but appeared to be in itself only a minor determinant of the outcome of pregnancy. Women who had consumed 10 units or more at one time in the first trimester were significantly more likely than other women to produce babies with abnormalities. Even so, once other variables were taken into account, alcohol use did not emerge as a substantial predictor of fetal harm. It is emphasised that 'moderate' (ie, up to 5 units per week) alcohol intake during pregnancy did not appear to cause any damage to the developing fetus. These conclusions have been supported by studies from several countries[30,31,32]. The last of these, by Forrest *et al*, indicated that there was no evidence of birth damage associated with maternal alcohol consumption up to 12 units per week.

Alcohol and breast cancer

The heavy consumption of alcohol is associated with cancers—notably those of the oesophagus and digestive tract[33]—and during the past 20 years, the possibility that it is also a cause of breast cancer has been raised. The extensive literature on this topic is flawed by badly-recorded alcohol consumption data, or by the use of inappropriate control groups, and, the results of research also need to be interpreted with caution due to the importance of a range of confounding variables. In spite of these limitations, and despite little evidence of a direct causal link between the two[34], the consensus is that alcohol consumption is weakly associated with breast cancer.

Alcohol education

Much activity has been invested in preventing alcohol misuse. Predictably, considerable attention has been focused upon the role of alcohol education. Sadly, available evidence is not encouraging. As noted by Bagnall[35] and Plant and Plant[21], past alcohol education initiatives have done very little to change the drinking habits of young people. The aetiology of alcohol use and misuse is complex and it would be hard for even well-designed education programmes to counter the influence of peer pressure, price, availability and the multiple factors which influence drinking habits.

Alcohol education initiatives have been conducted in widespread areas of the United Kingdom and elsewhere. Many have been targeted at adolescents, especially pupils in local authority secondary schools: only a minority have been assessed or evaluated. One evaluation, however, examined the use of a teaching pack in secondary schools in three regions—Berkshire (England), Dyfed (Wales) and the Highland Region (Scotland). Like many others, this indicated that although alcohol education programmes for young people may increase their alcohol-related knowledge and modify their attitudes to drinking, at least in the short-term, little, if any change in drinking behaviour is attained[35].

Alcohol education is important and can realistically be expected to influence public awareness and attitudes to alcohol use and misuse, but it is, as yet, experimental. At present there is no known educational means of preventing young people from misusing alcohol. Bland slogans and mass media campaigns, whether related to alcohol, or illegal drugs, have frequently proved ineffective or counterproductive.

Alcohol and nurses

The use and misuse of alcohol varies amongst people in different occupations[36,37]. Several theories have been expounded to explain such variations. **Risk factors** which have been suggested include:

Stress
Freedom from supervision
Separation from normal social/sexual relationships
Pressure to drink at work
Collusion by colleagues
Jobs which attract/recruit people predisposed to drink heavily
Availability of alcohol at work

26 Bagnall G (1991) Educating Young Drinkers, London, Tavistock/Routledge.

27 Jones K L and Smith D W (1973) 'Recognition of the fetal alcohol syndrome in early infancy', *Lancet*, **2**, 999–1001.

28 Rosett H L and Weiner L (1904) *Alcohol and the Fetus*, New York, Oxford University Press.

29 Plant M L (1985) *Women, Drinking and Pregnancy*, London, Tavistock.

30 Kaminski M, Franc M, Lebouvier M, Dumaxanbrun C, Rumeau-Roquette C (1981) 'Moderate alcohol use and pregnancy outcome', *Neurobehavioural Toxicology and Teratology*, **3**, 173–181.

31 Rosett H L, Weiner L, Lee A, Zuckerman B, Dooling E and Oppenheimer E (1983) 'Patterns of alcohol consumption and fetal development', *Obstetrics and Gynaecology*, **61**, 539–546.

32 Forrest F, du V Florey C, McPherson F and Young J A (1991) 'Reported alcohol consumption during pregnancy and infants' development at 18 months', *British Medical Journal*, **303**, 22–26.

33 Royal College of Phyicians (1987) A Great and Growing Evil, London, Tavistock.

34 Plant M L (1992) 'Alcohol and Breast Cancer: A Review', *The International Journal of the Addictions*, **27(2)**, 107–128.

35 Bagnall G M, Plant M A and Warwick W (1990) 'Alcohol, drugs and AIDS-related risks: results from a prospective study', *AIDS Care*, **2**, 309–317.

36 Plant M A (1979) *Drinking Careers*, London, Tavistock.

37 Hore B D and Plant M A (eds) (1981) *Alcohol Problems in Employment*, London, Croom Helm.

38 Morgan Thomas R (1990) 'AIDS risks, alcohol, drugs and the sex industry: a Scottish study', In: Plant M A (ed) *AIDS, Drugs and Prostitution*, London, Tavistock/Routledge, 88–108.

39 Plant M L and Plant M A (1988) 'Trading places: doctors, nurses and alcohol', *Social Pharmacology*, **2**, 327–342.

40 Plant M L, Plant M A and Foster J (1991a) 'Alcohol, tobacco and illicit drug use amongst nurses: a Scottish study', *Drug and Alcohol Dependence*, **28**, 195–202.

41 Plant M L, Plant M A and Foster J (1991b) *Journal of Advanced Nursing* (in press).

42 Plant M L (1990) *Women and Alcohol*, Copenhagen, World Health Organisation.

Address for contact

Moira Plant PhD, Alcohol Research Group, Department of Psychiatry, University of Edinburgh, Morningside Park, Edinburgh EH10 5HF.

2 Women and Alcohol

CLAIRE RAYNER, Nurse, Journalist, Broadcaster and Author

SUMMARY

This paper considers the uses to which women put alcohol (to release inhibition; to numb fear, loneliness, boredom and depression; to 'keep up with others'; and for simple social enjoyment) and the way these functions are affected by the heavy demands women feel are put on them to match up to a superwoman ideal. The effects of male drinking on women are outlined, and a consideration of the way women who drink are perceived by society is included.

Background

This chapter concentrates on why women, in particular, use alcohol. Women in Britain are profoundly affected by the misuse of alcohol; the incidence of marital breakdown, wife battering, child abuse and female poverty because of a heavy-drinking spouse is high, and something I know a good deal about. The letters written to me by women struggling to cope with homes and children when their partners use most of the family income on alcohol are very distressing indeed. Women who are beaten or whose children are abused by alcohol-abusing men write even more tragic accounts of their lives. And a good many women are suffering considerable distress because their sons are learning to be heavy drinkers in their early teens. If it is no more than dealing with wet beds every weekend for a drinking 16-year-old—I get a lot of letters about *that*—women are bearing the brunt of much male alcohol-prompted behaviour. Women's own use of alcohol may be overshadowed by such major problems, but it cannot be ignored.

Why women drink

What do women get from alcohol? I believe it has four main uses, though there may be subdivisions within each group.

1. Lowering of inhibition. A little alcohol not only makes the world seem to glitter a little more brightly; it makes our wits seem sharper also. As one girl wrote to me recently: 'I started to drink when I was 15 because when I'd had a cocktail, I found I wasn't tongue-tied any more and so stupidly shy, the way I usually was. I'm scared to talk in the ordinary way, but with a drink in me I could be witty and share in the giggles with the others. But now I'm getting even more tongue-tied because I get so depressed and ashamed after I've had a few drinks it makes it all so much worse.'

Shyness and fear of social failure in young girls is to a large extent inevitable—but few individuals going through that stage realise how *normal*

13

they are. They think every other girl they see who is bright eyed, bushy tailed and bouncy is that way naturally, and their self-confidence plummets. If they can give it a boost with a drink, 'Why not?' (they'll think).

Some girls deliberately use alcohol as a way of coping with **sexual fear**. Even in the post-AIDS era, there are some who see their virginity as a hurdle they have to get over somehow, and if they cannot manage it in cold blood, they will have a couple of drinks to make it easier. Some tell me they used alcohol this way deliberately; others say they did not mean to get involved but—and I quote— "The inevitable happened. I'd had a few drinks and I just couldn't say no."

Women with sexual problems are sometimes advised by professionals to use alcohol as a disinhibitor. I have lost count of the number of letters from young mothers who, finding they have lost their sex drive after childbirth, ask their doctors what to do. "Try a few drinks to relax you . . ." (and variations on the theme) is a popular response. It is also common advice from doctors faced with patients complaining of vaginismus (painful tightening of pelvic floor muscles which make sexual intercourse impossible). I am glad to say that, as under-standing of sexual disorders improves and becomes more widespread, this problem seems less common than before. But I also have to say that far too many doctors still seem to give such advice. Even more offer tranquillisers which are then often used much like alcohol. In many cases, these drugs have an even swifter dependency-causing effect, as well as the extra drawback of having been provided by prescription.

2. 'Numbing' properties. When someone is frightened, lonely, bored, or depressed, the short-term 'lifting' effect of alcohol can be seen as a benefit. The fact that the initial lift is rapidly followed by depression is forgotten or not realised, and because of this, dependency on alcohol may develop remarkably quickly. This is true for men and women of course, but women are more vulnerable, because they are still, in spite of changes in women's status in the UK, more likely to be less powerful than men; more likely to be poor; more likely to be exploited and bullied; and much more likely to be lonely and bored.

The classic example is the young woman who gives up a lively and interesting job to stay at home and look after a baby. Housework and childcare have long been grossly undervalued in this country. Oh, we pay lip service to the idealisation of motherhood—dewy-eyed girls gazing adoringly at perfect odour-free, smiling babies—but in real life, full-time mothers are too often dismissed as 'only housewives' and only those who have a paying job outside the home are described as 'working mothers'. **I never worked harder in my life than I did in the years when I was a full-time mother of young children at home**.

The effect of this common attitude is for the new home-based mother to lose not only the stimulus and satisfaction and income of a paying job—she loses her self-esteem too. The result can be very dispiriting indeed.

Unless such a mother has a good local support network of other mothers like herself, or someone to take on her baby's care from time to time (thus freeing her to seek some satisfaction for herself) she can become very isolated and very

Happy Hour

Monday to Saturday
6.00pm to 7.30pm

ALL COCKTAILS £2.50
DRAFT LAGER £1.00

Bar Snacks

Cocktails

Before Dinner Drinks

BLOODY MARY £3.00
Vodka, Lea & Perrins,
Tobasco, Salt & Pepper
with Tomato Juice

AMERICANO £3.00
Campari, Sweet Martini
and Soda

NEGRONI £3.50
Gin, Campari, Sweet
Martini & Soda

**CAFE CAFE
APERITIF** £2.80
Dry Martini, Lime Juice &
Lemonade

After Dinner Drinks

IRISH COFFEE £2.50
Jamesons, Coffee & Fresh
Cream

FRENCH COFFEE £2.50
Hennessy, Coffee & Fresh
Cream

ITALIAN COFFEE £2.50
Amaretto, Coffee & Fresh
Cream

MEXICAN COFFEE £2.50
Kahlua, Coffee & Fresh
Cream

SLOE COMFORTABLE SCREW £3.75
Sloe Gin, Southern Comfort, Vodka &
Orange with a Galliano and Amaretto top

BLUE LAGOON £3.50
Vodka, Blue Curacao
with Lemonade

LONG ISLAND ICED TEA £3.75
A blend of White Spirits,
Lemon & Coke

**HARVEY
WALLBANGER** £3.50
Vodka & Orange with a
Galliano Float

WHITE LADY £3.50
Gin, Cointreau with
Lemon Mix

BLUE HAWIIAN £3.50
Blue Curacao, Rum with
Coconut & Pineapple Juice

TEQUILA SUNRISE £3.25
Tequila & Orange with a
Grenadine Slip

MARGARITA £3.50
Tequila & Triple Sec
with Lemon Juice &
a Salt Rimmed Glass

**BRANDY
ALEXANDER** £3.50
Brandy & Dark Cacao
shaken up with Fresh
Cream

VELVET HAMMER £3.50
Cointreau & Light Cacao
with Cream

BLACK RUSSIAN £3.50
Vodka & Kahlua
with/without Coke

**SEX ON
THE BEACH** £3.50
Vodka & Midori with
Cranberry Juice

**PINA COLADA /
CHI CHI** £3.50
Rum or Vodka,
Coconut Cream
& Pineapple Juice

ORGASM £3.50
Vodka, Kahlua, Baileys
with a Cream Float

WHITE RUSSIAN £3.50
Vodka & Kahlua
with Cream

**STRAWBERRY OR
BANANA
BANSHEE** £3.50
Fruit Liquer & Creme
de Cacao blended with
Fresh Fruit & Cream

PINK SQUIRREL £3.50
Amaretto & Light Cacao
shaken with Cream
& Grenadine

We also carry a Large selection of Liquers & Brandy's

Virgins

SHIRLEY TEMPLE £3.50
Orange Juice & Lemonade
with Grenadine

VIRGIN COLADA £2.25
Pineapple Juice with
Coconut & Fresh Cream

PUSSYFOOT £2.25
A blended Fruit Punch

Figure 2.1: *Wine Bar Menu*

uncertain of how to get herself out of her trap. Alcohol can seem an ideal escape hatch.

One particularly vulnerable woman is the mother with long-lasting postnatal depression. Though a doctor or health visitor might be alert to the possibility of this in the mother of a four-week-old baby, they are less responsive if the child is a year-or-more old. I get many, many letters from such mothers who are using alcohol to deal with the symptoms of post-birth depression which they have hidden from everyone from the beginning. We need far more professional awareness of how very widespread this later post-birth depression is and support for these young women.

3. To be like others. Women who live in a society where it is normal for women to drink alcohol will do so. If drinking is not socially accepted, the likelihood is greatly reduced. I am of a generation which was reared to think that 'nice' girls did not go into pubs or drink in public. They could have a 'little something' on special occasions at home, or when being entertained in other people's houses. It was sometimes 'OK' to go into country pubs on holidays, because they were quaint and were not pubs anyway, but Inns or Hostelries, and therefore, more polite. As a result, I never set foot inside a pub until I was well into my twenties and I felt very wicked when I did. To this day, I feel uneasy in them—and to this day, I drink little alcohol. The old conditioning runs deep.

Now, though, this is the not the case. The young woman of today is emancipated and shares the same opportunities and aspirations as her brothers and boy friends. And that means she is free to drink like them if she so chooses. This is the downside of emancipation for women; they take on the less valuable aspects of male life, like smoking and drinking.

Another problem for many is the way the catering industry has reacted to their emancipation. Deliberate attempts to attract unsophisticated young drinkers are common. Figure 2.1 is based on a menu from a restaurant-cum-wine-bar I know.

I cannot imagine that a drink called '**Long Island Iced Tea**' is aimed at butch men. It contains gin, vodka, and white rum, lemon and coke. Similarly, a '**Sloe Comfortable Screw**' is made of sloe gin, Southern Comfort, vodka and orange with a Galliano and Amaretto top. I say nothing of the promise of sexual disinhibition here—I already have. But I will make the point that each of these drinks contains fully 3 units of alcohol. This information rarely appears on drink-counter guidelines.

Not only wine bars provide encouragement to drink. Supermarkets which stack alcohol containers just as they stack baby food and soap powder also contribute to a climate where alcohol is regarded by all as 'the norm'. And vulnerable women thus become more vulnerable.

I said women can choose to drink like men now—but I am not sure 'choice' is the correct word. There are pressures on women to behave in a very 'upfront' way, and not to be 'wimps'. Refusing alcohol can seem wimpish—especially in a work environment, where a woman has aspirations to be a 'high flyer'. Going out to entertain customers or contacts can turn into a heavy drinking event which a woman in the party will feel unable to resist. She might risk her status in her job if she does.

Another woman who might drink more than she actually wants to—and start to feel she *needs* to—is the one who is emotionally involved with a man who drinks. Working from the 'if-you-can't lick-'em-join-'em' principle, she accompanies him to pubs for his evening's entertainment, rather than sit at home, alone and angry. Because she's there, she drinks. How can she not?

4. Simple personal pleasure. The women in this group probably have the least risk of becoming problem drinkers. Their motive is simple and self-limiting. When they reach the point where alcohol stops being simple pleasure, they find it easier to stop using it. Now, with these four motives for drinking in mind, the next question to ask is

'What' must modern women be?

We hear a lot about 'role models' these days. It is not good enough for people to live according to their own ideas and feelings; they are made to believe they have to make themselves into an image acceptable for everyone around them. We have probably always been a competitive species, trying to imitate each other and to do 'it' better than everyone else. But I suspect that today we make it even harder for ourselves, because we have so many mirrors—newspapers, TV screens, films and records. All display appearances, lifestyles and attitudes which, whether we care to admit it or not, have a profound effect on the way we behave. A multi-million pound industry is dedicated to giving us role models and persuading us that to be *real* people, *successful* people, *happy* people, we must behave as 'It' says and use the things 'It' uses, in the way 'It' uses them. 'It' is called 'advertising'.

The net result is that a **modern woman has to be multi-talented**. She must be beautiful and look young—no matter what her age actually is—and thin and smooth and hairless (except on her head, where it has to be the glossiest and bounciest and brightest hair there is.). She must be highly intelligent and hard working, and career-minded and successful, and highly organised and capable, and sexy and motherly, and understanding and sweet, and . . . Well, I need not go on, the picture is very clear. Most of us are doing as much as anyone else to be like that.

It is an impossible goal of course. There might have been a time when women could *almost* manage it—ie, when the majority of them did not work. The highflyers thus had built-in support systems to make it easier for them. But those days are gone. There are few servants, maiden aunts, mothers and babysitters willing to take on the less-attractive parts of the superwoman job. Electricity in the kitchen and a multiplicity of 'labour-saving' machines do not help nearly as much as many people claim.

Altogether, the demands on modern women are insatiable. The fact that much of the pressure to be perfect comes from other women does not alter the effects of that pressure. It is small wonder that, when some feel their knees buckling under the load, they seek a crutch to help them keep up. Alcohol is often there, looking like a very agreeable crutch. At first.

'What' must modern women *not* be?

The implications of this question add even more to the impossibility of the superwoman image. A woman must *never* lose her head: she may drink, but on no account must she ever get drunk. Men who get drunk may be seen as amusing or even sweet in a puppyish sort of way, or just plain 'macho'; the response to their behaviour tends to be geographical. In parts of the British Isles a man who is not a heavy drinker is 'no man at all'. But there is no geographical differences in the way women who drink are regarded. The woman who drinks to excess is likely to be labelled with all sorts of other excessive behaviour—especially sexual. 'Drunken' and 'slut' are words which go together when women are being labelled. The rape victim who is discovered to be a drinker is considered to have 'asked for it'.

When it comes to the maternal role, the 'shalt-nots' get even more shrill. The woman who, against professional advice (see page 17), drinks when she is pregnant, is 'selfish'. The mother who drinks is seen as risk to her children. So, when a mother uses alcohol for *any* of the reasons already identified, she has to add the guilt of being that evil of all evils—the 'Bad Mother'. Quite a barrier against seeking early sympathetic and realistic help with the (underlying) problem!

Conclusion

As I see it, the problem some women have with alcohol is not due to the alcohol itself. It is often due to the lives of quiet desperation they are still forced to lead in these oh-so-emancipated 1990s. If we could support and encourage those valuable, vulnerable and unhappy women, the percentage able to use alcohol for simple pleasure and not at risk to themselves—already over 90%—would be even greater.

And it goes without saying that if we could also find a way to deal with male alcohol misuse, the lives of a great many women in this country would be transformed.

Address for contact

Ms Claire Rayner, Hollywood House, Harrow-on-the-hill, Middlesex HA1 3BU.

3 Résumé of paper, 'The Medical Background'

MARSHA MORGAN Clinician and Researcher, Royal Free Hospital, London

SUMMARY

Women achieve higher blood alcohol concentrations than men after comparable amounts of alcohol. Thus recommended levels of alcohol consumption for women, at 112 g/week (14 units), are lower than for men at 168 g/week (21 units). Women who are pregnant are advised to avoid alcohol in the early months of their pregnancy and then to limit their weekly intake to 32 g (4 units).

In both sexes consumption of alcohol AT ANY LEVEL is associated with an increased risk of injury, both accidental and non-accidental.

Consumption of alcohol IN EXCESS OF RECOMMENDED LEVELS is associated with the development of alcohol-related physical disease in men and women alike.

Men and women who abuse alcohol show excess mortality. The death rates from alcohol-related physical disease are similar in both sexes but the death rates from accidents are higher in women.

Résumé

Once drunk, alcohol is very rapidly absorbed from the gastrointestinal tract. It cannot be stored in the body and only very small amounts are excreted unchanged in the breath and urine. The remainder is metabolised, mainly in the liver, by what is essentially a very simple process. Following ingestion the blood alcohol concentration increases rapidly reaching peak values at approximately one hour. It can then take up to 8 to 12 hours for the alcohol to be eliminated from the body completely.

Women consistently achieve higher blood alcohol levels than men, after consuming comparable amounts of alcohol, even allowing for differences in body size. This occurs mainly because women have less body water than men so that the alcohol within the body is less diluted. In this respect, therefore, women are physiologically disadvantaged.

Individuals who consume alcohol AT ANY LEVEL increase their risk of injury whether accidental or intentional. Individuals drinking IN EXCESS OF 20 TO 60 G OF ALCOHOL/DAY (= 2.5 to 7.5 units) increase their risk of developing a wide variety of alcohol-related disorders.[1-3]

19

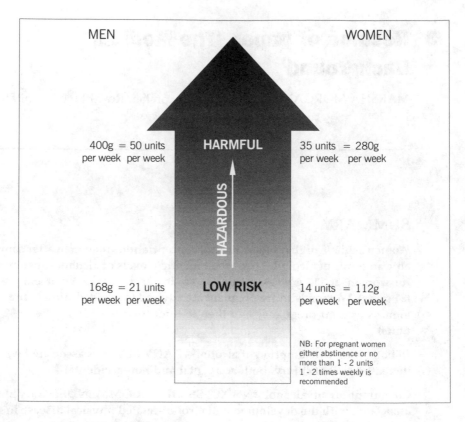

Figure 3.1: *Alcohol consumption and the risk of alcohol-related physical disease*

Table 3.1: *Adverse physical effects of alcohol consumption*

At any level

Injury
—accidental
—intentional

In excess of recommended levels

Nervous system
—tolerance/dependency
—chronic brain syndromes
—cerebro-vascular accidents
—peripheral neurolopathy
Liver disease
Pancreatitis
Gastritis/peptic ulceration
Cancer
Heart disease
Muscle disease
Infertility
Infections
Malnutrition

It has therefore been recommended[4-6] that weekly intakes of alcohol should not exceed 112 g (14 units) in women and 168 g (21 units) in men, preferably with 2 to 3 days kept entirely free of alcohol. The difference in the recommended levels of consumption for men and women mirrors the physiological differences in alcohol distribution between the sexes.

Intakes of alcohol in excess of these recommended levels constitute misuse or abuse of alcohol, depending on their magnitude (Figure 3.1), and are associated with a progressive increase in the risk of developing a variety of alcohol-related physical diseases (Table 3.1). A number of these alcohol-related disorders, for example, cirrhosis of the liver and brain damage, are well-recognised but the relationships between excess alcohol consumption and other disorders, for example, hypertension, cancer and infertility are generally unrecognised. Alcohol, when taken in excess, can produce damage in most organs or systems within the body to a greater or lesser extent. The importance of alcohol as a causal agent in accidental or intentional injury cannot be overemphasised.

It has been suggested that women who drink to excess are more likely to develop alcohol-related physical disease than their male counterparts. However, there is little or no evidence to support this contention. Equally, there is no real evidence that women who drink heavily develop alcohol-related physical disease more quickly or with lower tissue doses of alcohol than men. There is, however, anecdotal evidence that women with alcohol-related physical disease may be more floridly 'ill' than men with disease of similar severity.

Overall, individuals who drink in excess of recommended levels, over prolonged periods of time, are significantly more likely to die than sex-matched individuals who drink within recommended levels. The death rates from alcohol-related physical disease are similar in men and women but the death rates from all forms of accidental and intentional injury are significantly greater in women who abuse alcohol than men. Overall, therefore, the mortality rates amongst women who abuse alcohol tend to be higher then among men drinking similarly.

The recommended levels of alcohol consumption for women of 112 g (14 units)/week do not apply to women who are pregnant as consumption at this level during pregnancy may be associated with an increased risk of spontaneous abortion or, in pregnancies that survive, with the birth of smaller babies. Women who are pregnant are thus recommended to avoid alcohol in the first trimester of pregnancy and to limit their intake to 32 g (4 units) of alcohol a week thereafter. Women who drink in excess of the recommended levels are more likely to be infertile, more likely to suffer a spontaneous abortion and may give birth to infants who have been physically harmed by the alcohol.

References

[1] Durbec J P, Sarles H 1978 Multicentre survey of the etiology of pancreatic diseases. Relationship between the relative risk of developing chronic pancreatitis and alcohol, protein and lipid consumption. *Digestion* 1978; **18**: 337–350.

2 Coates R A, Halliday M L, Rankin J G, Feinman S V, Fisher M M. Risk of fatty infiltration of the liver in relation to alcohol consumption: a case-control study. *Clinical and Investigative Medicine* 1986: **9**: 26–32.

3 Norton R, Batey R, Dwyer T, MacMahon S. Alcohol consumption and the risk of alcohol related cirrhosis in woman. *British Medical Journal* 1987; **295**: 80–82.

4 Royal College of Psychiatrists. *Alcohol: Our Favourite Drug*. London, Tavistock Publications, 1986.

5 Royal College of Physicians. *A Great and Growing Evil*. London, Tavistock Publications, 1987.

6 Royal College of General Practitioners. *Alcohol: A Balanced View*. London, RCGP, 1986.

4 The 'Sensible Drinking' Message

DONNA MCLAUGHLIN, Assistant Operational Service Manager,
Oldham Health Authority

SUMMARY

As an individual's alcohol consumption rises, he or she is more at risk of a range of alcohol-related problems. The concepts of *units of alcohol* and *weekly recommended limits* which provide guidance on safer alcohol consumption have become popular messages for health educators. This chapter explains these terms; presents important information about the relative strengths of alcoholic drinks; and reports results of research on current levels of alcohol consumption and knowledge of these terms. Several ways by which the 'sensible drinking' message may be delivered to the public are suggested, and praise is given to a recent initiative by a major retailer who displays the total units of alcohol on the labels of individual containers.

Background

Several authors in this book show how the increased consumption of units of alcohol contributes to a wide range of medical and psychological problems. I will initially concentrate on the meaning of the terms *'units of alcohol'* and *'weekly recommended limits'*, and will then suggest how the public may be provided with safer drinking guidelines, to equip them to make informed choices about their personal drinking. The discussion covers both women's and men's drinking behaviour, as I believe that such information is pertinent to women as alcohol educators.

The Sensible Drinking Message

As far back as 1870, Anstie, a local physician, writing on the dietetic and medicinal use of wines in the diet of ordinary lives, stated that an intake of

> 'Three or four glasses of port wine a day . . . 1.5 ounces of absolute alcohol was about the limit of what can be habitually taken without provoking symptoms of chronic malaise.'[1]

Translated into modern UK limits, this would approximate to 28 units of alcohol per week. Over 100 years later, reports from the Royal Colleges of Psychiatrists (1986)[2], General Practitioners (1986)[3] and Physicians (1987)[4], have reached a consensus of agreement on sensible limits in terms of total weekly intake. Table 4.1 illustrates the relationship between alcohol consumption and alcohol-related ill health.

The term *sensible drinking* therefore relates to the lowest recommended level of consumption: ie, up to 14 units per week for women and up to 21 units per

Table 4.1: *Health risks and total weekly intake of alcohol*

Risk	Units of alcohol per week	
	Women	Men
LOW	Up to 14	Up to 21
INCREASING	15–35	21–50
HIGH	Above 35	Above 50

week for men. The units should be spread throughout the week, to leave two or three days completely alcohol free.

Are people drinking sensibly?

The Office of Population Censuses and Surveys (OPCS) survey *'Drinking in England and Wales in the late 1980s'* (1991)[5] reported that: 8% (one in 12 women) drink above 14 units per week; and 23% (one in 4 men) drink above 21 units per week. However, 16% of women and 33% of men, in the age range 18–24 years, were most likely to have exceeded those limits. The study also showed that whilst 6% of men drink over 50 units of alcohol per week, only 1% of women drink over 35 units per week.

In relation to these figures, the recent Government publication, *The Health of the Nation*, (1991)[6] suggested the specific target that, by the year 2005, fewer than one in 18 women and one in 6 men should be drinking more than the sensible limits. There is no doubt that, if everybody regulated their drinking according to the *'sensible drinking'* guidelines, the damage to public health due to alcohol would be dramatically reduced.

What is a unit of alcohol?

A unit of alcohol is equivalent to 8–10 grammes of pure alcohol. Units are based on the alcohol content of a drink (generally shown on a label as '% vol' which is the percentage of alcohol by volume (ABV) of the product). Table 4.2 shows one unit of alcohol translated into standard measures of alcoholic drinks.

Table 4.2: *One unit of alcohol translated into standard measures of alcoholic drinks*

ONE UNIT OF ALCOHOL=

1 pub measure of spirits (⅙ gill)*
1 small glass of sherry or fortified wine (2 fl ounces)
1 glass of table wine (about 4.5 fl ounces)
½ pint of ordinary strength beer, cider or lager
¼ pint of strong beer, cider or lager
1½ pints of low alcohol lager/beer (0.5%–1.2% ABV)

*This applies to the ⅙ gill measures based in most of England and Wales. But pub measures vary. In Northern Ireland, a pub measure is ¼ gill: in Scotland, it may be either ⅕ or ¼ gill.

The public should be made aware of the extra strength lagers and beers which seem to be growing in popularity (see Table 4.3). Of particular note, the OPCS research indicated that 45% of female and 37% of male beer/lager drinkers aged 18–24 drink beer or lager averaging 5% or more alcohol by volume[7].

Table 4.3: *Units of alcohol in beers and ciders*

Alcoholic beverage	Volume	Units
1. Ordinary Strength (3% ABV)		
Heineken, Carlsberg, Carling Black Label, Trophy	½ pint	1
Bitter	Can*	1.5
2. Export/Strong Strength (5.5% ABV)		
Stella Artois, Pils, Tennants Extra	½ pint	2
	Can	3
3. Extra Strength (7% ABV)		
Carlsberg Special, Skandia Special	½ pint	2.5
	Can	4
4. Super Strength (up to 9.5% ABV)		
Tennants Super, Kestrel Super	½ pint	3.5
	Can	4.5

*The mention of cans as well as ½ pints is deliberate. Research has shown that beer drinkers tend to recall the number of cans or bottles rather than glasses they have drunk.

How much does the public know about units of alcohol?

Research undertaken by the Health Education Authority (HEA) in 1990[7] showed that, although 75% of the survey population was aware of the term *'units of alcohol'*, 64% of, *'weekly recommended limits'*, only 15.3% of women correctly identified 14 units as their weekly recommended level and 13.8% of men, 21 units as the weekly recommended level for men.

The percentage of the population surveyed who correctly identified that one unit equals the following drinks was reported as: one glass of wine (24%); half a pint of beer (22%) and one pub measure of spirits (18%).

Interestingly, these figures are consistent with research carried out in Western Australia. Whilst 67.3% of the people surveyed had heard of 'unit' (or 'standard drinks' as they are classified in the article) only 17.9% could correctly define one unit[8].

How do we ensure that we have an informed public?

The general public should be given the opportunity to know more about the drinks they buy and consume, so that they can then make informed choices about their drinking. But what steps may be taken to inform people how much they can drink on a week-by-week basis, without jeopardising their health or doing other people long-term harm?

i. *Young people*

I believe that the education of young people is one of the most crucial areas for attention. The National Curriculum requires that health education, including alcohol education, must be taught as a core subject but the quality of the programmes delivered is patchy. Efforts to develop effective alcohol and similar health education programmes can suffer because the Departments of Health and of Education and Science may decide each is the other's responsibility. Could we not set the target that every pupil who leaves school will be able to state the number of units of alcohol in individual drinks, and will know the weekly recommended limits for sensible drinking?

ii. *General alcohol education campaigns*

Alcohol education campaigns can range from high profile, mass media initiatives, to local long-term, community-based programmes. Some may be directed at specific audiences (eg, women), others may be more general. The 'unit' and 'sensible drinking' messages can provide useful focal points for all such programmes.

iii. *Professional training*

Professionals—including GPs, health visitors, social workers and probation offices—have considerable scope for alcohol education in the daily interaction with individuals. But they may need further training about units—particularly those contained in extra-strength drinks. It is essential that they acquire this information so they can deliver a consistent, clear message to the public.

iv. *The retail trade and alcohol industry*

I believe that retailers and the alcohol industry can support education about units in a very precise way. At present, labels on canned and bottled alcoholic drinks display the strength of the drink as alcohol percentage content by volume (%ABV). This may enable consumers to make comparative judgments about the strength of drinks, but it does not help them to monitor accurately or objectively the total number of units in each drink. As I have shown, the alcohol content of beers and lagers can range from 3% to 9%, and estimating units may be difficult as 'special promotional sizes' are more common. If we want to ensure that members of the public have easy access to unit information, the confusing diversity of unit content on different containers and brands should be simplified.

One supermarket chain, Tesco, has begun to address this matter and is the first retailer to link units of alcohol directly to individual drinks: labels on the containers of their 'own-brand' alcohol products clearly indicate the total number of units of alcohol in each.

Research by the HEA indicates that people are very receptive to such initiatives. Around half of those questioned said that they would find unit labelling better, or as good as,the present system. Women and men aged 25–44 said that they would prefer the new system[10] and, most encouragingly, 91% of young people aged 16–19 also supported putting the number of units on alcoholic drink containers. This is particularly important, because young people are the least likely to be aware of the strength of individual drinks and are more at risk from alcohol-related harm. It is hoped therefore, that other retailers and off licence traders will follow Tesco's example.

In relation to the 'on licence' trade, research indicates widespread support for the display of more sensible drinking messages on units of alcohol in pubs[11]. Educating the public on the actual drinking environment (ie, at the point of purchase or consumption) is therefore an important consideration. Similarly, a standard glass size for wine sold in pubs and bars (see also page 24), which clearly showed the total unit content, would help people apply the messages of alcohol consumption more easily to their own drinking habits.

Conclusion

There is no doubt that the health education task in relation to delivering messages about sensible drinking will be a long one, but we have seen impressive results in changes in public attitudes to alcohol. Social norms are now strongly against drinking and driving, and there is an increasing aware-ness that drink and work do not mix. Providing the general public with clear, concise and accurate information about units of alcohol and sensible limits, I believe, is one of the most important steps forward.

References

[1] Anstie, F (1870) On the dietetic and medicinal uses of wine. Part 1. On the place of wines in the diet of ordinary life. Practitioner 4, pp219–224, quoted in Turner C (1990) How much alcohol is a standard drink? an analysis of 125 studies. **British Journal of Addiction** Vol 85 Number 9 pp1171–1177.

[2] Royal College of General Practitioners (1986) *Alcohol—A Balanced View* RCGP London.

[3] Royal College of Physicians (1987) Alcohol—A Great and Growing Evil. *The Medical Consequences of Alcohol Abuse.* Tavistock, London.

[4] Royal College of Psychiatrists (1986) Alcohol—*Our Favourite Drug.* Tavistock, London.

[5] OPCS (1991) *Drinking in England and Wales in the late 1980s.* HMSO.

[6] Department of Health. *The Health of the Nation.* HMSO. June 1991.

[7] Health Education Authority/RGSB 1990. Public Tracking Survey.

[8] Stockwell, T, Blaze-Tempell, D and Walker, C (1991). A test of the proposal to label containers of alcoholic drink with alcohol content in Standard Drinks. Health Promotional International. Volume 6 no 3 p 207.

[9] HEA/MORI November 1990.

[10] British Market Research Bureau/Health Education Authority. 1991.

Address for contact

Donna McLaughlin, Regional Alcohol Co-ordinator, Prevention Department, North Western Regional Health Authority, Gateway House, Piccadilly, South Manchester M60 7LP

B THE RECOMMENDED APPROACH

5 Women and Alcohol: Comments from the Chair

JOAN TROWELL, Hon Consultant Physician, John Radcliffe Hospital, Oxford

The speakers who opened our discussion on women and alcohol reviewed the social context in which women in Britain in the 1990s drink alcohol, and some of the differences in society's attitudes to alcohol consumption by women and men. Physiological differences lead to higher blood alcohol levels in women after a comparable amount of alcohol. About nine out of every ten women, if they drink alcohol at all, drink only occasionally and in moderation, and even by their presence on a social occasion, women may moderate the alcohol consumption of those around them.

They drink for many reasons. The advertisers aim to convince women that alcohol is associated with increased glamour and sexual appeal. On social occasions, alcohol is used to drink toasts and congratulate; to speed best wishes and create a sense of celebration. At times of stress and at the end of a long day, a glass of an alcoholic drink is a socially-acceptable 'drug' to aid relaxation and recreation. Some with personal problems and stresses consider that alcohol is a normal means of dulling the pain and rendering their lives more tolerable. In these circumstances, drinking in a normal social context may become a problem. Once the quantity of alcohol consumed rises, relaxation becomes difficult without alcohol and the woman's drinking becomes secretive and the problem hidden, the social, emotional and physical harm associated with problem drinking may result.

This is probably the commonest pattern of alcohol abuse among women in contemporary society, but, in the past, heavy-drinking women have been seen as social outcasts and the stigma attached to drunkeness in women is much greater than that associated with heavy drinking among men. In men, it may be seen as a sign of virility and enhance a macho image; in women it suggests promiscuity, even prostitution, and neglect of home and children. This stigma and the low self-esteem associated with alcoholism in women has led many women to make great efforts to hide their problem drinking. As a result, the patterns of alcohol abuse in our society are very different in the two sexes. Men certainly drink more than women, but the apparent absence of public drunkeness among women is compounded by the lengths to which a woman will go to hide the problem. Their families and friends may become co-conspirators in this attempt.

Women drinkers are more likely than men to be separated from their partners, and a woman who is drinking heavily is isolated and depressed and is less likely to seek help for her emotional, social and physical problems. This secrecy prevents early detection of alcohol abuse in women and means that the scale of the problem is frequently underestimated. Reliable estimates suggest that the incidence of problem drinking in women in Britain is of a comparable order to the incidence of cancer of the breast or cancer of the cervix. Perhaps comparable effort and expense should be directed at prevention and early detection?

The physiological dilution of alcohol in a woman's body is different from that in a man's body, due to the different proportions of water and fat in men and women and as a result of this a comparable amount of alcohol ingested leads to a higher level of blood alcohol in a woman. Although there may be other physiological differences in the metabolism of alcohol between men and women, these are less well understood or explained.

Problems associated with excessive alcohol consumption include many severe physical illnesses: diseases of the liver and digestive tract leading to gross malnutrition commonly exacerbated by neglect and inadequate diet; high blood pressure stroke; and an increased incidence of accidents of all kinds. Emotional and social problems interact with these. As these women do not readily come forward it is probable that they will come to medical attention only when the pathological processes are well advanced. Men are frequently questioned about their alcohol consumption at health screening arranged by their employers, or medical examinations for life insurance. Although women have less access than men to these screening contacts, they do have many other reasons for visiting health centres, such as family planning advice and cervical smear testing. A routine enquiry about alcohol consumption and a more active role for all those professionals who come in contact with women for any of a variety of reasons, could increase knowledge of the level of alcohol consumption which is associated with increasing risks. This information and an atmosphere in which alcohol problems are discussed on neutral territory could enable many women to gain help with their problems at an earlier stage.

Many of the speakers explained the 'unit of alcohol' but accurate knowledge of the alcohol content of the different beverages which are commonly drunk is not widely known or even widely available. With more adequate labelling of products which contain alcohol, it would be possible to monitor alcohol consumption. This would allow a woman to know more accurately the amount of alcohol that she and her family are drinking and by relating it to increasing risks, she would be better able to help increase the health and happiness of herself and those around her.

Address for contact

Dr Joan Trowell, Hon Consultant Physician, John Radcliffe Hospital, Oxford OX3 9DU.

6 Enjoying Sensible Drinking

JANCIS ROBINSON, Wine Expert, Broadcaster, Journalist and Author[1]

SUMMARY

There is no contradiction in the notion of enjoying sensible drinking. Drinking can and should be enjoyable. Ingested at sensible levels, alcohol can give the drinker a sense of euphoria without loss of control. A positive sense of enjoyment is rarely associated with excessive alcohol intake however. Drinking plays an important role in British social life. Increased awareness of the potential harm associated with alcohol misuse should not lead to increased guilt associated with normal social drinking, but rather to increased respect for alcohol and increased skill in choosing and consuming drinks, both alcoholic and non-alcoholic. The key to sensible drinking is education.

Background

In the last five years, the western world has seen an unprecedented increase in the dissemination of facts and opinion about the dangers of alcohol abuse and misuse. But there is another danger: that a necessary connection between the normal, social use of ethyl alcohol and guilt is established.

We have meanwhile inherited a social fabric in which alcoholic drinks have traditionally been seen as qualitatively different from non-alcoholic drinks in their social significance. There is a real need to break down customs which have in the past resulted in alcohol's being consumed unwillingly in response to a social obligation. Low-alcohol and non-alcoholic drinks deserve higher status as a perfectly valid option in all circumstances.

The concentration of alcohol in various drinks varies enormously, but is stated on all drinks labelled after May 1988. To drink sensibly, we need to know how to interpret this information and how to judge volumes and measures, as well, of course, as understanding the effects of different amounts of alcohol and how alcohol's effects can best be managed.

Drinking as a social act

We read and hear a great deal about drinking (alcohol) as an anti-social activity, but for the great majority of us—and the majority is even bigger for women than for men—drinking is a normal social act. We drink together to signify that we are playing rather than working. We drink together to celebrate, to cement an accord or agreement, to show that we are friends, to

---

[1] See Further Reading

relax inhibitions in an uninhibited state. In many religions, shared drinks have especial spiritual significance. The toast plays an important part in political and commercial life—both nationally and internationally. And, quite apart from the euphoric effects of the alcohol they contain, many alcoholic drinks taste rather good too!

In some societies, notably the United States of the 1980s, an increased awareness of the danger of alcohol misuse and abuse has been accompanied by diminished recognition of social drinking as a legitimate activity. This seems to have resulted in increased stigmatisation of drinkers, particularly female drinkers, and a dangerously defensive attitude among social drinkers, who have been increasingly regarded as belonging to the same category as problem drinkers—a development that is surely as illogical as it is undesirable.

It is important that we continue to view drinking with our friends and associates as the useful and enjoyable social activity it can and should be. A key element in maintaining legitimate status for social drinking is that we make the act a positive rather than a negative one. We can maximise our enjoyment of it through greater understanding of what we are doing and what alcohol is doing to us.

Drinking 'consciously'

Alcohol being a potent substance, it is a very obvious truth, that every time we consume alcohol, it will have some effect on us. Yet this very obvious truth is too rarely acknowledged. Better alcohol education is helping to spread awareness, particularly to the young, but it is remarkable how many people either choose or are persuaded to drink in entirely inappropriate circumstances, because they have not acknowledged to themselves that the alcohol in the drink will have an effect.

I am sure I am not alone in recalling occasions on which someone has persuaded me (often without much difficulty) to have a glass or two of wine with my lunch, which I later regretted. An example of drinking that was neither sensible nor, even in the medium term, enjoyable.

Enjoying sensible drinking **means drinking only in appropriate circumstances**. It seems to me extremely appropriate to drink with friends in the evening, either at home or somewhere from which I don't have to drive afterwards. It seems extremely inappropriate to drink just before taking the wheel, or before performing any other important physical task, or undertaking any major obligations to other people.

Drinking with enjoyment means drinking in full consciousness that you can afford to relax and enjoy that drink. It seems a useful, if somewhat trite, maxim to me that *every drink should be a consciously wanted one*, which is by no means always the case in practice. In certain social groups there are still strong pressures to consume only alcoholic drinks in the company of others drinking alcohol.

The 'soft', or low alcohol option

Bottled water may be regarded as the most chic drink possible among 30-year-old designers working in Soho, but most mature farmers of my acquaintance spend a considerable amount of their play time trying to persuade others in their company to drink as much alcohol as they are. When they offer a drink, they see 'the soft option', a glass of water or fruit juice, as something of an affront—even if a woman chooses it. Those who feel uncomfortable consuming alcohol with those who don't might learn something by examining their attitudes to their own drinking. Perhaps they have not yet looked their own drinking habits in the eye and arrived at a viable method of drinking sensibly and with enjoyment?

Many people are perfectly happy never to let an alcoholic drink past their lips, for all sorts of valid reasons which drinkers can have difficulty in accepting—a fact which reflects less honourably on the drinkers than the abstainers. (And it is surely particularly cruel to press alcohol on someone who has decided to give it up for health reasons.)

Others of us enjoy both the taste and the effect of alcoholic drinks, in appropriate circumstances, but would like to feel that a non-alcoholic alternative was viewed as perfectly acceptable, and tasted as good. I am personally unconvinced by non-alcoholic beer and wine taste-alikes for much the same reasons as I am suspicious of nut cutlets; why should the alternative be an unsatisfactory parody of the prototype? But this is a subjective quibble. More important is to validate the business of choosing a non-alcoholic drink in circumstances where alcoholic drinks are thought by others to be more appropriate. Perhaps we can all help with this process by being firmer when resisting alcohol. 'No means no', the slogan currently promoted in resisting another form of social approach, could even be useful here!

It is (still) rather more difficult to abstain from alcohol when playing host, particularly one-to-one, without seeming mean, miserable or both. Offering alcoholic drink is in many social groups inextricably bound up with offering hospitality—indeed the very word 'hospitality' is sometimes used as euphemism for 'free booze'.

How to handle alcohol

Considering how powerful, widely available and enthusiastically used alcohol is, it is surprising how little we are taught about handling it. As someone who, through my work, has been lucky enough to have been taught how to use my sense of taste, I happen to feel strongly that we should all be taught how to get the most, sensorily, from what we eat and drink, but that is rather a selfish skill. If everyone knew more about managing alcohol and its effects, society as a whole could benefit. Women, traditional educators within the home, could play an important part in this respect.

There are many ways in which drinkers can manipulate and control the effects of alcohol rather than finding themselves in the uncomfortable position of feeling that it is the alcohol that is controlling them.

Perhaps the single most important message for women is the very 'unfair' one that there are sound physiological reasons why they should drink less alcohol than men (see Chapter 3). Donna McLaughlin gives a full explanation of how to keep count of the number of 'units' of alcohol you consume in Chapter 4. What is less generally appreciated is the wide variation in alcoholic content of different drinks and within the same category (eg, see lagers, page 25).

Many women drink wine and the medical profession tends blithely to describe 'a glass of wine' as quivalent to one unit. Glasses in fact can hold anything from eight centilitres (in the case of the meanest pub wine glass) to more than 70 centilitres (in the case of some of the most grandiose burgundy glasses), and wine can vary in alcoholic content from six per cent (in the case of some fizzy Italian wines) to almost 15 per cent (in the case of some Italy's and California's strongest). Sherry and port can rise to 20 per cent.

The only constant in wine terms is the size of a standard wine bottle, 75 centilitres. All alcoholic drinks are now labelled with their alcoholic strength as a percentage by volume. A bottle of wine described as '12% vol' contains nine units of alcohol, so a unit is only just over eight centilitres of that wine—a very small glasss of wine indeed. A bottle of wine described as '10% vol' however contains seven and a half units of alcohol and a unit is therefore 10 centilitres of this weaker wine. A good general rule is that the cooler the provenance of a wine, the lighter it is in alcohol. As for judging the volume of your normal measure of wine, it may be worth just once pouring it, or its equivalent in water, into a kitchen measuring jug.

While spirits are almost all 40% vol and a unit of alcohol is almost equivalent to a standard pub single measure (or not more than half the usual measure poured in the home!), beers and ciders vary as much as wine in their alcohol content. One unit of alcohol is the equivalent of half a pint of standard bitter or lager at around 3.5% vol or only a fifth of a pint of the strong ales, barley wines or special lagers which are as strong as 8% vol. It can be worth studying the label closely, although it is not always easy when you are a guest!

It is also worth remembering what a useful role food can play in moderating the effects of alcohol. Drinking on an empty stomach is guaranteed to speed and maximise intoxication, while nibbling during, or eating fatty foods before, the consumption of alcohol noticeably softens its impact. It would be difficult to think of a less healthy drinking pattern than the 'Nordic', or young British male, model of drinking oneself silly and then staggering out in search of some solid matter to soak it all up long after the tastebuds have been pickled into insensitivity. Those of us who ingest our alcohol at the dining table, enjoying the interaction between the tastes of different foods and the drinks served with them, are on the other hand smugly convinced that we have discovered the sensible and enjoyable way to drink. We still need to monitor that consumption.

However an alcoholic drink is consumed, there are ways of making sure you get the most out of it. I find it a very useful rule *never to quench thirst with strong drink*. Whenever I drink or serve wine at the table, I always drink or serve water in a separate glass so that there is no temptation to gulp the alcoholic drink. It is a very standard social response, particularly at stand-up parties, to punctuate human interaction with gulps (or puffs, in the case of smokers) of whatever is to hand, but another useful rule for sensible, enjoyable drinking is to try to consciously *savour every sip*, and never to gulp unconsciously. (And those of us who know how the sense of taste works tend to smell things before we consume them—another useful brake on consumption.) The more slowly a drink is sipped, the less dramatic, and therefore more enjoyable, its effects will be. But, as one might expect, its effects last longer and it is not unusual after an evening's celebration to feel intoxicated the next morning—perhaps while driving to work.

Then there are ways in which the choice of drink shapes its effects. Fizzy drinks tend to accelerate the body's absorption of the alcohol they contain, while sweetness in a drink tends to slow alcohol's effects. There is also some medical evidence that drinks whose strength is between 15 and 30 per cent are most rapidly absorbed and result in the most dramatic intoxication. To put it another way, sherry, port and spirits diluted half-and-half with mixers, give a much quicker high than either neat spirits or heavily diluted spirits or beer or unfortified wine.

Conclusion

The art of enjoyable, sensible drinking is to know how much is enough; to drink only in appropriate circumstances; to know how to manage alcohol; and to get the most out of every drop.

Further Reading

HOW TO FIND OUT MORE ABOUT ALCOHOL
1   Jancis Robinson *The Demon Drink*, Mitchell London 1988 Beazley and Mandarin 1989.

Address for contact

Jancis Robinson, 24 Belsize Lane, London NW3 5AB.

7 Alcohol: Keeping Count

PATRICIA WILSON: Alcohol and Drugs Misuse Programme Manager, Health Promotion Agency for Northern Ireland

SUMMARY

Public awareness of the concept of "units" of alcohol and the recommended weekly drinking limits described in Chapter X is increasing.[1] Many people, however, can remain complacent about their own drinking because of a general tendency to underestimate the amount they drink. This section concentrates on showing how individuals can make a more accurate assessment of their drinking by using a Drinking Diary. By highlighting details of a drinking pattern this process can also assist people in modifying, if necessary, their drinking habits to keep within the weekly recommended limits ie 14 units for women and 21 units for men spaced throughout the week with two or three alcohol free days.[2] Various ways of cutting down are suggested.

How much do we drink?

This is often a difficult question to answer accurately. Some people have very regular drinking habits. They know definitely that they have two gin and tonics with friends on a Wednesday which is "Bridge Night" and two glasses of wine with Sunday lunch and never deviate from this pattern. Many people, however, are rather vague about the actual amount of alcohol they drink. A result of this vagueness is often delusion as to the real extent of their drinking.

Drinking can vary a lot depending on who we are with, what we are doing and how we are feeling. We often drink more at certain times of the year—at Christmas or while on holidays. An increase in salary, a change of lifestyle, a shift in social activities can influence how much we drink at one stage of our lives compared with another.

Often then, the answer to the question "How much do you drink?" is, "Well, it depends!" which is very vague and unhelpful. Even somebody with a fairly regular lifestyle and drinking habits might be quite unsure about the actual amount they drink.

Case histories

Take Mary:

Mary works in a busy office, is single and has a wide circle of friends. She meets her friends in a pub three or four times a week and they usually have several rounds of drinks before heading on to a disco or party.

Take Sue:

Sue is a single parent. She and a neighbour often get together to watch videos at home. They have several glasses of vodka as part of the evening.

Take Jane:

Jane is a buyer for a large department store. Her work involves many business lunches. She also unwinds in the evening with a large drink.

The context and style of their drinking is quite different, but in all areas the volume and units being consumed are never clearly considered. Units and recommended weekly limits give us guidelines to the nature of our drinking: low risk, increasing risk and high risk (see page 24). To find out where we stand within these guidelines we need to make an accurate assessment of our drinking.

The Drinking Diary

One way of doing this is to complete a drinking diary. Figure 7.1 shows an example of the diary format. People are invited to fill in from memory every alcoholic drink taken in the past week, or alternatively, to keep a daily record of their drinking over the coming week. There is space not only to note the type and quantity of drink taken (eg, two glasses of wine), but also to jot down some details of the drinking setting (eg, at lunch with Mary). Further columns indicate the units consumed at each occasion and the total for each day. At the end of the week all the units are added to give the weekly total.

Points to remember

When calculating the number of units consumed, it is important to remember that home measures are notoriously generous and would quickly bankrupt a pub landlord. The varying strengths of beers and ciders must also be remembered and the higher units in extra strong brands noted (see page 25).

The process of completing a drinking diary:

1   Reinforces information about the strength and unit value of different drinks.

2   Records the actual volume drunk in units and highlights whether the drinker is within or over the weekly limit recommended by the Royal Medical Colleges.

3   Identifies the style and pattern of personal drinking (eg, weekday abstinence and weekend binges; frequent lunchtime drinking; regular 'nightcaps').

Figures 7.2,.3 and .4 show what Mary, Sue and Jane's completed drinking diaries might look like.

MARY does not drink as heavily as some of her friends and feels that she is quite a moderate drinker. In addition to a busy social life she regularly goes to a local pub at lunchtime and usually has half a pint of beer with her lunch. Recently she has begun to choose a premium beer which is twice as strong as an ordinary beer (see page 24). Her diary shows how quickly units add up over

Figure 7.1: *The drinking diary*

Day	What	Where/When/Who with	Units	Total
Monday				
Tuesday				
Wednesday				
Thursday				
Friday				
Saturday				
Sunday				
Total for the week				

a week. She may be quite surprised to find that her total is 29 units, **double** the recommended low risk limit. She might also be surprised to see that she had something to drink each day during the past week.

SUE only drinks once or twice a week. However, her generous vodkas are twice as large as pub measures. As she usually drinks a substantial amount when she does have 'a drink', an extra occasion, such as a birthday party, increases her weekly total significantly.

Some people (like Jane) may feel that one week's drinking diary does not reflect their normal drinking pattern. Keeping a drinking diary over several weeks or routinely monitoring a week's drinking from time to time is obviously more thorough and more informative than a single week's 'snapshot' record. This is a useful thing for all drinkers to do, but is particularly important for anyone who may discover that they are exceeding the recommended low risk limits.

Figure 7.2: *Mary's drinking diary*

Day	What	Where/When/Who with	Units	Total
Monday	2 glasses wine	Met up with Tom & Sharon after work. Pub, then cinema	2	2
Tuesday	½ pt beer (strong) 1½ pts beer (strong)	At lunchtime With friends, in pub	2 6	8
Wednesday	2 large glasses wine	Meal at Sharon's flat. Brought along a bottle of wine.	3	3
Thursday	1 pt beer (strong) 2 vodka	In pub, with friends 9 pm At disco (10.30–12.00)	4 2	6
Friday	½ pt beer (strong)	At lunchtime	2	2
Saturday	2 glasses wine 1 pt beer (strong)	Wine Bar—8.30 pm with Tom. At Disco.	2 4	6
Sunday	2 glasses wine	Sunday lunch—with family	2	2
Total for the week				*29 units*

Figure 7.3: *Sue's drinking diary*

Day	What	Where/When/Who with	Units	Total
Friday	3 LARGE VODKAS	AT HOME WITH SALLY 9 pm–11 pm	6	6
Saturday	NOTHING	—	—	—
Sunday	3 LARGE VODKAS 1 CAN EXTRA STRONG BEER	JOANNE'S PARTY (SURPRISE BIRTHDAY PARTY FOR SALLY)	6 4	10
Total for the week				*16 units*

Figure 7.4: *Jane's drinking diary*

Day	What	Where/When/Who with	Units	Total
Monday	*Nothing*	—	—	
Tuesday	*1 aperitif* *2 glasses wine* *Large gin & tonic*	*Lunch with sales reps.* *7 pm at home*	*1* *2* *3*	*6*
Wednesday	*1 aperitif* *2 wine* *1 liqueur*	*Restaurant Business Dinner*	*1* *2* *1*	*4*
Thursday	*2 glasses wine* *1 glass wine* *2 gin & tonic*	*Lunch with colleague* *Fashion show, reception 7 pm* *Hotel Bar, later*	*2* *1* *2*	*5*
Friday	*Large gin & tonic*	*7.30 pm At home*	*3*	*3*
Saturday	*2 gin & tonic*	*At pub, with friends.*	*?*	*2*
Sunday	*2 glasses wine* *1 glass wine*	*With dinner 6 pm* *Later, watching TV.*	*2* *1*	*3*
Total for the week				*23 units*

Cutting down alcohol intake

The drinking diary is a very simple and practical starting point to cutting down. Keeping a tally of all drinking and noting the circumstances will increase awareness of drinking habits which are often unconscious. This alerts the drinker to areas where changes can be made, and from these the drinker can begin to decide on some personal rules which will help her to reduce her intake.

Keeping a drinking diary over a period of 10 to 12 weeks, writing in entries as soon as possible after drinking, also helps people to monitor their progress. Mary might decide to lower her alcohol consumption by having a low alcohol or non-alcoholic drink any time she has lunch in a pub. She may also decide to keep two or three days completely alcohol free. Sue could decide that she will try to stick to a limit of no more than 5 units on any accasion. Jane might decide

43

to drink mineral water instead of wine during business lunches and to invest in a drinks measure for pouring drinks at home. She could also explore other ways of unwinding after work—going for a short, brisk walk; a little gardening or listening to some favourite music.

Drinking pressures

There are many hurdles to changing a drinking habit.

i. **External pressures**. Offering and accepting a drink is often an expression of hospitality or a convenient ice-breaker. Sharing a round of drinks can be an expression of solidarity among friends. Drinking can be perceived as being sophisticated and cultured. These pressures can be acknowledged; personal attitudes and beliefs about drinking can be examined (eg, Do I really think that it is offensive to refuse a drink?); and thirdly, practical ways of handling different situations can be planned.

ii. **Personal pressures**. Drinking can become a trusted and convenient way of feeling good, lowering inhibitions and unwinding. Losing these positive effects can discourage people who are cutting down unless they are motivated by some strong personal reasons. It is helpful to make a note of two or three benefits of drinking less. These might be long-term benefits such as improving health, losing weight, checking a growing dependency. It is also important to have some immediate rewards as well, such as a sounder sleep, a clearer head, and extra money.

Figure 7.5 gives some further suggestions for ways of cutting down.

Self-help publications

Many excellent self-help guides are available ranging from small but comprehensive pamphlets such as 'That's the limit' produced by the Health Education Authority[2] to the more detailed guide 'So you want to cut down your drinking?' published by the Health Education Board for Scotland.[4] There has also been an increase in the number of publications now available in bookshops alongside other self-help guides dealing with a range of health issues.

Conclusion

Checking out how much you drink is neither time consuming nor costly. It is not difficult to do, given basic information and guidelines. Initially, people need to be invited to monitor their drinking. There are many opportunities to do this, including special *Drinkwise* promotions, Well-woman clinics, routine visits to general practitioners, and newspaper and magazine articles. The goal is to make people aware of how much they are drinking; of how this compares with the recommended guidelines of 14 units for women and 21 units for men over a week; and the significance of these levels for their general health. This would not seem inappropriate or impractical: people are already aware of other personal health information, such as weight and cholesterol levels, where targets are set and regular monitoring is used.

Figure 7.5: *Tips for cutting down alcohol intake*[3]

- Keep a drinking diary. Monitor your progress.
- Note benefits. Write down 2 or 3 good reasons for cutting down (eg, looks, weight, health, money).
- Set a limit for a day, an evening, a week and try to stick to it.
- Have 2 or 3 alcohol-free days.
- Choose low-alcohol or non-alcoholic drinks.
- Space alcoholic drinks with soft drinks.
- Dilute spirits with non-alcoholic mixers.
- Slow down, take smaller sips, put the glass down between sips. A held glass tends to be drunk more often.
- Change your drink. Changing the type of drink can help break old habits and reduce the volume drunk.
- Avoid rounds. If you drink with other people who regularly buy rounds for each other, it's easy to end up drinking more than you want. Try drinking more slowly so you can skip some rounds. Ask for a low or non-alcoholic drink now and then or a smaller measure.
- Start later. Start drinking later than usual. Go to the pub later.
- It's OK to say no. Have a 'No thanks' answer ready: 'No thanks, I'm watching the calories', 'No thanks, I've reached my limit for today.'
- Invest in a drinks measure for home. Use it when pouring drinks for yourself and others.
- Keep a supply of alcohol alternatives at home.
- Tell someone that you are cutting down. Invite a friend to keep a drinking diary.
- Reward successes. Drinking is a pleasurable experience. Find other ways of feeling good. If you manage to keep to your limits give yourself a treat—a visit to the cinema, new clothes.
- Remind yourself from time to time of the benefits to health, and purse, of not exceeding your drinking limits.

References

[1] *Results of Public Awareness Survey of main Drinkwise Campaign messages.* (1989–91). The Health Education Authority, 1991.

[2] *That's the Limit—A Guide to Sensible Drinking.* The Health Education Authority, 1991.

[3] *Adapted from Alcohol—A Balanced View.* Royal College of General Practitioners, 1986.

[4] Ian Robertson, Nick Heather. *So you want to cut down your drinking? A self-help guide to sensible drinking.* Health Education Board for Scotland, 1991.

Further Reading

Alan Maryon Davis. *Pssst. A really useful guide to alcohol*. Pan Books, 1989.

Ian Robertson and Nick Heather. *Let's drink to your health! A self-help guide to sensible drinking*. British Psychological Society, 1986.

Address for contact

Patricia Wilson, Alcohol and Drug Misuse Programme Manager, The Health Promotion Agency for Northern Ireland, 18 Ormeau Avenue, Belfast, BT2 8HS.

8 Seeking Help for an Alcohol-Related Problem: The Role of the Primary Care Team

Sarah Jarvis, General Practitioner, London

SUMMARY

The primary health care team—including the general practitioners, practice and district nurses, health visitor and social worker—forms an accessible starting point for people seeking help with alcohol-related problems. Given the general nature and continuity of primary care, most women will know one member of the team reasonably well and should have formed a relationship of trust with them.

It is important to seek help early for an alcohol problem, at a stage at which it may be most easily and effectively dealt with. Any woman can approach a health care professional directly to discuss a perceived problem. Asking for advice about sensible drinking levels may provide a useful opening to a discussion on alcohol problems, as may attending one of the health promotion clinics provided at most surgeries. Any approach will be treated in strictest confidence, which will mean that discussion of a partner's problem will be limited until that person can attend. The doctor can offer help and support, both by providing counselling and by appropriate referral to hospital or to self-help groups.

Background

Every member of the population has the right to register with a general practitioner (GP). Most practices have one or more health visitors or practice nurses working within the team and have direct access to district nurse and social work care. On average, women attend their GP more often than men, especially if they have children. If a woman has children she may know her health visitor especially well; if she lives in deprived circumstances, she may have regular contact with a social worker; and if she has sick or elderly relatives, she may be visited by the district nurse. A member of the primary health care team may thus be the easiest and most accessible person to turn to in order to discuss concerns about alcohol—not only should she be able to raise the question in a familiar environment with someone she trusts, but she may also feel more comfortable about broaching the subject in an informal manner when she attends for another reason. This article describes how a woman can seek help, and how she can ensure that she obtains the most appropriate help available.

How to seek help

Broadly speaking, help can be sought either directly or indirectly. Any patient may approach a health care professional to ask advice about sensible drinking levels or to seek help with an alcohol-related problem. Most surgeries hold health promotion clinics, run either by the doctor or by a practice nurse. A general health check will include questions about alcohol consumption and the types of alcohol drunk, as well as advice about sensible drinking limits. A large majority of patients drink within these guidelines and for them, such limits should reassure or act as an incentive not to exceed them. For others, this may be an appropriate entry into the subject of alcohol excess. If the health care professional feels that they cannot deal fully with the topic, they may refer the patient to another team member and may, with his or her permission, discuss the problem with them.

The GP may already have some idea that there is a problem, indicated by apparently unrelated visits. These include unusually high attendances at the surgery for very minor ailments; physical problems, which might or might not be alcohol related; social problems; psychological problems (such as depression or anxiety); recurrent minor accidents; or frequent requests for sick leave. If the possibility has crossed their mind, GPs may broach the subject or try to steer the conversation towards it.

The importance of confidentiality

The GP will not break confidentiality by discussing a patient's problem without that patient's permission, although he or she may wish to discuss the problem with professional colleagues in order to ensure that the patient gets the help they need. This does mean that the doctor cannot discuss details of medical problems with the patient's spouse or partner. Thus, if a woman wishes to discuss her partner or a relative with alcohol problems, the doctor will give general advice only and may suggest that the person concerned should himself attend, either alone or with his partner.

What the primary health care team can do

While all members of the primary health care team can offer initial guidance and support to a woman who approaches them with a problem, they will usually refer her to her GP. This is partially because the GP has more detailed knowledge of the patient's history; partly because he or she is trained to recognise the physical, as well as the psychological and social effects upon the patient; and partly because he or she is seen as the 'gatekeeper' to other services. An alcohol problem may have far-reaching effects on many areas of a patient's life and these should be tackled together. Thus, the GP is usually best placed to mobilise the different types of help which will be needed.

The practitioner's first aim will be to clarify the problem and to consider, with the patient, her overriding concerns. He will want to discuss the underlying reasons for the problem and to identify situations which are linked in any one case to drinking. This done, patient and doctor can together set about drawing up a plan to provide crisis support; to address the underlying problem; and to avoid drinking situations. The practitioner can provide counselling and support, as well as helping to manage withdrawal symptoms; if necessary, using drugs to modify the effects of withdrawal.

Working closely with other members of the primary care team, the practitioner will also aim to provide practical help to deal with other problems which already exist or which may arise. He may need to arrange social work support or to discuss with the local housing department the possibility of rehousing; the health visitor or social worker may be able to help with ideas for child care or contact groups for young mothers; and he may be able to provide sick leave while the patient is undergoing treatment.

It may become apparent that more formal treatment is necessary, referral for which is required from the GP. Depending on the problem, this could include referral to a hospital physician, to a psychiatrist or to a community psychiatric nurse. It may, however, be more appropriate for the patient to refer herself to one of the voluntary agencies, such as RELATE, Alcoholics Anonymous or Al-Anon.

The unsympathetic approach

Sadly, it is by no means unknown for a woman to be faced with an unsympathetic approach to alcohol-related problems. This may be related to time constraints and to the GP's unwillingness to become involved in a time-consuming problem. It may be because the practitioner is embarrassed, or wishes to avoid the conflict which may arise from tackling a sensitive issue. It may also occur because the doctor mistrusts the patient's drinking history, or has different perceptions from the patient about the scale of the problem.

Whatever the reason, it is important for the patient not to risk deterioration of the situation by failing to seek help again. It may be that booking a longer appointment will relax the time constraints often found in general practice and will allow a more open discussion. Alternatively, it may be easier to approach another member of the team. Some patients find it less awkward to discuss a potentially embarrassing topic with a doctor whom they do not know. At some practices, it is possible to make an appointment with a partner of one's own doctor. If necessary, women should feel free to contact voluntary agencies, who will be happy to help.

Conclusion

The primary health care team has a unique part to play in the recognition and treatment of alcohol-related problems. Its members provide continuous care for the whole family and have a detailed knowledge of a woman's home circumstances and family dynamics. By close cooperation, they can provide practical help, as well as support and counselling, which may be essential both to tackle the current alcohol problem and to prevent its recurrence.

Address for contact

Dr Sarah Jarvis, the Grove Health Centre, Goldhawk Rd, London W12 8EJ

9 Alcohol Services and Women

SUE BAKER, Divisional Director Services and Professional Education
Alcohol Concern

SUMMARY

Alcohol services, especially those which cater for women's particular needs are still 'patchy' across England and Wales. The recommendations of a succession of reports—from Kessel in 1978 to *Alcohol Concern's, Meeting the Need* in 1989—have still not been implemented. This paper outlines the range of services available; common difficulties which women face in gaining access to them; and ways to improve the present situation.

Background

In 1978, a landmark report[1] set the standard to which alcohol services should aspire; 'every person with a drinking problem should be able to find the help he or she needs' and (to paraphrase) 'there should be a range of services to cater for different needs and to enable people to choose'. It is ironic that in the same year, the then Secretary of State for Social Services, (whose Department sponsored the report) could state that: 'there is nothing manly or heroic or glamorous about those who drink too much. In men it is crude and embarrassing, in women it is plain sickening'.

Note that it is merely 'embarrassing' for men but 'sickening' for women. In a period of a few short months, two quotations encapsulated the debate about women and alcohol services; on the one hand women should have access to services which suit their needs but, on the other hand, the society which funds those services is much more critical of women who have alcohol problems than of men.

Have things changed since 1978? This paper attempts to summarise the range of services currently available to women, the difficulties women find in using those services, examples of good practice and how a system which was largely designed by male professionals for male clients could be changed to meet the needs of women.

The need for women's services

Women drink in different ways to men, drink different kinds of drinks at different times and in differing places[2]. Women consistently drink less than men, but over the last 10 years, while the average consumption for men has declined, for women it has, at best, remained constant. For young single women there is more definite evidence of an increase[3].

In comparison with the amount women drink, women are over-represented in measures of alcohol-related harm such as cirrhosis of the liver—particularly alcoholic cirrhosis. Death from this illness increased by 40% for women between 1979 and 1989, compared with a 6% increase for men. In 1989, men drinking very heavily outnumbered women by 6:1, but deaths by alcoholic cirrhosis were much closer than this, at less than 2:1 (men to women)[4].

In a 1989 survey, the women's group **DAWN** (Drugs, Alcohol, Women, Now) noted that: 'Although an increase in problem drinking among women is acknowledged by the alcohol field, the majority of agencies do not see proportionate numbers of women clients. It has been shown, however, that when agencies provide specific services for women, the number of clients increases[5]'. Individual experiences of women support this view[6].

'I was relieved to have a woman counsellor and feel that I couldn't have let myself trust a man in the same way.'

'One group I found very hard—it was controlled by two men (one well-established in psychiatry) and had a majority of men in it; it seemed obvious to me as a woman I wasn't going to feel comfortable . . . the two therapists . . . always colluded with the male members' sexist comments.'

There are few surveys which have asked women for their views of their treatment and hence anecdotal evidence is necessarily important. As Alcohol Concern acts as an umbrella organisation for many of the alcohol advice and counselling centres in England and Wales, this evidence is wide ranging.

The range of services

Help for problem drinkers can have a variety of meanings depending on the nature and extent of their problems. For some women it may be no more than one advice session where information can be given on sensible drinking, how to control their drinking, and/or avoid situations which are liable to lead to them drinking too much.

For others, it may mean weekly counselling sessions, perhaps combined with family or group therapy or assertiveness training; perhaps needing to give up alcohol altogether. Some women (a much smaller number) may need help with the physical and psychological symptoms of withdrawal from alcohol—detoxification—and some may need 'time out' in a residential setting in order to rebuild their lives.

Who provides alcohol services?

There is no statutory duty on local and health authorities to provide services to problem drinkers; approximately one third of district health authorities pro-vide no service other than hospital acute beds for alcohol withdrawal[7]. It is not surprising therefore, that the level of service is extremely varied across the country and that the voluntary sector should play such an important role in meeting the need.

The voluntary sector

Voluntary sector provision can be divided into three main categories:

i.   Advice centres/Counselling services
ii.   Residential care
iii. Self-help groups

i. *Advice centres/Counselling services*

There are currently 101 alcohol advice centres in England and Wales provided by the voluntary sector, ranging from small centres wholly staffed by volunteers, to those with a large staff from specialist disciplines. (A further 22 services which may also offer advice and counselling are provided through the NHS—see below). Of all advice and counselling services, only 32 (26%) offer a service specifically for women. There are 27 centres in Greater London and 96 in the rest of England and Wales. Of the 92 centres who are members of Alcohol Concern, between 60 and 70% use volunteer counsellors.

Figures 9.1 and 9.2 show the distribution of these services across the country. The growth in advice centres and counselling services has been 'organic' and often limited by availability of funds, which in part explains the 'holes' in the net of care. Parts of East Anglia (the fastest growing region in the UK), the whole of Central Wales, the East Midlands, Northern Lancashire and parts of Berkshire and Sussex have relatively few services. Certain charities are particularly strong in specific regions; ie **Turning Point** in Southern England and **Aquarius** in the West Midlands.

Existing alcohol centres have attempted to plug the gaps by providing sub centres which are frequently confined to very restricted hours (perhaps a half day a week or by request only). In 1990, a Government initiative enabled Alcohol Concern to award grants to 18 advice services in areas with no previous service, and a further 15 to extend other existing services.

What they offer

All staff (whether voluntary or not) will have experience in counselling people with alcohol problems. Alcohol Concern runs a scheme (VACTS) which aims to establish high standards for volunteer counsellors.

All counselling centres will be able to offer:

a free confidential service (some will have a policy statement making clear where confidentiality ends eg when others are thought to be at risk);

one-to-one counselling for problem drinkers or their family and friends (this could be in the day or evening or at weekends); assessment; establishing whether the client has a problem or not, and if controlled drinking or abstinence is the best approach; information on health risks;

assessing which other difficulties are contributing to the drinking problem;

knowledge of other treatments if necessary detoxification;

referral to the specialist services; eg residential care, doctors.

Many services will be able to provide women counsellors and telephone counselling. Some will be able to undertake home visits and have a wider range of therapies and women's support groups.

Figure 9.1: *Distribution of Advice/Counselling Centres in England and Wales*

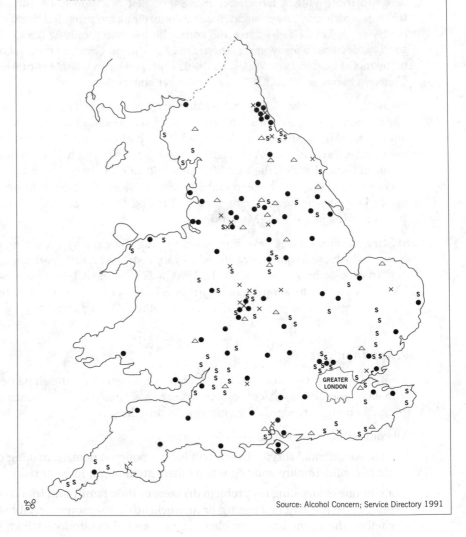

- ● Advice/counselling centre
- × Advice/counselling centre with specialist service for women
- s Sub-centre
- △ Planned new services

GREATER LONDON

Source: Alcohol Concern; Service Directory 1991

Figure 9.2: *Distribution of Advice/Counselling Centres in Greater London*

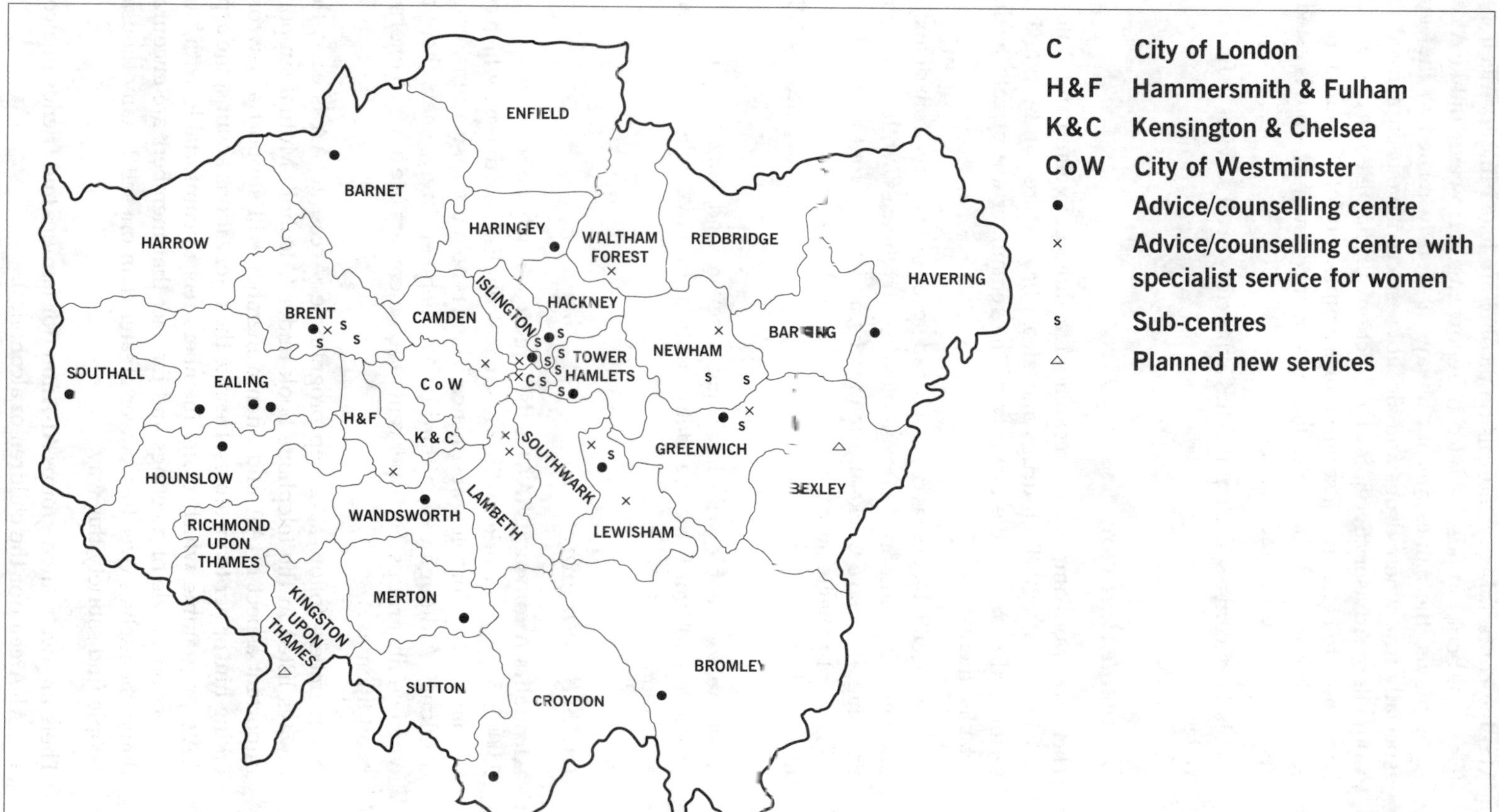

C City of London
H&F Hammersmith & Fulham
K&C Kensington & Chelsea
CoW City of Westminster
● Advice/counselling centre
✕ Advice/counselling centre with specialist service for women
s Sub-centres
△ Planned new services

Source: Alcohol Concern; Service Directory 1991

Making contact. Many councils on alcohol are listed under 'Alcohol' in the telephone book or under 'Advice' in Yellow Pages. However unlike Alcoholics Anonymous, the names are not always obviously related to the service—especially true where drugs and alcohol services have been merged to form 'Councils or Advisory Services on Addiction'. British Telecom does not always know how to categorise a service; for example, 'Suffolk Community Alcohol Service' is not listed under alcohol, Suffolk or community—but is listed in the Yellow Pages under 'advice'.

Alcohol Concern regularly publishes a directory of all services in England and Wales.

ii. *Residential care*

There are approximately 115 residential facilities in England and Wales (some of which deal with both drugs and alcohol); 73% are run by the voluntary sector and charities; the majority of the remainder are private health care establishments.

These residential facilities cover a broad spectrum of care, from detoxification (although in a minority of examples) to 'dry houses' with programmes of anything between 6 weeks and 18 months, and hostels for the homeless. Some will accept patients only when referred by a doctor or other professional, but most are happy to accept self referrals. Some residential facilities also offer day care and clinics.

Most are for people who have had a severe and long-standing drinking problem and most require detoxification to have taken place prior to admission.

iii. *Self-help groups*

Alcoholics Anonymous (AA) is the largest self-help network in the UK, with 2,000 groups. AA works on the basis that alcoholism is a disease which can *only* be managed by complete abstinence. There is no place for learning 'controlled drinking'. Although over a third of AA members are women, there are not women-only groups. Forty per cent of AA members use other alcohol services in addition to AA[8].

AA members follow a 12-step programme. Access to AA is easy; they are always listed in the telephone book under 'Alcohol'. Mutual support is an important aspect of AA and often a member will support a newcomer by taking him or her to meetings. Despite the reservations about some aspects of AA's programme which many members feel uncomfortable with,[9] (eg, the confessional style of meetings and the fact that members are encouraged to 'hand themselves over to a power greater than oneself') many thousands of people find sobriety this way.

There are two related groups **Al-Anon** (for families and friends of alcoholics) and **Al-Ateen** (for the children of alcoholics).

In South East England, **Libra** has a network of self-help groups dealing with drugs and alcohol.

The Women's Alcohol Centre (WAC) in London—an example of good practice—is the only exclusively counselling service in the country and is part of a larger voluntary sector scheme, the *Alcohol Recovery Project*.

WAC evolved because of demand by women and a willingness to listen to their needs. The Alcohol Recovery Project began 25 years ago and operates four shop-front advice centres. Women clients found several features of the ordinary advice centres difficult:

Signs which let the world know of their problem;

Dropping in without appointment (which many men preferred);

Mixed groups where women competed with men for time and where sexual sterotypical behaviour was common;

Concerns about confidentiality.

The Women's Advice Centre has addressed these problems by being an all-female space; using a discreet sign (with only the initial given); using appointments; and giving a statement of confidentiality to each client.

Low self-esteem is common to women attending WAC. In designing the interior there has been a conscious effort to ensure that the building does not reinforce this. (Too many centres, through lack of funds, look like relics of Departments of Health and Social Security offices). The WAC walls are not full of problem-centred posters on AIDS or alcoholism, but carry the artwork of women clients.

The decor is a balance between familiar homelike furniture (eg, pine tables and flowers) and efficiency. This is not just top-dressing. In the words of one counsellor: 'By the time a woman has come from the entrance to a private room, the building has said a lot to her about her worth.'

Many women choose group work in addition to individual counselling. Women tend to want to explore wider issues than simple alcohol problems, a tendency found by other workers[10]. Women also want to stay in groups for longer periods to deal with that range of problems. This could be construed as women's dependent behaviour; it could equally be seen as pragmatism—women choosing to stay with a system which works.

One of the topics which women are increasingly discussing is their difficulties with alcohol and sexual abuse. One counsellor reports that currently, six out of 10 clients were abused as children. This does not mean this is typical of the UK as a whole, although ISIS (the incest survivors network) reports a higher-than-expected level of addictive behaviour amongst their members. It does indicate that women's counselling may have additional problems to face.

Statutory services

The GP is often the first port of call for women concerned about their drinking; Sarah Jarvis discusses this topic more fully in Chapter [8]. However, two points are worth making here:

i. The GP might not feel able, or have time, to deal with an alcohol problem—even if the best course of treatment might be detoxification at home, supervised by a GP who knows the medical history.

ii. The GP might not be able to refer the patient to the most suitable treatment because it is not available.

iii. In essence, consumers of the statutory services have to play the same game of geographical Russian roulette as do consumers of voluntary sector provision. Clinical judgment may give way to geography.

Alcohol Treatment Units (ATUs)

ATUs were set up by the National Health Service in the 1950s and 60s to provide units, within hospitals, for patients needing detoxification, medical supervision and counselling. There are 23–25 (depending on definition) at present (see Figure 9.3).

In reality, ATUs vary greatly from district to district. The common denominator is that they **all offer detoxification programmes** to ease alcohol withdrawal, at the same time supporting any underlying medical condition. Some ATUs do much more than this, offering an excellent support service of extensive counselling, therapy and follow-up. Others do not, and patients are sent out ill-equipped to deal with the possibility of relapse and where to find non-ATU support.

Some ATUs will only admit patients who demonstrate their motivation to give up drinking—which might involve a waiting period to test their resolve—a process much debated by women's groups. Do lung cancer patients have to prove they will give up smoking before receiving treatment? Do women feel assertive enough in this situation to convince the service givers?

Beds in psychiatric and general wards

Where there are no other detoxification facilities (or home supervision), women can be referred to hospital wards—often gastro-enterology or psychiatric wards. Women are more likely than men to be treated as psychiatric patients[12].

Community Alcohol Team (CATS)

A CAT is a team of professionals (usually community psychiatric nurses, psychologists, counsellors, social workers) who provide a wide range of services. Some may provide home detoxification outside hospitals. There are at least 22 CAT teams in England and Wales. Many health authorities have moved from the in-hospital ATU approach to this community-based form of care. Evidence shows it to be equally effective[13].

Women fear the stigma of being branded 'alcohol patients' and 'being seen' at hospital clinics[14]. In this respect, CATs may be better geared towards meeting women's needs. For mothers, childcare can be a barrier to residential treatment. As women with alcohol problems sustain their homemaking skills longer than men and tend to drink when children are at school or asleep, CATs may be a particularly useful service for women problem drinkers.

Barriers to finding help

In surveying alcohol services, some of the barriers to finding help have been noted. At this point, it is perhaps useful to summarise and to add one or two issues not already covered.

General barriers

i. The social stigma attached to women and drinking which prevents women seeking help when they need it and at an early and more treatable stage.

ii. Women cannot easily give themselves permission 'not to cope' versus continuing to fulfil their other roles in life and putting the needs of others first.

iii. The fear of mothers with alcohol problems of having their children taken into care[17].

iv. Difficulties with childcare for women seeking treatment. Several advice centres have creches, not all of which are fully used. The Women's Alcohol Centre has discovered that women can feel distracted with their children so close. Getting children ready to go out, to unfamiliar childcare, may in itself be a barrier. A more creative response might be to give small grants to mothers to enable them to use their normal childcare system.

v. Concerns about confidentiality.

Voluntary sector barriers

Not all the country is well served; in particular, rural areas have a much poorer service, exacerbated by poor public transport, on which women are more dependent than men[18].

The name of the service: finding the service is poorly presented which puts off women and helps reinforce their low sense of self worth.

Limited funds mean limited times when counsellors are available. An answer machine is possibly the only immediate answer.

Lack of understanding of what counselling means. In a recent survey of three council estates, only 11 people in 900 understood the term[19]. Older women are the least likely to understand the term.

Statutory sector barriers

Specialist services not designed for women, notably in detoxification where women are more likely to be placed on psychiatric wards.

Limited services for home detoxification. If the GP is unable, or CAT is non-existent, to supervise this, the only choice may be a general/psychiatric hospital bed.

As with the voluntary sector, not all the country is equally well served and the same problems of access and transport apply.

What can be done?

So much in both the voluntary and statutory sector depends for success upon **funding**, but some aspects are as much determined by **attitude** and **understanding** as by money.

A statutory duty on local and health authorities to provide a range of alcohol services would ensure that women had a choice of service, making early intervention more likely and being more cost effective in the long term.

Planning alcohol services with women in mind by:
minimising social stigma by discretion in labelling advice/counselling centres;
making the service physically attractive;
offering a choice of 'women only' sessions/beds;
planning for more extensive issues being explored in counselling, particularly sexual abuse;
thinking creatively about childcare;
giving clear statements on confidentiality;
describing counselling and advice in ordinary language.

Reconsidering policies which place women, who have no previous psychiatric history, on psychiatric wards.
Giving thought to women needing to 'prove' sufficient motivation for treatment at ATUs.

Training ensuring that nurses and others in contact with alcohol dependent women have adequate training.

Research into women's experience of services.

Conclusion

Alcohol services (both voluntary and statutory care) are patchy across England and Wales; treatment may depend as much on geography as clinical judgement. Special consideration needs to be given to factors which put off women from seeking early intervention: social stigma, concerns about confidentiality and fears of children being taken into care. Women's needs in counselling are different from men's. Women may make a more successful recovery with counselling programmes which deal with a wide range of problems.

Although alcohol services for women are limited, there has been an encouraging increase in concern about women's needs and alcohol, of which the conference and the Government's grant programme (via Alcohol Concern) are evidence. Whilst there are shortcomings in provision for women (especially among lesbian women and women from ethnic minorities) there are examples of good practice and dedicated people on which to build for the future.

References

[1] *The Pattern and Range of Services for Problem Drinkers*, HMSO, 1978.

[2] *Drinking in England and Wales in the late 1980s*, OPCS by HMSO, 1991.

[3] Social Trends 20, Central Statistical Office; Drinking in England and Wales, op cit; General Household Survey 1988 (OPCS, 1990).

[4] Calculated per 100,000 men and women aged 16+: OPCS Mortality Statistics 1979 and '89.

[5] *Alcohol and Women: A Crisis in Detoxification Services* [London], DAWN, 1989.

[6] *Women and Dependency: Women's Personal Accounts of Drug and Alcohol Problems.* DAWN, 1986.

[7] Alcohol Concern 1991.

[8] Alcoholics Anonymous Survey, 1991, AA.

[9] Robinson D, *From Drinking to Alcoholism*; Chichester, John Wiley, 1976.

[10] Fanny Duckert, Inst., of Alcohol Research, Oslo, in *Women's Problems with Alcohol and Other Drugs* op cit.

[11] *Alcohol and Women: A Crisis in Detoxification Services*, op cit.

[12] *A Survey of Gateways to Treatment*; Avon Council on Alcoholism, 1982.

[13] Orford and Edwards, Maudsley Monographs No 26, 1977.

[14] Betsey Thom, Institute of Psychiatry, *Gateways to Treatment in Women's Problems with Alcohol and Other Drugs*, University of Kent, 1986.

[15] Sheehan and Watson, *Response and Recognition, Women and Alcohol*; Camberwell Council on Alcoholism, Tavistock, 1980.

[16] Mayer and Black; *Currents in Alcoholism, Vol 2*, Grune and Stratton.

[17] Betsy Thom, *British Journal of Addiction* 81 pp 777–8, 1986.

[18] Women's Environmental Network, Transport Briefing, 1991.

[19] To be published by Alcohol Concern 1991/2.

Address for contact

Sue Baker, Divisional Director Services and Professional Education Alcohol Concern, 275 Gray's Inn Road, London WC1X 8QF.

C GETTING THE MESSAGE ACROSS

The Conference Emblem

The Right Honourable John MacGregor

Baroness Hooper

Moira Plant

Claire Rayner

Marsha Morgan

Donna McLaughlin

Joan Trowell

Jancis Robinson

Patricia Wilson

Sarah Jarvis
General Practitioner

Sue Baker

Sara Edwards
Broadcaster, BBC Wales

Opposite:
Black Mime Theatre, formed in 1984, draws inspiration from cinema, television and comic-strip culture to create an engaging form of mime. The Women's Troop presented extracts from *Drowning* which portrays the stories of three women and their struggles to overcome alcohol-related problems.

Photographs by courtesy of Steve Speller

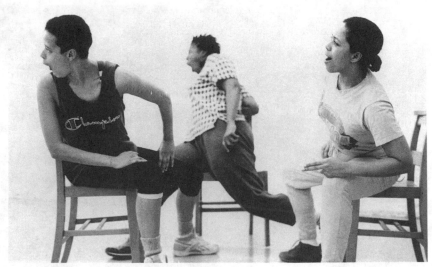

Terry Lawrence

Margaret Joachim

John Rae

10 Women and Alcohol: Examples of Local Agency Action and Drinkwise Campaigns

TERRY LAWRENCE, Regional Alcohol Misuse Co-ordinator, West Midlands Regional Health Authority

SUMMARY

On the whole, women use alcohol safely and sensibly. However, there is a need for local action, both to support women in their responsible use of alcohol and provide help, in the form of appropriate and accessible service provision. Several agencies at a local level can be involved in generating action, but a useful starting point is to get the issue of women and alcohol incorporated into local inter-agency strategic plans on alcohol, and on to the agenda of local women's groups. Examples are given of inter-agency work around the sensible drinking message of the Drinkwise campaign to illustrate what might be achieved.

Background

What is the problem?

One thing the problem is not, is women. Compared to men: women drink less (about ⅓ as much), and less often (women had on average 3.2 drinking occasions per week, compared to men's 4.4).

Women drink more slowly (women take on average just over half an hour to drink one unit of alcohol, whereas men drink one and a half units in the same amount of time).

Speed of drinking is important, because faster speeds lead to higher concentrations of alcohol in the blood, and in consequence to more acute short-term impairment.

Fewer women drink in excess of the recommended sensible weekly amounts (8% of women drink >14 units, and 23% of men drink >21 units of alcohol per week).

Fewer women are high-risk drinkers—consuming in excess of 35 units (for men, 50 units) of alcohol a week. (Only 1% of women, compared to 6% of men, drink at this level).

Fewer women are likely to binge or have a heavy drinking session—defined as 8 units of alcohol for a man and 6 units of alcohol for a woman—on any one occasion. Only 10% of women reported 'binge' drinking, compared with nearly 25% of men.

And in the workplace:

Women's work is less likely to suffer from the effects of drinking. Only 3% of working women, compared to 7% of working men, said they had been below par because of drinking at some time during the previous year.

The message from this information is that women, on the whole, drink responsibly and sensibly, and experience relatively few problems as a result of their *own* drinking.

Why (and what) action is needed

1 Action is needed to support and help the vast majority of women whose drinking is sensible, enjoyable and harm-free. We should be concerned to maintain the present situation of relatively few women experiencing problems as a direct result of their drinking—and to improve on it. We should make sure that women get appropriate information so that they can make informed choices about what to choose and how much to drink.

2 We need to identify some of the particular needs women may have to do with alcohol:

i. Accessible, appropriate service provision, counselling and help for women who are:

experiencing problems as a result of their own drinking;

drinking and using other drugs—many of them prescribed drugs like tranquillisers and anti-depressants;

victims of abuse—whether verbal, physical or sexual abuse as a consequence of another person's drinking;

carers, and have responsibility for the lives of people who are dependent, and in particular, may be protecting children from abuse;

in problematic and unrewarding relationships, and may be using alcohol to escape from or suppress painful feelings.

ii. Accurate, intelligible, accessible and consistent information for women in their many roles as educators and information givers—both to one another through sharing advice and support, and to others through relationships in the family, informally with colleagues, and in their professional working lives. Women have a right to know what alcohol is and how it will effect them and others. They have a right to particular information relating alcohol consumption to their physiological needs: information about drinking during pregnancy; the effect of alcohol on their moods and feelings at different times in the menstrual cycle; the increased risk of having unprotected and unsafe sex when they have been drinking.

iii. Proper information for women as purchasers of alcohol, both for their own consumption, and as part of the household stocks, in a context where women are the target of advertising. It has become more socially acceptable for women to drink in pubs than it was 15 to 20 years ago (see Chapter 2), and more women are drinking at home as a matter of course than previously. Women have a right to know the nutritional content of alcohol as much as of any other food and drink product they buy. They further have the right to know the strength of the product and the number of units of alcohol it contains (see Chapter 4).

How to develop local action

The idea of inter-agency action, both at national and local level, is not new. Ten years ago in *Drinking Sensibly*, a Department of Health and Social Services publication, the statement was made:

> "To control growth in alcohol misuse and in the harm it causes requires preventive action in which central government, local government, the health professionals and institutions, the business sector and trade unions, voluntary bodies, and the people of the United Kingdom as individuals can recognise and play their separate parts." (Drinking Sensibly, DHSS 1981: 65)

Local action: Whose responsibility?

Local action doesn't just happen. It requires someone to take the initiative to get things started. The starting point might be an individual woman, perhaps one for whom alcohol use (her own or another's) has had particular significance, and who is energetic and determined enough to galvanise people into action which will redress the balance.

But action doesn't have to be left to individuals. The systems and structures already exist at a local level for activity to be initiated, co-ordinated and implemented. Many local councils already have women's units, and some of these will have subgroups whose remit is to make policy and practice recommendations on women's health issues. If such a group exists, a good starting point would seem to be to get alcohol on to their agenda.

In the absence of any obvious co-ordinating group at a local level, health promotion units, community health councils or local specialist alcohol agencies might be the people to take a lead.

Local points of contact

The Government Circular on Alcohol Misuse issued in 1989[2], required that every health district or local area set up an inter-agency co-ordinating group to act as a forum to discuss alcohol-related issues and develop strategic plans for their locality. Such a group would be a good initial point of contact both for finding out what already exists in your local area, what plans there are for future developments, and getting the issue of women and alcohol on to their agenda, so as to have some influence in future decision making, particularly in the present context of service contracts and planning for care in the community.

Developing networks

At a local level there are a vast number of groups and services which might be involved in raising awareness, and getting information and service provision to women. Obvious ones include counselling agencies, (both alcohol-specific and others like RELATE, women's therapy groups, child guidance and Cruse, for example) community health and social workers, treatment teams, day centres, health education and health promotion units. But in addition to these 'obvious' services, local resources include a very wide range of less obvious institutions, groups and organisations which, if mobilised, could contribute to an overall local prevention strategy in relation to a vast range of local alcohol-related issues and situations.

Although this article is concerned with what can be done at a *local level* it is important, in the context of networks, to recognise the role of national organisations—like Alcohol Concern—in providing and disseminating specialist alcohol information; and the Health Education Authority (HEA) in its provision of materials and resources, and its ability to tap into the local networks of the 14 regional alcohol co-ordinators around the country. Other national organisations which link into networks of agencies at a local level include:

the **National Community Health Resource** which provides information, training, support and services to women's health workers in the community on a variety of issues, and which houses the Women's Health Network. The role of the network is to establish and develop local and regional links with women's projects. It has a database which can supply information on, and contacts with, women's health initiatives around the country;

the **National Association of Local Government Women's Committees** which has links with the women's committees of local authorities and thereby access through their mailing list to a host of community-based women's organisations and groups;

the **National Alliance of Womens' Organisations (NAWO)** has a membership drawn from voluntary sector organisations and trades unions, and is a central source for access to this network.

Adopting a 'bottom up' approach: taking account of what women want

Whilst national, regional and local groups provide useful mechanisms for planning programmes of local action, it is essential that these programmes reflect and support the needs of women in the community. Outreach and primary care workers from both statutory and voluntary sector agencies are strategically placed to be sensitive to what women are saying, and can both empower women themselves to take action to meet their needs in their own community, and facilitate access to formal policy-making and planning systems.

Developing local strategies and action plans

Once local needs have been identified, a strategic framework for action needs to be developed to ensure that initiatives are developed in a way which is compatible, coherent and relevant.

For maximum impact, a local prevention strategy needs maximum participation, and mutuality of interest from the agencies involved. It needs to agree targets, plan action, and make sure that messages are clear and consistent.

The *Drinkwise* Campaign

The *Drinkwise* Campaign is an example of a nation-wide initiative, operating at local level through inter-agency activity, and drawing on central support from the HEA and Alcohol Concern.

Drinkwise promotes the safer, sensible drinking message to the general public by raising awareness and encouraging people to think about their drinking

The *Drinkwise* Campaign operates through more than four thousand agencies at all levels throughout the country, getting its message across through the work of schools and youth groups, colleges and universities; health promotion and health education units, specialist alcohol agencies, the police, road safety, environmental, and occupational health, probation and social services, many employers and the Drinks Industry.

Drinkwise is a growth area. It gets bigger and better each year, and research shows[3] that it is effectively achieving its aims of raising awareness and knowledge about sensible drinking and safe limits in terms of recommended levels of drinking. Most people are probably familiar with the Drinkwise elephant logo—perhaps a reminder not to forget about drinking sensibly and keeping count of the number of units of alcohol consumed. Perhaps also a reminder that developing an awareness-raising compaign on a national scale is indeed a mammoth task!

Nationally, the campaign attracts considerable media attention, featuring 'stars', 'media personalities' and 'household names'. It is mentioned in many national magazines and one or two television soap operas. But it is important to remember that Drinkwise started off as a local initiative. The first Drinkwise campaigns were in Coventry, the South West Region and London. It was due to the success of these initiatives that pressure for a national campaign arose and Drinkwise, nationally, was born.

At local level Drinkwise activities designed for women include:

a. The Community Alcohol and Drug Service in Wisbech East Anglia, together with local health promotion and environmental health officers, targeted 'women and alcohol' as part of their *Drinkwise* initiatives. A series of articles appeared in local newspapers, and a display stand in the town centre provided information and drew public attention.

b. The Health Promotion Unit in Bromsgrove, West Midlands worked with local police, road safety and environmental health departments, and the landlord of a local Free House, to promote the *Pub of Tomorrow*, which illustrated ways in which the venue where we drink can become a source of information and health education by providing information about units and recommended safer levels, as well as creating a pleasant and secure environment for women and families to enjoy their drinking.

Nationally, Tesco supermarkets are to be congratulated as initiators of a strategy to provide information for their customers about the alcohol strength of their own brand drinks (see also page 26). Packaging contains information about the strength of the drink, in ABV, and also the number of units of alcohol in each container.

A Mori poll (HEA/Mori 1990) found that the majority of women say they would prefer a system of labelling all drinks containers with the number of units of alcohol they contain, to the current confusing system of giving information on alcohol by volume.

Year-round action is essential. Although the *Drinkwise* campaign focuses on one day in June, the message is promulgated throughout the year, in a concerted approach which targets areas such as the workplace, schools and colleges, primary care and the leisure industry. Examples of some of these initiatives include:

a. The Environmental Health Training Unit of Liverpool City Council has recently co-ordinated an initiative involving the local Alcohol Advisory Service (MLCAAS), road safety, city and health authority personnel departments, the district health authority, family health services authority and the *Healthy Cities movement* to launch an initiative called 'Survive the Christmas Party'.

The initiative is part of a wider campaign planned for 1992, but is promoting alcohol awareness at Christmas by giving employees in the participating organisations information about units of alcohol and advice about sensible, safer drinking, particularly pertinent as the festive season approaches.

b. The Probation Service in Worcester have taken a lead in declaring 1991 'Sensible Drinking Year' in the counties of Herefordshire and Worcestershire. The campaign involves health education and health promotion, police, road safety, the alcohol advisory service, probation and local industries, including the Midland Counties' Brewers Association and in particular, the Herefordshire cider makers (Bulmers) to promote the sensible drinking message through several venues and activities throughout the year. The campaign is closing with a series of conferences around the counties of Herefordshire and Worcestershire, which will provide a forum to discuss how the momentum can be continued into the future.

These two examples are drawn from the broader context of health promotion activity, and as such do not specifically target the needs of women. One example of inter-agency activity, supported by funding from a scheme set up by the HEA to assist regional alcohol co-ordinators develop initiatives in their regions, and which does address the needs of women is a scheme in Wolverhampton. The health education department, in collaboration with the local alcohol advisory agency, *Aquarius*, has developed a training package for voluntary sector workers, who work particularly with women, to develop the skills needed to identify and support women who may be experiencing problems related to their own, or another persons' drinking.

Evaluation and funding

Evaluation and funding are crucial to the success of any initiative.

Evaluation

Feedback is essential to gauge the effectiveness of any initiatives undertaken, so it will be necessary to plan a system for monitoring and evaluating the work. For example, it is essential to know:

Whether the distribution used for leaflets and information are accessible to all women, or whether specific distribution points might be more acceptable and accessible to some women;

How selected messages are being received. Are they clear, intelligible, sensitive, meaningful; or are there better, more effective ways of expressing what you want to say?

What do women themselves want? Do they want more services? And what kind of service? Do they want specialist advice, information and counselling? Do they want women's casual groups, couple counselling, support for partners of drinkers?

The best location for your initiative. Is the best location an alcohol advisory service, or are other locations preferable: for example, a GP surgery, family planning service, community centre? Would a telephone help line be useful?

How to involve the local media (newspapers, local radio and television) and assess the contribution they can make to help target women with specific information;

And so on . . .

Funding

Always a difficult issue, funding is vital to the success of any activity, so it must be confronted, and included in the planning process of any activity or project. Initiatives mentioned earlier have been funded from a variety of sources, and, in most cases, from contributions from several different agencies. Mostly, these are sources of local funding: eg local authority, health authority, local industry (particularly if it is the location for a large national distributor) and local benefactors. But there is also some national money available, for which a local initiative might be appropriate. Alcohol Concern funding, under the Grants Scheme, already distinguishes the need to increase and improve services for women. The Health Education Authority has funding, as I have mentioned, distributable through regional alcohol co-ordinators for small-scale pilot projects, the Alcohol Education and Research Council can be approached to fund projects of a perhaps somewhat more academic nature. Getting agreed initiatives to improve service provision around the issues of women and alcohol on to local inter-agency agenda, may well produce the necessary funding from local sources.

Conclusion

The most effective action will be that which is responsive to expressed and perceived need, delivered in a context sensitive to local demography and integrated with local policy making, planning and resource allocation processes. Although national organisations have a role in providing a strategic lead and direction, the activity which affects people's everyday lives and makes a significant difference is going to occur at a local level—the level of districts or areas in planning and service provision terms.

Many examples exist of innovative and effective local action to respond to the needs of women for alcohol-related information and help. This chapter has attempted to provide a few guidelines for initiating local responses.

References

[1] Goddard, Eileen, *Drinking in England and Wales in the late 1980s*. An enquiry carried out by Social Survey Division of OPCS on behalf of the Department of Health in association with the Home Office.

[2] Government Circular on Alcohol Misuse HN(89)4; LAC(89)6; HN(FP)(89)4

[3] Health Education Authority National Drinkwise Day 1991 Evaluation Research

Further Reading

Philip Tether, and David Robinson. *Preventing Alcohol Problems—a Guide to Local Action*—Tavistock 1986.

David Robinson, Philip Tether and John Teller. *Local Action on Alcohol Problems*—Tavistock/Routledge 1989.

Addresses of National Agencies (mentioned in the text)

The National Community Health Resource and Womens' Health Network, 57 Chalton Street, London NW1 1HU. Tel (071) 383 3841

The National Association of Local Government Womens' Committees, (ref: Marilyn Taylor). Tel: (061) 274 3684

The National Alliance of Womens' Organisations, 279–281 Whitechapel Road, London E1 1BY. Tel: (071) 247 7052

Address for contact

Terry Lawrence, Regional Alcohol Misuse Co-ordinator, West Midlands Regional Health Authority, 1 Vernon Road, Edgbaston, Birmingham B16 9SA.

11 Alcohol: What can be done at work

MARGARET JOACHIM, Instructor in Leadership and Professional Development, EDs; Member City Women's Network

SUMMARY

Employers' attitudes towards the use of alcohol are changing. Many have introduced workplace policies. Initially, this was usually for safety reasons, but when policies apply to all staff, efficiency and health have become significant factors. Employee Assistance Programmes, offering help with a multiplicity of problems, are a further advance. They make it easier to help those (particularly women) who are not themselves heavy drinkers, but are victims of alcohol abuse by others. Supervisors and line managers should be encouraged to monitor performance and absence from work; staff who fall below accepted standards can then be referred for help. Even when a welfare or assistance programme exists, employers, managers and counsellors must still be aware of the particular problems facing women, and approach them sympathetically and realistically. The alcoholic or abused woman whose employer condones excessive drinking or believes that she can 'just stop' faces very real difficulties.

Background

Attitudes to drinking

Not so long ago, workmen in many trades were not merely expected, but actually encouraged, to drink at work. Some were even paid in beer. Fortunately, attitudes have changed, but there is still wide variation. Workplace 'alcohol culture' now ranges from a complete ban on alcohol for all staff, to acceptance that, 'so long as you don't fall down or start fighting, it doesn't matter'. A recent survey from the Health Education Authority (HEA)[1] quotes comments from:

a southern manufacturing company:

  'We did have one person with a drink problem. We found him asleep under the table';

a government department:

  'We don't like people to drink in the office after eight, but that's because they're afraid they might be sick on the carpets"; and

a southern service company:

  'The consumption of alcohol by employees during the working day, including lunchtimes, is most strongly discouraged as it is detrimental to good working practices.'

When there are rules, or a sensible drinking policy, they have often been introduced for safety reasons, and may only apply to certain groups of staff, for example, drivers, machine operators or engineers. In such cases, misuse of alcohol is considered to be a disciplinary matter. If found to have been drinking, an employee can reasonably expect, at the very least, to be sent home and to lose pay; a serious or repeated offence will result in dismissal.

More far-sighted organisations have realised that business efficiency and staff health are important considerations. They have formulated more comprehensive policies on workplace alcohol consumption, and have often linked them to some type of welfare programme to help employees with problems. These employers expect consistent and reliable performance from all staff, and find that it is usually more cost-effective to help solve problems than to dismiss staff and then to recruit and train replacements.

The hallmarks of good practice in today's working environment are:
- A firm, well-publicised workplace alcohol policy
- Regular reminders
- Workplace-based alcohol-awareness campaigns (home-grown, 'Drink-wise', or similar)
- Equal expectations of, and equal treatment for, all employees (ie, no differences between office and shopfloor, men and women, or office-based and field staff).

If alcohol is allowed at all in the workplace (for celebrations or special events), an adequate supply of other drinks will also be provided. If the company arranges outside events, the same will apply. Women particularly appreciate this, as very few want to feel forced to drink 'with the boys'.

Recognising the problem drinker at work

Even if there are policies, problems will still occur. Nobody wants to interfere with normal, moderate social drinking. However, the occasional person moves gradually from normal to excessive drinking. He or she may not drink at work, but colleagues and supervisors will begin to notice the effects of heavy evening and weekend drinking (though they may not realise that alcohol is the cause). They might cover up for the addict, trying to help by making or accepting excuses for absence, completing unfinished work, or condoning poor performance in the hope that matters will improve. This behaviour, known as 'enabling'[2], actually makes matters worse because it allows the addict to continue to refuse to acknowledge the problem.

The role of managers

Recent management practice has moved away from centralised staff welfare offices to which people with difficulties could go or be referred. Instead, supervisors and first-level managers have been given more responsibility for overall staff welfare. They are now expected to know their staff as individuals. In theory, they should be able to recognise a drink problem and take appropriate action. However:

- Managers vary in quality and interest level;
- No manager can be an expert in everything;
- Even the best manager will vary in reaction to different employees;
- Many employees find it hard to talk to any manager, however good;
- The manager's principal task is to get the job done;
- First-level managers have least experience, but are best-placed to identify problems.

Managers should not pry officiously into the private lives of their staff. Nor should they try to be amateur psychologists, however good their intentions. Their responsibility is to ensure that staff are performing well, and that work of an acceptable standard is being produced on schedule. What they can and should do, on a regular basis, is to monitor the performance and attendance of all their staff. Increasing absenteeism, particularly on Mondays and after holidays, and deteriorating or wildly erratic standards of work, are danger signals. They may result from too much alcohol, but they may also be caused by drug abuse, domestic or marital problems, or the onset of illness. Whatever the problem, by the time it has gone this far, the employee needs help. The manager must encourage him or her to go to the welfare officer or use the employee assistance programme. If persuasion does not work, direct referral may be necessary.

Employee Assistance Programmes

An **Employee Assistance Programme** (EAP) is a broadly-based counselling and welfare programme available in complete confidentiality to all employees of the sponsoring organisation. The first EAPs appeared in the 1940s in the USA; more recently, their use has spread around the western world, partly because multinational companies felt obliged to offer similar facilities to all staff. Most employers now recognise that their staff cannot leave problems at the door on the way into work, and pick them up again on the way home. Many problems are not work-related, but may affect job performance; if so, assistance should be given. Furthermore, an apparent job problem may be only one symptom of a more complex cause. Expert help may be required to approach and deal with real difficulty: Figure 11.1 outlines the EAP approach to such problems.

A good EAP fulfils the following requirements[3]:
- An employee's problem which does not affect job performance is no business of the employer;
- The decision to use the EAP is made by the employee;
- Staff must be able to seek help voluntarily, and in complete confidence;
- A supervisor or manager may only monitor work-related parameters. When performance or attendance is substandard, the position must be discussed with the employee, who should be helped to regain a satisfactory standard (within normal disciplinary policy);
- Referral for counselling is made strictly on the basis of declining work performance. (This means that the manager does not have to identify or assess personal problems).

Figure 11.1: *Model of Employee Assistance Programme*

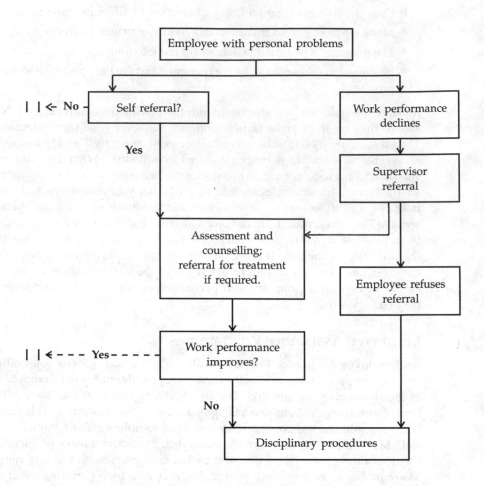

Source: Based on Buon and Compton, *J. Occup. Health Safety* Aust NZ 1990 (see reference 3).

The programme must be fully confidential, and it must not focus only on alcohol and drug problems. (If it does, people will soon work out what is the matter with anyone using the service.) Voluntary and compulsory referrals should be treated identically. For compulsory referrals, the manager may be told that the employee is continuing to use the programme, but no other details should be given unless the employee specifically requests this. An EAP is often linked to a health insurance scheme, and people may be referred onwards for medical, psychiatric or other treatment if necessary, either privately or via the NHS.

The aim of an EAP is to help the employee deal satisfactorily with the problem, and thus to become a reliable and productive person again. Many large industrial, commercial and public service organisations in the UK have already introduced such schemes, and have found them to be thoroughly worthwhile. Smaller organisations might not want to set up an in-house programme, but they can easily establish links with outside consultants who can be used when needed.

Women need special consideration

Women who misuse alcohol

Any policy or management practice must apply equally to both sexes, and women alcohol misusers can usually be spotted in the same way as men. However, because far fewer women drink to excess, many medium-sized and small organisations may never see a woman with this problem, or may be unwilling to recognise the true cause. The social stigma attached to women who drink too much may mean that the problem is covered up, or attributed to some other cause. Some women will have been prescribed tranquillisers by overworked GPs, which will exacerbate the problem but make it harder to identify. In any case, women who drink a lot frequently do so to escape from intolerable domestic, marital or financial pressures—drinking is a symptom of something else (see also page 13). Unless the cause is tackled and eliminated, drinking will continue.

The employer is faced with a difficult situation once a woman's drinking problem has been identified. Because women tolerate alcohol less well than men, they are likely to be more seriously ill by the time help is offered; they may already have been given inappropriate medical treatment. A woman may be unwilling to seek professional help because of fears that her children may be taken into care. In any case, when her family faces up to her problem they are likely to abandon her. Eight out of ten men with alcoholic female partners desert them; only one woman in ten leaves an alcoholic man. The woman will therefore need a strong support network for herself, as well as help with the children. Without this support, her chances of recovery are much less.

Women who are victims of alcohol abuse

A responsible employer will recognise that female staff are much more likely to be the victims of alcohol misuse by others than they are to be addicts themselves. Their partners or children can be violent, unreasonable or insulting when drunk. There may be grave financial problems because someone else in the family is buying large amounts of alcohol. The woman may be trying desperately to hold the family together, covering up for an alcoholic husband or trying to protect herself and the children from his violence. When at work, as well as showing poor or erratic performance, such a woman may display:

- Physical injury (often minor, but repeated)
- Depression, anxiety or agitation
- Absenteeism (to care for partner or children)
- Financial problems (borrowing money)

She probably needs very practical help to escape from the situation. Her partner needs professional help to confront his problem. It is usually quite useless to tell her to get her partner to seek help. He will be the last person to recognise that he needs it, and she may well be subjected to further violence if she tries. In any case, this is likely to create or reinforce her feeling that his drinking is her fault, and that it is her responsibility to take action.

This situation may create a real dilemma for the employer. He may be reluctant to help family members other than the employee, particularly when considerable time and expense is likely to be involved. What happens if the partner is unemployed, or is convinced that he would lose his job if his problem was revealed to his employer?

The unhelpful employer

Anyone with a serious drinking problem and an unsympathetic employer faces real difficulties. Revealing the problem may result in losing the job. Many people still think that an alcoholic can just stop drinking, and see failure as a lack of willpower rather than a symptom of disease. Smaller firms may be unable or unwilling to invest in any form of employee welfare, and may find it very hard to cope (for good business reasons) with an employee who is regularly absent for counselling or treatment. It may also be very hard to ensure confidentiality in a small company with a 'family' atmosphere.

Seeking help outside the workplace

In these circumstances, the alcoholic who is determined to conquer addiction will have to hope for a particularly sympathetic GP and a supportive family. Alcoholics Anonymous may meet locally and in the evening, but specialist treatment is not often available 'round the corner', and almost never outside normal working hours. For a woman with family and childcare responsibilities, as well as a job, it can be extremely difficult to work out how to manage everything. If there is no support at work, support from family and friends becomes even more vital.

Setting up workplace alcohol policies

The initial push for a workplace alcohol policy and some form of assistance programme need not originate from management. It can come from the staff committee, a trade union or a group of concerned staff who can show that such programmes are associated with tangible improvements in safety, efficiency, productivity and staff health. Early problem recognition can lead to higher retention of trained and skilled staff. There will be an overall improvement in loyalty and staff morale, because the organisation can be seen to be taking better care of its employees, and thus valuing them more highly.

Conclusion

The help that a woman (or man) can get at work depends entirely on the employer's attitude to alcohol abuse. Many organisations actively educate their staff, running alcohol-awareness campaigns linked to well-understood workplace alcohol policies. Some offer comprehensive Employee Assistance Programmes. Others still seem unaware of, or prefer to ignore, the damage that alcohol can do their staff and their efficiency.

Women with drinking problems are rare, but need particular support. Women who are victims of other people's drinking are much more common; they also need help and support, but many employers find this hard to provide. As with other drugs, misuse of alcohol creates problems for many people as well as the actual addict. In most cases, the employer can minimise his or her own difficulties and improve staff morale by taking a sympathetic approach to the welfare of each employee.

References

1 Health Education Authority, *Corporate Policies Towards Alcohol at the Workplace: Qualitative Research*, June 1991.

2 Brenda R Blair, MBA, *Supervisors and Managers as Enablers*. Johnson Institute Inc., Minneapolis, 1987.

3 T Buon and B Compton, The Development of Alcohol and other Drug Programs in the Workplace. *J Occup. Health Safety*—Aust NZ 1990, 6(4); pp265–277.

Address for contact

Margaret Joachim MA, PhD, 8 Newburgh Road, Acton, London W3 6DQ

12 Women and Alcohol

JOHN RAE, Director of the Portman Group, London

SUMMARY

The Portman Group is a drinks industry initiative against alcohol misuse. It was set up two years ago by the eight major drinks companies who realised that the industry had to become a major player in the task of combatting alcohol misuse. I recognise that there are bound to be some tensions between my brief, which is to combat misuse and to promote sensible drinking, and the legitimate commercial aims of the companies. But I think those tensions are worth resolving because I want to live in a mature society which knows how to handle alcohol without causing harm; and I do believe we shall never approach that ideal unless we have the genuine support and collaboration of the drinks industry. 'Fig leaves', 'acceptable faces', 'PR exercises', will not be enough.

Background

I speak first from the point of view of someone who understands the drink industry's position. But I also speak as someone who has spent most of his adult life in education and who believes that there is very much more that we can do to prevent people doing themselves or others harm by excessive or inappropriate drinking.

Marketing alcohol

In the last 20 years there have been a number of changes in the marketing of alcohol which may at first sight appear to have increased the pressure on women to drink.

1   **Alcohol is sold** in more outlets, such as supermarkets, that are user-friendly for women; and, what is often forgotten, in the supermarkets, alcohol is sold cheap. I must confess I regard with some irony, a supermarket which favours unit labelling to encourage the customer to monitor his or her consumption, but markets the alcohol on the basis of the more you buy the more money you save.

2   **Alcohol is drunk** in many more outlets that are user-friendly to women: wine, bars, brasseries, pubs that have lost their old male, spit-and-sawdust image.

3   **Alcohol advertising** has gone unisex. Whereas there used to be obviously male advertisements and only a few obviously female [remember Babycham and Cointreau], alcohol advertising, like most other advertising such as 'Do It Yourself' or motor cars, is now aimed at both sexes at a

particular 'life stage'; not at a particular sex. Double income and no kids (ie, 'dinkies') is the advertisers' favourite life stage. People in this category are targeted by many products: think of all those ads in which the young couple are stripping wallpaper or exchanging coffee. Alcohol advertising is just the same. Women are not targeted by alcohol advertising, but they are, with men, the target of life-stage advertising.

Women and alcohol

These changes might, as I say, appear to have increased the pressure on women to drink. But the fact is, that in the period when these apparent pressures have been effective (in the last 10–15 years) the percentage of women drinking above recommended sensible levels has not increased and, as the latest OPCS figures show, the actual alcohol consumption by women in the 18–24 age group, at which the advertisers aim, has fallen[1]. Greater temptation has not resulted in higher consumption. 'The good news, as the Health Education Authority reports, 'is that although working women now have more opportunities to socialise and drink and most do so, they remain sensible drinkers keeping well within health limits'[2].

This difference, between what we might expect to happen and what actually happened, suggests to me two conclusions: one speculative and one more down to earth.

The speculative conclusion is this. We have tended to assume that women's alcohol consumption was much lower than mens because there were cultural taboos against women's drinking. As those taboos broke down, it was assumed that women's alcohol consumption would increase as they tried to compete with men. But that has not happened. This makes me speculate about other reasons why women in Britain have been so moderate and sensible in their alcohol consumption. I am not dismissing cultural factors, only suggesting that they might not be the most important. Is it not possible that, while women are more vulnerable physiologically, they may be less vulnerable psychologically, to alcohol? If we say that women's low consumption is culturally dictated, aren't we ignoring the possibility that women are, and will always be, more sensible on most health matters and more aware of the risks of losing control? If that is true of women, might not the evolution of a more unisex social attitude to alcohol have a beneficial effect on the sometimes stupid, 'macho' drinking habits of men?

The more down-to-earth conclusion is intended to complement, not contradict it. There is one age group, and one age group only, in which the percentage of women drinking more than the recommended sensible level has risen. The age group is the 16 to 17-year-olds; and although the percentage has only risen from 7% to 8%[2], it should save us from complacency. Is there a delayed increase in the pipeline? That may be reading too much into one set of figures, but we should seize the opportunity, nevertheless, to put much more money and thought into alcohol education, particularly in the primary and early secondary years of schooling. I am amazed at the fragmentary, hit-and-miss, muddled nature of alcohol education in schools. There is even confusion about who is responsible: is it the Department of Health, which funds the Health

Education Authority, or the Department of Education and Science? This is not the place for a criticism of alcohol education, but my own view is that the Government should put much more emphasis on and provide much more funding for prevention and should ensure that one minister and one department is totally responsible for all alcohol education, in and out of school. And of course, for boys as well as girls.

Conclusion

There is no crisis in relation to women's alcohol consumption. Let's keep it that way and aim to reduce still further that small but *not* insignificant percentage of women who drink too much. A far greater emphasis on prevention is the most effective way to achieve this aim.

References

[1] OPCS, *Drinking in England and Wales in the late 1980s.*

[2] 'Women's Survey' in *Grapevine*, Health Education Authority Newsletter, 1991.

Address for contact

Dr John Rae, Director, The Portman Group, 2d Wimpole Street, London W1M 7AA

Appendix: Selected Bibliography and Resource List

General Reports on Alcohol

Alcohol—A Balanced View. Report of a working party of the Royal College of General Practitioners. Overview of alcohol related harm with guidelines for sensible drinking. RCGP 1986 £5.00

Alcohol. Our Favourite Drug. Report of a special committee of the Royal College of Psychiatrists. Overview of drinking, alcohol related harm and treatment, with guidelines for sensible drinking. Tavistock 1986 £9.99

Alcohol and the Public Health. The prevention of harm related to the use of alcohol. Study by a working party of the Faculty of Public Health Medicine of the Royal College of Physicians. Public health perspective on the prevention and treatment of alcohol related problems, including recommendations for action. Macmillan 1991 £8.99

Preventing Alcohol Problems. A guide to local action. Tether P and Robinson D. Practical guidelines to tackling various alcohol issues at a local level. Tavistock 1986 £4.95

Local Action on Alcohol Problems. D Robinson et al. Accounts of a variety of local prevention initiatives with the emphasis on practical advice. A follow-up to Preventing alcohol problems (see above). Tavistock & Routledge 1989 £4.95

Women and Drinking—specific

Statistical surveys

Women and drinking. OPCS 1985 Breeze E. HMSO £14.10

Drinking in England and Wales in the late 1980's. OPCS 1991 HMSO £12.50

Books/reports general

Alcohol Problems in Women. Wilsnack S C. et al 1984 Guildford Press New York.

Black women and dependency: a report on drug and alcohol use. DAWN 1988 £2.00*

Say When. Everything a woman needs to know about alcohol and drinking problems. Kent R. undated Sheldon Press £4.95

Women and Alcohol. Camberwell Council on Alcohol 1980 Tavistock £7.99

Women and Alcohol. A review of international literature on the use of alcohol by females. Plant M. 1990 WHO report EUR/ICP/ADA 020.

Women, Drinking and Pregnancy. Plant M. 1987 Tavistock £10.99

Women Under the Influence. Alcohol and its impact. McConville B. 1991 Grafton £4.99

Women and Dependency. Women's personal accounts of drug and alcohol problems. DAWN 1986 RAP Ltd Rochdale £2.50*

Booklets, leaflets, factsheets

Women and Drinking factsheet. Alcohol Concern 1988 £0.15 (305 Gray's Inn Rd WC1X)

Factfile: Women and Drink. Drinkwise, HEA. 1991

Women's Health and Alcohol broadsheet. WHRRIC. £0.30 (52 Featherstone St EC1Y)

Black women and alcohol. DAWN leaflet.* £0.35

Women and Drinking. 1990. HEA leaflet.

Women and Drinking. DAWN leaflet* £1.00

HEA produces a comprehensive resource list of alcohol education materials available, including publications for professionals, posters, and films/videos. The above represent a selection from this list which can be obtained from the HPIC, Hamilton House, Mabledon Place, London WC1H (free).

HEA materials are available from District Health Promotion Units or from HEA Distribution Department, Hamilton House, Mabledon Place, WC1H

*now available from GLAAS, 30–31 Great Sutton Street EC1V

Printed in the United Kingdom for HMSO
Dd294857 7/92 C15 G531 10170

CAREERS IN TECHNICAL THEATER

MIKE LAWLER

ABERDEEN COLLEGE
GORDON LIBRARY

ALLWORTH PRESS
NEW YORK

Portions of this book have been adapted from a series on technical theater jobs originally published in *Dramatics*.

For additional information about this book and the author, visit *www.mikelawler.com.*

11 10 09 08 07   5 4 3 2 1

Published by Allworth Press
An imprint of Allworth Communications, Inc.
10 East 23rd Street, New York, NY 10010

Cover design by Derek Bacchus
Interior design by Mary Belibasakis
Page composition/typography by Integra Software Services, Pvt., Ltd., Pondicherry, India
Cover photo by Paul Godwin

ISBN-13: 978-1-58115-485-6
ISBN-10: 1-58115-485-2

Library of Congress Cataloging-in-Publication Data

Lawler, Mike, 1973-
  Careers in technical theater / Mike Lawler.
    p. cm.
  ISBN-13: 978-1-58115-485-6
  ISBN-10: 1-58115-485-2
1. Theaters—Stage-setting and scenery—Vocational guidance. 2. Stage management—Vocational guidance. I. Title.

  PN2091.S8L299 2007
  792'.0293–dc22

                                                                    2007006840

CONTENTS

Introduction

PART I: Management

PART II: Scenery

PART III: Audio/Visual

PART IV: Costumes

PART V: Other Careers and Considerations

APPENDIXES

ACKNOWLEDGMENTS

◆

First, I'd like to thank the theater professionals who collaborated with me on this project. Each and every technician, designer, and manager featured in this book is a consummate professional, and this project would never have happened without them. Of special note are those who offered me their unique wisdom with enthusiasm, teaching me much about theater and art along the way, including: Eric Bass, Jim Guy, Rosemary Ingham, Lindsay Jones, Rick Thomas, and Susan Tsu. With this first round of thanks, I would also like to thank Don Corathers of *Dramatics* magazine, who first saw potential in this idea, as well as the other editors at *Dramatics* who did such justice to the articles on which much of this book is based.

Natalie George is another pro who appears within these pages, and she deserves her own acknowledgement. Her contribution to this book is really immeasurable, considering that she seemed to make it a point to keep me employed in the theater so that I could keep making money while trying to peck away at "my book." Her friendship and passion for theater have also helped me keep up my own creative resolve.

I'd also like to acknowledge Cindy Poulson, a veteran stage manager who helped me understand stage management in a way that made it possible to write about it concisely. Poulson, a longtime professor of theater at the University of Wisconsin-Milwaukee, passed away in the summer of 2006, as I worked on the book. She will be missed very much both within and outside of the theater community of which she was such an active member.

There have been many people I have learned from in my theater life, but a handful of them stand out above the rest, both for their contribution to my own growth and experience and for their superb knowledge, professionalism, and dedication to the theater. Those who have encouraged and taught me throughout my years in theater—in every regard, for I believe the best people in theater have broad experience and education in the art of theater—are, in order of appearance: Bob Brigham, Scott Grim, Richard Davis, and Bill DuWell.

Finally, I must mention the people who have supported me unconditionally in my personal life. My father, Jack, was always accepting of my passion for theater and the arts. A fairly conservative man born during the Depression, he could have easily chastised my pursuit of the theater (and writing) but instead encouraged me, and for that I am forever grateful. He passed in 2006, as I worked on this book, and his life and death have taught me much about the joy of life as well as the meaning and purpose we can find in our work. He also demonstrated how a person's simple gestures of kindness and understanding can change life for the better one moment at a time. I will miss him always.

My brothers and my sister have also been consistently supportive, even when they did not readily understand what it was I did in theater, and no matter how poor I was. (I hope this book gives them a better idea of what I've been doing all this time.) My extended family members (Charlie, Marianne, Ani, the Pattons, Scherner-de la Fuentes, Dixons, Griffiths, Waltons, and Weithes—among others) provided places to grow as a person and artist, never judging, always loving. In addition, I would like to thank my closest friends, the people who never pressured me and encouraged whatever wacky idea I may have had on any given day, including Jamie, Lisa, Matt, Reina, Robbie, Satia, and Tara. Their friendship has been invaluable to me.

In conclusion, I would like to say thank you to my partner in life, my best friend, and my wife, Dawn. Her undying support and encouragement has made this project (and so many others) possible. I love you.

INTRODUCTION

◆

Not long ago I was running a show that demanded very little attention from me. In fact, my primary duty was the maintenance and operation of two prop guns during the second act of a rather long Shakespearean play. This left lots of time to do nothing but wait for the second act to roll around. One night, while sitting in a production office in the backstage area, I heard a faint knock on the door. Turning around, I saw a young actor standing in the open doorway.

"Do you know where Ralph is?" he asked.

"The stage manager?" I said, sure that he was looking for someone other than the person currently at work in the theater's booth.

"Yes," he said. "Where can I find him?"

I laughed, not sure if the actor was pulling my leg. He stared blankly back at me. It wasn't a joke. "He's in the booth," I said, "calling the show."

"Oh," he said, unmoved by my response.

"Do you know what a stage manager does?" I asked, genuinely curious.

"Um, well, I guess they sort of keep the show together," he said, sounding as though he hoped he had arrived at the correct answer.

When he failed to supply a more specific response, I briefly explained what stage managers do during the performance of a show and advised the actor to look for Ralph during intermission or after the show had ended. I admit I was astonished that an actor who, I learned later, had recently graduated with a degree in theater did not understand such a basic element of production procedure.

This book is—in part, at least—for that young theater artist and others like him. It is a reference tool for those learning about the ins and outs of theater, as much as a guide for people seeking a career within it. With that in mind, I have this much to say about the information contained between these covers: Theater is art, and art, by necessity, is fluid, malleable, flexible, and adaptable. Therefore, while I have attempted to pin down each career or specialty in very precise and pragmatic terms, it is impossible to do so with complete confidence. In professional theater, you will find a world made up of innovative and creative individuals who perpetually shape theater in ways most conducive to their talents, as well as their limitations—especially those of their checkbook. In other words, it is common to encounter folks who perform not just the work outlined in any one specific chapter that follows, but also endless combinations: production managers who also do the work of a technical director; technical directors who freelance as designers; designers who work as technicians; and technicians who act or run the box office too.

Another aspect of this book that I believe is important is the information regarding the financial side of theater. As every professional and teacher featured in these pages will tell you, it is essential for students to become educated on the fiscal realities of living as a theater artist, rather than facing a litany of misinformation from parents, friends, and even teachers. I have attempted to take some of the mystery out of what people working in tech theater actually earn—and what you can expect to earn working in a given field. The potential may be limitless, but shouldn't people be given the background to make an informed decision about what type of work they want to do and where they want to do it? The romantic vision of the starving artist usually fades as we age, and the dreams of youth begin to be approached in a more pragmatic way. That doesn't mean they must be left unrealized, however. Money matters. And, increasingly, so do all of the other items that represent value for an employee or freelancer: health benefits, vacation time, and retirement options.

In the time it has taken me to compile and write this book, I have witnessed a handful of layoffs at theaters around the country (including a couple of folks featured in this book), as well as the unfortunate (and some might say unnecessary) closing of a prominent producing theater in the city in which I lived as I wrote this book. These events, while discouraging—especially for someone writing about the different ways to make a living in tech theater—are merely bumps in the road for theater in America. Such bumps may never disappear, and the only way they will be reduced is through the diligence of the next generation of theater artists, administrators, artistic leaders, technicians, and support staff. It is only with dedicated people, committed to theater in America, its accessibility and progress, that more and more people will be able to make a decent living doing what they love to do. Their dedication, however, must extend beyond the art itself and into the lives of the artists creating every facet of it—theater artists must learn better to look out for each other and recognize that we are all, as they say, in it together.

I'd like to make a note of my own small contribution to the information included here. Over the course of about three months in 2006, I conducted a confidential online survey that I call the "Tech Theater Earnings Survey." I contacted over one thousand technical theater pros and asked them to fill out a basic survey consisting of seven simple questions. The survey was by invitation only, in order to prevent those who may have stumbled upon the Web site from inputting false or misleading information. The survey received responses from theater pros in fields ranging from company management to prop artisans and master electricians. Nearly every category found in this book was covered—albeit some areas were blessed with more respondents than others. This is, in part, because many professional fields are more likely to be saturated with freelance artists and are not necessarily full-time staff positions. For this reason—and many others—it can be difficult to arrive at standardized, usable results.

For me, an important and revealing indicator in the survey was the final question, in which each respondent was asked to rate his income as "below average," "average," or "above average." While this is a purely subjective question, I felt that it would help to gauge the respondents' own views of their income. In this way it revealed not necessarily whether or not the respondents' income was indeed average, above, or below, but rather their perception of such. This is an important distinction that I think reveals a great deal about the situation, giving us information about how the professionals are paid versus how they think they should be paid.

There were about 400 respondents, of which approximately 350 provided usable data. While it may not be considered a scientific, concrete calculation of the realities of technical theater work, it is nevertheless a rather informative survey, giving both the working pro and the student a general idea of the income of a variety of career areas. I was pleased with the honesty of the survey participants and hope that the Tech Theater Earnings Survey will provide the reader with at least a glimpse of the real-world earnings of technical theater artists.

Fortunately, the theater community also has the Theatre Communications Group (TCG) to help us along on these fronts by conducting thorough research and providing us with useful, tangible information on all sorts of areas of theater. TCG's annual reports on income and benefits are a great resource for determining the realities of today's theater. It's also great fodder for effecting change in the future.

Labor organizations such as Actors' Equity Association (AEA), United Scenic Artists (USA), and the International Alliance of Theatrical Stage Employees (IATSE) have also been a focus of my research, and you will find that minor debates about their role in the business of theater crop up from time to time in certain areas of this book; however, it is difficult in a book of this kind to fully explore the sometimes odd and seemingly arbitrary decisions made in the theater community about which artists deserve to be represented by a labor organization. The worldviews (and industry standards) that inform these decisions are interesting, though, and the fate of theater artists are affected greatly by them. The viewpoint of technicians and artists on the subject of unions in the performing arts deserves inclusion where the featured pros of this book have found it of note, and this is the reason for its occasional appearance within these pages.

Collaboration is another key concept visited here. It is brought up time and again by the professionals interviewed for this book, and if you read each chapter it may seem that the notion of collaboration and its essential nature in theater is something that you have been beaten about the head with. For this I apologize, but it simply cannot be said enough. For the student about to embark on a hopeful life in the theater, it is an idea—in fact, a sometimes unwelcome necessity—that must be considered and confronted. In my talks with Rosemary Ingham, a talented designer and the wise author of books on costuming, she told me simply that if you are a creative person who thrives while working on solitary projects, the theater is not for you. It is a point that cannot be made strongly enough. But, enough of that.

There are areas of technical theater so convoluted and difficult to categorize that the question of their inclusion in this book was taken very seriously. While the specialties of wigs and makeup are elaborate art forms in their own right, it was at first thought that perhaps they should be lumped into the costume shop section of the book. But after investigating further, I realized that within theater the areas of wigs and makeup are so specialized and essential to so many theater productions that they deserved a more thoughtful presentation. However, depending on whom you speak with, it could be argued that these are such specialized areas that it is rare for wig masters and makeup artists to earn their living exclusively in the theater. Because of this rarity, and for other reasons, it felt odd to place them amid an array of specialties in which one could pursue one's passion for theater without feeling compelled to seek work in other areas of entertainment. This is not to pass judgment on such artists—for artists they are indeed—but rather an attempt to stay true to my goal for this book: to provide for future theater artists a guide to the theater, not a guide for dalliances with theater while supporting oneself making commercials in Los Angeles, films in New York City, or industrials in Seattle.

In closing, it might be appropriate after all of this talk of work and earning a living to say a few encouraging words. To do so, I'll mention an unlikely person, a person I interviewed for this book and who was laid off from his full-time staff position at a League of Resident Theatres (LORT) theater just before I spoke with him. Though this particular person has not been included in the book, I believed that his predicament was of special note, providing needed insight into the difficult nature of making a living in theater. So, we went ahead with the scheduled interview, and our discussion was enlightening and inspiring. He is a perfect example for the parents and other concerned folks that fear for the future of the young, hopeful theater artist in their lives. *You'll never make a living in the theater!* I know this admonishment well because I received it repeatedly when I was young. But not from everyone. And even the laid-off theater artist won't go so far as to say that. He knows what it means to have a passion for theater. He knows that for those of us that truly love the theater, there is always a way.

PART I MANAGEMENT

◆

I find it vital that any manager can speak intelligently about the art
and be able to respond to it wisely.

—PAUL HENGESTEG,
company manager, Shakespeare Theatre Company

My employees usually know more about their working conditions
than I do. If I don't listen to them, I'll never be able to do my job, and
in the end, neither will they.

—MICHAEL BROH,
production manager, American Players Theatre

A manager is a manager is a manager, right? Well, not if you're referring to managers in the theater. While they do conform to the general idea of most other managers, theater managers, like stage managers, production managers, and company managers are different—and not just because they're theater folk. You can look at the quotes above for an example of how they are the same *and* how they're different.

Production manager Michael Broh discusses schedules with American Players Theatre production stage manager Evelyn Matten. (Photograph by Sara Stellick.)

Broh demonstrates the traditionally ideal managerial outlook—one concerned with the conditions of the employees in his charge. Hengesteg, a company manager for almost a decade, shows us how theater managers must be in touch with the art they serve and thus how they differ from the kind of manager you would find lurking around your cubicle. It is the theater managers' devotion to the art form they make possible that distinguishes them from other managers. It wouldn't be a stretch to say that the people featured in this section are as much informed by the theater as the theater is informed by them. Just check out what Josh Friedman, another production manager, has to say at the beginning of the first chapter.

This section contains only the three technical theater careers mentioned above, but this shouldn't be taken as a sign that there are only three management positions in all of technical theater. In fact, you will likely find within these pages several careers that entail a great number of management duties, but the three careers highlighted here in the management section are first and foremost managers of people and information.

Each of these managers is responsible for a very different type of management, as you will see. They all, however, must manage people, and anyone pursuing similar career tracks must develop very good people skills in addition to any other expertise necessary to execute the job. Ask any manager, in theater or out, how important people skills are, and he will give you an earful on the subject, I assure you.

1

PRODUCTION MANAGER

A strong understanding of the artistic process allows a production manager to effectively communicate and understand the issues, pressures, and thought processes of directors, designers, and staff.

—JOSH FRIEDMAN,
production manager, Alley Theatre

A reliable way to determine what theater professionals actually do is to ask them what they say when their second cousin from Peoria approaches them at a family reunion and asks, "What d'ya do for a livin'?" Michael Broh, production manager of American Players Theatre since 2000, has his own canned response. "I say, 'I'm in charge of all the backstage stuff at the theater—you know, like costumes, sets, lighting, sound, props—that sort of thing,'" he says. "Usually, that's all someone wants to know. Then they start asking me about actors." Broh does not exaggerate with his cousin. Each and every person who is a part of the production team, including all of the areas Broh mentions, is under the jurisdiction of the production manager (PM).

Production manager Josh Friedman working the phone—something PMs do frequently.

In short, there is no technical theater without production managers. Even the smallest of theater companies has someone who does the job, though that person may have a different title. Sometimes the title is operations manager, director of production, production coordinator, or supervisor. In some cases, technical directors are responsible for what will be described here as the duties of a production manager. The thing is, the work a PM does must be done by someone, even if no one in the building is called the production manager.

"WAIT FOR THINGS TO GO WRONG"

"I do the stuff that our producing **artistic director** should not be bothered with," explains Rafael Castanera, production manager of Arkansas Repertory Theatre in Little Rock. "I really play the role of liaison between our administration and our production staff," he says. As with most technical theater careers, the duties of a production manager vary from venue to venue, depending on the size, location, and prestige of the theater, among other considerations.

Generally, production managers have a hand in most areas of a theater's operation but focus primarily on keeping the production team afloat. They coordinate and track budgets, labor, and staff to ensure that every technical aspect of a production and the entire season happens on schedule and within budget in a safe, reasonable manner. They are typically responsible for hiring technical staff, negotiating and drawing up contracts, creating and maintaining production budgets, and scheduling both personnel and stage use. As part of a collaborative effort involving designers, directors, the technical director, the administrative team, and the artistic director, they must decide, on the basis of reasons including safety, cost, and technical feasibility, which technical aspects of a production can actually happen. Ultimately, they are responsible for these decisions because they alone are aware of every angle: money, time, safety, quality, and—did I say this already?—money.

The modus operandi of a typical professional production manager is quite simple, according to Fran Brookes, who was until recently the production manager of Arden Theater Company, a classical **LORT** theater in Philadelphia. "Prepare as best you can," he says, "and wait for things to go wrong." Brookes is being candid when he says this, but realistic in his admission that something will probably not work out as planned. The skilled production manager learns how to adapt to the ever-changing realities of producing the technical side of theater.

For some production managers, working double duty as the technical director makes the job even more pressure-filled. At Virginia Stage Company, Stevie Dawson worked nonstop in her capacity as both PM and technical director. "It was not unusual for me to go from 9 A.M. to 6 P.M. without a pause in the meetings, phone calls, e-mails, and just plain questions," she says. "That means that any work that required concentration couldn't even begin until the business day was over and the building had begun to empty out." Some theater companies must structure their production team this way in order to work within their operating budget; however, this is uncommon among theaters above a certain level of financial ability, and Virginia Stage seems rare in this situation.

FROM STAGE TO PRODUCTION

It may seem odd to compare the duties and outlooks of people in such diverse areas as stage management, production management, and even company management by lumping them together under the broad umbrella of management, but anecdotal evidence seems to suggest that many production managers begin their careers in theater in stage management.

"Production managers are in the middle of facilitating a production process in the same way stage managers are the pivot to facilitate the rehearsal and performance process," explains Josh Friedman, the longtime PM of Indiana Repertory Theatre in Indianapolis and now the production manager of the Alley Theatre.

Broh, who was a stage manager for Second City in Chicago before pursuing a graduate degree at Yale, believes that the transition from stage to production management is a natural one. "Stage managers tend to be people that have brains built for organizing," he says. "I think many stage managers see these traits as being valuable in a production manager, and therefore see the job as something they could easily transition to." The career change is understandable, considering the odd hours put in by most stage managers. "The reasons for the transition tend to be about someone looking for more nights and weekends off, to spend more time at home, perhaps to raise a family," Broh says. A career trajectory that begins with stage management and leads to a position as a production manager may be a very desirable one, considering the issues of working hours and family time.

Another trait that is common to both stage and production managers is communication—good, open, and honest communication. One of the primary functions of a stage manager is facilitating information that pertains to the production, and a production manager must be good at distributing and coordinating information, too. For a PM, that generally entails the information for the production that is rehearsing or running, in addition to all the productions in the season and shows that are coming up in future seasons. As a result, production managers tend to think and talk a lot about how they handle the communication aspect of the job.

The notion of honesty and openness is critical. "Be honest and direct with every-one," Friedman advises. "You need to first acknowledge that everyone involved has a stake in the project and feels compelled to do their best work, then face the reali-ties of time, money, and creativity to get the best results."

"The best approach is honesty and transparency," says Broh. "Most people respond very well to honesty." Furthermore, production managers are privy to infor-mation of all sorts, much more than any one technician, director, or designer on the production team, and when one is responsible for keeping track of such a wealth of information regarding a show, honesty becomes a necessity.

COLLABORATING: THE ARTIST WITHIN

There are technical positions that theater folks consider artistic and those that they don't. Designers, for instance, are in the art camp. So, obviously, are scenic artists. The line gets blurry when talking about scenic carpenters and costumers because they actually build many of the beautiful things seen on stage. More easily placed across the line in the tech camp are management positions, and many designers do not hesitate to make that line clear. The necessary division between creation and technical implementation is a subject usually arrived at when a person in a manage-ment (or other nonartistic) position injects a bit of artistic input where it is not welcome. Ask a production manager—or stage manager—what he thinks, and you will likely get a very reasoned response. "I think everyone in the process should have a say," claims Brookes, before concluding that "one should be judicious about when one's opinion is voiced."

According to Friedman, the best work is always accomplished through fair and open collaboration. "The key to a successful team approach is for everyone to have input and for everyone to respect the decision-making responsibilities of each job," he says. "In other words, it's good to make suggestions to the set designer, but you have to respect that at the end of the day they make the decision."

Broh, one of the most reasoned and straightforward people I have ever known in professional theater, is characteristically precise when addressing the matter of managers and artistic input. "I do feel that a producing theater has a responsibility to evaluate shows aesthetically," he says. "Ideally, the artistic director is the person vested with that responsibility." For his part, Broh knows that his job goes beyond the aesthetics of the show. "It is my responsibility to evaluate if we can do it, if it is on schedule, and if we did it well," he explains. "It is not my job to say if it's ugly or not."

Understanding the acceptable bounds of a manager's input is critical to achieving cohesion among the production and design teams, and it is important to remember that without the pragmatic approach of production and stage managers, many art institutions, such as regional theaters, would simply cease to exist.

◇✦◇

Spotlight on a Pro

Michael Broh, production manager, American Players Theatre, 2000–present

Under Pressure

For a production manager, the ability to focus on details while remaining acutely aware of the (very) big picture is critical. The sheer number of decisions that need to be made in differing areas can be overwhelming for novice production managers and, at times, can push even the veteran beyond the ceiling of acceptable levels of stress. The best managers have the ability to deal with the stress of working with a multitude of personality types and being the final decision maker.

Production manager Michael Broh in his office at American Players Theatre.

Broh was a stage manager before returning to school to earn his MFA in technical design and production from Yale. His most noteworthy stage management gig might have been his six years with the notorious improv group Second City, in Chicago. During his time with Second City, Broh learned a lot about dealing with the stress of live performance. It also helped teach him how to be a decisive leader.

"One of my myriad of responsibilities as a stage manager was to take the lights out at the end of improvised scenes," he says. "This is an extremely high-pressure responsibility. If a scene is going well and you miss a potential out, then a scene will likely begin to fail," he explains. The other side of the coin was taking the lights out too early, disappointing the audience and the actors if the skit had potential left unrealized—a nerve-wracking responsibility. "I think that experience helped me to become more comfortable with my decision making and allowed me to take some pressure off of myself for self-preservation," he says.

◇✦◇

PATHS TO A CAREER AS A PRODUCTION MANAGER

Considering the essential nature of production management and the growing number of universities offering programs of study in theater management and technical production, it would seem that preparing for such a career would be relatively straightforward. And it can be. Having a solid background in theater is essential, but beyond that anything goes. There are many production managers who have little expertise in technical production, and many whose primary focus—in practical experience and training—has been in technical direction and design. Although there are many college programs offering concentrations in production and theater management, a general degree in theater arts may be just as desirable for a hopeful PM—especially as an undergraduate degree.

Castanera, for instance, grew up in Puerto Rico and came to the United States to study theatrical design at the University of Tennessee at Knoxville. His career took him to New York City, where he freelanced, designing window dressings, building costumes in a large shop, and working in film. "I always knew that I could do certain things," he says. "I just needed the opportunity." Eventually, recalling his roots in theater and longing to return to them, he found his present position—his first as a production manager for a theater. "The hardest thing about getting a job like this," he tells me, "is getting the first one."

There is also a large luck factor involved. Dawson may be the prime example of being in the right place at the right time. "I fell into it, more or less," she says of her dual role with Virginia Stage. In the midst of a complete artistic and business change, the production manager decided to leave only a few months into Dawson's stint as technical director. Dawson was offered the chance to take on the duties of the production manager. "The company was not, at that point, in a financial position to hire a new production manager, so I took on those responsibilities." Her situation was uncommon, of course, and most production managers come at the job in a more traditional fashion. But some theaters, especially small companies, combine the duties of the traditional technical director and production manager into one position without creating a special title for such an overworked person.

As advanced training in technical theater and design become more prevalent, there is no shortage of graduate programs for those wishing to pursue production management (see sidebar on page 9). But there is more than one way for a student or young technician to climb the ranks to management, and successful production managers have an earful of advice for up-and-coming managers.

"Work around a bit," says Friedman. "You need to understand what an electrician does, what a painter does, and what a TD does." Friedman is being brief, of course, because a production manager should understand each area of technical theater at least well enough to communicate effectively with the specialists doing the work. A broad base of experience coupled with the traits of a good manager are also essential. "Pay attention to the gripes you have as a technician and address them as a manager," says Broh. "Above all, remember that there is no such thing as being in charge," he says. "You just spend less of your time answering to your supervisors and more time answering to your staff."

Job Description

A production manager's work begins when he takes the job, and it doesn't end until there's a break in the season. It is much easier to speak of process in the case of theater artists that work on a show-to-show basis, such as designers, but for PMs the work overlaps in complex ways that are hard to pick apart. If we are to try to break a PM's job down into smaller bites, we should consider a production manager's approach to a single production.

The PM's first step, as that of any theater artist, would be to familiarize himself with the script. This enables him to communicate intelligently with any and all personnel working on the show, including the director, designers, technical director, costumers, and even performers if necessary. The PM will then discuss with the director and/or artistic director what their thoughts on design are for the production, so that the PM can help locate and hire designers (and any other personnel that might be necessary, including specialists) who best suit the project.

Production managers will then contract with any and all personnel needed for the production who do not already work for the theater. Once he has hired them, the PM will begin to meet with his staff and those hired on, like designers, in order to create schedules for completing each phase of production, including design, build, and install time. Coordinating schedules is a big part of a production manager's job, since he is the one person who has an eye on the overall project from beginning to end.

He will continue to stay in close contact with each and every member of the production team, coordinating budgets and assisting in technical areas when obstacles arise in the planned course. Once the show hits the stage and enters the **tech** process, the PM (or assistant PM) will be on hand to make sure that each component of the technical side of the production goes smoothly.

WHAT DO PRODUCTION MANAGERS EARN?

Although many professional production managers are former AEA stage managers, the union does not extend beyond actors and stage managers. For this reason, determining a profile of average earnings for production managers is a little tricky. The nature of production management dictates a wage that is generally superior to that of any other staff production team member; however, many production managers are the entire production team. As you can see in the table below, fifty-four production managers responded to my Tech Theater Earnings Survey, and, according to the results, they appear to be on the high end

TABLE 1.1. EARNINGS FOR PRODUCTION MANAGERS		
Total number of production managers surveyed = 54		
Where the production managers surveyed are working		
Type of theater	*Number*	*Percentage*
Academic	2	4%
Broadway	-	-
COST	-	-
Dinner	-	-
LORT	20	37%
Off-Broadway	1	2%
Opera	1	2%
Regional	23	43%
Resident	-	-
SPT	1	2%
Other	6	11%
How much production managers are earning		
Income range	*Number*	*Percentage*
Less than $10,000	-	-
$10,000–$20,000	2	4%
$20,000–$35,000	13	24%
$35,000–$50,000	14	26%
$50,000–$75,000	17	31%
$75,000–$100,000	7	13%
More than $100,000	1	2%
How production managers view their income		
Perception	*Number*	*Percentage*
Below average	14	26%
Average	28	52%
Above average	12	22%

Source: 2006 Tech Theater Earnings Survey.

of the earning scale of regional and LORT theaters. A slight majority of those responding reported an annual income between $50,000 and $75,000, with about 15 percent earning in excess of $75,000 per year. Over half of responding production managers believed that their annual income was average for a PM in a similar position, which is an indication that the results below may demonstrate typical statistics for earnings potential in the field of production management—especially in regional, nonprofit theater. (For definitions of the types of theaters listed see the glossary.)

FIVE SCHOOLS OFFERING PROGRAMS IN PRODUCTION MANAGEMENT OR SIMILAR FIELDS

AUBURN UNIVERSITY
  Degrees offered: BFA in Production Management
  http://media.cla.auburn.edu/theater/index.cfm
  Contact: Robin Jaffe, jaffero@auburn.edu

CAL ARTS
  Degrees offered: MFA in Management
  www.calarts.edu/schools/theater/programs
  Contact: Jillian Rothschild, Admissions, jroths@calarts.edu

CARNEGIE MELLON UNIVERSITY
  Degrees offered: BFA in Production/Stage Management
              MFA in Production/Stage Management
  www.cmu.edu/cfa/drama
  Contact: David Boevers, db4r@andrew.cmu.edu

EMERSON COLLEGE
  Degrees offered: MFA in Production/Stage Management
  www.emerson.edu/performing_arts/index.cfm
  Contact: Timothy Jozwick, timothy_jozwick@emerson.edu

UCLA
  Degrees offered: MFA in Design with concentration in Production Management
              and Technology
  www.tft.ucla.edu/dot_mfa
  Contact: Dan Ionazzi, dan@geffenplayhouse.com

RESOURCES FOR PRODUCTION MANAGERS

Books

Glover, Thomas J. *Pocket Ref.* Littleton, CO: Sequoia Publishing, 2002.

This compact booklet has all of the answers—from the physical properties of air to the tempering color of steel—and it is small enough to fit in your shirt pocket.

Rossol, Monona. *Health and Safety Guide for Film, TV, and Theater.* New York: Allworth Press, 2000.

A good resource for production managers to have on hand.

Sammler, Ben, and Don Harvey, eds. *Technical Design Solutions for the Theater.* 2 vols. Boston: Focal Press, 2002.

A collection of articles from Yale School of Drama's indispensable publication, *Technical Brief* (see below).

Periodicals

Live Design—www.livedesignonline.com

The convergence of three magazines that covered different aspects of live entertainment technology: *Entertainment Design, Lighting Dimensions,* and *Staging Rental Operations.*

Technical Brief—www.technicalbrief.org

A publication of the Yale School of Drama, *Technical Brief* provides articles that explain technical design solutions implemented by technical directors and other technical theater professionals.

Internet

"By far the most used reference material in my office is the Internet."
—Michael Broh, production manager, American Players Theatre

www.foghouse.com/PMForum—The online home of the Production Manager's Forum, this site can be used by professional production managers of LORT, regional, and educational theaters. The site features a member directory that lists dozens of theaters around the country with the contact information of their production managers—a great networking resource. The forum also has a great links page, full of useful online resources.

www.theatreproduction.com—The home of e-production, a free software program designed to facilitate the paperwork of a typical production manager or stage manager.

www.livedesignonline.com—The relatively new periodical *Live Design* has spawned a Web site that is full of information for the theater professional.

2

STAGE MANAGER

A good stage manager knows when to shut up.

—RICHARD COSTABILE,
production stage manager, Hal Holbrook's *Mark Twain Tonight!*

Years ago I was crewing a show in one of these big roadhouses in Southern California—the kind with a maze of basement-level service hallways and anonymous areas that provide space for dressing rooms, laundry rooms, greenrooms, trap rooms, and a myriad of others. The stage manager (SM) asked me politely to go down into the maze to buy a soda from a vending machine for him.

Student stage manager B. Elizabeth Manning at the helm.

"What do you want?" I asked.

"Um, I don't know, surprise me," he said.

As I wandered through the seemingly endless halls below the stage searching for a soda machine, a booming voice came through the PA speakers that hovered above me.

"This is God," it said, "and I want a diet Pepsi."

It was, of course, the stage manager. I learned early that respecting and obeying the stage manager goes a long way whether you are an actor, stagehand, designer, or director, but most SMs would never go as far as likening themselves to a god. Nor should they. In fact, stage managers will be the first to tell you that while their responsibilities are immense, they are as fallible and likely to mess up as the rest of us.

A MANAGER FOR THE STAGE

Stage managers, as a group, find it difficult to fully detail what their duties actually are because they do *everything*. "I am a manager like any company has a manager, only I do it for the stage," explains Michele Kay, a professional SM who teaches stage management at the University of Cincinnati. Lawrence Stern, author of *Stage Management*, a manual for stage managers and theater students first released in 1974 and now in its eighth edition, describes the stage manager as the person who ensures that "things run smoothly onstage and backstage, before, during, and after the production." Finding your way past vague explanations is tricky when it comes to a typical professional stage manager's job. At one point Stern advised me simply, "Read my book." (A line I plan to use on him soon.)

Above all, stage managers are responsible for tracking and coordinating information. "I coordinate everything that occurs within the rehearsal hall; I communicate that to those outside the rehearsal hall," Kay explains. "Then I call **cues** for various operators to run the show." Rick Cunningham, head of the stage management program for the University of Delaware's Professional Theatre Training Program (PTTP), views his primary task as facilitating information between the various artists involved in a production. "I see a play as a series of conversations and my job is to manage those conversations. I manage people, not things," he says. This makes paperwork a big part of the job.

In order to properly manage the many conversations taking place, the stage manager collects and tracks every detail pertaining to the production, including information regarding props, costumes, scenery, special effects, sound, lighting, blocking, backstage crews, dialogue, performers, and much more. Each aspect of the show is recorded and made into a list or report. Stage managers or their assistants, known as assistant stage managers (ASMs), will eventually compile a mountain of paperwork that includes props lists, costume tracking sheets, blocking notes, line notes, daily reports, and more. Much of this paper will end up in a stage manager's **promptbook**, or "bible," which also includes an annotated script. SMs will use this usually massive notebook binder to run the show. When the production closes, the "bible" is commonly handed over to the production manager for archival purposes, for future productions of the same show, or as a reference for future shows that may have similar needs.

Stage managers stay on top of this wealth of information by keeping each member of the production team as informed as possible throughout the entire process. The primary way they do this is by producing **rehearsal reports** after each rehearsal and distributing them to the designers, technical director, production manager, costume shop, props department, and all others involved in the production. Many stage managers will continue this process after the show opens by distributing performance reports following each performance. Communication and record keeping such as this is key to managing the large number of details that are changed or added daily during the rehearsal process. Because there are so many departments involved in a typical professional theater production, stage managers must keep on top of the progress and problems of each in order to facilitate communication among them all.

CALLING THE SHOW

A stage manager's duties shift once **technical rehearsals** and performances begin. This is when the SM will put to use all of the information that was so meticulously tracked during preproduction and will begin the task of "calling the show"—the term used to describe how the SM instructs crew members of a production, such as the light and sound operators. With the stage manager calling cues, all members of the technical crew will know exactly when to execute each of their assigned tasks. For crew members not in direct contact with the stage manager, alternative methods of "giving the go" are employed. One such alternative is known as a **cue light**, which the SM controls from the booth or wherever the SM is stationed during the show. The SM turns the light on to warn the person being cued, and when the light goes off, it is the equivalent of the stage manager saying "go."

The stage manager is also responsible for maintaining the look and feel of the show once the director has moved on from the project—usually when the production has officially opened. In addition to calling the cues properly so that all technical aspects of the show remain constant from show to show, the SM must also ensure the integrity of the show. This includes the look of each actor, the condition of every prop and piece of scenery, and the focus of all lighting instruments. In short, the SM is accountable for maintaining the show as it was directed and designed. When there are problems during a performance or there is preventative maintenance that should take place, the SM will put it in the performance report and distribute it to all concerned personnel.

◇ ◆ ◇

Tools of the Trade

The stage manager's tools are basic but varied. Though the contents may seem simple and even obvious, the trademark stage manager's kit is a very important part of any good SM's arsenal.

The kits are usually held in portable mid-sized tool or art boxes, and they should be kept organized for quick and easy access. The basic SM kit should include the following items:

◆ pencils
◇ pens
◆ markers
◇ highlighters
◆ paper clips
◇ push pins
◆ rubber bands
◇ binder clips
◆ safety pins
◇ matches/lighter
◆ scale ruler
◇ Scotch tape
◆ hole punch
◇ pencil sharpener
◆ small sewing kit
◇ glow tape

◆ small spike tape roll
◇ scissors
◆ small first aid kit
◇ tape measure
◆ stapler and staples
◇ straight line and chalk
◆ wrench
◇ speed square
◆ extension cord
◇ cube tap
◆ work gloves
◇ utility knife
◆ compass
◇ protractor
◆ glue stick

Most stage managers add to this basic list with items that they have found to come in handy, depending on the show and venue. "It can't all fit in one box, even a big one," Richard Costabile says. "So I carry a nice tackle box plus bring along a soft-sided bag with lots of the rest." Here's a partial list of the extras that Emily McMullen and Costabile keep handy:

◆ t-square
◇ small amount of tie line
◆ basic tools: both types of screwdrivers
                     hammer
                     pliers
                     Crescent wrench
                     Vice-Grip locking pliers
                     hacksaw
                     wire cutters
                     small level

◇ small assortment of wood screws, nails, eyes
✦ first aid: lozenges
               Tums
               Altoids
               Ace bandage
               pain relievers (ibuprofen, aspirin, Tylenol, Excedrin, etc.)
               small tube of Cortaid anti-itch cream
               Band-Aids
◇ 91% alcohol for cleaning
✦ plastic template with geometric shapes and another with lighting-design shapes
◇ envelopes (letter, business, manila)
✦ digital camera, with USB cable for downloading to computer
◇ pitch pipe
✦ extension cords
◇ string
✦ extra flashlight, bulbs, and batteries
◇ china markers
✦ extra lead and pencil erasers
◇ small metronome
✦ roll of gaff tape
◇ roll of masking tape
✦ rolls of miscellaneous tape

ZEN AND THE ART OF STAGE MANAGEMENT

If there is a book that all stage managers agree their colleagues and students should read, it has yet to be written. New Jersey–based stage manager Gregg Brevoort might have one up his sleeve though. "I have wondered if maybe I should write a book, *Zen and the Art of Stage Management*," he says. "I find that an even keel and levelheadedness best serves a stage manager."

Brevoort is not alone in this belief. Professional stage managers pride themselves on their keen ability to remain calm in the midst of a storm. Richard Costabile, a veteran New York City–based stage manager and production stage manager for Hal Holbrook's touring production of *Mark Twain Tonight!* knows from decades of experience that a stage manager must be careful not to let the stress of theatrical production become so overbearing that it affects one's sense of professionalism. "I constantly hear about SMs on tour who are high-strung and unpleasant, and it makes me sad," he says. "After all, 'it's only a show'—which is not to minimize the importance of doing the best job possible," he insists. "But, we don't have a patient on the operating table with his brains spilling out of his skull awaiting our ministrations. I say, if you work in theater and you can't have fun while working hard with your team, then you're in the wrong profession."

Michele Kay shares this belief and is also blessed with the talent to remain calm. "Even when I feel like there is steam coming out of my ears, I have the uncanny ability to remain calm," she says. The ability to perform and work with others calmly while dealing with the stressful situations typical of theater reveals itself as an important asset for successful stage managers. Even the most seasoned veterans find themselves in difficult situations that make it nearly impossible to remain calm. "When a friend fell backwards into an orchestra pit, that shook me," says Kay, describing one of the more harrowing events she's experienced. "But generally I'm very calm as a stage manager."

Because entire production teams look to the stage manager for support and guidance in stressful times, this is an important lesson for young stage managers to learn.

TEACHING STAGE MANAGEMENT

"No matter what the experience in college, the professional world is very different," says Emily McMullen, production stage manager of Merrimack Repertory Theatre in Massachusetts. According to the pros, practical experience is the most effective way to learn the craft of stage management. "I would rather see firsthand what works for other stage managers, than to look for guidance from a textbook," Brevoort says. Putting it plainly, Cindy Poulson, who, until her untimely passing in the summer of 2006, taught stage management at the University of Wisconsin–Milwaukee, said, "Practical experience beats everything else." And judging by the successive editions of his book, *Stage Management*, Lawrence Stern seems to agree. "Since initial publication in the early 1970s, my book has evolved from a manual for stage managers to a textbook for future stage managers," says Stern. "I believe that the most effective way to teach is to thrust the student into doing it."

The teacher should be cautious, however, about which students to thrust, according to Michele Kay. "A lot of stage management can be taught, but if someone doesn't 'have it,' they won't be successful stage managers," says Kay. The "it" is what Kay refers to as an "inherent ability." "All the classes in the world won't make me a better singer," she says. "The same can be said for stage managers."

ACTORS' EQUITY ASSOCIATION

Most professional SMs are members of Actors' Equity Association (AEA), a labor organization that represents theater actors and stage managers in the United States. Stage managers play a critical role in the union, commonly known as "Equity," and are responsible for seeing that its rules are followed during the entire production process. The definition of the duties of a stage manager (see sidebar on page 22) are a dos and don'ts list for every SM Equity member. Among other things, the list notes tasks much as calling rehearsals, maintaining a promptbook, and "maintaining the artistic intention of the director and the producer after opening." The list also states that SMs don't shift scenery, run lights, order food for the company, or handle outside art

When and if to join AEA is a big question for up-and-coming stage managers, and the advice one encounters from professional stage managers can be quite diverse. Cunningham, who has headed up PTTP's stage management training program for seventeen years, advises young stage managers to join AEA "as soon as you can." But Michele Kay disagrees. She advises students to avoid rushing into the first AEA gig that comes their way. "Just because it is there doesn't mean it should be taken," she says. "Once you make the choice you cannot go back." Both Costabile and Poulson offer similar advice. They agree, as does Kay, that being able to compete for AEA jobs is critical for determining when the time for joining AEA is right. "There is no right moment to join AEA," says McMullen. "It is strictly on a case by case basis," she says. "When a stage manager is ready to join." This seems to be the key. A young stage manager must gauge when he is ready to enter the competitive market of working Equity stage managers. Without proper qualifications and experience, vying with more experienced professionals for work at Equity theaters will be extremely difficult.

Furthermore, as Kay states, once you join AEA you can't go back. What that means is that, as a union member, in most cases you are prohibited from taking non-Equity jobs. There are exceptions to this rule. For example, Equity-member SMs are allowed in some cases to work under other union contracts, such as SAG or ACTRA. Working strictly nonunion productions, however, is not allowed once a SM joins AEA.

Poulson raises another important consideration: Where do you plan to live and work? She encourages novice SMs to research seriously how many AEA stage managers the community can support. All of the pros agree that consulting stage managers who work professionally in the city you want to live and work in is an important step. They will have the best information about how to proceed—both in terms of when to join AEA and how to find entry-level gigs in your area.

Working with professional stage managers or interning at a theater is another good way to hone skills and prepare for the leap into Equity. "There is no better tool than watching professional stage managers handle day-to-day situations and being able to ask questions as to why they made those decisions," McMullen says.

Another great resource is AEA itself. According to Maria Somma, an AEA spokesperson, a good way to gain experience as a stage manager while earning credit toward Equity membership is through Equity's Membership Candidate Program, or EMC. In this program, you can work for theaters under Equity contract while training to be a professional stage manager.

No matter what, the decision to join AEA should not be taken lightly. It can be a contentious issue, and, as McMullen reminds us, "Becoming union is a big step to take, and a big responsibility."

PRODUCTION STAGE MANAGER VERSUS STAGE MANAGER

The difference between a stage manager and a production stage manager (PSM) really comes down to circumstance. In terms of regional theater, a production stage manager usually exists in situations where there is more than one stage manager—either for a single production or for a theater working in **rep**. In such cases, the production stage manager is the senior SM and is charged with supervising and scheduling the stage managers and in some cases handling the budget for the stage management department.

"Production stage manager is a title that means many things to many organizations," explains Evelyn Matten, the production stage manager of American Players Theatre in Spring Green, Wisconsin, since 1998. "Some of that has to do with the size of the organization," she says, "and some of it has to do with how the organization itself is set up." Another kink in defining the role of a PSM is the role of AEA in stage management, because the union recognizes the term differently under certain types of contracts. In LORT theaters, for example, the position is not recognized by **Equity**, leaving such theaters to determine on their own how to compensate a member of their company doing the work of a production stage manager in addition to the normal AEA duties as an SM. "Sometimes, they're afforded that title because it sounds more impressive," Matten says, explaining why the term does not always accurately define the type of work being done by an individual.

On Broadway the title takes on a somewhat different edge because the role of a PSM is more like that of an assistant director. "It's a different and unique beast," Matten says, when comparing LORT stage managing to its Broadway counterpart. Costabile, who has spent a considerable amount of his stage management career on Broadway, is able to draw very clear lines between stage managers and production stage managers there. "The PSM is the executive instrument on a production on Broadway, much more so than in any other environment," he says. "The quality of the production is totally in the hands of the PSM, especially when the directing staff is out of the picture."

Moreover, acting as a production stage manager on Broadway requires a heightened awareness of the overall money matters of a production. "The production stage manager must keep the bottom line in mind when making all decisions," Costabile says, describing the most distinctive feature of the Broadway PSM. "One of the best reasons for a producer rehiring a PSM is when they know how to save the producer money."

◇✦◇

The Art of Net*work*ing

In theater, reputations precede everyone. There is rarely a person working on a production that found the job without someone else's recommendation or referral. "Most people don't want to hire unknown entities," says Costabile. The idea is to keep track of all of the people you work with whom you have found to be skilled and professional. It is a sort of back-scratching system—though one based primarily on merit—in which you must collect as many contacts as you can. "You will always, always, be looking for work," Costabile reminds future stage managers. "And that, more than anything else, is what causes people to leave the business."

But with a willingness to network, stage managers can stay in the game. If you aren't good at it or are uncomfortable doing it, you must do what you can to overcome your fear, for it doesn't dismiss you from the need to do it. Many tech professionals dislike the constant need to make contacts but admit that it is a necessary part of making a living in theater.

◇✦◇

PATHS TO A CAREER AS A STAGE MANAGER

Poulson's advice for how to become a good stage manager is direct. "You need to know how to think, ask questions, and solve problems. You need to understand literature, art, history, and so much more [because] you need to be able communicate articulately about so many things. Get a good education," she says. "Theater is not for dummies." As for the details of excelling as a stage manager, Kay believes you must have thick skin but also be capable of compassion. "Don't take anything personally; likewise, when you reprimand, attack the problem, not the person," she says. "Treat people with dignity, trust, and respect, and you will get the same in return."

As with every other field of tech theater, professional networking is a necessary skill for getting your foot in the door and maintaining a stage management career (see sidebar above). "You have to have a network so that the next job appears," Costabile says. "Those doors opening and phones ringing have to come from someplace."

It can be a very long road to a self-sustaining career as a stage manager, but it is certainly possible. "Take it slow," Kay says, "and you'll get to Broadway someday."

A Job Description

Since most professional theatrical stage managers are members of Actors' Equity Association, they are responsible for a list of duties detailed by AEA. For more info about AEA you can visit them online at *www.actorsequity.org*.

Definition of the Duties of a Stage Manager

A Stage Manager under Actors' Equity Contract is or shall be obligated to perform at least the following duties for the Production to which s/he is engaged, and by performing them is hereby defined as the Stage Manager:

- Shall be responsible for the calling of all rehearsals, whether before or after opening.

- Shall assemble and maintain the Prompt Book, which is defined as the accurate playing text and stage business, together with such cue sheets, plots, daily records, etc., as are necessary for the actual technical and artistic operation of the production.

- Shall work with the Director and the heads of all other departments during rehearsal and after opening and schedule rehearsal and outside calls in accordance with Equity regulations.

- Assume active responsibility for the form and discipline of rehearsal and performance and be the executive instrument on the technical running of **each** performance.

- Maintain the artistic intentions of the Director and the Producer after opening, to the best of his/her ability, including calling correctional rehearsals of the company when necessary and preparation of the Understudies, Replacements, Extras, and Supers when and if the Director and/or Producer declines this prerogative. Therefore, if an Actor finds him/herself unable to satisfactorily work out an artistic difference of opinion with the Stage Manager regarding the intentions of the Director and Producer, the Actor has the option of seeking clarification from the Director or Producer.

- Keep such records as are necessary to advise the Producer on matters of attendance, time health benefits or other matters relating to the rights of Equity members. **The Stage Manager and Assistant Stage Managers are prohibited from the making of payrolls or any distribution of salaries.**

- Maintain discipline as provided in the Equity Constitution, By-Laws and Rules where required, appealable in every case to Equity.

- Stage Manager duties do not include shifting scenery, running lights, or operating the Box Office, etc.

- The Council shall have the power from time to time to define the meaning of the words "Stage Manager" and may alter, change or modify the meaning of Stage Manager as hereinabove defined.

- The Stage Manager and Assistant Stage Managers are prohibited from handling contracts, having riders signed or initialed, or any other function which normally comes under the duties of the General Manager or Company Manager.

- The Stage Manager and Assistant Stage Managers are prohibited from participating in the ordering of food for the company.

- The Stage Manager and Assistant Stage Managers are prohibited from signing the closing notice of the company or the individual notice of any Actor's termination.

An Equity stage manager's contractual duties. (Courtesy of Actors' Equity Association).

The Assistant Stage Manager

Working as an assistant stage manager (or ASM) is an almost certain prerequisite for becoming a professional stage manager. It is in this role that the basics of stage management can be learned and valuable experience can be gained. Also, as noted in the section on AEA, it is possible to work as an ASM under Equity contract as part of the union's Equity Membership Candidate Program while earning credit toward membership. This can be a great way to learn while investing in a future career. (Check out the stage management resources listed at the end of this chapter for information on contacting AEA.) Once a member of Equity, ASMs earn wages that are only slightly below that of actual stage managers. (See table below.)

WHAT DO STAGE MANAGERS EARN?

Earning potential is greatly improved for stage managers who are members of AEA. Table 2.1 demonstrates the salary minimums for stage managers working under Equity contract in LORT theaters. LORT designations are based primarily on the seating capacity of the theater and run from A (the largest) through D (the smallest), with indicators such as B+ or C1 making room for more nuanced listings. The ranges below designate the difference between working in **repertory** versus nonrepertory. For example, working in rep in a LORT B+ theater, the Equity stage manager salary minimum would be $1,066 per week until February 2007, whereas working non-repertory reduces the minimum to $1,020. Remember, these are minimums, subject to increase at the discretion of the parties involved. The rates in table 2.1 also do not reflect other types of compensation, such as touring rates or per diem. There are exceptions to these salaries, which are based on weekly pay rates.

TABLE 2.1. ACTORS' EQUITY ASSOCIATION RATES FOR STAGE MANAGERS, LORT THEATRES, 2006-2008

LORT Category	Weekly Rates through	
	February 2007	February 2008
A	$1,181	$1,217
B+	$1,020–$1,066	$1,051–1,098
B	$851–$941	$868–$960
C	$794–$861	$809–$878
D	$661–$747	$670–$759

Source: Actors' Equity Association, "Agreement and Rules Governing Employment in Resident Theatres."

TABLE 2.2. ACTORS' EQUITY ASSOCIATION RATES FOR ASSISTANT STAGE MANAGERS, LORT THEATRES, 2006-2008		
LORT Category	*Weekly Rates through*	
	February 2007	*February 2008*
A	$967–$972	$1,016–$1,021
B+	$841–$905	$884–$951
B	$708–$833	$737–$867
C	$654–$719	$680–$748
D	$538–$613	$552–$628

Source: Actors' Equity Association, "Agreement and Rules Governing Employment in Resident Theatres."

Table 2.2 details the minimum weekly wages for ASMs working as Equity members.

When considering the earnings of stage managers, it is crucial to remember the sometimes contrary advice of professionals regarding when to join AEA. Without membership, none of the salaries listed here apply.

There were also a small number of stage managers, assistant stage managers, and production stage managers who responded to my Tech Theater Earnings Survey. For the sake of interest, and because there were twenty such respondents (more than

TABLE 2.3. EARNINGS FOR STAGE MANAGERS		
Total number of stage managers surveyed = 20		
Where the stage managers surveyed are working		
Type of theater	*Number*	*Percentage*
Academic	-	-
Broadway	-	-
COST	-	-
Dinner	-	-
LORT	6	30%
Off-Broadway	-	-
Opera	1	5%
Regional	7	35%
Resident	3	15%
SPT	-	-
Other	3	15%

How much stage managers are earning		
Income range	*Number*	*Percentage*
Less than $10,000	1	5%
$10,000–$20,000	4	20%
$20,000–$35,000	7	35%
$35,000–$50,000	6	30%
$50,000–$75,000	1	5%
$75,000–$100,000	1	5%
More than $100,000	*	
How stage managers view their income		
Perception	*Number*	*Percentage*
Below average	6	30%
Average	13	65%
Above average	1	5%

Source: 2006 Tech Theater Earnings Survey.

some other areas I was actually targeting), I have decided to include the data collected on stage managers (table 2.3). It is the only career in the book for which I managed to collect both union wage scales and usable survey data. Though the earnings data listed in the survey table is rather evenly spread among salary ranges, the SMs surveyed overwhelmingly believe as individuals that their incomes are representative of the average in the United States.

FIVE SCHOOLS OFFERING DEGREES IN STAGE MANAGEMENT

UNIVERSITY OF DELAWARE — PROFESSIONAL THEATRE TRAINING PROGRAM
Degrees offered: MFA in Stage Management
www.udel.edu/theater
Contact: Rick Cunningham, rickc@udel.edu

DEPAUL UNIVERSITY
Degrees offered: BFA in Stage Management
http://theaterschool.depaul.edu/schoolmain.html
Contact: Linda Buchanan, lbuchana@depaul.edu

UNIVERSITY OF IOWA
Degrees offered: MFA in Stage Management
www.uiowa.edu/~theater/programs/stagemgmt/stageinfo.htm
Contact: James P. Birder, elmono773@aol.com

RUTGERS UNIVERSITY
  Degrees offered: MFA in Stage Management
  www.mgsa.rutgers.edu/theater/MFAStageManagement.html
  Contact: Carol Thompson, cmthompy@rci.rutgers.edu

YALE UNIVERSITY — SCHOOL OF DRAMA
  Degrees offered: MFA in Stage Management
                      Certificate in Stage Management
  www.yale.edu/drama/admissions/sm.html
  Contact: see Web site for contact and application procedures.

RESOURCES FOR STAGE MANAGERS

Books

When it comes to stage management, there are plenty of books to look to for all sorts of information. This is a list of some of the more popular and well-known texts.

Fazio, Larry. *Stage Manager: The Professional Experience*. Boston: Focal Press, 2000.

Gruver, Bert. *Stage Manager's Handbook*. New York: Drama Publishers, 1972.

Kelly, Thomas A. *The Back Stage Guide to Stage Management*. New York: Backstage Books, 1999.

Stern, Lawrence. *Stage Management*. 8th ed. Boston: Allyn & Bacon, 2006.

Internet

www.stagemanagers.org—The Web site of the Stage Managers Association, which is a community of professional stage managers in the United States that provides resources, job listings, and, most notably, the ability to connect with other stage managers around the country. Costabile has this to say about joining this organization early in his career: "I credit that as the single most important move that I have taken in this career."

www.smnetwork.org—This Web site is an all-inclusive site for working stage managers. On it, you will find downloadable forms for use when stage managing, job listings, news stories relevant to SMs, recommended reading, and a whole lot more. Probably the most useful Web site a stage manager can access.

www.actorsequity.org—The Web site of Actors' Equity Association (AEA), a labor organization that also represents professional theater stage managers.

www.artslynx.org/theater/sm.htm—Artslynx has a great list of Web links that will be useful for stage managers and anyone wanting to learn about stage management.

3

COMPANY MANAGER

I was a stage manager in school, and while looking for stage management jobs,
I saw a job listing for a company manager. I said to myself, stage manager,
company manager . . . how different or impossible could it be?

—PAUL HENGESTEG,
company manager, Shakespeare Theatre Company

While Paul Hengesteg's
collegiate assessment of
company management may
seem naïve, it isn't too far off
the mark in many respects. Like
stage managers, company managers (CMs) spend most of their
time working with the creative
artists directly involved in production, such as performers,
designers, and directors or cho-
reographers. However, unlike
most stage managers, the role of
the company manager is one
that generally shifts according
to the particular theater or com-

Company manager Paul Hengesteg (left) meets with assistant general
manager Charles Phaneuf (right) in his office at Shakespeare Theatre
Company. (Photograph by Tselane Prescott.)

pany by which the manager is employed. The difference can be quite significant,
especially when comparing regional theater with Broadway, **SPT**s with academic

theater, and all of the other nuances of organization that reflects the differing needs and abilities of theater companies. Academic theater, for instance, is an area that rarely has a need for a company manager, and therefore specific training for such a position is hard to come by.

All of this has little to do with the inclusion of such a nontechnical position in a book about technical theater. Though it may seem a bit out of place, I have decided to include the job because I believe that the company manager is frequently the person who helps bridge the gap between the artistic, administrative, and technical teams of a theater. Like the production manager, the CM often sits on a line that separates distinct areas and therefore must be able to work and communicate effectively in all realms. Perhaps it is for this reason that most professional company managers come from such diverse backgrounds, as likely to come at the job from areas of tech theater as they are to be former actors or, in some cases, people with little or no training in theater whatsoever.

LEARNING CURVE

"This job is one of the coolest jobs in the theater in terms of the things you do, the people you meet, the networking, and the flexible work hours," exclaims Paul Hengesteg, company manager of the Shakespeare Theatre Company in Washington, D.C. "Yet somehow, the job is unsung and unknown."

In the corporate world we might call the company manager a human resources manager, though such a title would be incomplete. Inasmuch as they might be considered human resources managers, they do work on behalf of the well-being of company members and guest artists. But they spend most of their time dealing with the details of life outside of the theater and the various concerns of life—housing, food, travel—for those working for the theater.

"I think of my job as project based," says Hengesteg. "I do similar tasks for each project, but there are many projects overlapping each other, each at a different point in its life." As the person responsible for such things as contracting with artists, securing accommodations, and booking travel arrangements, he finds himself in a sea of budgetary and administrative details. Hengesteg, who held the same position with Indiana Repertory Theatre for several years, says, "The biggest learning curve a company manager will have is realizing just how much they have to sit on the fence on any given issue." As the go-between person, the company manager represents both the artists and the management and must be able to handle tricky situations with professionalism and aplomb. "The company manager usually knows the most information, the best gossip, and the true story," Hengesteg tells me, explaining the often delicate nature of his work.

The delicate side of the job is just one thing that makes it so tough. "A good company manager understands the needs of artists, the financial limitations of the company, and can diplomatically give everyone the best care possible under both of those extreme circumstances," explains Sophia Garder, CM of Shakespeare & Company. "It's an unsung position in theater land," she says, "but important enough that if you are good, rehearsals go well." And, Garder adds, if the company manager is not so good at the job, then rehearsals don't go nearly as well, and the company may suffer through rough performances and battling personalities.

"Many people wonder why I don't sit at my desk all day when they need to find me," Hengesteg says, describing the required fluidity of a company manager's work schedule. "I often respond that I missed seeing them at the airport at midnight the night before when the costume designer arrived." A company manager's flexibility is so central to the job that Hengesteg has found that it informs his life outside of work in a positive way too. "The real reward comes when I need something in my personal life," Hengesteg explains, "and my resourcefulness and creativity in the job gives me all the appropriate tools and knowledge to not panic about anything."

A company manager's resourcefulness is often put to the test, and sometimes CMs are asked to go above and beyond the call of duty. One of Hengesteg's favorite examples involves an actor recently dropped at the airport. "Later that day, I get a call from the actor," Hengesteg explains. It turns out the actor had forgotten to pack a few of his belongings—let's just call them "unmentionables"—leaving them in a drawer in his hotel room. "He was hoping I could put them in a package and mail them to him," Paul laughs. "Well, customer service being the keystone of company management, a package was on its way the next day!"

DIFFERENT THEATERS, DIFFERENT ROLES

The company manager's role will shift from theater to theater. Hengesteg's job, for instance, is different than Sophia Garder's. Whereas Hengesteg is the company manager of a large LORT B+ theater in the nation's capital, Garder is the CM for a small theater in the small western Massachusetts community of Lenox. It would be silly to assume that Hengesteg and Garder are dealing with the same type of people and the same budget numbers, but just how different is the actual work they do? Maybe not as much as one might think.

Working in dissimilar environments may mean that specific duties and responsibilities are not quite the same, but most of what Hengesteg and Garder do as company managers is quite similar. "I spend a good deal of my day listening, letting people tell me about their frustrations," Garder says, agreeing with Hengesteg's assessment of a company manager's part-time role as a facilitator of personal stories and problems.

"I am a nurse, mother, father, disciplinarian, consoler, counselor, psychologist, psychic, fixer-upper, friend, and all around go-to gal," Garder says, meaning every word.

Hengesteg himself made the transition from one regional company to another in 2006, and he shared with me the ways in which his role as company manager shifted when he moved from a Midwestern city to the nation's capital. "The mechanics by which I do my job are very different," he told me soon after the move. "During this transition period, I have learned that most of the 'magic' in a company manager comes from the general knowledge base about his or her surroundings," he says, referring to the information taken for granted after living and working in a large city, such as the roads, businesses, airport, hotels, restaurants, and much more.

The most pronounced difference, however, may be between resident companies and touring companies, as the CM will tend to take on far more duties on the road than he might while working solely in one physical space. "It seems to me that company managers on Broadway or on tour have to represent the company in other ways," Hengesteg tells me. "The company manager is in charge of settling with the box office, doing payroll, and representing the producer," he says, explaining what a touring CM might be responsible for in addition to what a nontouring position would encompass. "Regional theaters often break that job into other roles because the setting is different," Hengesteg explains. "They have their own box office staff, they have a business office, general manager, et cetera."

❖✦❖

Job Description

The title of the position would lead one to believe that the company manager is responsible for the extraordinary task of managing the entire company. And, in a way, that is what these managers are charged with.

Company managers usually attack their duties based on how their theater breaks down its season. For each production or season, a company manager will begin by receiving basic information on all of the artists and technicians who will be traveling to the theater for the given project or series of projects. Usually company managers do not concern themselves much with folks who are in residence at their theater, if there are any. Otherwise, any personnel, including actors, designers, directors, and technicians, will have their living needs arranged and managed by the company manager.

Once the CM has gathered information on all of the people he must take care of, he will contact them to assist with their travel and housing arrangements. By staying in touch with the traveling theater artists, the manager can both be kept apprised of their itineraries and needs as well as keep them informed regarding the theater's requirements.

Eventually, the company manager will arrange for transportation needs, including to and from the airport and within the community, especially if significant distance exists between the theater and the person's temporary residence. The CM must also make certain that contractual obligations are met, especially as concerns actors. Depending on the AEA contract under which they are working, actors are entitled to certain rights and privileges. For example, an Equity actor's housing must fulfill many specific requirements, and it is the job of the CM to ensure they are provided—before, but also during, the actor's stay if necessary. Naturally, such obligations frequently extend beyond members of Equity and may even include nonunion theater artists who have negotiated certain terms in their contracts that may apply to a CM's area of responsibility, including housing, transportation, and travel.

Because the company manager is charged with so many areas of an artist's life outside of the theater itself, his work can affect the vital workings of the theater. It is not unusual for CMs to go to great lengths to ensure the comfort and stability of a company's artists. "It's nothing to sneeze at," says Garder, a former actor and stage manager who understands the value of keeping the members of a production team comfortable enough to stay focused on the show.

Dealing with the arrangements for guest artists and company members alike brings with it a degree of involvement with the personal lives of people too, which calls for discretion and patience in equal measure. "A company manager is usually privy to some very confidential information," Hengesteg explains. "It is essential to use your powers for good, not evil," he says.

◇✦◇

WHAT DO COMPANY MANAGERS EARN?

Though company managers frequently work with unions to make sure that those represented are provided what is contractually due them, the CMs themselves are rarely members of a union. The world of company management also seems to be (through my own observations) one that is punctuated by transition and is often used as a stepping stone to other areas of theater management. Because of these things, it was difficult to find CMs who have been in their positions for an extended period of time to respond to my Tech Theater Earnings Survey. Of the nearly four hundred responses received, only eleven were from full-time company managers. As the table shows, each of them are employed by regional or LORT theaters, and over 90 percent earn between $20,000 and $35,000 annually.

TABLE 3.1. EARNINGS FOR COMPANY MANAGERS

Total number of company managers surveyed = 11

Where the company managers surveyed are working

Type of theater	Number	Percentage
Academic	-	-
Broadway	-	-
COST	-	-
Dinner	-	-
LORT	6	55%
Off-Broadway	-	-
Opera	-	-
Regional	5	45%
Resident	-	-
SPT	-	-
Other	-	-

How much company managers are earning

Income range	Number	Percentage
Less than $10,000	-	-
$10,000–$20,000	-	-
$20,000–$35,000	10	91%
$35,000–$50,000	1	9%
$50,000–$75,000	-	-
$75,000–$100,000	-	-
More than $100,000	-	-

How company managers view their income

Perception	Number	Percentage
Below average	5	45%
Average	6	55%
Above average	-	-

Source: 2006 Tech Theater Earnings Survey.

FIVE SCHOOLS OFFERING PROGRAMS IN THEATER MANAGEMENT

For those interested in theater management, which tends to include and focus on the business side of theater, company management can be a good way to learn about the inner workings of theater. For that reason, and because earning a degree in company management is unheard of, I have decided to include a few academic options in the field of theater management.

DePaul University
Programs offered: BFA in Theatre Management
theatreschool.depaul.edu
Contact: Leslie Shook, lshook@depaul.edu

Florida State University
Programs offered: MFA in Theatre Management
www.fsu.edu/~theatre
Contact: T. Lynn Hogan, lhogan@admin.fsu.edu

University of Alabama
Programs offered: MFA in Theatre Management
www.as.ua.edu/theatre
Contact: Thomas Adkins, tadkins@ua.edu

University of Evansville
Programs offered: BA/BFA in Theatre Management
theatre.evansville.edu
Contact: Sharla Cowden, sc75@evansville.edu

Wayne State University
Programs offered: MFA in Theatre with concentration in Theatre Management
www.theatre.wayne.edu
Contact: Anthony Rhine, au8164@wayne.edu

PART II SCENERY

◆

When you take on a show, it's sort of like doing a puzzle . . . trying
to juggle the pieces to come up with something that
ultimately you can take some pride in.

—BILL FORRESTER,
freelance scene designer and professor emeritus at
the University of Washington

cenery is a funny thing when you think about it. And I have. After spending a number of years building it, both in school and professionally, I grew to have a very conflicted relationship with the things I built for theatrical use. Mostly, I loved the act of creating new environments for the stage, but there was always the nagging concern about the

The Alley Theatre's scene shop. (Photograph by Joe Aker.)

amount of resources being burned through—and because theater is a business that is driven by extreme deadline pressure, there is seldom any attention paid to reducing waste or to using less toxic and more environmentally friendly materials. This concern of mine has little to do with the skills needed to pursue this kind of work, though, and I bring up the point primarily because it was raised by a couple of professionals featured in this section. Reducing waste and attempting to curb the environmental side effects of scenery production is also something that I believe future (as well as current) theater artists are obligated to consider in their creative pursuits.

For those who spend their days dealing in scenery, the notion of its temporal nature is something that can be overlooked only briefly, and one might argue that it shouldn't be overlooked at all. The designer and builder who embrace the fleeting reality of theatrical scenery are probably best suited for such work.

The pieces of the scenic puzzle, as Bill Forrester may call it, are many, and I have attempted to include them all here, though others might have split them into different categories. Susan Crabtree and Peter Beudert, in their indispensable text *Scenic Art for the Theatre*, divide the jobs found in this section into three areas: paint, properties, and scenery. For our purposes, however, keeping in mind the constant collaboration and frequent overlap of positions in these three areas, I found it more sensible to combine them under the single, broad heading of "scenery."

So, here you will find every type of position that has to do with the design, fabrication, and installation of all scenic elements in technical theater production. They are arranged loosely, based on the general order of how things get done and how scenery is handed down during the process from designer to builder, from builder to painter, to the stagehand who will install it and use it on stage.

4

SCENE DESIGNER

You learn from whatever you are doing in the theatre,
as long as you are paying attention.

—CHRISTOPHER McCOLLUM,
resident set designer, Theatre Memphis, and freelance scene designer

Scene design requires the seamless dovetailing of many skills. One must be exceptional at visualizing that which does not exist and be able to convert that vision into a conceptual image while simultaneously developing it as an engineering project. In this way, the scene designer is like a conventional architect. The difference is that scene designers create for the stage, accepting the temporal restrictions of their work. It is art made to be torn down—a fate accepted time and time again by the working scene designer.

A Moon for the Misbegotten at American Conservatory Theatre. Scene design by Robert Mark Morgan. Lighting design by Don Darnutzer. (Photography by Robert Mark Morgan.)

Acting as the architect of scenery, the scene designer often provides the conceptual foundation upon which all other designers will build. By so doing, the lighting, sound, costume, and perhaps projection designers will complement and highlight the environment created for the world of the play, musical, opera, ballet, or virtually any kind of live performance imaginable. The scenic concept, developed in concert with the director, and often at the behest of the director's original approach to the work, provides a physical space in which the performers can tell the story and develop the alternate reality of the stage

CONCEPTUALLY SPEAKING

"The theater allows designers to tweak reality into a more artistic and abstract environment," explains Robert Mark Morgan, a freelance scene designer based in San Francisco. "The result, I hope, is a kind of artistic ride for the audience: stepping foot into a theater, seeing a life-size sculpture onstage, and saying to themselves, 'This should be interesting,' " he says. Such an initial impression is created, in many ways, by the scene designer and can be essential for a production's success in conveying the story.

"The set designer has the biggest canvas, or broadest palette," says Bill Forrester, a freelance designer and professor emeritus at the University of Washington, speaking of the fundamental differences between scene designers and other theatrical designers. "You have basically an empty space, and you've got to do something to it," he says. "The set designer has the broadest range of possibilities of any of the designers."

Judy Gailen, a freelance designer based on the East Coast, considers herself an abstract or minimalist artist, focusing on "metaphorical things," and is thus driven by the concept of a production. "I feel that no matter how great you may be technically or how much technical resource you have, if the idea is uninteresting, the work will be uninteresting," she tells me, explaining her primary emphasis when designing and teaching design.

COLLABORATING: TAKING THE LEAD

"The beginning is always the best part, when the first conversations are happening and everyone is exchanging ideas," says Christopher McCollum, a freelance designer and resident set designer for Theatre Memphis. In an ideal situation, McCollum and his colleagues would sit down with the director and the other designers to hash out their ideas for the production. In practice, however, this rarely takes place due to the demanding schedules of most designers. As a result, scene designers generally take the lead, and the other members of the team take their initial design cues from the scene concept developed between a director and scene designer. "I sometimes feel like I'm out there alone, and everyone else is waiting for me to do something," says Forrester of this practice. It is understandable, however, that in situations where entire design teams cannot meet and swap ideas and where they may have limited access to one another, they might wait and use the ideas for the scenery to give them a reliable starting point. After all, the scene designer is the one who will in most cases dictate the physical environment of the piece and is therefore a critical piece of the puzzle affecting lighting, costume, and even sound designs.

This isn't to say that scene designers are noncollaborators. Such a thing would be nearly impossible. But more often than not, such collaboration takes place piecemeal, with the scene designer being the first to dip his toe in the pool of creation. "I think the collaboration is what keeps me doing it," Forrester says, fully aware that even under such fragmented circumstances, the collaboration among all members of the production team is essential to the creative nature of design. "Quite honestly," Gailen says, "my favorite experiences have been the shows where, in the end, we couldn't remember who had what idea; it just all worked."

"I always feel like hashing out a design with a director has to first get a visual language established," Morgan tells me. "Their idea of color or texture may be a lot different than mine," he says, so he first shares a variety of images with the director in order to communicate his own visual approach to the production. "Many times the best images are just abstract color images," he says. After sharing such images with a director, Morgan is able to establish a common vocabulary for discussing design ideas. "You get a really good dialogue going about concepts," he says, "and get to the core about how the set should feel to the audience."

Aside from working with the director and fellow designers, the scene designer must also work closely with many different technical staffers, including the TD, prop manager, and their related crews. "I have tremendous respect for the tech staff," Gailen says. Gailen, a designer with a varied background in art and theater, not only looks at working with technicians as a necessary step, but truly revels in the process. Designers have an acute understanding of how vital it is to have competent, talented, and hardworking tech support from any number of production departments. "If you have a shop that is not very interested or not very competent, then it just becomes a big pain in the butt," Forrester says, explaining that a design is only as good as those building and installing it.

But perhaps the most vital connection is between the scene designer and the scenic artist. Peter Beudert, a scene designer, head of Design and Technology at the University of Arizona, and the coauthor of *Scenic Art for the Theatre*, understands this potentially dynamic relationship well. "There is a bit of responsibility on both ends," he says, explaining the collaboration between designer and painter. "Part of what helps the process is that the scene designer needs to understand a little bit how the scenic artist may ultimately work on something," he says, indicating that scene designers should have at least some training and experience in the art of scenic paint-ing in order to better facilitate their collaborations—and their design work.

◇✦◇

Spotlight on a Pro

Bill Forrester, freelance scene designer and professor of design,
University of Washington, 1973–present

Filling an Empty Space

Bill Forrester has been designing scenery for a long time. After receiving his MFA from Yale School of Drama in 1969, Forrester was encouraged to move to Los Angeles, where he freelanced as a set designer in the televi-sion industry before being offered a position with the University of Washington in Seattle. When he did so, he recognized the pros and cons of moving into the academic world. He might have become a rich man if he had

Art at Arizona Theatre Company. Scene design by Bill Forrester. (Photograph by Carolyn Forrester.)

stayed in the television industry, but the opportunities to work in regional theater would probably have been far fewer. And Forrester enjoys the variety of theater—a variety not often found while working, for example, on TV series.

"I feel like if I don't learn something on every show I do, then it's probably a waste of time," he says, explaining what keeps scene design fresh for him after practicing it for over three decades. "Every time you go into a production, it's a slightly—or sometimes a wildly—different set of circumstances and it has a differ-ent goal, and so you are continuously trying to solve new problems," he says. "That and working with people who have skills that you don't—like the technicians and scenic artists—that's what really keeps it interesting."

Learning the craft of design in the 1960s, Forrester has also learned to accept the coming of new insights and ways of approaching the work over the course of his career. "I was brought up with the idea that you should prune and be careful in your selection of color, and just be careful and be tidy so that the audience wouldn't get confused," Forrester tells me while talking about his work on a show at Seattle's Empty Space Theatre two decades ago called *Gloria Duplex*. "We wanted the audi-ence to feel like they had truly walked into a strip joint in New Orleans," he says. The subsequent design altered many of his notions of design. "Well, we just pulled out all the stops and made a complete mess of the place," he says. And even though

Forrester had been taught and always believed that such an approach to design was unacceptable, he believes the experience convinced him otherwise. "What it taught me was that if you throw enough stuff into the mix, after a while it forms a kind of texture, and with decent lighting the performance can indeed happen; the audience's eyes will go where they're supposed to go, and it will work," he says. "For me, it was an eye-opening experience."

◇✦◇

PATHS TO A CAREER AS A SCENE DESIGNER

"I think a good liberal arts education; serious studies in drawing, painting, and sculpture; and life experience is the best start for a designer," says Gailen. As with no other field detailed in this book, scene designers seemed to dismiss the necessity of studying theater itself, especially for undergraduate students. McCollum also emphasizes flexibility and a wide range of skills. "Because I've never had a teaching position, I don't have any stability," he says, as he talks about the importance of remaining open and ever flexible. "One takes whatever work is available, which is why I'm glad I have lots of practical skills and why I think it's important for young designers."

Morgan, who has taught design at both the Art Institute of Colorado and the University of San Francisco, has a simple standard for students of design. Of his former students, he says, "I wanted them to be the 'yellow bloomers in a sea of suits.' " He believes this to be an ideal for all young designers. "It's a strange type of employment," he says. "You don't make widgets, and your client can't actually touch what it is they're paying for: your talent."

Speaking in purely pragmatic terms, Forrester, who taught design at the University of Washington for over thirty years, believes that young designers should be very careful about choosing their educational paths, if they insist on pursuing a life in theatrical design at all. "Avoid it if you possibly can," he says about his line of work. My laughter prompts a quick response: "I'm not kidding," he says. Forrester has some thoughts if you must follow your heart to design. "A graduate degree is not necessary," he says, "but it can be a helpful shortcut into the business." According to Forrester, a good graduate program can be hard to find, but it can teach you essential skills needed to find entry-level work in design. "It can also teach you, we hope, an approach to work which will serve you when you sit down with a director and try to envision a play," he says. However, Forrester believes strongly that young designers should not be coerced into thinking that without a graduate degree they won't succeed. "There is no magic thing about a graduate degree."

✦◇✦◇✦✦◇

A Job Description

The conceptual leadership provided by a production's director is vital to the scene designer's work. While the designer's initial ideas will be drawn from the text, the director will communicate the themes and conceptual underpinning of the work from his point of view. The director's concept may include a different time period, specific visual cues, the mood the production is expected to evoke, and textural ideas.

After several readings of the script, the scene designer will begin a thorough research process. The shape of the research will vary depending on the particular production and the designer's personal approach. Typically the designer will gather dozens of research sources, including material found on the Internet and in books and magazines, information on architecture and furniture styles, photographs and drawings depicting everyday life in the period of the production, and collections of images or objects that convey the color, texture, or mood that the designer has in mind for the production.

Having compiled the appropriate research and developed a design concept, the designer will then commit the ideas to paper. Sketches, paintings, collages, and clippings are all used to communicate the concept to the director and the other designers. Once the design ideas have been fine-tuned and agreed upon among the production team, the designer will move forward with the more concrete aspects of the work, planning how to translate the ideas into something that can be built. This step involves the preparation of technical drawings that will detail how scenery is to be constructed and specify what materials are to be used. Decisions about colors and textures are made, and the designer (or an assistant) will build a scale model of the set to assist all members of the production staff with visualizing the end product and bringing the design to life.

Throughout the build process, the designer will usually be available to the technicians and artisans creating the scenery in order to assist, troubleshoot potential design problems, and answer questions that may not be clear on paper. During the painting phase, the designer will also be available to verify any samples that the scenic artist has created to ensure that they have mixed color and texture as the designer has envisioned it.

Scene designer Robert Mark Morgan's scale model of *Arms and the Man*. (Photograph courtesy of Robert Mark Morgan.)

Being present for the tech process is also a vital part of the scene designer's job. This is the time when any complicated scenery movement or unforeseen technical difficulties will be addressed. It will also give the designer the opportunity to see the scenery in complete form at full scale and make any necessary adjustments before the show opens before an audience.

The designer will work closely with the technical director, as well as the production manager and prop

Arms and the Man at American Players Theatre. Scene design by Robert Mark Morgan. (Photography by Robert Mark Morgan.)

manager, during the build phase of a design project. Because the TD is the person charged with both building scenery to the designer's specifications and engineering the set so that it is safe and practical, it is important that the scene designer keep an open line of communication with him or her.

Following the construction and installation of the scenery, the designer will oversee any finish work to be done, including paint work and set decoration. The designer will also address any unforeseen issues that may arise with the scenery, working with the TD to modify, remove, or replace any components of the set that do not work—either practically or conceptually—for the production.

During technical rehearsals, the designer will be present to assist with set-related problems and will continue working with the scenic artist, TD, and prop personnel to bring the design to its completion and make it ready for performances.

◇◆◇

WHAT DO SCENE DESIGNERS EARN?

Scene designers, as well as those in the areas of lighting, sound, and costume, are represented in the United States by United Scenic Artists, Local 829. While it is not mandatory for designers to be members of the union, it does allow them to work in many theaters that work solely with union designers. "It is required if you want to design for the big gigs, such as designing for most regional theaters," explains Dunsi Dai, a freelance scene designer and associate professor of design at Webster University. Union membership can also have significant benefits, according to designers. "It establishes a baseline for fees that helps in getting better pay," explains McCollum. "It also offers benefits like health coverage and pension," he adds.

TABLE 4.1. UNITED SCENIC ARTIST RATES FOR SCENE DESIGNERS IN REGIONAL, RESIDENT, OR DINNER THEATER

Seating capacity	Number of sets			
	Single set	Two sets	Each additional Set	Unit set
Less than 199	$2,197	$2,473	$86.50	$2,561
200–299	$2,973	$3,444	$145	$3,556
300–499	$3,776	$4,422	$302	$4,702
500–999	$4,685	$6,044	$741	$5,621
More than 1,000	$5,175	$6,866	$763	$6,216

Source: United Scene Artists Local 829, "Minimum design rates 2006—Regional, Resident, Dinner theater, Schedule A."

For many designers, membership in USA Local 829 provides a degree of stability and offers them access to benefits that are not readily available to unrepresented freelancing artists. As a result, many scene designers today are members of USA.

The fees and daily rates agreed upon vary based on the type of theater, its location, and usually its seating capacity. On this page and the next, you will find tables detailing some of the more common rates for lighting designers who are members of USA.

Table 4.1 lists the 2006 rates for scene designers hired for work in regional, resident, or dinner theaters. These fees do not include daily rates, per diem, or fees for design assistants.

TABLE 4.2. UNITED SCENIC ARTISTS DESIGN RATES FOR SCENE DESIGNERS IN LORT THEATERS

LORT Category	Rates as of		
	July 2006	July 2007	July 2008
A	$7,125	$7,410	$7,744
B+	$5,825	$6,058	$6,330
B	$4,750	$4,940	$5,162
C-1	$3,563	$3,705	$3,872
C-2	$2,771	$2,881	$3,011
D	Negotiable	Negotiable	Negotiable

Source: United Scenic Artists Local #829: "2005 Memorandum of agreement between United Scene Artists, Local USA-829, IATSE and The League of Resident Theatres."

TABLE 4.3. UNITED SCENIC ARTISTS DESIGN RATES FOR SCENE DESIGNERS ON BROADWAY, 2006		
Type of set	Rates	
	Dramatic	Musical
Single	$9,549	$10,124
Multi	$13,566	$32,181
Unit	$17,492	$18,547

Source: United Scene Artists Local #829, "Broadway, Minimum Rates and Classifications, 2006."

Table 4.2 details the amendments to USA's Schedule C for design rates for LORT theaters. Designers working for a LORT theater work under contracts according to the theater's LORT designation, which is based primarily on the seating capacity of the theater. The designations run from A (the largest) through D (the smallest), with indicators such as B+ or C1 making room for more nuanced listings.

Table 4.3 is an example of the major leagues of theatrical design: the USA design rates for scene designers working on Broadway. While becoming a designer on Broadway is by no means impossible, young and beginning designers should rely on the first two charts for realistic earnings potential—especially considering that many New York–based designers must still work regionally and in off-off-Broadway theaters to earn a living.

◇ ◇ ✦ ◇ ◇

Ming's Clambake

Founded by renowned scene designer and artist Ming Cho Lee, the event (known officially as the Stage Design Portfolio Review) provides graduating design students an opportunity to present their portfolios and meet with established designers, directors, and producers. The invitation-only, annual event is held at (and partially sponsored by) the Lincoln Center Library and is a rare opportunity for young designers to hobnob with some of theater's big name designers. "You'd be surprised how many contacts you can make at a Clambake," wrote designer and one-time participant Brian Bustos in 2003. Since Ming's Clambake is not open to the public, aspiring designers should needle their professors about how to participate—it has the potential of being a career-making experience.

◇ ◇ ✦ ◇ ◇

FIVE SCHOOLS OFFERING DEGREES IN SCENE DESIGN

COLUMBIA COLLEGE
Degrees offered: BFA in Set Design
www.colum.edu/undergraduate/theater/index.php
Contact: Jackie Penrod, jpenrod@colum.edu

TEMPLE UNIVERSITY
Degrees offered: MFA in Scene Design
www.temple.edu/theater/
Contact: Daniel Boylen, dboylen@temple.edu

UNIVERSITY OF ALABAMA
Degrees offered: MFA in Scene Design/Technical Production
www.as.ua.edu/theater/
Contact: Andy Fitch, afitch@theater.as.ua.edu

TULANE UNIVERSITY
Degrees offered: MFA in Scene Design
www.tulane.edu/~theater/index.html
Contact: Marty Sachs, msaches@tulane.edu

UNIVERSITY OF ILLINOIS AT URBANA-CHAMPAIGN
Degrees offered: BFA in Theatre with concentrations in Scene Design or in
Scene Technology
MFA in Scene Design
MFA in Scene Technology
www.theater.uiuc.edu
Contact: Randy DeChelle, drandolp@uiuc.edu

RESOURCES FOR SCENE DESIGNERS

Books

Aronson, Arnold. *American Set Design*. New York: Theatre Communications
Group, 1985.

Focusing on the designer's process, rather than practical elements of design,
Aronson's book is now a classic. Aspiring designers should take a look.

Blumenthal, Eileen, Julie Taymor, and Antonio Monda. *Julie Taymor: Playing
with Fire*. 3rd ed. New York: Harry N. Abrams, 2007.

Bill Forrester calls this book—a history of theater artist Julie Taymor's career in pictures—"a real eye-opener" and lists it as one of his favorites.

Fisher, Mark. *Staged Architecture*. West Sussex, UK: John Wiley & Sons, 2000.

Fisher, the mastermind behind Cirque du Soleil's groundbreaking KA Theatre in Las Vegas, displays some of his most inspired work here. While it is mostly designs for rock music icons like the Rolling Stones, U2, and Pink Floyd, it is nevertheless a worthy entry in any collection on design concept and implementation.

Periodicals

Live Design—www.livedesignonline.com—The convergence of three magazines that covered different aspects of live entertainment technology: *Entertainment Design, Lighting Dimensions*, and *Staging Rental Operations*.

Internet

www.livedesignonline.com—The relatively new periodical *Live Design* has spawned a Web site that is full of information for the theater pro.

www.sceno.org—*Scenography—The Theatre Design Website* is run by the Online Society of Theatre Designers and Scenographers and offers a place to network with other designers and share protfolios and advice.

www.usitt.org/commissions/SceneDesign.htm—The home page of the United States Institute for Theatre Technology's Scene Design Commission.

5

TECHNICAL DIRECTOR

To be too proud to simply raise your hand and say, "I don't know how to do that," is ridiculous because that's what TDs do everyday—encounter things that they've never done before.

—BILL DuWELL,
technical director, American Players Theatre

There are a few areas of technical theater that grow increasingly complicated and difficult to categorize as technology and its applications in live entertainment continue to soar ever higher. The field of technical direction is certainly the premiere example of this. "The term 'technical director' is a very squirrelly term," says Drew Campbell, head of the MFA program in theatrical technology at the University of Texas at Austin. "People use it for all different kinds of jobs."

But no matter how their duties may vary, technical directors (TDs) are undeniably the backbone of technical theater. They are the ultimate problem solvers, the essential link between a director's vision and the realization of the design. TDs, as they are commonly known, are responsible for some of the most unglamorous work in the

The scene shop of the Alley Theatre in Houston, Texas. (Photograph by Joe Aker.)

arts, and yet without them little of the spectacle that today's theatergoers have come to expect would be possible at all. Every theater has one (or someone who does the work of one, no matter what the title), and each technical director faces a unique set of challenges. TDs work in vastly different organizations—struggling semiprofessional theaters, college and university theater programs, big resident companies, commercial producers, and everything in between. They oversee the building and installation of scenery in wildly varying shop facilities and load their sets into every imaginable kind of theater space and stage configuration. What they have in common is working under deadline and struggling with budget constraints, whether the budget is hundreds of thousands of dollars or whatever happens to be in the petty cash box.

BUILDING FOR THE ELEVATOR

Anthony Contello began working at the Alley Theatre in Houston as a high school student on the scene shop's **overhire list** ten years ago. Eventually, he became the technical director, where from 2003 to 2006 he oversaw a 17,000-square-foot shop that sits fourteen floors above the Alley's two theaters. (He recently left the Alley to become the TD for the University of Houston.) At the Alley, Contello supervised a crew of twelve that included his assistant, a shop coordinator, a lead carpenter, a stage supervisor, a paint charge, a scenic artist, and five scenic carpenters—a job probably as close to traditional as it gets for a professional technical director working in regional theater. At the Alley, one of the most important considerations is the size of the freight elevator that transports the scenery from a high-rise scene shop to the performance spaces below. "Almost all of our scenery has to be able to break apart and fit in our 10' × 14' freight elevator," he said of the Alley.

At Trinity Repertory Theatre in Providence, Rhode Island, TD Tom Buckland deals with similar obstacles. The theater's two stages have constrained access—one, like the Alley, is only accessible via freight elevator. "There is a lot of building on stage in each space," Buckland says. "Or, I get to design my build into very small puzzle pieces." Buckland, who has been the Trinity Rep's technical director for ten years, finds this aspect of his job one of the most challenging.

Though building scenery for transit in freight elevators can be challenging, it is not quite unconventional. Bill DuWell, the technical director at American Players Theatre (APT), on the other hand, has more than his share of the unconventional. APT does five shows in rotating repertory each season, which means the shows are all up at once and rotate on the stage throughout the season. The rotating rep, coupled with an outdoor stage, presents unique challenges for a technical director.

"The weather, combined with the rotating repertory, impacts everything we do," DuWell says. Many traditional approaches to scenery construction used in indoor theater must be altered to allow for the variety of weather that sets will be exposed to in the course of APT's June-through-October season. Most scenery is framed with light gauge steel, which must be rustproofed, rather than wood. DuWell's charge artist, who is responsible for single-handedly painting the five sets to the designers' liking, mixes sand into the paint used on all horizontal acting surfaces to provide traction during wet weather.

Another major concern is wind. "We get wicked storms here," DuWell says, and that means either eliminating scenery that is too tall or engineering creative ways to secure it. Accounting for all of this demands a lot of preseason analysis, and DuWell spends much of his time considering factors such as scenery storage and the time it will take to move one show off the stage and the next one on. In the same way that Campbell must keep his audience in mind, DuWell must build each show to break down into pieces that will install quickly and store easily in a limited amount of storage space.

HIGH TECH, BIG BUDGET

Throughout the country, interacting with constantly evolving technology has become an integral part of a TD's job. In an attempt to keep students in line with high-tech professional opportunities, new technologies are a major component of Campbell's program at UT. He has MFA students who have focused on multimedia, interactive video, and scenery automation. Campbell spent four years as a technical supervisor at Universal Studios in Hollywood and understands the importance of exposing his students to all aspects of technology used in the entertainment industry in order to keep them apace with the ever-changing job market. "The days of a technical director being able to grasp all of the skills that are necessary in a shop are gone," he says. "We are now in a situation where a TD is required to hire an expert who knows more about a particular area than the TD does."

Campbell, author of *Technical Theatre for Nontechnical People*, strives to give his students a broad overview so that they will be able to communicate effectively with specialists whenever their future jobs may demand it. In addition, he strongly encourages his students to focus on an area that they wish to specialize in. He wants his students to have the vocabulary and skills required to learn new technologies as they arise and to be able to communicate effectively with specialists that they may have to work closely with or manage one day. "As a TD you're going to be dealing with dozens of technologies: carpentry, welding, plumbing, networking, automated lighting, show control, pyrotechnics. The list goes on and on. So you've got to have really wide-ranging knowledge," Campbell says. And keeping up with change is as crucial to the technical directors' profession as it is to the medical profession or any profession that requires the continual absorption of new information. "Technical direction now requires a constant renewal of knowledge," Campbell says.

Ed Leahy, technical director of Chicago Shakespeare Theater (CST) since 2003, has become very familiar with using technology to produce spectacle. He's responsible for a seasonal scenic budget of $500,000 and regularly oversees productions full of impressive effects and complicated scenery. A graduate of the University of Delaware's Professional Theatre Training Program, Leahy had little previous exposure to the gadgetry needed for automating much of the scenery designed for CST, but has taken a proactive approach to learning about the safe operation of automated scenery. "It is an emerging field," he says, "and I ask a lot of questions during the build."

Leahy's job does differ from the work of many theatrical TDs in that he has no scene shop of his own. All CST scenery is built off-site by a Chicago area scenic house. Leahy admits that outsourcing scenic construction has advantages and disadvantages. The biggest downside is a lack of control during the build process, he says. "On the other hand, it's an asset because when difficult things need to happen, they come up with solutions." According to Leahy, the scene shop that does CST's work is frequently surprised by his willingness to admit ignorance to the technology they use from time to time. But, he says, there would be no better way for him to learn about the gadgets and processes with which he is unfamiliar.

With a seasonal operating budget of $13 million, CST can afford to try out innovative approaches to production. Leahy describes some of CST's productions as "outrageous in terms of spectacle" and says using new technology to work out creative solutions to the challenges that land on his desk keeps his work interesting. "I love my job," Leahy says. "I've got big budgets to do cool things in cool shows."

While keeping in mind the way automated scenery has become more prevalent in today's theater and in the work of technical directors, we should not forget about TDs like Bill DuWell, who use automation sparingly. This is important to remember when considering the role of the TD and technology.

"A lot of it comes from the type of theater that the institution decides to produce," Contello tells me, reminding us that the use of state-of-the-art equipment happens when the artistic leadership of a theater sees a need to create productions with a particular look or feel. "It's really about whether or not they choose to take us down that road or not," he says. "I'm not the person who decides."

"THE PRACTICAL SIDE OF THE STORYTELLER'S BRAIN"

For all their differences, TDs still share the same basic responsibilities. One of the most important aspects of technical direction is managing the scenic budget. To do this properly they must be able to estimate the costs of a production, including what materials are needed, how much they will cost, and how long it will take the shop crew to build the set. Sometimes certain scenic elements will need to be handled outside of the theater, and it's the TD's responsibility to obtain bids for this work. Production work always happens under deadline pressure, and the TD must also ensure that sets are installed and ready on schedule. Relationships with scene designers are also a crucial part of every TD's job. DuWell boils all of this down by describing his TD persona as "part of the practical side of the storyteller's brain."

With all of the logistics of set construction, most TDs don't spend much time honing their carpentry skills. Buckland, DuWell, and Contello build in their shops rarely, and Leahy will only occasionally need to build something on-site, in which case he employs CST's loading dock as a makeshift shop. "If I'm building it's as a last resort— or, I need to fulfill an urge," explains DuWell. Sometimes this is seen as an unfortunate turn of events by TDs who are used to getting their hands dirty when they worked as carps (theater slang for "carpenters"), but it is something that cannot be avoided due to all of the work that must go into a show before the build happens. "I'm envious of the ATD and carpenters," Buckland laments. "They actually get to build things."

The duties of the TD are plenty, but perhaps above all else is the ability of a TD to manage and work closely with a wide array of technicians, designers, and administrative people. Campbell says, in recent history "a TD has become more a manager of people and less the source of all technical information." DuWell, for example, is keenly aware of how he fits into the big picture at American Players Theatre and makes a point of keeping in constant contact with any member of the company that affects, or will be affected by, the work he does.

COLLABORATING: ENGINEERING ART

"I think a TD is the interpreter between art and engineering," Buckland says, describing the technical director's position as that charged with making reality from the conceptual work of a director and designer. In this process of bringing designs to life, the primary collaboration that technical directors encounter is with scene designers. It is the work of the designer that they will build and eventually install on stage. "They are all artists, and they all have a vision of their art and want it achieved," Buckland says, explaining what he's learned about working closely with designers over ten years as Trinity Rep's TD. "They each take their own kind of diplomacy." The relationship of most technical directors with scene designers is one of mutual respect for each other's craft. It is a relationship of reliance, too. "Most designers I have encountered are less interested with how the set gets built," Contello says. "The finished look is more important."

There are other critical areas of collaboration for TDs, though, and much of it is within their shops. Considering the size and quantity of scenery churned out in theatrical scene shops, the crew of the shop must be able to work closely, efficiently, and competently with each other and especially with the TD and ATD. Without respect among the often large crews involved, the atmosphere can be hectic, unnecessarily stressful, and, worst of all, unproductive.

◇✦

Spotlight on a Pro

Bill DuWell, technical director, American Players Theatre, 1998–present

A Stage in the Woods

In rural Wisconsin, about an hour west of Madison, is an outdoor classical company called American Players Theatre (APT). Founded in 1979, it has grown from a simple stage in a natural amphitheater in the midst of hilly farmland to an outdoor regional theater that seats 1,153. Bill DuWell began working for the theater as a scenic carpenter when the scene shop was nothing more than an old outbuilding of the farm that existed on the theater's 110 acres of land. They built most scenery outside because there simply wasn't enough room in the small shop. Since then, the company has grown substantially, and with that growth have come new facilities for every department, including a real scene shop.

TD Bill DuWell in his office at American Players Theatre. (Photograph by Sara Stellick.)

The stage, however, is still outside and nestled among the trees—and that presents challenges for all sorts of tech personnel at APT, including DuWell. The solution, for the most part, is the theater's intention to let the classic text they perform do the fancy stuff, while keeping the designs as complementary to the outdoor stage as possible. "We work very hard to preserve design integrity while remaining acutely aware of the limitations of our presentation style," DuWell says. With so many limitations and a modest seasonal scenic budget hovering around $30,000, the APT productions stay relatively simple. DuWell, who describes himself as an "old school dude," seems to like it that way. "I like telling stories in simple ways," he says, "and I am fortunate to be working at a place that really relies on the basics."

◇✦

PATHS TO A CAREER AS A TECHNICAL DIRECTOR

For students considering a career in the scene shop, college and professional experience as a scenic carpenter can be one of the best avenues to earning the title technical director. However, Contello began working full time soon after earning his diploma from a Houston performing arts high school, and he never attended university. His advice to students interested in becoming TDs is to get on the overhire list of a local theater. "This way you can experience firsthand how the business really works," he says. Buckland agrees and thinks that certain trades outside of theater are an ideal basis for much of the work a TD does. "Books are great, theater schools are great, but the real world can give you perspectives on theater tech that you will never get from a book," he says. "The practical world can only help you."

Learning on the job—whether it be in a scene shop or on a construction site—will also provide a solid foundation for understanding how to approach different tasks and it will give you practice at problem solving. "It's also a great way to learn the variety of ways things can get done," Contello says, explaining that variety is something that students of technical theater should embrace because an individual's ideas for tackling technical jobs may be the next ingenious technique. "There are a number of ways to approach the same project," Contello says. "One of the hardest things to do is teach someone a new way to build or approach a project. It's good to be aware of the variety of approaches that may exist."

Finally, Campbell notes that even without the goal of pursuing a career in the shop, being involved in theater in high school or college teaches valuable lessons. "It teaches you to work with other people, to be collaborative, to work on deadline, to be creative, to be comfortable being up in front of people," he says. "These are all really important skills for anything." Campbell also has some concise advice for young design and production students who are interested in entering the ranks of professional technical directors. "Be a jack of all trades and master of one," he says. "You need to have that one thing that you are an expert at, because that will be your avenue to jobs. And be a nice person. Seriously."

✧✦✧

A Job Description

A typical TD has responsibilities that reach far and wide. In addition to scheduling and supervising shop crews, the TD is held accountable for any activity related to the creation, maintenance, and cost of all scenic elements. This includes drafting the plans that will detail the method of construction for the carpenters and communicating as necessary with the scene designer in order to ensure that the progress of the build is conforming to the original design. Technical directors must also attend production meetings on a regular basis (usually weekly) to keep other theater personnel abreast of build progress and any unexpected problems with construction. Once the build is complete, TDs supervise the installation of the set and address any unforeseen problems. At this point, they will also complete any items that could not be finished in the shop.

After installation, a TD's work is still not done. All technical rehearsals will be attended by the TD in order to make certain that no problems arise with the scenery now that it is onstage and the performers are interacting with it. Usually, a TD and crew will make slight alterations to scenery after watching actors use the space. When the show has opened and is in performance, the TD will stay in contact with the production carpenter (sometimes known as a stage supervisor or deck chief) to help with any repairs that might need to be done during the run of the show. Then, the TD starts the process all over again.

The Assistant Technical Director

Most technical directors have assistants, known as ATDs. DuWell, Leahy, and Contello each work with assistants that help them keep up with the details and keep their shops running smoothly. Leahy describes his assistant's duties this way: "I keep an eye toward the future; the ATD keeps an eye on the facility as it is right now." DuWell looks to his ATD to provide fresh perspective and skills he can rely on both in the shop and behind a desk.

Assistant TDs generally handle technical drafting, purchasing, and carpentry work during the build process. If the ATD is spending most of his or her time in an office, the direct supervision of the scene shop will fall to a person known as a shop foreman, shop supervisor, or master carpenter (see chapter 4 of this section for more detailed information on those positions). For self-proclaimed old-school technical directors like DuWell, an ATD can serve as a vital link to new technologies and approaches. "Because they aren't behind like I am in using various technologies, I'll ask them," DuWell admits.

"As an ATD, you really deal with the shows and the nuts and bolts of it," explains Contello. In short, working as an ATD is an excellent way to learn the craft of technical direction, even for folks with academic training in the field.

◇◆◇◇

WHAT DO TECHNICAL DIRECTORS EARN?

Unlike designers, stage managers, and even many stagehands and other theater artisans, technical directors working in regional theater are rarely represented by a union. As a result, TD salaries are as varied as the type of theaters in which they work. Estimating an average income is therefore quite difficult.

As noted in the introduction, I spent about four months conducting an exacting, but informal, survey. Of the 350 usable responses, nearly 60 of them were technical directors. Of the TDs responding, 94 percent garner more than half of their earnings from work in theater and more than 20 percent work for more than one theater as technical director. Of the nearly 60 TDs that responded to the survey, almost half of them—the largest group—earn between $35,000 and $50,000.

TABLE 5.1. EARNINGS FOR TECHNICAL DIRECTORS

Total number of technical directors surveyed = 57

Where the technical directors surveyed are working

Type of theater	Number	Percentage
Academic	1	2%
Broadway	-	-
COST	-	-
Dinner	2	4%
LORT	14	25%
Off-Broadway	1	2%
Opera	-	-
Regional	30	53%
Resident	3	5%
SPT	2	4%
Other	4	7%

How much technical directors are earning

Income range	Number	Percentage
Less than $10,000	-	-
$10,000–$20,000	2	4%
$20,000–$35,000	23	40%
$35,000–$50,000	26	46%
$50,000–$75,000	5	9%
$75,000–$100,000	-	-
More than $100,000	1	2%

How technical directors view their income

Perception	Number	Percentage
Below average	22	39%
Average	29	51%
Above average	6	11%

Source: 2006 Tech Theater Earnings Survey.

Of the TDs that responded, 51 percent believed that their income was within the average range of technical directors in the United States.

FIVE SCHOOLS OFFERING PROGRAMS IN TECHNICAL DIRECTION

BOSTON UNIVERSITY
Programs offered: BFA in Technical Production
MFA in Technical Production
www.bu.edu/but
Contact: Stratton McCrady, stratton@bu.edu

UNIVERSITY OF CONNECTICUT
Programs offered: MFA in Technical Direction
www.drama.uconn.edu
Contact: Jack Nardi, jack.nardi@uconn.edu

UNIVERSITY OF DELAWARE—PROFESSIONAL THEATRE TRAINING PROGRAM
Programs offered: MFA in Technical Production
BA in Theatre Production
www.udel.edu/theater/unique.html
Contact: Peter Brakhage, brakhage@udel.edu

NORTH CAROLINA SCHOOL OF THE ARTS—SCHOOL OF PRODUCTION AND DESIGN
Programs offered: Technical Direction
Stage Automation
www.ncarts.edu/ncsaprod/designandproduction
Contact: Dennis Gill Booth, boothd@ncarts.edu

PURDUE UNIVERSITY
Programs offered: MFA in Technical Direction
www.cla.purdue.edu/theater/graduate/technicaldirection.cfm
Contact: Richard M. Dionne, rdionne@purdue.edu

RESOURCES FOR TECHNICAL DIRECTORS

Books
Carter, Paul. *Backstage Handbook: An Illustrated Almanac of Technical Information.* 3rd ed. Louisville, KY: Broadway Books, 1994.

The bible of technical theater, this book can be found on most TDs' book-shelves, desks, and workbenches, and in their tool bags and road cases. (Check out the hidden jokes—ask a TD to show you where they're at.)

Glerum, Jay O. *Stage Rigging Handbook*. 3rd ed. Carbondale: Southern Illinois University Press, 2007.

After a long interval, there is now a much-needed new edition of this book, keeping it the best resource of its kind. It should be within reach of any TD that routinely does any sort of rigging. Glerum's *Handbook* acts as a great reference for ensuring that your rigging is sound and it is a great primer on the basics of rigging, giving even the most budget-strapped technician the mental tools needed to rig safely.

Sammler, Ben, and Don Harvey, eds. *Technical Design Solutions*. 2 vols. Boston: Focal Press, 2002.

These books are collections of articles from Yale's *Technical Brief* (see below).

Ogawa, Toshiro. *Theatre Engineering and Stage Machinery*. Royston, Hertfordshire, UK: Entertainment Technology Press, 2001.

Periodicals

Live Design—www.livedesignonline.com

The convergence of three magazines that covered different aspects of live entertainment technology: *Entertainment Design, Lighting Dimensions*, and *Staging Rental Operations*.

Stage Directions—www.stage-directions.com

Provides a good look at the industry and focuses solely on theater, unlike other publications that spread focus across all aspects of entertainment.

Internet

www.livedesignonline.com—The relatively new periodical *Live Design* has spawned a Web site that is full of information for the theater pro.

www.patrickimmel.com/usitt/techprod/tech_prod_index.htm—The Web site for the USITT Technical Production Commission, the site includes useful resources, such as the Technical Source Guide, and contact information. The commission also has useful projects online, including the Tenured TD Mentoring Project and Women in Theatre.

6

THE PROP SHOP

The only rule in props: no rules. It's never going to be the same twice.

—JIM GUY,
properties director, Milwaukee Repertory Theatre

Props is in one sense a shortened version of the slang word "propers," a term describing the respect due an individual for any number of reasons. For a classic example of its use, just have a listen to Aretha Franklin's seminal soul rendition of "Respect." In the theater, though, "props" is an abbreviation of the word "properties," as in stage properties. And, as you will find in this chapter on the work of theatrical props departments, that is a fitting, if generally overlooked coincidence, because those toiling in the land of stage props certainly deserve their share of, well, props.

A scene from Milwaukee Repertory Theater's 2005/06 Quadracci Powerhouse Theater production *A Month in the Country*. Pictured (left to right) are Laura Gordon, Rose Pickering, Jonathan Smoots (all at the card table), Karissa Vacker (at the piano), and Brian Vaughn. (Photograph by Melissa Nyari Vartanian.)

THE PROPS DEPARTMENT

Theatrical or stage props may include **hand props** (items carried by performers), **set dressings**, costume accessories, furniture, and many other things that appear on stage.

A theater's props department is comprised of a department head (known variously as the master or mistress, manager, director, or designer) and any number of prop artisans who have diverse skills. The number and abilities of the prop artisans working in a shop will depend on the size and budget of the theater, the length of the season, and the skills and needs of the prop manager. If a theater has a small budget and a talented prop manager, it will likely not use any prop artisans. But the same manager, working for a theater with a larger budget, will be able to hire staff based on his own strengths and weaknesses. The manager must also have time to deal with the procedural side of the work, such as keeping track of budgets, communicating with other production personnel, and keeping an eye on future projects.

Jim Guy, properties director of Milwaukee Repertory Theatre, may be in these respects the envy of many prop managers. He has a full time prop staff of six talented individuals, including a carpenter, **shopper, soft props** specialist, crafts specialist, graphics specialist, and one person who roves, working in many different areas, including electronics. This enables Guy to concentrate on the bigger picture, dealing directly with designers, directors, budgets, and set decoration, which he admits is his favorite part of the job. "Set decoration can and should be really rich and detail oriented," he says of his affinity for putting the intimate touches on scenery. "It can be a major contributor to the effect that the play has," he says. Other props departments throughout the country are variations on Guy's setup at Milwaukee Rep, but many theaters do not have the budgets to retain such a diverse staff, requiring the prop manager to be more hands-on in the creation of props.

All props departments, regardless of the theater or the size of its staff, are responsible for a wide range of tasks. "I need to be a master of every trade," says Michelle Moody, properties manager of PlayMakers Repertory Company in Chapel Hill, North Carolina, from 2003 until 2006, and now a freelance prop artisan. "The ultimate properties manager is comfortable painting, building, welding, sewing, shopping, carving, electrifying, and going to meetings," she says.

Aside from the actors themselves, every physical item that appears on stage is covered by three departments: scenery, costumes, and props. Any prop that is carried by an actor (known as a "hand prop") is the responsibility of the prop shop; any piece of set dressing, including furniture, that is not built by the scene shop is built, found, or refurbished by the prop shop; any costume accessory not built by the costume shop (such as a walking cane) is provided by the prop shop. The prop shop is even responsible for food that appears on stage, including devising its preparation and storage routines for performances so that the **running crew** can recreate the same item for each show. Each and every prop must also be researched thoroughly to ensure its authenticity in terms of the era and specifications in the text.

A typical prop shop will have a fair number of stock props, often utilizing a large storage area with many standard prop items, including furniture, weapons, soft goods, and most everything else you can imagine. Ideally, it will have the area and tools to build items that may range in size from large furniture to the smallest bag or coin.

TECHNOLOGY AND PROPS

On the subject of high-tech prop gimmicks, Guy is unequivocal: "Low tech is best tech," he says. That said, Guy would be more than happy to tell you about the dozens of instances that technology—especially the use of computer graphics—has been integral to creating props for shows at Milwaukee Rep. "We do use a fair amount of radio control and pneumatics, and a little bit of hydraulics," he admits, "but we're not doing anything with computer-controlled devices. . . . When we start to introduce computerized stuff for use on stage, that adds a level of complication that I think we can generally do without," he says. "As far as using computers, though, we certainly use them."

Guy and his staff have found the use of computers to be the most beneficial in the area of graphics. They create custom newspapers and magazines, and even reproduce famous paintings—sometimes altering the images to fit the design concept. "We just morphed our leading lady's face into a pre-Raphaelite painting," Guy tells me while listing off the wonders of computer graphics and the many ways Milwaukee Rep has employed them recently.

Guy is probably not alone among prop managers when he says he believes that technology such as this is best used in the service of the performer, who can hold a realistic newspaper or periodical and feel more in the world of a period piece. "A few years ago we did *Last Night at Ballyhoo*, and that opens in Atlanta, Georgia, in 1939 on the weekend that *Gone with the Wind* premiered," he says, explaining one of his favorite uses of graphics. "We were able to exactly reproduce the December 22, 1939, *Atlanta Journal-Constitution*. So, the actor actually had in his hand the newspaper he would have had in hand had this been that day."

This is the sort of high-tech wizardry that Guy welcomes most. His work as a prop manager and artisan is always in service to the world of the play, supporting the performers, the designers, the director, and the play itself.

Sometimes, though, a show calls for something that demands a solution only found through the use of gadgets. In 2004, during a production of *Richard III*, a dead body created by Guy's staff was a prime example of how technology can be useful. "That body bled on cue," Guy says with the sort of almost contained excitement that pervades his conversations. "That was a combination of a small, almost silent twelve-volt pump, a blood reservoir hidden in the bier itself, and a radio control that ran the pump," he says. The body also had specially treated fabric to help the stage blood spread rapidly and was fitted with the cast face of an actor in the show. This is just one example of the lengths to which a prop manager like Guy will go to make the show the best it can be, even when it calls for a bit of prop gadgetry.

COLLABORATING: BEING PREPARED

In terms of the range of projects for which it is responsible, the props department has perhaps the most diverse work of a theater's production team. This department is faced with making decisions on how to handle sometimes very elaborate and difficult tasks that can cross over the lines of every major specialty of tech theater.

"Props is the area of theater that I believe more than any other crosses over or is affected by the other areas of theater," explains Guy, who has run the prop shop at Milwaukee Rep since 1998. The work of the props department can affect the running crew and stage managers ("Will the armoire fit through this door for the scene shift?"); the lighting designer ("Is the top of this coffee table too reflective? Does this have to be a battery-operated lamp on the desk?"); and the costume shop ("Does the sword goof up the hang of the coat? Is the gun too big or too heavy to put into a pocket?"). "We go every place," Guy says. As a result, the prop manager's job requires effective communication with designers, directors, stage managers, technical directors, production managers, and costume directors, among others.

It would seem that prop managers have their hands in more areas of technical theater than any other theater pros. And perhaps they do. This means that superb communication skills are a must. "I find that sharing information with everyone is usually the best approach," explains Moody.

Jennifer Stearns-Gleeson, prop manager for CENTERSTAGE in Baltimore, agrees that communication throughout the process is essential. "You have to stay on top of this or you will be wasting a lot of time working in a bubble that will burst once all the parts come together in tech," she says.

Props is all about being prepared. "There's no guarantee that when they ask for something in rehearsal and then say, 'Oh, but it's going to be all the way upstage, and nobody's ever going to stand on this chair,' " says Guy. "You get to third tech and all of a sudden [somebody says], 'wouldn't it be cool if . . .' " So, Guy makes certain the props coming out of his shop are built to exacting standards that will allow their use in virtually any situation. "Our assumption is that everything is going to be played as if the audience is going to breathe on it."

Similar to costume work, the props department also works closely with performers in order to meet their needs, at times altering designs in order to increase comfort and accommodate disabilities. According to Guy, the props department has the power to enhance an actor's performance and thus the power of the production itself. "It helps them get into and stay in character and feel supported by the stuff that's around them," he says.

THE SHOP

"Props departments are often forgotten when planning a theater, I've decided," Moody says. It is possible that an ideal props department does not exist, but good prop managers know what they need in order to supplement their skills as well as free their time so that they can deal with the logistics of running a props department. "My goal is to hire people who are better at what they do than I am at what they do," Guy explains. Having the right staff enables managers like Guy to give accurate cost and time estimates. It also gives the shop a reputation of quality and craftsmanship that lends itself to trust on the part of other production personnel such as the production manager and technical director. "My job is to know enough about what the people in my shop do to be able to ask them realistically to do things and know what their process is," says Guy. He also believes that fostering the proper creative atmosphere is essential to getting the most out of his prop team. "We respect these individuals as artists," he says. "They feel invested in what goes on stage."

But not all theaters can afford to hire a prop manager as well as the six full-time staff positions that Milwaukee Rep's shop employs. Guy is fortunate enough to work at a well-established LORT theater that has an annual operating budget of over $9 million. When Moody was the head of the shop at Playmaker's Rep, things were different. The theater, which is part of the University of North Carolina's Department of Dramatic Art, operates on a budget of just over $1 million and was only able to employ Moody and one prop carpenter/welder full time. "He takes all the fun projects," she joked. Otherwise she relied on work-study students and one student assistant.

The contrast between Guy's shop and Moody's underscores one of the concerns of this book, because it applies to virtually all career paths in theater. Finding work at a small theater with a modest operating budget is far more likely for the young technician or designer than landing the dream gig at a large, well-funded one. In fact, many theater professionals with years of experience find it difficult to move into more financially stable situations, so they decide to teach to supplement their careers. In the section that follows, we'll take a look at the realities of a theater education in props and the path to a good gig.

Spotlight on a Pro

Jim Guy, properties director, Milwaukee Repertory Theatre, 1998–present

The Prophet of Props

Writing this book kept me on a perpetual search for theater professionals who were willing to talk about the work they do. At times, I came across a personality so fervent and full of theatrical wisdom that it was nothing short of inspirational. Jim Guy was one interview subject who, simply put, I loved talking theater with. He was referred to me by Lindsay Jones, a sound designer (see chapter 12 for more on Jones) who told me that Guy was "the best props guy in the country." While that may be a subject open to debate, there is no question that Guy loves the work he does and hopes to inspire future prop artisans and help guide them toward the respect and passion that he has for theater. According to Guy, one of his missions in life; to "spread the gospel of props."

"Part of what we do is support the performances," he says, discussing the ins and outs of creating props that can be appreciated by the audience while adding to the world of the play in order to boost a performer's connection to the text. "I'm not the one that people are paying to see," he reminds me. "People aren't paying to see the furniture."

His beginnings in theater were auspicious. Coming from an undergraduate life that focused on becoming a librarian, his skill and training as a researcher gave him a leg up in the world of props, and after delving into the professional theater at the Cleveland Playhouse, he went on to earn an MA in theater from Kent State University in Ohio.

Eventually, he landed as a professor of theater at the University of Illinois at Urbana-Champaign and founded the MFA program for props design. But after seven years in this position, Guy began to worry that continuing indefinitely in academic theater would harm his students' ability to learn from a working professional, and it was keeping him from the regional theater he loved. "As soon as I had the opportunity, I went back to professional theater," he says. "It's different from doing any other kind of theater."

◇✦◇

PATHS TO A CAREER AS A PROP ARTISAN OR PROP MANAGER

"A good props person can always get work," Guy believes. On the other hand, what type of formal training, if any, a prop artisan should seek is a difficult subject. Guy, who began and headed the MFA props program at the University of Illinois at Urbana-Champaign from 1991 to 1998, admits to seeing the advantages of graduate studies. "If you go into the right program, you can benefit from the experience of someone who was or is a professional in the field," he says. "And, you have the instant safety net of the academic world; that is, you are allowed to fail." He explains that the diversity of training in a typical three-year graduate program can provide the student with a much broader base of experience than could possibly be gained in the same amount of time in the professional world. This, coupled with the fact that one's ability to, as Guy puts it, "pay the rent" will not be adversely affected by making mistakes in a university setting, leads one to accept Guy's premise that participating in a quality program of study may be the best approach for someone who is certain of the field he wishes to pursue.

"There are very few students who have more than a passing interest in props once they learn how much work goes into it," says Moody, who graduated from West Virginia University with an MFA in Scenic and Properties Design. "Those who *do* want to continue usually have a props temperament," she says, stressing the degree of commitment necessary to a life in props.

While finding your way into one of the handful of graduate prop programs in the country or one of the scene design programs may be ideal, it doesn't seem to be the way the average prop artisan becomes a pro. "Most prop people I have found probably have undergrad degrees from theater departments and then they earn while they learn," Guy tells me. "They learn the job on the job."

Whether you complete your academic training or not, Moody has some final advice: "Make sure you get paid for it once you're out of school," she warns. "There are too many people who will take advantage of your desire to learn, and the truth is, there are very few people who know how to do props."

Another consideration may be that two of the professionals with whom I spoke in the process of my research are no longer staff prop managers. I mention this not because it invalidates my interviews with them, but because I believe it is a testament to both the challenges of "propping" in theater and the limbo-like status that props departments retain. They exist in a decidedly gray area that lingers between nearly every other creative specialty of the theater, and they are typically staffed by folks who could easily toil in any one of the other shops or departments in the theaters for which they work.

It is this lingering existence, in some ways unrecognized as a discipline of its own (especially in academic settings), that makes one such former prop manager admit that the position is a "luxury position for many theaters." Guy also acknowledges the sometimes dicey chances for theater technicians but believes that a prop person with talent and adequate experience will always find employment with fair compensation.

✦✧✦✧✦✦✧✦✧✦✧✦✧✦✧✦✧✦✧✦✧✦✧✦✧✦✧✦✧✦✧✦✧✦✧✦✧✦✧✦✧✦

A Job Description

"Props are there every step of the way," says Stearns-Gleeson. The first step a prop manager will take is to read the play at hand, marking any area that will affect him and making lists of props that may be needed. This will include items that are not explicit in the text but that have been alluded to, such as characters dining ("What are they eating?" the prop manager will ask). The director and designer may also contribute to the list of necessary props, based on their concept. Once the final (or near final) list has been compiled, the prop manager must determine whether any props will be the responsibility of another department, like the scene or costume shops. Such decisions are based on many factors, like the size of the prop shop and the individual theater's structure of responsibility.

Then, the building and gathering process begins. By this time, the prop manager has determined what props will be built, purchased, pulled from stock, or rented. During the build process, the manager will provide any necessary rehearsal props to the stage manager to be used during rehearsal by the actors. These are nearly as important as the actual production props because actors will use this time to discover the physicality of using props during their performance. Therefore, the closer the prop is to the final product, the better.

Once the build process is over, the prop manager will turn the actual props over to the stage manager and/or assistant stage manager (the person usually in charge of props during performance). If there are prop weapons to be used, the prop manager is responsible for ensuring that any crew member or actor handling the weaponry has been fully trained and understands the safety precautions of the prop. He may also need to train crew members on the proper maintenance and care of certain props, including weapons.

The manager may also be responsible for creating prop tracking lists and other paperwork to assist the stage management team in working with the props. When the show is over, the props department will collect the props to be put into storage, returned to rental houses, or destroyed.

✧ ✦ ✧

WHAT DO PROPS FOLKS EARN?

As noted in the introduction, I spent about four months conducting an exacting, but informal survey. I contacted over one thousand theater pros and asked them to fill out a basic, confidential survey. The survey was by invitation only, in order to prevent people who may have stumbled upon the Web site from inputting false or misleading information. There were approximately 350 usable responses.

Of those 350, 35 of them were prop artisans—most in managerial positions. In fact, only a handful of the respondents were employed strictly as prop artisans. Ninety-six percent of the respondents garner more than half of their earnings from work in theater. Most prop artisans and managers reported earning between $20,000 and $35,000 per year, with only two respondents earning more than $50,000. Most of the 35 respondents were employed by LORT theaters.

Sixty percent of people working in theatrical props believed that their income was within the average range of prop artisans in the United States. Keep in mind that this survey does not necessarily account for prop artisans who may be represented by a labor organization, as some of them may be. Mostly, however, prop

TABLE 6.1. EARNINGS FOR PROP ARTISANS AND MANAGERS		
Total number of prop artisans and managers surveyed – 35		
Where the prop artisans and managers surveyed are working		
Type of theater	*Number*	*Percentage*
Academic	-	-
Broadway	-	-
COST	1	3%
Dinner	-	-
LORT	21	60%
Off-Broadway	-	-
Opera	-	-
Regional	11	31%
Resident	1	3%
SPT	-	-
Other	1	3%
How much prop artisans and managers are earning		
Income range	*Number*	*Percentage*
Less than $10,000	1	3%
10,000–$20,000	4	11%
$20,000–$35,000	19	54%
$35,000–$50,000	9	26%
$50,000–$75,000	2	6%
$75,000–$100,000	-	-
More than $100,000	-	-
How prop artisans and managers view their income		
Perception	*Number*	*Percentage*
Below average	14	40%
Average	20	57%
Above average	1	3%

Source: 2006 Tech Theater Earnings Survey.

artisans are not represented in their theater work. It may also be significant that of the remaining respondents, a full 40 percent believed their income to be below average. In this case, the response to this final question is revealing in that it may in fact demonstrate a belief on the part of props folks that they are undercompensated for their work, rather than below average in comparison with others in similar positions.

THREE SCHOOLS OFFERING PROGRAMS IN PROPS

BOSTON UNIVERSITY—COLLEGE OF FINE ARTS
  Programs offered: Certificate of Training in Properties
  www.bu.edu/cfa/theater
  Contact: Roger Meeker, rmeeker@bu.edu

NORTH CAROLINA SCHOOL OF THE ARTS—SCHOOL OF DESIGN AND PRODUCTION
  Programs offered: BFA in Theatre with concentration in Stage Properties
                       MFA in Theatre with concentration in Stage Properties
  www.ncarts.edu/ncsaprod/designandproduction
  Contact: Bland Wade, wadeb@ncarts.edu

WEST VIRGINIA UNIVERSITY
  Degrees offered: MFA in Scenic and Properties Design
  www.wvu.edu/theater/index.htm
  Contact: Joshua Williamson, joshua.williamson@mail.wvu.edu

RESOURCES FOR PROP ARTISANS AND MANAGERS

Books

James, Thurston. *The Prop Builder's Mask-Making Handbook*. Cincinnati, OH: Betterway Books, 2006.

_____. *The Prop Builder's Molding and Casting Handbook*. White Hall, VA: Betterway Publications, 1990.

_____. *The Theatre Props Handbook*. White Hall, VA: Betterway Publications, 1990.

_____. *The Theatre Props What, Where, When*. Studio City, CA: Players Press, 2001.

New York Public Library. *Desk Reference*. 4th ed. New York: Prentice Hall, 2002.

Wilson, Andy. *Making Stage Props*. Marlborough, UK: Crowood Press, 2003.

Internet

www.sourcebk.com/atac/—The Web site of the Association of Theatre Artists and Craftspeople.

www.proppeople.com—An online resource for prop artisans that's recently been reworked into a blog. It is still a site with useful resources, links, and a job board.

www.spamprops.org—The Web site of the Society of Properties Artisans and Managers.

www.ebay.com—An invaluable tool for tracking down and buying props, eBay was mentioned by almost every prop manager and artisan interviewed for this book.

7

THE SCENE SHOP

I'm envious of the ATD and carpenters. They actually get to build things.

—TOM BUCKLAND,
technical director, Trinity Repertory Theatre

There are only two jobs in the scene shop that have been separated from this chapter: the technical director and the scenic artist. Otherwise, we will consider all typical scene shop jobs here, including scenic carpenters, master carpenters, and assistant technical directors, in addition to touching on some affiliated or differently titled positions, like stage carpenters, stage supervisors, and shop foremen.

Scenic carpenter Emily Brainerd at work in APT's scene shop. (Photograph by Sara Stellick.)

Unlike the staff of a costume shop, the division of labor in a scene shop is usually more about delegation, supervision, and experience than specialization. Within the scene shop there will inevitably be those who excel at certain skills, such as welding or **CAD**; but, as any scenic carpenter or TD will tell you, the best members of a scene shop team are those that have the broadest experience and the deepest well of skill sets. This is because building scenery for theater requires people who are able to constantly shift between various types of materials and at times wildly different applications, depending on the production.

MASTER BUILDERS . . .

With the technical director acting as the head of the scene shop, there are several ways in which the leadership structure beneath the TD can be set up. Generally, the person (or persons) who assists the TD with office work, drafting, engineering, and budgetary concerns is the assistant technical director, or ATD. In some cases, the ATD will also act in the role of master carpenter and/or scene shop foreman, which means his duties will extend into the build process of the shop. In a traditional setup, however, the role of the master carpenter will be distinct from that of the ATD. A common hierarchy of a theatrical scene shop is as follows:

Technical Director
- ◆ Assistant Technical Director

    - ◆ Master Carpenter/Scene Shop Foreman
    - ◆ Shop/Construction Supervisor
        - ◇ Scenic Carpenter(s)
        - ◇ Stage Carpenter(s)
    - ◆ Stage Supervisor/Deck Chief

- ◆ Charge Artist

    - ◆ Scenic Artist(s)

This is a typical interpretation of responsibilities and lines of supervision, but this model is extremely flexible and will adapt to the individual needs of theaters and their staffs.

At the Oregon Shakespeare Festival, for instance, the structure above is roughly accurate, and the same basic hierarchy applies. But because of the sheer size of OSF (three theaters, eleven shows in rep, and a $20 million annual operating budget), the list fills out considerably and includes a shopper, two construction supervisors, two master carpenters, one master welder, and a handful of scenic carps.

However, the structure outlined above is certainly not how things always play out in the real world. Joseph Donovan, the ATD for Penobscot Theatre Company in Bangor, Maine, is just one example of how a life in the theater is sometimes not as straightforward as the diagram above (and the shop at OSF) may lead us to believe. "I am responsible for executing all aspects of lighting and sound design," he says, indicating how his duties extend into electrician work and sound engineering. "I am responsible for assisting all rentals with technical aspects and for assisting with teching out the scenic design, and I am part of a three-person crew for construction." Working not only as the company's ATD but also as its master electrician and the facilities manager of the theater company's venue, the Bangor Opera House, Donovan is what you might call a jack-of-all-trades. His ability to juggle all of these areas is remarkable and is in stark contrast to what an ATD at the Oregon Shakespeare Festival would be responsible for.

As a much more conventional example, there is Tony Lawrence, the master carpenter for Delaware Theatre. He explains his work in the simplest of terms: "I work on the floor [of the shop], building the plans that the technical director gives to me," he says. "I make sure all of the tools are in working order as well as quality control for the scenery that is made." Lawrence, a man of few words, makes his work in a rather traditional scene shop sound like a no-brainer, but in reality it is more complex than he lets on. For starters, a master carpenter must have the same sort of traits and skills a TD or ATD has: good people management skills and enough knowledge of building scenery to get just about any job done. This includes expertly working with wood, metal, plastics, hydraulics, automated systems, and computer drafting, and being able to accurately read a designer's or draftsman's plans. A typical master carpenter must also maintain and operate shop tools of all kinds. All of this, from the tasks of the ATD to those of the master carpenter and scenic carpenters, is hard work too. When I asked Lawrence what his least favorite part of his job was, he said, "carrying heavy things."

At Yale Repertory Theatre, Sharon Reinhart is officially a Theatre Technician II, Grade C. But that's just the bureaucratic title of a university-funded position. In plain terms, Reinhart is a scenic carpenter for Yale Rep, and she sometimes works for the School of Drama there as well. "The TDs of the shows at the Rep are students in the school's masters program in technical design and production," Reinhart tells me. "So, there's also an educational element to the carpenter's position." In this way, Reinhart's job—which she has held for over five years—turns the conventional hierarchy of scene shops on its ear. "We provide feedback on drafting and advice on construction," she says of her atypical interaction with a rotating roster of student technical directors. Otherwise, her work as a scenic carpenter is fairly conventional: working with all types of building materials to construct scenery for Yale's top-notch repertory company.

Union shops are another category of shops to consider here. In scene shops with employees represented by **IATSE**, the diagram above is clearly defined. "We are in an IA shop," says Mike Dombroski, the ATD for Seattle Children's Theatre, as he explains the more clearly defined processes and positions of union shops "So, my hands-on role is fairly limited." In other words, you won't find Dombroski out on the floor of the scene shop, wielding a staple gun, building scenery. His role is much more office-oriented than that. Because of the number of shows SCT produces each year, Dombroski also acts as the primary TD on about a third of their productions.

. . . AND OTHERS

The personnel covered in this chapter also extend beyond the confines of the scene shop. At Chicago Shakespeare Theatre, for example, there is no in-house scene shop (as those of you who read the chapter on technical directors may recall). Yet, even without an on-site shop, the theater still employs those necessary for the installation, supervision, and operation of scenic elements. The full-time crew includes a TD, an ATD, and a backstage supervisor named Jen VeSota.

VeSota, who has worked full time for Chicago Shakes since 2004, is the person responsible for keeping the lines of communication open between a production's running crew, stage managers, and the technical director, VeSota's boss. She is also charged with maintaining any and all technical aspects of the show that fall under the jurisdiction of the TD. "This job involves working with the stage managers and the director during tech rehearsals to determine what the show's needs are and then making sure that the crew can execute any needed scene changes, et cetera, in a safe and timely manner," VeSota explains. "While participating in scene changes and other show needs, I am also responsible for the repair of broken scenery or props, paint touch-ups, organizing changeovers, and hiring and training crew subs." VeSota also stays in contact with other tech personnel, such as the master electrician, keeping them apprised of any technical matters that need to be addressed during the run of a show.

While the people running shows are generally on their own in many ways, the TD will oversee this area of a theater's operation and be kept apprised of any and all technical-related matters. "I am in constant communication with the TD of the theater so that we are on the same page with what his needs from the stage crew are," VeSota says. TDs will never be completely disconnected from any production thanks to their stage supervisors, who will keep them up to date on matters such as maintenance, crew needs, and technical problems. "I am always discussing these issues with him," VeSota says of Ed Leahy, technical director for Chicago Shakes.

COLLABORATING: BRINGING DESIGN TO LIFE IN WOOD, STEEL, PLASTIC, AND FOAM

"My biggest connection is with the carpenters," explains Leah Blackwood, the scenic artist in residence at The City Theatre in Pittsburgh. Like the folks toiling in a costume shop, scenic carpenters must be trustworthy craftspersons, able to adapt to ever-changing design elements and comfortable working with a wide array of people and personality types. Scene shop personnel will regularly interact with managers (production manager, technical director, prop manager, company manager, stage manager), designers, and others, especially scenic artists and prop artisans. This is the case with most, if not all, of those working under the direct supervision of the technical director, including positions generally found outside the shop, such as stage supervisors.

For Dombroski, who is the ATD of a union shop, jumping in and lending a hand in construction is rare, so his job tends to be more about coordinating and collaborating with the principles of set design and construction. "The TD and I work very closely together," he says. "We will meet several times prior to the start of the build and come up with a build schedule, a list of materials needed, [and] how to approach any difficult or unusual elements."

Because Seattle Children's Theatre has two performance spaces, Dombroski finds himself as the primary TD for some of the shows. This means that he will meet and communicate regularly with scene designers in order to hammer out the details of their work. "We will start talking with our designers several months ahead of their final deadlines," he explains. "As we progress through the process, we'll give feedback on budget, materials, and labor, and brainstorm for solutions to any difficult challenges." Once a set is built and installed, Dombroski's duties as ATD extend into the tech process, which he shares with the TD of the theater. "We split up the coverage of work notes and rehearsals," he says, describing the almost egalitarian nature of his working arrangement with the TD.

At the Oregon Shakespeare Festival, the shop is run in a similarly conventional manner, with clear lines of communication and authority. "I'm kind of at the bottom of the heap," says Steven Blanchett, a scenic carpenter for OSF. "The construction supervisors receive drawings from the design assistants," he says, explaining the beginnings of how scenery is built in his shop, which is responsible for three diverse performance spaces: an outdoor Elizabethan theater, a large proscenium theater, and a smallish black box theater. "The construction supervisors then draft up working drawings and pass them on to me," Blanchett continues. "The TD keeps the machine running smoothly and oversees everyone in the shop."

However, such a smooth, conventional arrangement is not always realistic, especially in scene shops that are not unionized, allowing TDs and ATDs to get their hands dirty. "Being such a small shop, everyone does everything," Donovan tells me of the shop at Penobscot Theatre, a company with an annual operating budget of only about $500,000. "Sometimes the TD will be doing as much hands-on work as the rest of us," he says.

PATHS TO A CAREER IN THE SCENE SHOP

"You cannot be successful in tech theater unless you are fully devoted to it and are willing to work insanely long and crazy hours," says VeSota, whittling a complicated career down what she believes to be the basic building block of the theater profession: work ethic. "My advice would be to develop a very good work ethic A.S.A.P."

And while many of the folks toiling in this area of tech theater tend to be young in their jobs, the fact that nearly all of them have at least an undergraduate degree seems to indicate that following their lead may be the only way to break into the field. "College is a great place to get hands-on experience with a safety net," says Donovan, repeating the oft-heard mantra of the college educated. "A good education is so worthwhile," agrees VeSota.

Practical experience, however, can go a very long way—so much so that if you feel college is not for you, a path to work in technical production can certainly be paved. "Our TD had never done theater before coming to work here," Donovan says, admitting that a degree in theater is not essential for entering the trade. While this may be rare, there are plenty of carpenters, ATDs, TDs, and other shop employees without formal training in their field. As VeSota indicated, work ethic goes a long way.

For example, Anthony Contello, who was until recently the TD of the Alley Theatre and now the TD for the University of Houston, never went to college. Instead he began his climb into the chair of technical director by getting on the Alley's overhire list while still in high school. For many carps working in scene shops, the position of TD is the goal, but for many it is not. It is fulfilling, as many young TDs find, to spend the day on the floor of the shop, building scenery, and it can be a difficult transition to spending most of one's day behind a desk and in meeting after meeting trying to figure out the practical operation of a theatrical scene shop. That said, if becoming a TD is your goal, there is no better way to learn the ins and outs of a shop than working as a scenic carpenter on the floor of one.

◇✦◇

A Job Description

While this chapter focuses on several different jobs within a scene shop, the overall responsibilities of each are remarkably similar: the engineering, construction, and maintenance of scenery for theatrical productions in a safe manner that holds true to the vision and intent of the scenic designer. In a nutshell, that is what all scene shops strive to do. And now for the specifics:

assistant technical director—The right hand of the TD, the ATD is generally responsible for the day-to-day flow of a working shop. While the TD tries to keep an eye on the big picture, including future productions and annual budgets, and works directly with the production manager, directors, and designers, the ATD must keep a handle on such things as construction drawings, tool maintenance, crew supervision, and similar immediate demands.

master carpenter/shop foreman—Generally, this is the person or persons who are the lead carpenters on the floor of the shop. They are active in the build process as carpenters but are also responsible for the supervision of all other carps and for implementing the plans of the TD and ATD.

shop supervisor—This is usually a subordinate of the master carpenter who retains a supervisory position over other carpenters in the shop. (This position is also known as "construction supervisor").

scenic carpenter—The title couldn't be less ambiguous. That's what scenic carpenters do: build scenery. All day. Different carps will sometimes have different areas of specialty, such as welding and metal work, furniture or fine carpentry, or automated scenery, and this will determine the projects they are assigned.

stage/deck carpenter—This person is responsible for maintaining the scenery (and possibly props) during the run of a show. Any problems that crop up or unexpected breakages will be initially addressed and fixed by this person.

stage supervisor/deck chief—A position similar to that of the stage/deck carpenter (and often the same person), the stage supervisor, or deck chief, is responsible for the scenic elements of a production once the performances have begun. At this time, the TD will usually begin on the next project, relying on the stage supervisor to see the show through its run.

◇◆◇

WHAT DO SCENE SHOP STAFFERS EARN?

The table below represents every area of the scene shop discussed in this chapter, including master carpenters, scene shop foremen, carpenters, and stage supervisors. It's no secret that working as a carpenter in a theatrical scene shop is not the way to become a millionaire, and the survey does not refute that. However, one of the best paths to becoming a TD is through practical experience, which can only be gained in the trenches of a shop. It is also important to remember that the skills of a good carpenter are almost universally applicable, and there are many, many venues for such skills. Moreover, many such venues are similar to a theater's in-house shop—for instance, a scenic house that specializes in building scenery for all types of companies, including theaters without shops of their own (such as Chicago Shakes). Carpenters working in such a place will typically earn a better rate of pay, especially in entry-level positions.

TABLE 7.1. EARNINGS FOR SCENE SHOP STAFF		
Total number of scene shop staff surveyed = 22		
Where the scene shop staff surveyed are working		
Type of theater	*Number*	*Percentage*
Academic	1	5%
Broadway	-	-
COST	-	-
Dinner	-	-
LORT	9	41%
Off-Broadway	2	9%
Opera	-	-
Regional	6	27%
Resident	2	9%
SPT	-	-
Other	2	9%
How much the scene shop staff are earning		
Income range	*Number*	*Percentage*
Less than $10,000	-	-
10,000–$20,000	2	9%
$20,000–$35,000	14	64%
$35,000–$50,000	4	18%
$50,000–$75,000	2	9%
$75,000–$100,000	-	-
More than $100,000	-	-
How the scene shop staff view their income		
Perception	*Number*	*Percentage*
Below average	7	32%
Average	8	36%
Above average	7	32%

Source: 2006 Tech Theater Earnings Survey.

FIVE SCHOOLS OFFERING DEGREES IN SCENERY

BOSTON UNIVERSITY

Programs offered: Certificate of Training in Stage Carpentry
MFA in Design, Production, and Management
www.bu.edu/cfa/theater
Contact: Roger Meeker, rmeeker@bu.edu

SAN DIEGO STATE UNIVERSITY
Programs offered: BA in Theater with concentration in Design and Technology
MFA in Technical Theater
http://theater.sdsu.edu
Contact: Ralph Funicello, ralf3d@aol.com

SYRACUSE UNIVERSITY
Programs offered: BFA in Design/Technical Theater
http://vpa.syr.edu/index.cfm/page/drama
Contact: Helen Cochren, fcochren@syr.edu

UNIVERSITY OF ILLINOIS AT URBANA-CHAMPAIGN
Programs offered: BFA in Theatre with concentrations in Scenic Design or in
Scenic Technology
MFA in Scenic Design
MFA in Scenic Technology
www.theater.uiuc.edu
Contact: Randy DeCelle, drandolp@uiuc.edu

UNIVERSITY OF KANSAS
Programs offered: MFA in Scenography
www2.ku.edu/kuthf/
Contact: Dennis Christilles, dchrist@ku.edu

RESOURCES FOR SCENIC STAFF

Books
Carter, Paul. *Backstage Handbook: An Illustrated Almanac of Technical Information*. 3rd ed. Louisville, KY: Broadway Press, 1994.

Glerum, Jay O. *Stage Rigging Handbook*. 3rd ed. Carbondale: Southern Illinois University Press, 2007.

Raoul, Bill. *Stock Scenery Construction: A Handbook*. Louisville, KY: Broadway Press, 1998.
This text is a basic, nuts-and-bolts sort of resource, full of useful information for the novice but with enough knowledge for the expert to make it a worthwhile addition to any ATD's or master carpenter's bookshelf.

Sammler, Ben, and Don Harvey, eds. *Technical Design Solutions*. 2 vols. Boston: Focal Press, 2002.

Periodicals

Live Design—www.livedesignonline.com

The convergence of three magazines that covered different aspects of live entertainment technology: *Entertainment Design, Lighting Dimensions*, and *Staging Rental Operations*.

Stage Directions—www.stage-directions.com

Provides a good look at the industry and focuses solely on theater, unlike other publications that spread focus across all aspects of entertainment.

Technical Brief—www.technicalbrief.org

A publication of the Yale School of Drama, *Technical Brief* provides articles that explain technical design solutions implemented by technical directors and other technical theater professionals.

Internet

www.patrickimmel.com/usitt/techprod/tech_prod_index.htm—The Web site for the USITT Technical Production Commission.

8

SCENIC ARTIST

I am not only a fine artist and a house painter, a plasterer and a mold maker, not only a wallpaper hanger and a letterer. It is all these things and more that make up a scenic artist.

—LEAH BLACKWOOD,
resident scenic artist, City Theatre Company

Scenery can be impressive, it's true, even as it stands and lays disjointed about a scene shop—especially if it is on a grand scale. But, there is a leap of imagination needed to look at it sitting there, waiting for completion and installation, and visualize what the scene designer has intended. If we put ourselves in that moment, staring sidelong at pieces of scenery before the magic of the scenic artist has been applied, it's easier to recall just how crucial this final step in the process is. The work of the scenic artist can make or break a set design.

Paint shop at Cobalt Studios. (Photograph by Frances Key.)

Scenic artists make a living painting the ideas and designs of artists other than themselves. What if, as Susan Crabtree and Peter Beudert imagine in the opening pages of their comprehensive text *Scenic Art for the Theatre*, Michelangelo had stood by while a team of painters brought his ideas to life on the ceiling of the Sistine Chapel? More akin to Andy Warhol's Factory is the life of the scenic artist (and, in reality, the life of most theater artisans), whether he works on the staff of a regional theater or in the giant paint shop of a scenic house.

Of course, scenic artists are artists too, as redundant as that may sound. Many of them are accomplished visual artists and designers in their own right. Their trade demands that they understand not only the techniques and skills necessary to create the special looks necessary for different types of scenic elements, but also the historical and stylistic approaches to art.

PAINTING THE SET

The manner in which scenic artists accomplish their work differs depending on the artist and the type of organization for which he is working. But the painting of huge amounts of scenery, from backdrops to the tiniest scenic element, happens under deadline pressure that would amaze many conventional painters. According to Peter Beudert, head of Design and Technology at the University of Arizona and coauthor of *Scenic Art for the Theatre*, there are two distinct roles a scenic artist may have to fulfill on any given production. The first is that of the organizer, a role frequently performed, when available, by the lead painter or charge artist; the second, and perhaps more obvious role is that of the painter or artist. "[It's] a big logistical job, and a big creative job," Beudert says of the demanding combination of project managing and creating art.

"My main responsibility is to take the information I am given by a designer and make it work on a large scale," explains Leah Blackwood, scenic artist in residence for the City Theatre Company in Pittsburgh. She describes her routine: "First, plans come in from the designers. That is when I make my initial estimates for my paint budget; then, I like to get as much information from the designer [as I can] so I can get started doing paint samples and research." She will also spend time conferring with the TD and scenic carpenters to determine details about the scenery before it is built so that she can be fully prepared when it is ready for paint. "I need to know what the set is built from, and I gather materials from the shop for my samples," she explains.

THE CHARGE

The lead scenic artist on any project or within any organization is generally known as the charge artist, charge person, or simply the charge. This person is responsible for all aspects of the paint shop, including supervising the other scenic artists, budgeting both time and money, acquiring materials, maintaining equipment, and acting as the contact point between the shop and the scene designer, as well as any other personnel who may be involved in the project, including the production manager, technical director, stage manager, or prop manager, among others.

Tom Langguth is the charge artist of TheatreWorks in Palo Alto, California. "My primary responsibility is to see that the painting of the set follows the designer's vision," he says of his position as charge. "I also have the responsibility to get the job done based on the conditions of the shop and the time I have." Blackwood also acts in the capacity of a charge, in that she is the supervisory scenic painter, and would oversee any and all painters that may be brought in to work on a production—though that is not her actual title.

When scenic artists such as Blackwood act in the role of the charge artist as well as actually painting the scenery, the facility to perform the roles described by Beudert of both organizer and artist is crucial. "To find a scenic artist who is a successful charge artist is really great," Beudert says, referring to scenic artists who excel at both project organization and management, as well as the artistry of scenic painting. In some situations, especially in large theater shops or scenic houses, a many-tiered level of hierarchy will develop in the paint shop wherein one or more charge artists are the immediate supervisors of all scenic artists, with several lead artists directly below the charge, who will often work on the same scenery as the scenic artists under their supervision.

THE SHOP

The first thing you notice about a fully functional paint shop is the sheer size. Because it usually takes a lot of space to paint scenery and full-size backdrops, paint shops dedicated solely to painting are large, fairly nondescript open rooms covered with paint of all shades and texture.

Scenery is usually painted in one of two ways: **painting up**, or **painting down**. As the terms suggest, the former is when scenery is painted utilizing wall space or some other form of constructed vertical surface to paint the scenery with it standing upright. This technique is sometimes accomplished with floating frames. These frames are large enough to hold backdrops, and usually work by either raising and lowering the frame itself below the deck, or by placing the painter on a bridge that can be raised or lowered that spans the width of the frame. Painting down, on the other hand, is characterized by painting scenery on the floor

Rachel Keebler, of Cobalt Studios, "painting down." (Photograph by Cliff Simon.)

or horizontally, also known as "conventional style." Either technique requires large areas of space to paint comfortably.

Another concern in the paint shop is the quality of light available for work. It is vital that the light, its color temperature and intensity and its effect on color, be understood by the scenic artist working in the shop. If the quality of light is not ideal, the painter must be aware of this and be conscious of how it may affect the work being done.

"I work in a fairly large shop," Blackwood says. "We have a paint deck that is big enough for a backdrop," she says, suggesting that her shop is set up for "painting down." But for others, especially many regional theaters with limited facilities, it is not always so easy to find the space needed for painting scenery. Some shops share space with the scene shop, which requires a delicate balance and carefully orchestrated transfer of scenic pieces from scenic carpenter to scenic artist. But however large or small, the paint shop can be a messy place, and it is the responsibility of the painters to keep it clean and organized in order to facilitate efficient working conditions. If you train with a scenic artist, one of the first things you will discover is the meticulous care scenic artists devote to their equipment. This is necessary fastidiousness, because it is quite easy to ruin expensive brushes with one careless action, such as forgetting to clean them. Scenery can be easily damaged too, either by improper technique or accidental spills, causing setbacks in schedules and budgets. All of these things can weigh heavily on charge artists, and a well-run paint shop makes their life much simpler and virtually stress-free.

UNION WORK

Scenic artists are represented by one of two labor organizations in the United States: United Scenic Artists 829 (USA) or a local chapter of the International Alliance of Theatrical Stage Employees (IATSE). While both of these organizations exist as individual entities, USA has been absorbed by IATSE, and therefore their membership has seen the benefit of working under both unions in some locales.

There are many benefits to being a member of a labor organization as a scenic artist, but it can be difficult to secure membership. There are only three methods by which USA accepts scenic artists, each requiring the applicant to prove in some way that he has the requisite skills to perform the duties of a professional scenic artist, be it in theater, film, or television. One way to be accepted by USA is through participation in an apprenticeship program for those less experienced artists eager to work their way into the field. The other methods of acceptance are by examination, in which the applicant takes a complicated test in order to demonstrate his skill level, and the final process, most aptly described as "peer review," which provides established artists an opportunity to fast-track their union membership. The peer review process requires a higher initiation fee. The initiation fee and membership dues are cost prohibitive to the young artist to be sure; however, scenic artists who are members of USA/IATSE are broadly viewed as having proven their talent and skills in their chosen field. When working in a major entertainment city, such as New York or Los Angeles, union membership will also be helpful for finding freelance work. Overall, being represented as a scenic artist can be very desirable, but it can also be overly competitive and biased, according to some. As a result, not all professionals have made the decision to join either USA or IATSE. Blackwood, for instance, having worked as a scenic artist in theater for over twenty years and contributed her painting skills to over two dozen films (including *Silence of the Lambs* and *Night of the Living Dead*), has never joined a union. One factor affecting an artist's decision not to join a union involves the work she seeks, as well as the work she has managed to land. Scenic artists in residence like Blackwood are probably less likely to reap the benefits of union membership because they may not have the time or inclination to pursue the freelance work dominated by USA and IATSE members.

"I belong to United Scenic Artists as a scenic artist, not as a set designer," explains Laura Mernoff, a freelance SA and scene designer based in Providence, Rhode Island. "It's called a journeyman scenic artist," she says. This is an important distinction for Mernoff and other scenic artists who also design because it means that while she can earn union wages as a painter, she can only design nonunion gigs

In short, the matter of union membership for the scenic artist can be a difficult and complex one indeed. It is important that each individual consider the move, and I highly recommend that the texts cited in the resources section below (especially Crabtree and Beudert) be consulted. All scenic artists must decide for themselves whether or not joining a labor organization goes well with their personal and professional goals.

COLLABORATING: THE FINAL TOUCHES

Because they work with such a vast canvas, full of intricate detail, while adhering to the vision of the scene designer, scenic artists must be master collaborators. "The scenic artist is the one who can take the things I try to put on paper and really make them happen," explains Beudert, speaking from his perspective as a scene designer. "Designers vary in their presentations, requests, and personalities," Langguth points out, "so one has to be open to new approaches." As the primary link between the designer and the scenery's final form, the scenic artist must be able to maintain a good working relationship with the scene designer. "When it comes right down to it, what the scenic artist does is paint your show for you," Beudert says. "They have to be able to get inside your head and be able to understand your intention."

Generally speaking, this is a relatively easy relationship due to the training most scenic artists have received, whether formally or through work experience. The team of the scenic artist and the scene designer is also helped along by the fact that many scenic artists are talented designers in their own right. Being an accomplished designer is certainly not a prerequisite for becoming a scenic artist, but the manner in which the two artists must envision scenery lends itself to the frequent progression from scenic artist to scene designer. The collaboration between the two manifests itself in different ways, depending on the circumstance. At times, the scene designer has a longstanding relationship with a certain scenic artist and can therefore cater to the talents of the artist, rather than attempting to design scenery that does not jive with the artist's demonstrated talents.

But, more often than not—especially in regional theater—the designer and scenic artist have not worked together or have worked together only occasionally. For this reason, there are certain tools of the trade that make the communication of highly visual ideas much easier to convey. Perhaps the most useful such tool is the **paint elevation**. Though this visual tool may come in different forms, including painted models, computer-generated imagery, or hand-painted plates, it must accurately convey the three things vital to the scenic artist's trade: color, line, and texture. With well-crafted paint elevations, a scenic artist has a reliable guide with which to execute the look the designer is striving toward. The scenic artist will also refer to the common forms that designers use, such as three-dimensional models and any drafting used for set construction. If the designer feels it necessary, he may also provide the scenic artist with full-scale samples of certain elements.

Once the artist has received the necessary tools from the designer, he can begin the process of determining how best to create the looks and textures called for in the design. Blackwood, when in the planning stages of a project, consults frequently with the designer to be sure she is headed in the right direction. "I like to get an okay from the designer on samples before I start out," she says.

✧✦✧

Tools of the Trade

Professional scenic artists bring their own tools. When working with such delicate items as paint brushes, it seems to make more sense to be responsible for your very own implements. When working under union contract, SAs will usually be paid a daily rental fee for the use of their personal equipment, and rightly so. The tools of this trade—especially the ubiquitous paint brush—are rarely cheap.

There are many tools that scenic artists use every day, on every project. Perhaps the most obvious tool at the disposal of the SA is the brush. But, as with most mediums of art, there are a variety of specialty tools employed and countless tools that the scenic artist will find invaluable. Below is a brief example of the tools that an SA may have in his tool bag or that will be hanging in the paint shop when he shows up to work.

Brushes and other tools of the trade at Cobalt Studios. (Photograph by Cliff Simon.)

brushes—There are dozens of brush types used by SAs, including many common types that we might use to paint a room in our house, as well as highly specialized brushes with very specific uses. For a comprehensive listing of brushes, their names, and uses, see *Scenic Art for the Theatre* by Crabtree and Beudert.

sponges—Used to create texture, there are a nearly infinite variety available—not including sponges created on the spot by cutting or tearing them up.

rags—Any old rag can be used to great effect by a scenic artist to create certain strokes and textures.

flogger—Bits of rags affixed to the end of an old broom handle or stick are used to create texture and special strokes.

paint sprayers—There are many types of sprayers, including some that are not traditionally used for painting but have been utilized in scenic painting for different purposes. These include *garden sprayers* and *aerosol spray cans*.

brooms—Brooms have several applications in a paint shop, such as smoothing drops and applying large quantities of primer or other materials.

edgers—An edger is a tool used to guide the painter's brush in order to avoid painting a surface not intended for the paint or treatment being applied.

extenders—An extender is nothing but some form of extension of a scenic artist's brush. Extenders are used a lot when "painting down" so that painters do not have to bend over or squat over scenery.

rollers—There are all types of paint rollers utilized by the scenic artist, including patterned rollers.

stencils—Used to paint design elements that repeat, such as with wallpaper treatments, stencils can be made from a variety of materials, including paper, wood, metal, or plastic.

paint stamps—Also used for repeating designs, stamps are made of a variety of materials, such as foam. The paint is applied directly to the material and then stamped on the scenery.

◇✦◇

PATHS TO A CAREER AS A SCENIC ARTIST

There is no shortage of work for talented scenic artists, especially those willing to work for large scenic houses or for film and television productions. The sheer amount of scenery being constructed and erected in these areas is astonishing, and all of it needs painting. However, work in theater, especially regional theater, is considerably less abundant, but there is still plenty of it out there.

Langguth, who has held his full-time position as charge artist for thirteen years at TheatreWorks, a LORT C company in California, recognizes how fortunate he is to be able to hold a long-term position in regional theater. "It is very easy to break into this business from the standpoint of community theater, educational theater, and many regional theaters that utilize part-time work," Langguth tells me. "The nature of the business is that when the show is done the job is over," he says. "Most theaters are only budgeted for one full-time scenic artist." This fact makes it difficult to land such a position and even harder to hold on to one, which isn't to say that working as a freelance scenic artist is not feasible or financially rewarding—it certainly can be, especially if you are working in the right metro area. But, according to Langguth, the freelancing lifestyle can be tough. "The challenge would be to be happy jumping from job to job," he says.

But regardless of whether one decides to pursue a resident position or is content with the life of a freelance artist, there is still the question of gaining the skill necessary to augment any talent a hopeful scenic artist may already have. "I think hands-on experience is the best way to teach scene painting," says Blackwood. "Books can't possibly give you all the knowledge needed for this profession." At City Theatre, Blackwood regularly trains young artists through the company's internship program. "I let interns work alongside me doing whatever task I am involved in," she tells me. "I also have interns do samples of faux techniques like marble and wood graining to get them excited about painting." Blackwood encourages her interns to seek out real-life examples of what they are trying to paint so that they are aware of what they are attempting to recreate.

Seeking an internship with a company that has a skilled charge artist may be one of the best courses of action for learning the trade, but there are certainly an ample number of training programs too, if you are seeking something more definitively structured (check out the programs listed on pages 93–94). Such a program can provide a diversity of training that will probably not be found through an internship, but that also depends on the theater where one interns.

A Job Description

So, the scenery has been designed, engineered, and constructed, and it is now lying in bits and pieces of various sizes about the scene shop, looking like strange vehicle parts—all primer gray—and raw wood. This is where the charge artist and any of his or her scenic artists enter the long list of theatrical technicians and artists who contribute to a production.

Having spent much time preparing for the moment by testing paint samples on similar materials, mixing color, and discussing the design with the scene designer, the SA will step in and begin a many-layered process of paint and texture application. The scenic artist is responsible for the application of color and texture to all scenery as designed by the scene designer. This may also include items that fall under the responsibility of the props department, such as furniture.

On any given project, a scenic artist will be asked to employ various skills, including the recreation of specific styles of art as well as various realistic textures and finishes. Once the work of the SA has begun, the scene designer will usually be present to assist with any difficulties or changes that may crop up. The technical director and the scene shop crew will also be on hand to address issues that may affect the scenic artist's work, including work space and problematic scenery.

When the scenery has been installed in the performance space, usually the scenic artist will still have work to do on the set, especially on areas that can only be addressed once the scenery is in place, such as continuous lines and texture. Though the scenic artist's work is usually done by the time the tech process occurs, it is not unheard of for them to be on call to add details or touch things up before opening. Often, a member of the running crew such as the stage carpenter will be left with touch-up paint to keep the set in good condition throughout the run, and the SA will train this person on the use and application of the paint.

WHAT DO SCENIC ARTISTS EARN?

The earnings of a scenic artist are affected by several factors, including the role that IATSE and USA play in a particular scenic painter's employment. Most of the professional scenic artists with whom I spoke while researching this book were nonunion and were all paid according to the means of the particular theater for which they worked, which is sometimes the equivalent of "not much." However, union membership is usually desired by the freelancing artist because it can guarantee

TABLE 8.1. EARNINGS FOR SCENIC ARTISTS

Total number of scenic artists surveyed = 9

Where the scenic artists surveyed are working

Type of theater	Number	Percentage
Academic	-	-
Broadway	-	-
COST	-	-
Dinner	-	-
LORT	6	67%
Off-Broadway	-	-
Opera	-	-
Regional	1	11%
Resident	2	22%
SPT	-	-
Other	-	-

How much the scenic artists are earning

Income range	Number	Percentage
Less than $10,000	-	-
10,000–$20,000	4	44%
$20,000–$35,000	5	56%
$35,000–$50,000	-	-
$50,000–$75,000	-	-
$75,000–$100,000	-	-
More than $100,000	-	-

How the scenic artists view their income

Perception	Number	Percentage
Below average	3	33%
Average	5	56%
Above average	1	11%

Source: 2006 Tech Theater Earnings Survey.

highly competitive wages as well as health and retirement benefits. Below you will find two charts giving brief glimpses into the earnings of theatrical scenic artists. The first is the much-too-limited response to my Tech Theater Earnings Survey.

As an example of union fees paid in New York City, I will refer to a recent agreement between USA Local 829 and the New York City Opera (table 8.2). Keep in mind that most scenic artists working outside of New York City and nonunion painters will probably look at this table and drool a little bit. It is *not* a realistic guide for the earnings potential of most scenic artists in this country working in the live performing arts. It is, however, a reality and certainly something that can be achieved with the right mix of talent and ambition.

TABLE 8.2. UNITED SCENIC ARTISTS SCENIC ARTIST RATES AT THE NEW YORK METROPOLITAN OPERA	
Type of Cell	*Rate*
MINIMUM CALL (7 hours in 1one)	$303.98
REGULAR CALL (8 hours)	$372.73
HOURLY RATE (over 8 hours)	$68.83
OVERTIME HOURLY RATE (over 10 hours)	$86.84

Source: United Scenic Artists Local #829, "New York City Opera Memorandum of Agreement."

SCHOOLS OFFERING DEGREES IN SCENIC PAINTING

The programs listed below are probably the most prestigious in the country that offer programs and degrees specifically for scenic artists; however, pursuing an undergraduate or graduate degree in scene design or just theater or stage design will usually provide the student with quite a bit of training and potential for experience in scene painting.

BOSTON UNIVERSITY
Programs offered: Certificate of Training for Scenic Artists
             BFA in Design
www.bu.edu/cfa/theater
Contact: Diane Fargo, diane.fargo@goodspeed.org

CAL ARTS
Programs offered: MFA in Scene Painting
www.calarts.edu/schools/theater/programs
Contact: Mary Heilman, maryhei@aol.com

COLBALT STUDIOS
Programs offered: Scenic Artist Training program
www.cobaltstudios.net
Contact: Rachel Keebler, rachel@cobaltstudios.net

RESOURCES FOR SCENIC ARTISTS

Books

Blaikie, Tim, and Emma Troubridge. *Scenic Art and Construction*. Marlborough, UK: Crowood Press, 2002.

An older text, but still quite informative and useful.

Crabtree, Susan, and Peter Beudert. *Scenic Art for the Theatre*. Boston: Focal Press, 2005.

This is truly the "bible" for scenic artists. A comprehensive text, covering information on training, finding a job, joining a union, relations with scenic designers, scene shop staffing, painting techniques, painters' tools, as well as several interviews with teachers and professionals and so much more. Highly recommended.

Periodicals

The Painter's Journal—www.paintersjournal.com

A small journal for the scenic artist, containing tips, advice, features, and interviews with scenic painters.

Internet

www.paintersjournal.com—A limited but rare Web site dedicated to the art of scenic painting, including links to scenic studios and back issues.

www.usa829.org—The Web site of United Scenic Artists is a good starting place for those interested in joining.

9

STAGEHAND

The name says it all. Perhaps the most diehard theater technician imaginable, a stagehand (often known simply as a **hand**) is probably also the person with the broadest knowledge of technical theater—a fact few stagehands will let go undetected either through example or (at times long-winded) conversation. While it is not the most prestigious position or one that most theater artists and students would consider a viable career option, many stagehands make quite an impressive living. This is especially true in the larger urban areas that have a combination of union representation and plenty of work to go around. Regardless of their pay, all stagehands make today's huge productions possible and are relied upon to execute some of the most difficult tasks before a live audience. They deserve both recognition and consideration in this collection of technical theater career options.

Minneapolis stagehand Larry Kline operates the fly system at the Ordway Center for the Performing Arts. (Photography by Matthew Winiecki.)

JACK OF ALL TRADES, MASTER OF SOME

For Joe Hartnett, master electrician of the Pittsburgh Public Theatre, the veteran stagehands in the city have taught him the most about theater—and not just technical skills. "They are quick to remind you that we make people happy, sad, cry, and laugh for a living," he says. "And if we do it right, they don't even notice that we were there." It's no surprise that Harnett has spent so much time conferring with long-time stagehands, for they frequently participate in crew calls that find them working in each and every area of tech theater, including electrics. It is this ability to act competently in diverse settings that is the mark of the good stagehand.

Because of the variety of working situations, the title "stagehand" can be at once misleading and incomplete. It's important to remember that this is a generic title of sorts and includes any number of theater technicians with sometimes vastly differing areas of specialty and expertise. Some of these areas, such as electrics and sound, have already been addressed elsewhere in the book. Union stagehands also frequently cover wardrobe crew needs, discussed briefly in chapter 16, on costume shops. But there are other specialties that we will discuss only here in the chapter on stagehands.

✧ ✦ ✧

Tools of the Trade

An old stage manager friend of mine used to refer to the various items clipped to my belt when I worked as a scenic carpenter and stagehand as my "dork tools." And I suppose, if you aren't a stagehand (or something similar), having a multitool, flashlight, and other miscellaneous paraphernalia attached at the waist might seem a bit odd—or even dorklike. But, for the theater technician, having certain tools readily available at all times makes the job much easier. It's part of what keeps theater work so interesting; you never know what you're going to be doing next. Many electricians, riggers, and stagehands like to keep a rock climbing **chalk bag** clipped to their belt to use for stashing various tools, screws, instrument lamps or parts, or anything else they may need while working.

A stagehand's tool bag (or belt) should contain the following:

C-Wrench (Crescent wrench)—A good size is 8" because it accommodates sometimes unexpected uses, but a 6" wrench is lighter and will work for most everything a stagehand may use it for. Having both on hand is probably best. Many stagehands like to keep some sort of tether on the wrench they use to focus lights so that they can keep it attached to themselves in case they drop it or don't have a place to set it down while up in the air.

cordless screw gun (perhaps not in the tool bag)

electrical tape

flashlight—A small flashlight that you can carry with you at all times without taking up too much space is preferable. Compact LED flashlights are great, as are headlamps for hands-free light while working in the dark.

gaff tape—Don't skimp here; if such tape runs out on-site or isn't provided, this stuff is invaluable, and a roll goes a long way.

multitool—There are many brands of multitools now on the market and most of them are well-crafted and practical for stagehands, electricians, and many other tech professionals. A multitool with at least a knife, pliers, and screwdrivers is a good start.

pens and pencils—It is important to carry pens and pencils—including Sharpies and paint pens—because you never know what you need to write on.

screwdrivers

socket wrench and sockets—The best tactic here is probably a small, cheap set that can remain organized and self-contained. Why? If it is stolen you can replace it easily, and it won't fall apart and get lost in your tool bag.

tape measure—It is nice to have a standard 25' to 30' tape, plus a long, flat tape measure at least 50' in length.

◇✦◇

MASTER TRADE: RIGGING

Aside from typical deckhand duties, such as loading trucks, installing sets and lights, and running shows, the most notable area of expertise associated with stagehands is rigging. Rigging, a term that is used both as a noun and a verb in the theater, refers to both the workings of virtually any object that requires hanging from a point in the air and the work required to hang it. This includes traditional **fly systems**, as well as temporary positions for lighting, sound, or scenery. Because it frequently entails working high in the air, it can be dangerous and must be handled by professionals who take the responsibility of the trade seriously. A stagehand's contempt for a rigger proved incompetent is rarely hidden and frequently brought up at every possible opportunity. Stagehands have little use or concern for incompetent technicians in their ranks, especially when it comes to areas that are fraught with potential for physical harm and even death the way rigging is.

The qualified rigger is usually a union worker and has proven aerial skills. These skills are sometimes verified through the Entertainment Technology and Services Association (ESTA) via its recently conceived Entertainment Technician Certification Program (ETCP). The ESTA also certifies electricians and works together with other concerned organizations, including IATSE and USITT, to keep qualified, educated technicians working safely in areas of technical theater and the entertainment industry at large. In order to qualify to take the examination, an applicant is rated by the ESTA using a point system for prior experience and training. The test is relatively expensive to take, undoubtedly to ensure that only the best applicants with an actual desire for certification take it. (For more information on the ETCP, see the resources section at the end of this chapter.)

Working in the air also commands a higher rate of compensation, owing to the level of danger for both the rigger and those who will rely on the safely executed rigging, including crew and performers. Those working on the ground are known as "ground" or "down riggers," and they are responsible for working in concert with the rigger in the air (sometimes called the "up rigger") to provide support and complete any work necessary for rigging a point that must be done from the ground.

In addition to being skilled in the use of rigging equipment, understanding its proper use and under what circumstances to use or not use it, qualified riggers must also have an understanding of how certain disciplines, like mathematics and physics, apply to the work they do. They must also be able to put this knowledge into practice—often while hanging in rather precarious positions high in the air. This means that aside from technical knowledge, a competent rigger should have certain complementary personality traits, including an above-average comfort with heights, adequate strength, balance, agility, and a sharp ability to stay focused. It is not, to be sure, a gig for the faint of heart, and it takes years to learn it well enough to be trusted by co-workers and employers.

For an extreme example of a rigger, check out the final chapter of the book and the work that Jaque Paquin does for Cirque du Soleil.

OTHERS: FROM TRUCK TO STAGE AND BACK AGAIN

There will be, depending on the venue, all sorts of specialists on local crews, including electricians and sound engineers. Because these areas are covered in detail in other chapters, I won't go into them here.

Another common stagehand position is the loader. These folks spend their lives in trucks loading and unloading scenery, lighting and sound equipment, rigging gear, and any other bits and pieces that productions may bring with them. Unlike rigging, it's not technically challenging work, but there is a degree of skill involved that can make load-ins and load-outs go smoothly, rather than painfully slowly. Stagehands are often employed as forklift drivers when working as loaders too.

A UNION GIG: IATSE AND THE STAGEHAND

The specific duties and responsibilities of stagehands are something normally dictated by the IATSE local under which the hand works. Most locals are set up in a similar manner—at least for those representing theatrical technicians. Below the TD, the union hands will report to the **steward**, who is responsible for the supervision of all members of the local crew during a work call. Below the steward is a position commonly known as the "head carpenter." The person acting in this position is the supervisor of all union carpenters and also any personnel working as stage crew. It might be important to point out that when an IATSE local refers to a stagehand as a carpenter, it is generally referring to the hand assisting the TD, and possibly the outside crew, with the loading, striking, and installation of scenery.

Otherwise, each area of specialty will generally have lead positions, such as a head electrician and properties head. There will at times also be assistants to the heads, in order to split up a particularly large crew. One strange aspect of the union stagehand arrangement is the frequent inclusion of sound in the electrics department. As with any large organization, change is often slowgoing; however, there have been signs of progress on this front, with some locals developing a separate department for its members whose primary expertise is in sound.

And don't forget: There are those that do the work of stagehands who are not and never have been members of an IATSE local. Speaking purely anecdotally, it seems as common in regional theater for stagehands and other tech personnel to be nonunion as it does for them to be members of IATSE. While many of these nonunion theater technicians are not earning wages equal to IATSE hands in a comparable position, some might argue that they are also not regulated by the union's upper hand and stringent protocol. There are those too, though, who do make a decent living as stagehands, scenic carpenters, electricians, sound engineers, and riggers without membership in IATSE.

We should also keep in mind that theaters (and other houses) that require the work of stagehands frequently contract exclusively with IATSE so that the stagehands must be union workers or hired through the union. Such employers are commonly known as "closed shops," and if you are not a union member, you must sign up for the union's overhire list to get work there when they need more people than can be provided through the organization. There are states, however, known as "right-to-work states" that do not allow theaters to operate as "closed shops," or ones that require certain laborers to be members of a union. In such states—nearly half of all states—labor organizations are not allowed to require that workers join a union, even if the employer has a contract with the union. (For more information on "right-to-work states" go to the National Right to Work Legal Defense Foundation's Web site at *www.nrtw.org.*)

◇✦◇◇

A Job Description

What is included in a stagehand's job? In a word: everything. Stagehands are the go to technicians in all kinds of production settings. Though often they are the people sitting around waiting for the curtain to fall once a performance has begun, they are just as often running the essential bit of backstage machinery during the run of shows. They are also the backbone of the labor-intensive installation and **strike** of theatrical productions.

During a **load-in**, stagehands can be found hanging and focusing lights, operating fly systems, unloading trucks, installing scenery, setting up sound equipment, rigging points for equipment that will be in the air, and any other task deemed necessary. Their work is equally diverse during the **load-out** and at every point between the start of production through the end. Generally, stagehands will run the show, acting as the stage crew, executing cues that require human labor, filling the shoes of flymen, deckhands, spotlight operators, sound engineers, light board operators, and much more.

◇✦◇◇

WHAT DO STAGEHANDS EARN?

The various agreements that IATSE (the union that represents stagehands and their related colleagues) has negotiated in different cities make it difficult to assign a definitive number. The many types of venues that employ stagehands, including roadhouses and regional theaters, also create an incalculable diversity of pay ranges. Because few theater artists identifying themselves exclusively as stagehands responded to my Tech Theater Earnings Survey, I have chosen to list a range of union pay rates across the country for the purpose of demonstrating common stagehand earnings.

Suffice it to say that there are some stagehands (namely IATSE-represented hands in large metropolitan areas) who make a very good living, upward of $50,000 per year. There are also stagehands who make very little money, and they tend to be the men and women working strictly in regional or similar producing theaters. When working in this field, one must carefully consider the value of doing what you love to do versus doing what earns the highest dollar.

Listed below are a few tables demonstrating the diversity of wages earned by stagehands throughout the United States. As you can probably surmise, the size of the city and its proclivity toward the entertainment industry significantly affects the wage potential of its stagehands. (Keep in mind that IATSE usually enforces a four-hour minimum call, so a stagehand should never earn less than four times the hourly rate.)

TABLE 9.1. IATSE LOCAL #272, ASHEVILLE, NC—THEATRICAL WAGE RATES

Position	Hourly Rate
Stagehand, Wardrobe, Labor	$13
Spotlights, Sound, Fork Operator, Loaders	$15
Flymen	$17
Electrician	$20
Riggers	$20

Source: City of Asheville—Civic Center, "Theatrical Wage Rates in the Jurisdiction of Local 272, Effective July 1,2006," http://ashevillecivcenter.com.

TABLE 9.2. IATSE LOCAL #22, WASHINGTON, D.C.—RATECARD FOR WARNER THEATRE STAGEHANDS

Position	Hourly Rate
Department Heads	$43.21–$53.17
Assistant Heads and Keys	$37.68–$46.51
Others	$35.44–42.09

Source: Warner Theater, "Stagehands—IATSE Local 22," http://warnertheater.com.

TABLE 9.3. IATSE LOCAL #55, SALEM, VA—UNION STAGEHAND RATES

Load in/out Rates	
Monday-Saturday	Hourly – $13.73
	4-hour minimum – $54.92
Sunday & Holidays	Hourly – $20.60
	4-hour minimum – $84.20
Performance Rates	
Monday-Saturday	Hourly – $13.73
	4-hour minimum – $54.92
Sundays & Holidays	Hourly – $20.60
	4-hour minimum – $78.00

Source: Salem Civic Center, Salem, Virginia, "Local No. 55 IATSE Union Stagehand Rates," http://salemciviccenter.com.

TABLE 9.4. IATSE LOCAL #197, KNOXVILLE, TN—UNION STAGEHAND RATES	
Position	*Hourly Rate*
Stagehand	$13.50
Loaders	First Truck – $54.00
	Each additional Truck – $30.00
Riggers	Up – $45.00
	Down – $21.00
Fork Lift Driver	$15.00
Spot Light Operators	$55.00 per show
	$65.00 per show after first two shows

Source: Knoxville Civic Auditorium and Coliseum, "IATSE Local 197 Union Stagehand Rates," http://knoxvillecoliseum.com.

FIVE SCHOOLS OFFERING DEGREES IN TECHNICAL THEATER

UNIVERSITY OF GEORGIA
  Programs offered: MFA in Design and Technology
  www.drama.uga.edu
  Contact: Sylvia J. H. Pannell, hillyard@uga.edu

UNIVERSITY OF WISCONSIN–MILWAUKEE
  Programs offered: BFA in Technical Production
  www3.uwm.edu/arts/programs/theater/index.html
  Contact: theaterinfo@uwm.edu

VIRGINIA COMMONWEALTH UNIVERSITY
  Programs offered: BFA in Scene Design/Technology
  www.pubinfo.vcu.edu/artweb/theater
  Contact: Ron Keller, rkeller@vcu.edu

WAYNE STATE UNIVERSITY
  Programs offered: BFA in Theater with concentration in Production
                MFA in Production
  www.theater.wayne.edu/index2.php
  Contact: Fred Florkowski, ac8489@wayne.edu

WESTERN OREGON UNIVERSITY
  Programs offered: BFA in Theater with concentration in Technical Production
  www.wou.edu/las/creativearts/theater_dance/theater_dance.htm
  Contact: Scott Grim, grims@wou.edu

RESOURCES FOR STAGEHANDS

Books

Carter, Paul. *Backstage Handbook: An Illustrated Almanac of Technical Information.* 3rd ed. Louisville, KY: Broadway Press, 1994.

Glerum, Jay O. *Stage Rigging Handbook.* 3rd ed. Carbondale: Southern Illinois University Press, 2007.

Glover, Thomas J. *Pocket Ref.* 2nd ed. Littleton, CO: Sequoia Publishing, 1999.

Periodicals

Live Design—www.livedesignonline.com

The convergence of three magazines that covered different aspects of live entertainment technology: *Entertainment Design, Lighting Dimensions*, and *Staging Rental Operations.*

Stage Directions— www.stage-directions.com

Provides a good look at the industry and focuses solely on theater, unlike other publications that spread focus across all aspects of entertainment.

Technical Brief—www.technicalbrief.org

A publication of the Yale School of Drama, *Technical Brief* provides articles that explain technical design solutions implemented by technical directors and other technical theater professionals.

Internet

www.etcp.esta.org—The Web site of the Entertainment Technician Certification Program (ETCP), a program supported by several organizations with technical theater connections, including USITT and IATSE, the program aims to certify two major types of theater technicians: electricians and riggers.

www.iatse-intl.org—This is a good starting point if you are interested in getting into your local chapter of IATSE. If you don't already know how, finding the Web site of your local chapter may help you determine how to go about getting on the union's overhire list and eventually among the ranks of IATSE members.

www.patrickimmel.com/usitt/techprod/tech_prod_index.htm—The Web site for the USITT Technical Production Commission.

www.usitt.org—The homepage of the United States Institute for Theatre Technology, an important organization for all types of technical theater types.

www2.kcpa.uiuc.edu/kcpatd/physics/index.htm—The Physics of Theatre Project Web site, providing detailed information on the areas of common theatrical rigging and scenery.

PART III AUDIO/VISUAL

◆

As theater artists we all have an important responsibility to engage our audience, to make "magic" and not settle for the ordinary, the cliché, or the trite in our dramatic work.

—RICK THOMAS,
sound designer and head of the design and technology program,
Purdue University

While many careers highlighted in this book hold firmly to their roots in tradition and convention, the specialties we are about to examine are, for the most part, the newbies of the theater world. They rely on, and were derived from, technological progress in ways that continue to keep us all on our toes.

Waiting for Godot at American Conservatory Theater. Lighting design by Russell Champa.

While the term "Audio/Visual" does not usually include the field of lighting, it seemed an appropriate term to use in order to take a more holistic look at the specialties in this section. The addition of the projection designer to the ranks of theatrical designers in recent years seemed to call for further inclusion, especially considering the way projection equipment is now used by lighting designers as well. These ideas, not to mention the fact that sound is also frequently an important element of video in theater, seemed to lend themselves to a section that was all-inclusive. So, here they are: the tech theater folks that provide the light, sound, and projected imagery for stage production.

10

LIGHTING DESIGNER

Light needs application by the hand of those who transcend the mere technical application. The easel artist can have all the paint and brushes at his disposal, but they are useless without the soul of expression that makes the most minute detail of paint and stroke take on life.

—JOHN AMBROSONE,
lighting designer and professor of lighting at Virginia Tech

The actors might wear their own clothes and put on a show in an existing space with no modification. They might shout at the top of their lungs without reinforcement or music to set the mood. But before they begin the show someone must turn on the lights. In such a pared-down production, the basic elements of any theatrical lighting team will still be represented: the person manning the light switch on the wall is the light board operator; the person who screwed the light bulb in

A Theatre Arts production of *References to Salvador Dali Make Me Hot* at Virginia Tech. Lighting design by John Ambrosone. (Photograph by John Ambrosone.)

is the master electrician; and the one who decided where to put the lamp is the designer. But in the world of professional theater, there are a slew of talented and skilled people turning this oversimplified production into a feast of illuminated art. If you are putting on any kind of performance—dance, play, opera, concert—there is one thing you simply cannot do without: illumination.

Illumination, however, is just the beginning of theatrical lighting. "Lighting is the 'visual glue' that holds up and enhances all the other visual elements," explains John Ambrosone, freelance lighting designer (LD) and assistant professor of lighting at Virginia Tech. As a freelancer and former resident lighting designer for American Repertory Theatre (ART) in Boston for thirteen years, Ambrosone has been creating stunning and complicated light designs for theater, dance, opera, and other forms for almost twenty years. "Light is as accessible and expressive as an actor, but never should upstage or pull focus from the unified contributions of the whole," he says.

SHAPING A VISUAL ENVIRONMENT

"My role is to shape a visual environment for the play to take place in," explains Steve Woods, a freelance lighting designer and head of theatre design at Southern Methodist University. Woods works extensively with many types of performing arts organizations, including the renowned José Limón Dance Company, an ensemble he's collaborated with for more than seventeen years. "My responsibility is to the director's vision, the playwright, and my artistry," he says.

Like artists in other design fields, the designer who manipulates light walks the line between keeping up with cutting-edge technology and retaining the ability to think like a painter. It's a line that must be walked carefully while concentrating on supporting the vision of the production and working closely with the entire artistic team (see "Spotlight on a Pro"). "I live for the process and collaboration," admits Ambrosone.

Russell Champa, a freelance designer based in both San Francisco and New York City, does his best to experiment as an artist at every opportunity. "I think that part of the job is to challenge oneself on every project to try something new—a new color, a new type of fixture, new technology, or a whole new process," he explains. "There is tremendous technology going on in the lighting and entertainment world right now," Champa says. In today's theater, the new technology available to LDs is almost endless, increasing the way light can be used and manipulated. "Every time a new technology is introduced, regardless of how the application is used, it's a major advantage," explains Ambrosone. "It's always a good thing," he says, adding that technological advances in lighting, as with any other field in theater, require designers to practice restraint so that they not overdo it. "If an audience leaves the theater humming the sets or the lights," Ambrosone says, "then it probably wasn't a good show."

"There is certainly a need to have technology on a lot of projects and there is certainly a need to *not* have a lot of technology on certain projects," Champa says. With all of the technology at hand, it is easy for LDs to get carried away. Champa says that he is careful to keep in mind that his primary responsibility as a designer is ensuring that his lights lend themselves to telling the story. He explains his role this way: "To help the audience focus on what we want them to focus on. To not get in the way of the actors and their work. To make the space and the world visually exciting and make everyone else look good until you want or need them to look bad."

As an example, Champa tells me about a production of Caryl Churchill's *A Number*, which he designed in 2006 for the American Conservatory Theatre (ACT). While the creative team knew they wanted the action of the play to take place in what Champa calls "a very real and domestic space," they also wanted the areas surrounding the realistic elements of the set to represent a major theme in the play: science. "It's a play [in part] about cloning and biotechnology," Champa explains. "So we ended up with the idea that surrounding the set would be these two spaces that [we called] 'haze locks,' or 'fog chambers.'" In order to use the haze locks as transitions between scenes, Champa needed a way to create with his lights the feeling of a "scientific machine" or some sort of supercomputer. He turned to automated lights called Vari-Lites and various other tricks of the trade, including **gobo** rotators. "What we discovered is that it's very easy to make it look like a rock show," he says, expressing his struggle to keep a tight rein on the technology he employs.

Once the script has been studied, coordinating with other designers and the director is the essential beginning for any designer, and LDs are no different. "The first thing is to understand why the particular work is being done," says Woods, explaining his initial approach to design. "Being a designer is a lot like being a detective. You connect the dots to find the answer to the question posed by the work." In order to connect the dots, the lighting designer will meet with the director or choreographer, the design team, and sometimes even the playwright or composer to reach a visual understanding of the production.

"I always start with the script and then a big piece of paper and a pencil," says Champa. This can be a tough period for a lighting designer struggling to transform the production concept into a functional **light plot**. "Translating a bunch of great ideas into a practical solution can be very difficult, especially with lighting," he admits. "Often times nobody knows what you're talking about until you're actually in the theater and turn off the work lights and turn on some of your lights," he says. "This is when the real work begins."

Over time, Woods has grown to see the art of light design a bit differently. "Of course the move from paper to reality always brings surprises," he says. But, rather than waiting until the system is in the theater and hung, Woods believes that designers must make an active effort to conceive a lighting system that limits what he calls "the unpleasant surprises." Woods's design approach has evolved in direct relation to his effort to more fully account for the realities of each instrument he puts on a plot. By perfecting his initial plot and design tactics, Woods has been able to make his time spent in tech rehearsals much more flexible. "I no longer [see] the show in bits and pieces," he comments. "My research [has become] better [as has] my understanding of the script and the arch of the play." Woods now tries to storyboard productions with the director as well. "We need to be open to approaching our work not in a tried-and-true way but in a way that challenges."

✧✦✧✦✧✦✦✧✦✧✦✦✧✦✧✦✧✦✧✦✧✦✦✧✦✧✦✧✦✧✦✧✦✦✧✦✧✦✦✧✦✧✦✧✦✦✧✦✧✦✦✧✦✧✦✧

Spotlight on a Pro

Michael Peterson, freelance LD and resident lighting designer of American
Players Theatre, 2001–present

Lighting the Sky

American Players Theatre (APT) is an outdoor theater in rural Spring Green, Wisconsin, that focuses on performing classic plays in rotating rep. They usually mount five productions per season, and they use one light plot to serve each show. If you can imagine the difficulty in lighting *one* show in an outdoor space, where the appearance of each show shifts as the sun sets, imagine creating five unique light designs with the same set of lights. Michael Peterson, the general manager of Willamette Repertory Theatre in Eugene, Oregon, and a freelance lighting designer, has spent each summer since 2001 as the resident lighting designer for APT trying to do just that.

Fortunately, Peterson had plenty of experience working both in outdoor venues and in rotating rep situations. As the resident LD for PCPA Theatrefest in Santa Maria, California, for fifteen years, he gained invaluable insight that has helped him in his five seasons working with APT. "My first task at APT was to get the most from my rep plot design that I possibly could, while still leaving me enough flexibility with specials to light all five shows," he says. Specials are the lighting positions that LDs rely on to meet the unique needs of individual shows that may not be covered by general lighting. At APT, the use of specials takes on a new meaning. "The back wall of the theater is actually open to the woods," Peterson points out. "So, there are two additional washes that light the trees to create different looks for the backgrounds."

Another consideration is how to use color. For Peterson, this means instructing his master electrician (ME) to change the color between each performance. "The color in the rep plot is actually changed over in all of the washes except the backlight and two front **par** washes for each production."

"Since the shows actually begin before the sun has set during the first part of the summer, I actually stay late after each tech to review the cues that happen during the 'dusk' part of the show," Peterson says. He must do this in order to ensure that as the season begins to change and it becomes darker earlier, the show retains its intended look. With his years of experience, lighting the shows for APT has become a bit less daunting for Peterson. "My job is made somewhat easier by the fact that I have designed a very flexible rep plot that gets supplemented by specials for each show," he says. "But it is still a challenge to make sure that each show has its own signature look and feel."

◇✦◇

PATHS TO A CAREER AS A LIGHTING DESIGNER

Champa, who spent many years working as an electrician before being able to make the financial leap to full-time design work (see the next chapter for more on this approach), acknowledges that meeting and working with established designers is crucial for becoming one yourself. And it can be a struggle to keep up. "The biggest challenge," Champa admits, "was transitioning from the electrics and assisting work to be able to make a living and survive as a designer."

Experience and training in theatrical lighting shouldn't be hard to come by for those interested in the craft. There are hundreds of training options available throughout the United States, including undergraduate, graduate, and certificate programs, as well as apprenticeships and internships. Woods provides the potential lighting student with one critical caveat: Prospective students should be careful about choosing where to study if they are serious about pursuing a career in lighting design. "I have to say that a lot of programs use their students as a cheap labor force, pretending that these same kids are being trained by this exploitation while the faculty designers design the shows," he says, advising young theater students to be more particular about where they decide to attend university and pursue their theatrical futures. "The most important thing," he says, "is to attend a great school where your education will permit you to be employable upon graduation.

At Southern Methodist University, Woods focuses on teaching graduate students the skills they need to succeed in the professional design world. "I think designers need to learn how to read a play with understanding, how to discuss the play with the director and playwright, and how to manage their careers and lives in the theater as businesspeople and artists." Woods believes that learning how to make it as a freelancer is perhaps the most critical skill. "For someone just starting in the business, the challenge is making enough money to survive each month. Graduate school gives [designers] a chance to fail without disaster," he says, explaining why graduate study may be a good idea for many young designers. "They can't do that at a commercial theater and expect to move forward."

"You have to be passionate, patient, collaborative, and determined to live through the good and bad times," says Ambrosone. He also emphasizes the need for going to a school where you will get plenty of one-on-one attention from your professors. As a professor at Virginia Tech, Ambrosone believes strongly in allowing the personality and individual artistry of the student to inform the work the student does, both as a student and in the future.

On-the-job training is also a major part of learning the craft of lighting. Finding opportunities to get your hands dirty and work as an electrician in the theater—even if you'd rather be a designer—comes highly recommended from designers and electricians alike. "Lighting can be one of the most intangible ideas to grasp," says Ambrosone. "If you don't really put your hands on it and use it for real, it's hard to put in your mind," he says. "I find that students coming out of grad design programs may be great on paper, but they often don't understand the basics of an electrician's work," says Natalie George, production electrician of The State Theatre Company, an SPT in Austin, Texas. She encourages students to take time to learn the basics before attempting to step into the big leagues of design.

Working in professional theater before entering a grad program can be an excellent way to determine one's focus. "You will learn an extreme amount from others," Ambrosone says. Students also have the opportunity to reach a level of maturity and professional ethic when given the opportunity to work among pros before delving into an advanced degree program. "The student that has been out working for any given time between undergraduate and graduate school makes them more focused and mature," Ambrosone says, in reference to the students he has encountered.

But, not everyone makes it to grad school. Some find it unnecessary, and different opportunities arise for others. To be sure, grad school is not an inevitability for those seeking a professional career in lighting design. For Champa, it has always been about learning by doing. "Not having a degree or any grad school experience has meant that I came into design through the back door," he comments. "I spent a long time assisting and doing electrics work to supplement and finance my design career." Champa is now a successful theatrical designer who works regularly around the country, including at American Conservatory Theatre in San Francisco; Trinity Rep in Providence, Rhode Island; and various theaters in New York City. He's a good example of how one can overcome the inherent disadvantages of bypassing college in a business that relies heavily on creating and maintaining professional relationships. "The biggest challenge for me is marketing myself and my work," he says. In college and graduate school, students of theatrical design are able to connect with many working and aspiring theater professionals, a clear advantage when attempting to enter the workforce.

A combination of academic training and professional experience on some level is probably the best approach. One way or another, though, you have to get the training, find the experience, and learn the intangibles to master the technology and the artistry. And, as Ambrosone points out, artists never stop absorbing and learning. "I am proud of the fact that I'm still seeing and learning new things about what I do," he says. "Never think for one second that learning stops at the end of school, college, or your first Broadway show."

◇ ◆ ◇

A Job Description

The primary responsibility of a lighting designer is to ensure that a show's lighting fulfills the director's production concept. A good LD will strive to maintain cohesion with other design aspects of a production, including sound, choreography, and, perhaps most importantly, scenery and costumes.

The LD begins this process by drafting a light plot, a sort of floor plan for a production's lighting systems (see sample light plot on the following page). A typical light plot will show in detail the exact placement of all lighting elements in relation to the existing theater or performance space. It is crucial that the LD use the proper set of drawings for the preexisting space in order to clearly communicate his intentions. As an example of how difficult this can be, I always think of a spectacular site-specific dance piece which I was a part of in Austin, Texas, in 2006. The LD struggled a bit to draft a comprehensible light plot because the show took place on the five floors of an unfinished office building. In order to avoid confusing the ME on the project, it was important that he come up with a logical way to indicate the positions of lighting instruments on five huge spaces that had nearly identical footprints. He accomplished this by essentially creating separate light plots for each floor.

The lighting designer will also create an **instrument schedule**, a detailed list of all the information pertinent to each lighting instrument, including instrument type, **lamp** type, color, placement, purpose, **channel, dimmer**, and whether or not the instrument will need any accessories, such as an **iris** or gobo. Another important tool provided to the ME is the **channel hookup**. Sometimes known as a **magic sheet** (though a magic sheet is more often a diagram of focus areas with other essential information—see example on page 115), the channel hookup is a simple rundown of every channel the LD plans to use. Similar to an instrument schedule, it will also detail the individual aspects of each channel. The difference between the two is how the information is

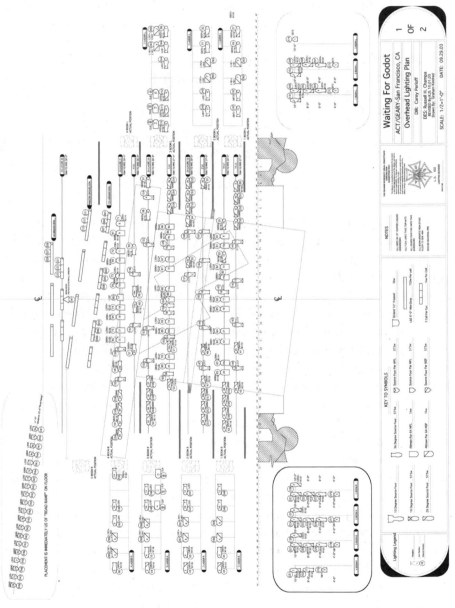

Russel Champa's light plot for *Waiting for Godot* at ACT's Geary Theatre. Note the details, which include information on instrument type, existing architecture, measurement scales to aid with exact placement, and channel and color notations.

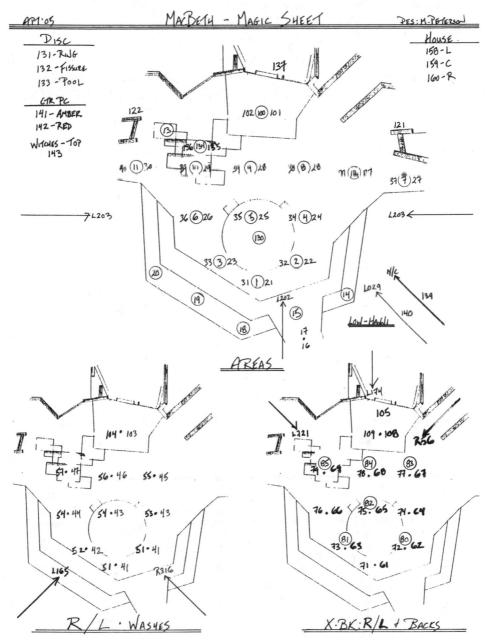

Michael Peterson's magic sheet for the 2005 production of *Macbeth* at American Players Theatre. Peterson uses three images of the stage for different types of lighting areas, indicating channel numbers, color, and direction of focus. (Courtsey of Michael Perterson.)

presented: the instrument schedule is generally in order of position, while the channel hookup is in chronological order of the channels.

All of the paperwork allows the master electrician and the lighting crew lead time to assemble and prepare the lighting system before the lighting designer is actually working on-site in the theater. This will help the ME plan in advance for any necessary renting or purchasing of equipment. "A good number of my shows go into empty theaters," says Steve Woods, "which require you to rent or buy everything you need."

The lighting designer will also make decisions regarding the colors to be used and what type of instrumentation to employ during the design phase. This is generally dictated to some degree by the budget and lighting inventory of the theater he is designing for. Like their counterparts in the areas of sound, scenery, and costuming, LDs will spend a fair amount of time researching and studying the script or piece for which they are designing.

Once the crew has hung, circuited, and patched the show, the LD will begin working in the theater, and instructing the crew during the **focus** and troubleshooting phase of the process. After the plot has been focused and all equipment is **patched** and operating correctly, the LD will write cues for the show. Some LDs arrive with cues already written, which they will then modify as necessary during the tech process.

◇✦◇

WHAT DO LIGHTING DESIGNERS EARN?

Generally speaking, lighting designers, like their colleagues in scenery, costumes, and sound, are members of United Scenic Artists Local 829 and are therefore entitled to compensation as negotiated through that union. However, not all designers decide to join the union. Michael Peterson is one notable example. He contends that at this point in his career he does not find it necessary to join because he is able to earn comparable fees on his own. It's hard to determine what sort of earnings such designers can demand, and we can assume that it varies from freelancer to freelancer.

Because most established designers are union members, I have included here the rates dictated by USA Local 829. Since such detailed information exists on the earnings of such areas of theater, I did not survey designers.

For those who have joined the union, the fees and daily rates agreed upon vary based on the type of theater, its location, and usually its seating capacity. Below you will find tables detailing some of the more common rates for lighting designers who are members of USA. For an explanation of the terms used in the charts, see appendix 3.

Table 10.1 lists the 2006 rates for LDs hired for work in regional, resident, or dinner theaters. These fees do not include daily rates, per diem, or fees for design assistants.

TABLE 10.1. UNITED SCENIC ARTIST DESIGN RATES FOR LIGHTING DESIGNERS IN REGIONAL, RESIDENT, OR DINNER THEATERS

Seating capacity	Rates	
	Single set	Multiple set or unit set with phases
Less than 199	$2,197	$2,561
200–299	$2,688	$3,556
300–499	$3,416	$4,702
500–999	$4,135	$5,620
More than 1000	$5,175	$6,216

Source: United Scenic Artists Local #829, "Minimum design rates 2006—Regional, Resident, Dinner theater, Schedule A."

Table 10.2 details the amendments to USA's Schedule C for design rates for LORT theaters. Designers working for a LORT theater work under contracts according to the theater's LORT designation, which is based primarily on the seating capacity of the theater. The designations run from A (the largest) through D (the smallest), with indicators such as B+ or C1 making room for more nuanced listings.

Table 10.3 is an example of the major leagues of theatrical design—the USA design rates for lighting designers working on Broadway. While becoming a lighting designer on Broadway is by no means impossible, up-and-comers should rely on the first two charts for realistic earnings potential—especially considering that many New York–based designers must still work regionally to earn a living.

TABLE 10.2. UNITED SCENIC ARTISTS DESIGN RATES FOR LIGHTING DESIGNERS IN LORT THEATERS

LORT Category	Rates as of		
	July 2006	July 2007	July 2008
A	$5,315	$5,528	$5,776
B+	$4,524	$4,705	$4,917
B	$3,760	$3,910	$4,086
C-1	$2,714	$2,823	$2,950
C-2	$2,262	$2,353	$2,458
D	Negotiable	Negotiable	Negotiable

Source: United Scenic Artists Local #829, "2005 Memorandum of agreement between United Scenic Artists, Local USA-829, IATSE and The League of Resident Theatres."

TABLE 10.3. UNITED SCENIC ARTIST DESIGN RATES FOR LIGHTING DESIGNERS ON BROADWAY		
Type of set	Rates	
	Dramatic	Musical
Single	$7,161	$7,593
Multi	$10,176	$24,137
Unit	$13,117	$13,908

Source: United Scenic Artists Local #829, "Broadway, Minimum Rates and Classifications 2006."

FIVE SCHOOLS OFFERING DEGREES IN LIGHTING DESIGN

INDIANA UNIVERSITY
Programs offered: MFA in Lighting Design
www.indiana.edu/thtr/academics/graduate/lighting.html
Contact: Robert Shakespeare, shakespe@indiana.edu

UNIVERSITY OF MASSACHUSETTS AT AMHERST
Programs offered: MFA in Lighting Design
www.umass.edu/theater/grad.html
Contact: Penny Remsen, remsen@theater.umass.edu

FLORIDA STATE UNIVERSITY
Programs offered: MFA in Lighting Design
http://theater.fsu.edu/academic/graduate/mfalighting.htm
Contact: Robert Coleman, rcoleman@mailer.fsu.edu

SOUTHERN OREGON UNIVERSITY
Programs offered: BFA in Theater with concentration in Stage Lighting
www.sou.edu/THTR
Contact: Craig Hudson, hudson@sou.edu

VIRGINIA TECH
Programs offered: MFA in Design and Technology with an emphasis in Lighting
www.theater.vt.edu
Contact: John Ambrosone, jambroso@vt.edu

RESOURCES FOR LIGHTING DESIGNERS

Books

Essig, Linda. *The Speed of Light: Dialogues on Lighting Design and Technological Change*. Portsmouth, NH: Heinemann Drama, 2002.

Morgan, Nigel. *Stage Lighting: For Theatre Designers*. London: Herbert Press, 1995.

Reid, Francis. *Lighting the Stage*. Boston: Focal Press, 1995.

Periodicals

LD+A—www.iesna.org/LDA/members_contact.cfm
   An abbreviation for *Lighting Design and Application*, it is the print and web publication of the Illuminating Engineering Society of North America (IESNA).

Lighting and Sound America—www.lightingandsoundamerica.com
   A magazine focusing on everything to do with lighting and sound within the entertainment industry, including Broadway, regional theater, dance, live music, and much more.

Live Design—www.livedesignonline.com
   The convergence of three magazines that covered different aspects of live entertainment technology: *Entertainment Design, Lighting Dimensions*, and *Staging Rental Operations*.

PLSN: Projection, Lighting, and Sound News—www.plsn.com

Internet

www.iald.org—The International Association of Lighting Designers Web site focuses mostly on architectural lighting, but is still an interesting resource.

www.iesna.org—The Illuminating Engineering Society of North America's Web site. The same organization that publishes *LD+A* (see above).

www.ldishow.com—The Web site of LDI, the largest trade show for people working in any area of lighting in the world.

www.lightingandsoundamerica.com—Web site of the print magazine *Lighting and Sound America*.

www.livedesignonline.com—The extensive Web site of the *Live Design magazine*.

www.plsn.com—*Projection, Lights, and Staging News* Web site.

www.usitt.org/commissions/Lighting.htm—The Web site of the USITT Lighting Commission.

11

THE ELECTRICIANS

I would go nuts working the nine-to-five cubicle lifestyle.

—JOE HARTNETT,
master electrician, Pittsburgh Public Theatre

Much the same way that a scene shop's scenic carpenters and technical director are responsible for building a set to the specifications set forth by a scene designer, the master electrician and the electrics crew are responsible for preparing the lighting for each production, as planned by the lighting designer. The crew, which may range in size from two to twenty (or more), is generally led by the master electrician (other titles include production or chief electrician, lighting supervisor, or, for short, the ME), who acts

Electrician and LD Natalie George. (Photograph by Mike Lawler.)

as the crew supervisor and is the contact point for the designer. On larger crews, there will also be assistant electricians that will help the ME in supervising the crew.

THE NUTS AND BOLTS

Bringing a lighting design to life entails the proper reading and interpretation of the designer's light plot. In order to do this, the master electrician must communicate effectively with the lighting designer and understand the designer's ideas. The electricians are also responsible for ensuring that the entire lighting system is operational and set up as the LD has designed it, and for keeping the labor and equipment costs in line with the budget. "The biggest challenge is being on top of your game and getting the job done," says Joe Hartnett, the master electrician for Pittsburgh Public Theatre. Being on top of your game means being comfortable with any and all equipment used in a light plot. When it is an in-house position, it is relatively easy for the ME to have good working knowledge of the theater's equipment and the idiosyncrasies of the system in place.

As the industry continues to evolve and technology becomes increasingly intricate and specialized, electricians need to be as well versed in programming moving lights and digital dimmers as they are with repairing instruments or focusing for a designer. And as a theater's inventory grows, electricians are often put in the strange situation of dealing simultaneously with cutting-edge equipment and instruments that may be twenty or more years old. For this reason, retaining a vast working knowledge of lighting equipment is essential. It's also worth pointing out that learning the ins and outs of older equipment is often a valuable experience because you never know what sort of instrumentation you may encounter in a theater.

An electrician who has the broadest knowledge of control systems, programmable lighting fixtures, and dimmer systems, as well as standard equipment, is the kind of technician most desirable. An ability to operate a range of light boards, retaining a firm grasp of the quirks of the software, will make an electrician worth a lot more to both lighting designers and master electricians. This is even more true for technicians who will not always be working in one facility with one type of control system. However, specialists are important in the industry too, and electricians who have very specific training in certain systems will also find themselves employable by the companies manufacturing and servicing lighting systems.

Beth Nuzum, the master electrician of Indiana Repertory Theatre for sixteen years, admits that keeping up with the ever-evolving technology of illumination has been the most challenging aspect of her career; well, that and being female. "When I became the master electrician in 1990, there were very few, if any, other female MEs," she says.

Tools of the Trade

An electrician's tool bag should contain (at least) the following:

amp meter
C-Wrench (Crescent wrench)—This is the tool that an electrician cannot do without. A good size is 8", because it can sometimes accommodate unexpected uses, but 6" is lighter and will work for most everything an electrician will use it for. Having both on hand is probably best. Many electricians like to keep some sort of tether on the

wrench they use to focus lights so that they can keep it attached to themselves in case they drop it or don't have a place to set it down while up in the air. There are other types of specialized wrenches that are touted as quicker because they have each size for quick, nonadjusting use, but nothing is as useful as a standard C-wrench.

flashlight—An LED headlamp is great for electricians who will often find themselves needing both hands while working on something in the dark.

Gamchek—This three-in-one electrical tester is the best on the market by far. With it, electricians can instantly check an instrument's lamp as well as test the circuit for power and correct wiring. The most useful version comes in stage pin, but it can also be found for edison and other electrical plug styles

multitool—There are many brands of multitools now on the market and most of them are well-crafted and practical for stagehands, electricians, and many other tech professionals. A multitool with at least a knife, pliers and screwdrivers is a good start. No need to get fancy—electricians will probably use those features the most.

pin splitter—A useful hand tool for electricians, the pin splitter simultaneously cleans and spreads the plug's pins for optimum performance.

screwdrivers

wire cutters

wire strippers

COLLABORATING: THE LD'S RIGHT HAND

"We always joke that we are the people that make the magic happen," says Hartnett. "As an ME, I enable the lighting design to come to life," he says, summing up his work in a more serious manner.

Like a technical director, master electricians usually have enough advance notice about an upcoming show to hit the ground running. As a show approaches, Nuzum likes to get to know everything about it that she can, including areas outside of lighting that she has learned have the ability to affect her work. "I go over the set plans with the TD so I can understand what the set designer is doing," she says. "Then, I talk to the lighting designer to find out if they have any special needs for the show." The ME must also be the eyes and ears for the LD before he arrives on the scene, making sure he is aware of any unforeseen issues that may cause problems later on. "If I hear of any changes to the script, set, props, et cetera," Nuzum says, "I make sure the lighting designer knows about them."

Even simple details about a theater may go unnoticed by an LD that has never worked there before, and the ME can be very helpful in such situations too. John Ambrosone, a veteran LD and professor at Virginia Tech, for example, loves it when an ME or electrics crew has the foresight to inform him of such problems.

"That way," he says, "when I show up for focus I don't have to say, 'Okay, we have to move these ten lights.'"

As an example of an untrusting relationship between ME and LD, Natalie George, the master electrician for the State Theatre Company in Austin, Texas, (until its recent closing) cites a production that featured as its primary scenic element a very tall tree that created quite an obstacle for the lights. To George's dismay, the lighting designer, who had never worked in the space before, forgot about the tree's existence when he completed the design and submitted the light plot. "He put stuff shooting right through this eighteen-foot tree," she says. She tried to explain the situation to him, even had the TD and production manager participate in a conference call with him, but he insisted and stood by his plot. "I was sitting in the theater the day he walked in the stage door," she laughs. "He stopped dead in his tracks and just stared at this big tree that he kept forgetting was there." Upon seeing it with his own eyes he made some last-minute adjustments to the plot and had George and her crew rehang many instruments to accommodate the tree.

According to George, there are two types of designers. "There are the designers who ask about the budget, and those that don't," she says. "You really have to learn how to handle the designers who don't, because they will push you and push you as far as they can to get everything they want—even things that they may never use." Nuzum agrees that crunching the numbers is often the most difficult part of a master electrician's job. "It is always a challenge to get the designers everything they want to execute their vision without going over budget," she says. "I try to never say no to anything a designer wants to try."

For the most part, designers understand that their collaboration with the technicians who hang, circuit, patch, focus, and run the production is of utmost importance. "There is no 'going it alone' in theater," notes Ambrosone (check out the previous chapter for more on LDs mentioned here). "A lot of what designers accomplish is due to technicians," he says. Lamenting how electricians are sometimes not appreciated by designers, Ambrosone makes a point of recognizing the contribution the technical staffs make to productions. "It's a common misconception that they too are not artists," he says. "They happen to be some of the most gifted artists I know." Ambrosone always makes an effort to contact the lead electrician as early in the design process as possible so that they are up to speed on the production and understand the design concept more thoroughly. "Oftentimes they are better at problem solving and have more successful budgeting solutions than I do," he explains.

Russell Champa, a prolific freelancing LD, summing up the tasks of the electrics crew as he sees it, says, "They do the heavy lifting." Champa is joking, but only partially, for they do indeed do a lot of heavy lifting. But electricians are responsible for a whole lot of other things too. "They figure out the circuiting and dimming, place the shop orders, schedule the crews, and often figure out how to achieve whatever crazy idea the designers come up with," Champa says.

Master electricians and lighting departments are forever adjusting to a constantly changing range of lighting designers. It can be a bit like having a new boss every month or two, and because the working relationship between an LD and an ME is very close and frequently strained under intense deadline and artistic pressure, the ME must learn how to get the work done regardless of how well he gets along with a designer.

"If you do your job," Hartnett says, "you will have very few problems—besides a conflict of personalities." When differences in personality crop up between a designer and ME, he emphasizes, the work must still get done properly. "There is nothing you can do but have your job done to the best of your abilities," he says.

Steve Woods, professor of lighting at Southern Methodist University in Dallas, agrees that the master electrician and the electrics crew are a critical element for realizing a great design. He also believes that a crew with a vested interest in the design will naturally be more inclined to do their best work. "I want them to take ownership of the work and contribute," he says.

PATHS TO A CAREER AS A THEATRICAL ELECTRICIAN

Many MEs are aspiring or working lighting designers themselves. George used her steady gig as a staff electrician to keep her design work financially feasible. Her position as both the master electrician of an SPT and as a freelance designer gave her a holistic perspective on the industry, as well as the opportunity to network with designers from around the country.

"Get experience," Nuzum advises, emphasizing that formal training is not as crucial as practical work experience. "I have an electrician who did not go to college but worked over a year with *Disney On Ice*," she says. "He is a master at moving lights, and he is only twenty-two."

For Hartnett, seven years into his gig as ME of the Pittsburgh Public Theatre, the basics are key to learning the trade. "Talk to all of the 'old-timers' and learn everything you can from them," he says. "They might not know all about moving lights or computer lighting consoles, but you can learn more about electrics, safety, and the business from them than any book or class."

Becoming a theatrical electrician is much different than what most people think of when they hear someone say, "I'm an electrician." There is no mandatory licensing or certification required to be hired as an electrician in the theater, even under union conditions. While there are usually anecdotal tests to be passed, such as proof of experience and competence, most union locals require nothing formal. There is a movement, however, spearheaded by USITT and IATSE, to make the certification of theatrical electricians (and riggers) more common in order to ensure the safety of those working in the entertainment industry. The idea has taken shape in the form of the Entertainment Technician Certification Program (ETCP), a comprehensive (and for now voluntary) examination process that aims to measure the practical knowledge of those who want to work in two of the most potentially dangerous areas of technical theater.

◇◆

A Job Description

Usually, a theater will have a staff electrician known as the "master electrician," or some other term that designates him or her as the theater's charge electrician. The ME is responsible for maintaining and operating the theater's lighting equipment, managing the lighting budget, and hiring the necessary crews to complete the tasks of hanging, focusing, running, and striking individual productions. Between productions, the ME will ensure that the electrics department and its equipment are organized and in proper working condition, guaranteeing that spare parts and replacement lamps are in stock. The ME must also be sure that all of the proper **gel** (or color) is available and any other materials specified by the designer, such as **templates** (also known as "gobos"), irises, and **sidearms**. If necessary, the ME will oversee any rigging that may need to be accomplished in order to successfully carry out the design.

During the planning stages and tech process, the ME is the LD's right hand, responsible for putting the paperwork of the designer into action. Supplied with a light plot, instrument schedule, and channel hookup, the ME compiles all of the necessary equipment and makes a plan for how to organize the work that will need to be done. (Many MEs will create informative flash cards known as **hang cards** so that electricians will have the information they need to complete their assigned tasks without having to periodically return to the usually centrally located light plot.) The ME is also responsible for deciding how much time and labor will be needed for a given project in order to ensure that the work is done on schedule. Generally, the LD will arrive for focus and preliminary notes once the electrics crew has fully hung, patched, programmed any equipment requiring it, and checked the entire system for problems. During focus, the ME will head up the crew, assisting the designer by making sure the proper lights are on at any given time.

Once the show has been focused, the ME will assist the LD in programming cues. If the ME is not also the light board operator, he will at least be on hand throughout the tech process in order to fix unexpected issues and change things that the LD has decided to adjust in order to accommodate the design more fully, such as the focus of an instrument. Obviously, the work of an ME is never done. "You work late, you work often, and during the holidays," says Joe Hartnett. "My only day off is Monday, so, going out with your wife, partner, or buddies on the weekends can get tough. But it can be done."

◇◆

WHAT DO ELECTRICIANS EARN?

Pinpointing a salary range for electricians across the United States is difficult primarily because of the diversity of working situations. The various agreements that IATSE—the union that represents stage electricians—has negotiated in different cities and metropolitan areas also make it difficult to nail down what an electrician or master electrician can expect to earn (see chapter 9 for examples of wages for IATSE electricians).

TABLE 11.1. EARNINGS FOR MASTER ELEVTRICIANS		
Total number of master electricians surveyed = 34		
Where the master electricians surveyed are working		
Type of theater	*Number*	*Percentage*
Academic	-	-
Broadway	-	-
COST	1	3%
Dinner	-	-
LORT	13	38%
Off-Broadway	3	9%
Opera	-	-
Regional	10	29%
Resident	4	12%
SPT	-	-
Other	3	9%
How much master electricians are earning		
Income range	*Number*	*Percentage*
Less than $10,000	-	-
$10,000–$20,000	4	12%
$20,000–$35,000	18	53%
$35,000–$50,000	10	29%
$50,000–$75,000	2	6%
$75,000–$100,000	-	-
More than $100,000	-	-
How master electricians view their income		
Perception	*Number*	*Percentage*
Below average	12	35%
Average	18	53%
Above average	4	12%

Source: 2006 Tech Theater Earnings Survey.

An anecdotal survey of my own reveals that electricians will earn anywhere from $15 to $45 per hour. While the low end of this range is sometimes lower for young electricians and those freelancing in a small city, this range generally seems to be accurate. Considering the demand for electricians with expertise in programming and automated lighting systems, potential pay can cover a very broad range.

Above is a table of results from the Tech Theater Earnings Survey mentioned in the introduction. Each respondent is a working master electrician. The majority of those responding work in LORT theaters. A large percentage (nearly 70 percent) of those responding work for more than one theater or venue in their capacity as electricians, but over 80 percent earn more than half of their income solely from work within theater, without venturing into other industries.

The most interesting figure in this survey is the high number of MEs reporting that they believe their income to be below the typical earnings of master electricians working in theater in the United States. While the bulk of respondents consider their income average, over one-third think they are earning below the average.

FIVE SCHOOLS OFFERING DEGREES IN LIGHTING

BOSTON UNIVERSITY
Programs offered: Certificate of Training in Electrics
BFA in Lighting Design
MFA in Lighting Design
www.bu.edu/cfa/theater
Contact: Mark Stanley, mws@bu.edu

CALIFORNIA STATE UNIVERSITY, LONG BEACH
Programs offered: BA in Theatre with concentration in Lighting
MFA in Lighting Design
www.csulb.edu/depts/theater
Contact: David Martin Jaques, djacques@csulb.edu

NORTH CAROLINA SCHOOL OF THE ARTS—SCHOOL OF PRODUCTION AND DESIGN
Programs offered: BFA with concentrations in Lighting Design or in Lighting Technology
www.ncarts.edu/ncsaprod/designandproduction
Contact: Eric Rimes, rimese@ncarts.edu

UNIVERSITY OF TEXAS-AUSTIN
Programs offered: BA in Theatre and Dance with concentration in Lighting
Design and Technology
MFA in Theatre Technology
www.utexas.edu/cofa/theater
Contact: Amarante Lucero, alucero@mail.utexas.edu

WEBSTER UNIVERSITY
Programs offered: BFA in Design/Technical Theatre with concentration in Lighting
Design
www.webster.edu/depts/finearts/theater/index.html
Contact: John Wylie, wyliejc@webster.edu

RESOURCES FOR ELECTRICIANS

Books
Cunningham, Glen. *Stage Lighting Revealed*. Long Grove, IL: Waveland Press, 2002.

Essig, Linda. *The Speed of Light: Dialogues on Lighting Design and Technological Change*. Portsmouth, NH: Heinemann Drama, 2002.

Reid, Francis. *Lighting the Stage*. Boston: Focal Press, 1995.

Shelley, Steven Louis. *A Practical Guide to Stage Lighting*. Boston: Focal Press, 1999.

Periodicals
LD+A—www.iesna.org/LDA/members_contact.cfm
An abbreviation for *Lighting Design and Application*, it is the print and web publication of the Illuminating Engineering Society of North America (IESNA).

Lighting and Sound America—www.lightingandsoundamerica.com
A magazine focusing on everything to do with lighting and sound within the entertainment industry, including Broadway, regional theater, dance, live music, and much more.

Live Design—www.livedesignonline.com
The convergence of three magazines that covered different aspects of live entertainment technology: *Entertainment Design*, *Lighting Dimensions*, and *Staging Rental Operations*.

Internet

www.etcp.esta.org—The Web site of the Entertainment Technician Certification Program (ETCP).

www.ldishow.com—The Web site of LDI, the largest trade show for people working in any area of lighting in the world.

www.lightingandsoundamerica.com—Web site of the print magazine *Lighting and Sound America*.

www.livedesignonline.com—The extensive Web site of the *Live Design magazine*.

www.usitt.org/commissions/Lighting.htm—The Web site of the USITT Lighting Commission.

12

SOUND DESIGNER

It's very important to sit in the back of the theater and observe
how the audience reacts to the theater piece, to assess and analyze whether
what you are trying to do is working, and to find ways to make the
communication better.

—RICK THOMAS,
sound designer, head of the design and technology program, Purdue University

For Rick Thomas, the fact that there is not a Tony Award for sound design confirms that the theater does not hold in very high esteem the design specialty practiced by what he calls "sonic artists." A theater sound pioneer and head of Purdue University's design and technology program for almost thirty years, Thomas has been struggling for decades to get sound designers the credit they deserve.

Sound designer Lindsay Jones at work. (Photograph by Michael Broh.)

Lindsay Jones, a Chicago-based sound designer who is in high demand throughout the country, concurs. Jones's long list of high-profile credits includes work at Steppenwolf, the Old Globe, and Actors Theatre of Louisville, as well as composing for world premieres of playwrights like Sam Shepard and David Mamet. "For some reason, sound is usually lower on people's priority lists," he says. "I'm not sure why this is. Maybe people think it's not the same amount of work as designing lights, even though it actually is."

Thomas admits, however, that industry recognition of sound design has improved, especially among the top designers and composers. "There was no such thing as sound design when I broke into it," he says. "You always had to fight to get yourself listed in the program as a sound designer. The fight to get on the title page with the other designers actually came later!" Thomas has designed all over the country and his credits outside the theater include composing music for ESPN's coverage of the Indianapolis 500. At Purdue, he leads one of the oldest and most highly respected sound programs in the country.

A PALETTE OF SOUNDS

Sound designers are responsible for a precisely defined set of tasks. Their primary function is to fulfill the production concept of the director in terms of any sound that is part of the show. They must do this for all audio aspects in a practical and efficient manner that works within the capabilities of the space and the available equipment. "Basically, if you hear it, it's my responsibility," says Jones.

Once the sound designer has become familiar with the script and the director's overall production concept, he will begin work on the design. The designer will consider practical matters, such as the possible need for sound reinforcement through microphones. This can be a difficult decision for designers who might prefer the natural, nonamplified sound of the performer's voices. But for some productions, especially musicals in big houses, microphones are an essential part of the sound design world. The designer decides what type of equipment should be used and will work with the director to set the mic levels that will be used during performances. The sound designer will also consider abstract elements of the design, such as mood and rhythm. "I try to gather a palette of sounds for the show," explains Thomas. "Examples of types of music that belong in the show, colors and rhythms, spatial conceptions, melodic lines, textures, that sort of thing."

Similarly, Jones focuses first on any incidental music that may be needed for a production that he is designing. "I start on the Internet, doing research about where the show is set and what the characters are like and what music might fit best into the environment," he says. As an avid music collector, Jones loves this part of his job. "Generally I try to buy fifteen to twenty research CDs per production. I may use some, none, or all of these in the final design, but I sit down and study these discs thoroughly. Then, from there, I usually select tracks if I'm using prerecorded music, or I begin composing melodies in the style that I've researched." Many sound designers spend a fair amount of their time composing original music for their designs. Thomas composes themes early in the process and tries to make them available during the rehearsal process so that they can be better incorporated into the show. "I'll often videotape scenes so that I can compose specific ideas outside of rehearsal," Thomas explains.

Another part of sound in the theater is, of course, the reproduction of realistic sound required by the script or the director's concept. Jones uses a variety of resources to find sounds that he may need. His already large CD collection includes most of the effects discs of both Sound Ideas and Hollywood Edge, two of the more widely used effects collections. When he can't find the exact sound needed, Jones will record it himself. "I carry around a mic with me everywhere so I can record things on the spot," he says. "I also collect weird ambient sounds from all over. I keep a fairly extensive library of strange and exotic sonic textures and I end up using these a lot."

ART AND HARDWARE

Both Thomas and Jones have backgrounds in acting but were lured away by the artistry of sound. "I definitely feel that actor training is a very valuable thing for sound designers," says Thomas, who believes that two very different personality types tend to gravitate toward sound design. Some designers are "pure artists," he says, who are primarily interested in creating an aesthetic experience for the audience. Others focus on gear and the highly technical aspects of sound. Fortunately, there is plenty of room for both personality types in the field, and they can complement each other quite well when collaborating on a project.

Jones falls into Thomas's "pure artist" classification. "There is an immediate visceral connection between performer and audience that is unique to theater," he says, "and I want the sound to have that same visceral impact." He sees his primary design responsibilities as both supporting and intensifying the mood and concepts of the production. "That's what I'm committed to," he says.

Andrew Keister, based in New York, has been involved in technical theater since he was in the seventh grade, studied theatrical design and production at the University of Cincinnati's College-Conservatory of Music, and could probably be considered a more technically oriented designer. "My designs tend to have a lot of technology involved in accomplishing the artistic mission," he says.

FLOODING THE STAGE

Sound designers, like their scenic and lighting colleagues, are problem solvers above all else. When they design a production, they must find ways to create a sonic environment for the show while overcoming obstacles like small budgets, limits on the capabilities of available equipment, and the physical space in which they are working.

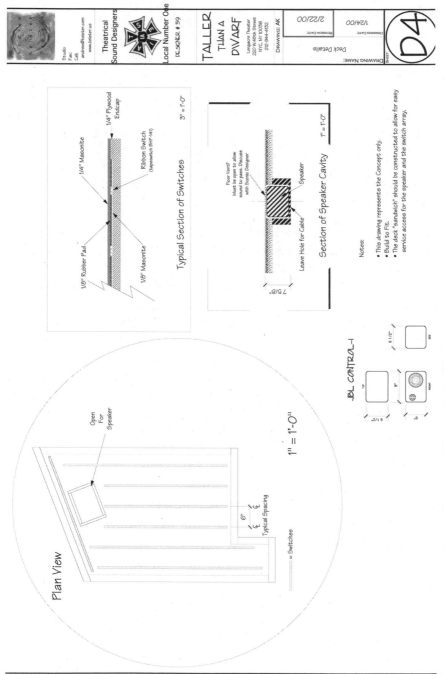

Andrew Keister's sound plot detail for *Taller Than A Dwarf*. (Courtesy of Andrew Keister.)

"I tend to get hired on shows that are very technically complicated," says Keister. As an example, he relates an interesting problem he ran into while designing Alan Arkin's Broadway production of *Taller Than a Dwarf* in 2000.

"Very early in the script, a pipe breaks in a bathroom that is offstage and water flows out and soaks the apartment over the course of the show," Keister says. "Obviously, we would have the sound of water flowing, but it's critical to the plot to establish that the floor in the apartment is getting drenched. We discussed lighting solutions; we discussed changing the carpeting during scene changes to make it look wetter. Then I had the idea that if every time an actor walked across the carpet in the 'wet' area we heard the 'squish' a wet carpet would make, the point would get across to the audience."

After Keister came up with the concept, he had to design a system that would make his idea come to life. "We built a matrix of switches into the deck and fed them into a computer," he explains. The wet carpet sounds were created using a semirandom set of **MIDI** notes. Keister experimented with several different realistic sounds that he recorded for the effect. He repeatedly encountered problems, however, when the sound in the recording studio differed significantly from the sound coming from the deck speakers in the theater. Eventually he found a series of "boot into medium-heavy mud" samples on a sound effects CD. "They sounded completely wrong when we listened to them in the studio environment," he explains. "But when played back through the speaker in the deck, they read correctly."

He continues, "The MIDI was fed into a sampler that was loaded with a few different sets of squishy sounds, which were then fed back into a speaker built into the deck so the sound would come from the correct location." Each time an actor stepped on a part of the set where there was a switch, it would trigger the computer to generate the squishy sound of walking on wet carpet that Keister was going for. "It's a very complicated solution to the problem, but it worked beautifully once we worked the bugs out."

LISTENING OUTSIDE THE BOX

Rick Thomas is a bold thinker, and he addresses his responsibilities as a trainer of up-and-coming designers with a great deal of energy. He has spent a career in the theater questioning the status quo and infusing Purdue's program with a spirit that challenges convention while searching for new ways of thinking and designing. Discussing theater with him is like talking politics with a veteran officeholder. He knows theater inside and out and has seen what works, what doesn't, and what *could*. As an example, he brings up a student production of *Picnic* produced at Purdue many years ago.

"At the time, our theater still had the sound board operator behind a glass booth, with a loudspeaker program system in one ear and a headset full of chattering run crew in the other," he explains. "I was standing in the back of the house with the artistic director for the theater during a performance when the sound cue of the horseshoe game played out of the proscenium loudspeakers rather than the offstage left one. The level was right, but the location was wrong—people were playing horseshoes over the heads of the audience. I turned to the director and said, 'You know the sound is wrong, I know the sound is wrong, everybody in the audience knows the sound is wrong. The only person that doesn't know the sound is wrong is the one person that can do something about it: the sound board operator.' "

Thomas convinced the artistic director that day that placing a sound engineer behind a wall of glass to mix a show made no sense, and eventually the board was moved out into the house. (Even now, nearly twenty years later, mixing sound in a closed booth is still practiced in some theaters.) Thomas also prefers to have two sound engineers running shows. One of them will act as the cue taker, in constant contact with the stage manager. The second operator is then free to mix the show without the distraction of wearing a headset.

A BRIEF HISTORY OF SOUND DESIGN

As Rick Thomas notes, theatrical sound design is a relative newcomer to theater. However, it's been a part of theater as far back as the historian can take us in the form of music, an essential accompaniment of performing and storytelling since the ancients first rose up in front of their communities to weave a grand tale.

In the late nineteenth century, Stanislavsky and Nemirovich-Danchenko began to revolutionize theater with the idea of realism, and sound was a part of their move-ment toward a more lifelike theater. Their production of *The Seagull* in 1898 used live offstage sounds in order to create a more realistic feel. But, according to Deena Kaye and James LeBrecht in *Sound and Music for the Theatre*, prerecorded sound was not something that was widely used until the 1930s when sound engineers began work-ing with turntables in a way that would be unimaginable in our digital age.

In terms of our modern theater, the notion of designing the sound for a produc-tion as one might design the lights or the sets is one that didn't really crop up until the 1960s. Dan Dugan is considered to be the first person credited as "sound designer" (at least in the United States) while working for ACT in San Francisco. A pioneer of theatrical sound, he also developed the automatic microphone mixer and now operates his own sound company. "Production stage manager Dorothy Fowler coined the term 'sound designer' to 'describe what Dan does,'" Dugan told me, confirming his status among the pioneers of theatrical sound.

The first Broadway designer credited for sound design was Jack Mann for *Show Girl* in 1963. For some perspective, we should note that scenic design and costume design have been Tony Award categories since the awards were first handed out in 1947, while lighting design was not recognized by the awards until 1970. Sound design has yet to be added to that list.

Of course, the technology used in sound production and design has changed radically time and again since the heyday of Dugan and Mann. It has evolved through new forms and taken on new meaning in the process.

Another major development in sound and music occurred in the early 1980s: Musical Instrument Digital Interface, or MIDI. It enables communication and synchronization between computers, electronic instruments, and other media by transmitting data in real time. MIDI revolutionized the sound and music industries, and it is used in theater in a variety of applications, including lighting and projections, which can both be linked and coordinated with a production's sound. Or, as discussed above in the case of Andrew Keister's design for *Taller Than a Dwarf*, MIDI can help a sound designer link sounds with specific actions onstage.

Now, in the first decade of the twenty-first century, the technology in use by sound designers to record, manipulate, and store sounds of all types revolves around the computer—so much so that Jones is able to show up at theaters with little but his laptop and a couple of external hard drives full of sound effects. Like Jones, any modern sound designer can call up sound very easily via his computer and proceed to alter the sound until it is a unique creature. So, while sound technology has come a long way since the ancients used it in the form of song and music, the essence of sound as a means of communication and expression has changed very little.

✧✦✧

Tools of the Trade

For a freelancing designer like Lindsay Jones—who works all over the country and designed a whopping forty-seven productions in 2005 alone and about thirty in 2006—the essential tool is a laptop loaded with tried-and-true audio software. Jones does virtually all of his design work on his laptop and enjoys the freedom and flexibility of working that way, especially considering how often he travels. (He estimates that he spent 250 days on the road during 2005.) He also travels with two Lacie 1.6 terabyte (or about 3200 gigabyte) hard drives on which he keeps his entire sound effects library, past shows, and music and sample libraries. "The idea being," he explains, "that you could say to me in tech: 'Hey, do you have the sound of an angry monkey with 'Hava Nagila' playing in the background?' and I can just say 'Yep, right here. I'll put it in the show right now,'" he laughs. "People seem to like that a lot."

Designers who work in a more, shall we say, stable environment enjoy more complex and sophisticated studio-type work spaces. Rick Thomas, for example, works primarily in his fully equipped private studio, Zounds Productions. "It evolves constantly as equipment and technology evolves," he says. Purdue also has a full studio, including a recording room, for recording sound effects, acoustic instruments, and other audio that the sound department may need.

◇◆◇

COLLABORATING: MERGING SOUND INTO PRODUCTION

A good designer will strive to maintain cohesion with other design aspects of a production, including lighting, choreography, and even scenery—especially in terms of what direction realistic sounds may come from. Above all, however, is the sound designer's collaboration with the director of the production. "When I first start working with a director, I always try to get them to understand that I am totally on their side," explains Thomas. "It's important for me to let them know that I intend to function as an extension of them, not as a separate, discrete entity."

The designer will examine all possibilities throughout the preproduction process, during which time he may be responsible for drafting a sound plot and creating other needed paperwork so that the production's sound engineer can properly prepare the system before the sound designer's presence is necessary. "I try to always have an assistant," Thomas says. "Their job is just about anything that keeps me out of the heart of the creative process, [such as] working with the directors and actors." Thomas's design assistant will typically help with research and complete detail work like drafting speaker plots, updating cue sheets, and even prebuilding sounds and cues.

The design should be malleable, Thomas believes, so that it fits as an element of a cohesive production when it's added to the show. "Almost always, I'll have the sound well integrated into the production about a week before the technical rehearsals begin," he explains. "For me, technical rehearsals should be times for getting all of the various components of a production to gel together, not a time to see if your contribution works."

Jones sees the up-to-the-minute capability of the constantly improving technology used by sound designers as a way to keep the final product of his designs flexible for as long as possible. "The concept of walking into a tech with all your cues as a fixed and finished product is now a thing of the past," he says. "You can think more abstractly in the creation and layering of sound—more like a painter and less like a technician. As a result, the creation of a cue is actually several levels that change and can shift constantly until opening night."

PATHS TO A CAREER IN SOUND DESIGN

"The first thing you should do is start seeing a lot of theater," Jones advises future sound designers. Then you need to get out and introduce yourself to a local designer and offer your assistance. "Sound designers are a surprisingly accessible bunch of people," Jones says, "and, believe me, we're always thrilled to have extra help." Once you've met designers in your area, keep in touch with them and pick their brains whenever possible.

Being persistent is very important. "Chances are not going to fall into your lap," says Ben Marcum, assistant sound designer in residence at Actors Theatre of Louisville. Marcum, who has broken into the field without the benefit of having completed a college degree, knows just how hard it can be. (Marcum is an exception in a field where most designers spend at least four years in an undergraduate theater program. He studied for a year and a half in Thomas's program at Purdue but decided that college wasn't a very good fit for him.) He has managed to keep his foot in the door and expand into a freelance career by both working hard and excelling at the art of networking. "Now that I know many more people, things are getting a little easier," he says, "but getting into new theaters is still a bit of a challenge."

With stories like Marcum's in mind, Thomas advises students to be sure to take a serious look at the financial side of the business before deciding to pursue a career in sound design. "If you are going to have a career, you need to understand what that means in terms of how you are going to live and how to survive," he says. "You have to be pretty sharp to understand all the difficulties involved and smart enough to figure out how to rise above the challenges," Thomas warns. He also notes that staying flexible will provide you with much more opportunity for doing the work you want to do *and* making a good living. "If you diversify," he says, "you may have a better chance of finding a better career path down any one of the roads you are likely to travel."

Keister, who has managed to sustain his sound career while living in New York, says simply, "Design work on Broadway is feast or famine." There are ways to make a good living in New York, according to Keister, but it takes an equal mix of strategy and luck. "The way a designer really makes his or her money is from royalties," he says. "For the royalties to really add up the show needs to be a hit and have a long, healthy run and have multiple companies—a tour or two, a London company, et cetera." Unfortunately, there is a better chance of a new production falling flat.

A good way for a talented designer to stay in the game is by working as a sound engineer (or sound operator) on other shows—preferably the hit shows. Keister recently worked as an engineer for *Hairspray* on Broadway with an arrangement that allowed him "significant time away from the show to do my design work," he explains. He has also paid his rent by running sound for *Aida, Titanic,* and *Bring in 'Da Noise Bring in 'Da Funk,* among others.

Thomas has this piece of parting advice to students who are drawn to a career in sound design: "Follow your heart," he says. "It will always lead you to the right places."

A Job Description

After discussing the design concept and audio needs for the production, the sound designer will examine all possibilities, including live sound or music, reinforcement, recorded effects, and prerecorded music. Throughout the preproduction process, the designer may be responsible for drafting a sound plot and creating other needed paperwork so that the production's sound engineer can properly prepare the system before the designer's presence in the theater is necessary.

Once the crew has prepared the equipment for the show, the designer will arrive to instruct the crew during the tech phase of the process. Sound designers generally arrive with already written and roughly edited cues, which they will modify during tech. The designer will work with other members of the design team, the director, the stage manager, and the sound engineer during techs and previews to develop the desired flow and execution of all sound cues (including levels, effects, reinforcement with mics, etc.) until the show opens.

WHAT DO SOUND DESIGNERS EARN?

Most professional sound designers are members of United Scenic Artists and are paid according to contract agreements negotiated through the labor organization that also represents other types of theatrical designers. Contracts vary depending on many factors, including where the work is being done. For instance, designers working for a LORT theater work under contracts according to the theater's LORT designation, which is based primarily on the seating capacity of the theater. The designations run from A (the largest) through D (the smallest), with indicators such as B+ or C1 making room for more nuanced listings.

Table 12.1 lists the minimum design rates for 2006 under USA's guidelines for regional, resident, and dinner theaters and are also contingent upon the seating capacity of the theater.

TABLE 12.1. UNITED SCENIC ARTIST RATES FOR SOUND DESIGNERS IN REGIONAL, RESIDENT, AND DINNER THEATERS	
Seating Capacity	Rate
1–199	$2,197
200–299	$2,688
300–499	$3,416
500–999	$4,135
More than 1000	$5,175

Source: United Scenic Artists Local #829, "Minimum design rates 2006—Regional, Resident, Dinner theater, Schedule A."

Table 12.2 details the contract fees for sound designers working under a LORT contract and it includes the scheduled increases through 2009. The rates listed do not include any applicable daily rates, which range from $100 to over $300. These fees are basic rates that do not necessarily include composition, studio work, effects, or royalties. Broadway pay scales, as well as pay scales for other regions and singly negotiated contracts, vary along these lines.

However, not all designers work under union contracts, so the way sound designers earn money varies greatly. If a designer works strictly as a freelancer, his income can fluctuate depending on the regularity and type of work he finds. Many designers (not just those of sound) find that a good way to supplement income is through teaching. It is not uncommon for a very successful designer to have a full-time gig as a professor—

TABLE 12.2. UNITED SCENIC ARTISTS RATES FOR SOUND DESIGNERS IN LORT THEATERS			
LORT Category	Rates as of		
	July 2006	July 2007	July 2008
A	$5,049	$5528	$5776
B+	$4,298	$4705	$4917
B	$3,572	$3910	$4086
C1	$2,578	$2823	$2950
C2	$2,149	$2353	$2458
D	negotiable	negotiable	negotiable

Source: United Scenic Artists Local #829, "2005 Memorandum of agreement between United Scenic Artists, Local USA-829 IATSE, and the League of Resident Theatres."

or at least as an adjunct lecturer—in a university theater program. Other sound professionals supplement design fees by working on sound design outside of theater. (This is the case with both Jones and Thomas, who have composed for TV and film.)

On Broadway and anywhere else that new work is being developed, sound designers can take advantage of the possibility of royalty payments for their original compositions—the method of producing income favored by Keister. But mostly a sound designer relies on design fees, which can range anywhere from nothing to several thousand dollars. This is a flat rate that theaters agree to pay the designer for all of his work, including attending meetings, rehearsals, and all of the work that goes into creating the design. Naturally, if not working under contract, the pay is based on a designer's experience and reputation, as well as the financial situation of the theater paying the fee.

It has been said before, but it simply cannot be emphasized enough: The value of a good reputation is immeasurable. In this business, word of mouth can make or break the livelihood of up-and-coming designers and technicians. If someone in a position to hire asks someone he trusts—whether a stagehand or a department head—and he hears something negative, it can decide a hiring decision on the spot. Never underestimate the importance of impressions. *Everyone knows someone.*

FIVE SCHOOLS OFFERING DEGREES IN SOUND DESIGN

CORNISH COLLEGE OF THE ARTS
Programs offered: BFA in Theatre with concentration in Sound Design
www.cornish.edu/perfprod
Contact: Dave Tosti-Lane, dtostilane@cornish.edu

NORTHWESTERN UNIVERSITY
Programs offered: Certificate in Sound Design
www.sounddesign.northwestern.edu
Contact: sounddesign@northwestern.edu

PURDUE UNIVERSITY
Programs offered: MFA in Sound Design
www.cla.purdue.edu/theater/graduate/sounddesign.cfm
Contact: Rick Thomas, zounds@purdue.edu

UNIVERSITY OF CALIFORNIA, IRVINE
Programs offered: MFA in Theatre Sound Design
www.drama.arts.uci.edu
Contact: Michael Hooker, drama@uci.edu

University of Cincinnati—College-Conservatory of Music
Programs offered: BFA
MFA
www.ccm.uc.edu/tdp
Contact: Chuck Hatcher, hatchece@ucmail.uc.edu

RESOURCES FOR SOUND DESIGNERS

Books

Ballou, Glen. *Handbook for Sound Engineers.* 3rd ed. Boston. Focal Press, 2002.
A comprehensive text, featuring detailed information on all types of sound media, techniques, and technology.

Bracewell, John. *Sound Design in the Theatre.* Englewood Cliffs, NJ: Prentice Hall, 1993.

Davis, Don, and Carolyn Davis. *Sound System Engineering.* Boston: Focal Press, 2006.

Davis, Gary D., and Ralph Jones. *Sound Reinforcement Handbook.* 2nd ed. Milwaukee: Yamaha, 1988.

Kaye, Deena, and James LeBrecht. *Sound and Music for the Theatre: The Art and Technique of Design.* 2nd ed. Boston: Focal Press, 1999.

Leonard, John A. *Theatre Sound.* London: A & C Black, 2001.

Moody, James L. *The Business of Theatrical Design.* New York: Allworth Press, 2002.

Walne, Graham. *Sound for the Theatre.* London: A & C Black, 1990.

Periodicals

FOH—www.fohonline.com
A news magazine that covers all areas of live sound, including theater.

Lighting and Sound America—www.lightingandsoundamerica.com
A magazine focusing on everything to do with lighting and sound within the entertainment industry, including Broadway, regional theater, dance, live music, and much more.

Live Design—www.livedesignonline.com
The convergence of three magazines that covered different aspects of live entertainment technology: *Entertainment Design, Lighting Dimensions*, and *Staging Rental Operations.*

Mix Magazine—www.mixonline.com
  A publication covering all things sound related.

Internet

www.aes.org—Audio Engineering Society. More information here than you could ever imagine. Check it out.

http://asa.aip.org—Acoustical Society of America Web site.

www.brooklyn.com/theatre-sound/index.html—The homepage of the Theatre Sound Mailing List. In their own words, "a forum for people who do audio for musical theater or plays, concerts, worship services, etc."

http://freesound.iua.upf.edu/index.php—The Web site of The Free Sound Project is a great online resource for just that: free sounds.

www.hollywoodedge.com

www.lightingandsoundamerica.com—Web site of *Lighting and Sound America* magazine.

www.livedesignonline.com—Web site of newly reformatted *Live Design* print magazine.

http://mixonline.com—Homepage for the online version of *Mix Magazine*.

www.richmondsounddesign.com—The site for Richmond Sound Design is a great resource tool in addition to being a commercial site for the design firm. The site includes a designer directory, as well as an extensive page of global sound resources.

www.soundfx.com

www.sound-ideas.com

www.usitt.org/commissions/sound/Sound.html—USITT's Sound Commission site. The Web site for USITT is a great resource for theater technicians and especially designers. "Everyone in theater sound should be a member," says Rick Thomas.

13

SOUND ENGINEER

I learned [early on] that knowing how to hook up a mic and a couple of speakers would get me out of class.

—BEN MARCUM,
assistant sound designer, Actors Theatre of Louisville

Sound has become a major part of theatrical production, and though it still lies in a bit of limbo with the status quo folks (see chapter 12 on sound designers), it nevertheless plays a critical role in today's theater, all the way down to the extreme budget level where one might simply put a boom box on a table, with a sound engineer releasing the pause button at

Sound engineer Ben Mitten at work in Austin, TX. (Photograph by Mike Lawler.)

the right spot. For professional sound engineers, however, it's a bit more high tech, and from what I can gather (and what I have witnessed), that's the way they like it.

BEYOND BOARD OPS

In theater, sound engineers are the technicians that set up and troubleshoot the sound system as designed by the sound designer and execute cues during performance under the direction of the stage manager. They are sometimes known by other titles, including audio engineer, sound technician, or simply sound tech, but there is one thing we should not call them. "Don't call them board ops," Lindsay Jones, a prolific sound designer based in Chicago, advises, showing his utmost respect for and acknowledging the breadth of responsibility and skill of the technicians that make his designs come to life night after night.

In fact, depending on the organization of the theater for which they work, some sound engineers don't even run performances, instead leaving that duty to their assistants or the staff board operators. Kevin Faulhaber, assistant sound technician for Studio Arena Theatre in Buffalo, New York, spends most of his time making sure that the changeover process between productions goes smoothly. "We do a seven-show season, and I come in and strike the closing show and tech the opening show," he says. "I am primarily responsible for the installation of locational speakers and for working with the designer to program our playback devices and console," Faulhaber explains. At Studio Arena Theatre, Faulhaber's supervisor is the lead sound technician, who will typically operate the sound system during performances. "I occasionally run the show when [he] wants time off," he says.

A more complex arrangement exists at Actors Theatre of Louisville, where Ben Marcum is assistant sound designer. "At ATL, we are unlike most other crews," he says. "We have a big crew consisting of designer, assistant designer, supervisor, engineer, and two techs [or] ops." A large crew organized in this fashion gives the resident sound designer as well as guest sound designers a well-oiled machine to implement their designs. Each member of the sound crew at Actors Theatre of Louisville understands how he fits into the puzzle and is assigned specific tasks in order to design, build, program, and operate the sound system for any production. This also gives the designer the luxury of stepping back from the engineering and programming of a design, which is not always the case in smaller theaters or in similarly sized companies with small sound crews.

UNION HOUSES

Another thing that may change the way a sound engineer does the job is the presence of a labor organization. At times the work of a sound engineer comes under the domain of IATSE, the union that represents most technical areas of theater (the most notable exception being stage managers, who are represented by Actors Equity Association). Faulhaber works in such a theater. "We are a rare LORT theater with combined IA and Equity contracts," he explains. This is, as Faulhaber indicates, an uncommon setup in regional theater. Most IATSE-represented sound engineers tend to be working tours, running Broadway shows, working as techs in roadhouses, or serving in other areas of performance altogether, such as live music.

COLLABORATING: "THE CONDUCTOR OF THE ORCHESTRA"

Considering the skilled work they do, it's no wonder that designers consider sound engineers a crucial part of their work. Jones feels very strongly about the people who control the sound he has designed. "People have an immediate reaction to sound," Jones says, "and so everything you hear makes an impression right away." This is where, according to Jones, a designer's reliance on the production's sound engineer proves critical. "They're the ones who have to recreate it night after night," he says. As a result, designers do what they can to elicit a sense of guardianship over the show from the engineers who will run it.

Because sound designers work hard to engender in their sound engineers such a connection to the work, the current system of sound operation during performances frustrates many designers. Rick Thomas, head of the sound program at Purdue University, believes that the way sound engineers are sometimes relegated behind glass is just one problem. Though this practice has become increasingly rare, it still exists in many smaller theaters. "Somehow a system for integrating sound into performance was developed that couldn't be more damaging to the performance," he says. Thomas sees the sound board operator as "the conductor of the orchestra." But, rare, he says, "is the theater group that treats sound in that manner." Another practice that is not necessarily conducive to proper operation of live sound is the way sound engineers must take cues from a stage manager over a headset system. "Sound is a live medium," he says, "and it must be performed with the actors and treated like the actors." At Purdue, where Thomas has control over such matters, he usually has two engineers operating sound for a show. One will wear the headset and take cues directly from the SM, while the other is headset-free in order to properly mix the show.

Such respect for the medium usually translates into respect for the sound engineer and thus a good working relationship between designer and technician. "The best way to approach working with any level of engineer is to be prepared and have a plan," says Jones, expressing an understanding gained through experience. It is the age-old idea of respecting a leader with vision and the ability to communicate that vision. "We've brought in designers from all over the country," says Faulhaber, as he describes the need for sound engineers to be open to the sometimes strange work routines of sound designers. "I try to get them to concentrate on what they want to be hearing and explain it to me in those terms so I can do my thing and make it a reality," he says.

PATHS TO A CAREER AS A SOUND ENGINEER

The educational opportunities available to sound engineers are diverse because of the wide range of employment opportunities available to competent engineers, including the recording industry, the touring concert circuit, the film and television industries, and innumerable theatrical possibilities. For this reason, the training of a theatrical sound engineer may not be based in technical theater. Michael Broh, production manager of American Players Theatre in Spring Green, Wisconsin, hires a sound engineer each season, and he admits it can be difficult to find competent technicians dedicated to his seasonal theater and eager to stay in the position for more than one summer. In his constant search, he has found a boon in sound engineers with nontheatrical training. "Full Sail Audio grads are, in many ways, more desirable than MFAs," he says, in reference to the vocational school famous for training professionals in all areas of sound. "They come in with the skills but are more willing to stick around for a few years."

There are benefits to both types of training, and students seeking an education in sound should carefully weigh their professional goals with the objectives of the program they choose to pursue. Attending a university while focusing on sound will enable the student to gain a more full and general training in theater, rather than the intensely focused atmosphere of a vocational school; however, many students are more interested in the specific, advanced training available at an institution like Full Sail. Hopeful sound engineers or designers must ask themselves how important a theater background will be to their future work; it is an important consideration and should be weighed carefully.

◇ ✦ ◇ ✦ ✦ ✦ ◇

A Job Description

Sound engineers are called upon to do more than operate the sound systems during performances, though that is usually their central duty. The engineer is also responsible for setting up the sound system, including speakers, monitors, microphones, the mixing board, and any computer or playback systems. When running the show, they are often referred to as sound operators, or sound mixers, and are responsible for controlling each element of the sound, including the mixing console (or sound board) and any sound reinforcement systems that may be in place. This can become very complicated when operating sound for large productions such as musicals, when large numbers of cast members are utilizing microphones that must be mixed live, muted, and activated on cue.

In order to be prepared to set up the system, the sound engineer must be in communication with the sound designer to determine the needs of the design, such as speaker placement, number and type of microphones to be used, instrumentation or other live sound elements, and what type of equipment is to be used for playback.

WHAT DO SOUND ENGINEERS EARN?

Many sound engineers are multitalented technicians, who have learned to ply their trade in as many areas as they can. The field in which they work presents many opportunities, including not only film and television work but also the gigantic music industry. Many sound professionals will spend as much time mixing live shows for local and touring bands as they will running theatrical productions.

Of the thirty-two sound engineers who responded to my Tech Theater Earnings Survey, most are employed in theater—either as staff engineers and resident assistant designers, or as freelancing technicians—though nearly half of them work for more than one theater. As you can see, a few of them make quite decent money, while the majority make a respectable living even if they're not getting rich.

TABLE 13.1. EARNINGS FOR SOUND ENGINEERS		
Total number of sound engineers surveyed = 32		
Where the sound engineers surveyed are working		
Type of theater	*Number*	*Percentage*
Academic	2	6%
Broadway	-	-
COST	-	-
Dinner	-	-
LORT	18	56%
Off-Broadway	2	6%
Opera	-	-
Regional	5	16%
Resident	1	3%
SPT	-	-
Other	4	13%

How much sound engineers are earning		
Income range	Number	Percentage
Less than $10,000	2	6%
$10,000–$20,000	3	9%
$20,000–$35,000	14	44%
$35,000–$50,000	10	31%
$50,000–$75,000	-	-
$75,000–$100,000	2	6%
More than $100,000	1	3%
How sound engineers view their income		
Perception	Number	Percentage
Below average	11	34%
Average	14	44%
Above average	7	22%

Source: 2006 Tech Theater Earnings Survey.

FIVE SCHOOLS OFFERING PROGRAMS IN SOUND

FULL SAIL

Programs offered: AS in Show Production and Touring
BS in Entertainment Arts
www.fullsail.com
Contact: See Web site for appropriate contact information.

MICHIGAN TECHNOLOGICAL UNIVERSITY

Programs offered: BA in Sound Design
BS in Audio Technology
BS, BA in Theatre and Entertainment Technology
www.fa.mtu.edu
Contact: Christopher Plummer, cplummer@mtu.edu

UNIVERSITY OF MISSOURI-KANSAS CITY

Programs offered: BA in Theater with concentration in Sound Recording
MFA in Theatre Sound Design
www.umkc.edu/theater
Contact: Tom Mardikes, mardikest@umkc.edu

younger audiences," she tells me. "At the same time, [it] embraces new and widely used forms of communication to express something to all generations."

Clark too sees the ubiquity of projected imagery in our society as one that can bring life and originality to almost any form of theater. "A lot of classic shows lend themselves to reinterpretation," he says, "and a lot of new scripts are really developed with media and concert in mind."

All of these may be reasons why video and other forms of projection have become a more common sight in live theater, but certainly another major cause for their rise in popularity is the very malleability to which Kibens refers. A theater director or playwright can use video to help tell a story in any number of ways, whether subtle or obvious. This flexibility is reflected not only in the imagery of video but also in its physical presence. The area it uses can be quite small, on a grand scale, or anywhere in between. It can easily be a part of a production with a small budget, using a projection technique as simple as a classroom overhead projector. It is also used in top dollar Broadway shows, like Billy Crystal's 2005 production *700 Sundays*, in which Clark integrated the projections into the scenery.

AN EVOLVING FORM

"It used to be that you didn't need computer tools," Clark says, laughing. "When I started I had my Exacto knife and my splicing block and I'd cut film all day." Now, of course, digital media rules the roost, and projection designers spend much of their time learning and using the computer programs necessary for graphic design work.

"I think the use of video in theater will depend more on the evolution of video technology than on the changes and advances in theater as an art form," explains Kibens. Video artists like Kibens and Clark have seen the field of theatrical video open up over the last several years, becoming more accepted by a wider range of theater artists and audiences alike. "As video [becomes] more widely accepted and embraced in the theater community, there seem to be fewer limits on creative ways to utilize the medium," Kibens says.

The possible ways to use projections in theater are only limited by the imaginations of the designers. "I think video will become more interactive," Kibens says. "It has already begun to be used that way, and as technology progresses this interactivity is explored further." A recent example of interaction between projected images and live performers is the Radio City Music Hall production *Frank Sinatra: His Voice, His World, His Way*, in which projections were used to create a virtual performance by the late crooner, singing and performing with a live orchestra and dancers. But what happened on the stage of Radio City Music Hall between live dancers and Ol' Blue Eyes, or even on Broadway, is generally a far cry from a typical regional theater production. "In many cases today, video is used almost outside of a theater piece in order to frame it and not integrated in the story the way lighting, set design, props, and even characters are," Kibens laments. But she sees hope in the new ways that projections are being used in theater today, and she is encouraged by the trends of integration and interaction. "Hopefully, the 4:3 box of the standard video frame will continue to be discarded, and the way images are projected will become more seamless with set pieces and props," she says.

With the constant evolution of technology, however, come the questions of how far it should be taken and when it is unnecessary. "I think right now, you're witnessing some examples that stretch beyond the boundaries of what we might call responsible," Clark tells me, speaking of the way some productions have managed to go overboard with the potential for spectacle in the theater. "In a certain sense, though, it needs to be done so that people know how far is too far," he adds. As evidence, he points to Andrew Lloyd Webber's *The Woman in White*, a recent production, designed by William Dudley, that employed projections for nearly everything that was not a live actor. "A lot of people found that very disorienting," Clark says. "It's one of those things that had to be tried, just to see how far you could take it."

COLLABORATING: CONVERGENCE

"My initial responsibilities are to understand, as best I can, what the director wants to achieve or enhance by adding video," Logan Kibens says, explaining the beginnings of her design projects and her subsequent collaboration with other designers. In many cases projection designers will find themselves working with other theater artists mostly unfamiliar with the work they do. This can leave them in the position of reacting to the work of other designers, rather than bringing wholly fresh ideas.

It is the overlapping nature of projection and video for the theater that affects collaboration for the projection designer. This is probably most true when considering the application of lighting and scene design, which are specialties that use the ideas of texture and illumination much like video and projections do. It is still common for the scene designer, for example, to design the projections for a production, since they are generally such an integral part of the scenery. Projection is also a form of lighting that is not too far off from much of the technology employed by lighting designers, which presents yet another reason that there must arise a close collaboration among designers of a production in which video projection is part of the concept.

"As recently as five years ago, there was this enormous conversation about what was called convergence," Clark says. "You'd have an über-designer or a production designer that would come in and say, 'Okay, I'm going to take care of not only set and costumes, but I'm going to do lighting and video too.'" But, according to Clark, things have become far too complex for one person to make a bona fide attempt at this in most cases—even to the point that a lighting designer would find it difficult to manage adding projections to the work. "Video production has become an incredibly technically challenging and time-consuming item that most American lighting designers really don't have time for," he says. "Space is being made for people who do what I do, as opposed to that position being overtaken by others."

For the projection designer to successfully integrate his art into other more established areas of theatrical design there are two major areas where special attention must be paid: the illuminating ability of the projection and the surface upon which the images will be projected. The former is a concern for (among others, of course) the lighting designer, while the latter is the primary concern of the scene designer. How will the light of projectors affect the look of the lighting design—and vice versa? How can the areas used for projection be stylistically integrated into the set? The answers to these questions will come first from the director or playwright and the concept for the production. While a pull-down movie screen may work for some shows, it won't work for all of them. This adds another element of consideration for the scene designer, especially if the projections are not used throughout the production but only in a limited amount.

"The funny thing is," Clark tells me, "the designer I feel most akin to most of the time is the costume designer." This he believes comes from the nature of projection design as a form of collecting, much the same way that costume designers gather bits of things to establish their designs. "A costume designer will hunt down pieces and bits and elements to compose a costume for an actor," he says. "You do that too when you work with imagery."

As an example of true design cohesion involving projection design, Clark mentions a 2006 production of *The Wiz* at La Jolla Playhouse. With Clark's design and the scene design using the entire theater, the production included projections on every wall and plasma screens. "The lighting designer used **LED** fixtures, so we were able to generate the same colors in our palette," Clark says. "So, even though I was doing imagery and he was doing lights, you wound up with this unified look that was really quite spectacular."

PATHS TO A CAREER IN PROJECTION DESIGN

Because of the relative newness of this area of theatrical design, professionals in the field tend to come at it from all over the map—both academically and professionally. "I came into theater completely by accident," explains Kibens. "I had skills that when I learned them had no obvious direction or usefulness other than commercial purposes, but came to be incredibly new and useful by the time I was in college," she continues.

"And because I focused on that, I was able to break into a wonderful art form and be one of the many people who got the chance to figure out first what this new design was all about." Coming into the world of theater through a little-used side door, as Kibens and many other projection designers have, presents its own set of challenges too. "I think the biggest challenge once I was there was understanding the world of theater," Kibens tells me. "I didn't know any of the basics of technical theater and that is something I continue to learn to this day."

Clark, however, had a distinct advantage in this area and one that I think is important to consider: He *is* a trained theatrical technician. Having graduated from North Carolina School of the Arts with an emphasis in stage management, he finds his solid background in technical theater has made his work in this emerging field much easier. "I find that it's a great help," he says. But it is rare. "I am one of the few people [in this field] that actually comes from a theater background," he says. "Most people seem to cross over from videography, or maybe they went to film school, or maybe they worked for an advertising agency," he says.

Kibens makes a point of valuing the path of individuality over the rigid suggestions of higher education. "People tell you that things should be A, B, and C, and the only way to get from point A to point B is via a straight line," she tells me. "But, secretly, everyone wants you to understand the rules and then creatively learn how to either build upon them or break them." This line of thought is probably quite appropriate when considering the use of video and projection in the theater, because the rules have yet to become concrete, giving artists like Kibens and Clark the ability to step in and create with little established theory dictating what may or may not work in production.

Above all else, such a career track proves that theater is the perfect place for innovators with new ideas, approaches, and techniques. As theater and related technologies evolve over time, Kibens thinks that it is important to remind young artists that there's no telling what will come next—which means students should follow the area that interests them most. You may be surprised where you find yourself in the future. "I think kids are in a perfect position to understand and intuit trends that others cannot," she says. "So, if you feel that something is important, I say pursue it even if no one else gets it yet. They'll catch up."

◇✦

Job Description

The process of the projection designer is like that of any other designer for the theater, in that all designers must approach the work from the point of view of the text and the director's interpretation of the work. According to Michael Clark, the acclaimed projection designer of such Broadway shows as *Jersey Boys* and *700 Sundays*, the next step is to meet with the scene designer. "Sometimes they have a very strong opinion about where they want the imagery to be," he says. He then moves on to locating the content of the projections and creating a storyboard, much like in the making of a film. Concurrently, Clark is considering the manner in which he will "get the image to the area of the stage that we want to see," which entails deciding what type of equipment and how much of it to use. It will also involve close cooperation with the lighting and sound designers, since the physical space they use often overlaps. "We're all sort of scrambling for that same aerial landscape," Clark says.

Once the design is in its final form on paper or in a "computerized visualization," the projection designer is ready to move into the space, place and focus instrumentation, make any adjustments necessary to correct for color or clarity, and transfer files to the local control system. During tech, the projection designer's work is very similar to that of lighting or sound designers: watching the cues, adjusting them as needed, and reworking focus or other technical aspects of the design based on how well they are or are not working within the performance.

◇✦◇

WHAT DO PROJECTION DESIGNERS EARN?

Unlike the other design fields covered in previous chapters, the theatrical projection designer is not part of USA's pay scale—*yet*. It seems likely, according to people within the industry, that by the time you are reading this, projection designers will be among those with union representation, giving them the right to specific pay scales and other benefits.

For now, the evolving nature of this particular area of design leaves it a wide-open area in terms of rates of pay. This can be both advantageous for talented designers and unfortunate for those just trying to start out.

The bottom line: Projection design is a wide-open field, and those practicing its art will earn based on their talent, skill, and the budget constraints of the company that hires them.

STUDYING PROJECTION DESIGN

There are no universities or colleges that provide a program in projection design for the theater. Finding a program focusing on theater that will allow you to pursue an area that interests you, with an ability to facilitate that pursuit, might be a student's best shot at studying theater while pursuing the area of video/projection design.

Studying film, video, digital media, and similar areas is also an option open to those interested in this field. The programs listed below are not all theatrically linked programs but instead institutions that have degree programs that focus on the areas that a projection designer must be well versed in. Keep in mind, too, that the brief list below is just a sampling of the possibilities if a degree is desirable to you.

THE ART INSTITUTES
   Programs offered: Media Arts
                        Fine and Performing Arts
   www.artinstitutes.edu
   Contact: See Web site for appropriate contact information.

CAL ARTS
   Programs offered: MFA in Integrated Media
   www.calarts.edu/schools/theater/index.html
   Contact: Carol Bixler, cbixler@calarts.edu

FULL SAIL
   Programs offered: Digital Arts and Design
                        Film
                        BS in Entertainment Arts
   www.fullsail.com
   Contact: See Web site for appropriate contact information.

UNIVERSITY OF ARIZONA
   Programs offered: BFA in Design/Technology
                        MFA in Design/Technology
   web.cfa.arizona.edu/
   Contact: Peter Beudert, pbeudert@mail.arizona.edu

RESOURCES FOR PROJECTION DESIGNERS

Books

The sheer number of books to be found on the vast subject of video and projections is daunting; however, I was not able to unearth a text focused specifically on using the medium for theatrical production. (If there is one out there, I apologize— if there isn't, there should be soon.) So, though the list is brief, it could easily have stretched the entire length of this book. Here you will find only a handful of books on a wide range of topics that cover areas of concern for the theatrical video designer, including books on art video as well as technical texts.

Holman, Tomlinson. *Sound for Digital Video*. Boston: Focal Press, 2005.

An area of video and projection for the theater that is essential for the designer to understand, this book is geared toward the novice primarily but provides useful information for all practitioners of digital video in any application.

Rees, A. L. *A History of Experimental Film and Video*. London: BFI Publishing, 1999.

While this book may not provide the technical knowledge needed to create video in this digital age, it does cover the areas explored by film and video artists of the past, which is always a good starting point for artists of today.

Rysinger, Lisa. *Exploring Digital Video*. 2nd ed. Clifton Park, NY: Thomson/Delmar Learning, 2005.

A well-rounded, comprehensive text for the digital video beginner, it covers topics ranging from editing software to camera techniques.

Periodicals

Live Design—www.livedesignonline.com

The convergence of three magazines that covered different aspects of live entertainment technology: *Entertainment Design*, *Lighting Dimensions*, and *Staging Rental Operations*.

PLSN: Projection, Lighting, and Sound News—www.plsn.com

Sound & Video Contractor—www.svconline.com

An industry publication, it is also online (see below).

Internet

www.plsn.com—*Projection, Lights, and Staging News* Web site.

www.projectorcentral.com—A simple Web site with features such as a projector search, which helps the user find a projector suitable for his project, and a list of suppliers of all things related to projections.

www.svconline.com—The Web site of *Sound & Video Contractor*.

PART IV COSTUMES

◆

I can't help making things.

—JOANNE MARTIN,
costume designer and costume shop supervisor, Santa Clara University

The world of theatrical costumes is full of so many intricate specialties that it is sometimes amazing that costume shops get anything done at all. A well-run costume shop working at full tilt is similar to what I imagine Santa's workshop might feel like on December 23—minus the wooden toys and elves. In place of the wooden toys are racks full of costumes; in place of the elves are the folks we'll find

Costume designer Rosemary Ingham (right) discussing a costume with cutter/draper Paula Buchert (left). (Photograph by Sara Stellick.)

in this section. A typical costume shop employs a variety of craftspeople to get the work done, including **stitchers, drapers, first hands**, milliners, wig masters, makeup artists, design assistants, and shop managers. Some of these specialists toil under the direct supervision of the costume shop manager, but others specialties often are departments in and of themselves, and the chapters have been divided along these common lines.

15

COSTUME DESIGNER

We don't make much money, but boy, the opportunity to meet new people, plumb their minds about the way they feel about the world in the process of putting on a play, that's just great. I just love it.

—SUSAN TSU,
costume designer and professor of costume design, Carnegie Mellon University

One recent summer, while visiting my wife's family in rural Wisconsin, I arranged to interview costume designer, author, educator, and all-around theater muse Rosemary Ingham. Shortly before I left my in-law's old farmhouse for a meeting with Ingham in the small town of Plain where she was staying while

Eliza - Acts 1 & 2   Eliza - Act 3   Eliza - Act 4   Eliza - Act 5

Costume designer Rosemary Ingham's rendering of the character Eliza Dolittle in American Player's Theatre 2003 production of *Pygmalion*. (Courtesy of Rosemary Ingham.)

costuming *The Play's the Thing* at American Players Theatre, my father-in-law asked an odd question: "Why would anyone need to design the costumes for that show?"

My wife and I had attended a preview of the show with her family the night before, and my father-in-law's question stumped me. The show, set in the 1920s, featured a cast costumed mostly in evening wear that seemed to transcend the era. When I sat down with Ingham, I shared my father-in-law's question and asked what she might have said to him if he had put it to her directly.

"I rather like that response," she told me. "I would say to him, 'Thank you.'"

She reveled in the idea that an audience member might find her costumes so natural to the world of the play that it would not occur to him that someone had painstakingly researched and designed them. But someone certainly had.

THE ACCIDENTAL COSTUMER

Supported by what is generally the largest team of workers assembled for the purpose of implementing a theatrical design—including an entire costume shop, a milliner, and a crew of wig, makeup, and wardrobe personnel—designers like Ingham are relied upon to clothe each and every person who sets foot on stage for a production. This work obviously includes performers but often extends to musicians and even crew members as well.

"Basically, I'm an on-the-job-trained costume designer and technician who worked in theater primarily to earn a living," Ingham tells me. A writer before she became a designer, Ingham has written three books about theater design. In fact, as I write this, an invaluable theatrical reference tool is propped open on my desk: *The Costume Designer's Handbook*, coauthored by Ingham and Liz Covey. It is an old, tattered copy that I used in college, yet the book remains an excellent resource for any student interested in pursuing professional costuming. Ingham and Covey also wrote the more recently released *The Costume Technician's Handbook*—an equally useful book. While Ingham spent years teaching costuming at the university level, teaching for a time at Southern Methodist University and later at Mary Washington College in Virginia, she currently focuses on writing and designing. "Now I'm strictly a freelancer," she says. "I like that."

Ingham's decades-long devotion to theater is, simply put, a happy accident. "I married into the theater," she explains. "I'd grown up with my grandmother who was a tailor and have always been able to stitch. One day in 1957, I volunteered to help with costumes for the Virginia Players at the University of Virginia. A tall, lanky, extremely interesting man was playing Captain Fisby in their production of *Teahouse of the August Moon*. We were married in 1959 and I soon found myself designing and building theater costumes—for pay!"

A founding member and resident designer of the new Great River Shakespeare Festival in Minnesota, Ingham has spent a career working in the trenches of well-respected and prestigious regional theaters, including the Long Wharf Theatre, Milwaukee Repertory Theatre, Arena Stage, and the Utah Shakespeare Festival. "I've never been interested in the for-profit theater, including Broadway," she admits. "I'm strictly a regional designer, dedicated to regional audiences."

BRINGING A SCRIPT TO LIFE

Though they share the common task of clothing the cast, costume designers have their own unique ways of approaching the process. For Ingham, also the author of *From Page to Stage: How Theatre Designers Make Connections between Scripts and Images*, successful costume design often comes down to fully realizing the artistic transformation from printed words to practical and inspired design elements. "I must understand a script completely—not just read it, but understand it," she says.

A big part of any designer's job is communicating design ideas clearly to the other people involved in a project. "I have to draw and apply color to my designs in such a way that the sketches can be read by all other members of the production team," Ingham explains, "and I must be able to direct, guide, encourage, and even inspire everyone who contributes to the costume process."

"I think I'm very practical," says Joanne Martin, costume designer and costume shop supervisor at Santa Clara University. "I see the whole play or characters in my head before I draw them," she continues. "To be a costume designer, you really need to think things through a great deal before the costume is made." Because a show's costumes are an essential part of how the production will look, Martin works closely with the other designers before committing to any one design idea. "I read the script, watch the dance, or listen to the music at least three times before I really design anything," she says.

The only way to contribute ideas that will mesh with the production concept is through research, according to Susan Tsu, costume designer and professor at Carnegie Mellon University. "I'm a designer who likes to do a lot of research before I begin. When I was younger, I didn't feel like I was doing anything until my pencil hit the page, but I would have pencil in hand, and all of a sudden feel like, well, gee, I'm not really sure what to draw here." As Tsu's career progressed, she discovered that her early approach to projects was missing the kind of thorough background necessary for good costume design. "It's through the process of research that I begin to gather some ideas and images to me, and pitch other ones out," she says. "The research is often visual, though often not exactly about the costumes."

After spending time collecting images and other research that relate to her vision of the production concept, she often finds that some people cannot make the link between her research and the costuming needs of the show. "It may be thematically linked to the material I'm working on, but not necessarily direct at first," she explains.

Tsu understands that different theater artists work in different ways, and sometimes she finds herself working with a director or designer who can't relate to her highly researched approach. "So then I keep it to myself—but I still do it," she says. "It is part of my process. It informs what I do. I feel that it allows me to approach work that I do on a much deeper level."

COLLABORATING: WORKING WITH THE SHOP

"I very rarely work with somebody that is cynical and that just doesn't want to put time into what we're doing," Tsu says. A designer's ability to work well with the artists and technicians who will implement her designs is critical in every field of design. "I've never done a show in which changes haven't occurred during the rehearsal process," Ingham says. "It's important to have the shop manager and tech staff in my ballpark in order to get not only the original designs done, but also to make changes."

A typical costume shop employs so many workers, with such varying degrees of specialization, experience, and personalities, that it is vital for the designer to enter the production process with an open and clear mind. Depending on the theater, the shop, and its management, costume designers may encounter a work experience ranging from effortless to impossible. "One must first understand how each theater likes to operate," explains Tsu. "Each theater is different," she says, "and each shop manager has differing skills and focus. It is important to ask questions and not make assumptions."

The divide between techies and designers that can arise is not a secret to anyone working in professional theater. The self-assured designer having to work closely with the resentful technician is an all-too-common scenario. It is easy to avoid, however, and when avoided can lead to the best kind of collaboration: designers working honestly and openly with technicians who feel invested in the production. "Perhaps," muses Tsu, "flexibility and sensitivity could be said to be the best characteristics to have." Tsu's favorite example of how a stellar costume shop can make all the difference takes her back many years to a production of Verdi's *Aida*. With costumes being constructed by Sally Ann Parsons, Fred Neida, and Janet Harper, Tsu marveled at the quality of work. "All of them were consummate artists, inspirational, and my designs were taken to a level possible only with collaborators of such a high caliber," she says. "When the costumes and accessories arrived at the Opera House, the work was so beautiful that upon opening the boxes, the project manager wept!"

The people most responsible for a good working environment are the designer and the shop manager, both of whom can imbue a shop with the right kind of energy and expertise (both with their attitude and their hiring practices). This relationship will also make it possible for the costume designer to interact with individual members of the shop if and when necessary, and the shop manager is the most practical contact point for the designer when dealing with the daily logistics of costuming a show.

Spotlight on a Pro

Susan Tsu, costume designer and professor of costume design,
Carnegie Mellon University

Letters to a Young Costumer

In her design classes at Carnegie Mellon, Tsu takes her work just as seriously as any of her designs. "I believe we have a moral obligation to expose and educate [students] in the profession," says Tsu. "Theater is not a lucrative or easy life and designers will often find themselves wearing many other hats while not designing." As a result, Tsu believes that costume design students should be exposed to every possible path their career might follow—including work in opera, dance, film, television, commercials, and industrials. "They should also have not only design and drawing capabilities, but also construction and craft expertise."

Tsu also makes an effort to train costumers who have an ability and desire to be innovative and bold. "As teachers, we can teach best what we know and believe," Tsu says. As a designer whose work is rooted in imagery and metaphor, she makes an effort in her classroom at Carnegie Mellon to go beyond the process familiar to most designers. "I do try to expose my students to different ways of approaching design. I try to give them enough opportunities designing different genres and approaching the work in different ways."

Inspired Designing

In 1996, Tsu took on the project of a lifetime, agreeing to design a cycle of Greek plays to be performed at the Kennedy Center the following year. The plays, performed in a cycle that spanned two days, required the costuming of more than one hundred performers. "It was a sizable project," she says with considerable understatement. "Preparations were along two different tracks at the same time. First, of course, I needed to familiarize myself with the stories and the information surrounding the stories."

While the technical challenges of the work were extensive, Tsu likes to talk about the effort that came after familiarizing herself with the stories to be retold—the second track. "I had the opportunity to explore what it means to be human with a really inspiring director," she says. "What was thrilling about the piece and the work was the material, because all of the great, unanswered questions were what we were dealing with."

Tsu's research for the project led her to delve into the potential for historical context as well as the larger, conceptual ideas of the production. "The first evening of plays was designed with the weight on ancient costumes, as perhaps influenced by the modern, whereas the second night flipped and it was modern influenced by ancient."

Tsu has also designed the opera version of Genet's *The Balcony*, performed in Russia during the politically turbulent 1990s. "In Russia," she explains, "they are so inventive with their fabrics and materials and throw nothing away, but make gorgeous things out of sweepings and bits and pieces of this and that. I thought, we in the United States are so wasteful."

Tsu was also a part the Long Wharf Theatre's foray into China, designing and building the 1993 production of *The Joy Luck Club* in collaboration with Shanghai People's Art Theatre. The production featured a close collaborative effort between Americans and the Chinese, with stage managers, actors, and costumers from each country. "We take so much for granted in the United States," she says. "Yet our designs are often less bold and deeply reflective than those of our colleagues [elsewhere] in the world."

PATHS TO A CAREER IN COSTUME DESIGN

Costumers know that a life in the theater is not for the faint of heart. "I have missed family weddings and funerals because I have been in dress rehearsals," Martin tells me. "This is hard to explain to nontheater people."

Tsu points out that what a young person usually finds exciting about the theater can be fleeting. "The high school experience is a first-time experience of infectious camaraderie and ego building. A lifetime in the theater can be lonely and not at all glamorous," she warns. But, Tsu wants to make one thing clear: "It can also be the most wonderful path one can take." She advises young theater students to take into consideration the reasons they want to pursue a theatrical career, and, just as she does meticulously with her own work, research everything thoroughly. Finally, she says aspiring costume designers will benefit greatly from a true understanding of their own artistic goals. "Read Rainer Maria Rilke's *Letters to a Young Poet*," she says. "Substitute your chosen field for anywhere he refers to the poet or poetry."

"Ask yourself quite frankly if you're happiest when you're working on a creative project all by yourself or with a group," adds Ingham. "If you prefer to work alone, you will not be happy working in the theater; we are a collaborative art," she says. "Always." For Tsu, such collaboration is the pinnacle of fulfillment as an artist. "The satisfaction of seeing my dreams realized on stage is powerful, but in the end, it is the people and my students who make the greatest contribution to my feeling of reward," she says.

The consensus among professionals is that opportunities for hardworking costumers of all kinds are abundant. "There is a huge need out there for really good costume designers, and, if you do a good job, meet deadlines, and work well with other people, you will always have work," Martin says. Remember, for each and every production going on at this very moment —plays, musicals operas, dance performances—someone is deciding what the performers will wear onstage, even if the folks in the audience don't realize it. In step with that of other designers, Martin's last bit of wisdom is something to keep in mind no matter what your field: "Do it only for as long as you really love what you are doing."

◇✦◇

A Job Description

As with any other theatrical designer, the central focus of a costume designer's work is finding a way to convey the overall production concept as articulated by the director of the production. The costumer's responsibilities encompass any and all elements that concern the look of the performers. This may include clothing, hair, makeup, and other accessories considered a part of the performer's costume. For instance, if a performer is to use a cane, it would be designed by the costume designer and built or otherwise found by the props department. Costume designers will attend production meetings, costume fittings, and technical rehearsals. Designers, at times with the help of an assistant or shop manager, shop for material needed or desired for their design and work with the costume shop to choose and find any pieces that may be used from stock or borrowed from another facility. Costume designers also work to solve problems that may arise with complicated costume pieces and devise practical ways to create any special effect that may involve a performer's wardrobe.

Once the production is in technical rehearsals, the costume designer will pay close attention to the use of costumes, continuing to make any necessary changes until the production opens. This may include working with the wardrobe supervisor and crew to modify and rehearse costume changes that take place during the performance and making any final alterations.

◇✦◇

WHAT DO COSTUME DESIGNERS EARN?

Like their colleagues in the areas of scenery, lighting, and sound, costume designers are represented by United Scenic Artists Local 829 and are therefore entitled to compensation as negotiated through that union. The fees and daily rates agreed upon vary based on the type, location, and seating capacity of the theater. In the case of costume designers, the number of costumes to be designed is also usually factored into the design fee. Below you will find tables detailing some of the more common rates for costume designers who are members of USA.

Table 15.1 lists the 2006 rates for costumers hired for work in regional, resident, or dinner theaters. These fees do not include daily rates, per diem, or fees for design assistants.

Table 15.2 details the amendments to USA's Schedule C for design rates for LORT theaters. Designers working for a LORT theater work under contracts according to the theater's LORT designation, which is based primarily on the seating capacity of the theater. The designations run from A (the largest) through D (the smallest), with indicators such as B + or C1 making room for more nuanced listings.

Table 15.3 is an example of the major leagues of theatrical design—the USA design rates for designers working on Broadway. While becoming a costume designer on Broadway is by no means impossible, up-and-comers should rely on the first two charts for realistic earnings potential—especially considering that many New York–based designers must still work regionally to earn a living. Also, table 15.3 does not include the breakdown for advances required or supplemental payments due for period pieces.

TABLE 15.1 UNITED SCENIC ARTIST RATES FOR COSTUMERS IN REGIONAL, RESIDENT, OR DINNER THEATERS, 2006				
Seating Capacity	*Number of costumes*			
	1–10	*11–20*	*21–30*	*More than 30*
1–199	$2,197	$47 ea.	$47 ea.	$44 ea.
200–299	$2,973	$81 ea.	$47 ea.	$45 ea.
300–499	$3,776	$99.50 ea.	$63 ea.	$54.50 ea.
500–999	$4,685	$137 ea.	$99.50 ea.	$70.50 ea.
More than 1,000	$5,175	$169 ea.	$112 ea.	$99.50 ea.

Source: United Scenic Artists Local 829, "Minimum Design Rates 2006–Regional, Resident, Dinner Theater, Schedule A."

TABLE 15.2. UNITED SCENIC ARTISTS DESIGN RATES FOR LORT THEATERS, 2005

LORT Category	Weekly Rates as of		
	July 2006	July 2007	July 2008
A	$7,125	$7,410	$7,744
B+	$5,825	$6,058	$6,330
B	$4,750	$4,940	$5,162
C-1	$3,563	$3,705	$3,872
C-2	$2,771	$2,881	$3,011
D	Negotiable	Negotiable	Negotiable

Source: United Scenic Artists Local 829, "2005 Memorandum of Agreement between United Scenic Artists Local USA-829, IATSE, and the League of Resident Theatres."

TABLE 15.3. UNITED SCENIC ARTISTS DESIGN RATES FOR BROADWAY, 2006

Number of performers	Rates	
	Dramatic	Musical
1–7	$6,758	$10,977
8–15	$8,754	
16–20 or 31–35	$404 per character	$515 per character
21–30	$11,958	$21,953
36 or more	$15,176	$32,181

Source: United Scenic Artists Local #829: "Broadway, Minimum Rates and Classifications 2006."

As I have noted in previous chapters, the Tech Theater Earnings Survey did not include designers that are typically represented by a labor organization, since such plentiful and detailed information is already available regarding the earnings of such artists.

FIVE SCHOOLS OFFERING DEGREES IN COSTUME DESIGN

BOSTON UNIVERSITY—COLLEGE OF FINE ARTS
Degrees offered: BFA in Costume Design
BFA in Costume Production
MFA in Costume Design

MFA in Costume Production
Certificate in Costume Crafts
www.bu.edu/cfa/theater/index.htm
Contact: Mariann Verheyen, msv@bu.edu

KENT STATE UNIVERSITY
Degrees offered: MFA in Costume Design
www.theater.kent.edu
Contact: Suzy Campbell, scampbe2@kent.edu

NEW YORK UNIVERSITY — TISCH SCHOOL OF THE ARTS
Degrees offered: MFA in Costume Design
http://drama.tisch.nyu.edu/page/home.html
Contact: Susan Hilferty, sh9@nyu.edu

NORTH CAROLINA SCHOOL OF THE ARTS — SCHOOL OF PRODUCTION AND DESIGN
Degrees offered: Costume Design
Costume Technology
www.ncarts.edu/ncsaprod/designandproduction
Contact: Pam Knourek, knourekp@ncarts.edu

NORTHERN ILLINOIS UNIVERSITY
Degrees offered: BFA in Theatre with concentration in Costume Design
www.niu.edu/theater
Contact: Lori Hartenhoff, lorijh@niu.edu

RESOURCES FOR COSTUME DESIGNERS

Books
Baker, Georgia O'Daniel. *A Handbook of Costume Drawing*. Boston:
Focal Press, 1993.

Bacalawski, Karen. *The Guide to Historic Costume*. London: B. T. Batsford, 1995.

Emery, Joy Spanabel. *Stage Costume Techniques*. Englewood Cliffs, NJ:
Prentice Hall, 1981.
    A dated but comprehensive resource for the costumer.

Ingham, Rosemary, and Liz Covey. *The Costume Designer's Handbook*.
Portsmouth, NH: Heinemann Drama, 1992.

―――. *The Costume Technician's Handbook*. Portsmouth, NH: Heinemann Drama, 2003.

This book, which I rate above the costume-writing duos first effort because it is more recent and a bit more comprehensive, has a fabulous annotated bibliography, chock full of useful resources for any costume designer or technician.

Kidd, Mary T. *Stage Costume Step by Step*. Cincinnati, OH: Betterway Books, 2002.

Pecktal, Lynn. *Costume Design: Techniques of Modern Masters*. New York: Back Stage Books, 1999.

A great source for reading what some of the most successful costume designers of our time have to say about their designs and their careers.

Wolff, Colette. *The Art of Manipulating Fabric*. Radnor, PA: Chilton, 1996.

Internet

www.clancy.uk.com—The Web site of British designer Deirdre Clancy and her online book, *The Costume Designer's World*. The e-book contains great information on subjects ranging from the history of costume design to employment options and it features an extensive listing of academic programs in costuming in both the United States and the United Kingdom.

www.heinemanndrama.com/ingham-covey—The Web site for Rosemary Ingham and Liz Covey's book *The Costume Technician's Handbook*, the site contains up-to-date resource lists, a comprehensive shopping guide, useful addresses, and more. This site is great for costumers of all kinds, and even has great links for any theater technician, regardless of her field.

http://pegasus.cc.ucf.edu/%7Ektollefs/—The USITT Costume Design and Technology Commission Web site, and one of the more useful USITT commission sites. It contains practical information and resources, including the Costume Program Survey, a useful tool in finding the right place to study—especially for grad school. The site has many other features too: a costume locator, costume plot database, research database, and commercial pattern archive.

16

THE COSTUME SHOP

We work together to make the costumes come alive on stage.

—JENN MILLER,
costume shop manager and costume designer, Signature Theatre

Robert Haven has been building costumes for a long time, but the theater moment that sticks with him most and informs his work ethic is one that found him running a show on the props crew many years ago during a production of *The King and I.* "Anna was out there singing her heart out," he begins. "About midway through the song she raised her arms and the zipper running up the back of the gown let go!"

Robert Haven's desk in the costume shop of the University of Kentucky. (Photograph by Amanda White Nelson.)

The actor managed to modify her choreography long enough to hide the slipping costume and get offstage quickly. "She exited into the arms of the costumers who did a quick change into another dress," Haven says. "To this day as a costumer I never trust zippers!"

With the possible exception of a large scene shop cranking out gigantic sets for full-scale operas, there is no department in technical theater that comes close to a costume shop in terms of crew size, detail work, specialization, and the amount of labor devoted to individual pieces by each member of the shop. And even the placement of zippers can make a big difference.

A costume designer's biggest asset is by far the skill level and talent concentrated in a theater's costume shop. To begin to understand what takes place in a costume shop, one must first consider the wide range of specialists who work there.

THE SHOP MANAGER

Supervising the whole affair is the costume shop manager (also known as the "costume shop supervisor" or "costume director"). "As the manager I try to keep the big picture," says Ann Emo, costume shop supervisor for Studio Arena Theatre in Buffalo, New York. Historically, shop managers have been folks with broad theatrical training, usually with extensive experience in costuming. In today's costume shop, however, many shop managers have found that striking a balance between costume experience and the facility to deal with lots of paperwork, lots of numbers, and managing people is essential. As costume shops have become more efficient and modernized, so their managers have become sleek amalgamations of talented artists and capable managers.

The Utah Shakespearean Festival, a LORT B+ theater with two performances spaces, employs a huge staff in its costume shop. Jeffrey Lieder, who has served as the costume director of the festival for twenty years, manages a shop that employs as many as sixty-five highly skilled costumers during the season, including two shop supervisors and one assistant costume director. "We also have between three and ten volunteers working with us during the build," he explains. The crafts department is likewise Lieder's responsibility, but it has a crafts supervisor and assistant crafts supervisor too. A separate department contains the wig and makeup personnel, adding another twelve people to the list of folks implementing every aspect of a costume design.

But not all shops are created equal. Costume shop size—both in terms of physical space and crew—varies greatly from theater to theater and is dictated by the size and scope of the theater's budget, production needs, as well as many other factors. Many smaller shops will employ only a handful of technicians to do several jobs at once. In some instances, the costume shop manager is the only full-time staff member.

At Studio Arena, a LORT B theater with an operating budget similar to Utah Shakes, Emo does not enjoy the super-sized support staff that Lieder does. She employs only an assistant and draper full time, hiring the first hand and all stitchers as needed. "This is not the best of all worlds," she says, explaining that she often must deal with a scarcity of stitchers who are not necessarily loyal to her shop.

The key responsibilities for any shop manager include hiring staff, dealing with budgets, and ensuring that designs are built on schedule and to the satisfaction of the designer and artistic team. "I am pretty good at getting into designers' modes fairly quickly," Emo tells me. "I have to facilitate realizing their vision," she explains. "I listen to how they describe things and go from there."

Today, many shop managers find themselves spending a great deal of their time sitting behind a desk rather than in the work areas of the costume shop. This is because pulling all of the pieces of a production's (or an entire season's) costume needs is very labor intensive, involving hours looking for materials, supplies, costumes, staff, and equipment and pricing options for such. What makes the position of shop manager especially challenging is that, in a moment's notice, one must be able to switch gears from desk work to communicating articulately about design, and then to efficiently planning staff and build schedules. And sometimes, the manager must jump in and help out with the build. "I try to keep the big picture, but will get in there and sew, drape, or do whatever is needed when things get tight," Emo says. "I like for my shop to see that I am not afraid to go the extra mile to get what I want or what is needed for a production."

The costume shop manager is, quite frankly, the technical director of costumes. And while costume shops may not build things as big or wide as the scenery of the scene shop, they certainly handle an equal volume of materials and deal with staffs that are usually even larger.

◇✦◇

Shop or Studio?

According to *The Costume Technician's Handbook*, the question of what exactly to call the space where costumes are created has cropped up in recent years. Should it be called a costume shop or a costume studio? Apparently, there is some dissent among costumers (not unlike that surrounding the use of the word "costumer"!). The argument goes something like this: The proper term for a place where works of art are created is *studio*, not *shop*. A shop, they say, connotes a place to go and pick up a child's Halloween outfit, not a place where artists and craftspeople toil to create new and original costumes for use on the stage. However, history and tradition have thus far trumped semantics, leaving costume *shop* as the term most commonly used. For now. Funny, I always figured that *shop* was short for *workshop*. So, don't be taken aback if you are one day asked to work in a costume studio. Soon after, we may see a rise in the use of terms like *scene studio* and *prop studio*. Either way, I presume the quality of work and the level of specialization and expertise in these *shops* and *studios* will not change much—it's already about as good as it can get.

◇✦◇

COLLABORATING: THE SUPPORTING CREW

Within a costume shop, there are a slew of specialty positions that typically fall under the supervision of the shop manager. These include cutters, drapers (commonly one position known as the "cutter/draper"), first hands, stitchers, crafts and dye personnel, and usually a wardrobe crew. It can also include wig, makeup, and millinery staff, but they are often under their own supervision. (For specific information about these jobs and others, please consult the descriptions below or the following chapters on milliners and wig masters and makeup artists)

Above all, each member of the costume shop staff must be able to work in harmony with designers in order to pull off successful productions. This is true from the assistant shop manager all the way down to the stitchers and crafts/dye people. As with any field of theatrical design, the technicians implementing the concepts must fully understand what they are striving to achieve as well as be able to communicate effectively with the designer directly if necessary. "Most designers consider themselves only as good as their shops are," says designer and educator Susan Tsu.

Designer and author Rosemary Ingham knows how essential the costume shop is when realizing a design, and she tells me that she is generally pleased with the work ethic of the costume shops she works with. "Most in-house shop managers and tech people are eager to make my show as successful as possible and have it look as close as possible to my designs," she says.

Sometimes, however, things that are out of the costume shop's hands go wrong. Martin recalls an incident involving an overzealous running crew, a **blood pack**, and a highly charged dramatic fight scene turned comic. "As costumers we carefully plan for blood," Martin tells me, setting up the story. "We put actors in clothes that can be easily cleaned shortly after the actor is done bleeding; we carefully place blood packs in specially made pockets; we make the blood darker or brighter depending on the lights. We don't want the actor bleeding too soon or the audience looking at the blood for too long," she says. During the fight scene the actor was stabbed by another actor in the right spot, but because the blood pack had been filled with an excessive amount of stage blood, things went awry. "The stage blood spurted and sprayed all over the first row of the audience," she says. And because of the excessive amounts of blood, the audience couldn't help but react to such theatrics with laughter. "The blood also went all over the other actor whose costume was not designed [for] blood," Martin continues, the story becoming simultaneously funny and unfortunate. Because the blood had reached destinations unforeseen, the nonbleeding costume, which had taken weeks to build, had to be remade in one day, and audience members with stained clothing were compensated for cleaning bills. "Thankfully, playwrights usually put these scenes close to a blackout," Martin laughs. Martin, who used to be less explicit with running crews dealing with stage blood, now makes the crews measure the blood. "Less is always better where blood is concerned," she concludes.

PATHS TO A CAREER IN COSTUMING

Robert Haven, assistant professor of costume technology at the University of Kentucky, values his work as a teacher of costuming, perhaps more than his work as a costumer. "I am first and foremost a teacher," he says. "When not in class I am in the costume studio building shows with all student labor. I am constantly teaching."

Haven is sure to make clear that he is not a designer. "There are very few positions like mine," he says, "I don't draw the pretty pictures. I turn them into three-dimensional garments that fit the performers." He prides himself on the positive atmosphere he has created in his shop in an effort to heighten the students' ability to absorb information and learn. "I like to think that we have a nurturing environment where students can feel comfortable while learning costume construction skills without being overly intimidated."

In addition to suggesting exposure to a broad spectrum of ideas and specialties by taking internships and working summer stock, Emo has some very basic advice for those thinking of becoming full-time costumers: "Stay fit," she says. "Treat yourself well, because it is hard work."

"There are more jobs for good theater technicians than there are for actors—or designers," Haven says. "Technicians, regardless of whether they are carpenters, electricians, stitchers, or milliners, always find work." He firmly believes that with the proper training, theater artists who want to make a living as costumers should have a relatively easy go at it if they aren't focused solely on design. "There are a few schools that focus on these areas," he says. Haven explains that unlike programs geared toward aspiring designers, good training in the nuts-and-bolts side of costuming is more valuable. It's simple supply and demand, he suggests. "Most undergrad and grad programs turn out dozens of designers a year."

In the end, what concerns Tsu most about the future of costuming is the type of training that young costumers are able to find. "There is a kind of old world guild discipline that must be inherent in the training," she says. "Most theater programs unfortunately expect the costume students to build the shows but don't leave them time to practice and perfect any craft before doing so." It is important to consider such things when investigating where one wants to study the art of costuming because, as Tsu reminds us, "the business is clamoring for good young drapers, tailors, dyers, and craftspeople."

◇✦

Job Descriptions

shop manager—The shop manager, also known as "shop supervisor" or "costume director," is responsible for the hiring, supervision, and, when necessary, instruction of the shop's staff, for budgetary concerns, and for quality assurance. The manager may also play an important role in the selection of plays for a theater's season by carefully reading any work being considered and reporting on expected cost and time needs as regard the costume department. The manager will also act as the contact point for the designer once the build begins and will keep the production manager (and other concerned personnel) apprised of the shop's progress. The manager will also consult with the production manager regarding budget and staffing needs for future productions.

assistant shop manager—The costume shop manager's assistant spends a lot of time behind a desk, dealing with the details of keeping the shop running: tracking receipts, rented costumes, and any other important items that the manager does not have time to keep up with while directly supervising the build and meeting with designers and other department heads. The assistant may act on behalf of the manager when the manager is unavailable. When necessary, and depending on the arrangements of the theater, the assistant may perform the duties of a design assistant as well.

cutter/draper—This person is responsible for making all of the patterns for any costume that the shop will build. The cutter/draper is a supervisory position as well, leading the first hand and stitchers through the build process. In certain situations the cutter/draper is known as the tailor and is responsible for aspects of the design requiring the skill and expertise of a costume tailor. The term "cutter/draper" is, in essence, a generic one, and this position may be called simply draper, cutter, or tailor. Rosemary Ingham and Liz Covey have this to say about how valuable a draper is: "A gifted draper is worth his or her weight in gold and will not only make the garment fit accurately but will interpret your sketch with sensitivity."

first hand—This position serves as assistant to the cutter/draper. Depending on the situation, this person may also cut patterns and/or supervise the stitchers.

stitchers—The stitchers do just that: stitch. A lot. They put the costumes together once the patterns have been made and cut.

craftsperson—Responsible for all types of crazy projects, the craftsperson builds specialized accessories and costume props, including any and all strange requests made by the costume designer and/or costume shop manager.

dyer/painter—Commonly a shared position filled by the costume craftsperson, this person modifies the color of fabric to be used as a costume or accessory, at times using chemical techniques to distress a costume. This person's responsibilities, like those of the craftsperson, are as wacky as the designer's imagination can be.

wardrobe supervisor—Also known as wardrobe chief or director, this person is charged with maintaining, repairing, and cleaning the costumes once the production goes into performance. He will also be responsible for supervising the wardrobe crew, often known as dressers. Along with the crew she will likely run the show, choreographing any quick changes that performers must make.

At the Guthrie Theatre, one of the nation's most prestigious regional theaters, Susan Fick is the wardrobe supervisor, heading up a full-time staff of eight and as many as twelve overhire crew members at a time. In this case, the crew works under an IATSE contract and is run independently of the costume shop. "I am basically an assistant stage manager dedicated to costuming," Fick says. "I'm the last line of defense between what the designer had in mind and what the audience sees."

dresser—This member of the wardrobe crew frequently assists performers with costume changes, especially in moments lacking in time known as "quick changes." Dressers are part of the team responsible for the maintenance and cleaning of the costumes once a show goes into regular performance. They are supervised by the wardrobe supervisor.

design assistant—This position, also known as assistant to the designer, is sometimes filled by the shop, using either a staff design assistant or the assistant costume shop manager. Other times, this person is hired directly by the costume designer. The design assistant's duties vary greatly and are dependent upon the needs of the individual designer and the unique situation of the costume shop. Working as a design assistant is an excellent way to learn about all aspects of the costuming world—from design to shop management to any one of the dozens of specialties found in a typical shop.

◇✦◇✦✦◇✦◇✦◇✦◇✦◇✦◇✦◇✦◇✦◇✦◇✦◇✦◇✦◇✦◇✦◇✦◇✦✦◇✦◇✦◇✦◇✦◇✦◇✦◇✦◇

WHAT DO COSTUMERS EARN?

"I hate that I can't pay people what they're worth," one costume shop manager told me. "I work hard to raise [the theater's] perspective on fair pay and advocate for higher wages constantly." The honesty of this costume shop manager says a lot about the earnings of costumers in general.

There were about fifty usable responses to the Tech Theater Earnings Survey from folks working in costume shops. About half of them were shop managers. The rest work in any number of shop staff positions. Taken together, lumping shop managers with their employees, almost half earn in the range of $20,000 to $35,000 annually, and nearly 60 percent believe they are in the average range of costume shop employees in the United States. However, there is a clear difference in income potential between costume shop managers, cutter/drapers, first hands, and other shop employees like stitchers. Therefore, it will be more informative to split this area up into two parts—one representing the costume shop manager and the other focusing on all other shop workers.

Intermixed within the survey respondents are probably union *and* nonunion costumers. Like many other areas of specialty, costumers are sometimes represented by IATSE and are therefore guaranteed specific wages. There are even costume shops that are "closed" and hire only union costume technicians.

TABLE 16.1. EARNINGS FOR COSTUME SHOP MANAGERS

Total number of costume shop managers surveyed = 27

Where the costume shop managers surveyed are working

Type of theater	Number	Percentage
Academic	1	4%
Broadway	-	-
COST	-	-
Dinner	1	4%
LORT	12	44%
Off-Broadway	-	-
Opera	1	4%
Regional	7	26%
Resident	3	11%
SPT	-	-
Other	2	7%

How much costume shop managers are earning

Income range	Number	Percentage
Less than $10,000	-	-
$10,000–$20,000	2	7%
$20,000–$35,000	13	48%
$35,000–$50,000	7	26%
$50,000–$75,000	5	19%
$75,000–$100,000	-	-
More than $100,000	-	-

How costume shop managers view their income

Perception	Number	Percentage
Below average	8	30%
Average	15	56%
Above average	4	22%

Source: 2006 Tech Theater Earnings Survey.

The Costume Shop Manager

Most of the respondents who identified themselves as costume shop managers were employed by LORT theaters. As with the overall look at costume shop workers, the majority of managers responding earned between $20,000 and $35,000. (See table 16.1 for more details.)

TABLE 16.2. EARNINGS FOR COSTUME SHOP STAFF		
Total number of costume shop staff surveyed — 33		
Where the costume shop staff surveyed are working		
Type of theater	*Number*	*Percentage*
Academic	3	9%
Broadway	1	3%
COST	-	-
Dinner	-	-
LORT	10	30%
Off-Broadway	-	-
Opera	2	6%
Regional	8	24%
Resident	5	15%
SPT	-	-
Other	4	12%
How much the costume shop staff are earning		
Income range	*Number*	*Percentage*
Less than $10,000	1	3%
$10,000–$20,000	14	42%
$20,000–$35,000	14	42%
$35,000–$50,000	4	12%
$50,000–$75,000	-	-
$75,000–$100,000	-	-
More than $100,000	-	-
How costume shop staff view their income		
Perception	*Number*	*Percentage*
Below average	11	33%
Average	21	64%
Above average	1	3%

Source: 2006 Tech Theater Earnings Survey.

The Costume Shop Staff

With only a slightly smaller number of respondents, this group was spread over a quite large area of expertise, experience, and job skills. Naturally, we would not expect an overhire stitcher to be earning as much as an experienced cutter/draper or first hand. The respondents listed as part of the costume staff portion of the survey include stitchers, design assistants, wardrobe supervisors and personnel, cutter/drapers, first hands, crafts specialists, and others.

The same number of shop employees reported earning between $10,000 and $20,000 as did those in the range of $20,000 to $35,000. Also worth noting is the large number of respondents who reported believing that their incomes were safely in the average range of those working in similar jobs in the United States. (See table 16.2 for more details.)

FIVE SCHOOLS OFFERING PROGRAMS IN COSTUMING

BOSTON UNIVERSITY
    Programs offered: BFA in Costume Production
                         MFA in Costume Production
                         Certificate in Costume Crafts
    www.bu.edu/cfa/theater
    Contact: Meg O'Neil, meoneil@bu.edu

CARNEGIE MELLON UNIVERSITY
    Programs offered: BFA in Costume Technology
                         MFA in Costume Technology
    www.cmu.edu/cfa/drama
    Contact: Susan Tsu, stsu@andrew.cmu.edu

SUNY-PURCHASE—CONSERVATORY OF THEATRE AND FILM
    Programs offered: BFA in Costume Technology
    www.purchase.edu/Departments/AcademicPrograms/Arts/TAF/default.aspx
    Contact: Dan Hanessian, dan.hanessian@purchase.edu

TEMPLE UNIVERSITY—SCHOOL OF COMMUNICATIONS AND THEATER
    Programs offered: MFA in Costume Construction
    www.temple.edu/theater
    Contact: Daniel Boylen, dboylen@temple.edu

University of North Carolina–Chapel Hill
Programs offered: MFA in Costume Production
www.unc.edu/depts/drama/index.html
Contact: Judith Adamson, jadamson@email.unc.edu

RESOURCES FOR COSTUMERS

Books
Emery, Joy Spanabel. *Stage Costume Techniques.* Englewood Cliffs, NJ: Prentice Hall, 1981.

Ingham, Rosemary, and Liz Covey. *The Costume Technician's Handbook.* Portsmouth, NH: Heinemann Drama, 2003.
    A one-stop reference for a costumer or costume student, this book has it all. An impressive and valuable resource.

Kidd, Mary T. *Stage Costume Step by Step.* Cincinnati, OH: Betterway Books, 2002.

Internet
http://pegasus.cc.ucf.edu/%7Ektollefs/—The USITT Costume Design and Technology Commission Web site.

17

MILLINER

As a milliner I thought everyone went to the theater to see the hats!

—MARGO NICKEL, FREELANCE MILLINER

At the very top of the actor, above the makeup and the wig, above all other costuming, there sometimes sits the handiwork of the milliner: a hat. The making of a fine hat, like that of a top-quality theatrical wig, is an art practiced by one of the most highly specialized artists working in, or in conjunction with, the costume shop.

Center Theatre Group milliner Dianne Graebner working on a hat in her shop.

The science of millinery is highly regarded and practiced by a relatively small number of theater artists in the United States, especially outside of New York City. You will find this chapter is probably the shortest in the entire book of technical theater careers. This is primarily the result of the relatively simple nature of what milliners do—which isn't to say how they do what they do is simple. On the contrary, it is complex, and it takes years of dedication to become a master milliner. However, to delve too deeply into the art of hat making here would be to do a disservice to those most qualified to explain its intricacies, and so I will only give you a bit of insight into the world of the theatrical milliners, because if millinery is your calling, you will find the people to teach and guide you through your hat-making career, that's for sure.

HATS, HATS, HATS

"One might not notice the hat, but without it one might be aware that something is missing in the context of the costume," says Margo Nickel, a freelance milliner based in Arizona. Nickel, who lived and worked for several years in New York City for a time as the assistant to the late Woody Shelp, the renowned milliner of Broadway and film fame, now works mostly in regional theater.

Milliner Kelly Koehn at work in her studio.

Building hats from scratch is an admirable skill and is an art passed down from generation to generation—mostly through well-respected schools and workshops run by some of the field's most successful artisans. "I still get a great deal of pleasure from turning buckram and wire and fabrics into three-dimensional objects," Nickel says. "Objects you can wear on your head!"

"Since you are working so close to the face, the hat is a prime focal point," says Kelly Koehn, a freelance milliner based in California who has spent twenty-two years as a milliner for the Oregon Shakespeare Festival. "A badly chosen hat is really grating and will usually get cut because it is so distracting."

A SMALL CANVAS

At the Center Theatre Group in Los Angeles—comprised of the Mark Taper Forum, Ahmanson, and Kirk Douglas Theatres—Dianne Graebner spends her days as the staff milliner. "My job shifts depending on what shows we're doing," she tells me, explaining the multifaceted nature of her work for one of the largest theater organizations in the country.

"It takes a special knack," Graebner says of theatrical millinery. "It takes a certain amount of anal retention as well." The requisite attention to minute detail, Graebner explains, is a result of a milliner's need to express something that is sometimes quite grand on a very small scale. "You have less of an area to make a statement with a hat," she says. The size of an artist's canvas, however, does not dictate the complexity of the art. "I have hats that I've had several assistants working with me for a week on," Graebner tells me while explaining the level of difficulty that frequently goes into millinery. It can, at times, be labor intensive to the point of causing budget crises. "The average producer isn't going to understand that or want to pay that."

Another concern is the physically demanding nature of the work. With a small canvas come small tools and intense physical movement requiring special strength, dexterity, and finesse. "You have to have really strong hands," says Graebner. "And you spend a lot of time bent over a table." As a result, milliners find themselves with cramped muscles from time to time and in general they admit that the hardest thing about their work may in fact be the physical toll it takes on their hands. "Find a really good massage therapist," says Koehn, advising any and all aspiring milliners who may be unaware of the stress it places on your hands, back, and other areas strained while constructing hats.

Beyond the muscles needed for the work, there is the question of what is wafting about in the air of the usually small shop of the milliner. "You work with a lot of chemicals," Graebner says, describing another hazard of the millinery world. "Things are getting better in that area," she says, and because many milliners are concerned about the toxic chemicals used in their trade, there has been an effort to develop products that are less toxic.

COLLABORATING: DESIGNERS AND HATMAKERS

"The most rewarding part of my work is getting it right," Nickel says, "and it isn't right until the designer says it's so." It's no surprise that milliners find collaboration with designers as one of the more enjoyable and challenging aspects of their work, for it is this cooperative effort that drives their creativity. "I've found that the best approach to working with designers is not to just look at the designs," Nickel explains, "but really listen to what they are saying." Nickel believes that working with a designer is a delicate balance between confidence and humility. "They came to you for your expertise," she says, explaining the unique nature of her trade and the knowledge milliners can provide to designers and costumers.

"Most designers—and some of my favorite designers—come in with their sketches. They show me the sketch and they say, 'Okay, I don't know anything about hats, you have to help me,'" Graebner says, describing a common scenario faced by milliners. But Graebner admits that this is one of the things she enjoys most about her work. The uncommon expertise of milliners often affords them the freedom to be creative within parameters set forth by costume designers. "Some designers will come in and say, 'Okay, look, this is a broad sketch and I want you to play and have fun,'" she says. "That's always a plus."

Besides costume designers, theatrical milliners must work with other artists involved in a production—at times delicately working to compromise with areas of design that may conflict with their handiwork. "We are constantly having a battle with lighting designers who are trying to put light on their faces," explains Koehn. "So, many times brim fronts have to be cheated back or curved up." And then, there are actors. "Actors who don't like to wear hats in real life can be a real challenge to work with," Koehn says. "They look very uncomfortable with one on their head even if it's a beautiful, well-fit hat."

PATHS TO A CAREER AS A MILLINER

Many professional milliners seem to come at the job from other areas of theater or fashion. "My education started while watching my mother make pheasant feather hats at our kitchen table," Nickel tells me. Years later, while taking costume classes at the Fashion Institute of Technology (FIT) in New York City, Nickel discovered that FIT offered a program in millinery. "Two years later I was out the door with a certificate in millinery techniques," she says. She admits, however, that even with the FIT certificate in hand, she only truly learned the craft of theatrical millinery after beginning her work with Shelp. "My *real* education began when I walked into Woody's showroom," she says.

Regardless of which professional theatrical milliner you speak with, one common thread becomes clear almost immediately: The likelihood of making a living solely as a theatrical milliner is slim, and all milliners have diverse costuming skills that keep them employable and financially stable. Koehn's advice to young milliners is to the point: "Don't pursue it as a career unless you think you will die if you don't do it," she says. "Have a lot of hat-making skills so you can find a 'real' job during the slow times."

◇ ✦ ◇

A Job Description

As Denise Dreher makes clear in the opening pages of her classic text, *From the Neck Up*, the distinction between craft and art, designer and technician, is often blurred when it comes to millinery. Like any other area of the costume shop, the milliner helps bring the costume designer's vision to life. As with wig masters and makeup artists, the milliner's expertise is often called upon by designers because the milliner's area of specialization is so concentrated that she will undoubtedly have valuable input into any design that employs headwear.

The basic pattern of a milliner's work is very similar to any other theatrical artisan in that he follows the specifications that a designer has laid out (unless she is responsible for the design—either all costumes or just headwear) and is called upon to create items to be used on stage in a timely and safe manner. The milliner's hats are in this way no different than the scenic carpenter's bits of scenery.

◇ ✦ ◊ ✦ ◇ ✦ ◇ ✦ ◇ ✦ ◇ ✦ ◇ ✦ ◇ ✦ ◇ ✦ ◇ ✦ ◇ ✦ ◇ ✦ ◇ ✦ ◇ ✦ ◇ ✦ ◇ ✦ ◇ ✦ ◇ ✦ ◇ ✦ ◇ ✦ ◇

WHAT DO MILLINERS EARN?

If you have your heart set on becoming a theatrical milliner, you may not want to read any further. The reality of the situation may be best expressed in the words of a working pro with many years of experience in the world of theatrical millinery: "Have a back-up plan." These words belong to Margo Nickel, who works primarily as an independent freelancing milliner in Arizona. "When theater work is scarce, look at other places to ply your craft," she says. "Teaching, hats for reenactors, even brides— it's all theater!"

The situation for milliners is probably most similar to wig and makeup artists— that is, it is a degree of specialty that regional theaters cannot always afford, thereby directing talented milliners into other arenas for work, including film, television, private design, and sales. I must report here that I have no set of data concerning milliners. The field is so spread out, with few of its practitioners working in any single media and most of them working as freelancers, that it was impossible to collect usable information on their earnings.

Milliners are also at times represented by local chapters of IATSE, which can improve their income potential.

SCHOOLS OFFERING PROGRAMS IN MILLINERY AND COSTUME DESIGN

FASHION INSTITUTE OF TECHNOLOGY
   Programs offered: Certificate in Millinery Techniques
   www.fitnyc.edu
   Contact: Ellen Goldstein, 212-217-7253

Many other schools offering programs in fashion and costume design have specialty courses in millinery. Those include the Art Institute of Chicago and the

College of Dupage, among others. If you are considering studying millinery as an undergraduate, a better course of action might be to major in theater at the school of your choice, so that you can study costume design and get a good overall education in theater arts. If, however, graduate studies are your next step, you might consider either pursuing an MFA in theater design, costume design, or fashion design, or simply attending one of the many private schools offering instruction in millinery. See the resources section below to find books and Web sites that can lead you to informed listings of such schools and programs.

CAL ARTS
   Programs offered: BFA in Costume Design
                        MFA in Costume Design
   www.calarts.edu/schools/theater/index.html
   Contact: Carol Bixler, cbixler@calarts.edu

NORTH CAROLINA SCHOOL OF THE ARTS
   Programs offered: BFA/MFA with concentrations in Costume Design and in
                        Costume Technology
   www.ncarts.edu/ncsaprod/designandproduction
   Contact: Pam Knourek, knourekp@ncarts.edu

RESOURCES FOR MILLINERS

From *agal* to *yeddo*, the language of milliners can sound like an alien tongue to those not used to it. Check out these books to find what you'll need to study this language and put the right words to the right techniques and materials.

Books
Albrizio, Ann, and Osnat Lutig. *Classic Millinery Techniques*. Asheville, NC: Lark Books, 1998.
   An excellent resource for learning the techniques of millinery as described by Albrizio, a veteran milliner with lots of wisdom to impart.

Dreher, Denise. *From the Neck Up: An Illustrated Guide to Hatmaking*. Minneapolis: Madhatter Press, 1981.
   Penned by Dreher, who admits to not being in the millinery business any longer, this book is still a great resource for hatmakers, and it was named as a fantastic resource by every milliner interviewed for this book.

Langley, Susan, and John Dowling. *Vintage Hats and Bonnets 1770–1970*. Paducah, KY: Collector Books, 1998.

Wilcox, R. Turner. *The Mode in Hats and Headdresses*. New York: C. Scribner's Sons, 1945.

Long out of print, difficult to find, and usually expensive when available, milliners love this book. "My most favorite book and the one I will never get rid of," says Kelly Koehn.

Periodicals

The Hat Magazine—www.thehatmagazine.com

A UK-based magazine about (you guessed it) hats.

Internet

www.millinery.info—A membership-based Web site devoted entirely to the art of millinery, including links to education programs, online references, hat-making glossary, milliner directory, and much more.

www.hathathat.com—An holistic millinery Web site, replete with resources for hatmakers, hat sales, millinery-related links, and lots of tidbits.

www.thehatmagazine.com—The Web site of the *Hat Magazine*.

18

WIG MASTER AND MAKEUP ARTIST

I am so used to finding hair everywhere that it doesn't bother me anymore.

—RALPH HOLCOMB,
wig master, American Players Theatre

While researching this chapter, I encountered varying attitudes about the career potential of wig and makeup specialists within theater. The professionals I interviewed—who span the spectrum within the field from academic to freelance to staff-positioned wig master and makeup artist—were especially frank about the realities of earning a living in the field without straying from theater. Many of them believed it impossible, and each of them acknowledged it was difficult at best. So, is it realistic to assume that folks specializing in wigs and makeup can earn a decent living while working strictly in theater and its related disciplines, such as opera and dance? The answer is not clear and perhaps is unimportant to many of you reading who may be considering employment or are already employed in the field.

A head block used for creating wigs at APT. (Photograph by Mike Lawler.)

Regardless of whether the career potential for theater artists interested in wigs and makeup exists for everyone, it is safe to say that it exists for some. The specialties detailed in this chapter are without a doubt an integral part of the art of theater, complementing the costume design field in some very crucial ways and at times usurping the role of costume design altogether. I have placed them together in one section because crossover between the specialties is common, and the training for one specialty is usually complementary to training for the other.

SPECIALIZING SPECIALISTS

"The wig and makeup industry is complicated and variable," explains Martha Ruskai, director of wig and makeup training at the North Carolina School of the Arts in Winston-Salem, a position she has held for eighteen years. Though the areas of wigs and makeup may sound quite different, they are frequently interchangeable and are often performed by the same people. Makeup artists are sometimes responsible for the care of wigs during production and are at times skilled wig makers and stylists in their own right. These artists, along with the milliner, are the people who look after the actor from the neck up. They do so, for the most part, in accordance with the costume designer's vision. Wigmakers may use wigs that are already built, having rented them or pulled them from a theater's stock, but they generally must still do a fair amount of maintenance and tweaking to make the wigs suitable for the design.

According to Ruskai there are six different skill sets applicable to both wigs and makeup: wig making, wig and hair styling, cut and color, makeup application, prosthetic lab techniques, and design. Most of these are self-explanatory; however, Ruskai explains that the art of one, makeup application, is very specialized. "Not all makeup artists can do all types and venues equally well," she says. There are several types of makeup application that require differing skills and training, including fashion, aging, prosthetics, and special effects. Again, Ruskai finds that even within these specialties there are stark differences between how they would be handled for the stage versus film, television, or print work.

The work of the wig master is also subject to the whims of other theater artists as they react to fashion and changing trends that seem to progress differently than they do with costumes and clothing. "Current taste and fashion affect hairstyles more than costumes," says Ruskai. "Audiences, directors, and performers accept that people in 1692 wore things that looked different but often have more difficulty in adjusting to a man in an elaborate, long wig, period makeup, and beauty spots," she explains.

Where Does Wig Hair Come From (and Where Does It End Up)?

"It's usually human hair," James P. McGough explains. As a wig master with over twenty years of experience, he's handled a lot of it. "It comes from hair merchants," he says. Such hair merchants are all over the globe, with the region determining the price, type, and quality of hair. McGough and Ralph Holcomb (see sidebar on Holcomb on page 204) have spent many summers building and maintaining wigs for the outdoor stage at American Players Theatre (APT) and point out that human-hair wigs will react to weather in predictably unfortunate ways, often necessitating restyling in certain conditions, like severe humidity. "There is never a hair shortage," McGough laughs. "They take it, color strip it, dye it," he says, explaining the process natural hair goes through before going to market. "They delouse it of course," he quips in all seriousness.

The hair is not always human hair, though. Frequently, theater companies use dyed yak hair as well as synthetic hair. These types of hair can be very useful for certain applications and are often preferred for building facial hair applications.

Whatever the source of the hair, it doesn't always end up where you'd think. "I am so used to finding hair everywhere," Holcomb says, dismissing my initial reaction to learning that he spends hours a day fiddling with real human hair. "If I'm in a restaurant and I sit down at a table and I see a hair," he says, "I wonder, did that come from me?" A question easily answered by most people, for we know what our hair is like, but wig makers like Holcomb work so closely with so many different types of hair that it's hard for them to know what they've brought to the table. Later, he tells a story of going home after work and finding a long human hair wrapped around one of his toes as though someone had taken the time to carefully secure it there. The thing is, wig specialists find hair everywhere. So, if you don't think you'd ever get used to that, wigs may not be the life for you.

WIG AND MAKEUP DESIGN

Design is yet another area that wig masters and makeup artists find themselves practicing. "While there are some costume designers who are skilled at drawing hairstyles and makeup, there are an equal number who are not," says Ruskai. "In addition, very few have been trained to apply makeup and style hair." The relationship between wig masters and costume designers is at times very complicated due to the high level of specialization involved and, according to some wig masters, the lack of expertise on the part of the designers. "A Costume designer is often stretched very thin and so may not want to take the time to think about hair and make-up until all of the costume pieces are under control, which can be right before the first dress rehearsal," Ruskai explains. "This shortens the amount of time available to build, have fittings, and make adjustments."

For these and other reasons, including the common understaffing of costume shops and the occasional lack

Wig master James P. McGough in the APT wig room in 2006. (Photograph by Mike Lawler.)

of a costume designer altogether, a specialized area of design has evolved: the wig and makeup designer. "We are more common in regional opera, Broadway, and film than in LORT theaters," explains Ruskai.

James P. McGough, wig designer and head of the wig shop at Virginia Opera for the past nine seasons, falls into such a category of wig and makeup design, though he admits his situation is uncommon. "What I have in Virginia is so rare," he says of his career. "Most opera companies don't have a resident wig person." McGough is also the retired wig master of American Players Theatre, where he spent fourteen seasons. While his title with APT was wig master, he did his share of uncredited design there, inasmuch as he has guided and assisted costume designers unable or unwilling to devote energy to wigs and makeup.

McGough has been followed by the next generation in the form of Ralph Holcomb, a character that seems unlikely in a wig shop. Holcomb, trained by a former pupil of McGough himself, has managed to create a career in theatrical wigs in a relatively short period of time. Turning thirty in 2007, Holcomb is an example of how fast one can excel with hard work and a talent for networking. He has demonstrated that one can create a niche and build a reputable career as a wig specialist in theater. However, Holcomb's career is probably the exception to the rule and by no means easily replicated. It takes a lot of work to build and maintain a life in wigs and makeup—especially if you are planning to stick to live performing arts.

THE REALITIES OF FREELANCING

"This work takes a lot of stamina," says McGough. "You're always looking for work," he exclaims. "Looking for work, looking for work, looking for work." But is that so different than any other freelance career or, for that matter, other career paths in theater? "Most theater companies don't use wigs," McGough tells me, suggesting one reason why it may be different for wig and makeup artists. "And when they do—and I hate to say this—they do them really badly," he says out of the corner of his mouth. "Good God," McGough chuckles, "is that Donald Trump playing Marian the Librarian in *The Music Man*?"

McGough may be joking, but he knows what he is talking about. As a wig designer, wig master, and makeup artist he has designed and built hundreds of productions in his twenty-plus-year career. By sharing what he believes the state of wigs in the American theater to be, he is hinting at a sort of catch-22 in the world of theatrical wigs and makeup. On the one hand, there is a saturated market of trained wig specialists, but really only a handful of theaters outside of the commercial world of Broadway can afford their skills. This leaves the wig and makeup artists fleeing for the financial rewards of Hollywood and New York (and other entertainment centers of the country). This seems to result in two distinct and vastly different pictures: one, a film and television market filled with employable artists—more, in fact, than the market can realistically employ on a regular basis; and, two, a mostly underpaid crew of freelancing theater pros, struggling to keep their schedules full while working for regional theaters and opera companies with ever-dwindling budgets.

Such an impression might be too gloomy though, and Ruskai reminds me of one very important thing: "I always have more job offers for my students than I have graduates of the program to fill them." This is an essential point and one well worth remembering when considering the ability of any theater technician to find work in today's theater.

FILM AND TELEVISION VERSUS THEATER

Work outside of theater is admittedly abundant, but different professionals see the opportunities in very different lights. "Monster, sci-fi, and gore get all the attention," Ruskai says, summing up her view of the dilemma faced by the serious theater artist.

"You make a lot of money in film," says McGough, who also freelances from time to time as a costume designer. "But there are a lot of sacrifices too." Besides the decisions that such artists make concerning relocating to one of the country's filmmaking centers, McGough views work in film and television as an entirely different ball of wax. "First of all, it's industry standard in film and television that you have to have a cosmetology degree," he says, referring to the training and licensing required by many states to work as a hairstylist or cosmetologist—regardless of where you have studied or earned a degree.

But according to Ruskai, who has been working with wigs for nearly thirty years, the debate is moot. "Very few wig makers don't work both industries," she says. "You can't really earn a living as a makeup artist in theater unless you run a Broadway spectacle." A realist, Ruskai is upfront with her students and other young people interested in pursuing wigs and makeup in the theater. "Be prepared to work very hard for very little payoff," she warns.

The labor organization that represents many artists in the field, IATSE local 798 is another determining factor in the building of a career. "The union requires that you specialize in hair *or* makeup," Ruskai says. "For me, the joy comes from creating a complete being or complete cast of beings." As a result, Ruskai is one of many working pros who are not affiliated with the union.

There is also ongoing pressure to require union members to hold a cosmetology degree, which puts veterans like McGough—who *is* a member of IATSE Local 798 and holds an MFA in costume design—in the unwelcome position of defending his expertise in the areas of both makeup and wigs. The debate surrounding the decision to join is a hotly contested one, and it should be considered carefully, weighing the pros and cons depending on how one wants a career to unfold.

And then there are the people in the industry who have aspirations that are all together different. I met one young wig stylist, a recent graduate from the University of Cincinnati with an MFA focusing on wigs and makeup, who had something entirely different in mind: the CIA. She hoped to one day land a gig designing and applying disguises for America's elite spy force.

COLLABORATING: ABOVE THE NECK

It's interesting to note that in over 250 pages of Lynn Pecktal's great costuming resource, *Costume Design: Techniques of Modern Masters*, the subject of wigs comes up in only two of the eighteen interviews the author conducted with some of the theater's most revered contemporary designers, and then only briefly. "Most people don't really understand what goes into good wigs," Ruskai says.

◇✦

Ventilating? What's That?

"Ventilating is what we call the process of knotting or tying the wig," McGough explains. "I have a friend who is in respiratory therapy, and she says, 'Every time I hear *ventilated* I think of something completely different,'" he chuckles. "A wig with a tube running down its throat!" But it's not as ominous as that.

"It's basically like doing a latch-hook rug," Holcomb says. "Or crochet." With a small tool called a ventilating (or tying) hook, Holcomb demonstrates the knotting technique he uses to tie the fine hair on the mesh that has been prefitted to a wig cap created from the actor's actual skull shape. The number of hairs tied together at a time depends on several factors, including where on the cap they are, and how many strands will be tied for each knot. Depending largely on the application and the wig maker, the back will often be tied thicker, with more hair per knot, while the front will be tied with a finer look in mind. "Once you learn, it's a very basic skill," he says as he shows me in extreme close-up how he ties each knot.

Ralph Holcomb demonstrates his ventilating technique. (Photograph by Mike Lawler.)

"Some people like really thick wigs, some people like thin wigs, and some people like it in the middle," Holcomb tells me, explaining how he has learned to accommodate the tastes and styles of the different wig masters and designers he has worked with.

❖ ✦ ❖

As a result, there is a tendency among those collaborating with wig masters and designers to have unreasonable expectations. "The biggest challenge is getting directors and costume designers to have thorough discussions and make timely decisions," she says. Many wig masters believe that costume designers rarely give the area above the neck much forethought. This sometimes leaves the wig master to take charge when it comes to the design and proper implementation of a cast's hair.

Aside from the folks that wig masters and makeup artists work with within a theater, an outside support network is also quite important—especially for problem solving. "You've got to build a network of people," McGough says, describing the common connection between like-minded wig and makeup artists. "And not be afraid to call them and say, 'Hey, I'm doing this, how do I do it?'" For wig masters, being able to contact other artists and brainstorm makes their jobs much more doable, in addition to providing a network of knowledge that any single person couldn't possibly retain. "You can't be one of these closed, tight-fisted people," McGough says, referring to his experience with some folks in the industry who closely guard their knowledge and expertise.

◇ ✦ ◇

Spotlight on a Pro

Ralph Holcomb, freelance wig specialist and wig master of American
Players Theatre, 2007–present

A Young Professional

When you walk into the wig shop of American Players Theatre, Ralph Holcomb seems out of place. If it weren't for the intent look on his face, staring down at the molded head in his lap while tying delicate strands of human hair through fine mesh squares, you'd think he'd stumbled in from the scene shop next door looking for a quiet place to think. Standing well over six feet, with closely cropped hair and a wild shock of red hair jutting from his chin, Holcomb cuts an imposing frame—especially when he stands up. Not the guy you'd imagine as the new wig master for the 2007 season of the classic theater in the woods, replacing the retiring veteran James P. McGough, with whom he worked for six seasons.

"If somebody told me when I started school, 'In ten years you're going to be sitting in a room tying hundreds of knots of hair every day,' I would have looked at them like they were crazy," Holcomb laughs. "But once I started getting into it, I fell in love with it." Now, after several years of supporting himself with his wig work, Holcomb knows how tedious the work may look to outsiders. And it is. Sometimes. "You can definitely see your progress," he says. "One of my favorite parts is when you put that finished, styled product on somebody."

"I started out as a film major, wanting to go into special effects," he says. And what sort of education does this unlikely wig master have? "My undergraduate degree is in dramatic theory, with a minor in film, figurative sculpture, and philosophy," he tells me in all seriousness.

Of course, his experience as a professional and the training he has received by working with some of the best in the field has made all the difference. When he talks about taking over for McGough, who has worked almost nonstop for APT since 1988, he demonstrates a guarded confidence. "Every single person has a different hand," Holcomb says, noting the delicate, hands-on, and often personal nature of the work. "So, I feel like I've got some big shoes to step into."

◇ ✦ ◇

PATHS TO A CAREER IN WIGS AND MAKEUP

So, what type of training should wig and makeup hopefuls pursue? It's hard to say. As you can see from the list of programs for wigs and makeup (below), formal training programs in a university setting are few and far between. But that doesn't mean that there is a shortage of trained wig and makeup personnel. This is because of the existence of private vocational schools focused on training in the field.

McGough is quick to point out the seeming overabundance of training for aspiring wig and makeup specialists. He tells the story of a friend who decided to become a makeup artist and visited a California training school for an interview. "The receptionist was a graduate of the program," he laughs. "What does that tell you?"

The decision about how to gain the necessary practical training for employment as a wig and makeup specialist is affected by many things. The primary considerations should be the following: (1) what industry you want to focus on, be it theater, film, television, or print; (2) whether or not you consider a liberal arts education valuable for your future; and (3) if you have access (or can gain access) to working professionals who are willing to teach you the trade in either a volunteer or entry-level capacity.

However one decides to pursue this field, it should be understood that there is no shortage of opportunities to learn about it thoroughly.

Job Descriptions

Wigs

Their process begins, as with most areas of theater, when they first read a script. "We're reading it with a completely different viewpoint than anybody else," McGough says. "I'm looking for any hair reference." As an example, McGough cites a recent production of *Tartuffe* in which the costume designer had overlooked a textual reference to Orgon's mustache. In this sense, it is helpful to have a wig master who takes the time to be familiar with the work.

The wig master must then determine how the desired hair and wigs will be accomplished for show. In doing so, the wig master will consult extensively with the costume designer who is, in most situations, responsible for the look of the performers' hair.

The wig personnel will schedule appointments with each of the performers to assess such things as head size, current hair length, hair color, and existing facial hair, if any. If it is not deemed necessary for certain actors to wear wigs, their hair length and style will be examined carefully so that any needed haircut or restyling can be determined and agreed upon. Actors requiring wigs will be measured and sometimes photographed so that the wig shop can create wigs that will fit their heads perfectly.

Often, wigs will be built from scratch. Other times a wig shop will use wigs that are already built, having rented them or pulled them from their own theater's stock. The shop must still do a fair amount of maintenance and styling to make existing wigs suitable for the design and the individual actor. The wig makers spend hours ventilating, a term used to describe the tying of the wig material (be it human hair, yak hair, or a synthetic material) to the mesh cap that will hold it together as a unit piece.

Once the wigs have been created in the style and manner necessary, the stylist will go to work manipulating the wig to match the desired look. During all of this, the wig shop may have the actors in for further fittings; for instance, a wig master would ideally want to have a fitting after the wig cap was built, after the wig was ventilated (or tied), and after the wig was styled. Depending on the theater or organization, this may or may not be possible based on the typically demanding schedules of the actors and the technicians.

When the wigs are complete, they will need maintenance during the run of a show and probably will also need periodic restyling.

Makeup

Though professional actors are usually responsible for applying the makeup created by the costume designer, there are times when specialized makeup is needed for a one or more of the characters in a production. If this is the case, a makeup artist will apply the makeup so that it is consistent at each performance in accordance with the design. (My favorite example of this was a costume design for Caliban in *The Tempest* that consisted of very little clothing and lots of body makeup. The makeup artist earned her wage every night for that one!) Because makeup is chemically based and in contact with a performer's skin for long periods of time, the makeup artist will also assess a performer's history of allergic reactions and ensure that all products used are safe.

Because makeup artists work in numerous venues and on a variety of productions, they must be able to make decisions about how makeup will "read" from the stage. They will do this based on many factors, including the performer's skin tone and the lighting, costuming, and scenery. The overall design and mood of the show are also critical considerations for a makeup artist, since the makeup they apply will reflect these ideals.

When necessary, makeup artists will also devise, design, and apply any prosthetic pieces or special-effects makeup applications, such as wounds, scars, or other modifying features that are required by the design.

As with any other tech theater position, the makeup artist will generally be present for technical rehearsals—either to apply the makeup as they will during the run of the show or to ensure that performers are properly using the makeup and fulfilling the demands of the design.

◇◆◇

WHAT DO WIG SPECIALISTS AND MAKEUP ARTISTS EARN?

Due to the nature of the wig and makeup fields, it was not only difficult to find professionals in the field who worked either solely or primarily in theater and opera, it was equally problematic seeking respondents to my salary survey. The table below is sorely lacking in useful information as a result, but it seemed appropriate to include anyway.

TABLE 18.1. EARNINGS FOR WIG AND MAKEUP ARTISTS		
Total number of wig and makeup artists surveyed = 7		
Where the wig and makeup artists surveyed are working		
Type of theater	*Number*	*Percentage*
Academic	1	14%
Broadway	1	14%
COST	-	-
Dinner	-	-
LORT	-	-
Off-Broadway	-	-
Opera	1	14%
Regional	4	57%
Resident	-	-
SPT	-	-
Other	-	-
How much the wig and makeup artists are earning		
Income range	*Number*	*Percentage*
Less than $10,000	1	14%
$10,000–$20,000	-	-
$20,000–$35,000	2	29%
$35,000–$50,000	3	43%
$50,000–$75,000	1	14%
$75,000–$100,000	-	-
More than $100,000	-	-
How wig and makeup artists view their income		
Perception	*Number*	*Percentage*
Below average	2	29%
Average	3	43%
Above average	2	29%

Source: 2006 Tech Theater Earnings Survey.

In order to provide more information on the matter of wig and makeup artist earnings, I have included an example of wages earned through IATSE Local 798 in addition to the Tech Theater Earnings Survey results.

Keep in mind too that (as Ruskai might point out) the respondents listed below earn over half of their income from work in the theater. Therefore, it is not at all representative of those earning higher dollar amounts in another medium, such as film or television.

TABLE 18.2. IATSE LOCAL #798 RATES FOR WIG AND MAKEUP ARTISTS AT THE FOX THEATRE			
	Rates as of		
Type of Rate	July 2007	July 2008	July 2009
Base Hourly Rate	$23.42	$23.89	$24.37
Overtime Hourly Rate	$35.13	$35.84	$36.56
Straight Time Performance Rate	$93.68	$95.56	$97.48
Overtime Performance Rate	$140.52	$143.36	$146.24

Source: Fox Theatre, "Hair & Makeup Wage Scale—'Commerical' Shows," http://foxtheatre.org.

FOUR SCHOOLS OFFERING PROGRAMS IN WIGS AND MAKEUP

NORTH CAROLINA SCHOOL OF THE ARTS—SCHOOL OF DESIGN AND PRODUCTION
Programs offered: Wig and Makeup Design
www.ncarts.edu/ncsaprod/designandproduction
Contact: Martha Ruskai, ruskaim@ncarts.edu

UNIVERSITY OF CINCINNATI—COLLEGE-CONSERVATORY OF MUSIC
Programs offered: BFA in Wig and Makeup Design
MFA in Wig and Makeup Design
wwww.ccm.uc.edu/tdp
Contact: See Web site for appropriate contact information.

WEBSTER UNIVERSITY
Programs offered: BFA in Design/Technical Theatre with concentration in Makeup Design
www.webster.edu/depts/finearts/theater/index.html
Contact: John Wylie, wyliejc@webster.edu

WIGS AND HAIR CHICAGO—IN PARTNERSHIP WITH DEPAUL UNIVERSITY, NORTH-
WESTERN UNIVERSITY, AND COLUMBIA COLLEGE
Programs offered: Wigs and Hair Production Certificate
Wigs and Hair Maintenance Certificate
www.learning.depaul.edu/c2k/headings/wigs_and_hair.asp
Contact: Moses Hudson, mhudson2@depaul.edu

RESOURCES FOR WIG SPECIALISTS AND MAKEUP ARTISTS

Books

Baker, Patricia. *Wigs and Make-up for Theatre, TV, and Film*. Boston: Focal Press, 1993.

Corson, Richard, and James Glavan. *Stage Makeup*. Boston: Allyn & Bacon, 2000.
Currently in its ninth edition, this book is a classic textbook used in
universities across the country.

Emery, Joy Spanabel. *Stage Costume Techniques*. Englewood Cliffs, NJ: Prentice Hall, 1981.

Morawetz, Thomas. *Making Faces, Playing God: Identity and the Art of
Transformational Makeup*. Austin: University of Texas Press, 2001.
A philosophical look at the idea of how makeup can transform a person into
a character. Interesting reading for those who do such things professionally.

Swinfield, Rosemarie. *Hair and Wigs for the Stage: Step by Step*. Cincinnati, OH:
Betterway Books, 1999.
Most useful for the novice, Swinfield's book is a simplified version of what
most wig masters do when creating period wigs. Recommended only for young
theater practitioners or for use in primary and secondary education settings.

Vinther, Janus. *Special Effects Make-Up*. New York: Theatre Arts Books, 2003.
Be prepared for some serious gore if you open this book, since Vinther concentrates
primarily on horror and sci-fi makeup applications here. The book is a must have if you
are planning on doing any special-effects techniques that call for blood and gore.

Periodicals

MakeUp Artist Magazine
Aimed at all types of makeup artists, it includes information on the film, television,
and print industries more so than theater.

Internet

www.costumegallery.com/hairstyles—The costume Gallery's "Hairstyle History"
page, with examples of hairstyles throughout the ages.

PART V OTHER CAREERS AND CONSIDERATIONS

◆

It doesn't matter if it's a big project or a little project. Everything you work on will hopefully help develop your skills and professional disciplines. Nothing could be more important than just getting out there and plying your trade.

—RICK LYON,
puppet conceiver and designer, *Avenue Q*

In the two chapters that follow, we will take a look at several areas of consideration for tech theater professionals, as well as some of what I have come to call "fringe careers," so-called because they are not connected directly to production but rather contribute to it from the outside. The first chapter covers the theater

Cirque du Soleil's *O.* (Photograph by Tomasz Rossa.)

consultant, a bona fide career but nonetheless one that lies outside the realm of technical production. It is, however, a career that is generally made up of folks who have a strong background in tech theater, and it is an important field that makes performing arts facilities as user-friendly and beautiful as they are these days.

The final chapter focuses on several things, including people who have created a niche for themselves over time—a common theme in the lives of theater artists and one of the reasons the structure of this book was difficult to nail down. I found it necessary to include such a chapter in order to consider the ways in which work in the theater is often specific to a particular job. Other fringe careers will be discussed briefly too, as well as the different types of working lifestyles that theater artists find themselves in, either through choice, luck, or, I suppose, misfortune.

One final note: Do not expect to find thorough information regarding the earnings of the professionals discussed in the following chapters. Since they either fall outside the area of tech production or retain such specialized positions as to be nearly unique, there were no related categories in my Tech Theater Earnings Survey.

19

THEATER CONSULTANT

It's not about hanging the audience from the roof just because it's different.

—ROSE STEELE,
principal consultant, Landry & Bogan Theatre Consultants

There is little that is more disappointing for theater artists than walking into an unfamiliar space in which they are going to work, only to realize that the facility is poorly designed and will present many technical obstacles to overcome: awful lighting positions, fly systems that do not suit the space, horrible acoustics—the list sometimes goes on and on. In an

Rendering of Portland Center Stage's recently completed Gerding Theater. (Courtesy of GBD Architects.)

ideal world, these issues will be well-known before anyone sets foot in a facility, but even then one can't help but feel a sinking heart at the prospect of having to deal with a space that could have been so much better suited to its purpose.

Fortunately, we now have an abundance of people known as "theater consultants," whose mission it is as much as possible to prevent that from happening. "A theater consultant assists architects and owners in the design of facilities for live performance," explains Rose Steele, a partner in the theater consulting firm of Landry & Bogan. She calls this her "elevator response" and admits that it is a bit more complicated than that. Many performing arts facilities owe their utilitarian design as well as their often graceful looks to consulting firms and consultants like Steele.

"GUARDIANS OF THEATRICAL FUNCTION"

Unlike any other career listed in this book, the work of a theater consultant is not for those who wish to be involved on a production level. But don't get me wrong. It cannot be stated enough how important their work is in the world of theater. It is especially so for those in the trenches—hanging lights, operating fly systems, and moving scenery—who must utilize the systems the theater consultant has designed.

Theater consultants like Steele, who holds a degree from Western Michigan University in theater with an emphasis in acting and directing, contribute to theater during the critical design phase of building and renovating performances spaces. In this way they become a part of each and every future production in the spaces they help to create. They lay the groundwork, so to speak, and once their work is done will be either cursed or praised mightily by generations of stagehands, designers, and directors.

"We are the guardians of theatrical function," Heather McAvoy, one of Steele's associates at Landry & Bogan, tells me, summing up a theater consultant's *raison d'être*. Aside from designing and consulting on integral technical theater tools and systems such as lighting, sound, and rigging, they will also typically assist with such things as interior design, seating configurations, ventilation, acoustics, and guiding the organization through building codes and compliance with the Americans with Disabilities Act (ADA). They may even handle such details as tool placement in the scene shop or, in the case of consulting firm WJHW, based in San Antonio, Texas, insulating building and street noise from the performance space. "Not all firms provide all services," Steele tells me, "but the range includes planning and feasibility studies, design and engineering services for theater systems including lighting, rigging, orchestra enclosures, pit lifts, curtains, acoustical canopies, sound and communication systems, and projection systems." And so much more. Basically, anything that may affect the functionality and proper operation of a theater or other type of performance space falls under the watchful eye of theater consultants. From figuring out the layout of dressing rooms to designing the best seating arrangement for the audience, consultants of some type have a hand in it all.

Theater consultants provide both the building architect and the owner or organization their expertise and experience in order to ensure that the performance space complies with safety regulations and building codes while retaining full functionality. The consultants will spend their time not only designing the systems of the theater but also coordinating with all of the different teams that participate in creating a new facility. "It's important to make sure that air conditioning ducts are not placed right in the center of the fly tower," says Fritz Schwentker, a consultant with WJHW, explaining the detail-oriented nature of such teamwork and the reason the expertise of theater consultants is needed. Consulting firms are usually hired by the architect to help guide him through the complicated maze of theater systems. "Sometimes we work for the owner of the building, and sometimes we work for the architect," Schwentker explains. "For most architects it's obvious that there are details that they are just not going to have familiarity with," he says. "If you think about a similarly complex kind of place like a hospital or something, how are you possibly going to know all of the things that need to go into such a building without the use of outside consultants?"

STILL CONNECTED TO THEATER

Steele lists her work for Oregon Shakespeare Festival as one of her favorite projects with Landry & Bogan; the firm worked with the festival on the Angus Bowmer Theatre, completed in 2002. "They are so knowledgeable, so technically proficient," Steele says of OSF. "To sit there and watch great, great theater and know that you contributed to it, even in a small way, is a thrill for me."

Theater consultants have the opportunity to do more than just give world-renowned theater companies fantastic, functional spaces—sometimes they are able to help provide a poorly equipped academic program with a facility that will improve the school's ability to serve its students. "I love the projects for an organization or educational program that has a make-shift building," Steele explains. "The difference it makes to the work they do can be dramatic, if you'll excuse the pun," she laughs. As an example Steele cites a recent project for Saratoga High School's McAfee Performing Arts and Lecture Center in California. The school's excellent music and theater programs were relegated to performing in a simple cafetorium, and since they lacked enough public funds to build a proper facility, parents stepped in with community support to raise the nearly $4.5 million needed. "We designed a very Spartan building but with a lot of options and alternates," Steele notes, including a full counterweight rigging system without a **grid**. "Eventually the parents group funded them all," she says, "but even with the extra money, we and the architect really worked hard to minimize the footprint and keep the project in budget."

Schwentker, who has a broad background in theater and holds an MFA in technical production from Yale, admits there have been times when he still misses "the intellectual stimulation of theatrical production." But, he also believes that his work as a theater consultant is not all that much different from his years working directly in technical theater. "The rewarding part is similar to the interest that I have in doing theatrical production," he says. "You sit down with an idea for a project and you work it through with a lot of different people." In this sense, Schwentker finds his work very much like working on an individual show for the theater. "Working with an architect in many ways is similar to working with a scene designer," he says, admitting that though the time frame may be quite different, the end result is equally satisfying. "It takes a lot longer to build a building than it does to build a show," he chuckles. "Most shows, anyway."

RAISING THE BAR

"Technology has had a huge impact, mostly for the good," says Steele. "[It] has led architecture and theater in some very exciting directions." As two prime examples of how theater design has evolved and expanded its conceptual limits in the recent past she mentions two mammoth projects she admires: first, the KA Theatre at the MGM Grand in Las Vegas, the latest production from Cirque du Soleil, for which designer Mark Fisher and the creative team of Cirque created a new space specially for the production, and, second, the Disney Concert Hall in Los Angeles, famous for its exterior architecture designed by Frank Gehry, a man with a penchant for creating buildings with unusual shapes. "Building technology allowed the Disney Concert Hall to be striking sculpture on the outside while still allowing the acoustician to create the right environment for the symphony inside," Steele says, explaining why the design is such a marvel to her and others in her field.

The KA Theatre and Cirque du Soleil itself, is of course in a league of its own. A company always on the edge, pushing technology and creativity in live perform-ance to the extreme, Cirque has created some of the most remarkable productions of our time. "Their vision and expertise have pushed performance and performance spaces into entirely new realms," Steele says. As for the KA Theatre itself, Steele imagines it as merely the tip of the iceberg. "It will influence other buildings and companies," she says. "But, it is an unusual organization and probably not a general model for many others." (For more on the KA Theatre and Cirque du Soleil, see the final chapter, "Specialization and the Theater Life.")

Keeping up with technological advances in the type of systems that theater consultants deal with, according to Schwentker, is not as tricky as it may seem. "You have to keep track of what the changes are," he says, adding that the primary way in which he and his colleagues do this is through the information distributed by the manufacturers of the equipment. "A lot of the innovation is from the people who are manufacturing and selling the gear that goes into the systems that we design." There are, however, certain areas of theatrical systems technology that theater consultants must understand on a fundamental level in order to do their jobs well. As an example, Schwentker cites the area of **ethernet** networks, widely used for lighting control systems in today's performance facilities. "Ten or fifteen years ago no one needed to know what an ethernet network was to design a lighting system, but now, of course, that's absolutely crucial," he says.

Most vital when a theater consultant is designing systems, however, is probably the type of facility under development and the people who will be using it. "It's more about the appropriateness and the needs of the users," says Schwentker, clarifying the need for consultants to properly address the client's intended use of the facility—and the skill level of its users—when considering what sort of technology to employ on a project. "A producing organization is going to have different needs for their facility than a large high school would," he explains. "What's going to happen in the space is different, the personnel that are going to use the space are different, so some of the choices that [theater consultants] make are based on that."

PATHS TO A CAREER AS A THEATER CONSULTANT

Becoming a theater consultant commonly seems to entail the gathering of a broad range of theater experience and training. There are not any set criteria for training for the field, and there are all types of professionals working as consultants. "It is fairly common that people who work as theater consultants would come from a theatrical background," Schwentker says. "Now, that's not necessarily as true for some of my colleagues who do audiovisual systems," he says, explaining that such professionals are just as likely to have training and experience in all types of related fields, such as concert sound and studio recording.

So, where do theater consultants come from? According to Schwentker, many theatrical technicians grow into the field. "For some folks, I think it's a sort of natural evolution," he says, detailing how there are specialists who find themselves working on projects that require massive temporary or touring installations, thus learning the basics of what theater consultants do every day. "So, for instance, if you've specified the gear for a touring concert and then somebody who is outfitting an auditorium in a museum or something says, 'Well, you should talk to this person I worked with on this project because they'll know what you need,'" Schwentker explains. The transition from certain projects in the world of production, in other words, to the world of consulting can be a relatively lateral one.

✧✦✧✦✦✧✦✧✦✧✦✧✦✧✦✧✦✧✦✧✦✧✦✧✦✧✦✧✦✧✦✧✦✧✦✧✦✧✦✧✦✧✦✦✧✦✦✧✦✧

A Job Description

The job description of a theater consultant is at once simple and complex. In one sense, the work can be easily summed up with an appropriate sound bite. An example might go something like this: *Theater consultants act as advisors on building and renovation projects in order to ensure that performance facilities are properly designed and equipped.* However, the work they do to fulfill this generalized goal is extraordinarily complex and involves a great deal of specialization. Theater consulting firms are full of specialists—people whose expertise usually only concentrates in one or two specific areas, such as rigging, lighting, or sound, among many others.

An accurate description of a theater consultant's job therefore is quite difficult to generalize beyond this. The consultants at a firm like Landry & Bogan or WJHW will use their experience, training, and background to collaborate with other consultants, as well as the architects and building owners, to guide the process of design and implementation. The scope of their work is dictated by many factors, including the type and size of the building, whether it is a renovation or new construction, the type of organization, and the budget of the project.

Many theater consultants are specialists too, or work for firms that handle only specific or limited areas of theater cosultation. For instance, Landry & Bogan does not offer consultation services in the area of sound systems. Generally, individual firms will have different requirements of those working for them, but retaining expertise in any area related to performance will be an asset if one decides to pursue a career in theater consulting.

◇✦◇

RESOURCES FOR THEATER CONSULTANTS

Books

Carlson, Marvin. *Places of Performance: The Semiotics of Theatre Architecture.* Ithaca, NY: Cornell University Press, 1993.

Fisher, Mark. *Staged Architecture.* West Sussex, UK: John Wiley & Sons, 2000.

Morrison, Craig. *Theatres.* New York: W. W. Norton, 2005
    Architect and historian Morrison has collected thousands of images, illustrating the variety of performance spaces over time and space.

Todd, Andrew, and Jean-Guy Lecat. *The Open Circle: The Theatre Environment of Peter Brook.* London: Faber, 2003.
    Working with renowned theorist and theater artist Peter Brook, author of *The Empty Space*, designers Todd and Lecat focus on creating performance spaces that best serve the art of theater.

Periodicals

Live Design—www.livedesignonline.com

The convergence of three magazines that covered different aspects of live entertainment technology: *Entertainment Design*, *Lighting Dimensions*, and *Staging Rental Operations*.

Protocol

The quarterly journal of the ESTA, with articles on all topics affecting those in the entertainment technology industry.

Stage Directions—www.stage-directions.com

Provides a good look at the industry and focuses solely on theater, unlike other publications that spread focus across all aspects of entertainment.

Internet

www.esta.org—The Web site of the Entertainment Services and Technology Association (ESTA). In the words of the ESTA, they are "dedicated to the core mission of building the business of show business."

www.oistat.org—International Organization of Scenographers, Theatre Architects, and Technicians.

www.theaterconsultants.org—The Web site of the American Society of Theatre Consultants, where one can find lots of information on theater consultants. The ASTC is mostly an advocacy group for its members.

www.usitt.org/commissions/Architecture.html—USITT Web site for its Architecture Commission.

www.usitt.org/commissions/Engineering.htm—USITT Web site for its Engineering Commission.

20

SPECIALIZATION AND
THE THEATER LIFE

I have been working in show business for thirty-some years, so I guess that
the vision formed itself as I was progressing.

—JAQUE PAQUIN,
acrobatic equipment and rigging designer, Cirque du Soleil

In the previous pages of this book, I have outlined nineteen potential career areas either firmly rooted in or, in the case of the previous chapter, intersecting the world of technical theater. As you may recall (for those who actually read the introduction), there is no set path in this industry, and it's probably best to gain as many varied skills as possible, especially as a high school or

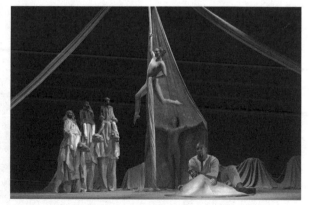

Sandglass Theater 2005 production *Between Sand and Stars*. (Photograph by Richard Termine.)

undergraduate student. It is the competent specialist, however, who is perhaps the most widely sought-after technician, precisely because there are so few of them.

In this chapter we'll take a look at some areas of theater that may or may not be strictly technical fields but that certainly have an element of technical theater within them. By way of one impressive example, we'll also explore the nature of highly specialized jobs that are tailored to the specific needs of certain organizations. None of these areas has been given its own section because to do so would be to imply that one could go out, study the field, and expect to land a job while earning a comfortable living. The disciplines found here are the kind that exist because the professionals who excel at them keep them alive and moving forward out of a love for the theater and performance.

We will also consider some different approaches to a career in tech theater and the different kinds of employment paths, such as freelancing, seasonal employment, and touring.

SPECIALIZATION

People usually become specialists either by deciding early on that their passions lie in a certain, specific area or by simply stumbling over the specialty while working in a field that contained it. Either way, the specialist is a highly prized commodity in technical theater, especially within organizations that require special attention to atypical details. If you stare off in the distance and think about this for a moment, one such organization that will probably pop into your head is Cirque du Soleil, a company so full of innovation and originality that its staff must abound with specialists. And it does.

RIGGING THE ACROBATS

Jaque Paquin is the acrobatic equipment and rigging designer for Cirque du Soleil. His projects for Cirque have included *Saltimbanco, O, Dralion, Varekai, Zumanity*, and *KA*. The thing about what Paquin does is that you won't find a training program set up and dedicated to churning out future Jaque Paquins. "To do it, you have to do it," he says of training for his line of work. He has worked in several capacities for Cirque since 1990, and he took on his current role in 1996.

When I ask him what he considers his primary responsibility, he says, "making sure that people literally trust me with their life." As the innovator of such technical performance marvels as the Bateau (or boat) in the Cirque du Soleil production *O*, which broke down previous acrobatic standards, Paquin has certainly carved a niche for himself with one of the most successful and respected performing arts companies in the world. And he insists that there is no way to reach such a position without putting yourself out there and working hard.

Paquin's Bateau

No one can argue with the notion that Cirque du Soleil is one of the most internationally successful performance companies imaginable. But, have you ever wondered what makes the work they do so particularly original and innovative?

Surely it must be not only the talented (and often strangely skilled) performers, but also the technical teams that make the elaborate shows possible, bringing the often outlandish designs to life.

Jaque Paquin is one of those people. He has spent nearly twenty years with Cirque and the last decade as Cirque's acrobatic equipment and rigging designer. One of his recent marvels of rigging was something called the

The "bateau" in Cirque Du Soleil's *O* presented new challenges for rigging expert Jaque Paquin. (Photograph by Tomasz Rossa.)

Bateau (or boat) in the Las Vegas production *O*. As you can see from the photos (see also the photo at the opening of this section), the Bateau is a floating acrobatic platform, enabling the performers to use it in nearly any way imaginable.

After the production's director, Franco Dragone, expressed a desire to see "parallel movement above the surface of the water" in *O*, Paquin went to the drawing board. Starting with a simple ladder structure rigged on four points so that it would lay flat, he quickly realized that more movement capability was needed. Once the company hit upon the idea of introducing a "vertical line in the parallel movement," Paquin began designing a structure that used a "rigid mast supporting the cradle" rather than employing cables for support, as in earlier versions. With the rigid mast, the Bateau would be stable enough to support the movement and the performers. "This process took six months and seven versions to get to a point where we had found what we were looking for," Paquin says.

"This trade cannot solely be learned in school," he says. "You have to be doing it in order to understand it," he continues. "You can do all the load calculations that you want, but if you're never out there in your harness installing, inspecting, you will end up missing a lot of the insight that comes from the hands-on relationship with the environment."

The work that Paquin does for Cirque du Soleil is probably the best example of technical specialization, as well as the way certain organizations and their unique needs tend to create niche fields that are inevitably filled by people who have gained special insight into the work by doing it. Most recently, Paquin contributed his expertise in rigging and acrobatics to Cirque du Soleil's ground-breaking KA Theatre in Las Vegas. "For KA, the rigging setup and the level of danger induced by the environment proved to be much more challenging than any previous show I had to work on," Paquin tells me. The KA Theatre, a site designed and constructed specifically for the new Cirque production, is one of the most state-of-the-art facilities built for performance, and Paquin's contributions were significant.

Due to the extreme complexity and danger of the production, Paquin developed new equipment in order to address very specialized needs. For starters, Paquin explains, the overall feeling of openness that the show's creators were striving for was achieved by removing the floor of the theater, leaving a "vast space that performers could fall into." "Some of the falls are intentional," he explains, "but I had to be certain that any involuntary falls could also be handled in a safe way." So, Paquin put in a very big net, stretching about sixty-five by ninety feet (about a quarter the size of a football field). "In the best of worlds," Paquin tells me, "a well-made net will safely catch you from up to twenty feet." But in the KA Theatre, Paquin was looking at choreographed falls of sixty feet and the potential for accidental falls from one hundred feet. So, Paquin added a giant air bag to the net. But adding to the complexity of the giant catch basin he created was the fact that it all needed to go away at certain points in the show, forcing Paquin to devise a way to safely strike the net and air bag and then redeploy it later—a task achieved through the use of eight high-speed, high-torque hydraulic winches. "We created the world's largest air bag and were able to meet my safety requirement and support the artistic intention of the show," he says. What more could anyone ask for?

"My designs also had to fit the specific themes and scenography of KA and blend with the aesthetics of the show as a whole," he says, "including the installation of the sound and lighting equipment throughout the theater." One significant aspect of KA that forced Paquin to take a new approach was the need for "single-point-failure devices." In other words, Paquin had to devise a rigging show that required a system with no backup devices in place. "In theory, this is not something that you want to do," he says. "Especially if human loads are involved." And they are. "It meant flying a performer on a single cable or rope," he explains. In order to make a theoretically unsafe system safe, Paquin planned a series of procedures, he says, in order to "validate the systems and the ability of the artist to perform on them on a daily basis." He devised stringent inspection and maintenance routines and hired an unprecedented fifty-seven-person rigging crew to handle the production. "It's looked at so regularly and closely that it will be seen and corrected before anything has a chance of going wrong."

It takes a special talent to pull off such technical equipment design, making sure to collaborate closely with the visual designers whose creativity has been given such free rein. Specialists like Paquin must set aside any preconceived notions of possibility under such circumstances. It takes a certain kind of person, with an ability to think in detailed (and abstract) ways, to accomplish projects on the cutting edge of performance.

PUPPETRY

"It's like a magic act of creation," says Rick Lyon, a veteran puppeteer who has worked on *Sesame Street* as well as originating roles for *Avenue Q* on Broadway . "You are conjuring a sentient being out of a lifeless block of wood or crumpled wad of cloth. It's a very powerful dynamic."

But the art of puppetry falls somewhere off the radar for most of us. Is it technical theater? Is it performance? Design? Or is it all

Rick Lyon performing with Nicky in *Avenue Q*. (Photograph by Jay Brady.)

of these things, and perhaps a little more? These questions struck me during my research each time I ran across a university that offered a program or course in puppetry. So I decided to look into the idea and found that it is at least an area of specialty worthy of inclusion in this chapter of odds and ends, precisely because it is so hard to pin down and categorize. It continues to grow as a field of specialty; opportunities for puppeteers and other theater artists interested in the form will surely continue to increase in the future. And, unlike most practicing puppeteers of today who are predominantly self-taught, young puppeteers now have a much wider range of training opportunities. "Puppetry is sort of a specialty art," Lyon explains. "It's on the fringe of legitimate theater, so the study of it is mostly done outside a formal institutional framework. Puppeteers largely learn their craft by working for established puppeteers or puppet companies, doing apprenticeships, and trial and error," he says.

Thinking Like a Puppeteer—A Conversation with Eric Bass

"Puppetry is a designer's theater form," says Eric Bass, veteran puppeteer and co–artistic director (with his wife, Ines Zeller Bass) of Sandglass Theater in Vermont. "We design our own actors," he says, and, as an example, Bass delves into one of the core ideas of puppetry: function. He explains how, when using puppets, the simple act of picking up a tea cup is one that informs all areas of performance in ways that would not be of concern otherwise. "How does the puppet pick up the tea cup?" he asks himself. "Does the [cup] have a separate rod so that the rod of the puppet's hand and the rod of the object being picked up are grabbed simultaneously? Does the puppeteer's hand come in and do it for the puppet? Does the puppet have a

Eric Bass in Sandglass Theater's *Sand*. (Photograph by Horst Huber.)

mechanical hand with a grasping thumb?" By asking such questions, Bass demonstrates the complex nature of puppetry and the necessary technical element involved in the art form. He also leads one to wonder how puppetry's technical aspects can create artistic and performance-related issues. "The technology opens up questions about how the performer, in this case the puppet, extends itself into space," he says, noting how a puppet's mechanics and its dramatic presence are both complex and intertwined.

Bass goes on to explain other ways in which the so-called technology of puppetry is central to the dramaturgical as well as imaginative needs of the puppeteer. He calls another essential theme the "technology of omission," indicating how the physical or technical elements of a puppet inform how the puppet can be used and also how it will interact with the puppeteer and its environment, and thus with an audience. He explains that what is left off of the puppet becomes crucial to how the performance develops—both physically and metaphorically.

Another key idea in the puppet theater, which relates to both its technical application and its contrast with "live action" theater, is scale. "As human beings," Bass says, "we come mostly in one scale." It is this predetermined scale, Bass believes, that keeps what he refers to as "actor theater" in a separate category. "One could do things to change that, but in effect when you do you're turning that human being into a puppet," he says. "With puppets the field is wide open."

Technical Theater Meets Puppetry

Puppets, in one form or another, have been around since the dawn of *homo sapiens*. As Eileen Blumenthal writes in her wonderful book *Puppetry: A World History*, "Before people had conceived of agriculture or animal husbandry, the earliest humans had taken the phenomenal conceptual leap to create miniature replicas of people." Puppets' ability to adapt to any sort of situation or performance type makes them a wonderful and fascinating part of today's theater too. They have been used to great effect on Broadway in shows like *The Lion King* and, more recently, in *Avenue Q*. They also are a part of more than just the performance world and are used as instructional aids and storytellers in classrooms around the world. Puppeteers would lament if we only recognized certain types of puppetry; we cannot forget about shadow puppets, marionettes, and even ventriloquism.

So where do puppets fit into technical theater? While it is true, according to Blumenthal, that many of the twentieth century's master puppeteers came from disciplines other than theater, there is no denying the inevitable merging of the two disciplines of performance and thus a serious involvement from those with a background in "live action" theater. Frankly, there are many aspects of puppet theater that can be considered technical theater, from the design and creation of the puppets themselves to the use of lighting (especially with shadow puppetry), sound, and scenery. The person operating the puppet is by necessity one part technician, one part designer, and one part performer. However, Nancy Cole writes in her book, *Puppet Theatre in Performance*, that puppeteers "sometimes seem to put their major effort into construction of figures, with little attention given to the dramatic vehicle that is to receive them," indicating that perhaps the technician part of a puppeteer is focused mostly on the technical aspects of the puppets themselves, rather than the lighting, sound, or scenery. Cole addresses some of these tech theater areas in her book and writes that the three critical technical areas of puppet theater are puppet design, lighting design, and scene design. At this point in history, though, a puppeteer would certainly consider such vital areas as sound and projection design and implementation as well. (Cole's book was published in 1978.)

Many contemporary theatrical productions that employ some form of puppetry rely on traditional design teams, replete with experts in lighting, scenery, sound, and perhaps video and projections. Puppets used in what we may call "conventional" or "live action" productions will probably be constructed by a props department or a specialized puppet-building shop, and they will likely be operated by actors or dancers, although they are also frequently designed, created, and operated by an experienced puppet artist.

"I think that sense of puppetry being a hybrid art form, one that draws on skills from all areas of theatre—design, performance, and technical theater—is what appeals to most people who become puppeteers," says Lyon. "Most puppeteers working in live performance do at least a little bit of everything," he adds. Lyon himself has extensive experience in each of these areas of puppetry, especially where his work on *Avenue Q* is concerned. "I designed the puppets, I built the puppets, and perform in the show," he tells me of the Tony Award–winning production. "Who else can say that about a Broadway musical?"

However, there are other technical considerations in puppetry performance aside from construction and design, and for some puppeteers they can be an added challenge. Having spent a considerable amount of time creating and performing the acclaimed production *The Story of the Dog* in close collaboration with Cambodian puppetry company Sovanna Phum, Bass is especially aware of how technical theater can be taken for granted by many theater artists.

"One of the things that had to change when we brought it from Cambodia to the United States was [the addition of] lights and sound technology," Bass says, explaining how the dynamic of the piece was transformed as bits of technical theater were established. "For the Cambodian artists, that was really introducing a new level," he says. As Bass points out, such changes were "simple for a technician," but affected the staging and puppetry as a whole. "It added another collaborator in the timing of the scenes," he says. Such a perspective is interesting to consider, because it is one that reaches beyond puppetry into all types of performance, and is reminiscent of a simpler theater, still practiced by puppeteers around the world.

In her book, Blumenthal also references several shows that have utilized puppets within a "live action" framework, including a production of *Spunk* in 1990, directed by George C. Wolfe, in which live actors worked onstage with a life-size human puppet. Other examples include *Bring in 'Da Noise, Bring in 'Da Funk*, Peter Brook's 1974 production of *Conference of the Birds*, *The Lion King*, and many others from such renowned theater artists as Richard Foreman, Robert Wilson, and the Wooster Group.

PATTERNS OF EMPLOYMENT FOR THEATER TECHNICIANS

Theater artists and technicians are often much like gypsies—or, at least members of some large, disjointed nomadic tribe if the reader has an objection to the comparison. Whether actors, directors, designers, artisans, or technicians, we tend to go where the work is, and once we find it, it often moves out from under us, and we either follow it, or get a desk job. Here, in the final chapter, we'll go over some common types of employment that you will encounter during your life in the theater.

Seasonal Employment
Many regional theaters are not year-round operations and retain only a small portion (if any) of their staff for full-time, year-round employment. This can leave a lot of talented, highly skilled theater technicians and artisans out looking for work for

sometimes over half of the calendar year. One might think that finding a full year gig somewhere would be a better option, but that ignores the value that a technician may find in the seasonal company for which he works. An ideal solution is usually to either freelance (see below) or find another seasonal operation that has a complimentary contract, such as spending part of the year at a summer theater, and the other part with a theater that runs a more typical season.

There are, of course, advantages and disadvantages to joining the part-time staff of a seasonal theater. One drawback may be the difficulty a technician working half of the year at one theater and either freelancing or spending the rest of the year at another theater may have in securing benefits such as healthcare, retirement options, and the other potential perks of a full-time position, such as the ability to remain year round in your chosen community. However, the ability to live and work in different environments with a reasonable assurance of job security could be considered an advantage too, depending on the lifestyle preferences of the technician or artisan. This is something that may have greater appeal for younger theater pros, but nevertheless, it is certainly in the advantage column if you like change coupled with security. "It can be fun to have a change in the summer and if you can live on nine months' salary, you can have a summer vacation," explains Sharon Reinhart, a scenic carpenter at Yale Repertory Theatre. "That's tough from a housing standpoint and from a family or community standpoint as well," she says. Another thing to keep in mind when considering seasonal employment is whether or not you want to build a résumé or gain more experience. If this is the case, it can be accomplished through an appropriate position with a seasonal theater.

Touring (and Broadway)

Touring is a world unto itself. Then again, so is Broadway. Job descriptions in these areas are sometimes nothing like those of regional or academic positions. The clearest example of a career highlighted in this book that falls in that category is the role of company manager, a job that tends to take on a much wider scope of responsibility when on Broadway or on tour than when working for a regional theater. The responsibilities of the Broadway stage manager are also greater than those of an SM in a smaller, or regional, venue, and the same could be said for just about every area of tech theater.

But the most important consideration when discussing work as a touring theater artist or technician is the touring itself. There are many folks out there who thrive under the working conditions dictated by the nature of touring, which include long, possibly sporadic hours (some have likened it to the cliché explanation of being in a war: long periods of boredom, punctuated by moments of sheer excitement and terror). Another potential drawback of touring is the way a tour turns all of life into a world that revolves solely around work.

Any of these considerations, however, can be looked at in a positive light as well—especially if you love to travel and are enthusiastic about the production you are touring with. The potential for earnings on tour can be great, but if you are headed out on a nonunion tour, it can be quite disappointing. It seems clear that because of the amount of work and time invested in a touring production, the compensation should be fair and competitive. Always be sure to carefully consider the pay of a tour in comparison to its length as well as the type and extent of work you will be expected to perform.

Freelancing

For many in technical theater careers, freelancing is the bread and butter. It can be the best way to maximize earnings, although is not always the most rewarding, due to the stressful nature of never being sure where your next gig will be. The perks of freelancing are the same as those for anyone else who works for themselves, including the ability to pick and choose projects and to have at least some control over your rate of pay. The drawbacks are the same too: stress, unpredictability, and the negotiating and tracking of your own finances. There are certain areas, such as design, that seem to necessitate freelancing, since most theater companies do not employ full-time resident designers and there are a finite number of academic jobs available. Other positions common in theater production, such as production managers or technical directors, are not jobs that lend themselves to freelancing—unless of course you consider those working in those posts on tour.

Academic Theater

Many theater pros eventually face the prospect of making the move into an academic environment. It can be a very attractive and tempting idea to designers, actors, directors, and even technicians who have spent considerable time bouncing about the country as freelancers or on tour, ready to settle into the relative comfort and security of the university life—or the similar world of primary and secondary education.

In the course of my research for this book, the subject of academic theater came up rather frequently, especially when speaking with designers and technical directors. Each and every professional interviewed for the book who also happened to hold a position at a university was very open when discussing the reasons for their move into the world of academia, and many were frank enough to admit that in many ways it was a compromise. At the top of the list of concerns for these folks was the need to maintain a professional career outside of the academic environment so that they could continue to provide their students with practical coursework that applies to the ever-evolving world of professional theater. This is especially true where technology is involved, as it so frequently is in theatrical design and production. Some of those interviewed expressed grave concern about the abundance of theater programs throughout the country, especially BFA and MFA programs, being taught by people who may not have spent much time outside of an academic environment. This concern is fueled by the potential for poor tech theater programs, churning out graduates with little practical experience or training to prepare them for the realities of professional theater. With this in mind, anyone who is preparing to enter college, either as an undergraduate or as a graduate student, should carefully consider the faculty and their connection with professional theater before making a final decision about whether or not to attend a particular school. At the other end, those considering a move into teaching should seriously consider their ability to maintain a foothold in the professional world in order that they might be better equipped to train upcoming generations of theater artists.

◇✦◇✦◇✦◇✦◇✦◇✦◇✦◇✦◇✦◇✦◇◇✦◇✦◇✦◇✦◇✦◇✦◇✦◇✦◇✦◇✦◇✦◇

Schools

General Tech

Earning a degree in technical theater gives the student a general background and training in tech theater without nailing down any one specialty. Folks who have a broad range of background are able to focus in on one particular specialty with the most facility.

For resources covering the areas discussed in this chapter, please see appendix 1.

CORNISH COLLEGE OF THE ARTS
Programs offered: BFA in Performance Production
www.cornish.edu/perfprod/default.htm
Contact: Dave Tosti-Lane, dtostilane@cornish.edu

ITHACA COLLEGE
Programs offered: BFA in Theatrical Production Arts
http://departments.ithaca.edu/theater
Contact: Colin Stewart, cstewart@ithaca.edu

SYRACUSE UNIVERSITY
Programs offered: BFA in Design/Technical Theater
http://vpa.syr.edu/index.cfm/page/drama
Contact: Maria Marrero, memarrer@syr.edu

UNIVERSITY OF ARIZONA
    Programs offered: BFA in Design/Tech
                      MFA in Design/Tech
    http://web.cfa.arizona.edu/theater
    Contact: Peter Beudert, pbeudert@email.arizona.edu

UNIVERSITY OF CINCINNATI
    Programs offered: BFA in Technical Production
                      MFA in Technical Production
    www.ccm.uc.edu/tdp
    Contact: Steven Waxler, waxlers@ucmail.uc.edu

UNIVERSITY OF GEORGIA
    Programs offered: MFA in Design and Technology
    www.drama.uga.edu
    Contact: Sylvia J. H. Pannell, hillyard@uga.edu

UNIVERSITY OF NEVADA-LAS VEGAS
    Programs offered: BA in Design/Technology
                      MFA in Design/Technology
    www.unlv.edu/Colleges/Fine_Arts/Theatre
    Contact: Brackley Frayer, theater@ccmail.nevada.edu

UNIVERSITY OF OKLAHOMA
    Programs offered: BFA in Technical Production
    www.ou.edu/finearts/drama
    Contact: mbuchwald@cox.net

UNIVERSITY OF WISCONSIN-MADISON
    Programs offered: MFA in Theater Technology
    www.theater.wisc.edu
    Contact: Dennis Dorn, dldorn@wisc.edu

Puppetry

There are many more schools than the four listed below that offer some level of training in the art of puppetry; however, these schools have programs dedicated to puppetry and are fully equipped to teach their students the often elaborate craft.

    For resources covering the areas discussed in this chapter please see appendix 1.

COSTEN CENTER FOR PUPPETRY AND THE ARTS AT CALARTS
www.calarts.edu/schools/theater/cotsen.html
Contact: Janie Geiser, jottay@sbcglobal.net

UNIVERSITY OF CONNECTICUT
Programs offered: BFA in Puppetry
                      MA/MFA in Puppetry
www.drama.uconn.edu/index.htm
Contact: Jack Nardi, jack.nardi@uconn.edu

UNIVERSITY OF HAWAII
Programs offered: MFA in Youth Theatre
www.hawaii.edu/theater/index.htm
Contact: Tamara Montgomery, tamarah@hawaii.edu

WEST VIRGINIA UNIVERSITY
Programs offered: BFA in Puppetry
www.wvu.edu/7Etheater/indcx.htm
Contact: Joann Spencer Siegrist, joann.siegrist@mail.wvu.edu

◇✦◇

Appendix 1: Resources

Here you'll find a list of every resource listed in each chapter, as well as some general resources not listed elsewhere.

BOOKS

Albrizio, Ann, and Osnat Lustig. *Classic Millinery Techniques*. Ashville, NC: Lark Books, 1998.

Aronson, Arnold. *American Set Design*. New York: Theatre Communications Group, 1985.

Baclawski, Karen. *The Guide to Historic Costume*. London: B. T. Batsford, 1995.

Baker, Georgia O'Daniel. *A Handbook of Costume Drawing*. Boston: Focal Press, 2003.

Baker, Patricia. *Wigs and Make-up for Theatre, TV, and Film*. Boston: Focal Press, 1993.

Ballou, Glen. *Handbook for Sound Engineers*. 3rd ed. Boston: Focal Press, 2002.

Beaton, Les, and Mabel Beaton. *The Complete Book of Marionettes*. Mineola, NY: Dover Publications, 2005.

Blaikie, Tim, and Emma Troubridge. *Scenic Art and Construction*. Marlborough, UK: Crowood Press, 2002.

Blumenthal, Eileen. *Puppetry: A World History*. New York: Harry N. Abrams, 2005.

Blumenthal, Eileen, and Julie Taymor. *Julie Taymor: Playing with Fire*. 3rd ed. New York: Harry N. Abrams, 2007.

Bracewell, John. *Sound Design in the Theatre*. Englewood Cliffs, NJ: Prentice Hall, 1993.

Cadena, Richard. *Automated Lighting: The Art and Science of Moving Light in Theatre, Live Performance, Broadcast, and Entertainment*. Boston: Focal Press, 2006.

Campbell, Drew. *Technical Theater for Nontechnical People*. 2nd ed. New York: Allworth Press, 2004.

Carlson, Marvin. *Places of Performance: The Semiotics of Theatre Architecture.* Ithaca, NY: Cornell University Press, 1993.

Carter, Paul. *Backstage Handbook: An Illustrated Almanac of Technical Information.* Louisville, KY: Broadway Press, 1994.

Cole, Nancy H. *Puppet Theatre in Performance.* New York: William Morrow, 1978.

Corson, Richard, and James Glavan. *Stage Makeup.* Boston: Allyn & Bacon, 2000.

Crabtree, Susan, and Peter Beudert. *Scenic Art for the Theatre.* Boston: Focal Press, 2005.

Cunningham, Glen. *Stage Lighting Revealed.* Long Grove, IL: Waveland Press, 2002.

Davis, Don, and Carolyn Davis. *Sound System Engineering.* Boston: Focal Press, 2006.

Dreher, Denise. *From the Neck Up: An Illustrated Guide to Hatmaking.* Minneapolis: Madhatter Press, 1981.

Emery, Joy Spanabel. *Stage Costume Techniques.* Englewood Cliffs, NJ: Prentice Hall, 1981.

Essig, Linda. *The Speed of Light: Dialogues on Lighting Design and Technological Changes.* Portsmouth, NH: Heinemann Drama, 2002.

Fazio, Larry. *Stage Manager: The Professional Experience.* Boston: Focal Press, 2000.

Fedorko, Jamie. *The Intern Files: How to Get, Keep, and Make the Most of Your Internship.* New York: Simon Spotlight Entertainment, 2006.

Fisher, Mark. *Staged Architecture.* West Sussex, UK: John Wiley & Sons, 2000.

Glerum, Jay O. *Stage Rigging Handbook.* Carbondale: Southern Illinois University Press, 2007.

Glover, Thomas J. *Pocket Ref.* Littleton, CO: Sequoia Publishing, 2002.

Gruver, Bert. *Stage Manager's Handbook.* New York: Drama Publishers, 1972.

Hamadeh, Samer. *Vault Guide to Top Internships, 2007.* New York: Vault, 2007.

Holden, Alys. *Structural Design for the Stage.* Boston: Focal Press, 1999.

Howard, Pamela. *What is Scenography?* London: Routledge, 2002.

Ingham, Rosemary, and Liz Covey. *The Costume Designer's Handbook.* Portsmouth, NH: Heinemann Drama, 1992.

_____. *The Costume Technician's Handbook.* Portsmouth, NH: Heinemann Drama, 2003.

James, Thurston. *The Prop Builder's Mask-Making Handbook.* Cincinnati, OH: Betterway Books, 2006.

_____. *The Prop Builder's Molding and Casting Book.* White Hall, VA: Betterway Publications, 1990.

_____. *The Theater Props What, Where, When.* Studio City, CA: Players Press, 2001.

_____. *Theatre Props Handbook.* White Hall, VA: Betterway Publications, 1990.

Kaye, Deena, and James LeBrecht. *Sound and Music for the Theatre: The Art and Technique of Design.* Boston: Focal Press, 1999.

Kelly, Thomas A. *The Back Stage Guide to Stage Management.* New York: Back Stage Books, 1999.

Kidd, Mary T. *Stage Costume Step by Step.* Cincinnati, OH: Betterway Books, 2002.

Kaluta, John. *The Perfect Stage Crew: The Complete Technical Guide for High School, College, and Community Theater.* New York: Allworth Press, 2003.

Langley, Susan, and John Dowling. *Vintage Hats and Bonnets.* Paducah, KY: Collector Books, 1998.

Latshaw, George. *The Complete Book of Puppetry.* Mineola, NY: Dover Publications, 2000.

Leonard, John A. *Theatre Sound.* London: A & C Black, 2001.

Moody, James L. *The Business of Theatrical Design.* New York: Allworth Press, 2002.

Morawetz, Thomas. *Making Faces, Playing God.* Austin: University of Texas Press, 2001.

Morgan, Nigel. *Stage Lighting: For Theatre Designers.* London: Herbert Press, 1995.

Morrison, Craig. *Theatres*. New York: W. W. Norton, 2005.

Ogawa, Toshiro. *Theatre Engineering and Stage Machinery*. Royston, Hertfordshire, UK: Entertainment Technology Press, 2001.

Pecktal, Lynn. *Costume Design: Techniques of Modern Masters*. New York: Back Stage Books, 1999.

Raoul, Bill. *Stock Scenery Construction*. Louisville, KY: Broadway Press. 1998.

Rees, A. L. *A History of Experimental Film and Video*. London: BFI Publishing, 1999.

Rossol, Monona. *The Health and Safety Guide for Film, TV, and Theater*. New York: Allworth Press, 2000.

Rysinger, Lisa. *Exploring Digital Video*. 2nd ed. Clifton Park, NY: Thomson/Delmar Learning, 2005.

Sammler, Don, and Don Harvey, *Technical Design Solutions for the Theater*. 2 vols. Boston: Focal Press, 2002.

Shelley, Steven Louis. *A Practical Guide to Stage Lighting*. Boston: Focal Press, 1999.

Stern, Lawrence. *Stage Management*. 8th ed. Boston: Allyn & Bacon, 2005.

Swinfield, Rosemarie. *Hair and Wigs for the Stage: Step by Step*. Cincinnati, OH: Betterway Books, 1999.

Todd, Andrew, and Jean-Guy Lecat. *The Open Circle: The Theatre Environment of Peter Brook*. London: Faber, 2003.

Vinther, Janus. *Special Effects Make-Up*. New York: Theatre Arts Books, 2003.

Walne, Graham. *Sound for the Theatre*. London: A & C Black, 1990.

Webb, Duncan M. *Running Theaters: Best Practices for Leaders and Managers*. New York: Allworth Press, 2005.

Wilcox, R. Turner. *The Mode in Hats and Headdresses*. New York: C. Scribner's Sons, 1945.

Wilson, Andy. *Making Stage Props*. Marlborough: Crowood Press, 2003.

Wolff, Colette. *The Art of Manipulating Fabric*. Radnor, PA: Chilton, 1996.

PERIODICALS

American Theatre—www.tcg.org/publications
The most comprehensive and well-respected magazine devoted to professional theater in America.

ArtSEARCH—www.tcg.org/publications
The best option for finding any type of work in theater. Even if you can't afford your own copy, it shouldn't be hard to locate one that you can peruse either at your school or workplace.

Dramatics—www.edta.org/publications/dramatics.asp
A publication of the Educational Theatre Association (EDTA), it is geared toward those creating and learning about theater in secondary education. *Dramatics* contains articles and educational information on all areas of theater, including tech, playwriting, and performance.

FOH—www.fohonline.com
A news magazine that covers all areas of live sound, including theater.

LD + A—www.iesna.org/LDA/members_contact.cfm
An abbreviation for *Lighting Design and Application*, it is the print and web publication of the Illuminating Engineering Society of North America (IESNA).

Lighting and Sound America—www.lightingandsoundamerica.com
A magazine focusing on everything to do with lighting and sound within the entertainment industry, including Broadway, regional theater, dance, live music, and much more.

Live Design—www.livedesignonline.com
The convergence of three magazines that covered different aspects of live entertainment technology: *Entertainment Design, Lighting Dimensions,* and *Staging Rental Operations.*

MakeUp Artist Magazine
Aimed at all types of makeup artists, it includes information on the film, television, and print industries more so than theater.

Mix Magazine—www.mixonline.com
A publication covering all things sound related.

New Theatre Quarterly—journals.cambridge.org/action/displayJournal?jid=NTQ
A scholarly journal that provides a forum for discussion regarding theater theory, innovation, and history.

PLSN: Projection, Lighting, and Sound News—www.plsn.com

Puppetry International—www.unima-usa.org/publications/index.html
A magazine filled with all things puppetry.

Sound & Video Contractor—www.svconline.com
An industry publication.

Southern Theatre—www.setc.org/publications/southern.asp
Devoted to theater in the southeastern United States, it contains all sorts of information for students and professionals alike.

Stage Directions—www.stage-directions.com
Provides a good look at the industry and focuses solely on theater, unlike other publications that spread focus across all aspects of entertainment.

Teaching Theatre—www.edta.org/publications/teaching_theatre.asp
Along with *Dramatics*, it is published by the EDTA and written with the secondary theater/drama educator in mind.

Technical Brief—www.technicalbrief.org
A publication of the Yale School of Drama, *Technical Brief* provides articles that explain technical design solutions implemented by technical directors and other technical theater professionals.

The Hat Magazine—www.thehatmagazine.com
A UK-based magazine about (you guessed it) hats.

The Painter's Journal—www.paintersjournal.com
A small journal for the scenic artist, containing tips, advice, features, and interviews with scenic painters.

Theatre Design & Technology—www.usitt.org/tdt.index
The quarterly journal of USITT provides coverage of varied topics relating to technical theater and the entertainment industry.

INTERNET

For more information about this book and its author visit, www.mikelawler.com.

www.aate.com—The American Alliance for Theater and Education (AATE), an organization dedicated to theater education and performance for young audiences.

www.actorsequity.org—Actors' Equity Association (AEA).

www.aes.org—Audio Engineering Society online.

www.americantheaterwing.org—American Theatre Wing, the organization best known for handing out Tony Awards to Broadway artists. It does other things that are perhaps more vital to theater in America, however, including producing "Working in

Theatre" seminars (broadcast on New York television and available on their Web site for download), presenting the lesser-known Hewes Design Award, sponsoring a theater intern program, and providing extensive resources via its Web site.

www.artscraftstheatersafety.org—Arts, Crafts, and Theater Safety (ACTS), a "not-for-profit corporation that provides health, safety, industrial hygiene, technical services, and safety publications to the arts, crafts, museums, and theater communities."

www.artslynx.org—An online base for all sorts of links pertaining to theater and the arts in general.

www.bimp.uconn.edu—The Ballard Institute and Museum of Puppetry (BIMP) at the University of Connecticut.

www.costumegallery.com/hairstyles—The Costume Gallery's "Hairstyle History" page with examples of hairstyles throughout the ages.

www.costumesocietyamerica.com—The Costume Society of America (CSA) Web site with lots of research links, a job bulletin, and more.

www.edta.org—The Educational Theatre Association in its own words: "We do a lot of different things—theater festivals for students, professional development programs for theater teachers, a magazine, a quarterly journal, and much more."

www.entertainmentsourcebook.com/atac—The Association of Theatrical Artists and Craftspeople (ATAC), a membership organization that exists primarily to enable theater artists to network with each other, as well as communicate on matters of importance to their trade.

www.etcp.esta.org—The Entertainment Technician Certification Program (ETCP), a program supported by several organizations with technical theater connections, including USITT and IATSE. The program aims to certify two major types of theater technicians: electricians and riggers.

www.foghouse.com/PMForum—A good resource for production managers that revolves around communication between PMs across the country.

http://freesound.iua.upf.edu/index.php—Yep, free sound effects for the designer can be found here.

www.hensonfoundation.org—The online home of the Jim Henson Foundation, this site is chock full of useful information for the young or veteran puppeteer, including access to the foundation's grants.

www.hollywoodedge.com—A Web site for those interested in obtaining sound effects.

www.iatse-intl.org—Home of IATSE International. A good starting point for finding your local chapter, if you don't already know what it is.

www2.kcpa.uiuc.edu/kcpatd/physics/index.htm—The Physics of Theatre Project Web site, providing detailed information on the areas of common theatrical rigging and scenery.

www.lightingandsoundamerica.com—*Lighting and Sound America* magazine Web site.

www.livedesignonline.com—The Web site of *Live Design* magazine, a publication that focuses on all things to do with design and technology in the entertainment industry.

www.lyonpuppets.com—Rick Lyon's Web site, featuring his life and work.

www.nrtw.org—National Right to Work Legal Defense Foundation Web site. Information on all aspects of "right to work states" for those concerned about their rights working with unions in such states. The site has a full list of all twenty-two such states and information regarding the laws in each.

www.nypl.org/research/lpa/lpa.html—The New York Public Library for the Performing Arts Web site provides many resources for researching all facets of theater, including an exhaustive list of online resources.

www.oistat.org—International Organization of Scenographers, Theatre, Architects and Technicians, host of Scenofest, an international festival highlighting the world's finest work in the fields of design, technical theater, architecture, and puppetry.

www.oneillpuppetryconference.com—Since 1990, the O'Neill Puppetry Conference has been a major part of keeping the traditions of puppetry alive in America while persistently pushing them forward. An invaluable resource.

www.patrickimmel.com/usitt/techprod/tech_prod_index.htm—The Web site for the USITT Technical Production Commission.

www.plasa.org—Professional Lighting and Sound Association Web site.

www.proppeople.com—A place for prop artisans to come together, this site is almost routinely rebuilt from the ground up.

www.puppet.org—The Web site of the Puppetry Center of America, an organization focusing on training and performance and headquartered in Atlanta, Georgia.

www.puppeteers.org—The Web site for Puppeteers of America, an organization that has been around since the 1930s, providing information and inspiration to puppeteers everywhere.

http://recreation-news.com/rec.arts.theater.stagecraft—If you need to know how to do something in tech theater and you don't have a book on the subject, this is the thread to go to.

www.sceno.org—*Scenography—The Theatre Design Website* is run by the Online Society of Theatre Designers and Scenographers and offers a place to network with other designers and share portfolios and advice.

www.smnetwork.org—An online forum for professional stage managers.

www.soundfx.com—Online sound effects library.

www.sound-ideas.com—Sound effects publisher.

www.spamprops.org—Society of Properties Artisans and Managers.

www.stagemanagers.org—Stage Managers' Association (SMA), which describes itself as "a network through which we can share our problems, ideas, and stories; educate ourselves and those with whom we work; eliminate that isolated feeling which strikes us all from time to time; make our crazy jobs just a little easier and help us to be better stage managers."

www.tcg.org—The Web site of the Theatre Communications Group.

www.theatrecrafts.com/glossary/glossary.shtml—The online "Glossary of Technical Theatre Terms."

www.unima-usa.org—The U.S. arm of the Union Internationale de la Marionnette (UNIMA) finds its online home here and is the best starting point for any research on puppetry in the world.

www.urta.com—University/Resident Theatre Association Web site. An organization designed to serve university theater training programs and the students in them, U/RTA is something that all young theater artist serious about pursuing the field should become familiar with.

www.usitt.org—United States Institute for Theatre Technology (USITT).

www.usitt.org/sightlines/home/Sightlines.html—The homepage of USITT's online newsletter, *Sightlines*, an informative insider's resource.

Appendix 2: On-the-Job Training

When I was in college, I took a summer internship as a scenic carpenter. It was a great experience that taught me an enormous amount not just about building scenery but also about professional theater as a whole. It gave me an opportunity to make critical contacts and helped build my résumé. The professor that I turned to for advice in seeking the internship encouraged me but let me know later that in his recommendation letter he had written that he would rather have kept me at the university for the summer to help with his own production. I'm glad he was willing to give me up for the summer.

Internships and apprenticeships are a great way to gain valuable, real-world experience. So whether you've just completed an undergraduate degree or are just trying to earn experience and make contacts, the tips in this appendix should help you find the experience that's right for you.

Here are some tips for finding the right internship, apprenticeship, or entry-level job for you.

QUESTIONS TO ASK

Some of these questions may not need to be asked directly of the theater but can be gleaned from some simple research.

What Type of Theater Is It?

Consider not only the type of experience you want to gain but also where you might like to work in the future. Should you look for a small theater or try to be accepted as an intern for a prestigious resident company? Would you like to work in opera or dance? Think carefully about these questions and make a list of priorities.

How Large Is the Company?

More specifically, how large is the production team? This will usually affect how many interns will be hired, and this will certainly make a difference to your experience. Naturally, there is much to be said for gaining experience in a large organization, but do not underestimate the value of interning with a small company. A smaller company with fewer interns can provide a good environment for the person still uncertain of an area of specialization and it will make one-on-one time with professionals more likely. On the other hand, if you know precisely what you want to do in the future, this may not matter as much as gaining experience with a well-respected, finely run organization and working with the best of the best.

Where Is the Theater?

Is there a region of the country (or the world) that you'd prefer to work in the future? This is important to consider, because you may be better off interning in that area so that you can build contacts and use the internship to network. Of course, traveling to a new, exciting place to intern can be a wonderful life adventure, giving you an opportunity to learn about a lot more than just theater. And who knows? You may find a new home in an unexpected place.

Is It a Paid Internship?

This is a huge consideration, depending on your situation. If it is paid, it probably won't be much, but—and again, this all depends on your outlook—something is better than nothing. And remember, experience working with talented, accomplished artists can be its own reward.

Is Housing Provided?

Another important detail. Many theaters provide some type of housing for interns, but it is important that you find out about the arrangements. Will you have your own room or will you be sharing? Where is the housing in relation to the theater? Will you need to bring your own transportation? These are all boring details, but critical for your comfort and enjoyment. Remember, you will most likely be working your butt off, so it is vital that you be happy and comfortable when you go to bed on your day off.

How Specialized Will Your Internship Be?

This is an especially necessary inquiry if you know exactly what you want to do and what you expect to learn about. Many internship programs use interns as a general cheap labor force and do not see the program as a training program. Be careful, and avoid this type of set up. Asking questions about what is expected of you will help you to do so.

How Old Is the Theater's Internship Program?

Another variation on this question would be: How long has the production manager (or person who oversees the internship) been conducting the program? Knowing this will help you understand the level of commitment the theater has to educating and training its interns. It also indicates a general understanding and comfort with interns.

QUESTIONS YOU WILL BE ASKED

It's important to remember that the theater you are considering for an internship (and certainly for an entry-level job) wants to be sure that you're a good fit for them too. The staff will interview you not only about your experience and education, but also about the details that they consider important to their theater and to a good working environment. An essential bit of advice when answering these questions: Be specific and be honest. Don't tell them what you think they want to hear, because neither you nor the theater will be well served by your customizing responses to your assumptions of what will get you the gig.

What Do You Expect to Get from the Experience?

You will know that the theater staff care about their internship program when they ask this question, and they want to be sure they can offer what you are seeking. Again, it is important to be honest. Consider your response to this question before you submit applications and résumés. Think about it critically and find the honest answer.

What Do You Want to Learn about Most?

This is an essential question, and if it is not asked of you in the interview, answer it anyway and inquire if it is realistic to expect to advance your knowledge in your desired area. Hopefully, the theater will be honest with you, because you should be able to work somewhere that has something to offer that is in line with your goals.

What Are Your Long-Term Goals?

Sometimes, when interviewing potential interns, theaters will ask this question in order to best place an intern. They may also be flexible with their internships and want to know how they may best serve you. If the only intern spot they have left is a carpenter position and you hope to one day pursue a career in sound, they may wonder why you would be interested in such a position. And rightfully so.

Why Do You Want to Work for This Theater?

Again, honesty is the best policy. If you are interviewing with a theater because you can't seem to get your foot in the door elsewhere, tell them that you hope to build your résumé and gain practical experience. This isn't spin, it's the truth. This question should be thought about in advance, and if you don't have a good answer for it, you should think about why you are bothering with the interview at all.

RESOURCES FOR FINDING THE RIGHT INTERNSHIP

The best resources for finding a technical theater internship or entry-level position are those that concentrate on theater. It is a unique world, and the more general resources on the market may help you establish basic goals and methods for preparing, but only those focused on the performing arts can offer you the detail you need. Just remember: make a list of priorities, and ask a lot of questions.

THE BEST RESOURCES

ARTSearch

www.tcg.org/publications

Available in print or online, this slim classified section for theater artists published by Theatre Communications Group is the best option for finding any type of work—period. For students, however, it is cost prohibitive. Fortunately, most university theater programs subscribe to at least the print version, and many theaters do as well. If you can't afford your own copy, it shouldn't be hard to locate one that you can peruse. TCG also offers a six month subscription as well as student rates.

http://teachingarts.org

This California-based Web site is a great resource for students looking for opportunities of all kinds in theater (and other art disciplines). The site does not limit itself to California or students in that state, and it is probably the most all-inclusive site I've found for theater students.

http://backstagejobs.com

Sort of a poor man's version of *ARTSearch*, this online resource is also quite valuable and has a section devoted to internships. The list of available internships is usually quite long. You should be able to find internship opportunities in all types of theater environments here.

http://playbill.com

Playbill's Web site has a fairly extensive jobs listing section and includes nationwide postings for paid and unpaid internships in theater.

OTHER RESOURCES

Books

Most books and other resources to be found on the subject of internships are designed for folks who are not pursuing the arts. As a whole they are very general, and while many of them have good information and sound advice, using such books for theater will not be very helpful. Though they may provide a decent argument for finding an internship that will boost your résumé upon graduation, you probably already are aware of that potential and have made up your mind about what type of internship to pursue. Now that I've given you that caveat, here are some general books on finding internships.

Bravo, Dario, and Carol Whitely. *The Internship Advantage*. New York: Prentice Hall, 2005.

Fedorko, Jamie. *The Intern Files: How to Get, Keep, and Make the Most of Your Internship*. New York: Simon Spotlight Entertainment, 2006.

Hamadeh, Samer. *Vault Guide to Top Internships, 2007*. New York: Vault, 2007.

Internet

There are regional Web sites, as well as the individual sites of virtually every theater company in the country, including the smallest of operations. If you know what city or region you are interested in, it may be simpler to seek out theaters in that area and see what they have to offer. There are also countless Web sites out there targeted at students looking for internships and other entry-level jobs. Here's a sampling:

www.monstertrak.com

www.internjobs.com

www.internweb.com

http://rsinternships.com

Appendix 3: Glossary of Terms

This section is for those readers who must know more. I understand them and want to accommodate them because I always find myself searching the back of reference books such as this, seeking even more knowledge about this or that small item noted in the corner of a chapter. Listed below you will find terms discussed in this book only. For an easy-to-use, thorough glossary of technical theater words, use the online "Glossary of Technical Theatre Terms" at www.theatrecrafts.com/glossary/glossary.shtml.

AEA—Actors' Equity Association, the labor organization that represents actors and stage managers in the United States. Frequently referred to as "Equity."

artistic director—the artistic leader of the company, responsible primarily for keeping the theater focused on its mission. Often, this position is filled by a person with a strong background in directing.

blood pack—container holding fake blood that is placed on a performer to create the illusion of bleeding.

CAD—computer-aided design.

chalk bag—a small, usually cylindrical bag with one open end designed to be clipped to the harness or clothing of a rock climber. Designed to hold chalk for the climber, chalk bags are also used by theater technicians to hold tools and other items that they may need access to while working in the air. Especially useful for riggers.

channel hookup—a document provided for the master electrician by the lighting designer that contains essential information about each channel for a production, including instrument type, position, color, circuit, and the purpose of the instrument.

costume accessories—usually small items such as jewelry or purses.

cue(s)—a signal for an actor or technician to say or do something. It is either a sound or a visual indicator of some kind. (See entry for "cue light" below for one example of a visual cue indicator.)

cue light—any type of light controlled by the stage manager and employed to give silent cues to crew and/or performers. The light is illuminated by the SM as a warning, and the cue is to be executed when the light goes out. I have noticed over the years that many people seem to be confused by this simple system. They usually think that when the light comes on it is their cue. Perhaps this is some tendency we have developed from spending all of our spare time in cars staring at traffic signals.

dimmer—a device used to control the intensity of lighting instruments. Because theaters have a limited number with specific wattage loads, dimmer systems are crucial to the size and scope of a lighting designers work.

draper—the person responsible for making all of the patterns for any costume that the costume shop will build. Also known as the "cutter" or "cutter/draper." See chapter 16 for a more detailed description.

ethernet—networking technology for local area networks (LAN) used in theater for dimming and lighting systems.

Equity—see AEA.

first hand—the costume shop staff person who assists the cutter/draper. (This is a tech theater job I knew of for years without understanding what the person did.) See chapter 16 for more information.

fly system—any system used to hang and travel a series of batons or pipes, upon which scenery, lighting, and other technical elements can be rigged. The most common style of fly system is known as a counterweight system. For detailed information see *Backstage Handbook* by Paul Carter.

focus—n. the period of time when lighting instruments are positioned and aimed with the proper beam size, color, and accessories for the production. v. the act of positioning, aiming, or changing the actual sharpness of the beam.

gel—a sheet of colored plastic, also known as "color" or "color filter," it is used to control the color of light. Short for gelatin, which is the material it was once made from.

gobo (also template)—usually a small, thin piece of metal with a certain pattern of holes, placed between the lamp and lens of a lighting instrument in order to project the pattern. They can also be made from materials such as glass and can project colored patterns. The term is probably short for "go between."

grid—an integral part of any counterweight fly system, it is the area at the top of the system where the weight is transferred from the control system (such as ropes) to the pipe or other item being moved through the system. For detailed information see *Backstage Handbook* by Paul Carter.

hand—stagehand.

hand prop—a prop carried by a performer.

hang card(s)—a diagram utilized by electricians when hanging instruments for a production. It is usually a condensed version, or detail, of the larger light plot so that the different members of the crew can carry information vital to the area of the plot that they are working on.

IA—see IATSE.

IATSE—International Alliance of Theatrical Stage Employees, the union for all theater folks not involved in other unions, such as stagehands, riggers, electricians, and sound engineers. It is not organized nationally (or internationally), but rather on a local basis, in order to better serve the diverse areas in which IATSE members work. It is also now the umbrella union of USA, and the abbreviation is frequently shortened to IA.

iris—an adjustable barrier placed in a lighting instrument to control the diameter of the beam.

lamp—in theatrical lighting, refers to what most folks would call the bulb.

LED—light-emitting diode. This technology is used in many practical applications, such as flashlights and even traffic signals. It is beginning to emerge as a useful tool in theatrical lighting design too.

light plot—a drafted diagram demonstrating the manner in which a lighting designer has decided the instrumentation should be laid out, including information about the type of instruments to be used, the precise placement of instruments, as well as information about the channel arrangement, color, and gobo selection.

load-in—a term used to describe the time dedicated to installing all technical systems, including scenery, lighting, sound, and costumes, among others.

load-out—a term used to describe the time dedicated to removing a production from a venue. See also strike.

LORT—League of Resident Theatres, an organization of approximately eighty regional theaters in the United States. The organization cooperates under contractual agreements with unions such as AEA and provides a communication and casting network for member theaters.

magic sheet—similar to a channel hookup, but usually more explicit, containing diagrams of lighting positions, including focus notes.

MIDI—musical instrument digital interface. See chapter 12.

overhire list—a contact list maintained by any organization with the ability to hire crews of qualified technicians who are not regularly employed by the organization.

Frequently used by technical directors of theaters so that they can increase their crews when needed, it is also used by unions such as IATSE for the same purpose. Getting one's name on such a list is an easy step toward becoming a union member or a regular employee of a theater.

paint elevation—a tool used by scene designers to demonstrate to scenic artists how they wish the scenery to appear in terms of color, line, and texture.

painting down—a scenic painting technique characterized by painting scenery, including backdrops, on the floor or on some other horizontal surface.

painting up—a scenic painting technique that entails painting scenery as it stands upright or is secured to a vertical surface.

par—also known as a "par can," it is a type of lighting instrument commonly used for wide washes of color and light.

patch or patched—the assigning of certain dimmers and/or circuits to specific channels so that the instruments can be arranged in a manner most useful for the lighting designer.

performance report—a report prepared by the stage management team following each and every performance to give all members of a production team any needed information in terms of scenery, props, costume, lighting, sound, and other areas, so that repairs can be made and problems solved.

promptbook—the book used by stage managers to run a show, it contains the most current script, blocking notes, cue placement, and most other information pertaining to the production. Frequently referred to as the "bible," the promptbook will be updated at the close of a production and kept on file for future use.

rehearsal report—similar to a performance report, the rehearsal report is a tool used by the stage management team to distribute pertinent information as a production evolves. It will include any information that may affect all ongoing work on the production.

rep—see repertory.

repertory (also rotating repertory)—denoting the process of producing more than one show at a time, typically on the same stage. The term is also commonly used by theaters producing several shows in the course of a season, though not necessarily concurrently.

rigging—(1) n. the actual workings of any fly system, or parts of a system assembled to hang an item or items. (2) v. the act of assembling a fly system, or parts of a system used to hang an item or items.

running crew (also run crew or stage crew)—any person or persons working the performances of a production in any technical capacity.

set dressings—the combined responsibility of the props department and the scene designer, these are items that decorate or enhance the look of scenery but are not interactive props used by actors.

shopper—a job category usually found in large shops, including costume, props, and scene shops. The person(s) in this position is solely responsible for buying any needed items for the shop's projects.

sidearm—a length of pipe used to extend the yoke of a lighting instrument in a certain direction.

soft props—prop items constructed of soft materials, such as fabrics and foam.

SPT—small professional theatre; a designation used primarily by Actors' Equity Association to identify certain theaters for contract agreements and terms.

steward—an IATSE designated position, in charge of local crew.

stitcher—a costume shop worker that assembles the costumes once the pattern has been made and cut. See chapter 16 for more information.

strike—the act of completely removing a production from the space once it has closed.

tech—often used as verb to describe the technical rehearsal process when each aspect of the show is finalized and organized into a workable set of cues for the production team. It is also used as an abbreviated form of "technical rehearsal."

technical rehearsal (also tech rehearsal)—rehearsals schedule to provide time for all members of a production team to add technical elements, such as lighting, sound, and costumes to a show.

template—see gobo.

unit set—United Scenic Artists describes a unit set as a set that remains on stage for the entire performance.

unit set with phases—A unit set that provides changes in locales and time through some scenic alteration of the set.

Appendix 4: Academic Programs in Areas of Technical Theater

By no means a comprehensive list, this table contains many of the institutions in the United States that offer one or more programs that focus on technical theater.

ARIZONA STATE UNIVERSITY
http://theatre.asu.edu/index.html

MFA in Intergrated Design Media
MFA in Performance Design
BA concentration in Design and Prod.

AUBURN UNIVERSITY
*http://media.cla.auburn.edu/
theatre/index.cfm*

BFA in Production Management
BFA in Design Technology

BAYLOR UNIVERSITY
www3.baylor.edu/Theatre_Arts

BFA in Design

BINGHAMTON UNIVERSITY
*http://theatre.binghamton.edu/
New/index.htm*

BA in Technical Prod. and Design
MA in Technical Prod. and Design

BOSTON UNIVERSITY
www.bu.edu/cfa/theatre

BFA in Design
BFA in Production
BFA in Stage Management
MFA in Design, Prod. and
Management
Certificates of Training for:
scenic artists, costumers, electricians,
carpenters, prop masters

CAL ARTS
*www.calarts.edu/schools/theater/
index.html*

BFA/MFA in Costume Design
BFA/MFA in Lighting Design
BFA/MFA in Management
BFA/MFA in Scene Design
BFA/MFA in Sound Design
BFA/MFA in Technical Direction

CALIFORNIA STATE UNIVERSITY,
LONG BEACH
www.csulb.edu/depts/theatre

MFA in Scene Design
MFA in Costume Design
MFA in Lighting Design

CARNEGIE MELLON
UNIVERSITY
www.cmu.edu/cfa/drama

BFA/MFA in Scene Design
BFA/MFA in Costume Design .
BFA/MFA in Lighting Design
BFA/MFA in Technical Direction
BFA/MFA in Prod. Management/
Stage Management
BFA/MFA in Costume Technology

CENTRAL WASHINGTON
UNIVERSITY
www.cwu.edu/~theatre

BA in Theatre with concentration in:
Design and Technology

CLARION UNIVERSITY
www.clarion.edu/departments/thea

BFA in Design/Technical Director

COBALT STUDIOS
www.cobaltstudios.net

Scenic Artist Training Program

COLLEGE OF SANTA FE
www.csf.edu/csf/academics/pad/index.html

BFA in Design/Technical Theater

COLUMBIA COLLEGE
www.colum.edu/undergraduate/theater/index.php

BFA in General Design
BFA in Costume Design
BFA in Lighting Design
BFA in Set Design
BFA in Technical

CORNISH COLLEGE OF
THE ARTS
www.cornish.edu/perfprod/default.htm

BFA in Performance Production

DEPAUL UNIVERSITY
http://theatreschool.depaul.edu

BFA in Costume Design
BFA in Costume Technology
BFA in Lighting Design

	BFA in Scenic Design BFA in Stage Management BFA in Theatre Technology BFA in Theatre Management
EAST CAROLINA UNIVERSITY *www.theatre-dance.ecu.edu*	BFA in Stage Management BFA in Design and Production
EMERSON COLLEGE *www.emerson.edu/* *performing_arts/index.cfm*	BFA in Production/Stage Management BFA in Theatre/Design Technology
FLORIDA ATLANTIC UNIVERSITY *www.fau.edu/divdept/schmidt/* *theatre/index.htm*	MFA in Technical Direction MFA in Costume Design MFA in Lighting Design MFA in Scenic Design
FLORIDA STATE UNIVERSITY *http://theatre.fsu.edu/index.htm*	BFA in Design/Tech MFA in Costume Design MFA in Lighting Design MFA in Scenic Design MFA in Technical Production MFA in Theatre Management
FULL SAIL *www.fullsail.com*	Recording Arts Show Production and Touring
GREENSBORO COLLEGE *http://theatre.gborocollege.edu*	BA/BS in Theatre with concentrations in: Stage Design Technical Theatre Costumes
ILLINOIS STATE UNIVERSITY *www.cfa.ilstu.edu*	BS/MS in Arts Technology BA/BS in Theatre with concentration in: Design/Production
ITHACA COLLEGE *http://departments.ithaca.edu/theatre*	BFA in Theatrical Production Arts

KANSAS STATE UNIVERSITY
www.k-state.edu/sctd/theatre

BA in Technical Theatre
BA in Theatre Design
BA in Stage Management

KENT STATE
www.theatre.kent.edu

BFA in Design and Technology
MFA in Costume Design
MFA in Scenic Design
MFA in Lighting Design
MFA in Theatre Technology

LONG ISLAND UNIVERSITY
C.W. POST
www.liu.edu/~svpa/theatre

BFA in Theatre Arts, Design and
Production

LOUISIANA STATE UNIVERSITY
www.theatre.lsu.edu

BA in Theatre with concentration in:
Design/Technology

MARYMOUNT MANHATTAN
COLLEGE
*http://marymount.mmm.edu/study/
programs/dfpa.html*

BA in Theatre Arts with
concentration in:
Design and Tech Prod.

MICHIGAN TECHNOLOGICAL
UNIVERSITY
www.fa.mtu.edu

BA in Sound Design
BA/BS in Theatre and Entertainment
Technology
BS in Audio Production and
Technology

MILLIKIN UNIVERSITY
www.millikin.edu/theatre

BFA in Design/Technical

MINNESOTA STATE
UNIVERSITY – MANKATO
www.mnsu.edu/theatre

BFA in Theatre with
concentration in:
Design/Technology
MFA in Design/Technology

MISSOURI STATE UNIVERSITY
http://theatreanddance.missouristate.edu

BFA in Theatre with concentration in:
Design Technology

MONTCLAIR STATE UNIVERSITY
www.montclair.edu/pages/
theatredance/index.htm

BFA in Theatre with concentration in:
Design/Production

MUHLENBERG COLLEGE
www.muhlenberg.edu/depts/theatre

BA in Theatre with concentrations in:
Directing/Stage Management
Design and Technical

NEW YORK CITY COLLEGE
OF TECHNOLOGY
www.citytech.cuny.edu/academics/
deptsites/enttech/index.shtml

Certificate in Sound Systems
Technology

NEW YORK UNIVERSITY
http://drama.tisch.nyu.edu/
page/home.html

MFA in Set Design
MFA in Lighting Design
MFA in Costume Design
MFA in Production Design

NORTH CAROLINA SCHOOL
OF THE ARTS
www.ncarts.edu/ncsaprod/
designandproduction

BFA with concentrations in:
Costume Design
Lighting Design
Scene Design
Sound Design
Wig and Makeup Design
Costume Technology
Scene Painting
State Properties
Stage Management
Technical Direction
MFA with concentrations in:
Costume Design
Scene Design
Wig and Makeup Design
Costume Technology
Scene Painting
Stage Automation
Stage Properties
Technical Direction
MFA in Performance Arts
Management

NORTHERN ARIZONA
UNIVERSITY
www.cal.nau.edu/theatre/index.htm

BA/BS in Theatre with
concentration in:
Design/Technology

NORTHERN ILLINOIS
UNIVERSITY
www.niu.edu/theatre

BFA in Theatre with
concentration in:
Design and Technology
MFA in Theatre with concetrations in:
Costume Design
Technical Direction
Lighting Design
Scene Design

NORTHERN KENTUCKY
UNIVERSITY
www.nku.edu/~powellt/destech.htm

BFA in Design or
Technology with concentrations in:
Technology and Production
Lighting Design
Scenic Design
Sound Design
BFA in Stage Management

NORTHWESTERN
UNIVERSITY
*www.communication.
northwestern.edu/theatre*

Certificate in Sound Design
BA in Theatre with concentration in:
Design/Technology
MFA in Stage Design

OHIO STATE UNIVERSITY
http://theatre.osu.edu

MFA in Design

OHIO UNIVERSITY
*www.finearts.ohio.edu/
theater/index.htm*

BFA in Production Design and
Technology
BFA in Stage Management
MFA in Production Design and
Technology

OKLAHOMA CITY
UNIVERSITY
www.okcu.edu/theater

BFA in Design and Production
MA in Technical Theater:
Costume Design
MA in Technical Theater: Scene
Design

OTTERBEIN COLLEGE
www.otterbein.edu/dept/
thr/index.html

BFA in Design/Technology

PENNSYLVANIA STATE
UNIVERSITY
www.theatre.psu.edu

BFA in Production
BFA in Stage Management
MFA in Design

PURDUE UNIVERSITY
www.cla.purdue.edu/vpa/theatre

MFA in Costume Design
MFA in Lighting Design
MFA in Scenic Design
MFA in Sound Design
MFA in Theater Engineering
MFA in Technical Direction

RUTGERS UNIVERSITY
www.masongross.rutgers.edu/
theater/thea.html

BFA in Design
BFA in Production and Management
MFA in Design
MFA in Stage Management

SALEM STATE COLLEGE
www.salemstate.edu/theatre_speech

BA in theatre with concentration in:
Technical Theater
BFA in Technical Theater
BFA in Design
BFA in Stage Management

SAN DIEGO STATE UNIVERSITY
http://theatre.sdsu.edu

BA in Theater with concentration in:
Design and Technology
MFA in Design
MFA in Technical Theatre

SHENANDOAH UNIVERSITY
www.su.edu/conservatory/scon/
Academics/Theatre/index.htm

BFA in Costume Design
BFA in Scenic and Lighting Design

SOUTHERN CONNETTICUT
STATE UNIVERSITY
www.southernct.edu/undergrad/
schas/THR

BA in Design and Technical Theatre

SOUTHERN METHODIST
UNIVERSITY
www.smu.edu/meadows/theatre

MFA in Design

SOUTHERN OREGON
UNIVERSITY
www.sou.edu/THTR

BFA in Theatre with
concentrations in:
Costume Design
Stage Lighting
Technical Direction
Scenic Design
Sound
Stage Management

SOUTHERN UTAH
UNIVERSITY
www.suu.edu/pva/ta

BA/BS in Theatre Arts with
concentration in:
Design/Tech

SUNY-FREDONIA
http://ww1.fredonia.edu

BFA in Production Design

SUNY-OSWEGO
www.oswego.edu

BA in Theatre with concentrations in:
Design
Technical Production

SUNY-PURCHASE
*www.purchase.edu/Departments/
AcademicPrograms/Arts/TAF*

BFA in Design/Technology
with concentrations in:
Scenic Design
Costume Design
Lighting Design
Costume Technology
Stage Management
Stage Management/Production
Management
Technical Direction/Production
Management
MFA in Design/Technology
with concentrations in:
Scenic Design
Costume Design

Lighting Design
Technical Direction/Production
Management

STEPHENS COLLEGE
www.stephens.edu/academics/
programs/theatre

BFA in Theatrical Costume Design

SYRACUSE UNIVERSITY
http://vpa.syr.edu/index.cfm/
page/drama

BFA in Design/Technical Theater
BFA in Stage Management

TEMPLE UNIVERSITY
www.temple.edu/theater

BA in Theater with concentration in:
Design/Technical/Stage
Management
MFA in Scene Design
MFA in Lighting Design
MFA in Costume Design
MFA in Costume Construction

TEXAS STATE UNIVERSITY
www.finearts.txstate.edu/
theatre/index.htm

BFA in Technology and Design

TOWSON UNIVERSITY
www.towson.edu/theatre

BA/BS in Theatre with
concentration in:
Design and Theatre Production

TULANE UNIVERSITY
www.tulane.edu/~theatre/
index.html

BFA in Design/Production
MFA in Scene Design
MFA in Costume Design
MFA in Lighting Design
MFA in Technical Direction

UNIVERSITY OF ALABAMA
www.as.ua.edu/theatre

MFA in Costume Design and
Production
MFA in Scene Design/Technical
Production
MFA in Stage Management
MFA in Theatre Mangement

UNIVERSITY OF
ALASKA-FAIRBANKS
www.uaf.edu/theatre

BA in Theatre with
concentration in:
Design/Technical Theatre

UNIVERSITY OF ARIZONA
http://web.cfa.arizona.edu/theatre

BFA in Design/Tech
MFA in Design/Tech

UNIVERSITY OF
CALIFORNIA, IRVINE
http://drama.arts.uci.edu

MFA in Stage Management
MFA in Scene Design
MFA in Costume Design
MFA in Lighting Design
MFA in Sound Design

UNIVERSITY OF CALIFORNIA,
LOS ANGELES
www.filmtv.ucla.edu/dot.cfm

BA in Theater with concentration in:
Design and Production
MFA in Costume Design
MFA in Lighting Design
MFA in Production Management and
Technology
MFA in Scenic Design
MFA in Sound Design

UNIVERSITY OF CALIFORNIA,
SAN DIEGO
www-theatre.ucsd.edu

MFA in Design
MFA in Stage Management

UNIVERSITY OF CALIFORNIA,
SANTA BARBARA
www.dramadance.ucsb.edu

BA in Dramatic Arts with
concentration in:
Theatre Design and Technology

UNIVERSITY OF CENTRAL
FLORIDA
www.cas.ucf.edu/theatre

BFA in Stage Management
BFA in Design and Technology
MFA in Design

UNIVERSITY OF CINCINNATI
www.ccm.uc.edu/tdp

BFA in Costume Design and
Technology
BFA in Lighting Design and
Technology
BFA in Makeup and Wig Design
BFA in Scenic Design

BFA in Sound Design
BFA in Stage Management
BFA in Technical Production
MFA in Costume Design and
Technology
MFA in Lighting Design and
Technology
MFA in Makup and Wig Design
MFA in Scenic Design
MFA in Sound Design
MFA in Stage Management
MFA in Technical Production

UNIVERSITY OF CONNECTICUT
www.drama.uconn.edu/index.htm

BFA in Design/Tech
BFA in Puppetry
MFA in Costume Design
MFA in Lighting Design
MFA in Scenic Design
MFA in Technical Direction
MA/MFA in Puppetry

UNIVERSITY OF
DELAWARE – PTTP
www.udel.edu/theatre

MFA in Stage Management
MFA in Technical Production

UNIVERSITY OF EVANSVILLE
http://theatre.evansville.edu

BA/BFA in Theatre with
concentration in:
Theatre Design and Technology
Theatre Management

UNIVERSITY OF FLORIDA
www.arts.ufl.edu/theatreanddance

BFA in Design and Technology
MFA in Costume Design
MFA in Costume Technology
MFA in Scene Design
MFA in Lighting Design

UNIVERSITY OF GEORGIA
www.drama.uga.edu

MFA in Design and Technology

UNIVERSITY OF HAWAII-MANOA *www.hawaii.edu/theatre*	MFA in Scenic Design MFA in Lighting Design MFA in Costume Design
UNIVERSITY OF IDAHO *www.class.uidaho.edu/irt*	BFA in Design/Technology MFA in Design/Technology
UNIVERSITY OF ILLINOIS AT URBANA CHAMPAIGN *www.theatre.uiuc.edu*	BFA in Theatre with concentrations in: Scenic Design Scenic Technology Sound Design and Technology Stage Management MFA in Costume Design MFA in Scene Design MFA in Scenic Technology MFA in Lighting Design MFA in Sound Design and Technology MFA in Stage Management
UNIVERSITY OF IOWA *www.uiowa.edu/~theatre*	MFA in Design MFA in Stage Management
UNIVERSITY OF KANSAS *www2.ku.edu/~kuthf*	MFA in Scenography
UNIVERSITY OF MARYLAND- BALTIMORE COUNTY *www.umbc.edu/theatre*	BA in Design/Production
UNIVERSITY OF MASSACHUSETTS- AMHERST *www.umass.edu/theater*	MFA in Scenic Design MFA in Lighting Design
UNIVERSITY OF MEMPHIS *www.people.memphis.edu/ ~umtheatre/td/index.html*	BFA in Design and Technical Production

UNIVERSITY OF MIAMI *www.as.miami.edu/theatrearts*	BFA in Stage Management BFA in Design/Production
UNIVERSITY OF MICHIGAN *www.music.umich.edu/ departments/theatre*	BFA in Design and Production
UNIVERSITY OF MINNESOTA *http://theatre.cla.umn.edu*	MFA in Design/Technology
UNIVERSITY OF MISSOURI-KANSAS CITY *http://theatre.missouri.edu*	MFA in Costume Design MFA in Sound Design MFA in Stage Management MFA in Technical Direction MFA in Scenic Design MFA in Lighting Design
UNIVERSITY OF MONTANA *www.sfa.umt.edu/drama*	BFA in Design/Technology MFA in Design/Technology
UNIVERSITY OF MONTEVALLO *www.montevallo.edu/thea*	BA/BFA in Design/Technology
UNIVERSITY OF NEBRASKA-LINCOLN *www.unl.edu/TheatreArts*	BFA in Design/Technical Production MFA in Design/Stage Tech
UNIVERSITY OF NEVADA-LAS VEGAS *www.unlv.edu/Colleges/ Fine_Arts/Theatre*	BA in Design/Technology MFA in Design/Technology MFA in Stage Mangement
UNIVERSITY OF NEW HAMPSHIRE *www.unh.edu/theatre-dance*	BA in Theatre with concentration in: Design and Technical Theatre
UNIVERSITY OF NEW MEXICO *www.unm.edu/%7Etheatre/td/ index.html*	BA in Design for Performance

UNIVERSITY OF NORTH
CAROLINA-CHAPEL HILL
www.unc.edu/depts/drama/index.html

MFA in Costume Production
MFA in Technical Production

UNIVERSITY OF NORTH
CAROLINA-GREENSBORO
www.uncg.edu/the/main1.html

BFA in Technical Production
BFA in Theatre Design and
Technical Production
MFA in Theatre Design

UNIVERSITY OF NORTHERN
COLORADO
*www.arts.unco.edu/theatredance/
default.html*

BA in Theatre Arts with
concentration in:
Design Technology

UNIVERSITY OF
NORTHERN IOWA
www.uni.edu/chfa/dep_theatre.html

BA in Theatre with concentration in:
Design and Production

UNIVERSITY OF OKLAHOMA
www.ou.edu/finearts/drama

BFA in Stage Mangement
BFA in Design
BFA in Technical Production

UNIVERSITY OF OREGON
http://theatre.uoregon.edu/start.htm

MFA in Scenic Design
MFA in Costume Design
MFA in Lighting Design

UNIVERSITY OF RHODE ISLAND
www.uri.edu/artsci/the

BFA in Design
BFA in Theatre Technology

UNIVERSITY OF SOUTH
CAROLINA
www.cas.sc.edu/thea/index1.html

MFA in Scene Design
MFA in Costume Design
MFA in Lighting Design

UNIVERSITY OF SOUTH DAKOTA
www.usd.edu/cfa/Theatre

BFA in Design/Technology
MFA in Design and Tech

UNIVERSITY OF SOUTHERN
CALIFORNIA
http://theatre.usc.edu

BFA in Design
BFA in Technical Direction
BFA in Stage Management

UNIVERSITY OF SOUTHERN
MISSISSIPPI
www.usm.edu/theatre

BFA in Design and
Technical Theatre
MFA in Costume Design
MFA in Lighting Design
MFA in Scenic Design

UNIVERSITY OF TEXAS-AUSTIN
www.utexas.edu/cofa/theatre

BA in Theatre and Dance with
concentrations in:
Lighting Design and Technology
Costume Design and Technology
Set Design and Technology
MFA in Theatrical Design
MFA in Theatre Technolgy

UNIVERSITY OF UTAH
www.theatre.utah.edu

BFA in Performing Arts
Design Program
BFA in Stage Management

UNIVERSITY OF VIRGINIA
www.virginia.edu/drama/index.htm

MFA in Costume Design
and Technology
MFA in Lighting Design
MFA in Scenic Design
MFA in Technical Direction

UNIVERSITY OF WASHINGTON
http://depts.washington.edu/uwdrama

MFA in Design

UNIVERSITY OF
WISCONSIN-MADISON
www.theatre.wisc.edu

MFA in Scene Design
MFA in Costume Design
MFA in Lighting Design
MFA in Theatre Technology

UNIVERSITY OF
WISCONSIN-MILWAUKEE
*www3.uwm.edu/arts/programs/
theatre/index.html*

BFA in Costume Production
BFA in Stage Management
BFA in Technical Production

UNIVERSITY OF WYOMING
www.uwyo.edu/th%26d

BFA in Theatre and Dance
with concentration in:
Theatre Design

UTAH STATE UNIVERSITY
www.usu.edu/theatre

BFA in Design
MFA in Design
MFA in Technical Theatre

VIRGINIA COMMONWEALTH
UNIVERSITY
www.pubinfo.vcu.edu/artweb/theatre

BFA in Scene Design/Technology
BFA in Costume Design
BFA in Stage Management
BFA in Lighting Design
MFA in Scene Design
MFA in Costume Design

VIRGINIA TECH

www.theatre.vt.edu

MFA in Theatre Design and
Technology
MFA in Stage Management

VITERBO UNIVERSITY
*www.viterbo.edu/academic/
ug/sfa/theatre/index.htm*

BFA in Design
BFA in Technical Production

WAYNE STATE UNIVERSITY
www.theatre.wayne.edu

BFA in Theatre with
concentration in:
Production
MFA in Theatre with
concentrations in:
Theatre Management
Stage Design
Lighting Design
Stage Costuming
Costume Design

WEBSTER UNIVERSITY
*www.webster.edu/depts/finearts/
theater/index.html*

BFA in Design/Technical Theatre
with concentrations in:
Costume Design
Lighting Design
Scenic Design
Sound Design
Makeup Design
Costume Construction
Technical Direction
BFA in Stage Mangement

WEST VIRGINIA UNIVERSITY *www.wvu.edu/%7Etheatre/* *index.htm*	BFA in Design and Technical Theatre BFA in Puppetry MFA in Scenic Design MFA in Costume Design MFA in Lighting Design
WESTERN ILLINOIS UNIVERSITY *www.wiu.edu/theatre*	MFA in Lighting Design MFA in Scenic Design MFA in Costume Design
WESTERN MICHIGAN UNIVERSITY *www.wmich.edu/theatre*	BA in Design and Technical Production
WESTERN OREGON UNIVERSITY *www.wou.edu/las/creativearts/* *theater_dance/theatre_dance.htm*	BFA in Theatre with concentrations in: Lighting Design Costume Design Scenic Design Technical Production Stage Management
WICHITA STATE UNIVERSITY *http://finearts.wichita.edu/* *performing/theatre.asp*	BFA in Design and Technical Theatre
WINTHROP UNIVERSITY *www.winthrop.edu/vpa/* *Theatre_&_Dance/default.htm*	BA in Theatre with concentration in: Design/Technical Theatre
WRIGHT STATE UNIVERSITY *www.wright.edu/academics/theatre*	BFA in Design/Technology BFA in Stage Management
YALE UNIVERSITY *www.yale.edu/drama*	MFA in Design (also Certificate) MFA in Sound Design MFA in Stage Management (also Certificate) MFA in Technical Design and Production (also Certificate)

Index

TODAY WE DROP BOMBS, TOMORROW WE BUILD BRIDGES

Peter Gill is a journalist specialising in developing world affairs. He has been South Asia and Middle East correspondent for the *Daily Telegraph* and has travelled widely in Africa and Asia as a current affairs reporter for ITV and the BBC. He covered the fall of Saigon for the *Daily Telegraph* and made documentary films on Afghanistan during the Soviet occupation. He led major media campaigns to combat AIDS and leprosy in India for the BBC, and has written four books on development themes, including a study of Oxfam's early work and two books on the politics of hunger in Ethiopia.

TODAY WE DROP BOMBS, TOMORROW WE BUILD BRIDGES

HOW FOREIGN AID BECAME A CASUALTY OF WAR

PETER GILL

Zed Books

LONDON

Today We Drop Bombs, Tomorrow We Build Bridges: How Foreign Aid Became a Casualty of War was first published in 2016 by Zed Books Ltd, The Foundry, 17 Oval Way, London SE11 5RR, UK.

www.zedbooks.co.uk

Typeset in Adobe Caslon Pro by seagulls.net
Cover designed by Jonathan Pelham
Printed and bound by CPI Group (UK) Ltd, Croydon, CR0 4YY

A catalogue record for this book is available from the British Library.

ISBN 978-1-78360-123-3 hb
ISBN 978-1-78360-122-6 pb
ISBN 978-1-78360-124-0 pdf
ISBN 978-1-78360-125-7 epub
ISBN 978-1-78360-126-4 mobi

CONTENTS

Conclusion: How Many Cheers for Neutrality?

ACKNOWLEDGEMENTS

My biggest debt is to the people and organisations that got me to the places I needed to reach to be able to tell this story. At my very first meeting in Kabul in October 2013, Benoit De Gryse, country representative of Médecins Sans Frontières in Afghanistan, started making the arrangements to fly me to Lashkar Gah and put me up with the MSF team running Helmand's provincial hospital. In Pakistan, Dr Fayaz Ahmad, country director for Islamic Relief, was equally helpful in acquiring the government permit I needed – and may not otherwise have got – to travel towards the Afghan border and see something of his agency's work on the ground. Without the help of Dawn Blalock Goodwin at the UN's Office for the Coordination of Humanitarian Affairs in Nairobi, it is likely I would not even have made it to Mogadishu. Her colleague Abdi Yussuf Noor organised my stay in the city superbly. To reach the world's biggest refugee camp at Dadaab on the Kenya–Somalia border, I relied on the help of Bogdan Dumitru, CARE Kenya's country director, and Rod Volway, CARE Canada's director of refugee operations.

I am grateful for many valuable introductions along the way. Khalil Rehman, chief executive of Doctors Worldwide in Britain, put me in touch with Syria Relief and Hand in Hand for Syria, two brilliant British Syrian organisations whose work I witnessed on the Turkey–Syria border. Lamees Hafeez, operations manager for Syria

Relief, linked me in turn to Syrian diaspora organisations in the US. John Penn, a former colleague with the BBC World Service Trust (now BBC Media Action), made many useful connections for me in Turkey. Sandrine Tiller, humanitarian adviser at MSF in London, fixed important contacts for me and has encouraged me in this project from the beginning. Two distinguished British aid experts – Myles Wickstead, formerly of the Department for International Development, and Mark Bowden, with the United Nations in Kabul – were generous with their introductions and insights. My thanks are also due to Ashley Jackson and Eva Svoboda at the Humanitarian Policy Group (HPG) of the Overseas Development Institute (ODI) in London. Ashley provided me with an impressive list of significant people to see in key countries, and both of them tutored me through their writings in this area. In its meetings, events and studies, the HPG leads the world in the quality of its analysis and discussion of the contemporary humanitarian scene. A good deal of its work is acknowledged in the book, and I want to thank David White from its communications team for his patience and his willingness to send me papers that I should have seen and read in the first place.

Press offices in the aid world are as varied in their responsiveness as they are anywhere else. Among non-government agencies, two individuals were consistently open-minded and generous with their help – Polly Markandya, head of communications at MSF in London, and Martin Cottingham, media and advocacy manager at Islamic Relief UK. Several government press officers went out of their way to make sure I got to see the right people and got my facts (I hope) right. I would like to thank Rebecca Gustafson, at the Office of US Foreign Disaster Assistance at USAID in Washington; Chris Kiggell, at the Department for International

Development in London; Kevin O'Loughlin, at USAID in Kabul; and Lloyd Jackson, at USAID in Islamabad. No one apart from me, of course, has any responsibility for errors of fact or judgement.

Good friends were kind enough to put me up on my travels around the aid capitals of the West. In Washington I stayed with George and Chrissie Griffin and with Rumu Sen-Gupta and Patrick Watkinson and family. In Geneva my hosts were Lori McDougall and René Véron and family. Their daughter Lili generously gave up her bedroom to me for a week. In Paris I stayed with Robin and Merrill Christopher. I loved being with them all.

When the manuscript was finished, I shared sections of it with aid people who had helped me along the way. It is better they remain anonymous lest they are thought to be responsible for anything that follows. I am nevertheless grateful to them for their inputs, including the spotting of factual errors. It was my additional good fortune that several leading authorities in this field were willing to read the manuscript as a whole. My thanks are due to Sara Pantuliano, who was already busy enough leading the ODI's Humanitarian Policy Group with such energy and skill; Fiona Terry, whose work is quoted in the book and whose stance is an eloquent reminder of the role principle should play in humanitarian affairs; and Myles Wickstead, whose knowledge and experience of the aid world overall is profound. Alex de Waal, at Tufts University, who has been generous to me on past projects, was helpful in getting this one off the ground and made a number of positive interventions along the way. Alex is closely associated with Zed Books, whose editorial director Ken Barlow picked up this project in 2013. I am grateful to him for that as well as for his detailed and incisive comments on the draft. Two very good friends, Sue Kyle and Ned Campbell, ran their literary slide rules over the manuscript and saved me from a number of lapses in spelling and grammar, punctuation and style. After all that, the book benefited greatly from the superb copyediting skills of Judith Forshaw.

Finally, I would like to thank my sister Frances for her very generous contribution to my research costs. I hope she thinks that the result was worth it.

Peter Gill, London, November 2015

INTRODUCTION

HUMANITARIAN ARMADA

When the United States bombed the Syrian town of Kobani in 2014 to stop it falling to Islamic State, the retired American general charged with building the military coalition against the jihadists, General John R. Allen, said he would not use terms like 'strategic target' or 'strategic outcome' to describe the action, then added, 'We are striking the targets around Kobani for humanitarian purposes.'

When President Vladimir Putin held a press conference in March 2014 and fielded questions about Russia's involvement in Ukraine and the Crimea, he told journalists that any military action he took would be aimed at protecting people with whom Russia had close historical, cultural and economic ties. 'This is a humanitarian mission,' he said.

Everyone is a humanitarian now. A word once used to describe principled civilian assistance to people suffering in natural or man-made disasters now provides a reassuring gloss for the actions of politicians and the military. This has both compromised and endangered the work of aid workers who had believed that their independence and impartiality would be enough to protect them.

1

The pattern was set during the war in Kosovo. The NATO air campaign against the Serbs in 1999 was declared a 'humanitarian intervention', and that led to the notion of a 'humanitarian war', even to 'humanitarian bombing'. A decade later humanitarianism reached its Final Frontier in Hollywood. In the Star Trek movie of 2009, a young James T. Kirk is being persuaded to join the Starfleet. 'It's important,' he is told. 'A peacekeeping and humanitarian armada.'

The starting point for this book was the big charitable aid agencies, the good guys of a $25 billion aid business, and how they handle the pressures and dilemmas of the war on terror. At home they rely on public reputation and private donations to sustain their humanitarian endeavours, but in the field many deliver aid on behalf of Western governments whose interest lies in countering terror.

Over the course of six months in 2013 and 2014, I travelled from Afghanistan, where the principal aid-funders have had boots on the ground for most of this century, to the Turkish border with Syria, where the West struggles to contain a jihadist threat far closer to home. In all four of the countries I focus on – Afghanistan, Pakistan, Somalia and Syria – the United States is conducting a bombing offensive, using either conventional warplanes or unmanned drones.

It is the war in Afghanistan that has defined the era for the non-governmental aid organisations, the NGOs. After 9/11 and the overthrow of the Taliban, most of them pitched in with enthusiasm to the huge and well-financed task of reconstruction. Afghanistan would be built anew, a beacon for what the West could do. But the old ways persisted, the war restarted, and the aid-givers lost their way. They were warned, as we shall see, that the drive for bigger budgets might be achieved only at the cost of their principles.

Afghanistan has widened a split in the humanitarian world. On one side are the big American and British agencies. Ever since the days of the Cold War, US non-profits have relied on government funding. More recently British charities have established a similar relationship. Oxfam now derives nearly half its income from governments and other institutional sources. For Save the Children, the proportion is closer to two-thirds.

On the other side of the divide are the direct descendants of Europe's greatest humanitarian institution. The International Committee of the Red Cross (ICRC) combines Swiss discretion with a solemn regard for the humanitarian principles it has formulated of independence, impartiality and neutrality. Governments may find it, but the uniqueness of its status is secured by its guardianship of the Geneva Conventions.

With French flair, Médecins Sans Frontières (MSF) began life as a rebellious breakaway from the ICRC. It is now the most widely admired aid agency in the world. MSF has a mighty annual income of $1.1 billion or £750 million, but gets less than a tenth of it from governments and takes none at all from belligerents in war zones. It does not even call itself an NGO, and once, in Pakistan, as we shall see, it went so far as to drop the tainted term 'humanitarian'.

As traditional NGOs try to balance their own priorities with those of their backers, they have been joined on the front line by a new breed of non-profit aid agencies for whom government contracts come first. In Washington they are the 'Beltway bandits' in search of a share of the official US aid funds that have gushed from the ground since 9/11.

I describe the extraordinary rise (and spectacular fall) of International Relief and Development (IRD), whose income grew 600-fold in 15 years. At the height of the Iraq and Afghan wars, IRD's earnings from the US government averaged $350 million a year. Then the investigations began and IRD was accused by its own funders of mismanagement and misconduct, of overpaying its executives and throwing lavish staff parties.

In Mogadishu, the capital of Somalia, I stayed at 'Airport Camp', which is owned and operated by an American firm called Bancroft. Here is an enterprise which cleverly combines profit-making in a war zone with NGO work that tackles Somali insecurity head-on. Bancroft Global Development hires ex-soldiers from around the world – along with a few ex-mercenaries – to 'mentor' the African Union troops deployed in the country to counter Somali jihadists. That qualifies as charitable education work. The expectation is that greater security will one day make Mogadishu safe again for business, which is the longer-term interest of Bancroft Global Investments in the city.

African Union forces are in Somalia with the authorisation of the United Nations, and that has pushed the UN's own aid workers onto the front line in the war on terror. Its great humanitarian institutions – the children's agency UNICEF, the refugee agency UNHCR and the World Food Programme – once enjoyed a measure of real independence from the UN's political institutions, but they are now formally 'integrated' into missions whose overriding task is to win wars for the Security Council in New York.

The UN has become a priority target for al-Shabaab jihadists in Somalia. In 2013 its Mogadishu headquarters was attacked and it was forced to retreat to the better-guarded airport. When four UNICEF workers were killed by a roadside bomb in northern Somalia in April 2015, the UN's head of humanitarian affairs, Valerie Amos, issued this bleak statement: 'Respect for the United Nations flag and the Red Cross and Red Crescent flag is disappearing.'

After Afghanistan, which remains the most dangerous country of all for aid workers, Somalia records the greatest number of hostile incidents. Around the world, the figures peaked dramatically in 2013 at 155 aid workers killed, 178 wounded and 141 kidnapped.[1] 'If you ask me today what is the greatest challenge for humanitarianism,' said

Manuel Bessler, head of humanitarian aid for the Swiss government, 'this is my first one, the security of my people. Without security for humanitarian workers, there won't be humanitarian aid.'

We were speaking in June 2014, a few days after a Swiss Red Cross delegate was shot dead in Libya. 'He was shot not because he was in the wrong place at the wrong time, but because he was targeted,' Bessler said. 'People wanted to kill him as a humanitarian.'

Manuel Bessler began his career with the International Committee of the Red Cross. He recalls asking his instructors on the introductory course, 'But what is our protection?' They told him, 'The cross. The cross is your protection because the emblem is protected.' 'Well,' Bessler says, 'today the Red Cross is more like the cross hairs.'

Aid worker casualties declined in 2014, but this was attributed more to their reduced presence on the front line than to any change of heart on the part of their enemies.[2] MSF produced a report that year which was sharply critical of the aid agencies. 'Risk aversion was pervasive within the NGO community,' it found, 'not only in relation to security but also to programming, meaning that agencies were choosing to prioritise the easiest-to-reach over the most vulnerable.'[3]

By withdrawing to a safer distance, the concern was that the risks involved in delivering aid were being 'outsourced' from international staff to local NGO workers. That might in turn account for an under-reporting of incidents and casualties. It was a Western manager with a leading Muslim charity, as I report in Chapter 3, who told me that it was 'morally wrong for aid agencies to transfer all responsibility and risk to local staff'.

I was on the Turkey–Syria border in March 2014 for the third anniversary of the start of the conflict in Syria. A senior British aid official was telling me how badly he thought the world's politicians and diplomats had failed the people of Syria. There had been neither effective peace-making nor any peace-keeping. 'When all else fails,' he said, 'let's go for humanitarian relief.' Humanitarianism had become the first and the last resort of governments.

The fallout from Syria will define the future of the humanitarian endeavour. Along with other crises, its enormity is already buckling the system. Towards the end of 2015 there were more than 4 million Syrian refugees outside the country, another 8 million displaced inside. Turkey alone was accommodating more than 2 million Syrians, overtaking Pakistan as the world's principal refugee host. Worldwide, 60 million people were displaced and on the move, 10 million more than at the beginning of 2014 and 20 million more than a decade ago.

The way aid gets delivered is also changing. With the advance of Islamic State fighters across northern and eastern Syria, there are no longer international aid workers on the front line. They have fallen back over the border, leaving the Syrians themselves to do all the work. Some of those Syrians are employed by foreign NGOs, but many are working for impressive diaspora start-ups from Europe and North America and still more are volunteers with local community organisations.

On the Turkish side of the border, it is Turkish NGOs and official Turkish aid institutions that shoulder the biggest burden. This has already propelled Turkey into the top rank of humanitarian aid-givers. Money from the Gulf is making ever larger, and largely unacknowledged, contributions to the international relief effort. The West still provides most of the money and much of the management, but on the ground the humanitarian initiative is beginning to slip away from Westerners and their institutions.

At its finest, the Western humanitarian movement is character-ised by its regard for the principles of independence, impartiality and neutrality. Utilising the freedoms that accompany democracy, foreign aid workers have been able to put the needs of all those who suffer ahead of political or strategic calculation. The war on terror has raised a set of high hurdles to the implementation of these ideals. Fundamental principles have been challenged, undermined and, in some cases, put to flight. For true humanitarianism to survive, they need to be revisited and reaffirmed.

PART I
FRONT LINES

CHAPTER 1

END OF THE
WHITE SAVIOUR

Turkey–Syria border, March 2014

Dr Mounir Hakimi stepped off the plane from Manchester looking every inch the British surgeon. He wore a navy blue suit, button-down shirt and sober tie. It was a Friday evening, and he had come straight from work at the Royal Bolton Hospital. His week on the orthopaedic ward had been busy with outpatient clinics and operations, often hip and knee replacements for the elderly of Greater Manchester. There would be a sharp change of focus this weekend. After a few hours' rest, Dr Hakimi would be heading for his homeland, over the border into Syria.

We met for dinner in a rooftop restaurant in Antakia, the biblical Antioch, about 25 miles from Turkey's frontier with Syria. Over the kebabs, Dr Hakimi confirmed my first impression of him as a hospital consultant in the making – an open and engaging manner, a ready laugh and a good appetite, kept in check perhaps by the consumption of cigarettes.

Allied to this personality is another – that of a skilled health professional bound up in the suffering of his people. Mounir Hakimi is the co-founder of Syria Relief, one of the diaspora charities started in the West in response to the outbreak of the conflict in 2011. As violence and brutality engulfed the country and blunted the outside world's capacity to help, it has been local relief workers and their overseas counterparts such as Dr Hakimi who have kept the humanitarian flag flying in the towns and villages of Syria.

In the first years of the crisis, Syria Relief developed an entire repertoire of aid roles, from food distribution to medical supplies, from schooling to sanitation. It established itself in parts of the country that no Western aid workers could dream of reaching directly. On the ground in this conflict, almost all the assistance is being delivered by Syrians for Syrians. With traditional aid-givers essentially confined to funding and management roles, a new model of aid delivery is emerging.

Hands-on medical care is at the heart of the Syria Relief operation, bringing the skills and standards of Western medicine to bear on the great humanitarian catastrophe of the era. Most of, the charity's trustees are British Syrian doctors. Dr Hakimi's purpose this weekend was to visit Bab al-Hawa ('The Gate of Winds'), the main crossing point on the highway to Aleppo, where Syria Relief and two other Syrian charities have set up a hospital in disused Syrian customs sheds. It would be a roundabout journey to get there. The hospital had already been hit twice in government air attacks.

Bab al-Hawa hospital was seeing 3,000 patients a month, almost all of them war-related. As one of the hospital's directors, Mounir was hoping for a quiet weekend on the war front so he could direct his energies towards administration – staff appointments, management discussions, the inspection of plant and supplies. They were also building a new operating theatre complex. 'It is being built to National Health Service standards,' he told me. 'It will be like Bolton Hospital.'

This was the seventh time since the war began that he had flown from Manchester to Turkey and crossed into Syria, a pattern of travel that had excited suspicious interest from the authorities at home. British Syrians and other Muslims bringing desperately needed humanitarian aid to this disaster have been surprisingly even-tempered about the level of attention, amounting on occasions to harassment, that they receive at British airports, in their UK workplaces, even at home. The authorities seem incapable of distinguishing between reputable aid workers (whom they support and increasingly fund) and other, suspect travellers. A few days before he left, Dr Hakimi had led a delegation of local Muslim charity heads to raise the matter with Sir Peter Fahy, head of Greater Manchester Police and of the government's anti-extremism 'Prevent' strategy.

'I am a trustee of Syria Relief and I am flying there on Friday,' was how he introduced himself to the Chief Constable. Sir Peter acknowledged the large number of government agencies, from the immigration service to the border force all the way to police counter-terror units and the intelligence services, each of them checking up for themselves on travellers to Syria. He also accepted that home visits raised particular anxieties among Syrians. Calls in the middle of the night were a common tactic of the regime from which some at the meeting had fled. 'Very nice man,' Dr Hakimi declared after the meeting, 'very intelligent.'

Early the next morning, Dr Hakimi and I travelled together to the border. He would cross; I would not. This was spring 2014, and the days of Western aid workers, Western journalists, even Western charity supporters crossing into Syria without immediate risk of kidnap, captivity and worse had passed.

We skirted the 3-mile truck queue at the main Bab al-Hawa crossing; we threaded our way through the border town of Reyhanli;

then we headed for the 'humanitarian crossing' at Atmeh that gives directly onto a large, informal refugee camp on the Syrian side. It was from here that David Haines, the first British aid worker to be gruesomely murdered by Islamic State jihadists in September 2014, was abducted.

We were in sight of the watchtowers at the Turkish frontier when Dr Hakimi's mobile rang. It was his Syria Relief colleague on the other side of the border. If the doctor was thinking of getting administrative work done, it would be best to avoid coming direct to the hospital. There had been an air strike earlier that morning on the nearby town of Maarat Masreen, and 'lots of wounded' were arriving.

Mounir's response seemed matter of fact. 'I have my scrubs with me this time,' he said. In fact, he had brought fresh surgical scrubs for the whole team, along with a pile of white coats with the Syria Relief logo stamped on the breast pocket. Then he paused and reflected, 'Every time I go, you know, it takes me a fortnight to recover – not just physically, but also mentally.'

We waited the best part of an hour at that informal border crossing. Names were checked, soldiers lounged, radio messages were sent up ahead and a Turkish official looked again at everyone's documents. Then suddenly there was movement and shouted commands. Two mighty Turkish Red Crescent aid trucks were the first to move, and then Dr Hakimi jumped back into his black Renault and was gone. 'See you Monday, *Insh'allah*,' he said.

Back in the border town of Reyhanli, there is a newly built stone and brick memorial to the 51 people who died in two large car bombs in May 2013. It was one of Turkey's deadliest terrorist incidents, variously attributed to the Syrian government and to the jihadist opposition. As for the cross-border aid effort, it triggered the retreat of the remaining international agencies to the greater security of Antakia. The overseas Syrian charities were the only ones left standing.

I saw the new offices acquired for Syria Relief's medical team, opening directly onto a gaping lift shaft on the sixth floor of a building still under construction. Then I was taken to a prosthetic limb unit they had opened with other Syrian British and Syrian American aid groups. There they had a list of 700 amputees waiting for new limbs, but many were stuck on the wrong side of the border. With their customary boldness, the diaspora agencies decided they would simply have to set up another unit inside rebel-held Syria.

At the Reyhanli unit a young man called Hassan told me he had been a carpenter in the city of Hama. He and his brother had been trying to disarm and dismantle a cluster bomb. The bomb exploded, and both men were injured. Hassan lost a leg. Nine months on I saw him learning how to tie the shoelaces on his new foot, and take his first nervous steps. Two young women technicians came out of the workshop to applaud, and smilingly urge him on. 'Faster, Hassan, faster.' He grinned with delight at his achievement. I asked the reporter's standby question: 'How does it feel, Hassan?' '*Alhamdulillah*,' he replied. 'Thanks be to God.'

Of all the British diaspora aid groups, the one that has probably made the biggest mark is Hand in Hand for Syria. Founded in Nottingham in response to the Syrian government's initial crackdown on protestors, it started out by distributing food parcels to families whose breadwinners had been jailed and transferring cash to those beyond the reach of this rudimentary distribution system. Its co-founders, Faddy Sahloul and Fadi Al-Dairi, left their Nottingham livelihoods – one running a fruit-packing business, the other in the finance department of an energy firm – to bring help to their countrymen.

Both men travelled widely inside Syria on their aid missions, often taking medical equipment such as portable anaesthetic and oxygen machines to makeshift clinics on the front line. Fadi Al-Dairi offered to take me in, if I wanted to go. He also told me of his anxious moments a year earlier when he took Gill Newman, wife of the Anglican Bishop of Stepney, in East London, over the border at the 'humanitarian crossing' at Atmeh, and well beyond. He had to remind himself that he had personally promised the Bishop that he would look after her.

It was Faddy Sahloul who accompanied a BBC film team to the Hand in Hand hospital at Atareb, near Aleppo, in September 2013. While they were there a school was hit by a 'napalm-like' incendiary bomb, and the TV team captured the scene of burned, gasping and traumatised children arriving at the under-equipped hospital. The Panorama film 'Saving Syria's Children' remains one of the most shocking eyewitness accounts of Syria's suffering to be aired on television. It was made all the stronger by the compelling witness of two British Muslim women doctors working as Hand in Hand volunteers. One of them, Dr Rola Hallam, a British Syrian intensive care specialist from London, complained about the role of the major foreign charities or INGOs (international non-governmental organisations). 'The bureaucracy of the big NGOs is just terrible,' she said.

Dr Hallam went on to be involved in a key study on the impact of the Syrian crisis on the aid system. It concluded that 'the formal humanitarian sector finds it extremely difficult to establish genuine, inclusive partnerships' with the estimated 600 to 700 'local' groups created since the start of the conflict.[1] 'Instead local/ diaspora groups are often seen as mere service providers, rather than genuine counterparts.'

Beyond the money they raise from their own supporters, diaspora organisations such as Hand in Hand depend on funding from bigger charities to run their programmes inside Syria, just as the big charities rely in turn on Western government money. By 2014, the British government, one of the largest official donors, had committed around £100 million to what it describes as 'undisclosed humanitarian agencies, not named for security reasons'.* Much of that was being routed via the big Western aid charities across the northern border. This means the British government had little or no direct link with Syrian NGOs and was also transferring responsibility for counter-terror security and monitoring to intermediaries.

The Hand in Hand hospital at Atareb was funded by the British medical charity Merlin but faced a crisis when Merlin became part of – was essentially taken over by – Save the Children in 2014. Save the Children gave Hand in Hand notice that it would not be extending its support for the hospital beyond the middle of the year. 'It was a painful decision to make,' one of their managers told me, 'because of course we'd all seen the Panorama documentary.'

Several reasons were advanced for pulling the plug. Save the Children's priority was more primary healthcare than front-line surgery. It was difficult to find a government backer for the project and then to monitor it properly. There was also, tellingly, Atareb's treatment of Free Syrian Army soldiers – apparently around 30 per cent of its patients – and the risk of falling foul of anti-terror legislation, even though these injured soldiers were from pro-democracy forces supported by the British and were, in any event, entitled to treatment under international humanitarian law.

'All these are rubbish excuses,' said Faddy Sahloul. 'Merlin pushed us to open a theatre for operations. Frankly, if someone comes into the hospital, and you say we're not treating you, they'll shoot!'

---

* By October 2015, the figure had doubled to £200 million.

For a time, Hand in Hand struggled to keep the hospital open by spending its own scarce funds on the monthly staff and equipment costs, but this could be only a temporary expedient. 'If we continue like this,' Faddy said, 'we'll end up either closing the hospital down or going bankrupt.' He was bitter about it. 'It's someone behind a desk saying it's got to close down.'

Atareb kept going into 2015, but then Hand in Hand's money ran out and it had to be closed. Several months on, the charity was approached again by a now desperate community in Atareb. Could nothing be done to reopen the hospital? At the time of writing, its emergency functions were being supported by a wealthy Syrian businessman, but there was no long-term solution in sight. Major Western funders were still apparently troubled by Atareb's treatment of wounded fighters.

The Overseas Development Institute report already quoted underlined the way in which the security imperative has consistently influenced the approach of Western aid-givers. There was particular reluctance to hand over cash to Syrian aid organisations. The report found that 'international aid agencies and donors tend to prefer in-kind rather than cash assistance, presumably out of fear of diversion, however impractical or risky it may be'.[2] Local NGOs pointed out that cash is often preferable to physical aid. It is easier to carry and can be spent on local rather than expensively transported goods. Insisting on sending aid over the border means that it goes 'where it can be most easily provided, not necessarily where it is most needed'.

Syrian NGOs also complained that they are given no latitude in adapting aid programmes to fast-changing circumstances on the ground. Even when local needs change, they must stick to the original plan. Charities from the Gulf are said to be more flexible, allowing local NGOs to switch aid to where it is most needed. The financial commitment of these new players from the Arab world is growing, but is yet to be properly quantified by the Western aid system. 'We had a conference the other day about "emerging actors",' a charity executive in the region told me. 'Some of these organisations have been around for as long as we have – except we don't know anything about them.'

At the end of his weekend mission to Syria, Dr Mounir Hakimi of Syria Relief returned to the border town of Reyhanli at nightfall on Monday. It was as well he had taken his surgical scrubs with him. His plan to devote his time there to routine administration was overtaken by the emergency of Saturday morning's air attack on the town of Maarat Masreen.

In my hotel room I had by now watched one of those fearful videos shot by opposition activists and swiftly uploaded onto the internet. To shocked exclamations of '*Allah o Akbar*' ('God is Great'), a camera phone walked the main street filming shattered shops, desperate rescue efforts, the dead and the injured.

Dr Hakimi filled in more of the detail. The air strike happened around 9am on Saturday, just as shops opened after the Muslim weekend. There had been three bombs, the second and third dropped to catch rescuers and witnesses out in the open. Maarat Masreen was regularly targeted like this. It had been one of the first communities to stage anti-government street protests in 2011. 'The people were resistant,' was how Mounir put it.

Twenty-five died in the attack and 15 were injured. Five of them were so badly wounded that they had to be transferred straight over the border to better-equipped Turkish hospitals. The rest were brought to Bab al-Hawa, the charity hospital opened and run by Syrian diaspora groups and backed by the big aid agencies.

There were two boys in theatre when the doctor from Manchester arrived. One, aged 13, had a piece of shrapnel lodged in his pelvis ('That big,' the doctor said, measuring 3 or 4 inches between thumb and forefinger) which had also damaged his penis ('Sorry about that'). The other boy was seven and had also been hit by shrapnel. They had already removed his spleen and his liver was damaged. He was so critically injured that he too was sent on to Turkey. 'Will he be OK?' I asked. 'I hope so,' said Mounir. 'Will he survive?' 'I hope so.'

Dr Hakimi was asked to operate on a third boy. A piece of shrapnel had smashed into his leg. This was a 'comminuted' fracture – the bone had been splintered to pulp. He was 11. The doctor managed to pin and realign the bone, but was seriously worried about infection. There was a lot of skin loss, and part of the bone was still uncovered. It would take months to heal, even if things went well. The boy was sent home the next day.

'In the UK, he'd be referred to a plastic surgeon,' said Dr Hakimi, 'and of course the standard of community care there is so much better.' Even if the wound healed, the worry was that he would end up with one leg shorter than the other, and a permanent limp.

As we drove back to Antakia that night, I asked Mounir what was next in his diary. He said he would be in Paris later in the week where he was to speak to French donors to the hospital. He had two operations scheduled at the Royal Bolton Hospital on Friday and was teaching on an orthopaedic course on Saturday. There was a trip to London planned the following week for more fundraising and a lecture at the Royal College of Surgeons on war surgery.

Sunday at least would be set aside for the family. He had a boy aged seven and a girl of five. Thoughts of them brought back images of those shattered young lives at Bab al-Hawa. The number and severity of the injuries had got to everyone at the hospital, he said.

'Our staff were very distressed. It keeps happening like this. The mood was really down.'

The Syrian civil war has presented an overwhelming challenge to the humanitarian aid world. The scale of the suffering numbs the senses. By late 2015, after four and a half years of conflict, the death toll exceeded 250,000. According to opposition monitors, the number of children killed, including those shot by snipers, was more than 12,000. Four million Syrians had fled to neighbouring countries, a sixth of the population, and most of those who stayed behind were in need of assistance, because they had been either displaced by the war or trapped by it. 'It's the worst crisis I never wanted to see,' one aid manager told me.

Access for foreign relief workers over the border from Turkey was risky enough to begin with, and then virtually extinguished in 2013 by the advances of Islamic State. Some of the big humanitarian agencies built up their own Syrian staff networks across the border, linking up with local community groups to extend their reach. They also relied heavily on Syrian start-ups from the diaspora. 'The amateurs have proved more effective than the professionals' was how one senior United Nations official put it to me.

Even those agencies determined to be on the ground, and in the thick of it, had their ambitions severely checked by the risk of kidnap and the ferocity of the conflict. Médecins Sans Frontières (MSF) – French in origin, international in character – struggled to sustain its vision of medical intervention without political confinement, truly Doctors Without Borders. It was one of their own experts who laid out the limitations on Western aid agency operations in Syria.

'In the short term,' wrote Fabrice Weissman, a former MSF country director now with the agency's Paris think tank, in 2013, 'the scaling up of aid can only come from Syrian networks of doctors, businessmen, local coordination committees, justice courts, and armed groups, amongst others …'³ He singled out the effectiveness of the diaspora groups, including a French Syrian organisation called the Union of Syrian Doctors that had 'certainly contributed much more to increasing access to medical services than all of the MSF sections combined'. He concluded that the 'only realistic way to increase aid in the rebel zones today is to support Syrian diaspora networks, even if this results in some cases in aid diversion and the strengthening of political networks'.

In the first phases of the Syria conflict, MSF succeeded in creating its own network of hospitals and health posts in opposition-held territory. This was makeshift medicine at its most inventive. Private houses, sometimes neighbouring properties, were taken over and converted into field hospitals. For reasons of safety, one of their hospitals was set up first in a cave before it was moved into a chicken farm.

Existing medical facilities had to be avoided because they were deliberately targeted by the Damascus regime. 'My enemy's doctor is my enemy' was the Syrian government's perverted and ruthlessly applied principle. Six hundred medical personnel are reported to have been killed in the conflict to December 2014. A young Syrian surgeon working for MSF in Aleppo was abducted in 2013, and later found executed. 'Being there, but at what cost?' was the question posed by a senior MSF manager.

The agency's international presence across the border exceeded that of any other Western body. By the end of 2013 it had seven projects strung out in the north and west of the country, deploying some 70 expatriate medics. There was also indirect support for scores of locally run hospitals and medical posts. This was the way MSF wanted to operate – bringing the best of Western medicine to the world's ugliest tragedies; monitoring standards and finances directly, not remotely; and bearing witness to the political realities behind the suffering. In August 2013, it was MSF that provided some of the evidence that the Syrian government was using chemical weapons against its own people – the famous red line that the West drew and the Syrian regime crossed with impunity.

Maintaining a presence in the Syrian interior involved constant negotiation between MSF managers and rebel groups. With the forces of Islamic State pushing westwards from the Iraq frontier, what had first been a familiar political challenge in a war zone now became knife-edge, life-and-death diplomacy. Sometimes the agency benefited from being the only foreign group in the area and managed to establish a level of wary trust with local Islamic State leaders.

'Remember, we were in there for 18 months,' a senior MSF staffer told me. 'There was some tension, but we were working with their doctors, and we found they kept their word. They weren't worried about our being Westerners, being aligned in that way. What they were really worried about was spies. So that's the promise we have to make, that we are not spies. I say to them, "I'm honest," and they have to trust me as well. "Allah knows what's in my heart, and that I'm telling the truth."'

Then, on 2 January 2014, Syria suddenly changed for MSF. A five-strong MSF team was taken hostage from living quarters close to their hospital in Idlib, north-west Syria.

The team comprised a Belgian, a Dane, a Peruvian, a Swede and a Swiss. Two of them were released after three months, the remaining three after another month of captivity. Like governments in the West and other aid agencies, MSF says nothing for public consumption about hostage negotiations or ransom payments. The team's release in Syria came at around the time when other Europeans were being freed, several of them journalists, and before the serial murders of American and British hostages whose governments do not, on principle, pay ransoms.

The upshot of the kidnapping for MSF was the abrupt withdrawal of their international teams from Syria and the adoption of 'remote management', something they try to avoid. Instead of highly qualified foreigners attending directly to patients and standing at the shoulder of local colleagues, they sit instead in offices in Turkey, even in Europe, and advise them by Skype and by telephone.

A month before the kidnapping, Jérôme Oberreit, Secretary General of MSF International, underlined just how undesirable such an outcome would be. In a lecture at the Overseas Development Institute in London, he stressed that MSF was not a donor organisation but a direct implementer. It believed that, in the midst of conflict, international staff brought a specific added value. 'Blind work', he said, was too much of a compromise.

In the field, I was told that remote management was simply 'not in MSF's DNA'. Even after the kidnapping, some senior MSF field workers were eager to get back. 'If I had the word of the ones I was dealing with, I'd walk into Syria tomorrow,' said the senior staffer quoted earlier. 'We don't want to lose our surgical capacity. We do believe in the double mandate – emergency medical intervention and *témoignage* [bearing witness].'

The larger reality in Syria is that emboldened Islamic State jihadists present an overwhelming challenge to the bravest of international humanitarian initiatives. MSF was still running seven of its own medical units in rebel-held Syria, ranging from a burns unit to a full hospital, and supported more than 100 local Syrian facilities with cash and medical kit, but the direct engagement of Western aid workers in this phase of the war on terror was in retreat by 2014. 'It's not surgical gloves on the ground,' another senior MSF staffer told me, 'but it's the best we can do.'

For MSF, the gravest impact of the crisis has been in areas under direct Islamic State control. 'What we talk about – our branding – is that we go where other people don't,' said the MSF staffer. 'That's no longer the case in Syria.' As a direct consequence of the 2014 abductions and continued Islamic State threats directed against aid workers, the agency has no access at all to the estimated 3.2 million Syrian civilians in territory occupied by the jihadists. 'The world has changed,' the MSF staffer told me. 'The white saviour complex is finished.'

The scale of human need in Syria can be gauged from the dimensions of another aid agency's cross-border operation. By 2014, Mercy Corps, an impressive American non-profit founded in response to the Cambodian emergency 35 years ago, was disbursing around $90 million a year in aid through its offices in eastern Turkey. Its funds come mainly from the big Western donors – the US government, the British government and the European Union. Mercy Corps was on the ground in Turkey in 2012, within a year of the civil conflict in Syria beginning to escalate.

The agency employs a staff of over 200 – some 150 Syrians on front-line work, 50 Turks and 20 international staff concentrating on back-office operational and financial management. They are Pakistanis, Indians, Americans and Britons. Their task is a big one – to help feed the people of northern Syria, many of them already refugees in their own country, and to make sure that hunger alone will not be the factor that drives them over the border into Turkey.

Mercy Corps was reaching 1.2 million people when I travelled to eastern Turkey in 2014. They were distributing 400,000 food baskets a month. This was much more than a charitable contribution to a better diet; it was intended to supply families with the basics they needed until the next food basket. A 'basket' comprised a sack of rice; boxes of pasta and lentils; and tins of sardines. Each week

Mercy Corps was also transporting an astonishing 900 tons of flour across the border to 70 small bakeries in and around the shattered city of Aleppo.

Bread is fundamental to Syrian existence, as I was reminded time and time again. Without it, people are inclined to give up and leave. Big bakeries and flour mills, which had often been in public ownership in peacetime, soon fell under the control of combatants in the civil war. They were then used to feed fighters and loyalists or forced to close down and feed no one at all. 'If you control bread supplies, you control the population,' said Rae McGrath, the Mercy Corps area director for northern Syria. So the agency decided to try to fix this state of affairs for the poorest people around Aleppo. 'We set out deliberately to manipulate the price so that the most vulnerable can still afford to buy their bread,' he said.

Running a supply operation of this magnitude in the world's worst civil war requires strong nerves and intricate planning. For Mercy Corps, the process begins with twice-daily security reports that analyse routes and road conditions. To get relief supplies through to the smashed city of Aleppo, for example, it became necessary first to cross-load them into smaller vehicles to negotiate the rubble-strewn back streets, and then to know where the government snipers were that day. Staff safety is paramount.

Mercy Corps has 45 drivers responsible for aid supplies and personnel travel. They are specially trained in conflict driving, including how to deal with multiple roadblocks. They have what was described to me as 'proper first aid', which involves instruction on how to use a trauma kit.

'You look at a lot of organisations and at their drivers and guards,' said Rae. 'Their managers don't really know who they are. But they're very important. You rely on them to protect you and keep you safe. Take the drivers. They travel the roads, and they see what's happening. They talk to fellow drivers. When you're in some meeting or other, they're outside – talking, observing and learning. As for the guards, they're the ones who are going to keep you alive, so of course you take them seriously. Our drivers are some of the best trained in the world, and that's no exaggeration.'

Rae McGrath is himself very well qualified for the tasks facing humanitarian aid workers in an era of proliferating conflict. After 18 years as an engineer in the British army, he moved to the NGO world and founded the Mines Advisory Group, which was soon engaged in mine clearance in Afghanistan and Cambodia. It was Rae who helped persuade Princess Diana to get involved in the landmines cause, and it was his organisation which earned a share of the 1997 Nobel Peace Prize for the campaign to ban these weapons. Rae delivered the Nobel acceptance speech in Oslo.

He had no interest in climbing higher up the greasy pole as a charity boss, and returned to fieldwork in the 2004 Asian tsunami. For four years he was a disaster response manager with Save the Children and in 2013 joined Mercy Corps, where he brought a lifetime of experience to bear in the worst conflict of the era. Rae's knowledge of inhumane weaponry gained as an army engineer and through his Mines Advisory Group brought our discussion round to the Syrian government's use of barrel bombs, the horrific munitions rolled out of helicopters on rebel-held residential districts in the country's towns and cities.

It is rare, Rae said, for conventional bombing to lead to a building's total collapse, so it is best for civilians under attack to stay indoors or in shelters. Barrel bombs are different. In the narrow streets of an ancient city such as Aleppo, these weapons often bring a building down completely. 'Leaving aside the high level of deaths, people simply cannot patch up their houses again after they have been demolished in this way.'

What is worse is the way the Syrians make these bombs. Mixed in with 1,000 kilograms or so of explosives are lengths of 'rebar', the fluted steel rods used to reinforce concrete and encountered in clanking piles on building sites. These rods are chopped into 4- to 6-inch pieces and then loaded in with the high explosive. As an economy measure and as further cruel refinement, 'rebars' are often reclaimed from demolished buildings, and have lumps of rotten old concrete still stuck to them.

'They are the sort of thing that just tears chunks out of people,' said Rae. 'Those injured by them will cling on for a while, but they tend to die in three or four days anyway. This is the quite deliberate use of a terror weapon. This is a crime in many, many ways, even in a war like this.'

As Rae spoke about the barrel bombing in Syria, I thought of Guernica, the attack by German and Italian aircraft on the Basque town during the Spanish civil war. This was the first large-scale 'terror bombing' of civilians, and it foreshadowed the aerial excesses of the Second World War. Guernica lives on in infamy. Such is the Western world's contemporary sense of detachment from inhumanity occurring beyond its borders that Syria's barrel bombs may soon barely be recalled.

In addition to the physical dangers facing Mercy Corps staff operating over the Syrian border, for a time the agency also ran a political risk. Almost alone among the cross-border operators, Mercy Corps succeeded in mounting a parallel aid programme from the capital Damascus. Syrians in government-held or disputed territory were also suffering high levels of distress, and they were sometimes just as difficult to reach.

The humanitarian answer was simple – aid-givers should be free to help civilians in need, wherever they were, on whichever side of the border. Damascus took the opposite view. To the extent it troubled at all about the suffering of its own people, the Syrian government declared that aid across its frontiers supported its enemies and infringed its sovereignty, and was therefore illegal. It had to cease.

For more than a year, Mercy Corps got away with this double life. They kept the lowest possible profile on their cross-border operation. There was certainly none of the national and international branding that accompanies modern aid-giving. Damascus surely knew what was happening, Mercy Corps reasoned, and perhaps the human need would be tacitly acknowledged.

Not a hope. In April 2014 the Syrian government insisted that Mercy Corps follow the rules, and stop helping the enemy. The agency responded by closing down its Damascus programme. The decision was distressing, but clear-cut. Mercy Corps had been assisting some 350,000 Syrians on the government side, but was reaching a number several times greater across the Turkish border.

On both sides of the conflict, the Syria crisis has presented aid-givers with a series of major obstacles. Principal among them are security and access. Only the boldest of the agencies are able to work effectively across the lines, and in that they rely almost entirely on Syrian aid workers to take the physical risks. That much is recognised by the big agencies, but not always by their official funders for whom counter-terror strategy is the priority.

The unyielding brutality of Islamic State has barred inter-national aid workers – the 'white saviours' of past decades – from reaching most of Syria's most vulnerable people. Contacts continue, but the distrust is profound. No reassurances as to safe conduct or aid monitoring are offered by the jihadists. After 15 or more years of the war on terror, all Westerners are suspect. There is no longer a humanitarian exception. The long war in Afghanistan has seen to that.

CHAPTER 2

DEVELOPMENT
AT GUNPOINT

Lashkar Gah, Afghanistan, November 2013

I arrived outside the big allied base in Lashkar Gah in a white Toyota Land Cruiser flying the flag of Médecins Sans Frontières. After driving for a mile or so around the perimeter wall I got out and walked towards the entrance. Four British soldiers in camouflage battle kit slipped swiftly out of the base and took up defensive positions. Wrong entrance.

The pedestrian gate was half a mile further on and reached down a long sandbagged walkway. The sentries had my name at the desk. 'What are you doing here, then?' one of the soldiers asked. I told him. 'Why don't you write about the plight of the 2nd Royal Anglians?'

Main Operating Base, Lashkar Gah, was the home of the provincial reconstruction team (PRT) for Helmand, a coalition force in its own right. There were PRTs throughout Afghanistan during the years of the Western war. Their composition mirrored the make-up of the West's armies on the ground, and like the military they were now packing up and going home.

For ten years the PRTs spent big money in Afghanistan. The West's official aid bodies, led by the United States Agency for

International Development (USAID) and Britain's Department for International Development (DFID), added millions more on their own accounts. In the name of WHAM – Winning Hearts and Minds – the military had their own large aid budgets. Their money was spent on projects close to army bases – 'force protection' – or on quick impact projects (QIPS) intended to impress the locals.

British unit commanders were given a monthly sum of £40,000, which they forfeited if they did not spend.[1] The parallel American system was likened to an ATM machine that never ran out of cash. US officers had $100,000 a month and an army handbook to help them spend it entitled *Commander's Guide to Money as a Weapons System*. They were told that aid was a 'non-lethal weapon' to be used to 'win the hearts and minds of the indigenous population to facilitate defeating the insurgents'.[2] The US commander, General David Petraeus, declared money 'my most important ammunition in this war'.

The PRTs needed good relations with the private aid agencies. The latter were in the field and much closer to the Afghan people, and many of them took PRT money to get their job done. Some did not, on principle. Others chose carefully in which provinces and in what circumstances they would take it. Even then, a fateful confusion was created between Western military boots on the ground and Western aid workers. For independent humanitarianism, this confusion would prove to be the Afghan war's most lasting and costly legacy.

In the years after 9/11 and the overthrow of the Taliban, there was a mighty Western collaboration to rebuild and to try to refashion Afghanistan. Every player of consequence in the overseas aid world wanted a hand in the game. Hard and fast distinctions between humanitarian endeavour on the one hand and the realisation of political and military objectives on the other proved hard, if not impossible, to maintain.

Some aid agencies kept their distance from the military, others did not; the Afghans themselves, whatever their view of foreign intervention, could hardly be expected to separate out Western charity in all its shades from Western government aid channelled through the military, through the big contractors, through international organisations, or through the charities themselves. The provincial reconstruction teams, often but not always civilian-led, were embedded with the military and represented the toughest affront to the notion of aid independence.

PRTs 'blur the distinction between humanitarian and military actors', said Save the Children in a 2004 report: 'the very presence of a PRT can instil or reinforce a perception that aid workers are "agents" of the military'.[3] Oxfam took up the theme in a joint agency briefing to NATO in 2010. It warned of an increasing number of attacks on aid workers, and added: 'If urgent efforts are not made to re-establish the civil–military distinction in Afghanistan, the operational reach of expert humanitarianism and development agencies may be even further reduced.'[4]

Once through the pedestrian gate and on the base in Lashkar Gah, I saw the Union Jack at half mast. It was for the 446th member of the British armed forces to die in Afghanistan. His Warrior had been rammed by a suicide car bomber. I was escorted past rows of other armoured vehicles, Foxhounds and Mastiffs, to the fast-emptying offices of the PRT. Framed photographs of the British and Danish queens, the President of the United States and the President of Estonia hung in the Portakabin lobby to mark the international composition of Helmand's military and civilian aid coalition. Those portraits too would soon be packed up and flown home.

British officials were blunt in their justification for the big sums they had spent in Helmand. These were the 'badlands of the south' where the Taliban insurgency was at its worst. 'We did it because we had boots on the ground,' one British official told me. His colleague spoke of the need for 'increasing government legitimacy' by improving local services and for tackling the heroin trade by encouraging Helmand's farmers to cultivate 'pomegranates not poppies'.

What troubled some of the humanitarians was that British aid money was supposed to be spent on the poorest people in the world. 'Eliminating World Poverty' was the Department for International Development's founding objective when it was prised from the Foreign Office in 1997. For a time, DFID did set its face against aid motives beyond that of poverty reduction. Then al-Qaeda in its Afghan caves and the attacks of 9/11 led to the progressive undermining of that principle. DFID became a welcome partner with the Foreign Office and the Ministry of Defence around the policy table in Whitehall. What it brought to the meeting was a sizeable and rising budget. For its critics, the British aid programme had been captured by Britain's national security interests.

'In strictly development terms,' said a former DFID official who had followed the British aid effort in Afghanistan for a decade or more, 'there was no justification for choosing Helmand. It was one of the richest provinces in Afghanistan. DFID got lost in terms of the development agenda. There was nothing really about poverty reduction. Everything was focused on the "stabilisation agenda".'

Oxfam broadened the charge against British and other Western aid programmes in the age of terror. 'Skewed aid policies and practices threaten to undermine a decade of government donors' international commitments to effective, needs-focused international aid,' said a report of theirs in 2011.[5] Disproportionate sums were going to the war-on-terror countries. In Afghanistan, Oxfam found that more than 70 per cent of official aid was being spent either in the capital Kabul or in just three of the country's 34 provinces. They were not the poorest; they were the ones at the centre of the West's counter-insurgency operations: Helmand, Kandahar and Herat.

As the provincial reconstruction teams prepared to follow their uniformed compatriots out of Afghanistan, other development principles were being jeopardised. Aid programmes are supposed to be 'sustainable'. They were certainly not supposed to follow a military timetable of advance and retreat. Unsurprisingly, the PRTs found that other agencies were reluctant to take over their projects. The United Nations was resistant and private aid organisations turned them down flat because of the implications for the safety of their staff. 'NGOs just do not want to take on an anti-insurgency role,' I was told by one of their senior managers in Kabul.

The British-led PRT tried hard, for instance, to persuade Save the Children to come and work on education in Helmand. Save the Children declined.

Western governments and the military could not be blamed alone for blurring the lines between counter-insurgency operations and civilian aid. The NGOs did much on their own account to promote close relations with coalition forces. It was not only that most of them depended on government money to go to work in the first place. It was not even that they had to acknowledge the reality of the Western occupation on the ground. They had gone much further than that by issuing their own rousing call to arms to NATO.

In June 2003, 18 months after the fall of Kabul, 85 overseas humanitarian organisations put their name to 'Afghanistan: A Call for Security'. Looked at now after a further ten years of costly and wearisome warfare, it makes for extraordinary reading.

This gung-ho document demanded that NATO be given a 'robust stabilisation mandate in Afghanistan'. It said that international forces should expand 'to key locations and major transport routes outside Kabul'. Training for Afghan security forces 'must be accelerated'. The newly established PRTs were not enough, as they 'lack[ed] the resources to really address the security threats posed by warlords and other armed spoilers'. NATO's expansion beyond Kabul to the rest of the country would make sure that 'democracy can flourish' and 'improve the prospect for peace and stability for the Afghan people and the world'.

All the big American non-profits signed up to the call to arms, as did the large British charities. Signatories extended beyond the relief and development agencies. Even the very liberal-minded Human Rights Watch was there. There was a heavy Anglophone bias to the group, and there were some important agencies that did not sign up, as we shall see.

From the very beginning of the Afghan war, the Western allies made it plain that they were going to fight it on the humanitarian as well as the military front. As soon as the bombing began in October 2001, the United States started dropping tens of thousands of emergency ration packs along with propaganda leaflets to make sure, in the words of President George W. Bush, that 'the oppressed people of Afghanistan know the generosity of America and our allies'.

Western leaders intended to occupy the humanitarian space in Afghanistan as surely as they occupied the political and military ground. In a speech leading up to Britain's participation in the war, Prime Minister Tony Blair spoke of the need 'to build a humanitarian coalition to deal with the humanitarian crisis in that region' in the same way they had built their political and military alliance in the weeks after 9/11.

Colin Powell, the US Secretary of State, laid out the same vision in more soldierly terms, as befitted a retired general. 'Just as surely as our diplomats and military, American NGOs are out there serving and sacrificing on the front line of freedom,' he told a meeting of aid agency bosses in October 2001. He went on: 'NGOs are such a force multiplier for us, such an important part of our combat team.' This observation was to haunt the US NGOs for the rest of the war. Yes, they needed US government money, and yes, they needed a relationship with the US military in the world's top trouble spots. But 'force multiplier'? 'Part of our combat team'? Was that how America's enemies were to view the private US aid agencies? And what of the British NGOs and those from other coalition countries? Were they also to be seen as 'force multipliers'?

NATO was every bit as clumsy. In March 2010, the Secretary General, Anders Fogh Rasmussen, made a speech about how the West should respond to new crises around the world. His conclusions were based, he said, on the alliance's experience of Afghanistan. There needed to be better civil–military relations, and he wanted 'a frank and open dialogue' with the NGOs. The military was no longer the complete answer, only part of it, he said. He ended with this flourish: 'Hard power is of little use if it cannot be combined with soft power.'

Here was another challenge to independent humanitarianism. NGOs were really not interested in – or surely *should not* be interested in – power of any sort, either hard or soft. Worse than that, how were the Western world's enemies supposed to see humanitarian aid workers, unarmed and often still unprotected, when they were publicly identified not as the expression of a principled humanitarian tradition but as an extension of Western power?

On the ground in Afghanistan, there was the same dangerous confusion. As often as not it involved the provincial reconstruction teams, the coalition's aid-givers with links to private agencies in the field. The Afghanistan director of one international charity told me of the occasions when PRT officials would arrive at his offices in provincial towns to talk about budgets or progress on a favoured aid project. They would be wearing helmets and body armour, quite likely accompanied by troops, and would emerge from the back of a roaring armoured vehicle. What were the locals to think of that – and of the foreign charities in their midst?

Aid for intelligence-gathering was another contentious area. One well-researched report spoke of a scheme to distribute blankets to the disabled where the blankets had telephone numbers printed on them for locals to ring if they had information on al-Qaeda. 'That really put those who had received the blankets in danger,' the report writers were told.[6] In another blanket distribution, this time to displaced people, a PRT official was quoted as saying: 'The more they help us find the bad guys, the more good stuff they'll get.'[7]

There was also the question of deploying white vehicles, which by custom are associated with civilian aid-givers, but in Afghanistan could provide a usefully low profile for the military. Agreement was reached that coalition forces would distinguish their vehicles as military, although it was never specified exactly how. Researchers spoke to one witness who had watched Afghan workers at a coalition base in Kabul applying a single khaki stripe to the sides of otherwise white vehicles.[8]

Where to draw the line between military and civilian efforts in Afghanistan exercised the military as much as the civilians. This was a new world for them, too, in which the politicians at home wanted a 'joined-up' approach to delivering aid and a military victory at the same time. The two sides spoke different languages, but had to reach a common understanding. The process had been initiated in the Balkans in the 1990s, where it was eloquently documented by the American writer David Rieff. It was at the end of the Kosovo war that Rieff came across a report to the US military in which one section was headed 'Does Anyone Here Speak Civilian?'[9]

American NGOs took the lead in trying to define the relationship with the military. Their representatives started negotiating formal guidelines with the Department of Defense in 2005. The process took two years and was not easy for either side. Responding at one point to NGO demands about protecting civilians in war zones, an exasperated US army officer exclaimed: 'We hear you when you say "Stay in your lane," but we don't know what our lane is any more.'[10]

Joel Charny, Vice President of InterAction, the Washington body that represents American NGOs, led on these discussions and found it very hard to get humanitarian independence recognised. 'The military kept saying to us, "We're all part of the same fight." When we pushed back at that, they questioned our patriotism. This was almost un-American.' He characterised the attitude of the military as: 'We're the biggest institution in the world, and we'll just go out there and do what the hell we want.'

It was nevertheless essential to reach an understanding. 'We've got to be talking to the military,' Charny said, and, in an echo of Colin Powell's notorious observation already quoted, added: 'Hello military, don't call us "force multipliers", please.'

Mr Charny was as sharp a critic of the NGOs he represents as he was of the military. By custom and practice through the Cold War, US non-profits saw eye to eye with their government's view of the world far more consistently than did their European counterparts. In Charny's view, too much of that common purpose had been sustained into the war on terror, and with it a disinclination to stand up for independent humanitarianism.

'NGOs are just not seized of these issues,' he told a meeting in London in 2013 to launch a report on civil–military coordination. 'People at the top of NGOs are not properly engaged.' Similar criticism could be levelled at the big British NGOs. In the past, they may have displayed a more rigorous independence from their government than the American non-profits, but in the wars of the new century they have been prepared to forfeit some of that independence.

Money is likely to be at the root of this. The big US NGOs have always depended substantially on government funds, but British NGOs are catching up fast. InterAction gave them all this piece of advice: 'NGO leaders need to ask themselves hard questions about whether the drive for ever-expanding budgets has undermined their ability to adhere to humanitarian principles, and what the costs of a pragmatic approach may be.'[11]

It was with the help of Médecins Sans Frontières – which takes no money at all from belligerents in Afghanistan or in any other conflicts – that I was able to visit Lashkar Gah. I flew one morning from Kabul on a flight that MSF operates with the International Committee of the Red Cross. Our call sign was 'Red One', and there were big red crosses and the initials ICRC on the wings and fuselage. Of all the foreign relief agencies at work in Afghanistan in the fearful times at the end of the Western war, it was the ICRC and MSF that identified themselves most openly. Flags flew and logos were flourished. 'We would prefer to be targeted for who we are,' the MSF country representative in Kabul coolly told me, 'rather than because we were thought to be someone else.'

Benoit De Gryse, Belgian and in his thirties, had to be cool to manage an ambitious front-line agency in one of the world's most enduring conflicts. He told me the story of MSF's latest project, an 80-bed maternity hospital in Khost, on Afghanistan's eastern border with Pakistan. Khost is the focus of cross-border operations by the Haqqani network, named after a Taliban leader who was once a favoured jihadist ally of the United States and later became a much-feared enemy.

The MSF hospital in Khost was due to open in March 2012. Six weeks before the opening, two small bombs exploded at the front gate. The incident was put down to a rival health establishment's resentment over the free service that MSF offered. This was Afghanistan, after all, where bombs often do the talking. No one was hurt and MSF pressed on. A month after the opening, it got worse. A bomb went off in a lavatory inside the hospital and blew it apart. Seven people were hurt. The hospital was closed.

The story of Khost hospital, though, had only just begun. In August, MSF took the remarkable step of convening its own tribal assembly to help them decide what to do next. One of the wards was cleared, and 80 bearded elders in black turbans sat down on the concrete floor. Benoit flew in from Kabul; his boss flew in from Brussels. As Westerners unused to sitting cross-legged on the floor, they were given a low bench to sit on instead.

Top of the agenda was the bombs. The elders expressed their regret, and explained that they lacked control over some of these 'bad' elements, particularly in the towns. Didn't you have the same problems in the West, they asked? Besides, they were only small bombs, and this *was* Afghanistan. The maternity service was still very much needed and MSF was urged to reopen. The elders would do their utmost to see that there was no more trouble. A document was drawn up and signed: 80 signatures with 80 thumb prints, the combination apparently lending it particular force.

MSF announced that it would reopen Khost hospital in December 2012. Still the drama was not over. On 10 October, another small bomb was planted at another of the gates. What now? MSF decided to hold its nerve, and reopened on schedule. Khost maternity hospital was recording 1,100 admissions and conducting 1,000 deliveries along with 45 surgical operations every month in 2015.

As this book went to press, I checked again on the story of Khost hospital. There had been another bomb – a small one left at the perimeter wall and attributed once again to rival medical interests in the town. No one was hurt and it did not shift MSF's resolve. 'The problem has not gone away,' I was told, 'but we're better equipped to deal with it because we have such strong support from the community.'

The MSF team I joined in Lashkar Gah was running the agency's biggest single project anywhere in the world. This was Helmand's main hospital and one of only two referral hospitals in the whole of southern Afghanistan. (The other was run by the ICRC in Kandahar.) It employed a staff of more than 600. There were 14 international staff on duty when I stayed there.

Those who imagine that foreign aid is still dispensed by white people saving the world need to adjust their vision. The largest grouping among the MSF expatriates in Lashkar Gah when I stayed there was African. The head of the project and the medical team leader were both Africans (from the Democratic Republic of Congo), and so were the nursing director (from Congo-Brazzaville) and the midwifery supervisor (from South Sudan). The fifth African was a nursing coordinator from Zimbabwe. 'I am quite happy and proud to be part of this story,' he said.

What their African nations had in common with Afghanistan was trouble, sometimes catastrophic trouble. All of them had begun by helping their own people in times of crisis – some as junior employees of foreign aid organisations – and had then moved on to bring their experience to bear in other emergencies. Sitting with them in the team dining room at the end of the working day, I heard stories of the 'Camp of Death' and the 'Triangle of Death' in eastern Congo – 'We recruited someone just to count the bodies'; of emergency evacuations in Somalia; and of minefields right outside hospitals in South Sudan. 'As Africans, our coping mechanisms are very good,' said Germain Lobango, the Congolese project head, in a neat use of development jargon.

'I used to think that Afghan people just wanted to kill everyone,' Emma Zoba, the nursing director, told me. She had begun her career with a French charity in Congo-Brazzaville during fighting there in the late 1990s. 'Now everyone I work with here is good; they are my friends. We have a very big welcome here.' After a moment's pause, she added this reflection on the troubling threat posed by suicide bombers: 'What I fear is that people can have a bomb and explode themselves.'

MSF operates a 'no roads' policy in Helmand, limiting car journeys to the town and then only for essential travel. For most of the expatriates, this means just two journeys a day, each of about a mile – one in the morning from their residential compound to the hospital and the other back home in the evening. Everyone squeezes into a three-vehicle convoy of Land Cruisers, with an oversized MSF pennant flying from each of the radio aerials. In the era of roadside bombs, the route taken each morning is varied deliberately.

Like a lot of other agencies, MSF first went to work in Afghanistan during the Soviet war of the 1980s. They brought medical relief across the border from Pakistan into areas under the control of the West's then allies, the jihadists fighting a modernising communist regime in Kabul. After 9/11 and the Western coalition's overthrow of the Taliban (the latest incarnation of the jihadist movement the West had fostered), MSF restarted operations in a new Afghanistan under Western domination. They sought – as they always seek – to remain independent of competing political forces and scrupulously neutral in the conflict.

When the 85 NGOs came together in June 2003 to issue their stirring call for NATO to expand military operations throughout the country, MSF's signature was absent. The ICRC does not sign such documents. Nor do several other French NGOs.

As it turned out, their missing signature did MSF little good. Security beyond Kabul was deteriorating and MSF was working in some of these tough areas. In late 2003, the agency announced that it was pulling out of a refugee camp near Kandahar where it had been caring for thousands of Afghans. The reason was the increasing number of attacks on aid workers, which they condemned. But they did not leave the matter there.

MSF complained in a press statement issued on 4 December 2003 that the 'Call for Security' from the aid agencies to NATO 'may also have contributed to the erosion of the image of NGOs as independent and neutral actors'. MSF emphasised that its own call was 'NOT for the Coalition Forces, NATO or the Government to scale up military intervention to provide security for our workers'. Instead, the call was for all parties 'to respect the neutrality and impartiality of humanitarian workers'.

Worse was to follow. In June 2004, exactly a year after the NGOs called for NATO's expansion, five MSF workers travelling in north-west Afghanistan – national and international staff – were stopped, shot and killed by the roadside. The Taliban claimed responsibility. 'Organisations like Médecins Sans Frontières work for American interests and are therefore targets for us,' a spokesman was quoted as saying. Despite the claim, MSF had credible evidence that government security personnel were complicit in the murders. In any event, no action was taken against the perpetrators, which only added insult to the dreadful injury.

MSF now pulled out of the country altogether. At a press conference in Kabul in July 2004, they expressed outrage at the accusation that they were working for American interests in Afghanistan. This charge was 'particularly unjustified as MSF honours the separation of aid from political motives as a founding principle'. They returned to what they saw as the now fatal confusion over

43

the motives and objectives of humanitarian aid. 'MSF denounces the coalition's attempts to co-opt humanitarian aid and use it to "win hearts and minds",' they said. 'By doing so, providing aid is no longer seen as an impartial and neutral act, endangering the lives of humanitarian volunteers and jeopardising the aid to people in need.'

Divisions within the aid world on matters of principle had never been starker. Western humanitarian workers viewed their role and purpose in distinctly different ways. In one corner were the Anglophones, comprising most of the big US and UK agencies. In the other were the Francophones, led by the ICRC, the longest-established of humanitarian actors, and MSF, a relative newcomer. It was the war on terror that sharpened this division, and Afghanistan that defined it.

MSF was absent from Afghanistan for five years. When it returned in 2009, it came back with a renewed will and vigour. The fighting had intensified, security had worsened, and civilian needs had increased dramatically. In offering its services again, MSF needed to impress. It would deliberately take on large and difficult projects. It would continue to take no funding from government sources, spending only its own money from private donations. Its 2014 Afghanistan budget alone was €25 million. It would stick to its humanitarian principles, including on neutrality, and negotiate with both sides to the conflict.

In the middle of a war claiming heavy American and British casualties, Lashkar Gah probably presented the biggest challenge of all. To make sure that it would be able to run the principal hospital in Afghanistan's most violent province, MSF arranged meetings in Washington with the State Department and in Florida with US Central Command. There were meetings in the Gulf with Taliban representatives, and with the British at the Ministry of Defence in London and at the embassy in Kabul.

The main purpose of these meetings was to keep armed men out of Lashkar Gah and other MSF hospitals. There would be a strict 'no weapons' policy. MSF also needed assurances that patients were not to be arrested by security forces during treatment nor interrogated until a doctor had declared them medically fit. The negotiations seemed to pay off. 'This is a civilian hospital,' said an appreciative patient frightened of going to his own district hospital because it was staffed by military doctors. 'I don't see any weapons here. That means you don't have any problems with the opposition or the international forces.'[12]

Regular contact was maintained at local level with 'the other side'. MSF managers in Lashkar Gah spoke to representatives of a shadow Taliban administration, including its shadow Minister of Health. Unlike most jihadist movements, the Taliban had experience of both exercising state power and being thrown out of it. Navigating their way through the who's who of an insurgency was never easy. 'There are 12 different commanders out there on the other side of that river,' said an MSF hospital manager, gesturing towards the fast-flowing Helmand.

MSF's efforts to secure the safety of its hospitals provided no protection at all in the early hours of Saturday, 3 October 2015, when its trauma centre in the northern town of Kunduz was repeatedly struck in bombing and strafing raids by a US Spectre gunship. At least 30 died in the attack, including 13 MSF staff and 10 patients. Two patients were killed on the operating table and several more burned to death in their beds in the intensive care unit. It was the biggest loss of life that MSF had sustained in Afghanistan and had ever suffered in an air assault.

The trauma centre had been open for four years and was the only such unit in the whole of north-eastern Afghanistan. In the days that led up to the attack, staff had treated almost 400 Afghan casualties from the fighting that erupted after the Taliban captured Kunduz on 28 September, the first time a provincial capital had fallen to the jihadists since the start of the American war in 2001. Patients included government troops and Taliban insurgents as well as civilians. The raid destroyed all the hospital's main surgical facilities and it was forced to close.

For the US military, the attack was simply a tragic accident. After a six-week inquiry, it provided some detail: malfunctioning equipment on board the aircraft; a lack of proper briefing and other human errors; and the 'fatigue' of US Special Forces on the ground. For MSF, it was a war crime. Not only had the agency provided the military with the hospital's exact coordinates during the fighting for Kunduz, it had also made contact with US officials and with NATO in Kabul and in Washington while the raid was going on. The bombing runs lasted for over an hour, five of them at 15-minute intervals, and continued for 30 minutes after US officials had been told who and what their aircraft was hitting.

Claims that the Taliban were 'holed up' in the hospital and firing at Afghan government troops were vehemently refuted by MSF. The agency continued to demand an independent international inquiry to establish all the facts and the circumstances. How had their hospital come to forfeit its protected status under international law? 'This was not just an attack on our hospital – it was an attack on the Geneva Conventions,' said Jason Cone, head of Doctors Without Borders USA. 'There are no "mistakes" under humanitarian law … Today we say: enough. Even war has rules.'

MSF embarked on what was described to me as a 'very fierce fight-back' over the raid. For its senior managers, the attack fitted a pattern in which respect for international humanitarian law had been steadily eroded during the years of the war on terror. Here was a tragic opportunity to try to restore some of its status and provide a measure of protection for those who go to work in its name.

When coalition forces stood down in Helmand province in 2014, they withdrew all the medical care they had extended to local Afghans caught up in the war. This left civilians dependent on a desperately under-resourced government health system or on the boldest of overseas aid-givers.

In this single respect, the people of Helmand were fortunate. Not only did they have access to MSF's skills and resources at the main provincial hospital in Lashkar Gah, provided they could reach it in an emergency, but, for those who had lost limbs, there was also a prosthetic unit opened recently by the ICRC, part of a remarkable national programme that I shall describe in the next chapter. Thirdly, there was Emergency, an Italian charity specialising in war surgery. Emergency represents the European humanitarian ideal at its finest.

The Emergency trauma centre was right next door to the MSF hospital. Its flag flew from the water tower – similar to the MSF logo, each paying graphic respect to the original Red Cross, that great emblem of nineteenth-century humanitarianism. Along with ICRC representatives, Emergency and MSF now comprised Lashkar Gah's resident international community in its entirety.

My meeting at Emergency was with Dr Alberto Landini, its medical coordinator. A surgeon in his sixties from Milan, he had been volunteering with the agency for 15 years, on missions to Cambodia, Sierra Leone and Libya and many times to Afghanistan. I was with him for two hours that afternoon. In between answering my questions, he attended calmly to messages on his mobile phone about fresh casualties around the province; he spoke to junior colleagues who sought urgent clinical guidance; and he rounded off our interview while overseeing the admission of a young man with bullet wounds.

There was a framed cartoon on the wall of Dr Landini's office. It showed a crazy soldier shooting at a blank gravestone, chiselling out the words *'La parola pace non si scrive con le armi'* – 'The word peace is not written with weapons.' Emergency is pacifist, and has campaigned loudly against Italian involvement in all the wars on terror. It was the creation of Dr Gino Strada, a heart specialist who became a war surgeon. When he started his charity, it was to send surgical teams into hospitals on the front line. They saved many lives, but found that their patients were still dying because of poor aftercare. They concluded that they would have to build their own hospitals.

It did not require a professional eye to see that Emergency's hospitals in Kabul and Lashkar Gah were providing superb care. No corners were cut, no concessions made to the sometimes grim surroundings. As coalition forces withdrew their medical services in Helmand, the British took to passing on civilian war victims to the Emergency hospital. 'It's as good as Camp Bastion,' I was told at the PRT offices in Lashkar Gah, 'and Bastion is the best in the world.'

The most extraordinary part of Emergency's operation is its network of first-aid posts around Helmand. Their locations read like a roll call of British and American battle honours – Musa Qala, Sangin, Garmsir, Marjah, Gereshk, Nowzad. The busiest clinic was in Sangin, close to the fiercest fighting of the war. Emergency's managers lost count of the number of times its windows had been blown in – it happened again while I was in Helmand – but the insurgents otherwise left it alone. 'We tell them it's like a mosque for prayer,' said Emanuele Nannini, Emergency's programme director in Kabul, 'so please don't touch.'

The first-aid posts have to be close to the front line on the principle of the 'golden hour' – if casualties are stabilised rapidly, they will survive. Once stabilised, Emergency's little Suzuki ambulances bring them to Lashkar Gah. The young man who arrived at the hospital on the afternoon of my visit was from Sangin. His bullet wounds were to the buttocks, and Dr Landini was worried about infection and damage to the spinal cord. The young man had surgery that evening and I checked up on him the next day. He would be fine.

Completing this network of real foreign care in the midst of the Helmand conflict is another exceptional initiative. The ICRC has introduced a system of its own to bring wounded civilians through the lines from troubled corners of the province. Sometimes the traffic is in the other direction – bodies being returned from hospital mortuaries to their families for burial.

The ICRC has contracted and trained local taxi drivers to do the job. They are given Red Cross identity cards to get them through the checkpoints. One of the drivers I met at the ICRC office in Lashkar Gah had brought a man with a bullet in his leg from Marjah to the Emergency hospital the day before. He was a farmer who had been irrigating his fields when the shooting started. He was caught in the crossfire because he went to turn off the generator in order to save electricity.

In addition to the risks of roadside bombs, the drivers complained to me about the treatment they received from international forces, from the Afghan army, the Afghan security department and local police. Despite their Red Cross ID cards, and often with a casualty stretched out in the back, the two drivers I spoke to had both been arrested a number of times. They would be separated from their patient and taken away for interrogation – by the Afghans or by the foreigners. Both drivers had seen the inside of the British base at Camp Bastion.

'They say we are Taliban, and our passenger is a Talib,' one of the drivers said. 'But we are helping war victims. Talib or anyone else, he is a human being.' I asked him whether he wanted to keep doing the job. 'Yes,' he replied. 'It's not just for the money. Helmand is our province and we are working for our people.'

Front-line aid agencies in Helmand are set apart by the special focus of their work – medical in the case of MSF; trauma surgery in the case of Emergency; protection and rehabilitation in the case of the ICRC. Many other agencies follow a much broader remit that stretches from meeting welfare needs to managing education programmes to running economic development projects. It is this more extensive focus that aligns aid workers with the priorities of local and national government and then directly with their funders in the West. They are then at risk of being seen as 'force multipliers', in Colin Powell's notorious phrase.

The challenge of operating in much of Afghanistan is simply no longer within everyone's capacity. In a contested environment, development itself becomes a hazardous undertaking. Those who succeed against the odds do so not because of the quality of their analysis or even the wholesomeness of their projects. They do so because they have gained enough local trust to overcome the hazards of alignment. Their success is defined by human factors such as cultural sensitivity, experience on the ground and fine leadership.

CHAPTER 3

MEETINGS WITH REMARKABLE MEN

Kabul, Afghanistan, October 2013

Kabul is a pretty sight at night. Look out over the city, and you see the surrounding hills embroidered with twinkling lights. Behind the sparkle, the reality is anything but pretty. Most of the people on the edges of Kabul are refugees in their own country, IDPs – internally displaced people – from the years of conflict. Since the Afghan capital is the largest, best-provisioned and, in its fashion, one of the safest places in the country, a majority of its inhabitants now live in these 'informal settlements'.

There is no running water on those bare hills and no sewage system. The lights you see are because ingenious refugees have hooked up some wires and managed to steal electricity. If they had chosen to squat on flat land closer to the city centre, the government would have sent in the bulldozers to flatten their shacks. Bulldozers don't work on steep hillsides.

Life may be tolerable for Kabul's swelling refugee population in the warmer months, but the Afghan winter can kill. One hundred children were said to have perished in January 2012 when temperatures fell to minus 20°C. They died of the cold or from hunger, with most freezing to death. Families had to choose between heating and food because they could not afford both.

My own encounter with Afghanistan's internal refugees took place a few days after the great Muslim festival of *Eid al-Adha*, which commemorates Abraham's sacrifice of a ram in place of his own son and the end of the pilgrimage season. As well as being a family feast, well-off Muslims are under a religious obligation to distribute some of the meat they slaughter to the poor. It is a tradition that has been institutionalised by Muslim charities in the West – an Islamic equivalent of the Christmas appeal.

Fadlullah Wilmot is the head of international programmes for Islamic Relief in Australia. He was in Kabul to review the agency's work with orphans and its recent distribution of meat to displaced people. I joined him and his Islamic Relief colleague Parwaiz and we drove out one morning from the city centre, off the main road, and skirted ramshackle settlements on corners of waste land. At one point the drive took us up and over an active rubbish tip baking in the autumn sunshine.

Parwaiz pointed to one settlement that had just become home to hundreds fleeing the rising tide of insecurity in Helmand. The drawdown of international forces had only magnified civilian nervousness. They were not yet receiving any assistance in the new camp in Kabul; there had first to be a proper assessment of their needs, and their leaders had refused entry to the survey teams because that might involve their womenfolk being questioned by men.

Our destination was *Bag-e-Daoud* – Daoud's Garden – named after the man who ruled Afghanistan in the 1970s. Here was an echo of the first phase in the country's contemporary descent into disorder. Mohammed Daoud was successively a general and prime minister who overthrew his cousin the king to take power himself. Daoud was close to the old Soviet Union, but not quite close enough. In 1978 he in turn was removed from power – then murdered – by Afghan communists. After months of intensifying conflict between the regime and a new generation of jihadists, the Russians stepped in directly to try to save the revolution. Afghanistan's modern wars had begun.

Daoud's Garden had once been attractive parkland, but all the trees had been felled long ago to turn it into an army exercise ground. One corner was still being used as a tank park by the Afghan army, but buildings that had been offices and accommodation were now occupied by displaced people. This is where we met Bibi Khara, a widow of 40 who looked very much older, and several of her five children. They all lived, ate and slept in one decent-sized office.

Bibi Khara comes from a town on what was once the tourist route to Bamiyan, home to the monumental Buddhas destroyed by the Taliban in 2001. The family had fled to Kabul six years earlier, and there was no question of their going back. The situation was still very bad, Bibi said. Only the day before yesterday, she heard that Afghan army soldiers had been involved in a big fight there.

Fadlullah's task was to establish how well Islamic Relief had organised the meat distribution and whether its consumers were satisfied. This family of six had been given 4 kilograms of meat and had made several meals out of it over the Eid holiday. Bibi explained that it was the only time in the year when they got to eat any meat at all, adding, for the sake of clarity: 'It's not like we don't like meat ...'

There were follow-up questions. How long had her teenage son had to wait in line to exchange the family's Islamic Relief voucher for their meat? The answer was that any wait seemed reasonable in the circumstances. And had she been told who to complain to if anything was not satisfactory? This good 'accountability' question caused some puzzlement. 'Why would I want to complain to anyone?' she asked.

After the interview, there was a photo call with the family, and Bibi was asked to record her thanks to Islamic Relief donors on video, which she did very well. The son who had queued for a while to collect the meat was also asked to say something. He sat cross-legged on the floor, looked straight into the camera and was equally eloquent in his thanks.

I had encountered these Eid gifts of meat once before – also from Islamic Relief, as it happened, in the Horn of Africa. I was rather disdainful of the initiative. It was, I thought, hardly 'developmental'. I have revised that opinion. At a time when grand visions of Western-led development fail so often to bring about the promised transformation, the case for individual acts of rich-world charity becomes all the stronger. For a family such as Bibi Khara's to be able to eat meat once a year is surely, in the language of development, a very good outcome.

Islamic Relief is the biggest of the Western world's Muslim charities. It owes its creation to the same impulses that triggered the great aid explosion of the mid-1980s in Britain and elsewhere in the developed world. Television pictures of Ethiopia's famine and the crisis in neighbouring Sudan prompted a group of Muslim medical students in Birmingham to mobilise their own community to help the hungry. Over the past 30 years, Islamic Relief has brought off the impressive feat of being closely allied to mainstream development while remaining firmly rooted in its Muslim identity.

With funding from the United Nations and some of the major Western donors, Islamic Relief has been spending around £8 million a year in Afghanistan. Unusually among Western NGOs, it has established programmes in each of the country's most troubled southern provinces, including Helmand. I located its offices one afternoon on the outskirts of Lashkar Gah, and met up with Abdul Ghani, its man in the hotspot.

'So many people come only to the centre of Kabul,' he complained. 'The presence of NGOs is too limited because they stay
in their offices at the centre. When they come to Afghanistan,
they should visit programmes in the south of the country. That is
my position.'

Islamic Relief's key project in Helmand is 'Food for Education'.
The idea is simple – to make it worthwhile for parents to send their
children, particularly their daughters, to school. The UN World
Food Programme, along with the Afghan Ministry of Education,
contracts Islamic Relief to hand out high-energy biscuits to the
boys and cooking oil and flour to the girls. The scheme operates
in some of Helmand's toughest districts, with the oil and flour a
particular inducement. It represents real money and makes a big
contribution to the family's kitchen expenses.

Abdul Ghani jumped up from his seat at this point to show me
pictures on his phone of little boys clutching packets of biscuits and
little girls smiling broadly next to big cans of cooking oil. From the
figures, the scheme appears to be making a difference. In Lashkar
Gah itself, there are almost as many girls in primary school as boys.
There has been progress in rural areas, too, but the proportion here
drops off steeply, with boys at primary school outnumbering girls
by three to one.

The man who recruited Abdul Ghani to take on Helmand
was Fadlullah Wilmot, my Kabul companion in the camps for the
displaced. As Islamic Relief's country director in Afghanistan in
2012–13, he pushed hard at the boundaries governing NGO work
in the midst of conflict and insecurity. He had previously been
the country director in neighbouring Pakistan, and before that
had served in other posts in the Muslim-world. Even those jobs
represented a late career break. Fadlullah was a strikingly energetic
70 when we met.

He was born of a Scottish father and an English mother. He left England as a boy when the family emigrated to Australia as 'ten pound poms' in 1950. He converted to Islam as a university student in Tasmania in the 1960s. Almost 40 years later as an aid worker in the thick of the war on terror, he forcefully reflects both his own dual heritage and the distinct role of Islamic Relief in promoting Western-based Muslim aid. Too many Western governments, he would tell Australian audiences, are too ready to link such charitable initiatives to terror and this has restricted the important humanitarian contribution Islamic charities can make.

Fadlullah's Muslim colleagues in Afghanistan and Pakistan were awestruck by his determination to go places. He certainly preferred the field to the office. His favoured transport was not the aid worker's customary white Land Cruiser, but an elderly Mitsubishi Pajero. He had travelled all over Afghanistan in it. On one visit to Helmand, he became the first expatriate country director to drive to Nad Ali, one of the province's most violent districts. 'He was very brave,' said Abdul Ghani, the local Islamic Relief representative. Others were more troubled by his daring. 'From a professional point of view, it was too risky,' I was told in Kabul. A senior regional colleague was blunter: 'If I'd been his line manager, I would have sacked him.'

What Fadlullah certainly demonstrated was leadership from the front. This quality has traditionally characterised the work of the aid agencies, but it does so much less today. There may be more professionalism and better-qualified aid workers, but the systems and the requirements of head offices tend to take precedence over initiatives in the field. In the age of terror, security is the watchword, with good reason, but senior field workers complained consistently to me that they were ruled and often overruled by security concerns. Fadlullah said to me that he regarded it as 'morally wrong for aid agencies to transfer all responsibility and risk to local staff'.

The most sustained humanitarian initiative I witnessed in Afghanistan has defined one man's entire career. He is an Italian physiotherapist called Alberto Cairo and he works for the International Committee of the Red Cross. Back in the 1980s, he was engaged on a charity project for disabled people in South Sudan when a colleague told him that the ICRC was looking for physiotherapists. The initials ICRC meant nothing to him, but he applied for a job nevertheless. 'I didn't choose Afghanistan,' he told me. 'I would not have turned down China, and I would not have turned down Papua New Guinea.'

The ICRC had been ordered to close its Afghan operations after the Russian invasion in 1979, and, as the war with the jihadists raged on through the 1980s, they relocated across the border in Pakistan. It was there in the frontier cities of Peshawar and Quetta that they established their first artificial limb centres for wounded Afghans brought out over the frontier. Eight years later, with a Soviet withdrawal in prospect and a more stable government in Kabul, the ICRC was at last able to return.

There were no Afghans who could make artificial limbs, so the Red Cross brought in foreign technicians to do the work. It was Alberto Cairo's job to get new legs to the war-wounded and then to help them walk again, on whichever side of the shifting front lines they found themselves. Cargoes of artificial limbs were driven regularly through government and rebel checkpoints, and the ICRC's bold Red Cross was consistently respected. 'We are all human,' said Alberto. 'I have seen that even the hardest Taliban were touched by this. Some of them were really affected. I played quite a lot on that.'

The worst of times came with the ailing Soviet Union's withdrawal of support for its communist allies in Kabul in 1992, the collapse of yet another Afghan government, and the outbreak of a ferocious contest among the rebels for the prize of Kabul itself. At one point, the main road on which the ICRC's prosthetic limb centre is located became the hottest front line in the city. One well-armed militia held the hills behind the centre and a rival group occupied Kabul University buildings opposite.

'This was when the risk of rocketing rose,' Alberto explained. 'Sometimes we just had to leave and close the place. Often the fighting was so intense you just couldn't get out. So we stayed the night.'

Of all the independent humanitarian agencies, it is the ICRC that most often hangs on in there. They have their status as the guardians of the Geneva Conventions and their formal agreements with governments to help them, but conventions and treaties do not stop rocket fire. In the face of major threats, they cut back on their relief operations and slim down their staff, but they very rarely, if ever, close down and pull out. They have important protection work to do in the middle of a war – for the wounded, for prisoners, for civilians caught up in the conflict – and they get on with it in their undemonstrative Swiss fashion. Then, when they are able and without fanfare, they start up their programmes once again. So it was with Alberto Cairo's war work for the limbless.

He took me on a tour of the workshops turning out the artificial limbs. I was shown the latest-model callipers and a new alignment machine capable of producing 15,000 limbs a year. The Red Cross has 320 workers on the payroll here and emphasises positive discrimination towards the disabled. Looking around, I saw all these men in *shalwar kameez* moving purposefully from workbench to workbench. 'Apart from you and me,' Alberto told me in one of the workshops, 'everyone in this room is an amputee.' Of its 320 workers, 295 have lost limbs.

In fluent Dari, Afghanistan's Persian, Alberto bantered good-naturedly with his Afghan workers. He went up to one smiling, heavily bearded man who had lost a leg in a mine explosion 20 years ago. 'You were *mujahid* [a jihadist fighter], weren't you?' he said. 'And you were a very bad one.' The man took mock offence, and they both laughed. 'In fact,' Alberto confided to me as we moved on, 'he's a very heavy hashish smoker.'

Not all the patients treated in the ICRC's Kabul orthopaedic centre are war-wounded. Over nearly 25 years in Afghanistan, Alberto has developed a broader mission towards the disabled. 'We realised that all the people were the victims of war – the child infected by polio, patients who could not get their medicine because of the war, patients sent home from hospital who got worse again through lack of treatment.' He talked of vocational training and of jobs. His latest focus was on sport and the wheelchair basketball teams he ran. 'Sport is the perfect combination,' he said. 'It represents physical rehabilitation and social reintegration at the same time.'

Alberto Cairo offered this humanitarian perspective on Afghanistan's endless fighting: 'Dignity cannot wait till better times.'

Outside Kabul, the ICRC went on to establish six provincial orthopaedic centres. The last to open, in Lashkar Gah in 2010, soon became one of the busiest. So intense did the fighting become in Helmand and so great the need for artificial limbs that the Red Cross centre had to restrict its work to the war-wounded. On the day I visited there were ten patients on rehabilitation programmes: eight of them had first been treated at the town's two other exceptional foreign facilities – the provincial hospital run by Médecins Sans Frontières and the trauma centre built by the Italian charity Emergency.

At the ICRC unit that afternoon, I watched three men learning to walk again, slowly and awkwardly, up and back again, on the parallel bars. One was a shepherd from Gereshk who had followed his sheep into a fire fight, and had lost his leg to shrapnel. The second was a driver on an ambushed NATO supply convoy. The convoy was under Afghan army escort, but had been abandoned by its supposed protectors. 'They are good at running away,' said the driver bitterly. The third man on the bars was a policeman who had lost a leg in a mine explosion in Sangin. He had been flown to Bagram air base near Kabul for treatment by coalition medics and then sent home to Helmand. The best news I heard all afternoon was that he at least was still being paid his police salary.

The ICRC man in charge of the Lashkar Gah centre is Ismatullah Qazi Zada. It was only when he got up from his desk that I saw he had a limp. Like everyone else working for the injured in this unit, he is an amputee. His own story goes back to an earlier phase of the Afghan tragedy. In the Soviet war of the 1980s, his family fled to Pakistan yet would still cross back into Afghanistan to check up on their home and to review the prospects for a permanent return. It was on one of those journeys that the schoolboy Ismatullah stepped on a mine and lost a leg.

It was the ICRC in Pakistan that gave him a new one – and more new legs as he grew towards adulthood – and it was the ICRC that opened the door to a decent education in Peshawar. No wonder that when Ismatullah finally returned to Kabul he should have gone straight to Alberto Cairo for a job. No surprise, either, that he should have benefited from the ICRC's policy of positive discrimination. He was soon put in charge of the paraplegic section in Kabul and was then sent to Lashkar Gah to run the new centre there.

Would he always work for the International Red Cross? 'I shall work for them as long as Alberto Cairo is working for them,' Ismatullah replied.

For Alberto himself, Afghanistan has changed all over again during the years of the Western war. For a time after the removal of the Taliban in 2001, he said, it was a new life, everything seemed possible and security was good. The deterioration set in as early as 2004. As for providing disabled people with the services they need, things have got steadily worse since then.

Take the ICRC's programme for tetraplegics, people paralysed from the neck down with injuries to the spinal cord. Once discharged, they need to be visited at home and trained along with their families to get the best out of their lives. In the early years of the West's war, ICRC teams were able to travel widely and securely. 'Now, slowly, slowly, these areas have gone off limits,' said Alberto. 'Today we have problems close to Kabul. We can't work in some areas which are very close to Kabul.'

He spoke of other changes he had witnessed over his 25 years in Afghanistan. 'I always felt that the Red Cross was respected. They even stopped shooting when we passed by. I never had the feeling that I was a target – humanitarian organisations were respected.'

And now? He shook his head. 'It's changed,' he said, referring to relations between the Afghans and foreign aid workers. 'There have been good people who have come, but the bastards have come as well, people who have just come to make money and get out. People's perceptions have changed. I am sometimes insulted in the street – not by everyone, of course; some still have the old attitudes, but many people have changed.'

A big part of that change was linked to the West's view that, as well as a military campaign, it was also fighting a 'humanitarian war'. Alberto Cairo had witnessed this process unfold over the first decade of the century. 'It was [once] very clear what the job of a soldier was, and what was the job of a humanitarian,' he said. 'But the military has tried to invade the humanitarian area, and many of the humanitarian organisations have been seen to cooperate with the military.

'Humanitarian activity by the military is fine, but it's got to be clear that it is not humanitarian activity for its own sake. The

Afghans are not stupid. Today you are dropping bombs. Tomorrow you are building a bridge. Excuse me …?'

As the Western war wound down in Afghanistan and the post-war analysis got into its stride, it was commonly observed that our diplomats and army officers had known extraordinarily little of the country they came to pacify. On their short tours of duty, many were then said to have learned precious little more about the country and its people, its traditions and its languages. Similar charges can be laid against aid workers. In Alberto Cairo we have seen one exception, and there are others. Some of them, through their length of experience and personal qualities, run aid programmes that respond directly to the challenge that Alberto posed – can Western nations fight in a country and aid it at the same time?

Paul Barker is an American Quaker who, over the course of two lengthy Afghan tours for the US agency CARE, dealt first with the Taliban as they consolidated power in the late 1990s and then with the American-backed government which emerged after the 2001 invasion. Later still, in 2012, he was plucked from East Africa by Save the Children to return to Kabul and to work through the nervous years of transition and the final withdrawal of international troops. When I met him he was in his eleventh year in the country.

His first experience of the Taliban was sitting cross-legged on the floor with them, drinking their tea and negotiating an access agreement with two of their senior mullahs. It was March 1996 and he had travelled over the border from Pakistan to meet the Taliban mayor of Kandahar and the head of the Taliban's Foreign Relations Office. Paul and his CARE colleagues assumed that this would be only the first of several tortuous discussions. In fact, the two sides reached formal agreement in less than 48 hours. Each recognised the status of the other and CARE was given specific permission to carry relief supplies through the Taliban lines into Kabul, which had yet to fall under the Taliban's control.

In another cross-border operation, CARE ran community schools in Khost, which led to a series of sharp arguments with the Taliban. The rule at CARE was that they would support a school provided a third or more of its pupils were girls. When the Taliban took over Khost, they said that girls must be sent home. 'No,' objected the locals, 'these are our schools and our students and we are paying for the teachers. We want our children to learn.' The upshot was that the schools around Khost stayed open, and the CARE programme expanded to other provinces under Taliban rule, with a close to 50–50 girl–boy ratio.[1] It was a textbook example of the community outflanking the extremists.

With Taliban forces in control of Kabul, internal security improved while relations with outsiders became more fraught. As CARE's country director, Paul Barker had to respond to a number of ugly incidents. In one of them a squad from the Taliban's Department to Promote Virtue and Prevent Vice stopped a bus carrying female CARE staff, ordered them out and beat them with leather straps as they disembarked. Verbal protests and the suspension of aid programmes gained assurances that these actions were not sanctioned by the Taliban leadership and would not be repeated.

On another, bizarre occasion, the Taliban Minister of Justice personally led a dawn raid on a CARE sub-office overlooking one of the southern highways out of Kabul. He commandeered half the office and turned the basement into a prison for men who had defied the law by trimming their beards. The men from the ministry then set up a roadblock on the highway and sent offenders up the hill to what Paul called 'the CARE office/Taliban prison'. Even one of CARE's own engineers was arrested and detained, in his own office. It took weeks of negotiation to get an official decree from

Kabul that the office should be handed back to CARE and more weeks still to have the order implemented.

Throughout these and other ordeals, Paul Barker showed what can surely be described as true Christian spirit. 'Principled engagement was not fast, but it did work,' he wrote in the *Friends Journal*. It was 'possible through patience, respect and tact to work with Taliban leaders at different levels to address some of the most egregious aspects of their policies and practices'.

He provided this eloquent expression of Quaker philosophy for a fractured world, spiritually more wholesome and practically more useful than simply branding all Muslim jihadists as evil terrorists: 'To believe that there is "that of God in everyone" is to believe and to act as though the Taliban leadership is worthy of respect, to appeal to and to seek to nurture that responsible side of their being.'

On his return to Afghanistan for Save the Children in 2012, Paul continued to focus on education. Save the Children's country programme ranged from school building to teacher training to the fast-tracking of senior high-school girls into teaching jobs. Close to the front line, the agency took on both health and education projects in Uruzgan, Helmand's eastern neighbour and another violent province. It was the agency's single largest programme in the country, directly funded by the Australian government. The Australians had troops on the ground in Uruzgan, as did the Americans and the Dutch.

The story of Timo's School exemplifies Save the Children's capacity to stay at work in a hostile environment. Timo Smeehuijzen was a 20-year-old Dutch soldier killed in June 2007 when a suicide bomber rammed his armoured personnel carrier in the provincial capital of Tarinkot. Ten Afghan bystanders also died. The troops had been escorting a Dutch aid team on visits to girls' schools.

Timo's father wanted to honour his only son by raising money to build a school in Tarinkot, and linked up with a local NGO to get the job done. A contractor was hired and the school duly built and opened. One night soon afterwards, the school was destroyed in a bomb explosion. Timo's distraught father started fundraising all over again and this time teamed up with Save the Children. In 2012, Paul Barker accompanied Timo's father to Uruzgan to see the school open once more and full of children.

The dangers facing aid workers in Uruzgan remain dreadfully high, with the worst impact falling, as always, not on the foreigners but on the local staff. In March 2015, five Afghans working for Save the Children to bring clean water to rural Uruzgan were abducted by Taliban gunmen and later murdered when the provincial authorities refused to negotiate a prisoner exchange. All five were men in their twenties; four of them were married.

The capacity of foreign NGOs to work effectively in Afghanistan's most troubled provinces often parallels their length of service and their level of acceptance by locals. The Uruzgan murders were attributed to a breakdown in relations between Taliban hotheads and community elders who wanted to see their province develop. Despite the appalling human costs, development work done properly remains the best way to tackle suspicions that the NGO's backers are interested only in gaining political or military advantage.

The same argument applied in reverse when Save the Children came under official British pressure in 2013 to take over development projects in Helmand. They resisted. 'The issue is acceptance,' Paul Barker said. 'If you've had a long presence somewhere, you're going to be accepted. But we were not interested in going to new places.'

The most prominent NGO at work in Helmand with direct Western government backing was Mercy Corps. As we saw on the Turkey–Syria border, the agency lives up to its motto 'Saving and Improving Lives in the World's Toughest Places'. Longevity and familiarity accounted for its success in Helmand. Having started work on the Pakistan side of the border in the 1980s, by the 1990s Mercy Corps was working under Taliban authority in several Afghan provinces and had established its biggest country office in Helmand. Some of the insurgents it dealt with in 2014 had been involved in running the province when the Taliban was the government 15 years earlier.

Mercy Corps' official partner in Helmand was Britain's Department for International Development, which funded its vocational training programme in Lashkar Gah. The training on offer ranged from computing and information technology all the way to tailoring and motorcycle maintenance. The project recorded impressive results, including 40 per cent female graduation and 80 per cent post-training employment.

Mercy Corps describes itself as impartial, but does not claim to be neutral. 'We work with local communities,' said David Haines, the agency's British country director in Afghanistan. 'We're not neutral because we do take money from protagonists to the conflict. But the people and the communities we work with range from the pro-Karzai to the pro-mullah.'

Unlike some NGOs, Mercy Corps steers away from the overtly political, notably the West's sustained enthusiasm for 'nation-building'. Mercy Corps doesn't do 'governance' and it doesn't do 'democracy training'. Nor does it do mine clearance, 'however admirable that work may be', as David Haines put it. 'The development needs of a community, that's what we do.'

Political or not, gender equality is the bedrock of aid agency work in Afghanistan. 'Despite the Talibanisation of much of the countryside in Helmand, we have trained thousands of young women,' David Haines continued. 'There's no doubt that's a sensitive issue – taking women out of the home for training. We still seek the buy-in of all these groups.'

My final field trip in Afghanistan took me back to school with Save the Children. We drove out of Kabul one morning and turned off the Jalalabad highway to reach some of the agency's new community schools. The programme was introduced in order to locate schools closer to families and persuade parents to send their youngest children, their six- to nine-year-olds, off to school rather than keep them at home. A walk of 3 or 4 miles to the nearest government school and all the way home again was discouraging enough for young children, particularly for girls in Afghan culture. Worse, I was told, were the twin dangers of kidnap and dog attacks.

Save the Children had made 20 of these little schools happen so far. That was 600 children, of whom 450 were girls. Local communities had to find suitable sites, but Save the Children did the rest. They paid the teacher's salary and handed out the uniform rucksacks. They provided the exercise books, the teaching aids, the pencils and sharpeners and the colourful wall hangings for classrooms. Since desks were expensive, Save the Children sent them plastic carpets instead and everyone sat happily on the floor. This was a pilot project to drive up school enrolment and the plan was to launch the initiative across the country in 2016.

My first visit was to School Number 5, where I interrupted an all-girl class. Several nine-year-olds, their faces framed in white veils, read very creditably to me in English and showed off their writing and arithmetic on the blackboard. I asked them how they would use their schooling in adult life. 'Teacher' and 'doctor' were the stock replies, although one girl firmly answered 'jobless'. I said

I would return in ten years' time to see how they were doing. One bright child said she thought I should wait 20 years.

The highlight of my day was meeting Miss Ghotai, the teacher in the second community school I visited. Her life to date and her nervous hopes for the future seemed to me to sum up Afghanistan's troubled past and uncertain prospects.

Miss Ghotai was born in Kabul and was a high-school graduate. She did two years of an agricultural degree but left university to come to her new husband's home here in Dehsabz. Over the next decade she gave birth to her four children and taught at the girls' high school 3 miles from home. Then the Taliban came to power, and the school closed.

There was no question of girls being allowed to continue their education. They were all sent home, along with their women teachers. Things were worse for Miss Ghotai because her brothers lived in Kabul and had had jobs under the previous regime. In Taliban eyes that made them communists. Miss Ghotai was at risk too, and so the whole family fled to relatives in Khost.

Five years later came 9/11 and the Taliban's ejection from Kabul. Within three days of President Hamid Karzai coming to power with the backing of the West, Miss Ghotai and her family were back home in Dehsabz. The local girls' high school reopened and she resumed teaching. She also offered rooms in her mud-walled family house for a community school and declared that she wanted to be its first teacher.

So six days a week Miss Ghotai is very busy indeed. Every morning at 6.30 she walks the 3 miles to the girls' school, teaches for four hours and walks home again. There is rarely time for lunch. The little ones arrive at 1pm for their four hours of community school in the afternoon – an hour each for the Koran, Dari, arithmetic and drawing.

'I have been very happy during the Karzai government,' Miss Ghotai told me. 'Foreign troops have come here and they have helped build a better situation.' We were talking at the end of 2013 and Miss Ghotai had clearly not been keeping up with the West's waning interest in Afghanistan. 'I hope these troops never leave Afghanistan,' she told me. 'Maybe if they leave someone like the Taliban will come again.'

Save the Children's community schools are a vivid example of how the West contributes to a country's development even as its troops are fighting a major war around the next corner. It requires the same strong nerves and leadership that medical charities display closer to the front line. Safety is never guaranteed, but tightly focused programmes and sustained engagement with local communities offer a measure of protection.

In the years after 9/11, Afghanistan became a full-scale Western experiment in projecting military power, building government institutions and delivering development. Now that the West has moved on again, a measure of social progress will outlast the military and institutional impact of the occupation. Yet the country and the region remain in turmoil after 40 years of conflict and foreign invasions – one from the Soviet Union, the other from the West. Nowhere have the consequences of these interventions been more marked than in neighbouring Pakistan.

CHAPTER 4

TAKING A BULLET
FOR POLIO

Rawalpindi, Pakistan, November 2013

There is nowhere in Pakistan you can't get to from Rawalpindi bus station – down the M2 motorway to Lahore, then on past the towns and cities of Punjab towards Karachi on the Arabian Sea. Up the M1 you reach Peshawar, and further on (if you care to) you can twist up through the Khyber Pass into Afghanistan. This is one of history's great invasion and migration routes. It became one again towards the end of the twentieth century, with refugees from Afghanistan's modern wars. Today the journey crosses the dangerous frontier between a settled and a profoundly unsettled world.

On the morning I went to the bus station at the end of 2013, the polio vaccination teams were at full stretch. And with good reason. The city serves as the principal transit point for Pushtun people travelling out of their tribal homeland on the Afghan frontier into the rest of Pakistan. Polio infections are higher than anywhere else in the world in these Pushtun areas and Pakistan was then one of only three countries in the world where polio was still endemic (the second was neighbouring Afghanistan; the third was Nigeria – what they all had in common was a jihadist insurgency). The residential quarter around the bus station was a particular concern. This is where Rawalpindi's own Pushtun migrants have settled, and their children must also be protected from a paralysing and crippling disease.

The eradication of polio became a global objective in 1988 with a target deadline of the year 2000. That was missed through a simple lack of political application, but international efforts were redoubled in the new century, and slowly – very slowly – the virus was being extinguished. It really did seem that a generation after smallpox had been finally eradicated in 1980 there would at last be a corresponding success with polio early in the twenty-first century.

The optimism was premature. A global programme colourfully described as being on a 'war footing' found itself on the front line in a real war. Young men and women in Pakistan equipped with nothing more offensive than cold boxes full of children's vaccines were being gunned down in the streets because they had dared to volunteer to help stop a preventable disease from blighting young Pakistani lives.

In trying to derail international and national efforts to eradicate polio, the Taliban were challenging one of the fundamental tenets of humanitarianism – that children around the world should not face crippled lives simply because of poverty, politics or geography. Aid workers – not Westerners but Pakistanis, most of them young women – were paying the price for 30 years of jihadist violence and clumsy superpower interventions. In spite of the intimidation, the resolve of these humanitarians did not falter. As this book went to press, there was a real chance that they would soon be contributing to a triumph in the cause of humanity – and a rare victory in the war on terror.

The challenge on the ground in Pakistan in 2013 was laid out to me by Bushra Ajmal, my guide and companion in Rawalpindi that day. Bushra works for the United Nations children's agency

UNICEF in support of the local health authority. 'It's very difficult with these high-priority populations,' she said. 'There's resistance. They don't like vaccinations, they don't trust vaccinations.'

There were four vaccination teams at work in the bus station, all of them wearing green 'polio' baseball caps and each with a blue cold box full of mouth drops. Their job was to find children under five, check from special pen marks whether they had been vaccinated recently, give them the drops, mark their fingers, enter their names on a list, and move on.

The apparent randomness of the process was countered by the frequency of these nationwide campaigns and the high level of coverage achieved in all but the most difficult areas. I saw several families approached at the bus station, inside and outside vehicles: none refused and their children were duly vaccinated. The residential colonies beyond the bus station would be more difficult. As we headed into their littered streets, Bushra drew her black scarf more tightly around her head to emphasise a feminine modesty in this conservative community. 'Unfortunately, I didn't bring a bigger shawl,' she said.

In Foji Colony I met Saiqa and Rabia, one a medical student, the other a school leaver, each covered in a *niqab* revealing only their eyes and each receiving just £7 a week for pounding the streets with cold box and tally sheet. They had covered 200 households that week and had vaccinated some 600 children. 'They are a little bit conservative, they refuse a little bit,' said Saiqa mildly. Her more anxious colleague Rabia added that five households had refused point blank to admit them. That meant that 30 children had not been vaccinated.

As the young women moved swiftly from shuttered house to shuttered house, they were observed by the calm figure of Constable Asif Hussain from New Town Police Station. All 11 teams out on the streets in the colony that day had an armed policeman as escort. The danger was real. As a specific defence against drive-by shootings, the police had also banned motorcycles from streets where vaccinators were working.

The Pakistan Taliban issued their ban on polio vaccinations in 2012 and began enforcing it in the areas they controlled. Some of their sympathisers claimed that the anti-polio drive was not aimed at eradicating the disease at all, but was a Western plot to sterilise a troublesome Muslim population. The Taliban leadership itself asserted that vaccination was a cover for Western espionage – not a fanciful suggestion at all, as we shall see – and one of their leaders insisted that the ban would be lifted only when the United States stopped its drone strikes in the tribal areas.

On a single day in December 2012, the Taliban shot and killed five volunteer health workers, all of them women, in the Pushtun colonies of Karachi. They murdered two more in the frontier city of Peshawar and close to the border with Afghanistan over the following 24 hours. In total that month, nine volunteer health workers were killed. The programme went into shock. Vaccinations were temporarily suspended and security arrangements enhanced. Policemen were brought into the line of fire. From July 2012 to February 2015, 80 polio workers and their security men were killed, and a further 54 were seriously injured.

I travelled to Pakistan a year after the start of the Taliban campaign, and read daily press reports of security incidents around the vaccination programme. One polio team escaped unhurt in a bomb blast in the frontier town of Charsadda; 11 teachers were abducted by gunmen in the Khyber area because their school had been used in the vaccination programme; in Peshawar, doctors went on strike to protest about lax security after the kidnapping of a colleague who was in charge of the local polio campaign.

'Taking a bullet for polio' was the headline in my *Express Tribune* newspaper on 2 December 2013. 'Slain security official is remembered as a great cricketer and supportive friend.' It told the story of Zakir Khan Afridi, a 22-year-old policeman, shot dead in Peshawar as he was going off duty after a day of protection work with polio workers. 'A young man with a smiling face, he was known to almost everyone in Shareefabad,' the newspaper said, 'mainly because he played good cricket. His big sixes would always attract a crowd ...'

The impact of the Taliban campaign on the prospects for the early eradication of polio in Pakistan was devastating. There were more than 300 fresh cases of the disease recorded in the course of 2014. That was a tripling of the caseload of 2013 and represented 85 per cent of all new cases around the world. The clock was being turned back to the beginning of the century, perhaps even beyond that to a time when the extinction of the disease was a matter of hope rather than realistic expectation.

The rest of the world could take no comfort from the uniqueness of Pakistan's troubles. It was the Pakistan strain of the polio virus that was tracked from one of the Pushtun quarters of Karachi to Egypt, and then on to the Occupied West Bank, Israel and Syria. It was identified among Syrian child refugees over the border in Turkey, an area that had recorded Europe's last major polio outbreak in 1998.

In the Pushtun colonies behind the bus station in Rawalpindi, the talk was of the safety of polio workers. 'From the television and the newspapers I came to know there are problems and threats,' said Rabia, the volunteer school leaver doing her best, on her £7 a week, to convert 'refusals' into 'acceptances' by banging on the doors all over again. 'I was worried when I came here and my parents were worried also, but today we have security,' she said, looking over her shoulder at the reassuring figure of Constable Hussain.

Fahmeeda, the medical officer stationed in the area, said she had thought a lot about security and concluded that there should be women police officers to escort female polio workers into people's houses. There was no question of a male policeman entering private family quarters. 'Sometimes we enter these places, we see arms and guns,' she said. 'If they refuse to have their children vaccinated, what happens then? That could lead to physical assault, and, God knows, murder.'

At international and country level, the anti-polio programme is the responsibility of two United Nations humanitarian bodies, the World Health Organization (WHO) and UNICEF. For the mouth-drop vaccine to be fully effective, every child must have at least four doses. If a child is malnourished or has diarrhoea, yet more doses will be needed. Only wave after wave of vaccination and the resulting immunisation of every child will ever squeeze the virus out of waste water and stop its onward transmission. That day around the bus station, I witnessed the area's third campaign in a month. Such is the expense of the international polio programme – put at $1 billion a year – that the Bill and Melinda Gates Foundation, one of its principal backers, has declared that it is not sustainable in the long term.

As the death toll mounted among polio workers and their escorts in Pakistan, the desperate repetitiveness of the campaign was a constantly expressed concern on the ground – and the basis of suspicion and complaint among its intended beneficiaries. I recorded these comments in my notebook.

From a doctor in her private clinic: 'Repeated campaigns are a real problem. This has to be tackled. People need careful counselling if they are to be convinced. Even educated people have been refusing this time round.'

From a local health official: 'Campaign fatigue is there on our technicians, on parents and volunteers. I may suggest one campaign in a month. Also the quality of the campaign is declining. It is a very taxing job.'

Suspicions creep in at street level. Campaign coordinators relayed these comments from residents: 'Why do you keep coming back to my children? These vaccines obviously do not work.' 'We are from Waziristan [a border area where the Taliban formally banned vaccinations] and all you are doing is collecting data on us.' 'Why do you only give us vaccines? Why don't you give us food and bread?'

Then they raise the universal bogeyman of the United States: 'This vaccine comes from the US. Why doesn't the US give us food?' 'The Americans are not vaccinating their own children. Why should they vaccinate ours?' Often it comes back to the feverish politics generated in Pakistan by the West's war on terror: 'They are killing us through drones. Then they are treating us here. What is this?'

What makes it tougher for people wanting to protect their children in a conservative, religion-bound society are the *fatwas* issued by Muslim clerics against the vaccination campaign. 'I do not have a problem with vaccinating my children,' one mother said, 'but since the imam at my mosque has issued a *fatwa*, what can I do?'

With Bushra from UNICEF helping with translation, I talked to Farid Khan outside the joint family house which he and his wife shared with six other families in Habib Colony, near the bus station. These families still accepted the regular range of childhood immunisation and, until the current campaign, had agreed to polio vaccination as well. Public controversy around the drops then prompted a big family argument and it was decided that they would refuse entry to the vaccinators. There were 18 children in the household.

Farid said he had been reading articles in the Peshawar newspapers about the polio campaign and had been studying declarations from local imams who denounced the vaccinations as an American plot to sterilise Muslims. I understood the words 'Ameriki' and 'dollar' in his answers. 'Why is America spending $10 on one vaccine?' he asked. 'Why don't they invest in us?' UNICEF's counter-effort of assembling and publishing a score of scholarly Muslim endorsements of the campaign had had no effect. The vaccinators were still not going to be allowed in.

'We are responsible for all our children, for good or for bad,' Farid continued. 'We trust in the will of God. These two drops obviously do nothing.'

By the time our street conversation ended, we were in a sea of children, some of them from among the 18 living in Farid's joint family house. 'It's certainly not having any effect on the fertility here,' a young Pakistani woman on the UNICEF team observed sharply as we walked on. 'It's well known how many children we have!'

At the top of UNICEF and the WHO in Pakistan there was no disguising the scale and seriousness of the battle they had on their hands. On its outcome hung the prospect not just of eliminating a terrible disease, but of maintaining momentum towards a healthier global future. To fail, even to suffer a sustained setback, would undermine confidence that Western-led aid institutions were capable of building a better world. UNICEF and the WHO had addressed the challenge by deploying some of their best field officers to direct this 'war of the worlds' in Pakistan.

Per Engebak is a Norwegian who thought he had retired. For years he had run whole regions of the world for UNICEF – all of Latin America and the Caribbean for four years, all of East and Southern Africa for six. When I met him in Islamabad, the Pakistan capital, he was in his first year in charge of a single unit tackling a single disease in a single country.

'Very few people know how serious this is,' he said of the violent opposition to polio vaccination. 'There is clearly a campaign going on that is well planned, well executed and at a certain scale. This campaign has caused considerable anxiety – the concern that we will not be in a position to get the job done.'

Engebak had ordered changes to the UNICEF programme. Instead of a noisy, media-driven campaign, he wanted the polio message to be integrated into the broader sweep of health promotion. Priority had to be given to protecting the 72,000 'volunteers' – teachers, health workers and other government servants in addition to the medical students – whose lives were on the line whenever they went out with their cold boxes and tally sheets.

Particular attention was paid to the areas where the Taliban held sway. UNICEF was mapping the political geography of North Waziristan, the most rebellious of the Pushtun border areas. Distinctions had to be made between different Taliban groups. Could the health authorities work with any of them? At this point they learned that several Taliban leaders were travelling many miles to hospital to acquire polio drops for their own children. 'If that's happening,' exclaimed Per, 'why don't we build on it?'

When I met Per Engebak at the end of 2013, he said he was committed to leading the Pakistan polio campaign until 2015. By then he hoped recent reverses would have been halted and progress resumed towards national and global eradication. As the crisis deepened in 2014, that turning point seemed to be still further off. 'We haven't given up,' he told me. 'Ultimately we will get this job done.'

Dr Elias Durry is an Ethiopian who does not mince his words either. He has been working on polio eradication for 20 years. He has tackled it in Nigeria, in South Sudan and in Somalia, with major achievements to his credit in each. This track record led him to his current role as the WHO's polio emergency coordinator in Pakistan. He described the situation in the country as 'unprecedented'.

When he worked in Somalia, it was a failed state with no government, inter-clan warfare, and what he described as a '24/7' security problem. In South Sudan there was a war going on and an almost total lack of infrastructure. Factors like that had slowed the progress towards eradication. Pakistan was different – and worse. 'Now we have polio as politics with direct attacks singling out the vaccinators,' said Dr Durry.

He described polio eradication as a programme in local hands where the West's interest lay in tackling the disease once and for all. It could be a bridge between East and West, between the rich and poor worlds. 'Now it is not being used as a bridge any more, but as a tool,' he said. 'The bridge is broken.'

The Taliban were trying to make sure the West never finished the job of eradication. 'They're fighting against their own children,' said Dr Durry, 'but they understand that it won't just affect their own children. It will derail a global programme that has been championed by the West. The virus will go out of these [Pushtun] areas into Punjab and to other countries. Eventually it will affect the whole globe, including the West.'

Dr Durry believed that there was method, not madness, in the Taliban ban and the attacks on health workers. He summed up their approach as: 'Stop the drones and we will let you vaccinate.' It was payback time for the American air campaign against the Taliban and it was the strongest card in their hand. Taliban efforts to convince villagers that the true purpose of the vaccinations was to sterilise Muslims were just a tactic, he said. 'They can't openly say they are anti-West, so they argue it's anti-Islam.' The Taliban campaign, he added, amounted to biological warfare.

Standing behind Elias Durry at WHO headquarters in Geneva is the modern architect of the drive against polio and its unrelenting champion. He is Bruce Aylward, a Canadian doctor who has been in charge of the programme since it was scaled up at the end of the 1990s. The number of countries where polio is endemic fell from 20 to three in the years to 2014 and fell again to two in September 2015 when Nigeria was removed from the list. In each of these countries it was Islamic extremism that presented the principal obstacle to finishing the job.

'You have a lot of bad days in a programme like this,' Dr Aylward said to me by way of candid introduction when we met in Geneva. 'We're ten years late and ten years over budget.'

As the WHO official responsible for health emergencies, he said the range of threats faced by medical workers in the world's trouble spots was now unprecedented. 'I have to say in 30 years of doing this work, we've never been in the position we're in now, where we are the targets. It's not just Pakistan. It's hospitals being blown up in Yemen and in Syria; our convoys being attacked; our ambulances being misused. We're in a position which was unimaginable 20 years ago, even ten years ago.'

He posed this question in relation to the polio campaign: 'When do you quit?' And here was the answer. There could be no question of ever giving up on reaching every child. 'It is not an acceptable idea,' he said. 'You have to reach every kid. If we give up on polio today, it will be measles tomorrow. If we give up on protecting health workers today, it will be school teachers tomorrow.'

It is under Dr Aylward's determined leadership – backed by the work of the courageous men and women we have met in the field – that the prospects for polio eradication have changed once again. With a renewed Pakistani commitment to the campaign (imagine the shame of being the last country on earth to harbour this ancient virus), the earth seemed to move in 2015. Humanitarians began to turn the tables on those in the Taliban who would play jihadist politics with the rights of even their own children to protection against disease and disability.

On the Afghan border, the Pakistan army first cleared the way for the revival of effective medical interventions. In June 2014 they launched a major military operation in areas of Waziristan where the Taliban were at their strongest and where the ban on polio vaccination was at its tightest. Prior evacuation of civilians from the region and subsequent access for aid workers enabled tens of thousands of children to be reached by vaccinators for the first time in several years. The results were astonishing.

According to UNICEF statistics published in July 2015, the number of unreached children in the tribal frontier fell from 300,000 in July 2013 to fewer than 60,000 in February 2015. Other militant-influenced Pushtun communities got the message. In Karachi, in the nine months to April 2015, the number of unreached children fell from 250,000 to just 10,000. The figures for children paralysed by polio showed a correspondingly dramatic decline. Cases recorded in the first five months of 2015 were a third of those in the previous year.

Pakistan was 'getting back on track to stop transmission of polio in 2015', declared UNICEF in July 2015. They added with a flourish: 'Pakistan has the extraordinary opportunity to take the world over the finishing line for polio eradication.'

At the WHO in Geneva, Dr Aylward was more circumspect, less triumphant. 'You've got to get to zero,' he told me. 'You've got to sustain coverage long enough to halt transmission. The question remains, will we get to that level of pragmatic perfection? I would say, "Yes." If you asked, "When?" – well, that I don't know.'

As long as the polio virus remains unvanquished, every unvac-cinated child in Pakistan is in danger, and the recent spike in cases brought with it more suffering for the young and more uncomprehending anxiety for parents. In a country where medical care is patchy, it is fortunate that there is a well-focused aid project to respond to their needs.

One morning before dawn I set off down the M2 motorway into the agricultural heartland of Punjab. 'Good clean air here,' said my driver. 'The whole thing is natural.' My destination was the district of Hafizabad, close to Lahore, where I met Shehzad Hassan who covers Punjab for the Polio Rehabilitation Initiative. This WHO project was funded initially by the charity Islamic Relief and is now underwritten by the Gates Foundation. It supports schooling for young polio victims and provides specialist care to counter the disability that follows paralysis. Shehzad himself is a specialist in orthotics – the provision of mechanical aids for weakened limbs – and came well prepared for his field trip. In the back of his car he had several pairs of very small splints.

Our first stop was at Genius School in the village of Lot Sarwer. Like the other schools we visited that day, it was privately run in a country where parents scrimp and save to afford a better education than the government schools provide. Aziza Farheen was the woman behind Genius School and was keen to talk about one of her pupils, seven-year-old Huzaifa – she had persuaded his parents to send him to school, despite his disability.

'I've not started the school from a business point of view,' said Aziza. 'I have started it because of my belief.' Thirty of her 130 pupils were paying discounted fees. 'I was thinking that Huzaifa was special and that I would give him the education at half fee. This is a very backward area, and education is my passion.'

Huzaifa lives on a farm 3 miles out of the village and is brought to school every morning on his Uncle Babur's motorbike. He sits up front on the fuel tank and the breeze blows through his hair. He was ten months old when he contracted the fever that led to paralysis in his right leg. Now his Uncle Babur carries him over the broken ground into school. Once there, he is able to walk around. He can also stand to play little games of badminton.

The two other children I met that day both contracted polio at six months. The pattern was the same – high fevers, visits to unsuspecting doctors who charged for an injection to reduce the fever, and then the paralysis set in. Muneeb was partially paralysed in his left leg. He can walk for short distances, but he can't run. A smiling little girl called Samreen has paralysis in both legs. She can walk a little, too, and tries to play but keeps falling over.

Muneeb was doing well at the Fairy English Medium School. 'I am hoping he will continue with his studies to university level and get a job so he can support a family,' his mother said. At the Al Munir Public School I asked how Samreen was doing in class. Her teacher was summoned from the classroom to speak to me. 'She's okay,' said the teacher dismissively. 'But her parents are illiterate, so she's not brilliant.'

We travelled on to the farmhouse where Huzaifa, the little boy from Genius School, lives with his extended family. Shehzad, the orthotics expert, performed his most important task of the day. It is vital that small limbs are straightened and kept straight while a child with polio grows up, otherwise they contract, and significant contracture means the child will not walk. Splints must be worn at night and there need to be frequent new fittings.

Huzaifa climbed onto one of the rope bedsteads outside in the compound and lay down. He had done this before. Shehzad rolled up the boy's corduroy trousers and tried on the splints. Small adjustments were made. The adults standing around watching were reminded how important it was that the splints were always worn at night. And the job was done.

Pakistan's Polio Rehabilitation Initiative is caring for several hundred children like Huzaifa. That is not a huge number. After all, the disease had been in decline until the recent sharp increase in cases led to a greater demand for specialist services. Even from Taliban-controlled communities along the Afghan frontier, parents were now travelling to seek medical care for their children. It was just as well that Bill Gates, the programme's main funder, had deep pockets.

During the day I spent with polio vaccinators in the streets of Rawalpindi, several references were made to a place called Abbottabad and an individual named Afridi. Abbottabad is the Pakistan hill station where Osama bin Laden, architect of the 9/11 outrages, was tracked down and shot dead by US Special Forces in May 2011. The individual is Dr Shakil Afridi, a Pakistani physician recruited by the CIA to assist in the operation. It is one of the gravest breaches of humanitarian trust that any government has ever publicly owned up to.

One of the Pakistani polio workers accompanying me that day described it as 'a propaganda gift to the other side'. She went on: 'The Americans are very generous with their gifts. Things are going well, and then along comes another gift!' In a further street-corner conversation, a polio team member turned confidentially to me and said, 'Mr Peter, this Dr Afridi caused us a very big problem.'

Dr Shakil Afridi was Pakistan's senior health officer in Khyber district, which borders Afghanistan. Among his responsibilities were vaccination programmes, including the local response to polio. This work enabled him to travel widely across the sensitive frontier region and brought him to the attention of American intelligence. His eyes and ears would be valuable assets for the CIA in its long search for the leader of al-Qaeda.

His last job for the Americans would be the big one. He was to set up a phoney vaccination campaign in the town of Abbottabad, many miles to the east of Khyber, where US intelligence believed Osama bin Laden was hiding. They wanted confirmation that America's most wanted man was living there, and DNA samples were one way of getting it. It had to be an injection-based programme where blood was drawn – polio mouth drops would not do the trick – and so they settled on a hepatitis B campaign.

Members of Afridi's team did gain access to the bin Laden compound, although they failed to get the proof the Americans were seeking. The US Navy SEALs assault in 2011 was nevertheless the triumph that President Obama was looking for, and for America it wrote a decisive concluding chapter in the story of their war in Afghanistan. The enormous fallout of the operation in Pakistan, including the damage done to the reputation of the Western world's humanitarian efforts, was a secondary US consideration, if it was considered at all.

For Pakistanis, the attack was a national humiliation. They had not been consulted about it and had not authorised it. For several years, it turned out, Osama bin Laden had been holed up less than a mile from the country's top officer training establishment, the Pakistan Military Academy, and the Pakistani authorities apparently knew nothing about it. In response to this political disaster, Pakistan intelligence swiftly detained Dr Afridi; the government announced a formal commission of inquiry; and the story of the bogus hepatitis B campaign, orchestrated by foreign intelligence, began to emerge.*

---

* Hollywood got into the act at this point. The 2012 film *Zero Dark Thirty* suggested it was a polio campaign, not hepatitis, that helped track down bin Laden. Its stars joined in efforts to have Dr Afridi freed as 'America's abandoned hero'.

The use by US intelligence of a humanitarian endeavour as a cover for espionage had a major impact on the world's efforts to eradicate polio. The Taliban seized upon it and cited it in its September 2012 statement that preceded all the murderous attacks on health workers. It was now plain, they said, that vaccinators were spies. In the United States, the deans of 12 leading public health schools wrote to President Obama in January 2013 reminding him that, 50 years ago, his predecessor John F. Kennedy had stepped in to prevent the new US Peace Corps from being used as a front for covert CIA work.

The deans condemned the killing of Pakistani health workers as 'unforgivable acts of terrorism', but went on to make this judgement on the CIA's Abbottabad operation: 'While political and security agendas may by necessity induce collateral damage, we as an open society set boundaries on these damages, and we believe this sham vaccination campaign exceeded those boundaries ... public health programmes should not be used as cover for covert operations.'

It took the Obama White House 16 months to respond to the deans' complaint. When the letter came, signed by Lisa Monaco, the president's adviser for homeland security and counter-terrorism, it said that the US strongly supported 'efforts to end the spread of the polio virus forever' and, without elaboration, added that a decision had been taken that the CIA would 'make no operational use of vaccination programmes, which includes vaccination workers'. The stable door had been closed, the harm done tacitly acknowledged.

The Abbottabad operation exacted its heaviest price on the humanitarian community in Pakistan. The reputation of NGOs sank further in popular esteem, and one major agency faced a crisis that threatened its very presence in the country. With an annual budget of around $100 million, Save the Children is the biggest international NGO in Pakistan. It had worked in the country for over 30 years, ever since the Russian invasion of Afghanistan provoked a major refugee crisis on the border.

It was Afridi himself who did the damage to Save the Children. By now he was in jail facing a 33-year sentence for spying, but the government's commission of inquiry wanted chapter and verse from him on his links with the CIA. Behind closed doors, he told them all about the fake hepatitis B campaign, provided figures for what the CIA had paid him over the years, and claimed he had originally been recruited into the agency through Michael McGrath, Save the Children's then country director in Pakistan. His handlers had gone by the names of 'Kate' and 'Sue', he said, and added some exciting detail about being driven into the US embassy in Islamabad hidden in the boot of a car.

The truth was less colourful. Dr Afridi was indeed known to Save the Children. He had attended a number of the agency's training and management workshops. He had also applied for several jobs at Save the Children but had never been successful. David Wright, the new country director, went before the inquiry commission to express Save the Children's outrage at the rest of his allegations. He said that the agency was a 'fervent defender of the principles of impartiality, neutrality and independence to which every staff member had to commit'.

To *The New York Times*, David Wright added this about the intelligence operation of which his charity had fallen foul: 'The CIA needs to answer for this. And they need to stop it.'

As soon as stories began to circulate about Dr Afridi's evidence to the inquiry, the pressure on Save the Children mounted. Pakistan's powerful intelligence establishment needed to blame someone for its embarrassment, and Save the Children fitted the bill well. A suspicious and credulous public would believe the worst of any Western NGO, and, in September 2012, the Pakistan government gave Save the Children's expatriate managers just a week to leave the country. A short stay of execution was negotiated, but the axe duly fell and the foreigners were expelled. In the months that followed, the agency's country programme was taken forward by its senior, and notably competent, Pakistani staff.

The fallout of the Afridi affair continued. Nine months after the expulsions, Save the Children managed to negotiate a temporary 30-day visa for a new country director. David Skinner is a former diplomat and experienced front-line aid worker. He needed that varied experience in the new post. Waiting for his flight to be called at Heathrow airport, he checked his email. There was a message to say that a final draft of the 336-page Abbottabad Commission report had been leaked in its entirety to the *Al-Jazeera* television network and was ready for him to download.

'It was awful,' he told me. 'It didn't say we were OK!' In fact, the Commission report gave little credence to Dr Afridi's contention that he had been directly recruited by the CIA through Save the Children, but it did conclude, somewhat contradictorily, that NGOs were open to such infiltration, 'as almost certainly happened in the case of Save the Children'.

The report went on to say that the US decision to use the institutions of aid as a cover for intelligence-gathering had 'done incalculable harm to the environment in which perfectly respectable and indeed renowned NGOs seek to assist the government in discharging its development and humanitarian obligations to the people of Pakistan'.

David Skinner was in the eye of a media storm from the moment he touched down in Islamabad. One television show that week was devoted entirely to a discussion of how untrustworthy the Western aid agencies were. Despite popular and political agitation against Save the Children, Skinner still managed to extend his visa several times and successfully led the organisation in Pakistan for 18 months. By the end of 2014, Save the Children was once again being run by Pakistanis, not foreigners.

That was not enough to protect the charity from further official assaults. In June 2015, a notice issued by the finance ministry ordered Save the Children to 'wind up its offices/operations in Pakistan forthwith'. Its premises around the country were padlocked and a police official spoke darkly of 'anti-state activities'. Although its offices did reopen over the following weeks, the ministry ban was never lifted and permits to resume normal operations around the country proved stubbornly elusive.

Save the Children found itself in an organisational limbo, living on borrowed time, at the mercy of an antagonistic government. That placed in jeopardy three decades of charitable service to the country and the dedication of a 1,200-strong staff in providing education and welfare to several million Pakistani children and their families.

Pakistan itself was as much the victim of tumultuous developments in the region as it was the architect. From the 1980s onwards, it had struggled to control the forces of jihadist revolt that US arms and money had unleashed in the final Cold War contest with the Soviet Union in Afghanistan. When the tables were turned in the new century and the jihadists took on the West, the United States came to view Pakistan less as a long-term ally and more as a threat to its interests.

Intelligence operations played a key role in the US engagement in Pakistan, and Pakistanis were outraged at the implications of this American focus for their nation's honour and dignity. Hiring Dr Afridi to run a sham vaccination programme to help catch Osama bin Laden was just one intelligence operation among many. It was also a grave affront to the humanitarian ideals that the United States espouses and proclaims.

CHAPTER 5

FRONTIER MANOEUVRES

Jalozai, North-West Pakistan, December 2013

The lives of foreign journalists in Pakistan, like those of overseas aid workers, are ruled by a set of initials. NOC stands for No Objection Certificate. You must have an NOC to travel anywhere near the border with Afghanistan. Objections may come from a number of quarters. It could be the provincial government; or the federal government; or the military; or it could be the powerful Pakistan intelligence services in one of their manifestations. NOCs are difficult to get and the system provides increasingly effective control over those who want to find things out or, in the case of aid workers, do something about them.

The Pakistan high commission in London was charming and optimistic, the foreign ministry in Islamabad politely reassuring. No NOC was forthcoming. One big aid agency was happy to have me travel with them, but there was still no NOC. I was told of the recent visit of a senior aid executive on a tour of his charity's projects in Pakistan. He had acquired, with difficulty, a one-month visa, but within that time he never received an NOC to travel within Pakistan. So, at the end of the month, he just went home again. In a country whose suspicion of foreign aid borders on hostility, the NOC is a brilliantly devised catch-22.

This is part of a new pattern governing the foreign aid effort and applies well beyond the borders of Pakistan. Aid agencies in South Asia in particular have witnessed more and more assertiveness on the part of governments, acting, as they see it, in defence of their national sovereignty. As a country once free of the need for foreign welfare and foreign aid workers, Pakistan has taken its modern dependence badly 'They're asserting their sovereignty in such a way,' a regional aid chief said to me, 'that independent and neutral humanitarian action is facing many more constraints and many more challenges.'

It was the agency Islamic Relief that finally sorted out an NOC for me. With its roots in the Pakistani community in Britain, it has its biggest single programme in Pakistan. Islamic Relief runs projects around Jalozai, one of the world's largest and longest-established refugee camps. Just off the motorway to Peshawar, I linked up with my armed police escort for the day and with the jovial figure of Lieutenant Colonel (Retired) Zia ur Rehman, Islamic Relief's security officer. 'There is nothing to worry about, Mr Peter,' he beamed. 'From here you are my baby.'

Jalozai bears witness to the human cost of three decades of shifting conflict in the region. The camp was established in the 1980s for refugees fleeing the Soviet war in Afghanistan. The Americans were then arming the rebels to enable them to attack Russian convoys and bring down Russian aircraft with ground-to-air missiles. In the 1990s, there were further refugee flows from the ugly civil war that followed the Soviet withdrawal, and there were yet more refugees from Taliban rule.

Having satisfactorily humiliated its Russian foes, the Western world turned its back on Afghanistan until the dawn of a new century and the attacks of 9/11. The Taliban rebellion against Western occupation spread violence beyond the borders of Afghanistan to envelop Pakistan's frontier communities. A fresh generation of refugees was driven into Jalozai.

The sector of the camp I toured had been established only six months earlier. It was occupied by families from the Khyber district where the Pakistan army was taking on the Taliban. The recent civilian exodus had been triggered by the intensified fighting. Oxfam was engaged here in Jalozai in one of its familiar roles as a provider of clean water. I was shown the neatly engineered tube well, all locked away in its brick-built shed, drawing the water that was pumped twice a day to hundreds of standpipes around the camp.

Oxfam's local partner was an agency called Lasoona, which means 'hands'. Lasoona had direct experience of instability on the frontier. When, in 2007, the Taliban took over the Swat Valley, not far to the north, there was an immediate confrontation with the Pakistani NGOs based there. Lasoona was told to abandon its work on women's empowerment, a central plank of development and a priority for NGO funders. The agency could no longer hire any women staff and had to sack all those already working for them. It was ordered to limit itself to environmental work.

Next, the Taliban threatened to commandeer Lasoona's offices for their own use. One evening they ostentatiously parked their vehicles outside the front door, and it was clear a takeover was imminent. The Lasoona team packed up as many of their computers and files as they could manage, and fled overnight to Islamabad.

Outside Jalozai, there was another community of the displaced. Almost as many refugees were staying with their clansmen or renting rooms in the surrounding towns and villages as were living in tents in the camp. This imposed immense burdens on already stretched local services and was where Islamic Relief was concentrating its efforts.

As soon as I entered the 'basic health unit' in Misri Banda, I could tell it was a well-motivated, well-ordered project. The clinic was supported by Islamic Relief USA, which had assembled the extra personnel and skills needed when several hundred additional families arrived in the town in 2013. Refugees now accounted for nearly half its patients.

Two encounters confirmed my positive impression. They were with young Pakistani health professionals building significant careers with foreign aid organisations. Dr Hakeem Orakzai was matching his patients to the paperwork when I interrupted him. He began his career as a houseman with UNICEF, moved to the French agency Médecins du Monde, and then to Islamic Relief. His postings had been to some of the toughest places on the Afghan frontier. 'I wanted to work with the IDPs [internally displaced people],' he said. 'Humanitarians have to work for the poorest people.'

Sumaira Hussain started out with a psychology degree and became a child protection officer with Save the Children. Her job now was to counsel women refugees struggling to survive the traumas of war, loss and displacement. In fact, she confided, her real job was to convince the men that their wives and daughters should be allowed to receive proper professional support.

Pills were no good, Sumaira insisted, her eyes expressive behind the veil; these women needed proper counselling. 'They need this too much,' she said, 'but as females they are not allowed.' She went out to meet the refugee families, to talk to the women and to confront the men. I had little doubt of her persuasiveness from behind that veil. Having built up psychological services at the health unit, Sumaira was working on an expansion proposal to present to Islamic Relief South Africa for funding.

The most prominent figure I met that day was a malik, or tribal chief, called Mir Akbar Afridi. He had come to Jalozai with his clansmen to get away from the frontier fighting between the Pakistan army and the Taliban. To make the point crystal clear, he handed me his visiting card, which carried his name, his photograph and all four of his mobile telephone numbers. It also had a little picture of the famous Jamrud Gate at the foot of the Khyber Pass, to show where he had come from; and there was another little picture of a tent, to underline his current misfortune.

I wondered what the prospects were of a return to Khyber. None at the moment, he told me; there was still too much fighting. 'But we are hoping for the best,' the malik said. He spoke highly of Islamic Relief because they showed him and his people the respect that came of a shared identity. He singled out the quality of medicine now available at the hospital. It had been very poor, apparently. 'With the arrival of Islamic Relief, we are getting excellent quality medicines.'

The malik praised what he saw as the sustained quality of Islamic Relief's commitment. Other agencies had helped with one-off distributions of goods, even cash, but had then gone away again. 'Only Islamic Relief is still working,' he said. 'I hope they will continue working with us.'

At Islamic Relief's head office in Pakistan, its country director Dr Fayaz Ahmad also led the Pakistan Humanitarian Forum, which represents the 50 or so international NGOs at work in the country. Security was the first problem facing both foreign and local aid workers. When we met late in 2013, he told me that 19 Pakistani aid workers had been killed so far that year. Unlike their foreign counterparts, local organisations 'don't have the means and no one really listens when they shout about casualties', he said. Here was yet further evidence that it is now local aid workers, not their Western counterparts, who are most exposed on the humanitarian front line.

The other problem was the widespread Pakistani suspicion of NGOs. As far as government officials were concerned, the very idea that foreign aid should be independent of the authorities was preposterous. That made them little better than the terrorists themselves. But there was a corresponding distrust among the Pushtun communities of the frontier. NGOs were identified with an army that often brought strife in its wake. Aid workers were also making a fat living from the troubles. 'Even within my own extended family, it is difficult to say that I work for an NGO,' said Dr Fayaz. His family is from the frontier tribal district of Mohmand, where his great-grandfather once proudly fought against the British.

On the face of it, Islamic Relief should be better placed than other Western NGOs to straddle the divide between the Islamic Republic of Pakistan and its jihadist insurgents. With its community ethic, its historical links with Pakistan and its strong Muslim identity, the agency's status is surely enough to provide a passport through the lines. Dr Fayaz said otherwise. 'We have to be careful,' he said. 'From our experiences in Pakistan and also in Somalia, we now know that Islam is not enough.'

As for the international NGOs, Dr Fayaz spelled out the broader challenge they face. There was a danger they would become no more than contractors to major Western funders. Humanitarianism had turned into 'service delivery' and that way lay the loss of independence. The process was already under way, said Dr Fayaz, with funders looking to work with NGO consortia rather than with individual agencies setting their own agendas. NGOs could end up following the lead of a new generation of US aid contractors, some with charitable NGO status, which the war on terror had promoted.

Dr Fayaz of Islamic Relief singled out Médecins Sans Frontières as the NGO that had held most tenaciously to the principles of independent humanitarianism. No wonder, he remarked, that the

Pakistan government had a 'down on the French NGOs'. MSF had never made money the deciding point in embarking on an aid project. That contrasted with the outlook of many other international NGOs. 'Most of us live in the grey area,' said Dr Fayaz.

I heard similar praise for MSF during my day with the refugee communities around Jalozai. Dr Orakzai, the doctor from Islamic Relief whom I met at the basic health unit, said MSF's reputation was very good in his Pushtun homeland. 'The community is supporting them,' he said. 'That is why they can work here.'

Médecins Sans Frontières has gone to extraordinary lengths in Pakistan to distinguish itself from the generality of foreign NGOs. So distrusted is the motivation and alignment of these aid agencies on Pakistan's tribal periphery that MSF no longer wishes even to be associated with NGOs in the public mind. NGO has itself become a tainted set of initials in Pakistan.

MSF wants to be known for something that it is, not for something it is not – a 'non-governmental organisation'. For a time in Pakistan, MSF called itself simply a 'private medical organisation', resisting even the term 'humanitarian', another word that has been blemished, perhaps corrupted during the years of the war on terror. Only when MSF restarted its programme in neighbouring Afghanistan in 2009 and adopted the 'humanitarian' mantle there did the agency, for the sake of logic on the border, become once again a 'medical humanitarian organisation' in Pakistan.

MSF takes great care to underline its individual status. Here, for example, is an MSF press release about its response to a bomb blast on the frontier. It says that '55 injured patients were treated by the independent medical humanitarian organisation Médecins Sans Frontières' and it ends with this firm declaration: 'MSF relies solely on private financial contributions from individuals around the world and does not accept funding from any government, donor agency or military or politically-affiliated group for its activities in Pakistan.'

So determined is the agency to distance itself from the foreign aid establishment in Pakistan that it even keeps the United Nations at arm's length. It sees the UN system, including its humanitarian agencies, as so aligned with Western governments in the war on terror that its capacity to bring impartial aid to communities locked in conflict has been seriously compromised.

As a general rule in the world's humanitarian crises, MSF sets itself apart from the UN's aid coordination mechanisms. In Pakistan it goes an exceptional step further. It expressly forbids the UN from including MSF aid statistics in its public accounting of international relief efforts. Any formal association with the international aid system, as MSF sees it, taints the organisation in the eyes of Pakistanis.

On 8 October 2005, a great earthquake struck the mountains and valleys of Kashmir, along Pakistan's disputed border with India. Around 75,000 people were killed, including in many communities where an entire generation of schoolchildren was caught in poorly constructed schools. More than 3 million people were affected by the disaster, and the world joined Pakistan in mounting what was seen at the time as a selfless and committed relief operation. It saw, for example, the deployment of large numbers of heavy-lift helicopters from the Western armies stationed over the border in Afghanistan.

For some, though, this human tragedy was an opportunity. A few years on from the start of the Iraq war, the CIA at the time was refocusing on America's unfinished business in Afghanistan. The Kashmir earthquake was identified as a key entry point. 'The

US intelligence community took advantage of the chaos to spread resources of its own into the country,' said a study published in *The Atlantic* magazine. 'Using valid US passports and posing as construction and aid workers, dozens of Central Intelligence Agency operatives and contractors flooded in without the requisite background checks from the country's Inter-Services Intelligence (ISI) agency.'[1]

Others appear to confirm this account. According to Mark Mazzetti, national security correspondent for *The New York Times*, Pakistani intelligence officials 'suspected that the aid mission might be a Trojan horse to get more CIA officers into the country, but amid the devastation in Kashmir and the urgent need to maintain the stream of humanitarian relief, Pakistan's military and intelligence officers were not in a position to challenge the credentials of all the Americans arriving in Pakistan'.[2]

Mazzetti's book sets out the historical flexibility of American judgements as to who could – and who should not – be recruited to spy for the United States. From the 1970s, the CIA had a policy of not hiring journalists, clergy or Peace Corps volunteers as spies, but the rules were never 'cast in stone', he explains. One CIA director said there might be instances of 'extreme threat to the nation' when they might abandon the policy. John Deutch told a Senate Intelligence Committee hearing in 1996: 'I believe it is unreasonable to foreclose the witting use of any likely source of information.'

American officials had 'long understood the dangers of using humanitarian workers as spies', Mazzetti observes, but then America's world had changed after the attacks of 9/11. 'Expanding the categories of who can be recruited to spy was just another tactic of a CIA in the midst of an enduring war.'

Further confirmation that aid was no longer off limits to the spies or to the military has come from other sources. The practice long predated the CIA's decision to hire Dr Afridi to conduct a bogus vaccination campaign to help find Osama bin Laden. In April 2009, not long into a new US administration, the late Richard Holbrooke, President Obama's special envoy to the region, spoke candidly on the subject during a visit to Islamabad.

He publicly bemoaned America's lack of intelligence on the Taliban. 'I am deeply, deeply dissatisfied with the degree of knowledge that the United States government and our friends and allies have on this subject,' he told journalists. The Associated Press account of the briefing went on: 'Holbrooke said the US would "concentrate on that issue, partly through the intelligence structure" and partly through private aid groups that provide humanitarian and other services in Afghanistan. He estimated that 90 per cent of US knowledge about Afghanistan lies with aid groups.'

Another insight into the uses and abuses of humanitarian intervention came with the publication by WikiLeaks of a 2008 diplomatic cable sent jointly from the US embassies in Islamabad and Kabul. Special Forces Command in the United States had been asking the missions for information on 'camps along the Pakistan–Afghanistan border which are housing Afghan refugees and/or Internally Displaced Persons (IDPs)', the cable said. The military wanted to have the names of the camps, their locations, their numbers, their ethnic breakdown and details of 'NGO/ humanitarian relief organisations working in the camps'. The purpose of these requests was unclear, the cable complained: '... some emails have suggested that agencies intend to use the data for targeting purposes, others indicate that it would be used for "No Strike" purposes.'

The United States does not have boots on the ground in Pakistan, but it is most certainly at war there. President Obama's weapon of choice has been the drone. In his first ten months in office, he authorised as many drone strikes as his predecessor George W. Bush had done in his entire eight years in office.[3] The agency selected for prosecuting this war was the CIA. 'The CIA gets what it wants,' was how President Obama apparently concluded one meeting in the White House Situation Room.[4]

The word most frequently used in Pakistan press headlines to sum up popular and political reaction to American drone warfare is 'fury'. In the early years of the campaign, the US had the Pakistan government's backing for the attacks, but that was forfeited as their intensity increased. Again, the Bush–Obama comparison is instructive. George W. Bush authorised around 50 drone strikes in the Pakistan frontier region from 2004 to 2009. In his first term alone, Barack Obama gave the go-ahead for six times that number.[5]

Hardening Pakistani attitudes towards the aid-givers played out in another humanitarian emergency. In 2010, five years on from the Kashmir earthquake, torrential monsoon rains in the Indus Valley flooded an area the size of Italy. Some 20 million people were made homeless. This time the Pakistan authorities set out to make sure it was they, not foreigners, who were in charge of the relief exercise. The United Nations itself was caught out in the anti-aid backlash.

At the centre of the UN's response to natural and man-made disaster is OCHA, the Office for the Coordination of Humanitarian Affairs. Its team in Pakistan began to mobilise an emergency response on behalf of the flood victims – what they call a 'flash' appeal – and seemed to have the support of Pakistani officials. That was an illusion. Other official voices asserted themselves, and the UN was ordered to delay the appeal.

This presented OCHA with a dilemma. 'You need the money quickly,' one senior official said. 'The needs are imminent. On the other hand, you have a national government you can't neglect.' A sympathetic aid manager outside the UN system in Pakistan made the same point more crudely: 'Either you piss them off inside Pakistan or you sit back and wait for three months.'

OCHA chose the first course, and went ahead with its 'flash' appeal anyway. At more than $1 billion, it was the first time this landmark figure had been reached, though it would soon be dwarfed by the needs in Syria. The UN paid a price for this initiative. There were 'robust discussions' with the government and Pakistan came close to expelling the head of OCHA in Islamabad. The OCHA office was, in the words of one official, 'effectively closed down' the following year. When it reopened fully, it would do as Pakistan told it. In future, international aid would be subject to local control.

Of all the world's humanitarian organisations, the one with the longest and most impressive record of service in Pakistan is the International Committee of the Red Cross. The ICRC was present at the violent birth of Pakistan in 1947. It was on hand when East and West Pakistan broke up in 1971 and 90,000 Pakistani troops were held in Indian prisoner of war camps. For decades it has attended to the conflict between India and Pakistan in Kashmir and served people across the borderlands between Pakistan and Afghanistan.

In recent years the ICRC's Pakistan operations commanded an annual budget of close to $100 million. Much more was forthcoming in times of crisis. Since 2012, though, that figure has shrunk dramatically to around $15 million. Staffing has been reduced from 1,300, which made it one of the biggest ICRC teams in the world, to 300.

The sequence of events was this. The ICRC suffered a savage murder near Pakistan's frontier with Afghanistan. Aside from the shock and trauma felt at the killing, there was widespread dismay over the inadequacy of efforts to catch the perpetrators. The ICRC's special role in Pakistan's story seemed to count for little. Along with other aid agencies, it was considered a threat to Pakistan's sovereignty. 'Organisations like the ICRC harbour spies,' I was told by an aid agency chief in Islamabad. 'That's the allegation.'

In January 2012, an experienced British aid manager working for the ICRC in Quetta, the capital of the Pakistani province of Baluchistan, was abducted by insurgents as he drove home in a marked Red Cross vehicle. He was Khalil Dale, a Muslim convert and former nurse who was running an ICRC health programme in the city.

Khalil was no stranger to the risks involved in working on the humanitarian front line. He had already served tours of duty in Somalia, Afghanistan and Iraq. 'I just get on with the job,' he told one interviewer. 'I believe in destiny. But I'll put it this way: I've made my will.' Four months after his kidnap, his beheaded corpse was dumped by his captors in an orchard on the outskirts of Quetta. There was a note with the body saying that he was killed because ransom demands had not been met.

'There are no words to convey the sorrow shared by so many around the world,' said the ICRC's South Asia chief Jacques de Maio. Their operations in Baluchistan were suspended, and those in the rest of Pakistan were put on hold pending a review. This meant, among other things, the closure of a big Red Cross surgical hospital in Peshawar and the suspension of much of their protection work under the Geneva Conventions, including visits to detainees.

'We want answers,' Mr de Maio said of the crime that had halted so much of their work in Pakistan. 'We expect a proper investigation to take place and justice to be served.' Three years on from the crime, the ICRC had received few answers and little enough justice. There had certainly been no arrests. Much of its protection work under the Geneva Conventions was still suspended, and it had received no permission to reopen its major hospital in Peshawar. The Pakistan authorities seemed in no hurry at all to re-establish its strong working relationship with the ICRC.

One more natural disaster in the catalogue of twenty-first-century calamities to befall Pakistan provides a further indication of the state of relations between the government and the overseas aid community. In September 2013 two powerful earthquakes struck southern Baluchistan. The world at large learned little about them and Western aid organisations did little to respond to them. That was exactly how the Pakistani authorities wanted it.

Baluchistan is a remote and underpopulated region, but for all that, the earthquakes killed about 350, injured 800 and made some 140,000 people homeless. By any reckoning, this was a significant disaster. Top provincial politicians and senior local officials reacted as you would expect, and called on the outside world to help. These appeals were then countermanded.

The Pakistan military had problems of its own with Baluch insurgents, and did not want foreigners coming in and treating them with anything like impartiality and neutrality. Civilian bureaucrats were sensitive to the connections between Western aid and Western intelligence, and may not have wanted to stoke up yet more public agitation.

The consequences were serious for the locals who needed help – and for the aid-givers. After its bruising battles with the government over the floods appeal in 2011, the UN's emergency team OCHA said little on this occasion and did less. Big Western government funders sat bitterly on the sidelines. The major NGOs were told that Quetta, the provincial capital, was closed to those who were not already there, and travel beyond the city was banned anyway. The work was left to local NGOs, backed in some of their interventions by Kuwaiti and Saudi Arabian charities.

Western aid-givers had been frozen out of a significant humanitarian disaster. 'It was a big slap in the face to the international community,' one international NGO chief told me in Islamabad, 'but we didn't acknowledge the slap.' It also signified that the overseas aid community was no longer trusted to confine itself to its humanitarian mission. Such was its record – including accusations of links to the West's security and intelligence services – that, instead of enabling aid workers to go about their work in Pakistan, the authorities set about deliberately frustrating them. Western conduct in Pakistan had done much to bring about this outcome. The cost would be borne by the poorest people in Pakistan.

CHAPTER 6

BLUE UN, BLACK UN

Mogadishu, Somalia, February 2014

After a security briefing on the current threat levels in Somalia, the early morning flight from Nairobi to Mogadishu was with UNHAS, the United Nations Humanitarian Air Service. In *Black Hawk Down*, the book that became the film about America's disastrous engagement in Somalia in the early 1990s, our destination is described as 'the world capital of things-gone-completely-to-hell'. The pilot who flew us to Mogadishu that morning was called Moses.

One immediate sign of the country's fracture is the mobile telephone system. Somalia has two main phone companies, Hormuud and NationLink, but there was no connection between the two. Somalis either had to have two phones or a single phone allowing them to flip from one SIM card to another. I was helped out by a resourceful Somali driver with the UN who lent me two of his own cards.

I stayed at Airport Camp, which was close enough to be able to see the tail fins of parked aircraft over the blast-proof walls. The camp looks like a trailer park, except the trailers are old shipping containers which have been turned into rooms. A window and a door have been cut into each container and a further opening houses the air conditioner.

Every inch of every structure in the camp is protected by stacks of industrial-sized sandbags. The airport is a prime target for al-Shabaab rocket and other attacks. 'Action in the immediate aftermath will vary,' says a notice to guests, 'and may include dealing with shocked and injured people, evacuation to a safe area and the arrival of armed police and military.'

Airport Camp is owned and operated by one of the world's most unusual aid enterprises. It is part profit-maker, part charity. Bancroft Global Investments makes money in Somalia from ventures such as war-zone accommodation. Its sister organisation, Bancroft Global Development, is registered as a non-profit NGO in the United States and locally in Somalia and Kenya. What they share is an interest in conflict and insecurity – which also happen to be the predominant concerns of the modern aid establishment – and the business opportunities that arise from them.

Bancroft's charitable work in Somalia is focused on the relationship it has built up with African Union troops who are on the ground to support a desperately weak central government. These AU troops are not peacekeepers. They are in the country on United Nations authority as peace-enforcers to tackle al-Shabaab, and they have made some significant progress since the jihadists were ousted from Mogadishu in 2011.

Bancroft personnel – mostly ex-military from Europe, North America, the Middle East and South Africa – numbered more than 70 when I visited. They are not exactly trainers and they emphatically reject the label 'mercenary'. The term they prefer is 'mentors'. Under US law, they also qualify as charity-sector educators. Their task is to improve the anti-terror skills of AU troops from Uganda and Burundi, along with those of the newly formed Somali defence forces, and to foster better relations between the military and Somali civilians caught up in the fighting.

An African Union tank had recently been blown up by a road-side bomb south of Mogadishu. Here was an opportunity. Bancroft advisers got African Union soldiers to secure the area, and then used it for two weeks of on-the-spot training. In Mogadishu itself, Bancroft worked to reduce the extent of indiscriminate AU firing into civilian localities from which al-Shabaab had launched attacks. They then embarked on a publicity exercise in the hospitals to persuade the families of civilian casualties that they were more likely to have been hit by al-Shabaab gunmen than by the African Union.

Bancroft sees no contradiction in its intimate collaboration with the military and its status as an NGO. It says it 'does not accept the premise that humanitarian assistance, development and security are mutually exclusive', and contests the relevance of at least one long-held humanitarian principle: '… we find that in many modern conflicts, the policy of neutrality no longer affords the level of operational security that organisations seek.'

There is certainly business to be done on the front line in Mogadishu and there will be more of it if African Union troops and their Somali allies achieve long-lasting improvements to security. Bancroft runs another, less basic accommodation unit called International Campus on the seafront, and the local produce it buys for these enterprises puts cash in people's pockets. If proper peace ever returns to Somalia, the firm's property holdings will surely rise in value.

When journalists and aid workers ask Bancroft who is paying for its NGO work in Somalia, it likes to reply 'you are' because of the $2 million a year it makes from its war-zone hotels. Bancroft's main source of charitable income remains the direct and indirect funding it receives from the US government, much of it paid via African governments, and from the United Nations for its 'mentoring' work with African Union troops. In 2015 that amounted to $35 million over two years.[1]

The conflict in Somalia, now well into its third decade, has put overwhelming pressure on the main humanitarian organisations. For several years, agencies had no direct access to South Central Somalia, which was the neediest part of the country and the epi-centre of past famines. Agencies often had to break their own rules to be able to carry on at all in Somalia. They found themselves making payments to insurgents to ensure that relief supplies reached the needy, and foreign aid workers never sensibly ventured out in Mogadishu or in most other parts of the country without fully armed escorts.

An al-Shabaab attack on the UN compound in Mogadishu in June 2013 severely checked any international optimism that Somalia might at last be on the point of re-joining the community of orderly nations. It was the sort of assault in which Somali jihadists specialised. A truck bomb was detonated at the front gate, and, in the terror and confusion that followed, gunmen entered through the breach to wreak more havoc. Eight people at the site were killed and the immediate effect was to drive UN personnel back from the city into the better-guarded airport complex.

'That attack broke a lot of spirits at the UN and in the NGOs,' an aid security expert told me in Nairobi. 'They were naive to think there would be a new peaceful Somalia. All that has crumbled. It was a big warning to them. They realised that these people can hit us and get away with it.'

There were other attacks around the same time that were also directed at foreign targets. Then, in January 2014, al-Shabaab intensified its campaign – not this time with bombs and bullets, but with chilling words of warning. It was the most explicit threat it had ever made against aid agencies in Somalia and ranks as one of the most alarming jihadist statements of the whole war on terror.

'Muslim people should be especially on their guard against those claiming to be humanitarian agencies,' the statement read. 'People should not be misguided by those claiming that they are supporting the country. People should extend their hand to Allah and beg him if they need anything ... we are saying that the Muslim people stay away from what is called the humanitarian agencies that bring bad things, people should not work for them, people should not go to their offices because they are invaders, they are people fighting against us ...'

The reference to national staff ('people should not work for them') was particularly troubling. As the aid security expert in Nairobi explained, large NGOs tend to pay more attention to the safety of their international staff than to their locally hired colleagues. Yet it is the latter, here as everywhere else in contemporary conflicts, who are exposed more consistently to danger. 'This campaign against national staff could seriously undermine the NGO effort,' the security specialist said.

In these circumstances, my efforts to visit any of the few big overseas NGOs with a base in Mogadishu came to nothing. One agency, Save the Children, was all too willing to help at local level, but head office refused to let me visit its Mogadishu office, let alone any of its projects. Other agencies were more helpful than Save the Children's famously uncommunicative press office, but the answer was the same. The Norwegian Refugee Council said that 'the security situation in Mogadishu remains critical and we cannot take responsibility', and the Irish agency Concern told me with regret that they were not allowing their own international staff to travel, so they could hardly facilitate my visit.

Had it not been for the UN's Office for the Coordination of Humanitarian Affairs and its determination to keep the blue flag flying, I might not even have made it to the city. The pressure on UN humanitarian agencies in Somalia was by now intense. Not only did their staff face the daily risk of living and working in Mogadishu, they were also expected to follow on the heels of African Union troops into towns and regions from which al-Shabaab had been freshly expelled.

The jihadists make no distinction between the UN's humanitarian role – its work for children, for refugees and for the hungry – and its political and military objective of taking on and defeating al-Shabaab. Their attack on the UN compound was a direct riposte to a Security Council decision to establish an 'integrated mission' in Somalia in which all UN agencies would work for one common purpose. This controversial process, central to the UN's modern role, has been resisted by some of its own agencies and now only adds to their vulnerability in the field.

'Because of the work we do, we used to say that we would not be a target,' one staffer with a UN humanitarian agency told me in Mogadishu. 'Then came the attack, and we knew a message was being sent, and that we were part of a new UN. With an integrated mission, they are merging the blue UN and the black [military] UN and we feel more vulnerable when we wear that hat because it has a political element.'

'That June attack hit us deep in our soul,' said another senior UN humanitarian worker. 'It killed friends we laughed with every night. Between ourselves, we are really not happy that we are part of an integrated mission.'

The pressure is worst of all for locally recruited staff. Unlike UN expatriates who return at the end of the working day to a secure compound, national staff drive off to their homes in the city. There they risk being marked down by the jihadists as targets. The result is that local UN workers go to great lengths to avoid any public association with their employers.

On journeys out of the office, UN staff have to follow 'standard operating procedures' and wear helmets and flak jackets. These civilian aid workers drive out of their compounds in armoured Land Cruisers with a 24-strong security detail and three additional escort vehicles – two from the UN plus a Somali security team driving a 'Mad Max' pickup with a heavy machine gun mounted in the back.* Local staff have no wish to be linked with such a show of weaponry and often choose to reach the location independently and unprotected.

Western NGOs in Somalia follow the same security protocols, but also vary them in the field. One charity director insists that full armoured protection be worn while on the road, but relaxes the rule during project visits. 'You can hardly wander up and start talking to children in body armour and helmets,' he told me. Nevertheless, that is exactly how most official aid workers are expected to dress in many of the wars of the twenty-first century.

Senior UN officials acknowledge that Somali perceptions of its humanitarian role might be compromised by what it sees as its larger international purpose of defeating terrorism. They stress, however, that the UN Security Council resolution mandating the new 'integrated' mission underlined that 'when it comes to humanitarian assistance to the population, this assistance has to remain impartial, independent and neutral'.

The United Nations stance on Somalia has triggered argument and dissension among the NGOs that congregate in Nairobi, some with their own forward bases in Mogadishu, others at work in

---

* These vehicles are known as 'technicals', a term that is said to have originated with the international NGOs in Somalia. When insecurity forced the agencies to hire such protection, it went down in charity accounts as 'technical assistance'.

cross-border partnerships with Somali organisations. Major official donors in the West fund much of their Somali aid effort through the UN, so NGOs have to be part of the so-called UN 'cluster' system if they are to win contracts and stay in business. Save the Children became so troubled by UN partisanship in Somalia that it pulled out of the coordinating body overseeing the choice and allocation of projects and said it would not be returning. It marked an unusual stand on principle against UN integration of its humanitarian and military roles.

For aid workers who subscribe to fundamental humanitarian principles, the issue raised by the UN's 'one mission' in Somalia is one of simple practicality. 'This political solution has firmly locked the United Nations out of half the country,' was the way one experienced charity director put it to me in Nairobi. 'There is no attempt to talk to al-Shabaab. All we are told is that we have just got to defeat them.'

He went on: 'I'm not being naive about this. They are thoroughly nasty people. So it's not going to be easy. But the world has got to recognise that these guys exist and that they're seriously committed to this fight. The UN has now become a "Western Nations" organisation. It's no longer a United Nations. They're not coordinating anything; they're just on one side.'

For this NGO director, it seemed that Western politicians, with Americans and Britons in the lead, have been busily reframing humanitarianism for the modern era. It was close to becoming just another component in contemporary anti-terror warfare. He quoted a senior UN humanitarian executive as declaring on a recent visit to East Africa: 'Humanitarianism as we understand it no longer has any political support in the West.'

Of all the humanitarian agencies that have wrestled with the chaos and complexity of Somalia over the decades, it is the International

Committee of the Red Cross – as so often – that emerges with the greatest credit. The ICRC dates its formal presence in the region back to 1977, when war broke out between Ethiopia and Somalia in the Ogaden desert. The ICRC established a permanent presence in Mogadishu in 1983 and since then has played a life-saving role in two of the great famines of the modern era, in 1991–92 and in 2011.

Somalia made history in the early 1990s, not just for the depth of its suffering but also for the character of the foreign intervention. When political meltdown and clan violence threatened a humanitarian catastrophe, almost the entire independent aid world called for Western military intervention. The United Nations Security Council declared the crisis to be a threat to international peace and authorised the use of 'all necessary means to establish as soon as possible a secure environment for humanitarian relief operations in Somalia'. This became the US military's 'Operation Restore Hope'.

Sticking to its principles, the ICRC was alone among major humanitarian agencies in not joining the chorus for a military invasion. Then, in the company of a few other big players – CARE, World Vision, Save the Children and Médecins Sans Frontières – it remained on hand to bring relief to a stricken population. Working through the Somali Red Crescent, it deployed many thousands of volunteer aid workers in some of the least secure parts of the country to run emergency feeding centres. Its work is recognised to this day by Somalis. I heard it said more than once that the International Red Cross 'saved the country', no less, in 1991–92.

Twenty years on, when another famine struck – compounded once again by severe drought and desperate insecurity – the ICRC mounted a similar rescue operation. At one point it was feeding more than a million people, and because of its strong local reputation was accommodated by the al-Shabaab militias that controlled the worst-affected areas. That understanding did not last. In January

2012, local insurgents seized a large Red Cross food consignment and the ICRC suspended its relief operations. Not long afterwards, in May 2012, the ICRC joined other Western aid agencies on al-Shabaab's banned list.

In Mogadishu, the ICRC continues to function as it has tried to do for the past 30 years. Although no expatriates were based in the city in 2014, there were frequent visits. When I was there, a team was conducting a series of prisoner visits in Somali jails in fulfilment of the ICRC's role as the guardian of the Geneva Conventions.

Somalia's gun-toting culture has imposed specific constraints on the way in which even the ICRC can work on the ground. In Afghanistan and Pakistan, it still relies, just, on its familiar and distinct identity – those big red crosses – to stay safe. There are no weapons on its premises or on board its vehicles and there are no armed escorts for ICRC travellers. Somalia has required a practical adjustment to these principles, as the conflict in Chechnya did in the 1990s.

When the ICRC regretfully concluded that its offices and staff needed armed protection, it asked its own long-term head of security, a Somali, to do the job for them. He in turn set up his own private security firm and made all the vital balances of clan and family in appointing his team. On journeys away from the office, ICRC personnel are now accompanied by the ubiquitous 'technical' with its heavy machine gun and its six or seven uniformed men bearing Kalashnikovs.

Security concerns came close to overwhelming the Western world's aid efforts in Somalia, and that went for its diplomatic presence as well. The British became the first – and, in 2015, still the only – Western nation to re-establish an embassy (and a permanent aid presence) in Mogadishu.

Their return came after a 20-year gap in which most of the world had kept well away from the country. Prime Minister David Cameron sought to take the international lead on Somalia and to counter the deadly combination of piracy, kidnap and terrorism. He went one step further in September 2015 in announcing that he would deploy 70 British soldiers to Mogadishu to help train African Union troops. In an echo of past glories, the British Foreign and Commonwealth Office describes these initiatives as 'expeditionary diplomacy'.

Britain trebled its aid budget to Somalia. The Department for International Development declared Somalia to be 'the world's most fragile country' and said it would fail to meet any of its current development goals. Next to expenditure on emergency relief and health, the big British priority has been to find ways of tackling Somali disorder. They have spent money on the police and justice system, on human rights, and on the central prison in Mogadishu. There was a 'Conflict Pool' and a separate 'Counter-terrorism Fund'. The purpose of it all, one diplomat told me, was to try to 'drain the swamp'.

The British did not return to their original embassy. That was a ruined shell near the port which they abandoned in the early 1990s. Instead, they put up single-storey prefabs behind a succession of tall wire fences in a distant corner of the airport complex. I was told that the European Union, one of Somalia's biggest aid-funders, was eyeing a possible office site next door and that the French and Italians were in competition for another plot, but neither had shown up yet.

The most curious diplomatic representation of all in Mogadishu is the American. If you went online in 2015 you were welcomed to the 'United States Virtual Presence Post' in Somalia. The US had also evacuated its Mogadishu embassy more than two decades earlier, and, like the British, had concluded that the famine of 2011 combined with fresh military pressure on al-Shabaab had set Somalia on a new course. Yet so searing were the memories of 'Black Hawk Down' in the US consciousness – as well as the more recent killing of the US ambassador and three other Americans in Libya in 2012 – that Washington was in little hurry to re-establish its embassy there. 'That is still one of our primary mission objectives,' said US officials in 2014, 'but we're not there yet.'

Along with its political relationships, America's aid programme in Somalia is run from its embassy in Nairobi. US officials are permitted to travel to Mogadishu, but such visits are limited in duration and generally confined to a few well-protected buildings at the airport. Somali ministers and officials have to drive all the way out there and undergo the most rigorous of security checks if they are ever to meet American aid-givers face to face.

At a briefing I attended in the US embassy in Nairobi in 2014, a senior US diplomat was not able to join us because there had just been a bomb in Mogadishu and it was his job to make sure that the US Special Representative for Somalia, who was on a visit to the city, returned safely to Nairobi. To add drama to the occasion, the embassy chose that afternoon to stage a 'duck and cover' anti-terror drill.

'Duck and cover,' boomed the public address system. 'Get away from the windows, take cover and await further instructions.' Pause. 'Secure all classified documents and evacuate the building using the nearest exit.'

Probably the most effective aid-giver to Somalia is not generally counted among the world's major donors at all. Turkey has Islam in common with Somalia and historical links with the Horn of Africa that predate the coastal land-grabs and arbitrary colonial borders of the European period. In the modern era of aid as 'soft power', Turkey has adopted an approach in Somalia that differs sharply from that of the big Western institutions – the United Nations, the European Union, the Americans, the British and others. The Turks believe that they do aid better than the rest, certainly more economically; they take bigger risks; and they have little interest in liaising with the 'aid community' at large.

The Turks do not sit behind the lines in Nairobi. They are in Mogadishu. Their embassy is not at the international airport; it is in the city proper. When I was first in touch with the ambassador, he told me he had no reason to travel to Nairobi and never went to meetings at the airport. I was most welcome to visit him at the embassy. The upshot was an airport rendezvous one morning with a convoy of blacked-out armoured Land Cruisers bristling with Turkish security men who would escort me to my appointment.

Dr Kani Torun was appointed ambassador in August 2011, just a few days after Recep Tayyip Erdoğan, the then Turkish prime minister, became the first non-African leader to travel to Mogadishu in two decades. Al-Shabaab had only just pulled out of the city and the Turks staged a prime ministerial visit of real theatrical impact. Erdoğan arrived in the country accompanied by his wife and daughter and half his cabinet. 'The tears now running from Somalia's golden sands into the Indian Ocean must stop,' he declared.

The man chosen to be ambassador was well qualified for the job. As a doctor working in Britain in the late 1990s, Kani Torun was inspired by the suffering in Kosovo to start a medical charity of his own. For a decade he ran Doctors Worldwide from Manchester; as other groups had done, it set out to harness the skills and commitment of Britain's Muslims in the overseas humanitarian field. Doctors Worldwide flourished in Britain, and when NGO regulation was eased in Turkey it established a branch there in 2005. The offspring now outstrips the parent in size.

The Turks in Somalia embarked on a raft of significant aid projects, concentrating first on the capital. 'Mogadishu is the place where the Somali state collapsed,' Dr Torun told me. 'A capital city should be the mirror of a country and so we want to change the image of Mogadishu. If Mogadishu becomes better, it will spread. We have plans for other top cities.'

Turkey's most eye-catching early project was to cleanse Mogadishu of its swollen, city-wide rubbish tips. After years of chaos brought about by al-Shabaab's occupation of much of the city, the place stank. 'You should have come here two years ago,' the ambassador said to me, 'and now see the difference. The city becomes cleaner and cleaner.' Instead of looking for African subcontractors around the region or waiting to foster local Somali 'capacity', the Turks called up the Istanbul municipal authority. They built a waste treatment plant near Mogadishu airport and Turkish garbage trucks went out on their rounds in city streets.

It was thanks to the Turks that street lighting made its important contribution to security once again; that Turkish Airlines started serving Mogadishu as soon as Turkish repairs to the airport had been carried out; and that Turkish engineers were out on the streets over-seeing a road-building programme. I was told by grateful Somalis that better roads led to better road discipline and thus a more orderly city. They added that it was surprisingly difficult to plant a bomb without detection in a well-constructed stretch of tarmac.

Starting work at the height of the 2011 famine, the Turkish Red Crescent opened and ran a camp for 30,000 displaced people near the airport, and their kitchens in the city produced 10,000 hot meals a day for orphanages, schools and hospitals. Big infrastructure projects opened the way for other welfare and development work. The Turks built or refurbished several hospitals, including a modern 200-bed unit that the ambassador claimed was 'better than anything in Nairobi'. New schools had been built, including a technical college concentrating on fishing skills. There were some 2,000 Somali students on scholarships in Turkey.

Turkey's overseas aid programme funded most of the running costs of these projects, but the capital sums invested were the result of the generosity of the Turkish public. After his visit to Somalia in 2011, Prime Minister Erdoğan returned home in the holy month of Ramadan, which is also the season of Muslim giving. With his wife and his ministers, he went on television and started campaigning to raise money for Somalis suffering in the famine and to finance Turkish development schemes. The initiative raised a remarkable $300 million.

The Turks believe in a direct, hands-on approach to aid-giving rather than the contractor model adopted by the Europeans and North Americans. They deal with Somali institutions – official and voluntary – and do not route their funds through the coordinating mechanisms of the United Nations. They are certain they get far better value for money this way and avoid the huge administrative overheads of a UN system still substantially based in Nairobi.

To make his point, the Turkish ambassador quoted the mayor of Mogadishu, Mohamed Nur, who told this story to a journalist in 2013: 'If I request computers from the UN, they will take months and require a number of assessments. They will spend $50,000 to give me $7,000 of equipment. If I request computers from Turkey, they will show up next week.'[2]

Turkey's aid effort in Somalia also benefits from a significant expatriate presence on the ground. The ambassador, among many others, is sceptical about the level of trust that Western donors and NGOs are prepared to place in their local partners, particularly those in parts of the country controlled by al-Shabaab. 'Some of these so-called NGOs are managed by very corrupt people,' said Dr Torun. 'They get their money from Western organisations and they are very good at preparing fancy reports for their donors. Somali people know this.'

Turkey has paid a heavy price for its prominence in Mogadishu. Turkish civilians were targeted twice in 2013. In April that year it was a car bomb attack on a Turkish Red Crescent convoy near the airport. A Somali driver was killed and three Turks were injured. In the aftermath of the bombing of the UN compound in June that year, a copycat assault was mounted against a Turkish staff residence close to the embassy. It was late afternoon and the Turks were preparing the evening meal that breaks the Ramadan fast. A suicide car bomb was blown up at the gate, and then there was a ground assault with small arms and grenades. One Turkish security man died in the attack and three were wounded.

'We're not going anywhere,' was the defiant response of Kani Torun, the ambassador. 'We're here, and that's where we'll stay.'

He accepted that these attacks had had an impact on the Turkish aid operation. 'It affects our mobility – not for myself, but for the NGO people,' he said. Yet the programme continues and the Turks still take risks. 'Turkish people know this is done by al-Qaeda affiliates and this is not the Somali people,' he went on, adding a reference to Turkey's own troubles with Kurdish militants. 'We're very much immune to terror because we've had 30 years of it in eastern Turkey.'

He had a final jibe at the more risk-averse West. 'Western governments are waiting for stability to invest in Somalia,' he said. 'Our approach is to invest in that stability.'

I sought a qualified Somali view on Turkey's role as an aid-giver. Abdi Aynte is a Somali American journalist who became head of the country's first independent think tank and was later appointed

Somalia's minister of planning and international cooperation. We met at the Peace Hotel in Mogadishu, which is all of 50 yards from the airport's main gate, the last 20 of which are on a heavily barricaded side street. Security arrangements were nevertheless required, and Bashir Osman, the hotel owner, generously dispatched two vehicles and five armed men to fetch me.

Abdi Aynte described the Turkish aid model as unique and remarkable and praised the Turks for their direct engagement with Somalis. The programme was quick and impactful, and taking out the UN middlemen saved on costs and bureaucracy. 'In a short span, they've proved themselves qualitatively different,' he said. 'There's a lesson here for our friends in the West.'

When I was to return to the airport gate, a series of single shots rang out from the direction of the checkpoint, and I was asked to wait for a while in the quiet of the Peace Hotel compound. I was assured the shots were probably no more than a traffic-calming measure conducted by jittery African Union troops at the gate. It was a stretch of road frequently targeted by jihadists.

The coast was soon clear, and the hotel's vehicles and security men took me on the 50-yard return journey to the airport check-point. I smiled broadly at a Burundian army officer and, after a long pause for effect, he let me back in. I told my UN driver about the shots at the gate. 'You will hear many shots,' was his reply. 'What we hate is explosions. A bullet can kill only one person. An explosion kills many.'

The impact of Somali disorder is not confined to Somalia. It has spread to neighbouring countries and to nations contributing troops to the African Union force. Somali jihadists have conducted a series of devastating terrorist assaults over the border in Kenya, prompting politicians and the public to question the presence of a huge number of Somali refugees in their country.

For the world's aid-givers, the Somali conflict has also exposed the shortcomings of Western counter-terror laws in the face of humanitarian disaster and has erected yet more barriers to effective relief work on the ground. Even the boldest of aid agencies have suffered reverses and retreat in Somalia.

CHAPTER 7

DELAY COSTS
LIVES

Dadaab, Kenya, February 2014

The German television station RTL responded to the East African famine of 2011 by mounting its own special appeal for the victims. The company added some of the cash it raised through its telethon that year and ended up giving nearly €2 million to the international charity CARE for its work among Somalia's child refugees.

Wolfram Kons was the star of the show. He is a lead presenter on *Guten Morgen Deutschland* and fronts the annual telethon. 'They chose me because I can go without sleep,' he says. Wolfram is also head of the station's charitable foundation *Wir helfen Kindern* – 'We Help Children'. After several postponements because of security concerns, he and his cameraman Vinni were at last on their way to Dadaab, close to the Somali border in north-eastern Kenya and site of the world's largest refugee camp. He would now report on how the viewers' money had been spent.

From the dusty airstrip, we drove 12 miles to the furthest corner of this strung-out refugee settlement in the bush. Our CARE convoy was preceded by a team of Kenyan police reservists specially trusted because of their local connections. Kenyan police regulars brought up the rear. They were considered the more likely targets of local jihadists, so putting them right at the back, with a big gap, was thought the safest option.

The whole party was now travelling on a tight German television schedule. Wolfram had allowed himself only six hours on the ground to find and film everything he needed for his report. He had flown into Nairobi the previous night and would return to Germany later that day so as to get back into the studio the next morning. By contrast, I was on a writer's schedule, and it is an invariable media rule that television takes precedence over print.

At the school where RTL money had built classrooms for 800 pupils, Wolfram went into animated action for the camera. He handed out the midday meal of corn-soya porridge (knocking back some of it himself), he washed his hands and drank fresh tap water from CARE-installed boreholes and even managed to say something upbeat as he emerged from the boys' latrines. He clambered to the top of a water tower for a wide shot of the camp in its scrubland setting. 'We were told not to spend too much time up here,' he said. 'Snipers or something like that ...'

Wolfram interviewed the school's head teacher, met pupils in their classroom and joined a meeting of the parent–teacher association. There was well-drilled appreciation from them all. The parents underlined the importance of education. 'This will mean that the new generation of Somalis will contribute to the life of the nation,' they told him, adding that no early return across the border to Somalia was possible. 'Still the situation is not stable, so we will need continued help from the international community,' they said.

Responsibility for Dadaab refugee camp lies with the United Nations High Commissioner for Refugees (UNHCR), but day-to-day management is in the hands of the Canadian section of CARE International. The Canadians look in turn to funders such as CARE Germany to manage such vital relationships as those with ECHO, the European Union's humanitarian aid organisation, and the German government. At the start of this funding stream are television reports like Wolfram's which help maintain public interest when the news media have moved on to other crises – and have taken the politicians with them.

CARE has been in Kenya since the 1960s, and in Dadaab for as long as there has been a camp here. In the grim world of refugee statistics, Dadaab used to be runner-up in size to Jalozai, the camp for Afghan refugees I visited in Pakistan. Now Dadaab exceeds Jalozai as the world's biggest. The human catastrophe of Syria has put many more people to flight than Somalia's war and hunger, but the Syrians have ended up in camps and communities much smaller than Dadaab. These strung-out settlements in the Kenyan bush still constitute the world's largest concentration of refugees.

Food supplies, health and education, shelter and sanitation are the basics of camp life, but there is also room for more imaginative initiatives. Such was the idea conceived by two young Kenyan women working for CARE as they noted the approaching third anniversary of the start of the Syrian civil war.

'I am telling them not to take part in the war, to work hard and to respect their leaders,' explained Fathi, a pupil at one of the CARE-run schools in Dadaab. The local CARE team of Mary Muia and Reshma Khan had decided to encourage Somali boys and girls in Dadaab to write letters to their Syrian contemporaries in the camps in Jordan. Reshma would deliver the letters to Amman and bring back the replies.

'I am not a Kenyan by nationality but I am a Somali girl who is living in Dadaab refugee camp and there had been a civil war in my country for at least 23 years consecutive,' wrote Hibo to Syria's schoolchildren. 'I am really encouraging you not to lose hope you will get peace and stability.' Hibo drew a dove of peace at the top of her letter.

'Our beloved brothers and sisters, go and work hard in schools, be the stars and the new presidents of Syria,' wrote Dahir. 'First I am giving a special thanks to the agencies who care about the refugees,' added Abshir in his letter. 'Second I hope your country to be peace and settled well.'

Then there were the responses from young Syrians. 'When I receive the letter from other refugee children,' one wrote, 'it touch my heart that someone strange is encouraging me and can feel my pain.' He added: 'If God sends you down a stony path, may He give you strong shoes.'

Dadaab refugee camp lays out the stark human geography of Somalia's collapse as a state. It also tells the story of two terrible famines 20 years apart. So total has been the disorder in whole regions of the country that in the famines of 1991 and 2011 – and lesser crises along the way – Somalis were not only incapable of feeding themselves, but also unable to rely on outsiders to bring any food to them. The aid simply never reached them. From 90,000 refugees 20 years ago, in Somalia's first big convulsion, Dadaab's numbers grew to more than 500,000 in 2011 and were still close to 400,000 when I visited three years later.

The story of Dadaab underlines the enormity of the challenge that the war on terror has presented to the aid agencies – and how far they have fallen short in their response. Two years on from the 2011 famine, experts concluded that 250,000 had died as the world stood by. United States counter-terror laws – and their echoes in the rest of the West – played a significant part in creating the delay. On the other side in this war, Somali jihadists showed themselves to be so inhumane towards their own civilians and towards outside aid workers that even the bravest agencies are now in retreat.

The first the world at large knew of the 2011 emergency was, as always, from television news. TV teams made the journey from Nairobi to Dadaab to record the arrival of thousands, then tens of thousands, of starving families from the Somali interior. Those who reached the camp had not eaten for days. Parents had lost children on the march, and had buried them where they collapsed. Some of those who survived the journey died before they could be nourished back to health. This was what the media called a 'walk of death'.

Aid agencies had known about the developing crisis for months. The Horn of Africa was where so many of the worst famines of the late twentieth century had taken place – Ethiopia in 1973 and 1984, Sudan in 1985 and 1986, Somalia itself in 1991 – and as a result there was a sophisticated system in place to predict fresh emergencies. FEWS NET, the Famine Early Warning Systems Network, is funded by the United States, and predicted a crisis from the moment it first recorded drought and crop failures in 2010.

The Somalia emergency of 2011 was the first big famine of the twenty-first century. It was also the most political. It was the product of poor rains, but also of conflict and inaccessibility. Responses to it reflected long-lasting divisions within Somalia, but also in the region and among forces further afield. The major aid agencies scrambled belatedly to give assistance, but tended to emphasise their few successes, not their glaring failures.

It took another two years for the scale of the disaster to be revealed fully. In May 2013, the United Nations and the US government agency USAID, which paid for all the early warnings, published a report compiled by British and American public health researchers. Based on calculations of 'excess mortality' – deaths above the number expected over such a period in such poor communities – it estimated that a shocking 258,000 Somalis had died in the famine, the majority of them (133,000) children under five.[1]

The study said that it could not attribute these deaths to a single cause; rather, 'our estimates should be viewed as the combined impact of drought, reduced humanitarian assistance, high food prices and civil strife in the affected regions'. Consequences such as disease had to be seen in 'a context of persisting and/or worsening insecurity'.

These figures bracketed the 2011 Somalia famine, in its human cost, with some of the worst African tragedies of the last century, including even the 1984 famine in Ethiopia. Although drought and crop failure had a widespread impact throughout East Africa, the UN/USAID report concluded that 90 per cent of the deaths occurred in south and central Somalia bordering Kenya.

As the emergency unfolded inside Somalia, charity appeals for its victims were based on television pictures from the refugee camp in Dadaab. A lot of money was raised and much good work was done. But direct engagement in southern Somalia eluded most of the aid world. Such was the suspicion of al-Shabaab towards a hostile West that almost all the aid-givers had already been expelled. At best there was a modest, poorly monitored flow of assistance through the lines to local Somali groups working under the thumb of al-Shabaab. The jihadist message was pitiless and accounted for yet more lives. 'If people are hungry,' they said, 'they must pray harder – or move.'

It was never going to be popular to draw attention to the limitations of NGO efforts in the famine. Far better, the agencies thought, to get on and spend the money as well as they could – in the refugee camps, in more peaceful parts of Somalia – than underline the hurdles they faced in trying to operate in one of the harshest theatres of the war on terror.

It was, unsurprisingly, Médecins Sans Frontières that broke ranks. With the famine at its height, Dr Unni Karunakara, MSF's international president, returned from a visit to the region to declare that charities should start treating the giving public as adults. 'There is a con,' he said. 'There is an unrealistic expectation being peddled that you give your £50 and suddenly those people are going to have food to eat. Well, no. We need that £50, yes; we will spend it with integrity. But people need to understand the reality of the challenges in delivering that aid.'[2]

Trying to access those at the 'epicentre' of the disaster was proving slow and difficult. 'We may have to live with the reality that we may never be able to reach the communities most in need of help,' Dr Kurunakara said. He criticised other aid organisations and the media for 'glossing over' the reality in Somalia in order to convince people that money alone could fix the problem.

MSF's intervention drew attention to one of the enduring divisions in the aid world – between 'humanitarian' and 'developmental' approaches to extreme poverty and hunger. Sometimes, as is the case with leading British aid charities, tensions between the two can exist even within the same organisation. As the food crisis in Somalia persisted into 2012, Oxfam and Save the Children came together to produce a joint report offering their own findings on the disaster.

Entitled *A Dangerous Delay* and published in January 2012, it produced what was then a reasonable estimate of the number of famine deaths – between 50,000 and 100,000, drastically fewer than the 258,000 whom the UN/USAID public health researchers later concluded had died. Whatever the final figure, the aid agencies had failed. 'If an early response had saved even a small proportion of these lives, then thousands of children, women and men would still be alive,' Oxfam and Save the Children concluded.[3] 'The scale of death and suffering, and the financial cost, could have been reduced if early warning systems had triggered an earlier, bigger response.'

The two agencies acknowledged that they themselves had been slow to respond. 'Many agencies, including Oxfam and Save the Children, had begun a small-scale response in December 2010,' their report said, 'and tried to focus international attention on the impending crisis.' But 'most agencies did not adapt their programming on a sufficient scale to meet the level of need over the next six months' and did not 'respond at scale' until even later.

The report singled out for praise the US Christian charity World Vision as having declared a 'Category III' emergency in February 2011, a trigger that mobilised its Global Rapid Response Team. Oxfam and Save the Children did not give the emergency that level of priority until 'the end of June and early July respectively', four to five months later.

What also stood out in the Oxfam–Save the Children report was its determination to stress the technical and 'developmental' over the desperate and violent politics of the Horn of Africa. It was as if the implications of contemporary conflict had yet to be properly absorbed by influential aid agencies. While drought and potential famine affected East Africa as a whole, countries at peace in the region could be assisted to deal with food shortages and so avoid widespread death from starvation. Yet nine out of ten of all the deaths from hunger had occurred in that part of Somalia where the West was at war with jihadists. Here, the agencies were largely absent.

Using all the appropriate 'development' terminology but otherwise without much conviction, the report declared the answer to Somalia's tragedy to be 'a fundamental shift to integrated, long-term, flexible programming that aims to reduce the risks faced by people whose livelihoods are extremely vulnerable'. Long-term development work was best placed to respond to drought, with 'established programmes, experienced staff, an understanding of vulnerabilities ...'

As for civil war in Somalia, 'Reducing Armed Violence and Conflict' was down at item number 5 in a newly proposed 'Charter to End Extreme Hunger'. The world, it stated, had done 'too little to address the vicious mix of poverty, poor governance and violence that sustain conflicts'. Governments and aid agencies would now commit themselves to providing 'timely, appropriate and sufficient humanitarian assistance based on need where insecurity is destroying the chances of life and sustainable development'. But the charter offered little or no assurance that south and central Somalia would become any more accessible in the near future than it had been in the recent past.

Beyond the special pleadings of the aid agencies, there is little doubt that Somalia's famine victims were direct casualties of the war on terror. For its part, al-Shabaab put its hostility towards the West, specifically its suspicion of Western charities, way ahead of the welfare of the people under its control. On the other side in this war, the United States, the world's biggest aid donor, was intent on pursuing its counter-terror agenda at the expense of any humanitarian obligation.

The story began in February 2008 when the US listed al-Shabaab as a terrorist organisation. This meant that any case of diverted aid or cash payments that ended up in the wrong hands in Somalia was a crime under US law. Diligent precautions against such occurrences were no defence. Even USAID itself – along with its private partner agencies – was liable to prosecution. The impact in areas of Somalia under jihadist control was apparent within months.

The figures are glaring. Between 2008 and 2010, just as famine conditions were building up, US humanitarian aid to Somalia fell by 88 per cent – from $237 million in 2008 to $99 million in 2009 and then to $29 million in 2010. US funding in the region as a whole under President Obama was reported to be $500 million lower than that committed by the Bush administration. Deprived of money, major NGOs were forced simply to stop work on programmes in southern Somalia. It is reasonable to attribute many of the 250,000 deaths recorded by the UN/USAID researchers in 2013 to these actions of the US government.

The US government's most trenchant critic at the time was Jeremy Konyndyk, who was then director of policy and advocacy at Mercy Corps in Washington. When others in the American NGO world seemed fearful of speaking out in public, Konyndyk voiced his frustrations at Congressional hearings and in the press.

'Avoiding aid diversion is a reasonable goal, and one that humanitarian groups like Mercy Corps share,' Konyndyk wrote in early July 2011.[4] 'But the US's overzealous approach to this challenge now threatens to write off millions of Somalis who face the very real risk of starvation. As things stand now, the US has withheld hunger assistance to the nearly 2 million desperately hungry civilians in areas that the militants control.'

Interventions such as Konyndyk's, combined with the television pictures of starving refugees arriving in Dadaab, forced a late-in-the-day climbdown by the US government. The media spotlight then promoted a frenzy of tragically belated assistance. 'Many humanitarian actors interviewed described a shift from a cautious environment to one where aid was delivered at all cost,' observed the single most impressive study conducted into the Somalia emergency.[5]

'One NGO increased its budget by a factor of 15 within a few months. It was asked by its donor to deliver plane-loads of unidentified goods it had never ordered and whose contents it could only check when the plane landed in Mogadishu.' The same study observed that it was probably the public scrutiny that had 'prompted donors to be more flexible and humanitarian actors less risk-averse'. No such flexibility was evident when US-funded experts manning the regional early warning system first accurately foretold the famine in 2010.

The events of 2011 turned the Somali civil war into larger-scale regional warfare. Two of Somalia's neighbours, Ethiopia and Kenya, sent troops over the border in an effort to smash al-Shabaab and halt the spread of jihad. The Kenyans suffered most by way of retaliation. Two of the war on terror's most infamous outrages took place on Kenyan soil over the following years – the attacks on the Westgate shopping mall in Nairobi in September 2013, which killed 67, and on Garissa University College in April 2015, which killed 148. There were other mass killings in between.

Dadaab itself was on the front line in this war. The porous Kenya–Somalia frontier presented no obstacle to jihadist infiltrators, and al-Shabaab could rely on a measure of support from among the refugees. The first roadside bomb at the camp was recorded in November 2011, just three weeks after Kenyan soldiers crossed the Somali border. In the weeks before I visited in February 2014, two more bomb attacks struck at CARE's operations in Dadaab – one during refuelling operations at one of the camp's boreholes, the other aimed at the long staff convoy that races each morning from one settlement to the next in the strung-out encampment.

CARE Canada did not flinch, for the moment. They believed it was their Kenyan police escorts, not themselves, who were the target. Next in the firing line, they thought, would be the UN because of its military engagement in Somalia. CARE had been working with Dadaab's refugees for 20 years, and reasoned that they still enjoyed the relative security that comes of long-term community engagement. Hence the strict convoy etiquette that ruled for a gap of 100 metres between one of their own vehicles and the Kenya Police Land Rovers following behind.

'It's still an attack on our humanitarian space,' said one senior CARE official. 'And make no mistake, if something really bad happens, the NGOs will withdraw and CARE will withdraw, too.'

Bigger than the bomb threat in Dadaab was the risk of kidnap. Among the reasons for the growing hostage trade was the international success against Somali pirates in the Indian Ocean. This had had the effect of encouraging pirate gangs to move to the interior in search of alternative targets and income. Dadaab was one of the hostage hunting grounds. CARE's security briefing for the camp declared the kidnap risk 'to be very high for INGO staff'.

'So we're damned if we do use police escorts,' said the senior CARE man in reference to the roadside bomb attacks, 'and we're damned if we don't' – because that lays them open to abduction if they are not protected.

CARE had already suffered one tragic loss from kidnapping. At the height of the famine in Somalia in 2011 they had been showing a group of visitors around Dadaab. The party had stopped to look at the freshwater system installed for newly arrived refugees. James Gichuhi, their Kenyan driver, was waiting outside for his passengers to return to the vehicle when he was overpowered and abducted. James has not been seen or heard of since.

The biggest prize for the kidnappers is expatriate personnel, with Westerners at the top of the most-wanted list. In June 2012 they targeted a team from the Norwegian Refugee Council (NRC), well accustomed to front-line work in hostile environments. Elizabeth Rasmussen, the NRC's secretary general, was visiting Dadaab from Oslo in the company of senior regional colleagues. They were fortunate both to survive the attack and to avoid lengthy captivity.

The NRC seems to have decided against armed protection for the visit, choosing instead to use nondescript vehicles as cover. It didn't work, either because news of the visit had leaked out or because they were travelling in a prominent three-vehicle convoy. As they emerged from an NRC compound in the camp, they were blocked front and rear by vehicles full of armed men. One NRC driver escaped from the ambush with Ms Rasmussen and others on board. A second driver, Abdi Ali, was shot and killed. A third was injured.

Four expatriates – a Norwegian, two Canadians and a Filipino – were taken hostage and then driven and marched over the border into Somalia. There is reticence at the NRC over what happened next, but within 72 hours the four were free again, in an operation apparently mounted by local Somali militiamen and Kenyan forces. The incident was one of the worst that the NRC has ever faced and had a significant impact on its security procedures. The agency is one of several NGOs that have opted to buy expensive armoured vehicles to protect staff at risk in exposed locations such as Dadaab.

'We're no longer living in the 1970s, the 1980s or even the 1990s, when humanitarian workers were greeted with respect,' one senior aid manager told me in Nairobi. 'Now humanitarian workers are at as much risk as anyone else. In a way it's worse because they are such soft targets. Part of the problem is that aid has become so much more political, so the neutrality of humanitarian work is at risk of being undermined and neglected.'

Another NGO country director observed how 'heavily militarised' Dadaab had become, with fences topped with razor wire and its entrances obstructed by concrete blocks as protection against suicide truck bombs. 'In all the larger camps there's now a gap between aid-givers and their beneficiaries,' he complained. 'You think about the days when you could go into the community and sit down and drink tea with our beneficiaries. Those days are over.'

With each fresh terrorist attack in Kenya – in the north-east, in Nairobi or on the coast – domestic pressure intensifies to kick the refugees out. Kenyan politicians and officials step up their rhetoric against the Somalis in their midst, accusing them of harbouring jihadists. 'According to the Kenyans, every single refugee is a terrorist,' I was told by one international refugee manager. Somali refugees, said senior Kenyan officials, were the biggest single threat to Kenyan security – the talking had to stop; it was time they all went home.

The pressure boiled over after the Garissa college massacre in April 2015. Kenya would now change, said the country's deputy president William Ruto, 'the way America changed after 9/11'. He demanded that the UNHCR close Dadaab and remove its 350,000 refugees within three months – by July that year – or 'we shall relocate them ourselves'. This was the most extreme threat issued so far in the tense and protracted international negotiations over the refugees' future.

Towards the end of 2013, the Kenyan and Somali governments had come together with the UNHCR to sign a special tripartite agreement governing repatriation. Detailed planning was left in the hands of the UNHCR and its specialist NGO partners such as the Norwegian Refugee Council. Provision was made for the supply of thousands of special travel packs for the journey, and cash was handed out for bus travel within Somalia. 'Is it safe for me to return to Somalia?' was one of the questions posed on leaflets handed out to refugees. 'Return to Somalia is voluntary,' said the handout. 'No one should force or intimidate you to return.'

There was an early uptake for the assisted repatriation programme, but it was largely confined to recent refugee arrivals, to those who had fled in response to the approaching famine of 2010–11. Dadaab's core population, refugees who had crossed the border in the 1990s and had built their lives in the camp, were much more reluctant to trust assurances that security was returning to Somalia. Kenya's impatience with the slow progress was met with an unusually strong response from the United Nations and the voluntary refugee agencies. There was to be no coercion to return, not even any formal encouragement. Again and again the watchword was 'voluntary'.

The aid world was frankly sceptical that Somalia was in any state to accommodate an accelerated return. There were still 300,000 or so displaced people in the capital Mogadishu whom the authorities were unable to send back home, and while African Union troops had recaptured many of the big towns from al-Shabaab, the militants still controlled the countryside from where most of Dadaab's residents had fled.

Despite critical underfunding of the camp at Dadaab – leading to 30 per cent cuts in food rations, for instance – the principles underlying refugee welfare are well established. There is a body of international law underpinning them and there are remarkably well-qualified individuals in positions of authority whose job is to implement them. It was not by chance that the senior UN official in Dadaab and the Norwegian Refugee Council chief in Nairobi in 2014 should both be Somali refugees.

Ahmed Warsame, UNHCR's head of operations in Dadaab, fled Somalia because of the civil war and became a Canadian citizen. His home is in Winnipeg. Hassan Khaire, regional chief of the Norwegian Refugee Council, was born and raised in Mogadishu before he too became a refugee. He is now a Norwegian citizen. Their appointments underscore the emergence of a new generation of front-line aid executives who, emotionally and practically, may be rather better qualified to deal with a harsh new world than their European and North American counterparts.

Next to food and water, medical care is the most basic need for refugees and civilians caught up in conflict. Many in Dadaab, as in Somalia itself, had for decades been able to rely on Médecins Sans Frontières. MSF's big budgets and its established independence from governments provided the agency with exceptional access, although nothing in contemporary Somalia offers any guarantee of safety. In the course of just a few weeks in the famine year of 2011, MSF was hit by two grave security incidents that had life-threatening consequences for its entire programme.

Montserrat Serra and Blanca Thiebaut were young Spanish women working on MSF logistics in Dadaab. In October 2011, they were ambushed in the camp, and their driver was shot and injured. The women were then driven over the border into Somalia. This incident, along with a string of other kidnappings, preceded the major Kenyan cross-border military operation against al-Shabaab. The women's ordeal lasted a full 21 months before they were released in July 2013. Kidnap negotiations, along with any ransom demanded or paid, are one of the very few matters that MSF never addresses in public.

Some weeks after the abductions in Dadaab, and quite unconnected with that incident, two members of MSF's international staff based in Mogadishu, the Belgian emergency coordinator Philippe Havet and Dr Kace Keiluhu from Indonesia, were shot dead in their offices. Their killer was a Somali member of staff and the dispute involved a complex mix of theft, sackings and clan allegiances. In 20 minutes of firing in the compound, not a single Somali was hurt.

Faced with these incidents, MSF's various national sections either scaled back on their activities or withdrew their teams entirely. Security precautions were redoubled. But there was another factor at play which provoked greater outrage at MSF and led to more drastic action. Over bitter months of discussion and negotiation, senior MSF managers concluded that the Somali leadership – government as well as insurgent – was simply contemptuous of humanitarian practices and principles and of the need for basic staff security.

The man who shot dead the two MSF expatriates in the capital Mogadishu was called Ahmed Nur. He was eventually overpowered and arrested, then tried and sentenced to 30 years in prison. Three months after his conviction, he was allowed to go free and return to his home town. Somali officials offered MSF no explanation for this other than to point out that it had all happened during a period of political transition in the country.

MSF staff told me that neither the outgoing nor the incoming Somali government, neither the Ministry of the Interior nor the Ministry of Health nor any government minister ever expressed a word of regret about the killings or their aftermath. Trust between aid agency and government was utterly undermined.

The kidnapping of the Spanish women from across the border in Kenya led to a similar collapse of understanding between the aid agency and al-Shabaab insurgents. As MSF pursued its contacts and negotiations during the long months of the women's captivity, it became clear that local al-Shabaab leaders were either conniving – or actively colluding – in the women's detention.

'You can accept the risk of being shelled,' one senior MSF manager told me, 'but parties that welcome us and then target us for financial gain are a different matter. Continuing in these circumstances becomes a suicide mission. It's not a possibility that you'll be killed or kidnapped; it's a certainty that you will be.'

For as long as they were held captive, MSF could not jeopardise the women's safety by taking precipitate protest action. But within weeks of their release, the agency announced it was pulling out of Somalia entirely. It was a huge step to take – and one with appalling consequences for the suffering and innocent civilians of Somalia, as we shall see later.

The agency nevertheless concluded that a basic understanding with Somali political authority as to the role and status of humanitarian work had been undermined. It was summed up for me like this: 'We help you and you don't harm us.' Except in the case of

Somalia it was different. 'It's been replaced by a terrifying new principle in Somalia,' an MSF veteran said to me. 'We help you, and we then put up with any sort of shit you throw at us.'

The close-down extended throughout Somalia, even to parts of the territory considered relatively secure and peaceful. In neighbouring Kenya, the Spanish section of MSF shut down its Dadaab operation in the immediate aftermath of the October abductions. That left just one MSF outpost in the camp – a hospital run by MSF's Swiss section and staffed by Kenyans and Somalis. It received only occasional 'flash' visits from expatriate personnel travelling the 250 miles from Nairobi by the astonishingly expensive expedient of hiring helicopters.

When I visited the hospital, local staff spoke to me about the deteriorating security situation in Dadaab – kidnappings, shootings and roadside bombs – and the impact this had had on expatriates and locals alike. The sudden departure of foreign experts had been particularly unsettling. 'It was very traumatic,' said one of the Kenyan managers. 'We had been working together as friends, and then we were told they were leaving. They had left their home countries in order to help the refugees, so they were not happy to be going at all, and many cut short their missions with MSF.'

When international staff arrive on one of their 'flash' visits, the helicopter drops them right into the hospital compound in a cloud of sand and dust. The only road travel permitted is in order to avoid a 2-minute walk to and from their living quarters. It was now Kenyan and Somali staff who were on the front line. 'Of course, anything can happen at any time,' said a young Kenyan woman staff member visiting from Nairobi. 'It's always at the back of my mind. Perhaps it should be at the front.'

In May 2015, MSF reduced its links with Somalia yet further. A month after the college massacre in Garissa and in response to rising insecurity in north-eastern Kenya, the agency said it was pulling 42 of its Kenyan staff out of its remaining mission in Dadaab. The hospital would remain open, but health posts would close. Antenatal care and other services would also be suspended. If one of the boldest and most resourceful of Western aid agencies was beating such a retreat, the prospects for other Western humanitarians staying close to the front line in the war on terror seemed very poor indeed.

CHAPTER 8

ACTS OF FAITH

Reyhanli, Turkey–Syria border, March 2014

It was described to me as a 'really very delicious bakery'. It is in fact a big modern bread-making plant owned and operated by a Turkish NGO on the outskirts of Reyhanli, a few miles from the Syrian border. 'Bakery with NGO attached' was what I wrote in my notebook. It is built on an industrial park and dwarfs the offices of the NGO next door. Everything the Turks have done in response to the overwhelming human disaster in Syria has had to be massive, and by general agreement they have done it magnificently.

On a fairground ride of a conveyor belt the bakery turns out 180,000 flatbread loaves every day, six days a week. A proportion goes to Syrian refugees in Turkey; the rest are trucked over the border to help feed north-western Syria. The benefactors who make the operation possible are rich Arabs from Kuwait and Qatar. 'The Sheikh Abdullah Nouri Charity' was stamped on some of the bread packages, with a saying from the Prophet about securing merit for the Sheikh and his family until Judgement Day. 'Gift of the Qatari People to the Syrian People,' said others. 'Free distribution. No selling inside.'

Bread is more than a dietary staple for Syrians; it is fundamental to the Syrian way of life, as we have noted before. Dr Mounir Hakimi, the British Syrian doctor with whom I travelled to and from the border at the beginning of this book, was eloquent on the subject. 'Bakeries are as important as hospitals,' he told me, 'flour is as important as polio vaccine. Education, medicine and flour – these are the priorities.' Then he grinned. 'You will see Syrians eating rice with bread.'

The absence of bread inside Syria could have created even greater tides of refugees. 'Syrians who don't have bread see themselves as starving,' an aid director told me on the border. 'It's more than just eating. It's a cultural thing. We can take a month's food rations into Aleppo for these families, but they would turn round and say, "But look, there's no bread."'

There is a moment in a BBC television documentary about the children of Syria when a Palestinian boy called Kifah is being interviewed after the siege of the Yarmouk refugee camp near Damascus was lifted briefly. He is asked through an interpreter what life was like inside the camp. 'It was good, normal, but there was some hunger,' he replies solemnly. The interviewer prompts him a little. 'There is no bread,' he says with anguish, and his face crumples into tears.[1]

The Turkish NGO that runs the bakery in Reyhanli is called, in rough translation, the Humanitarian Relief Foundation, but is known by its initials İHH, pronounced 'Ee-Ha-Ha'. İHH was founded by young Turkish activists in the 1990s in their outrage over the fate of their fellow Muslims in Bosnia, notably in the Srebrenica massacre where the instruments of international protection so utterly failed the civilian victims of war.

'The Serbs were killing Muslims in the middle of Europe and the world just watched,' said Hüseyin Oruç, one of the original founders of İHH and now its deputy chairman. 'We told the whole world what was coming. Everyone knew there would be a massacre, but the world did nothing to stop it. That was a huge disaster for us.'

İHH turned its attention next to the desperate fighting in Chechnya. Here it set out its approach to aid-giving. 'We have always chosen conflict areas,' said Mr Oruç. 'Because of the security problems, there's a very limited number of organisations able to operate. Yet it is the people in these areas who are suffering the most.'

İHH deliberately engages with the politics of conflict, and, like some Western European NGOs, sets store by speaking out. 'Public relations and advocacy are as important as relief in the long run,' Mr Oruç went on. 'We cannot conduct relief operations for ever. There has to be more support from outside if there are going to be solutions to these problems. It helps people if we can support them in a crisis, but if we can save a life by trying to resolve the conflict then that is the equivalent of helping all of humanity.'

When I met Mr Oruç in Istanbul, he had just returned from putting this principle into practice. Unusually for an NGO, İHH had been appointed to an international monitoring group whose task was to broker a long-term peace agreement between the Philippines government and Muslim separatists on the island of Mindanao. This project committed Oruç to travelling to the Far East for two weeks every two months.

İHH now commands an annual budget of around $100 million, from a mixture of private and government sources, and is ranked the most influential NGO in Turkey. From its modest start-up in the Balkans, it now has programmes in 130 countries. It has succeeded in aligning Islam's aid-giving traditions to the personal and corporate wealth generated in the years when the Turkish economy boomed.

In a world of regional and national assertiveness, İHH has also contributed a generous measure of soft-power influence to Turkey's re-emergence on the world stage. It was Mr Oruç who introduced me to the phrase 'New Ottomans', although he added hurriedly that his commitment was to creating a strong new civil society in Turkey, not to rebuilding an empire.

İHH retains the activist, risk-taking edge that characterised its earlier interventions. In the agency's office in Reyhanli, next door to the bread ovens, Muhammed Yorgancioğlu, its area director, was telling me about its trucking operation into Syria. On the table between us was the model of a boat. It was the MV *Mavi Marmara*, the ferry that the NGO had acquired so that it could sail with the 2010 Gaza Freedom Flotilla in a well-publicised effort to break the Israeli blockade of the Palestinian territory. The *Marmara* was boarded by the Israelis, and nine Turkish civilians were killed in the confrontation that followed. Many Turks and Israelis were also injured in this audacious, even reckless, example of humanitarian activism.

I was asking Mr Yorgancioğlu for more detail of İHH's current Syrian operations when he suddenly stopped me. 'Will you write this in your book?' he asked. 'All the international media and all the international governments are blind and they are deaf. They don't like to see the bullets being fired in Syria; they don't like to hear all the voices being raised from inside Syria. There are a few organisations that come here with a strong offer of help, but after that they do not come back.'

This frustration with the response of global aid institutions to the Syrian tragedy was forcefully echoed at İHH headquarters in Istanbul. Mr Oruç singled out United Nations agencies for criticism. Diplomatic regard for Syrian sovereignty meant that the UN had not at that point authorised any cross-border assistance for Syrian civilians. 'I've had a very senior UN official in this office saying we cannot help in liberated areas because we have staff in Damascus. So if we help over here, then our staff will face real difficulties. But that is not fair and it is not humane. That leaves the suffering of the Syrian people out of account,' Mr Oruç told me. 'The notion that you have to have "permission" from the host government to give aid to people represents a very big failure.'

Mr Oruç was more broadly critical of the Western aid response in Syria. He accepted that the advance of Islamic State extremists had imposed constraints on the relief effort, but questioned whether enough had been done in the earlier phase of the conflict. 'For two years, they closed their eyes to Syria,' he said. 'Everyone said there was no access, but there was access. We were there and we are still there. Many of these barriers were in their minds.'

Tensions in the humanitarian field between new players such as Turkey and longer-established Western players will be one of the keys to the future course of aid. Mr Oruç spoke positively of his exchanges with the International Committee of the Red Cross, and said he was a personal admirer of Médecins Sans Frontières, but he was scornful of some of the others. For their part, Western aid officials complain that the Turks and other new players are reluctant to coordinate their efforts with mainstream agencies, with the result that there is often duplication and confusion.

As aid-givers prepared for the World Humanitarian Summit in Istanbul in 2016, it was the lessons of Syria that were uppermost in Turkish minds. The first 263 refugees from Syria crossed into Turkey on 29 April 2011 and were directed to specially built refugee camps near the border. They were described as 'guests' and treated like guests. Turkey decided that it would dig into its own pocket to pay for the emergency rather than call on the United Nations. In October 2011, it extended 'temporary protection' to the refugees, the only country in the region to do so.

What Turkey and the rest of the world thought would be a manageable and temporary crisis turned into a steadily escalating humanitarian catastrophe. In late 2012, Turkey's open-door policy shifted to one of limited entry, which led in turn to the creation of a series of makeshift camps on the Syrian side of the border. Those who were admitted into Turkey as refugees continued to be remarkably well accommodated.

'The camps resembled well-established towns with primary and secondary schools, health clinics, community centers, supermarkets, playgrounds, and even laundry rooms,' reported one visiting group of international experts.[2] 'Refugees were given refrigerators and stoves; accommodation had hot water and, in some cases, televisions and air conditioning.'

Instead of coming to an exhausted end, the conflict in Syria only intensified, particularly along the country's northern border with Turkey. Islamic State advances in Iraq brought the Middle East conflagration and its refugee crisis to another of Turkey's international frontiers. By 2015, Turkey was accommodating 1.7 million Syrian refugees, making it the world's largest refugee-hosting country. It was running 22 refugee camps for Syrians with more under construction.[3] At both official and community level, Turkey's response contrasted sharply with the miserly attitude of many European countries to the Syrian exodus, and there was additional exasperation in Turkey over the lack of international financial help.

Only in response to Europe's own refugee crisis did the European Union decide on a significant increase in its humanitarian aid to Turkey. The link was explicit: political pressures on European governments at home would ease if only the Turks could be persuaded to use this aid to keep Syrian refugees in the region and stop them reaching Europe. Turkey had already spent $2.7 billion on its own response to the Syrian crisis between 2011 and 2013, yet had received far less in external assistance than Lebanon or Jordan for hosting many more refugees.

Once again, Western aid experts demonstrated their skill at assessing levels of need and generating polished reports, but proved much less capable of following this up with action. 'In its field trip,' reported the Brookings study quoted earlier, 'the team was struck by the complaints received about the large number of Westerners who visit the area to talk to local authorities, refugee representatives, Turkish NGOs and Syrian National Council (SNC) representatives with little concrete assistance resulting from these visits.

'The problem was best expressed by an official of the education board of the SNC who remarked that "it is all talk, talk, talk and then bye-bye" as he waved his hand at the team.'

Everywhere I went along the Turkey–Syria border and whoever I spoke to among foreign aid officials on the ground, the verdict offered on the quality of the Turkish response was uniformly positive. There was praise for the way in which the Turks gave priority to humanitarian needs and gratitude for the quality of the actions they had taken.

A senior US government official told me: 'I've done a lot of disasters in my time and I wish they had all been next door to Turkey ... When you have a problem, 99 times out of 100 they will help you solve it ... The amount of money Turkey is spending on refugees in this country is simply astounding, amazing, you can use any number of words for it ...'

The medical coordinator of a European NGO commented: 'The Turks have kept the border open and the result is that they have treated many more wounded than anyone else. We've been able to stabilise the wounded and bring them to the border. Their efforts on the humanitarian front have been absolutely fantastic.'

A humanitarian adviser to the Syrian opposition said this: 'If the Turkish government had behaved like Jordan or Iraq, the disaster for Syrians would have been even greater ... Iraq and Jordan have had complete control of the border crossings ... Jordan has even stopped the injured coming.'

The regional director of a leading US NGO made this observation: 'In the region I'm working in, I only wish we had more host
governments like Turkey ... They're the fourth-largest humanitarian donor and their cost-effectiveness and value for money is far
greater than the rest.'

'Independent of its refugee hosting contributions,' said the 2015
Global Humanitarian Assistance Report, one of the aid world's chief
compendiums, 'Turkey has grown in profile as an international
humanitarian donor in recent years, contributing to a number of
responses, including in Somalia through direct presence, when
many other international actors were absent.'[4] The report concluded:
'Given the nature of its role and the scale of its contributions,
Turkey is a key global strategic actor in humanitarian preparedness
and response ...'

Turkey has been ascending the ranks of the world's aid-givers
for 30 years. It dates the inception of its aid programme to June 1985,
when the Ankara government designed a $10 million assistance
package for seven, mainly Muslim, countries in West and East
Africa. Over the following quarter of a century, its annual aid
budget grew towards the $1 billion mark, and by 2010 Turkish aid
was reaching most of the countries of Africa. Turkey had emerged,
as its Ministry of Foreign Affairs put it, as 'a new and dynamic
player in the international development cooperation architecture'.

Some faulted the Turks for identifying future commercial
advantage in their aid to poor countries. Others objected that there
were strategic calculations behind the programme and that dreams
of empire were being revived. If such motives did influence its aid
programme, then Turkey would be behaving in a similar fashion to
most of the other big national aid donors.

Just as Western governments financed their own national
NGOs, so the Turks provided funds for a younger generation of

local aid organisations. In both cases, the piper was expected to play the right tunes. In the case of Turkish NGOs, there was an urge to create organisations capable of defining humanitarian objectives for themselves. The Turks borrowed some of the best characteristics of NGOs in Europe and North America and applied them on their own terms to tasks that they themselves set.

Doctors Worldwide (DWW) is a British charity originally headed by Dr Kani Torun, a Turkish doctor in the North of England. It started by raising money from the Muslim community in Britain and mobilising Muslim professionals to bring medical care to civilians suffering in the Balkans. A decade later, as we have seen, Dr Torun went on to become Turkey's first ambassador back in war-ravaged Somalia, where he established and directed his country's ambitious aid programme.

One of DWW's senior officials in Istanbul, a pharmacist called Muhammad Karabacak, underlined to me how he had been personally inspired by the example of European aid workers. He recalled an aid mission to Gaza as a volunteer and how the 15-day trip had involved five days of waiting on the Egyptian border. He was an Arabic speaker and had gone there, he told me, in order 'to show solidarity with my fellow Muslims and with the Arabs'.

In Gaza he met a French doctor and they spoke of what had prompted each of them to volunteer. 'I came here because I am a human being,' the French doctor told the Turkish pharmacist, and that made Muhammad consider his own motives. 'In my view, his purpose was bigger than mine, and I have changed my thinking about the work we do. We must be prepared to help all humanity without any further expectations.'

In common with other Muslim aid organisations, Doctors Worldwide found that a common religious identity provided no guarantee of security on the front line of contemporary conflict.

Some of the greatest challenges were in Somalia, where decades of fratricidal war had blunted sensibilities and where any aid project aimed at restoring civil structures was likely to face violent resistance.

DWW's big initiative in Mogadishu has been to provide medical expertise for the al-Shifa hospital, purpose-built by the Turks to serve the needs of local residents and refugees. Turkish officials declared it to be the best hospital in the city. Opened in 2012, it was first targeted by jihadists in 2013. Gunmen killed the hospital's Somali director as he left a mosque after Ramadan prayers, and then a week later bombers struck the hospital itself. The targets on that occasion were Turkish visitors, although none were hurt. 'The Turks are part of a group of nations bolstering the apostate regime,' said an al-Shabaab statement claiming responsibility, 'and attempting to suppress the establishment of Islamic *Shari'ah*.'

Faced with this level of hostility, DWW pulled its Turkish project manager out of Mogadishu and suspended visits by Turkish medical personnel who had been passing on their skills to Somali staff. 'Working in Somalia is difficult, we understand that,' Muhammad Karabacak said after these attacks. 'We want to survive this and we will continue to monitor the situation from here. But there are no Turkish doctors there at present.'

On the front line of the Syria conflict, Doctors Worldwide has used its 15 years of experience to guide and mentor the next generation of Muslim aid workers. In the border towns of Turkey they joined forces with Syrian NGOs to run courses for doctors travelling out of the country to acquire new surgical skills. At the original home of Doctors Worldwide in Manchester, there was training of a different kind. DWW staff worked with several Syrian start-ups, including Syria Relief and Hand in Hand for Syria, on how to make grant applications and how to satisfy the requirements of British charity law.

'Just wait and see,' a senior Syrian aid worker said to me in Turkey, not entirely in jest, 'it'll be Syrians who take over the market in the charity sector.' What is certainly true of the evolution of humanitarianism is that each new era of conflict inspires important new aid institutions. The most challenging conflicts are now breaking out in the Muslim world and on the frontiers of the religious divide. Their victims are overwhelmingly Muslim and it is Muslim aid efforts that are playing the largest role in bringing relief to where it is needed. The conduct and character of international humanitarianism are changing.

In straddling the divide between East and West, Muslim and Christian, developed and developing world, Turkey has articulated some important new perspectives on the future of aid. Turkish NGOs are as much a part of this process as Turkey's official aid institutions. They speak the language of the Western aid community, but they do not accept that the West will retain its easy predominance in the field.

'Turkish philanthropists on duty: new actors on the LDC [least developed country] aid map', was the headline in the journal *Turkish Review*.[5] After reviewing the growth of Turkish aid from the 1980s onwards, it spoke of Turkey's $200 million aid commitment to the world's poorest countries and its intention to invest $10 billion in these countries by 2020. It concluded with this striking sentiment: 'It seems Turkey has set its sights on being the "good white men" of the new millennium.'

If Turkish aid-givers have adopted some of the approaches of their European and North American counterparts, Muslim charities based in the West have gone much further in embracing developments within the Western humanitarian movement. One researcher has charted the emergence of what she terms 'secularised aid' among Muslim organisations in Europe, a stance that draws a rigorous distinction between aid work and faith promotion. This secularisation has taken place, Dr Marie Juul Petersen argues, in the years since 9/11 and mirrors similar developments within Christian NGOs in the 1990s.[6]

Dr Petersen's study identifies two British Muslim charities as examples of this trend. She writes that 'by framing themselves as professional organizations, addressing material poverty based on values of universalism and neutrality, organizations such as Islamic Relief and Muslim Aid have tried to promote an aid that resonates with the values of the mainstream aid culture'. These agencies respond to 'conceptions of poverty as material, not spiritual ... best fought through economic development projects and humanitarian aid, not through Islamic education or mosque instruction'.

Islamic Relief, whose work so impressed me in Afghanistan and Pakistan, now rates itself the biggest Muslim NGO in the world, with an income in 2013 of £175 million. Its funding shot up in the early years of the new century, with much of the increase coming from official donors such as Britain's Department for International Development and the European Union. British officials in particular were keen to reach out to Islamic aid organisations in the post-9/11 world.

Dr Petersen concludes that 'the mainstream aid culture, led by government agencies such as DFID, came to perceive a quasi-secular, invisible religiosity as a sign of "good aid" and "moderation", while a visible orthodox religiosity is a sign of "bad aid", "fundamentalism", and perhaps even "extremism"'.

The genius of Islamic Relief in Britain lies in its capacity to retain strong community links while offering its official funders an avenue to meet the needs of the poorest in the most hostile environments. As conflict rages in the Muslim world and Western societies feel threatened at home, the challenge facing both parties – official and charitable – is to sustain and build on an important relationship. The future of Western humanitarianism may depend on it.

The encouragement offered to Islamic Relief by Britain's official aid-funders has not always been extended by the rest of the British government. When this home-grown British aid agency was designated a terrorist organisation by Israel and also, remarkably, by the United Arab Emirates, the support it received from the British Foreign and Commonwealth Office was described to me as, in the first case, 'less than fulsome', and, in the second, 'resoundingly silent'.

Muslim aid workers, even those from the risk-averse West, believe in operating on and, if need be, across the front lines of modern conflict. In April 2014, at a time when almost no Western aid worker – and almost no Western journalist – was crossing into Syria, two of Islamic Relief's most senior executives took a trip to visit their relief projects around Idlib, in north-west Syria.

Jehangir Malik, Islamic Relief's UK director, and Anwar Khan, chief operating officer of Islamic Relief USA – both Pakistani by heritage, friends from Birmingham, one travelling on a UK passport, the other on a US passport – calculated that they would probably be all right provided they did not open their mouths in the wrong company. English or Urdu would immediately mark them out as foreigners.

Because of threats of arrest from the British authorities for even entering Syria, the visit might also have proved awkward on the return journey. 'It's quite murky as to whether this was an offence in Britain or not,' said Jehangir Malik. 'As humanitarians we don't feel we are committing an offence until and unless we work with a proscribed organisation. Under international humanitarian law, we have a mandate to fulfil in places like Syria.'

The real aid millions in the Muslim world come from the Gulf. Spurred on by the severity of modern emergencies, an increasing share of oil revenue is being converted into foreign aid. In the five years to 2013, four leading Gulf donors – Kuwait, Qatar, Saudi Arabia and the United Arab Emirates (UAE) – accounted for more than a third of global aid funds from outside the Western world.[7]

Syria was the priority. When the United Nations held its Syria aid-pledging conference in Kuwait in early 2014, the hosts made a mighty $500 million payment to the cause. Kuwait additionally coordinated an NGO and private philanthropic initiative that contributed another $207 million. Further payments totalling $180 million were pledged by Saudi Arabia, Qatar and the UAE – at $60 million each. This total of close to $900 million lent perspective to even the biggest commitments from the Western world – $380 million from the US, $225 million from the European Union, $164 million from Britain.

Saudi Arabia has emerged as the largest single humanitarian donor outside the Western world. The Saudi record was underpinned with an exceptional commitment to Pakistan at the time of the Indus floods in 2010 – $220 million, a figure that exceeded the contributions of all the European donors put together.[8] Not to be outdone by the Kuwaitis on their pledges to Syria, Saudi Arabia announced shortly afterwards that it was contributing $500 million to an appeal for the humanitarian crisis created by Islamic State advances in Iraq. From 2013 to 2014, a year in which international assistance increased across the board, Saudi contributions shot up by 219 per cent. That rise was beaten only by the UAE, whose aid increased by 317 per cent.[9]

Well-financed NGOs in the Gulf, as in other parts of the Arab world, represent a sharp challenge to the rest of the humanitarian world. They are described, politely, as 'conservative' and 'old-fashioned' compared with 'moderate' and 'progressive' Muslim charities in the West. Gulf charities are often headed by senior members of ruling families or other figures close to royal palaces. They give out relief supplies, they dig wells and they hand over sewing machines. But building mosques and *madrassas* is also a big priority.

Heavy-handed regimes in the region have little or no interest in fostering independent civil society. Egypt, for instance, gave birth to the first Arab Red Crescent Society and promoted its own independent humanitarian movement. It flourished again during the 'Arab Spring' between 2011 and 2013, when thousands of new civil society bodies were created. But most of them were abruptly closed down again when the revolution was snuffed out by the military. I asked a leading Muslim NGO executive in Britain whether the rich Arab regimes of the Gulf were supportive of independent Muslim charities. 'Shall I give you an honest answer?' he replied. 'Governments just don't want this to happen.'

In an era of violence and need in the Muslim world, aid-givers from the West will need to build sturdy bridges with local organisations if they are to deliver effective assistance. Well-established charities such as Islamic Relief have done the job well enough over the years to grow into major enterprises – so big, in fact, that they sometimes ignore smaller Muslim players, as they did in the early phase of the Syria conflict. Syrian start-ups from the diaspora were right to insist on their independence and have become the mainstay of aid efforts across the border. They, in turn, have helped promote a non-governmental civil society network in Syria that did not exist before.

Western NGOs are already absorbing lessons from the world's new conflicts – that they need local people, local Muslim agencies and links with the diaspora if they are to work there at all. The same lessons should be learned by official Western aid-givers in their overwhelming focus on foreign terror and domestic security. Official suspicion of Islam and of the Muslim community should not be allowed to obstruct humanitarian aid. This would have a cost well beyond a failure to meet needs on the ground. It would undermine the West's record for principled humanitarian endeavour.

PART II

HOME FRONTS

CHAPTER 9

WITH ALL THOSE WHO SUFFER

Geneva

'I was a mere tourist with no part whatever in this great conflict,' wrote Henry Dunant about the Battle of Solferino in June 1859, 'but it was my rare privilege, through an unusual train of circumstances, to witness the moving scenes that I have resolved to describe.' The book he wrote, *A Memory of Solferino*,[1] is a brilliant piece of first-person reporting that changed the world and led to the founding of one of its greatest institutions.

Towards the end of his book, Dunant poses this question: 'Would it not be possible, in time of peace and quiet, to form relief societies for the purpose of having care given to the wounded in wartime by zealous, devoted and thoroughly qualified volunteers?' The answer led, with astonishing speed, to the creation of the modern humanitarian movement. *A Memory of Solferino* was published in Geneva to popular acclaim in November 1862. Within a year the Red Cross was born and within two years the First Geneva Convention was signed.

Henry Dunant was a determined Christian and a restless visionary. He had already, in his twenties in Geneva, founded the

YMCA, the Young Men's Christian Association. He was also a bit of a chancer. His presence on a battlefield in northern Italy had nothing at all to do with humanity and everything to do with a shaky business venture he had launched in North Africa. One way to promote it, he thought, was to get the backing of his hero the Emperor Napoleon III, and since the French Emperor was at that moment leading an army against the Austrians near Lake Garda, he decided to go there and present his scheme in person. What he stumbled on was the aftermath of a terrible battle.

Solferino was the bloodiest engagement in Europe since Waterloo. Two great armies, 300,000 men in all, fell on each other over 15 hours of fighting; 40,000 were killed and 40,000 were left dying, wounded and largely uncared for. There were more veterinarians on hand for the horses than there were doctors for the men.

'The stillness of the night was broken by groans, stifled sighs of anguish and suffering,' Dunant recorded. 'Heart-rending voices kept calling for help. Who could ever describe the agonies of that dreadful night! When the sun came up on the 25th, it disclosed the most dreadful sights imaginable. Bodies of men and horses covered the battlefield; corpses were strewn over roads, ditches, ravines, thickets and fields; the approaches to Solferino were literally thick with dead.'

Dunant possessed neither medical nor nursing skills, but he did what he could for the wounded. He bought up all the cigars and pipe tobacco he could find and took them around the churches where the soldiers lay. 'Only tobacco could lessen the fear which the wounded men felt before an amputation,' he wrote. 'Many underwent their operation with a pipe in their mouths, and a number died still smoking.' He learned later that the men called him 'the white gentleman' because that was how he was dressed.

Dunant also organised others to help. The women of Lombardy 'entered the churches, and went from one man to another with jars and canteens full of pure water to quench their thirst and moisten their wounds,' he recorded. 'Their gentleness and kindness, their tearful and compassionate looks, their attentive care helped revive a little courage among the patients.' He added that they 'followed my example, showing the same kindness to all these men whose origins were so different, and all of whom were foreigners to them. "*Tutti fratelli*," they repeated feelingly.'

The 'mere tourist' of today in Geneva can trace the footsteps of Henry Dunant and his fellows as they went about building the foundations of modern humanitarianism. In February 1863, just three months after the publication of *A Memory of Solferino*, a plan to care for battlefield casualties was presented to the Public Welfare Society of Geneva, one of the city's leading philanthropic organisations. There is a modest plaque commemorating the meeting on Rue de l'Evêché, in the shadow St Peter's Cathedral in the old city.

There then had to be proper international engagement. A conference was planned in Berlin, but never happened. Dunant instead canvassed his way around Europe to secure decent attendance back in Geneva, and 14 countries were represented when a 'Conference to Study Ways of Overcoming the Inadequacy of Army Medical Services' opened in October 1863. It was held in the Palais de l'Athénée, the beautiful new home of the Geneva Arts Society, a ten-minute walk down the hill from St Peter's.

Some of the big powers of the day were not at all keen on these proposals. The French said it was unacceptable to have civilians on a battlefield, and the British insisted that looking after wounded soldiers was the responsibility of the army, not unattached do-gooders.[2] One British delegate went a shameful step further when he proposed that the best way to deal with the wounded was to shoot them so they would not die 'with a fevered brain and blasphemy on their lips'.[3]

Despite these crass objections, the conference had a surprisingly positive outcome. Resolutions were passed that provided the underpinning of the International Red Cross as it is today. It was also at this meeting that the Red Cross emblem – the Swiss flag in reverse – was adopted, first of all as an armband to be worn in the field to mark out the volunteers as non-combatants. Dunant and his fellow committee members were now able to press on with their next objective – to ensure that care for the wounded was formally underwritten by international treaty.

A few hundred yards along the cobbled street from St Peter's Cathedral stands Geneva's town hall. It was here in a specially redecorated reception room in August 1864, still less than two years on from the publication of Henry Dunant's book, that delegates from 16 states came together to agree on arrangements for the wounded in war. The agreement they signed became the First Geneva Convention, described by Swiss Red Cross delegates at the conference as 'a step forward in the law of nations, namely the neutrality of wounded soldiers and of all those looking after them'.

Article 1 laid down that 'Ambulances and military hospitals shall be recognized as neutral and, as such, protected and respected by the belligerents …' Article 2 said that 'Hospital and ambulance personnel … shall have the benefit of the same neutrality when on duty …'

In 2014, the one hundred and fiftieth anniversary of the original Geneva Convention, visitors to the headquarters of the International Committee of the Red Cross above Lake Geneva found a badly shot-up ambulance outside reception. It was not a real vehicle, but a compelling work of art commissioned by the Australian

Red Cross for a 'Health Care in Danger' campaign. It was also a forceful reminder of how twenty-first-century belligerents, notably but by no means only jihadist insurgents, have ignored the civilized principles supposedly governing war.

There was one more location for the 'mere tourist' to visit in Geneva in 2014. The Rath Museum is within a few hundred yards of the other locations that tell the story of the early Red Cross. The Rath was built in the 1820s as Switzerland's first museum of fine arts, but was handed over in both World Wars to the ICRC as office space for its prisoner-of-war tracing agency. For the one hundred and fiftieth anniversary of modern humanitarianism in 2014, it housed a special exhibition on the history of the Red Cross.

The opening exhibits comprised a first edition of *A Memory of Solferino* and the four Nobel Peace Prizes earned so far by the Red Cross, including the first Nobel Peace Prize ever awarded – to Henry Dunant himself in 1901. The prize meant a measure of rehabilitation for the 70-year-old whose role as founder of the Red Cross had by then been assiduously written out of the record by his colleagues. The reason for that was the dubious North African business venture for which Dunant had gone to get the backing of Napoleon III at Solferino. The venture went bust within a year or two of his early humanitarian accomplishments, and that drove him, his family and even his bank into bankruptcy. Dunant was accused of deceit and left Geneva in disgrace at the age of 39, never to return.

Two more of the Nobel Peace Prizes on display were awarded to the ICRC for its work for prisoners of war during the First and Second World Wars. Testimonials from European governments in the 1940s were glowing, but at the ICRC itself there is now little but regret and apology for its conduct in the Second World War.

Nazi Germany's attempted extermination of the Jews – the Final Solution – remains the twentieth century's single most grotesque assault on humanity. The ICRC's own exhibition at the Rath Museum acknowledged that its response to the Holocaust was 'not sufficient' and that it had 'abandoned its neutrality, voluntarily or not, in playing into the hands of Nazi Germany'. The section on its role in the Nazi era was headed 'Powerless and Doomed to Fail'.

An historian of the Red Cross, Professor David Forsythe, concluded that in its dealings with Germany the ICRC had simply put the national interests of Switzerland before the demands of humanity. The ICRC had been told more than enough about the concentration camps to oblige it to act, but Geneva headquarters had left the issue in the hands of a 'thoroughly Nazified German Red Cross'.[4] No senior ICRC official visited Germany during the war, and the organisation decided at one point against issuing a public appeal that would have dealt at least in part with the Holocaust.

Professor Forsythe found that the ICRC had allowed its approach to Nazi Germany to be dictated by the Swiss government so as 'to forestall any thoughts in Berlin about an invasion of Switzerland'. Its efforts 'can generally be characterised by lack of dynamism. It is perhaps intermittently persistent. It is certainly discreet.' The organisation had tended to believe that 'Swiss nationalism was fully compatible with Red Cross humanitarianism. The Second World War showed that this was a false and damaging assumption.'

There were other lessons for the ICRC from the wars of the twentieth century. For a humanitarian agency on the front line of the world's conflicts, the most vulgar lesson of all was that war was very much better for business than peace. After the First World War – 'the war to end all wars' – the organisation faced a dramatic slump in income that threatened to become, in the view of its own historians, 'a question of survival'. This led to its first steps in a process that continues to the present day – an extension from war work focused on the welfare of combatants to meeting the needs of civilian victims of conflict and natural disaster.

The ICRC faced another slump after the Second World War. It was largely frozen out of the Communist world, and had only a modest presence on the ground in South Korea during the Korean War. The early conflicts of a postcolonial world, such as the Biafra war in Nigeria and the Cold War blowing hot in Vietnam, would become major preoccupations, but the 1950s and early 1960s were, to quote Henry Dunant's *A Memory of Solferino*, a 'time of peace and quiet'. It was a period when the ICRC's greatest thinker set about defining the purpose and principles of the institution.

The ICRC's fundamental principles are encapsulated in the mnemonic NIIHA, standing for Neutral, Impartial, Independent, Humanitarian Action. It is easy enough to say and a surprisingly large number of aid workers say they subscribe to it. Impartiality and independence, commonly defined, may present no overwhelming challenge. It is neutrality that splits the humanitarian world. Some proclaim it, fewer strive for it, and fewer still manage to achieve it.

In the early 1990s, the Red Cross took the lead in an effort to draw up a code of conduct for independent humanitarian agencies. The code was published in 1994, in the aftermath of the genocide in Rwanda, a human catastrophe in which the ICRC was one of the few agencies to stay in the country. Médecins Sans Frontières stayed behind as well, but could do so only by working under the banner of the Red Cross.

I could find no record of the discussions that led to the adoption of this ten-point code. What can be surmised from the text is that, while the signatories articulated many important principles – aid to be given on the basis of need; aid not to be used to further political or religious objectives – the 500 or so agencies that have now signed up to it are very shy about using the word 'neutral'. They go only as far as this: 'We shall endeavour not to act as instruments of government foreign policy.' That is the palest possible reflection of neutrality.

Jean Pictet, the ICRC's greatest jurist and the man who did most to codify its principles, was brilliantly plain-spoken on the subject. He joined the ICRC in 1937 and for more than 40 years was engaged in formulating humanitarianism for the modern world. He brought the Geneva Conventions up to date in 1949 when a fourth convention was added to cover civilians detained in war. The fundamental principles of the Red Cross on which he wrote the definitive book in the 1950s became the charter of the movement in 1965 and are now formally recited at the start of the International Red Cross conference every four years. His commentaries on these texts remain startlingly to the point in the conflicts of the twenty-first century.

'Neutrality manifests itself above all in relation to politics, national and international,' Pictet wrote in a layman's guide to the fundamental principles published in the 1970s, 'and Red Cross institutions must beware of politics as they would of poison, for it threatens their very lives. Politicisation constitutes the greatest danger now confronting the Red Cross.'[5]

Pictet acknowledged that, like other humanitarian agencies, the Red Cross operates in a world of politics. 'Indeed, like the swimmer, it is in politics up to its neck. Also, like the swimmer, who advances in the water but who drowns if he swallows it, the ICRC must reckon with politics without becoming part of it.'

Pictet's view was that the pressures on the ICRC were mounting and that the world of politics 'is characterised by struggles that reach the pitch of savagery'. Still, he argued, the Red Cross 'cannot compromise itself in this wild turmoil'. With stunning prescience, he posed the very question that President George W. Bush put to the world two decades later in the aftermath of the 9/11 attacks and at the start of the West's war on terror. Pictet had the answer ready, too.

'If anyone presents the Red Cross with the well-known and destructive dilemma embodied in the phrase, "whoever is not with me is against me," may it always reply, "I am with all those who suffer, and that is sufficient."'

The conduct of the United States in the war on terror was a consistent challenge to the principles and practices of the International Red Cross and to the workings of the Geneva Conventions, of which the ICRC is guardian. Of all the many infamous texts that these conflicts have thrown up, the memo sent by Alberto Gonzales, the White House Counsel and future US attorney general, to President Bush in January 2002 ranks among the most notorious.

'The war against terrorism is a new kind of war,' Gonzales wrote. 'In my judgement this new paradigm renders obsolete Geneva's strict limitations on the questioning of enemy prisoners and renders quaint some of its provisions.' This was one of the so-called 'Torture Memos' in which Gonzales' 'new paradigm' challenged Jean Pictet's drafting of the Fourth Geneva Convention. Obsolete and quaint conventions were viewed as 'old Europe' at work, in the phrase of Donald Rumsfeld, then US Defence Secretary.

George Bush's challenge – 'either you are with us or you are with the terrorists' – set the scene for a series of tussles between the US government and the ICRC, staged almost entirely behind closed doors. The denial of prisoner-of-war status to the Taliban – they were declared instead to be 'illegal enemy combatants' – did not put them entirely out of sight, but it restricted Red Cross access to them along with its capacity to monitor their treatment. In the case of the CIA's 'rendition' programme – where suspects were picked up, put on aircraft and dispatched around the world to secret jails – the ICRC was given even less access, or none at all.

The status and treatment of these detainees prompted a rare public intervention from Jakob Kellenberger, the ICRC's president, on a visit to Washington in 2004. He said that the ICRC was 'increasingly concerned about the fate of an unknown number of people captured as part of the so-called global war on terror and held in undisclosed locations'. He appealed, mildly enough, 'for information on these detainees and for eventual access to them'.

America's conduct of the war in Afghanistan presented the ICRC with a sharp political challenge. Here was the organisation's largest funder insisting that neutrality should play little or no part in the international humanitarian response to the conflict. Here, too, was most of the rest of the Western world – including other major funders of the ICRC – aligning itself with the US in sending troops to Afghanistan. Many of the major Western NGOs, surely the ICRC's natural bedfellows, also appeared to view this conflict differently. In their 'governance' and 'nation-building' roles in Afghanistan, they too seemed to be on one side in the war, even, as we have seen, appealing to NATO to intensify its military operations.

There was no formal review of Red Cross principles in the early years of the Afghan war, but behind closed doors senior ICRC staff debated them anxiously enough in light of the US stance. Were insurgent groups – armed non-state actors, or ANSAs in the jargon – and the civilians under their control entitled to the same protection and humanitarian care as others engaged in the fighting? Jean Pictet and his generation had done their work well, and the answer was clear.

In the words of one senior ICRC official, the basic tenets of humanitarian law were reaffirmed as a result of these internal discussions, and the upshot was that 'the church was put back into the village'.

As Geneva faced its war-on-terror challenges at home, the physical risks run by ICRC staff in the field began to become tragically clear. In March 2003, little more than a year after the United States and its allies overthrew the Taliban, insurgents in Uruzgan province stopped an ICRC vehicle and executed the only non-Afghan on board. His name was Ricardo Munguía, a water engineer from El Salvador who had been a local Red Cross volunteer during the war in his own country and went on to work for the ICRC in Colombia, Angola and Congo-Brazzaville.

Ricardo was the first aid worker to be killed in Afghanistan in more than five years, and his murder was burdened by a dreadful irony. The Taliban gunman who killed him wore an artificial leg. It would almost certainly have been fitted at an ICRC prosthetic unit in Afghanistan – or by the ICRC over the border in Pakistan. The gunman took the final order to kill his captive in a satellite telephone conversation with the Taliban commander Mullah Dadullah. He, too, wore an ICRC prosthesis.

As the sense of shock at Ricardo's killing sunk in, most of the aid agencies in Afghanistan drew only one conclusion – that there needed to be much more security in the country and that it should be provided by a larger Western military presence. Within a few months of the murder, the NGOs issued their stirring appeal to NATO, 'Afghanistan: A Call for Security', which I discussed in Chapter 2. It demanded that the Western military should implement 'robust stabilisation' in 'key locations and major transport routes outside Kabul'. The ICRC was not a party to this appeal, and drew wholly different conclusions from their colleague's murder.

For a start, they did not pull out of the country. In the violent southern provinces they adjusted their programmes and tightened their internal security arrangements, but their presence in Afghanistan continued. As guardians of the Geneva Conventions, they needed to maintain their relationship with the Afghan government – for prisoner visits, family link-ups and other aspects of their protection work – and that could not be achieved from outside the country. Instead of relying on the Western – or any other – military for safety, they continued to promote even-handed neutrality. Despite the murder, in part perhaps because of it, they redoubled their efforts to build relationships with the Taliban.

'The ICRC persevered,' wrote Fiona Terry in *International Review of the Red Cross*, 'and through some innovative and sometimes risky initiatives managed to show both sides the benefit of having a neutral intermediary in the conflict.'[6] I have quoted already from Dr Terry's work on Afghanistan and will do so again in relation to Somalia. As well as being an authority on humanitarianism, she has worked in the field for both the ICRC and Médecins Sans Frontières. She is also a trenchant critic of the generality of NGOs.

'Neutrality as a guiding principle of humanitarian action was roundly rejected by most actors in Afghanistan's latest conflict,' she wrote, adding that mainstream aid organisations were 'deeply embedded culturally, politically and financially in the western sphere'. The vast majority of international NGOs 'embraced a role of "post-conflict" reconstruction and development efforts and joined the political project to extend the government's legitimacy throughout the country.

'By supporting one side, however legitimate it might have seemed,' Dr Terry concluded, 'aid agencies tarnished their image in the eyes of opposing forces, and not only compromised their chances to help civilians in contested areas, but also faced increasing difficulties even in "secure" areas.'

A decade on from 9/11 and the US-led invasion of Afghanistan, senior ICRC officials reached a settled view on the lessons learned. Pierre Krähenbühl, director of operations at the ICRC, looked back on the now 'commonplace' attacks on humanitarian aid workers. 'They are clearly illegal and unacceptable and must be condemned in the strongest terms,' he wrote in an article for the ICRC website, but added:

> The rejection of humanitarianism is, however, also the by-product of policies that integrate humanitarian aid into political and military strategies. For some time now, this has been known as the 'blurring of the lines' debate ... When humanitarian action becomes part of strategies aimed at defeating an enemy, the risks for aid agencies in the field grow exponentially. This is when a bright red line must be drawn.
>
> I note a growing pessimism in the aid community and nostalgia for what is often called a shrinking 'humanitarian space'. In fact our experience tells us that there is simply no such thing as a pre-established, protected 'humanitarian space' ... The ICRC, for one, believes in consistent neutrality and independence as a way to build trust.[7]

With its network of national Red Cross societies and Red Crescent societies in Muslim countries, the ICRC is better placed than any other Western humanitarian agency to get help to those in need in the savage wars of the early twenty-first century. In 2015, 70 per cent of the ICRC's global operations were focused on the Muslim world. In the pitiless violence of the Syria conflict, it was additionally shocking that in the first four years of fighting the Syrian Red Crescent Society lost 40 dead. They were all killed, said Geneva, 'while carrying out their humanitarian duties'.

Yves Daccord, the former journalist and director general of the ICRC, told me:

Being close to people directly affected by war is central, but just look around us today at Syria, Iraq, the Central African Republic, South Sudan, Nigeria, the Sahel, Somalia – you would say there are very few humanitarian actors that are able to maintain a close proximity with people.

I really want to insist that close proximity means that you move away from an idea that you come in and then you leave again. It means you stay because it's the only way to understand the changing nature of people's needs and try to provide a response that integrates their own coping mechanisms. People expect this. They are more demanding and more challenging than they were, they expect you to provide a real relevant response.

Syria's expanding crisis presented the ICRC – and the humanitarian world in general – with its biggest challenge of all. Alongside its vital relationship with the Syrian Red Crescent, the ICRC had 300 staff in the country at the end of 2014 and a budget for 2015 of $170 million, its largest programme anywhere in the world. Because of its formal, nearly 50-year relationship with the government in Damascus, the organisation worked only from one side in the conflict – from offices in Damascus, Aleppo and Tartus – which was a serious limitation, but also an opportunity.

ICRC officials talked of an incompatibility of approach on humanitarian needs between themselves and the Syrian regime, but they nevertheless held their noses and did business with the government because, like the United Nations, they would not work clandestinely across international borders. That put all the more pressure on them to run effective relief programmes on the government side and, wherever possible, to cross civil war battle lines to deliver their aid.

In October 2013, a joint ICRC and Red Crescent team taking medical assistance to Idlib, close to the Turkish border in north-western Syria, was seized and held. Four out of its seven team members were released the next day. The remaining three were still being held at the time of writing. The ICRC disclosed neither their nationalities nor the identity of the group holding them.

'Syria is the place which is most daunting, where the gap between what we can do and what we should do is biggest,' said Yves Daccord. 'It's much tougher, much more complex than Iraq, or Afghanistan. Are we doing the right thing? We chose one road – step-by-step negotiations. So far it's interesting we have been able to do what we wanted to do, really cross the lines and reach people controlled by the government or by the opposition.'

The ICRC issued a stream of statements on the unfolding Syrian disaster, but there were no formal denunciations of the regime. Appeals and reminders in the name of humanity were painstakingly even-handed. I looked in vain for specific references to those horrifying 'barrel bombs', the oil drums packed with high explosives and metallic debris that have done such terrible damage to people and places in Syria's towns and cities. The regime's barrel bomb raids over Aleppo reached a peak in the spring of 2014 when, on one day, 38 such weapons were dropped on the city.

At that point the ICRC issued a news release saying that they were 'appalled by a sharp escalation of violence in Aleppo, where parties have in recent days carried out indiscriminate attacks against civilians'. In the fifth and final paragraph of the release, they went so far as to call 'on all parties to refrain from using imprecise weapons in densely populated areas'. This was not a news release designed to make much news.

In his book on the ICRC quoted earlier, Professor Forsythe refers to the organisation's 'discreet neutrality'. As for actually looking for publicity, Forsythe wrote, 'the ICRC seems almost congenitally opposed to this option. The majority of ICRC officials say that most of the time efforts at publicity do little good.'[8]

With the advance of Islamic State jihadists across northern Syria, the humanitarian aid world faced a new dimension to its challenges in the region – an ideologically driven guerrilla group intent on occupying territory and controlling population. In the following months there were corresponding actions from Boko Haram in northern Nigeria. Major aid organisations struggled to address the refugee fallout across international frontiers. The ICRC wanted to go further. This was an important new test of their purpose and principles.

'Are we able to work in territory controlled by Islamic State?' was the question Yves Daccord, the director general, asked himself. 'That will be our biggest challenge. Governments are not able to provide services to their people, and you have to have a principled response to humanitarian need.'

Islamic State aggression represented a grave challenge, said M. Daccord, 'but it's got control of territory with a population of 10 million people. We have to find a way to connect with them on a pragmatic and humanitarian perspective, and then create a level of trust. I think it is possible. In a sense they have to connect with us. If they don't, they will have to take care of their people, so it's up to us to find the right channels and find a way to work with them.'

Behind the barriers erected by jihadists, there are entire communities of displaced and frightened people in desperate need of help. Assertions of neutrality might in time enable the ICRC to reach them, and allow for the European tradition of independent humanitarianism to play its front-line role in the worst of twenty-first-century conflicts. Jean Pictet's question about taking sides – in our era it has become 'either you are with us or you are with the terrorists' – will have been answered once again. 'I am with all those who suffer, and that is sufficient.'

One hundred and fifty years from its foundation, the ICRC remains the leader of global humanitarianism. It is still the organisation by which other humanitarian aid-givers should be judged. The ICRC continues to exercise Swiss discretion in its dealings with states and armed movements, and that will not change. A lot is probably achieved without shouting. In the age of terror, though, there is another area where the ICRC might choose to be more outspoken – in its judgements on the compromises made by other agencies providing humanitarian relief.

CHAPTER 10

WHEN AID BECOMES A CRIME

Washington, DC

They call it the 'chill factor' – the impact of US counter-terrorism laws on American aid agencies working in the most troubled corners of the world. 'Chill' is a mild term for their level of anxiety. International non-governmental organisations (INGOs), the household names as well as smaller ones, all of them relying on public support for their existence, exhibit real institutional fear when asked to discuss the most important set of challenges they face.

Some are reluctant to talk at all. Almost every conversation I had was either 'on background' or 'off the record' – or both. Nervousness at US headquarters extends around the world to their country offices. A national director in Africa for one US agency referred me to his 'media risks' adviser. An email from another laid down these conditions for my planned meetings with staff and aid recipients: '… the participants are to remain anonymous and [name of agency] is not to be mentioned in any subsequent text or documentation. The conversations remain on background and off the record.' The meetings never took place.

The biggest inquiry conducted so far into the 'chill factor' was commissioned by the United Nations and the Norwegian Refugee Council (NRC) and uncovered 'a high level of self-limitation and self-censorship, in some cases going beyond what was requested by the donor or the law'.[1] Researchers were particularly worried about the impact of counter-terror laws on Muslim agencies. 'The risk of criminal prosecution, as well as of significant reputational damage, appears to be leading in some cases to over-compliance. This appears to be stifling the principled push-back that might normally be expected from humanitarians.'

The implications of US legislation for aid in the world's conflict zones made agencies dependent on their lawyers more than ever. The UN/NRC study told of one charity that was refused legal advice by a private law firm on the grounds that the firm itself might be in breach of counter-terror laws if it so much as offered a professional legal opinion. In London, a British charity chief told me of visits from his American counterpart. The latter was accompanied by the agency's lawyer, who, it was explained, had the final word on where funds from the US could and could not go. People's needs and priorities were subsidiary.

Washington DC was not as frightened as some cities I visited in what they call the GWOT – the 'global war on terror' – but corporate anxiety among the US aid agencies was nearly universal. For an outspoken voice in the humanitarian world I had to look beyond the fundraisers, the media offices and their lawyers and heard it loud and clear, to my surprise, at InterAction, the umbrella body representing American relief and development organisations.

I first encountered Joel Charny, head of humanitarian policy and practice at InterAction, when he spoke by video link to a London conference about the relationship between aid agencies and the Western military in the war on terror. He was critical of US NGOs for what he saw as their failure to grasp the principles at stake in these wars. When we met later in Washington, he found it difficult to contain his exasperation with the organisations he spoke for.

Joel had worked for Oxfam America in Cambodia in 1980, at the time of the famine that succeeded Year Zero, the Killing Fields and the country's 'liberation' by North Vietnam. Then, as now, Oxfam America was on the radical wing of the US NGO community and it had joined Oxfam Great Britain in standing out against the Western consensus that insisted on recognising the defeated Khmer Rouge as Cambodia's legitimate government. He went on to run Oxfam America's programmes in South East Asia and became successively the organisation's overseas and policy director.

With his experience in policy roles and in the field, Joel believes that US NGOs should be using their public standing to resist the 'chill factor' and speak out in the name of humanitarian principle. Joel has a grave and studious manner, but the language he uses in describing what he sees as the craven posture of InterAction members is vehemently to the point.

I put to him what the big NGOs were telling me – on background – that they could not take American public support for granted in the war on terror; that the US Congress was turning Republican; that humanitarian principles were difficult to promote; and that it was altogether easier in Europe where there was greater awareness of the issues. 'Bull!' Joel exclaimed:

What's happening is that we're afraid of our own shadows. It's like we've decided that the water is too cold to get in. Well, why not try getting into the water first and finding out how cold it really is? You're talking here about World Vision, CRS

[Catholic Relief Services], CARE, Mercy Corps. They have hundreds of thousands of supporters in the US. They are so unclear about the level of respect they have among the general public. They have a halo effect and yet they refuse to utilise it. That's completely wrong.

If they say, 'we can stop these children dying and keep them alive, and the US is preventing us from doing it,' then 90 per cent of their constituents are going to support them. This is driving me crazy, and it's been going on for the whole of the last decade. No one is going to accuse CRS of being soft on terrorism! In a tough environment, we're supposed to stand up – not cower.

There is a textbook example available of how standing up for humanity led to a major US government climbdown: the Somali famine of 2011. As I set out in Chapter 7, the tragedy here comprised three elements. It lay in the 250,000 who died in spite of all the early warnings; it lay in the callous indifference of the al-Shabaab militias that controlled most of south and central Somalia; and it lay in American fears that food for the starving might fall into the hands of jihadists.

Food is currency in Somalia, and in 2010 a devastating United Nations monitoring exercise confirmed that its supply chain in the country, run by the World Food Programme, was subject to corruption and diversion. Much of the food was going to poor and hungry people, but some was going to the jihadists. In addition, food aid was subject to tax at checkpoints on the road, and much of that cash was also getting into jihadist hands. The upshot was that the United States slashed its food aid to Somalia and people went hungry. When harvests failed shortly afterwards, they starved to death.

The clear humanitarian imperative was that people should be fed, and so a public relations battle was fought out in Washington. Newspapers and television were reporting from Kenya and Ethiopia as weakened Somali families struggled over the border on their 'walk of death'. NGO voices were raised. 'The approach of the US government, up to now, has been so absolutist,' Joel Charny complained on National Public Radio. 'They're basically saying that the diversion of almost, literally, a cup of rice constitutes grounds to more or less shut down an entire aid programme for hundreds and thousands of vulnerable people.'

A key figure in the campaign was Jeremy Konyndyk, policy and advocacy director at Mercy Corps in Washington. In testimony before Congress, in blogs and newspaper articles, he marshalled the arguments for a change of heart in government and the granting of special licences for food shipments to Somalia. The result was that, in August 2011, two weeks after the United Nations formally declared a famine in Somalia, the United States announced it was lifting its ban on aid to the victims.

At a press briefing at the State Department, officials confirmed that they would not prosecute NGOs for aid diversions to al-Shabaab as long as 'good faith efforts' were made to prevent them.[2] Aid agencies knew it was not the State Department but the Justice Department that would launch any such prosecution. Justice officials were apparently present at the briefing, but remained silent.

The special licence issued by the government did not open up any sort of general exception to US sanctions. It was issued only to USAID, the government's official aid agency, and licence requests from individual NGOs continued to be refused. Agencies that did not accept funds or food from USAID remained at risk of prosecution if they tried to help. It even took USAID lawyers themselves several months to be satisfied that their own colleagues would not end up being prosecuted by a neighbouring government department.

Little more than a year after promoting a humanitarian break-through on Somalia, Jeremy Konyndyk moved from Mercy Corps to take up a top position at USAID. He became head of the Office of US Foreign Disaster Assistance, which in 2014 commanded a budget of more than $1.1 billion. Other senior NGO officials made a similar switch into government during the Obama years.

Reflecting on the government's 2011 change of heart from his new vantage point, Mr Konyndyk acknowledged that the NGOs had waited too long to sound the alarm bells. 'It's always difficult to find that media sweet spot when you actually have a megaphone and concern can be raised. If we'd gone out in April when that [early warning] data came in, we wouldn't have got traction. What enabled the traction that the NGOs and the United Nations achieved had a lot to do with the fact that the media picked up on the story that people were beginning to stream over the border from Somalia in very bad shape.'

The lesson of Somalia – from its 250,000 victims – was nevertheless clear to the NGO policy director turned senior government official. 'When you have a sanctions regime and a major humanitarian emergency,' Jeremy Konyndyk said, 'there does need to be a way forward to enable both to coexist. It was a matter of anti-terrorism not automatically trumping all.'

Joel Charny, the outspoken voice of InterAction, was characteristically sharper in his comment on the Obama administration's conduct. 'The lesson of Somalia is scary,' he said. 'They've done exactly the same as the Bush administration. The only difference is that they feel bad about it.'

At issue in Somalia and on all the other fronts in the war on terror was the crime of giving 'material support' to terrorists. After the 9/11 attacks, the scope of this law was extended by the Patriot Act so that anyone supplying anything that ever reached a terrorist group was liable to prosecution, whatever the circumstances and however innocent the motive. The maximum sentence was 15 years' imprisonment, which was extended in 2015 to 20 years. Here was the single biggest constraint facing humanitarian agencies in parts of the world where their intervention was needed most desperately. The law allowed them no quarter. Court cases over the years had served only to emphasise the catch-all quality of 'material support'.

Aid agency discussions focused on the consequences, for example, of terrorists drinking at a well built by an aid agency. Would the aid-giver be guilty of a crime? The decisive ruling came from the US Supreme Court in 2010 when it upheld the government's view that 'all contributions to foreign terrorist organisations (even those for seemingly benign purposes) further these groups' terrorist activities'. The Court considered the legality of an initiative such as peace promotion among insurgent groups and concluded that even 'material support meant to promote peaceable, lawful conduct can be diverted to advance terrorism in multiple ways'.

These across-the-board provisions led to a terrible timidity on the part of the NGOs, and many acknowledged it. 'We're one misstep from going out of business,' said a policy adviser for one of the major agencies, 'and I'm talking about a simple mistake, even a clerical error. That's why everyone is mindful of where and when they'll bite the hand that feeds them.'

Aid agency lawyers were given the final word on day-to-day programming, and that made life uncomfortable both for them and for the senior executives they advised. 'One error or one transgression and we could find the organisation closed down,' a young lawyer with a middle-ranking NGO told me. 'We need to fight this off, but humanitarian space is getting smaller and smaller. We could face a shutdown. Let's just hope it never happens.'

Once again, Somalia 2011 was the textbook case: a country so 'fragile' that national institutions held no national sway and insurgents controlled access to hundreds of thousands of starving people. 'Who knows how many lives were really lost in Somalia?' said the lawyer. 'Our people were all poised to go, but the question was, "Is this one intervention worth risking the organisation's life for – making sure we kept our doors open? Do we save 1 million Somalis now, at the price of not being able to help 20 million later?"'

If 'material support' was an intimidating hurdle for the aid agencies at home, another counter-terror measure was a direct threat to their independence and safety in the field. The 'partner vetting system' was an invention of the war on terror designed to ensure that no aid agency, however inadvertently, had any financial connection with anyone classified as a terrorist. The easiest way to achieve this was to get the NGOs themselves to do the legwork for the intelligence services.

The seeds of US partner vetting were sown in the Occupied Palestinian Territories in 2007 – to assist in the efforts to contain Hamas – and saw their fullest flowering in Afghanistan at the end of the decade. Congress had formally authorised pilot studies in five quite different countries, but the twin presence in Afghanistan of US troops and US aid-givers led to pressure on the State Department and the US embassy for the full roll-out of the system in Kabul. 'You don't say no to a guy in uniform,' was how one NGO staffer explained the process.

The US embassy's mission order on partner vetting in Afghanistan runs to 18 pages. It spells out how NGOs must collect information on their colleagues and their partners right the way down, in some cases, to the individual Afghans benefiting from American aid. By way of example, the document explains that a charity giving drugs to a hospital or repairing a children's playground must provide full personal details of all the Afghans involved in running these projects. It does formally draw the line at having to name the sick or the children playing on the swings: 'Vetting is not required, however,' the order explains, 'for patients of the hospital ... or users of the recreational facilities.'

Among America's big NGOs, there was first resentment and then some honourable resistance to partner vetting. 'It is very onerous,' said one country director in Kabul. 'All these anti-terrorist checks require a lot of information on people's identities and bank accounts. We simply don't want to become part of a collection agency for US spying.'

From the moment this data is passed on to government, the process becomes secret. Details are checked against classified databases, and if a terrorist link is found, funding is promptly halted. No appeal is allowed and no explanation ever accompanies the withdrawal of funding. The US embassy in Kabul tries to be as encouraging as possible as it relays the bad news: '... while we cannot disclose specific vetting issues,' says the pro forma letter in the mission order, 'we hope your organisation will overcome such issues in future awards.'

Senior NGO staff argue that they have always conducted 'due diligence' on their projects and partners. They also emphasise the real risks they run in implementing an elaborate and secret partner vetting system. Instead of exposing US government employees to retribution and possible danger, it is now expatriate and Afghan aid workers who have to collect all this sensitive information. The UN/ NRC report already quoted explains that partner vetting 'promotes the perception of NGOs as intelligence sources (and thus increases the security risk for aid workers); and that it is detrimental to the US' foreign policy objectives as it undermines the trusted relationship with USAID's partners ...'

At meetings in Kabul, USAID chiefs and NGO country directors tried to see if they could reach agreement on a way forward on partner vetting. USAID wanted to keep working with the leading private agencies and the NGOs had important projects for which they needed government money. The two sides kept talking, but there was often no agreement between a government agency helping to prosecute a war and humanitarian organisations guarding their independence. Breakdown led to damaging cancellations in the American aid programme in Afghanistan.

Mercy Corps was one of several agencies not prepared to go through with the collection of intelligence data on their partners and beneficiaries. As a consequence they were forced to close down a $40 million USAID-funded project for economic development in northern Afghanistan. There was still 18 months to run on the four-year contract and the prospect of renewal after that. Instead, 300 Afghan staff and two expatriates were made redundant overnight – not to mention the impact on the many thousands of Afghans benefiting from the project.

How did Mercy Corps' own employees respond to the closure? 'I take my hat off to the way staff made redundant took it,' said David Haines, Mercy Corps' British country director in Kabul. 'They were unanimous in supporting the protest.' Here was an ironic comment on the effects of a decade of Western engagement in Afghanistan – that a group of Afghan aid workers should show more attachment to the principle of humanitarian non-alignment than the US government.

The US introduced partner vetting in other theatres of the war on terror. It was applied, for instance, in the Dadaab refugee camp in northern Kenya, home to nearly 400,000 Somali refugees.

Here, the Norwegian Refugee Council turned down money from the Bureau of Population, Refugees and Migration, an aid agency within the US State Department. The grant had been intended for a water and sanitation project in the world's largest refugee camp.

Without naming the US government, Jan Egeland, secretary general of the NRC, complained that they had been 'asked by a donor – which is a very good donor, in general – to do something bad, which is to hand over bio data on all the staff involved in this project, and all of our partners on this project, so that they, this Western donor, can vet these people. That is prohibited by our board; we cannot do that. We have to avoid being seen as an instrument for any political or other actor in this world ... That's counterintuitive to every fibre in our humanitarian body.'[3] Egeland added that he did not think it was the intention of US counter-terror legislation 'to make it difficult to dig latrines for refugees'.

Just outside Washington at Glen Echo on the Potomac River stands a monster of a house that serves as a monument to early American humanitarianism. It was partly a home, partly an office, partly a dormitory and partly a warehouse. It was built in the 1880s for Clara Barton, America's first great modern humanitarian, and redesigned thereafter to suit her changing needs. It is now an historic site run by the National Park Service.

Clara Barton was working as a clerk in the US Patent Office in Washington when the Civil War broke out in 1861. 'I'm well and strong and young,' she declared, 'young enough to go to the front. If I can't be a soldier, I'll help soldiers.' In the aftermath of the battle of Cedar Mountain, an admiring field surgeon named her the 'Angel of the Battlefield' when she appeared in the middle of the night with a wagonload of supplies drawn by four mules.

Miss Barton was honoured for her work during the Civil War and honoured once again for the years of service she devoted to her post-war tracing service 'Friends of Missing Persons'. She and her assistants answered 63,000 letters and identified 22,000 missing men from the Civil War. Then, suffering from exhaustion and one of her periodic depressions, she was ordered to Europe on a rest cure and chose to stay on the lakeside in Geneva, the beating heart of the European humanitarian movement.

Clara Barton had been tending the wounded at the Civil War battles of Wilderness and Cold Harbor when Geneva's leading citizens were organising the conference that led to the First Geneva Convention in 1864. Five years on, her philanthropic reputation preceded her to Geneva, and members of the new Red Cross were keen to meet her. Apart from anything else, they wanted to know why, despite three formal approaches and the accession of 32 other nations, America had still shown no interest in signing the treaty.

Miss Barton's brisk response to them was that she had never heard of the Red Cross or of the Geneva Convention, and she was equally sure that the American people knew nothing about them either. Her visitors handed her a copy of Henry Dunant's *A Memory of Solferino* so she could read up on the history. She marvelled that the United States could have 'carelessly stumbled over this jewel and trodden it underfoot to the astonishment of all the world, and in its young American confidence never dreamed that it was doing anything to be remarked on'.[4]

In Europe she returned to the front line by joining the Red Cross as a volunteer during the Franco-Prussian War of 1870–71. She worked in Paris, Strasbourg and up and down the border, overcoming what her biographer Elizabeth Brown Pryor calls 'demure Swiss objections to battlefield nurses'. She declared that she loved the colour red and had been impressed by the big Red

Cross warehouse she saw in Basle. It may well have lent something to the design of the house in Glen Echo.

Back in Washington, Miss Barton founded the American Red Cross Society and started lobbying for US accession to the Geneva Convention. Here she met with exceptional resistance. The first president on whom she pressed her case, Rutherford B. Hayes, rejected the Convention as 'an entangling alliance'. The second, James Garfield, was assassinated. The third, President Chester Arthur, finally signed the treaty in 1882, close to 20 years after the European powers had done so.

Under Clara Barton's leadership, the American Red Cross concentrated as much on natural disasters at home as on man-made disasters abroad. That was why she needed a barn of a house: to provide storage space for relief supplies, offices for staff and sleeping quarters for volunteers. That was also why, at a conference in Geneva in 1884, the Red Cross adopted an amendment to the Geneva treaty, extending its remit from soldiers on the battlefield to the victims of natural calamities. It was named the 'American Amendment' in her honour and set the seal on America's full participation in international humanitarian affairs.

Along with American fighting men and American arms, the great conflicts of twentieth-century Europe brought American charity across the Atlantic. In the First World War, the future President Herbert Hoover, born into a Quaker family, began to build his reputation as 'The Great Humanitarian' with food programmes that reached 6 million war victims. When his American Relief Administration went to work in the famine that overtook Bolshevik Russia after the war, he had to face down obstruction from communist officials – 'Starvation does not await the outcome of power politics,' he said – and then objections from Americans back home for wanting to help the communists. 'Twenty million people are starving,' Hoover declared in his classic affirmation of humanitarian principle, 'whatever their politics, they shall be fed.'

The Second World War saw the establishment of several of today's biggest US private aid organisations. America's Roman Catholic bishops formed their National Catholic War Council in 1941 and two years later Catholic Relief Services began its response to Europe's refugee upheavals. The first CARE packages to reach Europe arrived in France in May 1946 when those initials stood for Cooperative for American Remittances to Europe. Later that year, British families, schools and hospitals started receiving CARE packages of their own.

With a global income of $2.7 billion, World Vision has grown to become the biggest US NGO of them all. It was founded by an American missionary called Bob Pierce who encountered great human need in pre-revolutionary China – 'Let my heart be broken by the things that break the heart of God' – and expanded his work steadily through America's anti-communist wars in Korea and in South East Asia. When the communists won in Vietnam and Westerners pulled out of Indo-China, World Vision switched its anti-poverty crusade to Africa and South Asia.

World Vision remains firmly Christian and Evangelical at the top. 'It's the glue that holds us together,' a senior executive told me. At the same time it has opened its doors to full-scale internationalisation in the field. The agency's single largest employee group is now African. 'Twenty years ago when I joined I would never have thought I could get to this level,' one of World Vision's African country directors told me. 'Number one, I'm a Roman Catholic; and number two, there's my national identity. Here I am in charge of 307 employees and there are 47 expatriates under me, including five Americans and two Germans. These are things I never believed in. I never believed I would get to this level. History has proved me wrong.'

At a time of increasing religious tension around the world, World Vision's Christian identity can be a challenge. It was a hurdle that had to be surmounted in Afghanistan when the agency applied to join the body coordinating all the relief and development NGOs. 'They had to persuade us that they weren't proselytising,' I was told by someone involved in those discussions, 'and they did persuade us.'

There is also the sensitive question of whether in conservative Muslim countries it is better for a Western aid worker to be a practising Christian or avowedly secular. The consensus among World Vision staff is that it is worse to be an agnostic and worst of all to be an atheist.

One of the agency's managers told me of how he was in the vanguard of relief efforts after the big earthquake that hit Pakistan Kashmir in 2005. It was the month of Ramadan and at intervals on the long trek through the hills to the worst-affected areas his Pakistani companions would stop and pray. So he, too, a Christian, stopped and prayed. 'It was certainly better to do that than to sit on a rock and smoke a cigarette,' he said.

The most serious impact of the war on terror on US aid agencies has been felt by Muslim charities. They grew up as a modern expression of the Muslim tradition of aid, but, as in Britain, they have adopted the character of Western charities to deliver it. Not one among them contests the case for scrutinising aid to conflict zones, but the evidence in the United States suggests that Muslim charities have been unusually and unfairly targeted.

A brave and struggling non-profit on Capitol Hill called the Charity & Security Network (CSN) has done an exceptional job in documenting this process in the years since the attacks of 9/11. In its review of the decade to 2011, CSN listed the problems faced by US Muslim charities as 'opaque and unfair procedures to shut down charities, indefinite freezing of funds intended to relieve human suffering, and a general view that charities are a threat to national security rather than a source of confronting terrorism through their humanitarian work'.[5]

In the course of the decade, reported CSN, the US government shut down nine US-based charities for supporting terrorism; seven of them had Muslim affiliations. One other Muslim charity was closed when its leaders were charged with tax fraud. Despite this level of scrutiny, 'only one American Muslim charity has been convicted of supporting terrorism and it was not represented at trial,' the report said.

Specific complaints were levelled at the US Treasury Department and its Office of Foreign Assets Control. Once a charity is accused of providing 'material support' to a 'foreign terrorist organisation', its property and assets can be frozen – without notice, recourse or time limit. Federal courts have found these processes unconstitutional because they allow for neither adequate notice of the allegations nor a meaningful opportunity to respond.

CSN concluded that government actions had 'caused serious harm to civil society and freedom' and that the fear of guilt by association and investigation had 'caused some Muslims to forego their religious obligations'. That finding is vividly borne out by the experience of one leading Islamic charity in the US.

Anwar Kahn, the British-born chief operating officer of Islamic Relief USA, has a fund of stories to illustrate how nervous American Muslims have become about giving money for overseas humanitarian work. He recalls how, not long after 9/11, a man cycled up to him in the street and wordlessly handed him a wad of dollars before pedalling off. Nowadays he has to plead with people to give him cheques, and he told me how he had recently turned down $10,000 in cash. 'No, no, please,' they begged him, 'no receipts, no nothing!'

At the time of the 9/11 attacks, Islamic Relief USA had an income of $6 million a year. By 2014 it had grown to $50 million, almost all of it from private donations, with an additional $30 million worth in gifts such as medical equipment. 'Our income has gone up every year,' said Anwar Khan, 'but it would be much higher if people weren't so scared to give. They're even scared to go to the mosque and give money that way.'

Islamic Relief has received no funding from the US government so far, although it has submitted applications. 'We would love to have institutional funding if it doesn't compromise our work,' Anwar said. The charity already has to satisfy arduous US compliance procedures. 'It's not like it was before 9/11,' he said. 'We've had to hire more and more lawyers and accountants.'

I asked him about the closure of other Muslim charities and the impact on Islamic Relief. 'It spreads fear in the Muslim community,' Anwar replied. 'What we do is to explain aggressively how we spend the money, but it means that we get less, and we are less able to help hungry people around the world.'

One consequence of US government pressure on Islamic charities is that more and more Muslims are finding ways of sending money home directly. 'That's underground cash and you don't know where it's going,' he said. 'It's very difficult to monitor and there are many security issues. That's the situation that's been created.'

Islamic Relief has its US headquarters in Arlington, Virginia, and Anwar Khan told me about its bulging police file. Not a file of its misdeeds, but of the threats made against it. Again he explained how things changed on 9/11. That day alone there were 40 telephone death threats made to the Islamic Relief office. All such calls are now formally logged and passed to the police.

There are personal pressures, too. As a frequent flyer to the front line and other destinations, many within the US, Anwar told me how regularly he is 'randomly' selected for extra security searches. It is unusual for him *not* to be 'randomly' selected, he said. His cheque book, address book and credit cards are 'routinely' photocopied, gifts for the family are 'accidentally' scattered on the floor and luggage is 'unfortunately' ripped open. Flights are sometimes missed. 'I just smile when they are rude to me,' he says.

Not for the first time in my meetings with senior Muslim aid workers in the US and Britain, I was struck by their apparent lack of bitterness over the petty and not so petty harassment they face. 'We believe America is a wonderful country,' Anwar said to me at the end of our meeting. 'For every hater, there are many, many good people. Our staff abroad risk their lives in the field. Sometimes we have to take small risks here to get the money we need.'

Optimistic sentiments like that continue to inform a modest pushback against the great weight of US counter-terror legislation. The Charity & Security Network saw a 2014 Obama memorandum on civil society as a hopeful sign, and pressed on with its efforts to lessen the impact of restrictions and penalties on humanitarian aid. It looked for support from leading US NGOs to make sure that there are better policies in place by the end of the Obama administration than there were at the beginning. But the 'chill factor' persists in Washington and a price is paid in the reputation and effectiveness of global humanitarianism.

CHAPTER 11

DOING WELL BY DOING GOOD

Washington, DC

During the war in Afghanistan, the Americans sent in the aid as soon as the fighting was over. One of their schemes, on which USAID spent $140 million, was to assist Afghan civilians caught in the crossfire between international forces and the Taliban. If not a 'feel good' project, it was certainly intended to make people 'feel better' about the war. It applied only to engagements between foreigners and Afghans, not to those where the Afghan army was engaged against the Taliban, and the project was handed over to the United Nations when Western combat troops stood down in 2014.

In the final years of US engagement, the Afghan Civilian Assistance Program was run by International Relief and Development (IRD), a huge US NGO contractor that had grown and grown during the war on terror. On the day IRD took over the assistance programme in December 2011, a Taliban truck bomb struck the entrance to a NATO base south of Kabul. One Afghan worker died, several policemen were wounded and around 70 locals were hurt. IRD's job was to assess the needs of the civilian victims and get immediate help to them.

USAID paid out $200 per household for food, kitchenware and repairs to damaged homes. Where there were fatalities, the programme covered the cost of rebuilding family livelihoods: grants to set up small businesses or to buy livestock. Two hundred people were helped in this way after the bombing of the NATO base, including a little boy who received specialist surgery after his sight was imperilled by shrapnel in his eye.

The 'feel better' diplomacy of the project was most needed when foreign forces, not the Taliban, were directly responsible for civilian casualties. As the war intensified, mistakes made by the Western military increasingly antagonised Afghan civilians and Afghan politicians. The records of IRD's assistance programme revive some of these now forgotten incidents:

> A US drone attack kills three civilians and injures six in Kunar; a child's face is badly disfigured. A NATO airstrike in Kapisa kills seven children and an adult. An F15 airstrike in Laghman kills eight women and girls collecting firewood and picking nuts in the hills. Another seven are injured. President Hamid Karzai is furious. NATO offers its sincerest condolences.

IRD in Afghanistan drew substantially on ex-military personnel for its staff. 'It's very exciting out here,' a former US Marine Corps officer working with the agency told me in Kabul. 'But you know what? Helping people who can't help themselves is what makes this job. Everyone loves us. It's a "feel good" programme because we're there to help.'

In neighbouring Pakistan, USAID funds a similar project for communities affected by the Taliban war on the other side of the border. The Conflict Victims Support Program is aimed at helping the civilian victims of Taliban attacks who do not have the protection of government employment. Once again, its political purpose is to help win 'hearts and minds' for the US cause – a particular challenge in Pakistan – and once again the $25 million contract was won by International Relief and Development.

The project covers the Pakistani frontier province of Khyber Pakhtunkhwa and the tribal areas directly bordering Afghanistan. The impact of the insurgency and the needs it generates were spelled out in a study funded by the United Nations and conducted by a local NGO called the Paiman Alumni Trust. It dealt only with the district around the provincial capital of Peshawar and was bluntly entitled *Bomb Blast Survey*.

The population of Peshawar district is a little over 2 million, with rural and city people more or less equally divided. In the three and a half years from 2006 to 2010, the *Bomb Blast Survey* recorded 11,401 civilian casualties in this single theatre of the war on terror. Of these, 3,624 were killed and 7,777 were injured.

Since then, there has been an escalation in the conflict, notably with the attack on All Saints Church in Peshawar in September 2013 (the most savage ever on Pakistan's Christian minority, with 87 killed and 170 injured) and the massacre at the Army Public School in December 2014 which left 145 dead and 130 injured. The latter was Pakistan's single worst terrorist outrage.

The *Bomb Blast Survey* summed up the effects of such violence on the people of Peshawar. 'In the past couple of years, life has not [been] as good as it was a few years back in Peshawar,' it said. 'The hustle and bustle, the happiness, the fun and the joy, everything has vanished in thin air. Peshawar now gives an image of a graveyard with countless "living dead".'

On the ground, the Conflict Victims Support Program funds community first-aid training and provides support for frontier hospitals in trauma care and mass casualty management. There are immediate assistance packages worth $400 for bomb blast victims, including for the families of those killed and wounded in the murderous attack on All Saints Church.

With more men than women killed in terrorist attacks, the long-term burden usually falls on wives and mothers who are left without an income, or often, in a conservative society, any means to earn one. So the IRD programme concentrated on providing scholarships for the children and home employment such as garment-making for the widows.

At this level aid can work wonders. It transforms lives, as its publicists claim. The video testimonies delivered by IRD's war victims in Afghanistan and Pakistan are heartfelt in their gratitude. But Western aid in these war zones has grander ambitions than helping individuals and families to live better lives. Along with 'winning hearts and minds', it is aimed at creating peace, building democracy and binding these countries to their benefactors. That is where the really big money comes in.

Like most of the West's humanitarian enterprises, International Relief and Development had its origins in war. It was the creation of Dr Arthur B. Keys, a Christian minister and missionary who first travelled to the Balkans in the years before the collapse of the Soviet Union and the subsequent dismemberment of Yugoslavia. Dr Keys became a fluent Serbo-Croat speaker and was on hand with his Bosnian wife Jasna when the world began to take a serious interest in the state of the Balkans.

With his background in missionary relief work, Dr Keys and his wife started a small consultancy to advise aid agencies on all the humanitarian needs that had to be met. 'We were writing these proposals for other companies,' Mrs Basaric-Keys told me in 2014. 'Why would we not do it for ourselves?' IRD was born as an independent agency in Washington DC in 1998.

Its reputation with US government aid-givers was cemented in that early post-communist era in Europe. It grew from modest beginnings with a child health project in western Georgia to running a $40 million reconstruction programme in Serbia. It was well placed for a generous share of the avalanche of US aid money that swept down on Iraq and Afghanistan during the war-on-terror enterprises of the new century.

Arthur Keys was one of the first NGO bosses to reach Baghdad after the destruction of Saddam Hussein's regime in 2003. He recalled taking a ride in a Chevrolet across the desert from Amman, in Jordan, and being greeted at the Iraqi border by GIs. He shared the vehicle, he said, with the German ambassador and 'a couple of shooters' in the back for protection. It was worth the journey.

Among the projects that USAID commissioned from IRD was the Community Action Program, aimed ambitiously at changing the way Iraq was governed. Its objective, grimly ironic in the light of Iraq's later struggles with Islamic State and its virtual break-up as a country, was to model 'innovative approaches to decentralised democracy and governance in Iraq'.

Another of IRD's major Iraq undertakings was a Community Stabilisation Program to provide work for the unemployed, specifically for young men who might otherwise have been tempted to join the anti-US insurgency. The project put them to work clearing rubbish, digging ditches and rehabilitating schools and playgrounds. At one point IRD claimed to have 65,000 day labourers on its payroll. 'What the community wanted, the community got,' IRD said. The contract was worth $675 million.

This project was dogged by controversy. There were allegations that payments were going to bogus workers, even directly into the pockets of insurgents. But IRD and its government backers stuck resolutely with the programme. 'Most of the diplomats and the military strongly supported our doing job creation for young men as an alternative to violence,' said Mrs Basaric-Keys, who became IRD's head of operations. 'The world still needs development and we could provide that. Our commitment was that by doing development in the middle of a conflict, you can help resolve it, too.'

In Afghanistan there were even bigger opportunities awaiting IRD. Helping war victims and their families was one small pro-gramme in a portfolio of huge projects that ranged from agricultural development schemes to road-building. Along with the US troop surge in Afghanistan from 2009 came a surge in civilian aid aimed at achieving pacification through development. IRD was contracted to build 400 miles of provincial roads in the south and east of the country – more than 120 Afghan workmen were killed in Taliban attacks during construction – and a national voucher scheme for poor farmers was rolled out in Helmand and Kandahar. Together, the two contracts were worth close to $1 billion.

'There is a need for a group of organisations like ours to do the heavy lifting in conflicts,' Dr Keys told me. 'CARE and World Vision don't do that and I can't see them coming our way, either.'

I met Dr Keys in April 2014 at IRD headquarters in Arlington, Virginia, across the Potomac River from Washington. American combat troops had pulled out of Iraq 30 months earlier and were now close to leaving Afghanistan. Aid budgets were getting tighter and the political focus was switching westwards to the Middle East. As well as a smaller appetite for armed intervention, the Western taste for enforced constitutional remodelling had also diminished.

The husband-and-wife team that started IRD retired from their positions in summer 2014, a few months after our interviews. Their departure was preceded, probably hastened, by a *Washington Post* investigation into the agency's affairs entitled 'Doing Well by Doing Good: The High Price of Working in War Zones'. The

Post reported that 'IRD finds itself falling out of favor with the agency that was once its most ardent patron. Because of concerns about performance, USAID is considering whether to continue its relationship with IRD ...'[1]

From its analysis of USAID figures and IRD's own accounts, the newspaper established that IRD's annual revenue had increased over 15 years from $1.2 million to $706 million. In the seven years to 2014, IRD received almost $2.4 billion from USAID, with 82 per cent of it earmarked for spending in Iraq and Afghanistan. No other NGO earned as much from the US government.

Whether prompted by the newspaper investigation or not, USAID and other official investigators now subjected IRD to a level of scrutiny that it had never faced in the boom years of 'boots on the ground'. The dramatic upshot was a USAID statement in January 2015 announcing that a review by its Office of Inspector General 'revealed serious misconduct in IRD's performance, management, internal controls and present responsibility'.

The statement went on: 'USAID has a zero tolerance policy for mismanagement of American taxpayer funds and will take every measure at our disposal to recover the funds.' IRD was suspended as a USAID contractor, which meant that it could complete existing contracts but was barred from bidding for new ones.

The Washington Post pressed on with further revelations. In March 2015, it published an account of staff parties and retreats that IRD had charged to USAID at the height of the wars in Iraq and Afghanistan. Just three of the bills added up to $484,338 for retreats at a five-star spa and resort in the Allegheny Mountains, north-west of Washington. The expenses were billed as 'training' and 'staff morale'.[2] USAID told the newspaper that 'waste, fraud and abuse of American taxpayer funds are completely unacceptable' and that every measure was being taken to 'recover misspent funds'.

Exceptional pay and benefits packages received by senior staff were also under scrutiny. High salaries were a distinctive feature of USAID's contractor classes, but IRD was unusual in having the tax-exempt charitable status of an NGO.

When I met Dr Keys, he was unapologetic about the level of his own salary and benefits. His annual pay, he said, was $472,000. There was also a bonus system in operation and payments were made into his pension. 'We don't have the socialist system that you have in Europe,' he explained.

'First of all, this is a big job. There are 3,500 people working here and 100 projects. You can earn a lot of money as an economist at the World Bank, but you don't have to manage anything ... Our salary levels are on a competitive scale with top executives at the NGOs and other non-profits. Our pay scales are in line with other groups.' (In fact, they were appreciably higher.)

Tax returns filed with the US authorities in November 2014 put the total compensation due to Dr and Mrs Keys at the time of their retirement at $690,000 and $1.1 million respectively. The *Post* reported that Dr Keys was expecting an additional $900,000 contribution to his retirement fund.[3] But with multiple investigations under way, IRD's new management held back $1.7 million of the retirement money that had been awarded to them.

I asked Dr Keys about pay levels for staff in the field. He described them as 'very healthy' at between $140,000 and $180,000 a year. On top of that, he said, there was a 70 per cent bonus for working in a war zone rising to 90 per cent to cover housing and allowances – a near doubling of the basic pay. The tax returns for 2013 showed that six of IRD's best-paid staff were working in Afghanistan. Their average annual pay and benefits package was $315,000.

IRD's prospects seemed bleak in the aftermath of the USAID suspension. A new chief executive had taken over, board members were removed, and 90 of a headquarters staff of 170 were laid off. Many more lost their jobs in the field. 'The suspension was a death sentence,' a member of the new management team told me. 'In 20 years no other organisation that's been suspended by USAID has ever survived. The view here was that IRD was being dismembered.'

Then a US federal judge found in IRD's favour when it mounted a court challenge to the suspension order. USAID's procedures had been flawed, the judge found; the suspension must be lifted and IRD could bid for new contracts until proper procedures were adopted and the investigation re-run. In the meantime, IRD's income, which had risen so spectacularly during the wars in Iraq and Afghanistan, collapsed from $587 million in 2010 to $78 million in 2014. Survival was still not guaranteed. 'We may not even be called IRD a year from now,' said the manager from the new team.

On the ground in Afghanistan, there was constant tension between traditional charity-based humanitarians and the new breed of NGO contractors and aid corporations. What was it that came first for the contractors, the charities asked? Was it getting the contract, spending the money, growing the business and moving on? Or was it making sure that there was lasting development?

Nor was this only an American phenomenon. The British and the Australian governments have handed over increasing proportions of their aid budgets to contractors. So much Australian aid money, including big sums earmarked for projects in Afghanistan, remained in the hands of Australian managers, Australian consultants and Australian suppliers that the local monitoring group AidWatch coined the brilliant Aussie term 'boomerang aid' to make its point.

'I try to be sympathetic, but I find it very difficult,' said a British NGO director in Kabul. 'Take a $100 million project. They'll keep

$30 million back in management and overheads, they'll spend another $30 million on security and close protection, and maybe there's something left to spend on the ground. Sometimes it amounts to bugger all ...' That rough breakdown into thirds is commonly quoted by aid officials. In 2010, a senior USAID officer told the American journalist Rajiv Chandrasekaran in Afghanistan that 'security management and overhead costs have grown to almost 70 per cent of the value of most contracts'.[4]

At project level, charities complained that contractors were so eager for rapid results – and the rapid disbursement of official funds – that they undermined the painstaking process that is supposed to underpin 'sustainable development'. One contractor in Afghanistan provided free cattle vaccinations in an area where established international NGOs were charging for the service. Vaccination should bring its own reward, argued the charities; subsidies should then be reduced and farmers would stand on their own feet. When the contractor in question stopped giving the vaccines away, local farmers found themselves back at square one.

It was a similar story with vocational training programmes in Helmand, where young people were being taught a trade in the middle of the insurgency. A well-established Mercy Corps project in Lashkar Gah charged a small fee for its courses while a major US contractor actually paid its students to attend. Mercy Corps claimed that their own results were better. Their students were several times more likely to get jobs than those from the contractor's colleges.

An important division has opened up in the US between commercial aid contractors and traditional NGOs. Each looks for a big slice of the USAID pie and the two are often in direct competition. The difference between them is the way they expected to be funded – through grant in the case of the NGOs or by contract in the case of the aid corporations. Faced with fewer and fewer officials to administer its huge programmes, the US government has progressively favoured the contract route. That in turn has diminished the capacity of NGOs to operate independently of their paymasters in government.

'With a grant we're funding one of the NGO's own programmes,' a USAID mission chief explained. 'When we have control, it's easier to shift emphasis on a project – to run it and manage it how we want.' The mission chief said that he made it plain to NGOs that they now had to compete directly with contractors. 'If you want it,' he tells them, 'you go bid on it.'

Aid enterprises are as varied in their character as they are in their origins and history. The initials DAI stand for Development Alternatives Inc., which suggests American capitalism red in tooth and claw. DAI certainly makes money, and is consistently in the top ten of USAID's biggest aid disbursers. In 2010 it was at number three with $486 million – only the UN World Food Programme and the Global Fund to Fight AIDS, Tuberculosis and Malaria were higher. In 2014 it was at number eight, as the aid squeeze in Washington pegged its revenue back to $262 million.

Unusually, DAI's origins lie neither in conflict nor in emergency humanitarianism. It is the product of a Cold War focus on Third World development grafted onto the idealism of the Kennedy era. The 1960s were the UN's first 'development decade' and witnessed the start of both USAID and the Peace Corps.

Towards the end of that decade, three young men met at the Kennedy School of Government at Harvard. Their backgrounds were varied: the military in South East Asia, aid work and Peace Corps volunteering. To that was added a strong dash of American entrepreneurship, what DAI describes as 'doing economic development on a competitive, cost-effective, best-value basis that was self-sustaining because it was profitable'.[5]

Founded in 1970, DAI first made its mark when it was commissioned to study 36 of USAID's agricultural projects in Latin America and Africa. This was a time when development priorities were shifting from large-scale infrastructure to small-scale rural enterprises. DAI's 'Strategies for Small Farmer Development' led to hands-on contracts in Zaire and Sudan and it has retained a strong agricultural bias ever since.

James Boomgard, the present CEO, has a doctorate in agricultural economics, and in Kabul I met Juan Estrada, highly qualified in the same field, who headed up Afghanistan's Agricultural Development Fund for DAI. It is unusual that two such senior aid agency executives should be equipped with advanced degrees in something as practical and relevant as agricultural economics. The modern aid business is more commonly staffed by those with academic qualifications in development itself.

Dr Estrada is a Guatemalan who had already served for three years with DAI in Afghanistan when he was offered the new position. 'It was too big a challenge to pass on,' he said. The project was a nationwide credit scheme for Afghan farmers, underwritten by USAID with $100 million in lending capital and $50 million for administration. When I met him at the end of 2013, other Western donors were on the point of putting up a further $60 million in loan capital.

In their search for partners to run the loan scheme, Dr Estrada told me that they had approached 15 banks in Afghanistan. Not one of them showed an interest. Too many of the loans were too small for the banks to bother with. So DAI developed its own lending arrangements – compatible with *sharia* law – and teamed up with farm cooperatives and agri-businesses ranging from food processors to fertiliser importers. By 2014, there were 30,000 Afghan farmers on the scheme, and they recorded a very low level of default on their loans.

'It's always the little people who repay,' said Dr Estrada, 'and it's the fat guys who sign the papers without ever intending to pay.' The 'fat guys' had met their match in Juan Estrada. He told me how a prominent businessman in Wardak province, the head of an apple-growing association, had taken out a big loan that he was refusing to pay back. The 'fat guy' was well connected, and it would have taken many years and a great deal of money to pursue him through the courts.

So Dr Estrada pulled rank on him. He went to the provincial governor and told him that unless immediate action was taken there would be no more loans to anyone in Wardak. Within hours the 'fat guy' was arrested and on his way to jail to consider his options – accompanied by Dr Estrada.

'When I was growing up in Guatemala I used to see myself working for Oxfam,' said Dr Estrada. 'I never thought I'd be in a job like this and sitting next to one of our clients in handcuffs on his way to the police station, but for development to be effective there needs to be structure and discipline.'

I asked him what difference he thought his Guatemalan upbringing had made to his running this major project. 'I think it's taught me not to be too naive,' he replied. 'You should never believe what a lot of people say. I know when people are lying to me.'

When I interviewed Dr Estrada, the loans scheme was close to being handed over to Afghanistan's Ministry of Agriculture. Already the number of expatriates employed on the project had fallen from 20 to seven, and within months it would be slimmed down to three. Dr Estrada thought he might be the one to lock the office door behind him.

'What keeps me here is the challenge,' he told me. 'I want to tell you that this is the biggest thing I will ever do. I'm extremely pleased and honoured to work with the team I have here, and I want to see it through.'

Aid offices in the field often reflect the character of their headquarters at home, but not in the case of Bancroft Global Development. Bancroft's main overseas operation, as we have seen, is run from sandbagged shipping containers in the Somali capital Mogadishu. Its headquarters in Washington is a grand and sombre mansion on Massachusetts Avenue, in among all the embassies.

Bancroft is an NGO start-up and the brainchild of Michael Stock, scion of an American banking dynasty and a modern-day adventurer – financial and otherwise – in the world of conflict, aid and development. He was barely out of Princeton and in his early twenties when he put some of the family money into starting Landmine Clearance International, whose mission was to 'rehabilitate populated areas in the aftermath of armed conflict ...' That was 1999. Since 2007, Mr Stock's big project has been Somalia, and his starting point was on the front line.

Bancroft's ex-military personnel act as 'mentors' to African Union troops who have the UN-appointed task of defeating the jihadists in Somalia's civil war. Bancroft people are not doing any of the fighting, but nor are they safely at the rear. They comprised 16 nationalities when I visited, including former US Special Forces and British SAS soldiers, and some of them have an African mercenary background.

All are regularly exposed to danger along with the troops they mentor, and several have been wounded, a few of them twice. On Christmas Day 2014, they suffered their first fatality when Brett

Fredricks, a 55-year-old American who had served with US Special Forces, was killed in a shoot-out with al-Shabaab insurgents inside the airport compound in Mogadishu.

Bancroft's mainstay relationship in Somalia is with the Ugandan army. The arrangement was secured by a retired US army colonel called Greg Joachim, once US defence attaché at the American embassy in Kampala and later a military adviser at the State Department. At Bancroft he was the lead on African and strategic affairs.

When Burundi decided to send a force to join the African Union operation in Somalia, Bancroft was asked to 'mentor' them as well. 'They called us,' said Colonel Joachim, 'and they said, "We just found out our head of state has signed up for a UN mission. Will you come join us?"'

In an era when the US government fights shy of 'boots on the ground' – past experience in Somalia had been particularly bitter – the option of funding Bancroft at arm's length had real attractions. Formally, the firm is paid by the African governments whose troops they mentor, but most of that money is reimbursed by the US State Department. The UN's Department of Peacekeeping Operations also funds Bancroft, and there was a separate State Department grant for working alongside the new Somali defence forces.

'You have to have somebody doing it,' I was told by Rick Barton, the US diplomat heading the Bureau of Conflict and Stabilization Operations at the State Department. 'If you have the Burundians there or whoever the fighters are and they need an upgrade, you might as well get the upgrade on the spot. We've invested in some of these African forces before, but there's a lot to be said for this way of doing it.'

What drew Bancroft's founder Michael Stock to Somalia was precisely its reputation for extreme violence and disorder. Here was a country that appeared, as he put it, to have 'fallen off the bottom of the development ladder. You were going to die as soon as you got off the plane. Life in Somalia was as wholly incompatible as life on the surface of the moon.'

As Bancroft saw it, addressing insecurity by making African Union and local Somali forces better at fighting and defending themselves was part of the aid task. So, too, was ensuring that these troops were responsive to Somali civilians. Without better security there could be no development. Colonel Joachim described the local Somali outlook to me this way: 'Until me and my family are safe, we're not going to be worried about any of your *frou-frou* development projects.'

Twinned with its non-profit role as an NGO was Michael Stock's money-making initiative, Bancroft Global Investments. This, as the company explains on its website, 'makes speculative allocations of capital … in opportunities that emerge as a consequence of Bancroft Global Development's success but that would otherwise remain disconnected from global markets.'

This was the virtuous circle Mr Stock had identified to make Somalia safe for capitalism. When he started out, he said, the real risks of doing business there were as great as the perceived risks, but with improving security there was a chance to earn big money while the rest of the world continued to keep its fearful distance. 'There's the potential to reduce the risk rather quickly from extreme to moderate,' he said, 'and that's where one would find entrepreneurial opportunities of one sort or another.'

Conventional aid workers deprecated Bancroft's NGO status and showed even less sympathy for its military role and the proximity of profit to its Somali operation. Yet violent and disordered countries – the far-fetched aid euphemism is 'fragile' – have now moved to the very top of the development agenda and no one has come up with a more persuasive approach. US failures in training and motivating

Syrian volunteers to fight in the moderate cause – revealed in 2015 – served to emphasise the point.

For its own part, Bancroft rejoiced in being outside the humanitarian aid fold. 'These organisations have had two decades to achieve something,' said Mr Stock of the conventional NGOs, 'but the way they are set up precludes any outcome. The problem is their structure. They only have one activity – and that's delivering more relief. They have a vested interest in the perpetuation of the problem. That's historically myopic and morally wrong.'

The Bancroft operation is a modest one by the standards of the aid business. Its links with the military set it apart from other agencies whose disapproval it has attracted. Yet the sort of work that Bancroft does in promoting stability in Somalia is an essential prerequisite for development – even for the safe delivery of relief. For almost a quarter of a century the country languished in disorder, neglected by the outside world until the West's own security interests were threatened.

Bancroft's emergence and growth underline a broader truth about modern aid – that this mighty, money-spinning industry now accommodates the widest variety of organisations and approaches. Corporations vie with NGOs for Western taxpayer funds, and the NGO contractors have it both ways. Charity may still inspire a lot of aid work, but government funding and institutional growth are big drivers as well. That leads to such a close embrace between official funders and the charities they underwrite that a further cost is incurred to humanitarian independence.

CHAPTER 12

THE POLICE, NOT THE STASI

London

Addressing a meeting of development experts after he left office, Tony Blair said that one of the things he was proudest of as prime minister was the creation of the Department for International Development (DFID). Among the very first acts of the New Labour government when it took office in 1997 was to prise Britain's overseas aid ministry from the Foreign and Commonwealth Office and re-establish it as an independent department.

To make his point, Mr Blair told a story about visiting Africa and his encounter with a British civil servant. 'So you're with the British government here?' he said by way of introduction. 'No,' was the reply, 'I'm with DFID.'[1]

DFID was formally committed to 'eliminating world poverty' – once the theme of all its big policy pronouncements – and saw its exclusive purpose as meeting the long-term needs of the poor. It was accordingly viewed with some hostility by the Foreign Office – which saw aid as serving objectives well beyond that of poverty reduction – and was dismissed by some in government as 'that NGO down the road'.

The attacks of 9/11 and the West's long war on terror have steadily altered the focus of British aid. Until 2002, neither Iraq nor Afghanistan was among Britain's top 20 aid recipients. By 2004, Iraq was the largest single recipient, and by 2006 Afghanistan was in the top three. Ministers championed the new course. 'In recent years DFID has begun to bring security into the heart of its thinking and practice,' said Hilary Benn, Secretary of State for Development, in 2005. 'But we need to do more.'

By the time it lost office in 2010, New Labour had committed itself to 'allocating at least 50 per cent of all new bilateral country aid to fragile and conflict-affected countries', and the incoming coalition of Conservatives and Liberal Democrats made the connection between Britain's foreign aid programme and British national security more explicit still. An internal DFID paper leaked in August 2010 spoke of how development projects would be expected to make 'the maximum possible contribution' to Britain's national security. 'Although the NSC [National Security Council] will not in most cases direct DFID spending in country, we need to be able to make the case for how our work contributes to national security,' the DFID paper said.

Far from pursuing its own course in trying to eliminate world poverty, DFID was now playing a large and, to the relief of other government departments, welcome role in Britain's war on terror. Its budget rose dramatically because of the coalition's undertaking not just to ring-fence aid expenditure at a time of austerity but to drive it towards the United Nations target of 0.7 per cent of national income. Four-fifths of British humanitarian aid was now earmarked for conflict-related programmes. In London and overseas, DFID officials were working alongside the Foreign Office and the Ministry of Defence; on the front line – in Afghanistan, for instance – they were described to me as being 'embedded' with the military.

The provincial reconstruction teams (PRTs) in Afghanistan were originally conceived as a means of providing military protection for civilian experts sent to the field on reconstruction and development projects. Once established around the country, they came to 'epitomise the civil–military approach in Afghanistan', in the view of Barbara Stapleton, a leading authority on the subject. Their work would be 'a primary means of expanding the central government's authority beyond Kabul and would provide a security dividend'.[2]

British aid's exclusive focus on poverty reduction was now tempered by the need to try to win the war. As Ms Stapleton described the process, 'the civil–military approach towards development was increasingly geared towards an expanding insurgency rather than towards the long-term development agendas also being supported by the donors'.

In Helmand province, the main theatre of Britain's war from 2006 to 2014, British officials took over the management of a provincial reconstruction team that had been set up and led by the US military. The Helmand PRT was located inside the main allied base in Lashkar Gah, although London made a point of putting a succession of civilians in charge. Three of its eight PRT chiefs over the years were women.

Big efforts were made by the PRTs to attract working partners from among the international NGOs and UN humanitarian agencies, but few wanted such a direct link with coalition forces. The PRT experiment faced similar problems when British forces pulled out of Helmand and took their aid managers with them. There was little enthusiasm among civilian agencies still at work in Afghanistan for stepping into Britain's desert boots.

Early in 2015, Britain said it was spending 30 per cent of a much increased aid budget – development expenditure as well as emergency humanitarian funding – on fragile and conflict-affected states. That represented a near doubling of its commitment over four years, from £1.8 billion to £3.4 billion. If anything, these figures underplayed the new emphasis on security. They reflected only direct country-to-country aid, not the large sums that Britain sends to international bodies such as UN agencies which in turn are directed towards states in conflict.

Later in the year – in response to the escalating Syria conflict, Europe's own refugee crisis and the terrorist attacks in Paris – the government once again recast its aid policy. At least half of a still rising budget would now be spent on 'stabilising and supporting broken and fragile states' in addition to helping 'refugees closer to their homes'. David Cameron, the prime minister, said this shift would 'make our spending an even more fundamental part of our strategy to keep our country safe'. It would also 'help to maintain Britain's position as number one in the world for soft power'. He added, in a chest-thumping aside: '... I can tell you that soft power packs a real punch.'

As Britain reshaped its aid programme, the number of poor countries receiving British assistance fell by around half in the course of a decade. By 2015, DFID's priority fragile countries numbered 21, with officials suggesting that in another decade the figure would fall by half again. By then, they say, British government aid work will be largely humanitarian and emergency-related.

'At a bilateral level, DFID has become an organisation specialising in fragile states,' said the government's Independent Commission for Aid Impact in a report published in 2015.[3] But it concluded with this sceptical judgement: 'It is not clear that the scale-up in funding is yet matched by an increased impact on overall fragility.' The commission uses a dinky little 'traffic lights' system – from green for good to red for bad through several combinations of amber – to report its conclusions. For its work on fragile states, DFID received an amber/red score, which translates as the programme 'performs relatively poorly overall' and 'significant improvements should be made'.

The biggest ever commitment of British humanitarian aid has been to the Syria conflict, which by March 2015 had been raging four years. The £800 million spent to that point already exceeded Britain's response to the next three major world disasters put together – the Asian tsunami of 2004, starvation in the Horn of Africa in 2011 and the Ebola crisis of 2014.

The refugee crisis in Europe prompted the British in September 2015 to increase their financial commitment to Syria further to £1.1 billion. Ministers kept emphasising the '£1 billion' aid figure in their determination to hold the line against accepting more than a very limited number of refugees. Their commitment to Syrians who stayed in the region put Britain second only to the United States as an aid-giver and well ahead of the European Union. British officials liked to point out that they have given 12 times as much as the French.

From this £1.1 billion, three major UN agencies (the World Food Programme, UNICEF and the refugee agency UNHCR) shared £462 million. Two leading American NGOs (Mercy Corps, with close links to the Obama administration, and International Rescue Committee, run by the former British Foreign Secretary David Miliband) received £80 million. Another £200 million was allocated to what DFID describes as 'undisclosed humanitarian agencies, not named for security reasons (operating outside the UN led response)'.

This money has funded significant aid operations over the Turkish border into 'liberated' areas of northern Syria. Here, as

British officials put it, DFID is the 'wholesaler' and the 'retailers' are the household name NGOs. Many 'retailers' insist on anonymity because the Syrian government is flatly hostile to cross-border operations and the United Nations itself had only recently been authorised to develop any sort of cross-border programme.

When Britain's contribution stood at £600 million on the third anniversary of the conflict in March 2014, Foreign Office and DFID ministers issued a joint statement saying that 'the people of the UK can feel proud that we are at the forefront of the international humanitarian effort'. Britain was then providing clean water to 1.4 million people, medical help to nearly 250,000 and food for up to 320,000 refugees a month.

At this point a specific international request was made to Britain – that it should accept a modest number of Syrian refugees as a token of burden-sharing with countries at the centre of the crisis. Lebanon and Turkey were already hosting more than a million refugees each, and Jordan was accommodating 600,000. The initial target proposed for the whole of the rest of the world by the UN refugee agency UNHCR was that 30,000 refugees be accommodated by the end of 2014.

Instead of agreeing to any particular number – Germany had set an early example by saying it would take 10,000 – Britain announced an initiative called the Vulnerable Persons Relocation Scheme, which was unveiled with a parliamentary flourish by Theresa May, the Home Secretary, in January 2014.

Mrs May spoke of 'appalling scenes of violence' in Syria, of 'simply sickening' torture and starvation, of millions 'in desperate need' and of 'staggering' numbers of refugees. She quoted Prime Minister Cameron as saying that 'our country has a proud tradition of providing protection to those in need' and said that the British scheme would focus on those who had survived sexual violence in the conflict, which was a recent policy focus of the British Foreign Office.

In the run-up to a general election in which immigration was a prominent and divisive issue, there were those who wondered how hard the Home Office would look for Syrians who qualified for the scheme. The answer was soon apparent. After six months, a paltry 24 Syrians had been admitted. After a year of the scheme, the total had risen to 90.

With a Conservative government returned to power in the general election of May 2015, the unyielding line on migration was maintained. By then Europe was facing an enormous tide of refugees risking their lives to reach southern Europe by sea and then struggling on northwards through the land borders of the Balkans into the European Union. Syrians were joined by many others fleeing conflict and disorder in Asia and Africa. By far the majority were refugees from the conflicts of the war on terror.

Under pressure to respond, in September 2015 London announced an expansion of its 'vulnerable persons' scheme. So far, the commitment had barely exceeded 200 Syrians over 20 months. Now it would take in 20,000 over five years – just 4,000 a year. Considering the hundreds of thousands who had fled to Europe, it was the most modest of gestures.

As for Britain's record aid budget, it was now performing two functions beyond its humanitarian and anti-poverty purposes. In the conflict states themselves, it was being used directly to help fight the war on terror. At home it was presented as an alternative to accepting refugees. Conservative politicians who had opposed a ring-fenced and expanded aid programme can never have imagined how useful it would turn out to be.

Muslim charities in Britain were focused on Syria from the start of the crisis in 2011. Their managers recall how for more than two years British aid convoys heading for northern Syria were not only officially tolerated, but positively encouraged. This was the era of the 'Arab Spring' and the regime in Damascus was in line as the next dictatorship to be overwhelmed by a tide of Western-inspired democratic protest. Britain was unequivocally aligned with the Syrian opposition and wanted to help in every way it could.

The charities dated the change of heart to the House of Commons vote against military action in Syria at the end of August 2013. Neither the West nor the moderate Syrian opposition was in control any longer of events in the region and Islamic State jihadists seized the opportunity to expand their presence across northern Syria. A full-scale terrorist threat to Europe emerged over the following months and Muslim charities soon became suspect in the eyes of politicians, press and public.

For David Cameron, this 'existential terrorist threat' became a 'generational struggle' and Downing Street briefed on the growing number of arrests for what were described simply as 'Syria-related activities'. Official anxiety was underpinned internationally by the Paris-based Financial Action Task Force, created to tackle money-laundering but since 9/11 in hot pursuit of terrorist financing as well. 'Terrorist organisations and non-profit organisations have very different objectives,' declared the Task Force, 'but often rely on similar logistical capabilities.' Since terrorists sought the same resources as NGOs, this made NGOs 'vulnerable for abuse by terrorists or terrorist networks'.

Early in 2014, Sir Peter Fahy, Chief Constable of Greater Manchester Police and head of the government's anti-radicalisation 'Prevent' strategy, made the direct link between charitable endeavour in Syria and terrorism at home. He told BBC radio that the problem was with those 'who may be driven because of the huge concern over there – some for humanitarian purposes – naively to go out there'. He warned firmly against doing so. 'We are saying for the protection of the country that anybody coming back will be stopped and may well be arrested.'

What the police and politicians had in mind was that British Muslims wanting to help should be content to contribute to a charity already at work in the region. UNICEF was mentioned along with established NGOs such as Save the Children. This left out of account the desire of many British Muslims, Syrians in particular, to respond in person to the desperate need of their countrymen and co-religionists. It also ignored the fact that the big NGOs were themselves in partnership with Syrian start-up charities established in Britain and elsewhere in the West to get aid to where it was most needed.

When I visited the Turkey–Syria border in March 2014, I spent my time with British Syrian NGOs founded specifically to respond to the crisis. Their essential task was to work on the other side of the border. One of the most resourceful, as we have seen, was Hand in Hand for Syria, which was running medical, educational and emergency food programmes throughout the country. Its income had risen steadily to around £4 million a year by 2014, with the increase attributed to its partnerships with big international NGOs. It was trusted to spend large sums of Western government money in Syria, but not trusted enough to come and go from Britain without a burdensome level of challenge and scrutiny.

At a meeting in London after my visit, Faddy Sahloul, one of Hand in Hand's founders, told me how incensed he was over the treatment of a young woman colleague who had just returned to Britain after a two-month posting to the charity's office in Turkey. She had been stopped at airport immigration and questioned for four hours on what she knew about events in Syria and who she had met. Her mobile phone and tablet were taken away, everything on them was downloaded and the phone returned to her, broken.

'They make no distinction between what is humanitarian and what is not,' Faddy complained. 'This is happening to people of Syrian origin, but it's worse for others. They're given far more hell. It's much tougher for Pakistanis.'

The British media and the UK authorities were 'only highlighting the bad stuff about Syria', he continued. 'They don't highlight all the good work that the British people are doing for Syria.' One consequence of the suspicion was that the charity was finding it hard to sustain its early levels of private donations. That was why they had to rely on funds from Western governments directed to them through the NGOs.

Banks were another problem. 'People are terrified of making bank transfers to Syrian charities or to charities in the name of Syria,' said Faddy. HSBC had recently closed down Hand in Hand's account because a donor had made an online payment to them using the reference 'Syria'. The bank had told the charity that it couldn't handle Syrian payments because of anti-terrorist embargoes. 'What do you mean?' asked Faddy. 'The UN has helped me. The British government has helped me. They replied, "No, that's it."' The account stayed closed.

As the head of the government's anti-radicalisation programme, Sir Peter Fahy acknowledged to me that there had been confusion in the British official response to the Syria crisis. This still had to be addressed within government. 'Overall,' he said, 'it's clearer to say to British people that they should not go and engage with foreign conflicts.'

His was a 'safeguarding message', he said.

We are concerned about vulnerable young people. Whether they are Muslims or not has got nothing to do with it. They are British subjects. It's the same way we tell people not to get involved in drugs or gangs; this is an incredibly dangerous thing to do.

They will be stopped, they will be questioned, because part of that is to try and understand the situation and gather intelligence and information and try and work out if people are genuinely involved in the humanitarian effort.

Muslim charities are under pressure on several fronts. The press and public are suspicious of them and the authorities bear down on them as more and more stones are turned in search of terrorists. Yet their own communities expect them to take the lead in efforts to get aid to people in real distress.

As I found throughout my research, Muslim charity executives remain remarkably even-tempered in their reaction to these challenges. They have the satisfaction of honouring Islam's charitable demands while creating effective NGO hybrids on the Western model. They display a vigorous moral focus on the job in hand – very often a dangerous one – that is no longer always apparent inside the West's big aid bureaucracies.

I have already told the story of the Anglo-Turkish charity Doctors Worldwide (DWW) from Manchester and its founding chief executive Dr Kani Torun who became Turkey's first ambassador back in Somalia. The present chief executive of DWW in Britain is Khalil Rehman, a strong-minded British Kashmiri who switched career from investment banking to the charity sector to work in the fields of homelessness, blindness and medical aid overseas.

Doctors Worldwide experienced the unfolding Syria crisis at first hand through its mentoring relationship with start-up charities within Britain's Syrian community. After guiding them on fundraising and charity regulation, it went on to advise them on longer-term development work in areas such as mother and child welfare. 'Life goes on,' as Khalil put it.

He described the British government response to Muslim charity work in Syria as 'an attempt to scare the *bejesus* out of us' and summed up official attitudes like this: 'We don't want you as a Muslim anywhere near that environment, just in case you come back here and do something bad. We don't care for any of the niceties here, we just want you to stop this. To hell with it if this puts a stop to voluntary activity.'

Khalil said that the upshot was real nervousness about working in Syria. Muslim donors were being pushed to send aid underground through unofficial channels. 'People say they don't want to help through charities anymore,' he told me. 'We won't register,' they tell him. 'We don't need to bother.'

He foresaw longer-term consequences for the British humanitarian movement. 'I'm British and I love this country,' Khalil told me. 'The problem is that this is suffocating people here, and this will have an impact down the road. Turkish and Gulf players will end up predominating in this area, and where will that leave UK humanitarian influence?'

At the heart of the official network governing NGOs in Britain is the Charity Commission, a uniquely British institution that acts as both regulator and cheerleader for the sector. In Washington I was told several times how fortunate the British were to have this light-touch system in contrast to the United States, where government departments and law enforcers compete to threaten aid-givers with legal retribution. In Britain, too, the pressure had steadily built up on the Charity Commission to become less of a supporter of the sector and more of a scourge.

Politicians set the scene. Interventions from Downing Street and from House of Commons committees in 2013 and 2014 made it plain that the Charity Commission needed to toughen up. The prime minister's Task Force on Tackling Radicalisation and Extremism recommended that its powers should be strengthened and the Home Affairs Committee said it should 'be granted extra resources and stronger legal powers to counter the abuse of charities by terrorists'. After another parliamentary inquiry, Margaret Hodge, outspoken chair of the Public Accounts Committee, declared flatly in February 2014 that the Charity Commission was 'still performing poorly', with 'no coherent strategy', and was 'not fit for purpose'.

The man appointed by the government to steer the Charity Commission through these perilous waters was William Shawcross. As a journalist and author, he had personal experience of the aid world. His book *The Quality of Mercy*, published in 1984, set out to make sense of the complex politics and aid relationships surrounding the Cambodian emergency of the late 1970s. As a communicator, he was given to the use of vivid language.

In an interview in April 2014 with *The Sunday Times*, he described his first 18 months as commission chairman as a 'rollercoaster' ride 'with IEDs going off'.[4] He went on to emphasise the counter-terrorist dimensions of his job. In places such as Syria and Somalia, he said, it was 'very, very difficult for charities always to know what the end use of their aid is, but they've got to be particularly vigilant'. The problem of Islamist extremism was 'not the most widespread problem we face in terms of abuse of charities, but it is potentially the most deadly. And it is, alas, growing.'

Face to face with Muslim leaders, Mr Shawcross said that the Commission had to police the charity sector, but it was not going to be the Stasi. By way of illustrating how high the stakes were, he told them that if there was another atrocity like the murder of Lee Rigby, the off-duty British soldier murdered in south-east London in May 2013, which could then be linked in some way to a Muslim charity or to someone who had travelled to Syria under charity auspices, the consequences for the agencies would be catastrophic.

A succession of statistics emerged from the Charity Commission emphasising how seriously it was now taking the risk of terrorist association with Muslim NGOs. Some 200 British charities working in Syria had been registered since the conflict began, Shawcross said. 'Some of them are inexperienced and obviously more vulnerable to exploitation than bigger and more established charities, the household names.'[5] By the end of 2014, five Muslim NGOs were under formal investigation by the Commission, including the organisation for which the British taxi driver Alan Henning was working when he was taken hostage and savagely murdered by Islamic State. It was further reported that the Commission had flagged up 55 charities with an 'extremism and radicalisation' warning in the 17 months to May 2014. The charities themselves had not been informed.[6]

The Muslim mainstream among British charities was troubled by what it saw as the Charity Commission's remorseless concentration on the risks of terror and the downplaying of its support and advisory role. At a working level, there was a close and respectful relationship between the Commission and the charities and there were fears that this would be jeopardised if giant steps were made towards accommodating pressure from politicians. A study conducted by the Overseas Development Institute referred to 'the government's explicit involvement of the Charity Commission in its counter-extremism and counter-terrorism strategies' and voiced international NGO fears that this was 'resulting in a major shift in the Commission's focus to counter-terrorism and counter-extremism, with greater policing of charities on behalf of the government'.[7]

Pointers to this shift were plain to see. Consider the Commission's new board members appointed in 2013 after William Shawcross became its chair. The most prominent of them was Peter Clarke, formerly head of the Metropolitan Police Anti-Terrorist Branch and national coordinator of terrorist investigations. Mr Clarke had conducted investigations into the London bombings of 2005 and the 'Trojan horse' controversy involving Islamist influence in schools in Birmingham. It was clear where he would be directing his gaze as a Charity Commission board member.

Then there was the matter of finance. The Commission had lost staff and capacity as a result of government cuts and Shawcross admitted that it no longer had the means to 'provide as much support for charities as [it] did in the past'. It had to 'prioritise [its] resources on holding charities to account and tackling serious abuse'. Towards the end of 2014, the government found a fresh £8 million for the Commission, but this was not to help it advise charities on how to perform better in risky conflict zones, but to tighten the regulatory screw. Downing Street specified that the money would 'boost the Charity Commission's ability to tackle abuse, including the use of funds for extremist and terrorist activity'.

In polarised times, it was as well that Britain's Muslim charities had a clear collective voice of their own. The Muslim Charities Forum (MCF) came into existence in 2007 as the representative body of organisations still only a few years, at most a few decades, old. The man who inspired and co-founded the forum was Dr Hany El-Banna, an Egyptian-born doctor from Birmingham whose attendance at a medical conference in famine-hit Sudan in the 1980s led directly to the establishment of Islamic Relief.

MCF scrutinised developments at the Charity Commission and was worried by what it found. 'The Charity Commission is supposed to be a neutral entity and not influenced or affected by the policy-makers,' said Abdurahman Sharif, MCF's executive director. 'Its neutrality is a bit affected at the moment and I'm not sure how neutral it really is.' He went on:

> Some people believe there has been a change of strategic direction at the Commission, which they believe is coming from higher up. One of the concerns is that it is slowly losing its role of support for the sector and is acting like a policing entity: 'If you do anything wrong, we will damage you, close you down and so on and so on.'

As others have warned, one consequence of a tougher line could be disenchantment and disengagement on the part of Britain's Muslim voluntary workers. 'We've done a lot of work in recent years to get community-based groups and mosques to be registered,' said Abdurahman. They are now faced with people saying, 'Why should we do this?' The risk is that more Muslim charity efforts would be directed through unofficial, unscrutinised channels. 'We want to be aware of what's happening,' Abdurahman added, 'and the Charity Commission should be supporting that.'

It would be a perverse upshot of British anxiety over possible links between Muslim charity and jihadist terror if a community's charitable giving became less rather than more subject to oversight. It would also represent a setback to the development of the British humanitarian movement. Muslim charity workers are already at the forefront of Britain's aid efforts in the ugliest conflicts of the era. They will form an important component of the next generation of British overseas aid-giving. That is a process that needs to be fostered, not stultified.

CHAPTER 13

MAKING POVERTY HISTORY?

London and Oxford

Oxfam and Save the Children are Britain's biggest private aid operators. Each is several times larger than any other UK agency in the field. As global brands, they rank high among international aid donors. Save the Children International and Oxfam International each runs an aid operation comparable in value to that of a small- to medium-sized country – a little less than Belgium or Switzerland, on 2011 figures, but a bit more than Austria or Ireland.

In their origins, the two organisations have a great deal in common. They were both conceived and born in times of war – Save the Children in the First World War, Oxfam in the Second. Both took on the British government of the day and mounted sharp challenges to contemporary political and public attitudes. Their stance was the same – a principled objection to British naval blockades that were turning deprivation and hunger in parts of Europe into mass death from starvation. Pacifist Quaker influence was significant in the foundation of both.

Save the Children was the creation of two amazing sisters from Shropshire, one educated at Oxford, the other at Cambridge. The elder was Eglantyne Jebb, who ran Save the Children from soon after its foundation in 1919 until her early death less than a decade later at the age of 52. Her younger sister Dorothy married into a family of Quaker reformers, became a Quaker herself, and drove the internationalist vision that inspired the new organisation. It was Dorothy Buxton who coined the phrase 'Save the Children' and it was she who brandished a tin of condensed milk at a rally in the Albert Hall as she tore into the politicians and churchmen of the day. 'There is more practical morality in this tin than in all their creeds,' she cried.[1]

Through the First World War, Dorothy and her husband, the radical MP Charles Buxton, had contributed 'Notes on the Foreign Press' to the *Cambridge Magazine*. They received special permission to import 25 'enemy papers' from Scandinavia. What they translated from the Swedish, Swiss and German press made for grim reading. The war's impact on civilians, aggravated by the British blockade, 'was creating a humanitarian crisis across Europe on an unprecedented scale, which was neither morally justifiable, nor in the long-term interest of a safer or more stable Europe'.[2]

Worse followed when the war was over. Instead of relaxing the blockade, the British kept it tight for eight more months to force Germany to accept the terms of the Treaty of Versailles, thus sowing the seeds of the next European war. Eglantyne Jebb summed up British policy as 'submit or starve'. In an essay entitled 'Save the Child!' published after her death, she provided this description of the immediate post-war period in Austria and Germany: 'Mothers killed the babies they could not feed. Parents sent their children to the hospitals when they could no longer give them any bread, but in the denuded hospitals they were simply placed in rows to die.'

Eglantyne also wrote of the outright hostility she encountered as Save the Children began to take root. People 'considered it an unpatriotic act to feed the children of enemies'. 'These children had much better die,' she was told. 'They will only grow up to fight us.' On the other hand, she could count on encouragement from some of the great figures of the day. George Bernard Shaw was one of Save the Children's early supporters. 'I have no enemy under the age of seven,' he said.

The Jebb sisters utilised the most modern forms of protest. They organised 'Ban the Blockade' meetings and they marched on Downing Street. In April 1919, Eglantyne was arrested in Trafalgar Square for distributing 'starving baby' leaflets with a photograph of an Austrian child that had not been cleared by British censors. There was a special poster produced at the time of her trial under the wartime Defence of the Realm Act. 'What does Britain stand for?' it asked, and provided this answer: 'Starving babies, torturing women, killing the old.'

Eglantyne was found guilty and sentenced to 11 days in prison, but fined a charitable £5 with no costs. Save the Children filled the Albert Hall thanks to all the publicity and the money raised was spent in Austria by Quaker relief workers. After the post-war emergency was over, funds dried up, but a dreadful famine then loomed in Russia and the sisters' efforts had to be redoubled. On this occasion, 'persons in humble positions sold the produce of their gardens or wild fruits'; a man sent in £100 – 'half the savings of a lifetime'; 'an aged woman collected 15 shillings in farthings'.[3]

Even the British government got caught up in this street-level generosity and agreed to match Save the Children's funds pound for pound. There was, as usual, no accounting for the lack of humanity shown by the British press. 'Huge sums for a dubious famine: what of England?' said one headline in the *Daily Express* in November 1921. 'Moment ill-chosen to appeal for funds: needs at home,' said another.[4]

Not long after the establishment of Save the Children, and partly to avoid these politics at home, Eglantyne Jebb left Britain to live in Geneva. Her move confirmed the city's status as the international capital of humanitarianism. If the world really was to be changed for the better for children, she reasoned, this was the place she had to be. She would be close to the new League of Nations, forerunner of the United Nations, and a neighbour of the International Committee of the Red Cross. As a consequence of her presence, the 1920s in Geneva became as creative a period in the evolution of humanitarianism as the 1860s had been when the Red Cross was founded and the First Geneva Convention was signed.

In the very room at the Geneva Arts Society building where the ICRC had come into being 60 years earlier, Save the Children and Red Cross delegates met in January 1920 to create the International Union of Save the Children. Eglantyne – this 'daughter of the ICRC', as her biographer Clare Mulley describes her – repaid their patronage by encouraging them to see beyond wounded soldiers on the battlefield to the civilian and child victims of war. Here began the process that led to the Declaration of the Rights of the Child, drafted by Eglantyne and endorsed by the League of Nations, which today is enshrined in the Convention on the Rights of the Child, the most widely ratified human rights treaty in history.

Despite her fierce promotion of children's rights, Eglantyne Jebb's own feelings towards them were far from sentimental. She had taught for a time after leaving university, and wrote in her diary: 'I have none of the natural qualities of a teacher. I don't care for children, I don't care for teaching.' At one point she calls them 'little wretches', and on another writes to a friend: 'I suppose it is a judgement on me for not caring about children that I am made to talk all day long about the universal love of all humanity for them.'

She was also, by her own account, a poor public speaker and a rotten fundraiser. 'Friends told me that I appealed for money so badly that it positively pained them to hear me trying to do so.' Yet she drove herself remorselessly on, steadily undermining her already poor health. 'It was strange,' she wrote, 'that I knew perfectly well I was killing myself and that I was killing myself for nothing.'

As she lay dying in a Geneva nursing home, she was at work on what would today be called the bigger development picture. Her purpose was to spread the message of childcare and child rights to other parts of the world. She was planning a conference of 'non-European races', which duly took place in Geneva in 1931, three years after her death, as the International Conference on African Children. Its focus on infant mortality, child labour and child marriage underlines how very little has changed in 85 years.

There were other areas where Eglantyne showed astonishing prescience in anticipating the practices and principles of modern aid. From the early 1920s, Save the Children ran child sponsorship schemes where individual donors were linked with poor children. An early schools project connecting British and East European children produced a thank-you letter saying they 'used to eat grass' and now 'eat bread and do not suffer any more'.

Eglantyne articulated the very point of modern development when she declared that 'relief alone cannot save the children. If we really want to save them we must add to our work of relief other activities.' Aid had to be 'constructive, self-sustaining [and] should stimulate self-help'. Three things were required to save children from misery, she concluded. 'Money. Knowledge. Good will. We have the money, but we spend it on other things. We have the knowledge, but we do not apply it. Can we not cultivate the good will …?'

The founder of Save the Children is buried in an unadorned grave in St George's Cemetery in Geneva. There was just a pot of weather-bleached plastic flowers on it when I visited. She had lived a life of exceptional frugality and had shown a puritanical disregard for wealth. One section of her posthumous essay 'Save the Child!' is entitled 'The crime of luxury', in which she quotes the early Quaker William Penn, founder of Pennsylvania: 'The very trimming of the vain world would clothe all the naked ones.' She added crisply: 'This remains true today.'

There would be many things that would surely impress Eglantyne Jebb about the modern Save the Children and its work in the world's toughest places. The charity's high pay levels would probably not be among them. Jasmine Whitbread, who moved in 2010 from heading Save the Children in Britain to running Save the Children International, was paid $401,000 in 2013. Her successor at the UK arm, Justin Forsyth, was paid £168,000 in 2012. Press criticism and dismay among Save the Children's supporters over such large sums seem to have had an effect. Mr Forsyth's pay was pegged to £140,000, that important benchmark representing the prime minister's salary, and Ms Whitbread's salary was reduced in 2014 to $368,000, less than President Obama's.

If the historical record could identify a single person as the inspiration for Oxfam, it would be another woman and another Quaker. Her name was Edith Pye. She had worked in Austria in the aftermath of the First World War as a 'War Vic', a member of the Friends War Victims Relief Committee. She would have utilised funds that the Jebb sisters raised in England.

The experience left an indelible impression on her. 'I think it is my recollection of what those children looked like which makes me anxious to help now,' she said in 1942, in the middle of another World War when another generation of children faced death from starvation as a result of a British naval blockade. What Edith Pye did to help was to form a national Famine Relief Committee, similar in many ways to the Fight the Famine Council that became Save the Children.

The major humanitarian concern at this point in the Second World War was the fate of women and children in German-occupied Greece. The International Committee of the Red Cross was reporting that mortality had increased six-fold in just two months and that 2,000 had died of starvation in Athens and Piraeus alone. In all, some 200,000 Greeks perished in the winter of 1941–42. 'Send bread or coffins' was the stark message from one of the Aegean islands.[5]

In July 1942, Miss Pye travelled to Oxford to mobilise local Quakers, fellow churchmen and others in the cause of feeding Greece. Later that year, in October, a group of them met again at the University Church in the High Street and the Oxford Committee for Famine Relief was born. It had swift success. Five thousand pounds was collected in the first half of 1943 and a 'Greek Week' in October raised another £12,700 – hugely impressive sums in wartime. The money was handed over to the Greek Red Cross in exile and utilised by the ICRC on the spot.

With the Germans and the Allies waging 'total war' in Europe, there was no inclination on Britain's part to relax the blockade. Edith Pye was given courteous hearings by ministers, but variously told that 'it is not always understood that food is contraband' and that 'the innocent must suffer in time of war'. It was only under American pressure that the British eventually agreed to allow food to reach Greece – Canadian wheat on board Swedish ships flying the flag of the International Red Cross.

After the war was over, most of the famine relief committees were wound up, but the Oxford Committee stayed on to extend its objectives, first to post-war suffering in Europe and then, in 1949, 'to the relief of suffering arising as a result of war or any other cause in any part of the world'. One of its earliest non-emergency grants was to Greece in 1948 – £200 to a domestic training college in Salonika, run by Quakers.

From these modest beginnings, Oxfam acquired a global ambition to change the world. Its projects and programmes were aimed at helping individuals, families and communities, but that was never enough. Whole societies had to be transformed; poverty itself had to be overcome. In the 1990s and 2000s, alliances were formed that enshrined these objectives. When the New Labour government set about, in its own phrase, 'Eliminating World Poverty', its friends and allies in the NGOs undertook to 'Make Poverty History'. No other country in the world, of whatever size or influence, would have dared put it quite like that.

Maggie Black, Oxfam's historian and a one-time staff member, marked the agency's fiftieth anniversary in 1992 by writing that Oxfam, in common with other aid agencies, 'had a tendency to convey a grander importance of Oxfam projects in the scheme of things, and a greater belief in Oxfam's ability to solve the problems of world poverty, than was realistic'. She added that: '… it had to be clear to the thoughtful mind that a typical Oxfam grant could exert no conceivable influence on the problem of poverty.'[6]

The rhetoric of aid was one problem; the other was the state of the world. Time and again Oxfam was brought back to the wretched realities of global division, civil turmoil and international conflict, which obstructed the peace and stability needed for development. The agency continued to set great store by its political interventions at home, and in many of its early responses displayed a readiness to confront authority that is much less apparent today.

Oxfam's strong stance on disarmament was linked to its anti-poverty purpose through the slogan 'Bread not Bombs'. Two grants of £10,000 to the World Disarmament Campaign strained relations with the Charity Commission, but were declared legitimate on the grounds that they might also help to end poverty. There was bigger trouble over Oxfam's connections with the Campaign Against Arms Trade, and then the Commission launched a full-dress inquiry into its agitation against apartheid South Africa and in favour of sanctions.

Here, the regulator found against Oxfam and the campaigning had to cease. The Commission went on to review other Oxfam campaigns of the late 1980s and concluded that they, too, had overstepped the mark. It ordered that 'unacceptable political activities of the charity must cease' and, while imposing no financial penalties, forced Oxfam to withdraw all the offending campaign material.

Inside Oxfam there was often a tussle between 'development' and the need to mount 'relief' responses. The most striking example of getting it wrong was over Ethiopia at the time of the great famine. Oxfam's trustees chose 1984, the year of Band Aid of all years, to declare that 'relief projects should be avoided and development projects sought'.[7] News of hundreds of thousands dying of starvation broke in October, although the famine had been building for nearly two years, and Oxfam's staff on the ground quickly acknowledged the scale of their error.

'In retrospect, Oxfam should have moved in much earlier,' said Hugh Goyder, its field director in Ethiopia at the time, 'and placed less reliance on the judgements of our long-established projects in areas which, it transpired, knew too little about the growing hunger on their own doorsteps until it was too late.'[8]

A similar conjunction of drought and conflict in 2011 led to the biggest famine so far of the new century, with hundreds of thousands dying in Somalia. Senior Oxfam managers were quick to denounce global aid institutions for their failures and insisted that the answer was more development. Yet their own report on the famine, as we have seen, produced jointly with Save the Children, found that, while some major NGOs had reacted swiftly to the crisis as early as February 2011, Oxfam and Save the Children let a full five months pass before scaling up their response.[9]

The wars prosecuted by Tony Blair as prime minister put fresh and unwelcome strain on the big British NGOs. Tony Vaux, an Oxfam emergencies coordinator for many years and later its manager for Eastern Europe and the former Soviet Union, describes in his book *The Selfish Altruist* the impact that the war in Kosovo had on him and the agency. He speculates as to whether Oxfam would have been able to take the stand it did on the allied blockade of Greece in 1942 'if it had then relied on widespread public support'. His chapter on Kosovo is entitled 'The loss of impartiality'.

Despite its early history, Oxfam found itself formally supporting military intervention in Kosovo – 'Oxfam believes action to enforce a ceasefire must be taken' – although internal arguments meant that it did not publicly endorse NATO's 1999 bombing campaign. 'In Kosovo, we let our human concern be exclusively directed as politicians wished,' Vaux said afterwards. 'Taking tea with French soldiers, putting up tents and water systems for refugees alongside NATO troops; we had not behaved as impartial humanitarians, but as if we were part of NATO.'[10]

In his book, Vaux points out that Médecins Sans Frontières did not work with the military in Kosovo, but adds that 'it was a competitive environment in which plenty of others were even less thoughtful than Oxfam'. His conclusion on the conflict is that Oxfam 'should have learned the value of impartiality' and that 'by failing to take a principled stand it became co-opted'.

The 'blurring of lines' between civilian aid-givers and governments at war became more contentious during the West's lengthy engagement in Afghanistan. Oxfam and Save the Children both accepted funding from Western belligerents, either directly or through multilateral agencies such as the World Bank and the United Nations, and there was no doubt as to which side of the conflict they were on. In the case of Save the Children, senior staff argued that it was quite different from MSF and the ICRC, which focused on emergencies and could thus avoid official alignments. By contrast, Save the Children had a broader development mandate with major ambitions in the areas of education and child rights, and that meant working alongside the Afghan government and its backers.

Oxfam was more tortured in its responses, with staff emphasising how funding decisions were always taken on a case-by-case basis. In Afghanistan, the issue became doubly sensitive. A strong-worded Oxfam report entitled *Whose Aid is it Anyway*, published in 2011, was critical of the big donors for skewing assistance from the most needy to areas of military priority, but was reluctant to scrutinise too closely the role of the international NGOs themselves, including Oxfam, or to question how impartially they behaved.

Like Save the Children, Oxfam stoutly defended its support for aid in the cause of Afghan 'nation-building'. Senior staff proudly emphasised that it had not been 'neutral' in the war. 'What's wrong with espousing and promoting liberal values?' one of them asked me. 'What's wrong in defending and promoting women's rights in a place like Afghanistan?'

Oxfam spent some £17 million in Afghanistan in the 12 years to 2013, with most of the money coming either directly or indirectly from Western governments engaged in the war. Funds were often channelled through the World Bank and the United Nations and then paid out by the Afghan government. Of all Oxfam's official backers, one of the few to be able to claim neutrality in the conflict was the Swiss government's Agency for Development and Cooperation.

In recent decades, major British NGOs have come increasingly to rely on official funds. In most parts of the world this has little bearing on agency independence, even when the NGOs are engaged in broadly political rather than humanitarian projects. Only when Western security interests are directly at stake, as they now are in more and more foreign conflicts, do tensions arise between principled humanitarianism and the priorities of official aid-givers.

Dame Barbara Stocking, who was Oxfam's chief executive for most of the Western war in Afghanistan, recalls the anxious debates over when and where to draw the line between independence and alignment. Having flatly rejected British government money in Iraq after the 2003 invasion, Afghanistan was thought to be different – a country in need of wholesale reconstruction after decades of war, invasion and extremism. Ms Stocking now accepts that mistakes may have been made along the way.

In 2003, Oxfam was a signatory to 'A Call for Security', which pressed NATO to embark on a major military expansion outside Kabul so that 'democracy can flourish' and 'the prospect for peace and stability for the Afghan people and the world' could be improved. 'I can see exactly why we did it, because we really wanted to have security so we could get development going,' said Ms Stocking. 'In retrospect, I don't think that I thought this through enough – about the fact that a war was still going on with the Taliban and therefore that we were effectively taking sides.'

After 28 years at Oxfam, Tony Vaux went on to become an aid consultant in the area of conflict and humanitarian operations. The conclusions he reached on the Kosovo war have been forcefully underlined by the war on terror. 'The money that Oxfam is taking has come through a highly political and military filter before it comes to Oxfam,' he told me. 'So the government is saying "We want to do this in Afghanistan; we want to stabilise this province; we couldn't care less about other provinces; we'll offer people money in this place, but not in that place, for this kind of thing, but not for that kind of thing."' However inadvertently, Vaux maintains, Oxfam and other big NGOs became 'force-multipliers' for the military, in the words of Colin Powell, US Secretary of State, in the aftermath of 9/11.

> Ultimately it's an issue of resources. If you want to keep yourself separate from the UK government agenda, you would have to refuse its money, and if you refuse its money, you can't do all that much. So end of story – you just have to live with it as best you can and avoid any extreme situations and maybe argue a bit about it, but that's basically the way it is.

When I first wrote about Oxfam, it received no funds at all from the British or any other government. Research for a book on Oxfam's work in the 1960s took me to West Africa to look at its response to a refugee crisis in southern Senegal. The governor of the province asked me where Oxfam's money came from. 'Entirely from the public,' I said. 'How much do you collect?' 'About £3 million a year.' There was a long, low whistle.[11]

The first grant Oxfam received from the British government was for £130,000 in 1976. By the end of that decade it was getting £1 million a year. The figure for 2014–15 was £46 million out of the £192 million received from governments and institutions as a whole. Such funding now adds up to almost half of Oxfam's income and is nearly twice the amount the charity receives in private donations and legacies. The other major source of income is the Oxfam shops.

The charity's historian, Maggie Black, put it like this to me: 'In the 1970s we still boasted that we took no money from government. That enabled us to be properly free. It meant we could say what we wanted to. We might only be a gnat's bite or a bee sting, but we could stand up to power.' She added: 'Now, of course, Oxfam would never really attack DFID.'

Over the years, Oxfam has imposed ceilings on the amount of money it accepts from governments. In the early 1990s this funding was restricted to 10 per cent of income; that was later relaxed to 20 per cent, and the present restriction is lighter still – funding from a single official source should not exceed 20 per cent of the total charitable spend. At £46 million, DFID's total commitment to Oxfam in 2014–15 represented 15 per cent of its charitable expenditure and was a rise of £11 million over the previous year.

Oxfam's top management has consistently emphasised the importance of keeping a check on the level of official funding. One former director who insisted on sticking to the 20 per cent overall ceiling told me that they 'didn't want to become subject to other people's agenda' and that it was 'very easy to slip into self-censorship'. Mark Goldring, who took over as Oxfam's chief executive in 2013, said that there was a risk in getting too close to government. 'As long as the big NGOs seek to do large-scale service delivery, the more risk there is,' he said.

Crisis and conflict in the contemporary world once again raise the historical dilemma of relief versus development. Oxfam has always strived to move on from emergency aid to concentrate on the bigger, brighter picture of making poverty history. Its development work includes a range of rights-based and social justice programmes, but these are often modest in size and difficult to scale up. It also concentrates on campaigning and advocacy – £20 million in 2014–15 – and that is sometimes criticised within the organisation for being insufficiently rooted in its experience in the field.

Along with the British government's Department for International Development, Oxfam prides itself on its 'thought leadership' of the aid community and wants to be less operational and more engaged in local partnerships. 'Overall,' I was told at Oxfam, 'we need to do less and influence more.' Even Oxfam's traditional commitment to the provision of water, sanitation and hygiene services – the famous WASH – is said to have diminished in recent years. On several of my field trips I was personally asked, 'Where's Oxfam?'

If the world enjoyed a greater measure of stability and people were not suffering grievously from the lack of it, Oxfam's commitment to reducing its operational capacity might be justified. It was based on a calculation made around 2005 – the high-water mark of British aid ambitions, when the level of international violence was declining – that global conflicts would continue to diminish. In fact, since 2007 they have steadily proliferated and intensified.[12] 'Some of the assumptions we made a decade ago turned out not to be correct,' I was told at Oxfam, and this had left them ill-placed to respond more fully to the humanitarian fallout of conflict.

When al-Shabaab militants were pushed out of Mogadishu and a measure of order was restored in the city, international aid agencies began to return to the Somali capital. The United Nations took the lead. Oxfam decided against reopening an office there and relied instead on funding Somali partners. That decision was defended at Oxfam's Oxford headquarters, where I was assured that partnerships with local organisations had performed very well.

A different view was taken by key Oxfam staff in the field. 'We need a presence on the ground,' one of them said to me. 'If we don't have one, we can say what we like about what's being done there, but we can't be sure.' When I visited East Africa in 2014, there was no one from Oxfam in Mogadishu and very few flying visits. 'Oxfam needs to decide if it can afford to stay out of Mogadishu and still reckon itself a player,' another senior staffer told me. 'We will have to decide soon if we're going to change the travel schedules and have more people visiting or follow the process of the other NGOs and have our own office.'

There were also, I was told, the views of Oxfam supporters to consider. 'If you did a survey on the high street,' a senior field manager told me, 'you would find that the majority of people who give money to Oxfam give it to save lives and reduce suffering. That's where the money comes from and you can't ignore that.'

Similar circumstances arose in Afghanistan, where Oxfam ran both humanitarian operations and development programmes, with the emphasis of the latter on rights and social justice. I spent a morning in Kabul in a well-fortified hotel with one of Oxfam's local NGO partners witnessing efforts to sensitise a group of senior city police officers on gender matters. Outside Kabul, Oxfam had had no presence for several years in any of the country's troubled southern provinces.

Some field managers argued that this needed to change. 'By being there and being involved you can help stabilise the situation,' one of them said. 'You can say this is part of terrorist reduction because if we don't do things like this, what are people going to do? They'll end up queuing at the local Taliban office, saying "Please give me a gun."'

In his second year as Oxfam's chief executive, Mark Goldring told me that 'Oxfam is there' could not mean 'Oxfam is everywhere'. 'There's no policy behind that,' he said. 'It's just the limits of what we can do.' He also pointed to places such as South Sudan, where most

NGOs pulled out in the murderous meltdown of 2013 and Oxfam stayed put. Its confidence and capacity were linked to Oxfam's 30-year presence in the region. Long-term development projects were rapidly transformed into emergency programmes, with Oxfam spending £20 million in South Sudan in 2014 alone.

The tensions between 'feel-good' development and 'band-aid' relief played themselves out on British television screens. At Christmas 2013, Oxfam launched a 'Lift Lives for Good' advertisement which showed smiling villagers with healthy and productive cows and a growing milk business. Here was development at work. 'It bombed,' said Mr Goldring. 'It wasn't forceful enough in telling the story and saying, "We have to have your money now!"'

So Oxfam pulled the advert off air and replaced it with an emergency appeal for South Sudan. This was filmed without any special effects in an Oxfam warehouse and showed a staffer just back from the country asking urgently for £3 donations towards the cost of providing clean drinking water for thousands of displaced people. Oxfam did not regret the switch. The South Sudan appeal made seven times more than the 'Lift Lives for Good' advertisement.

At a meeting early on in the Syria crisis to discuss how Save the Children and other NGOs should respond to the suffering, Gareth Owen, its humanitarian director, wrote in the margins of his notes: 'Syria is too hard for today's aid world.' After the politicians and the diplomats had failed Syria so badly, it was left to aid agencies to pick up the pieces. The United Nations was restricted by diplomatic protocol as to where it could deliver aid; the West's big government donors had long ago ceased to be operational. That left NGOs on the Turkey–Syria border to face the most ferocious conflict of the century.

Gareth Owen was able to travel across the border in the early days of the war, but with the advance of Islamic State across the north that was no longer practicable. From its base in south-eastern Turkey, Save the Children moved to deploy a staff of around 150 Syrians inside the country and to link up with Syrian NGOs – locals and diaspora – to bring British and other international aid to bear. By mid-2015 it had received funding commitments of around $70 million for aid work that ranged from health and education to child protection.

'Beware the last mile,' was the warning to charities from British government officials safe in their London offices. DFID and the Charity Commission wanted to know exactly who was getting British aid and to be assured that none of it ever reached anyone with a terrorist link. In vain did the charities point out that there was a war going on. 'So they steal a tenner from us which they shouldn't,' Gareth Owen complained, 'but they're getting millions, billions probably, from their allies around the region.'

In Syria and elsewhere, Save the Children decided that its proper place was at the front. It wanted to be in many more of the most difficult places. By 2014, over half its income was being spent on humanitarian interventions, a sum that had doubled in seven years. I was told by senior managers in London that the development of Save the Children's humanitarian capacity was going to be 'central to the next 15 years'.

At the heart of this plan was an unusual charity takeover. In 2013, Save the Children merged with – or, put bluntly, took over – the £60 million British medical relief agency Merlin. The inspiration for Merlin was a private aid initiative undertaken in Romania after the fall of the communist dictatorship in 1989. It might at that point have become the British operational arm of Médecins Sans Frontières, but MSF rejected the approach, and so for 20 years Merlin remained an independent charity.

Cash-flow problems propelled it into the arms of Save the Children, although Save the Children had to find £2 million from wealthy private donors to secure formal British government backing for the takeover. The man who masterminded the Merlin deal was Save the Children's chief executive Justin Forsyth, who had intimate knowledge of the ways of Whitehall. With a background as an Oxfam policy and campaigns director, he had worked in Downing Street for both Tony Blair and Gordon Brown before taking over at Save the Children after Labour lost office in 2010.

Forsyth arrived at Save the Children with big ambitions. Playing a more significant role in the humanitarian field was the biggest of them. In a world caught up in conflict, he saw how many young lives were being blighted. Children were being killed and injured, their health compromised and their education sidelined. 'The reason we've decided to get much more into the field is our analysis of what children need,' he told me in February 2015. 'If our job at Save the Children is to make sure the most neglected and most vulnerable children are helped in this world, we have to do the really tough stuff as well as the development stuff.'

The merger with Merlin helped put Save the Children back on the humanitarian front line. It enabled them to start a hospital in Sierra Leone that became the centrepiece of Britain's response to the West African Ebola epidemic of 2014. It also gave them an emergency medical presence in the collapsed countries of South Sudan and the Central African Republic. 'We haven't taken Merlin over and shut them down,' Forsyth said. 'We've kept them and taken them to greater heights.'

There was another strand to Save the Children's humanitarian ambitions. The agency put £500,000 of its supporters' money into starting a Humanitarian Leadership Academy to train aid workers in the global South. The purpose of this investment was to leverage far larger commitments from the big donors. After 'incubating' this international academy, Save the Children expected the real funding to flow from DFID in Britain (£20 million over five years), from the Dutch and Norwegian governments, and from private corporations.

When he took over at Save the Children, and in common with other modern NGO bosses, Forsyth adopted what is termed an 'insider–outsider' approach to running a twenty-first-century charity. It means that NGOs are broadly supportive of their governments, take lots of their money, and are measured in their criticism. Voices are raised within and beyond the agencies that this arrangement is altogether too cosy, a long way from founding principles and based far too obviously on financial calculation.

Justin Forsyth himself is the very embodiment of the 'insider–outsider'. Indeed, he is a master of the art. He schooled himself in the approach in Washington in the 1990s, where he set up an Oxfam International office and converted Oxfam's previous antagonism towards the World Bank into something of an alliance over Third World debt.

In Downing Street in the 2000s he was Tony Blair's key strategist in promoting the relationship between government and the NGOs, an embrace that reached its passionate climax in the 'Make Poverty History' campaign and the G8 Gleneagles summit of 2005. This was the 'Africa' summit that made real progress on the key development issues of aid, trade and debt. On the down side, a close working relationship with Tony Blair was not always an asset in Forsyth's other role – that of the outsider.

There was furious upset in November 2014 when Save the Children in the United States decided to confer a 'Global Legacy Award' on Tony Blair at a gala dinner in New York. British members of staff signed a letter saying that the award was 'morally reprehensible' and should be withdrawn to protect the charity's 'credibility globally'. Save the Children in Britain logged an extraordinary 3,372 complaints from supporters over the award – 'negative feedback', as it was described by the organisation.

Forsyth's excuse was that he had had nothing to do with it beyond forwarding the invitation to Tony Blair's office. He also stressed that Save the Children was not honouring him for everything he had done as prime minister ('That would have been wrong,' he told me) but specifically for Gleneagles and for 'Make Poverty History' – the very focus, of course, of Forsyth's own work in Downing Street.*

The 'insider–outsider' strategy was pursued further in a series of senior appointments at Save the Children. At executive director level there were further arrivals from Downing Street, from the Department for International Development and even from Tony Blair's offices in Africa. More 'insider–outsider' skills went on display as Save the Children negotiated the transition to the Conservative-led government after 2010. The agency lavished praise on David Cameron for his aid initiatives and appointed his wife Samantha as one of its global ambassadors.

I asked Justin Forsyth what he thought Eglantyne Jebb, Save the Children's founder, would make of the charity's present direction. He knew her story and suggested that he was following in her footsteps, even, he claimed, down to the 'insider–outsider' strategy. 'What I like about her was that she was a radical, but also appealed to middle Britain,' he told me. 'I know people think in a way I'm doing the opposite, but I want to take Save the Children back to its values and roots in that radical and middle Britain. At the same time I want to use very modern techniques on how you achieve change.

---

* The original plan had apparently been to give the 'Global Legacy Award' not to Tony Blair, but to his successor as prime minister Gordon Brown, a powerful advocate of aid in government who later became the UN Special Envoy for Global Education. That would have been a more imaginative and certainly a safer choice.

'I think this is very much in the spirit of Eglantyne Jebb. She thought out of the box, and she challenged ways of doing things from the very beginning, even in the way she campaigned, the way she took on the Establishment. But then she was extraordinarily practical at the same time.' I asked him how close she would have got to government. 'I think she would say you're critical of them sometimes and at other times you work with them,' he replied. 'In the end it's about how you achieve the best results.'

In financial terms, proximity to government certainly paid off. In Forsyth's years as chief executive, Save the Children's income from the British government increased more than six-fold, from £19 million in 2010 to £120 million in 2014. This rise underpinned a performance in which total government and institutional grants rose to £228 million, over 60 per cent of the charity's record income in 2014 of £370 million. In the troubling terminology of the modern aid business, Save the Children became the British government's 'contractor of choice'.

Corresponding efforts were made to drive up the charity's private income. Save the Children broke ranks with British and other aid-givers in its use of distressing images of prone and starving African babies for fundraising purposes. These 'apocalyptic or pathetic images' had once been formally condemned by the NGOs as 'images which fuel prejudice'.[13] Aid radicals went a step further and called them 'development pornography'. They nevertheless helped increase individual donations to Save the Children by £20 million over five years.

Corporate Britain was another target of the charity's fundraisers. When he was at Oxfam, Justin Forsyth had organised noisy protests against the British pharmaceutical giant GSK (GlaxoSmithKline). Now Save the Children and GSK became partners in researching and developing child health interventions in Africa. For Forsyth, this was the 'power of the private sector' in action. Save the Children's corporate funding more than trebled over five years to £27 million.

Dramatic growth attended by frequent controversy characterised Justin Forsyth's five years as head of Save the Children. Then, in October 2015, suddenly and unexpectedly, he announced he was resigning and would be leaving the agency early in 2016. His resignation followed the hurried and unexplained departure of another senior figure, Brendan Cox, director of policy and advocacy. Like Forsyth, Cox had worked both at Oxfam and as an adviser in Downing Street. He had directly followed Forsyth to Save the Children. These upheavals are unlikely to alter the strong emergency humanitarian focus developed since 2010, although the highly profitable 'insider–outsider' relationships developed with government might well falter.

Tie-ups with industry, hard-core advertising, more and more funding from government: this is the modern aid charity at work. Save the Children's approach under Justin Forsyth can be justified by the results – more money to spend on quality programmes and quality people in the field. But a price is paid, sometimes in reputation, sometimes even in principle. Striving for independence, impartiality and neutrality has helped sustain the European humanitarian movement for the past 150 years. In recent decades, the British have distanced themselves from that tradition. In a word, the big British charities have become more American.

CHAPTER 14

FRENCH LESSONS

Paris

On the cramped fifth floor of its offices in the 11th arrondissement of Paris, Médecins Sans Frontières houses a small think tank called Crash. It got the name as a joke, as a play on all those *comités révolutionnaires d'action* with which French history abounds. In this case, the initials stand for *centre de reflexion sur l'action et les savoirs humanitaires*, or 'centre for reflection on humanitarian actions and knowledge', and there is nothing quite like it anywhere else in the NGO world.

Crash is very largely independent of the organisation that houses and supports it. It is as critical of MSF as it is of other aid bodies, often more so, and its existence goes some way to account for MSF's distinctive spirit and personality.

When I visited Crash early in 2015, it was engulfed in the bitter fallout of a 'letter to the MSF movement' which was marked 'internal' but did not remain so. Entitled 'Ebola: a challenge to our humanitarian identity' and signed by eight of the organisation's top doctors, including a research director at Crash and other senior figures from MSF in Paris, it was a 3,000-word account of MSF's failings during the public health crisis in West Africa.

While the world at large stood in awe of MSF's achievement in leading the way on Ebola and in shaming the UN's World Health Organization and other humanitarian agencies into belated action, the organisation itself was struggling to absorb the most painful lessons of all from the epidemic – and being very harsh on itself. The letter suggested that the agency's approach had led to unnecessary deaths.

'Haunted by the fear of staff contamination, MSF repeatedly overlooked the features of our intervention that needed improvement,' it said. 'Consequences were and are still dramatic – resulting in a high number of presumably avoidable deaths.' What the letter's authors had scrutinised was whether the safety of MSF health personnel had been placed ahead of patient care in the testing, monitoring and rehydration of patients.

'MSF collectively failed to demonstrate that – even in an Ebola outbreak – the survival of every individual patient is a battle worth fighting for,' the letter said. 'It is, arguably, an institutionalised form of non-assistance to persons at risk of dying, a serious infringement of commonly accepted and morally binding codes of medical ethics.

'This open letter intends to raise awareness that MSF should never shy away from treating every individual patient as well as possible – this is our core mission anchored in humanitarian values and medical ethics ... We must change our mindset.'

Many in MSF were troubled and upset by the vehemence of the criticism. They included staff and managers who had been on the front line in West Africa and who resented what they saw as an armchair assault from Europe. The Belgian section of MSF gave back every bit as good as it got in its letter of response.

'The accusatory tone and simplification of dilemmas – or even lack of acknowledgment that the dilemmas exist – lead to dogmatic conclusions of a lack of patient focus,' said eight senior signatories from Brussels. 'We do not accept that this open letter can be considered as a constructive contribution to the debate. When the authors repeatedly throw the worst possible accusation in a humanitarian association – that of leaving people to die – they make constructive dialogue rather difficult.'

Particular bitterness was directed at MSF's French section in Paris, which, the letter complained, had not intervened in the Ebola crisis 'on a significant scale'. The French had 'therefore unfortunately missed every opportunity to mobilise the most well-resourced operational centre in this fight. In effect, the largest operational and medical departments of MSF have remained unused. But this epidemic needed Paris – its creativity and operational capacities were missed.'

By any standards, this was a ferocious and ultimately, surely, an unfortunate argument. Yet the instinct to speak out – and a determination to be heard – has been part of MSF's make-up from the start, and a taste for public controversy in the area of human suffering must be better than an unquestioning corporate consensus. The French started MSF and, as *Charlie Hebdo* reminds us, they make a habit of saying the unsayable.

In its origins, MSF was a fusion of front-line medicine and free speech. A group of doctors and journalists – nine of the former and four of the latter – brought the organisation into being in the offices of a doctors' magazine called *Tonus* in Paris in December 1971. When the think tank Crash was formed many years later, its objective was not only to stimulate critical reflection about humanitarian action inside MSF but to share it with the outside world.

'You can't have a relevant discussion if it's kept entirely internal,' said Rony Brauman, a former president of MSF and a leading light at Crash. 'It has to spill over the borders of the institution. It has to touch a broader audience.' With this anti-corporate attitude towards scrutiny and disclosure, it is no wonder MSF receives such an admiring press.

Crash itself is rooted firmly within the French section of MSF. Its core staff come from the French section, although it sometimes brings in outsiders from the wider movement. It is overseen by a committee of ex-presidents and other senior figures from MSF France, but determinedly follows its own path. It has created many tensions on many fronts over the years, not least in the era of the war on terror, but has resisted formal supervision. 'We have the final say on what we say' was how Rony Brauman put it.

MSF's founding commitment to combine *témoignage* ('bearing witness') with humanitarian action sprang from the Nigerian civil war in the late 1960s. A number of French doctors had volunteered for service with the International Committee of the Red Cross and came face to face with horrific civilian suffering in the breakaway state of Biafra. Official ICRC discretion meant that it would not speak out publicly and the organisation imposed a similar vow of silence on its volunteers.

'I had signed; I was a perjurer,' wrote Bernard Kouchner, one of the youngest doctors in the group and a future French foreign minister. 'Upon my return to France, I formed a committee against genocide in Biafra. My reasoning was simple. I did not want to repeat the mistake of the ICRC, which, during the 1939–45 war, had not condemned the Nazi extermination camps. That was the origin of Médecins Sans Frontières and Médecins du Monde.'[1]

If the horrors of Biafra were the key inspiration for MSF, it also owed a lot to the radical ferment of the times in France. Bernard Kouchner travelled twice to Biafra in 1968, the year of the May uprisings, and Rony Brauman, who joined MSF a decade later as one of its first paid employees, judged its creation as a sign that France had finally joined 'the group of so-called "founder democracies"'.[2]

MSF combined relief practices 'learned from the Red Cross' with efforts to mobilise public opinion, using strategies 'invented by Amnesty International'. The French section of Amnesty was established the same year as MSF.

In tone and personality, MSF marked a vivid departure from the British outlook on aid. The United Nations had declared the 1960s the 'development decade' with an emphasis on economic and social advance, and then there was the 'second development decade' to carry on the work through the 1970s. Brauman complained that aid agencies had 'almost ignored wars' and identified the difference between the French and the British approach as 'we French tend to value controversy and debate whereas our British colleagues tend to look for consensus'.

As with the Ebola controversy, 'speaking out' was a matter of sometimes fractious controversy within MSF. Its original 1971 charter laid down that members refrain from 'any interference in states' internal affairs' and neither judge nor express opinions on local events or politics. Such constraints were regularly ignored by MSF's own leadership, which roundly denounced the authorities in Cambodia and Ethiopia, for instance, for ignoring famines in the 1970s and 1980s.

The expansion of MSF in Europe promoted a more conservative approach to public commentary, but that too was to change. 'With the end of the Cold War, speaking out publicly and defending human rights began to gain some legitimacy within the other four sections of MSF,' observed Fabrice Weissman, the Crash coordinator in Paris.[3] 'Created during the 1980s in Belgium, Holland, Spain and Switzerland, they had until then resolutely opposed the French practice of bearing witness, which they accused of politicising MSF in violation of its statutes. After bitter debate, in 1992 all of the sections decided to remove the provisions in the charter committing

MSF to confidentiality and prohibiting it from any involvement in a country's internal affairs.'

Since then, MSF has gone further than any other major aid agency in speaking out, both inside and outside the movement. Until security concerns in the war on terror began to restrict open dialogue – ransom demands, for example, are 'not up for discussion' – the movement sought to live by one of its essential texts, the pronouncement by Bernard Kouchner that MSF must guard against becoming just the 'bureaucrats of misery and technocrats of charity'.[4]

Now an international humanitarian enterprise with an annual income in 2014 of €1.3 billion, MSF underpins its independence by relying almost entirely on the money it raises privately from supporters. Less than 10 per cent of its funds comes from governments and public institutions, and in conflict zones it takes no money at all from such sources. It never accepts funds from the US government, and MSF France receives nothing at all from the French government.

Today, its four-paragraph charter remains resoundingly to the point. After setting out its purpose to provide 'assistance to populations in distress', it undertakes to observe 'neutrality and impartiality', claims 'unhindered freedom' to do its work, and demands of its staff that they remain completely independent of 'political, economic or religious powers'.

The fourth and final paragraph of the charter was the only one posted on the noticeboard in the MSF hospital in Lashkar Gah, Afghanistan, when I visited in 2013. It was a telling reminder of the sacrifice that aid work has involved – and would continue to involve – for MSF staff in the country. 'As volunteers,' it reads, 'members understand the risks and dangers of the missions they carry out and make no claim for themselves or their assigns for any form of compensation other than that which the association might be able to afford them.'

Such expectations of service are reflected in pay levels at MSF, which are appreciably lower than NGO earnings in Britain and the United States. MSF financial reports provide figures for the highest and lowest paid in all its headquarters offices. Top pay at MSF France in 2014 was €81,000 and bottom pay was €24,000. At MSF UK it was £62,000 at the top and £24,000 at the bottom. At MSF USA it was $169,000 top and $46,000 bottom. That puts the highest MSF salaries in France and Britain at half or less of what their senior Oxfam and Save the Children counterparts receive.

'When I speak to MSF donors,' one of the agency's regional managers said to me with feeling, 'I have no difficulty in assuring them that their money is certainly not being spent on me!'

Reviewing the evolution of the world's big NGOs in 2002, the American author David Rieff singled out Oxfam for praise among British agencies. '[Its] history of confrontation with its own government provides a revealing counterpoint, emblematic of the British humanitarian tradition generally, to the American tradition of collaboration with government,' he wrote.[5] While American NGOs 'became more deeply involved in the Cold War as adjuncts to their government, British NGOs ... increasingly acted from a desire to support various liberation struggles and insurgent governments as much as to undertake specific aid projects'.

While British NGOs have since forfeited their radical edge, MSF has retained much of its original spirit. Writing in 2002, as the war on terror got under way, Rieff declared MSF to be 'the most important humanitarian NGO in the world. Its medical protocols have become the model for other relief organisations, and it is both envied and resented by other groups. It is, in an important sense, the conscience of the humanitarian world.'

Its reputation rests on those demanding charter principles. If independence is constantly claimed by aid agencies and impartiality can sometimes be demonstrated, the sticking point is neutrality. Its meaning seems as plain to the layman as it is to the jurist. It stands for not taking sides and for dealing with both sides. Many in the aid world proclaim their neutrality. Few exercise it.

Within MSF, its former president Rony Brauman once made serious efforts to remove its charter commitment to neutrality. In the 1980s and throughout the 1990s he argued that MSF had shown itself so consistently opposed to totalitarian regimes – in Afghanistan under the Soviets, for instance, or in the Balkans under Serbian domination – and so much in favour of liberal Western intervention that it would be more honest to abandon the pretence of neutrality altogether.

'I thought we'd betrayed so constantly this notion of neutrality by taking public positions, by denouncing this power and standing up against this or that government that it was ridiculous to claim we were neutral,' he said. 'So it was better to drop the notion.'

The idea was debated heatedly at several MSF general assemblies, but resisted. Dr Brauman said he is now glad he lost the argument. 'It was rejected, and rightly so,' he said. 'They did a good thing; they did the right thing.' In the war on terror, MSF's commitment to neutrality has played a valuable role in its political and public positioning.

'Listening to the discussion I got convinced that it would be really uncomfortable, not to say dangerous, to drop this notion,' Rony Brauman told me. 'It's something we need when we discuss with governments, with political powers in general. It's important that it's in our charter and to be able to show it to the people we work with.' He went on:

Neutrality is not a compass; it's a flag and a very useful flag. You can brandish it and explain to your interlocutors that you are not acting on the grounds of religion or politics, but just for the sake of helping your fellow human beings. That is something that is widely understood. There is a decent pragmatic view of this notion of neutrality.

The war on terror has presented progressively harsher challenges to the practice and principle of the humanitarian movement. I was witness in the field to the wide range of agency responses to these conflicts, to their varied approaches to front-line work, and to the distinct role of MSF. These days MSF still often aligns itself with the International Committee of the Red Cross, from which it sprung, while remaining much less inhibited by the need for diplomatic discretion.

In Afghanistan, MSF inveighed noisily against the Western world's 'blurring of the lines' between its humanitarian and military endeavours. The agency paid its own fatal price for this confusion when five of its workers were murdered in 2004 and it left the country. Its return five years later, as we have seen, marked a bold initiative based on detailed prior negotiation with all the warring parties. Contacts were nurtured and sustained down to local level.

Such understandings offered staff and patients no protection at all when MSF's trauma hospital in Kunduz was repeatedly and shamefully bombed by a US warplane in October 2015. This 'tragic mistake' was attributed by the US military to malfunctioning equipment, to 'avoidable human error' by aircrew, and to 'fatigued' US troops on the ground. MSF continued to describe this 'catalogue of errors' as 'gross negligence' and as 'violations of the rules of war'.

In many ways, neighbouring Pakistan has presented a more severe set of challenges. So distrusted and unpopular has the apparatus of Western aid become there that MSF seeks to protect itself by having as little as possible to do with the rest of the humanitarian community. For some years it called itself just 'a private medical association', rejecting even the term 'humanitarian', and it has issued standing instructions to the United Nations that its data should not be incorporated into UN reports on international aid efforts in the country.

The Pakistan government has intensified the pressure on independent-minded aid agencies by controlling their access to sensitive border areas, and sometimes blocking them from such areas altogether. When they do go to work there, they are expected to subscribe to such prejudicial notions as 'non-cleared' areas and 'terrorist populations' to describe the civilians they want to help. MSF has summed up this approach in the terrifying phrase 'counter-insurgency humanitarianism'.[6]

The advance of Islamic State insurgents across northern Syria has been the most serious challenge to the humanitarian aid community in a generation. Towards the end of 2013, MSF had the largest expatriate presence of any agency in the 'liberated' north. Along with a Syrian staff of more than 500, there were 70 overseas medics and managers running a string of hospital projects. That was besides its network of remotely supported Syrian-run facilities.

Then, in January 2014, came the kidnapping of five MSF expatriates from their hospital in Idlib followed by several months of harrowing captivity. The consequence was the withdrawal of all international staff and the closure of all MSF facilities in IS-controlled areas.

'It's just impossible to work with these people, just as it was impossible to work with the Khmer Rouge – or with the Nazis,' declared Rony Brauman at Crash. He specified the three areas of 'humanitarian space' that had to be open before principled aid work could be resumed. They were the freedom to speak openly to the people who needed help; the capacity to be able to verify medical and other needs on the ground; and the need for access to monitor the use of goods and services provided by MSF. None of these conditions were being met in areas controlled by Islamic State.

There were also the kidnappings. 'An explanation is not enough,' Brauman said. 'There has to be recognition that it was a big mistake. They had promised to protect our teams, and they did the contrary.' If a ransom was paid, it should be paid back. 'That money was for the Syrian people ... and they are using it for another purpose.'

Security concerns restricted what Crash could research and publish about this latest phase of the war on terror. Its decision to work on a book covering kidnap incidents caused predictable consternation within the organisation and an article on events in northern Syria during the Islamic State advance had to be significantly edited. The article in question was by Jean-Hervé Bradol, one of the research directors at Crash who had worked in northern Syria – once in 2012 as head of an assessment team and again in 2013 as a project manager.

Dr Bradol's article provides important insights into front-line relations between humanitarian aid-givers and the Muslim world's most violent jihadists. The period it covers was from late summer 2013, when Islamic State forces moved into the town of Qabasin, north-east of Aleppo, where MSF was running a hospital and supporting mobile health teams.

After the IS takeover, Dr Bradol recorded, 'the group's commanders could not have been more clear when they asked MSF's teams to continue working'.[7] At a meeting in the MSF office, the senior local commander 'guaranteed our safety and put his word in writing in an official letter from ISIL [Islamic State of Iraq and the Levant] delivered to the office a few hours later. He considered it crucial that his takeover of power would not lead to the closure of the town's only hospital.'

From MSF's past experience of dealing with jihadists, Dr Bradol characterised this phase as the 'honeymoon'. It would be followed by 'disappointment' – economic dislocation and the imposition of strict Islamic codes of behaviour – and then descend into 'disaster': from 'purges, schisms and restructurings' to 'horrific violence against non-combatants'. Except for those in Kurdish-controlled areas, the last MSF expatriates left northern Syria in February 2014; as soon as the five expatriate hostages were freed in May, the rest of the MSF programme in IS-controlled territory was also closed down.

Yet local jihadists still wanted medical aid from MSF. 'When, in response, we demand that IS explain the arrest, detention and extortion suffered by our team,' recorded Dr Bradol, 'they retort that it is too dangerous for them to pass on our grievances and demands to their superiors.'

If MSF is ever to return to Islamic State areas, said Dr Bradol, it would need an official invitation and 'a public commitment to guarantee our safety'. The jihadists respond that it is 'unrealistic' to expect such a reassurance and reiterate their request for drugs and medical supplies, 'saying that a refusal by MSF serves to confirm our support for "Western" policy'.

Dr Bradol concludes that MSF has 'little hope of coming to an acceptable humanitarian compromise with the Islamic State in the near future'. But they have not stopped talking to them, 'demonstrating that we are willing to negotiate impartially with all the belligerents'. He added: 'We know from experience that the groups who are least inclined to accept humanitarian aid often end up changing their tune.'

In contrast to northern Syria, where MSF swiftly built up its presence within two years, the agency had worked in Somalia for over two decades, ever since political collapse and civil war first brought famine in their wake in the early 1990s. Continuing and chaotic violence forced the closure of individual projects and on occasion the withdrawal of international staff, but MSF never pulled out entirely. Sixteen MSF staff died over those 22 years in Somalia – many more if one counted those indirectly employed by the agency – yet MSF stuck it out to become the most important outside health provider in the country.

Such was MSF's role in propping up Somalia's battered health system that alone among the big overseas aid-givers it was able to maintain a presence in areas of south and central Somalia under the direct control of al-Shabaab insurgents. US drone attacks and Kenyan military advances magnified local suspicions of foreigners and led to al-Shabaab's expulsion of 16 agencies in the famine year of 2011. That was followed by additional bans on the International Red Cross and Save the Children in 2012. MSF remained in place.

By the middle of 2013, MSF had 1,500 staff in Somalia. Its annual budget was €25 million. All of it, as usual, came from private sources and none from governments. It was running ten hospitals, eight health clinics, which handled child nutrition and maternal health, a tuberculosis centre and a 40-bed inpatient therapeutic feeding centre.

Then, suddenly, MSF decided to close everything down. I have described the two incidents that led to this – the long hostage ordeal of two Spanish women abducted from the Dadaab refugee camp in Kenya in October 2011 and the killing of two expatriates in the MSF compound in Mogadishu a few months later. Grave insult was added to terrible injury by the indifference shown by the Somali authorities to the murders in Mogadishu and the likely complicity of al-Shabaab insurgents in the prolonged hostage crisis.

In justifying its withdrawal, MSF loaded all responsibility for the suffering that followed onto Somali leaders. 'In choosing to kill, attack, and abduct humanitarian aid workers,' said its international president Dr Unni Karunakara in the press release announcing the pull-out, 'these armed groups, and the civilian authorities who tolerate their actions, have sealed the fate of countless lives in Somalia.'

In a later commentary, Dr Karunakara reassured MSF supporters that contingency plans had been put in place to minimise the stress on hospital patients whose care was suddenly removed. There was specific concern for those suffering from tuberculosis, whose incidence in Somalia is one of the highest in the world. Provision had been made for them to receive drugs to complete their course of treatment, and MSF had handed over the equipment and medicine they would need. 'MSF teams strived to ensure a responsible discharge of patients under very difficult circumstances,' said the MSF president.[8]

The reality of the pull-out from Somalia was much more distressing than those comforting observations suggested. It was to MSF's credit, once again, that it did not seek to hide what actually happened. The agency's inclination to scrutinise its own conduct and to debate its actions would help inform its judgements in future crises.

As soon as MSF announced its withdrawal, local al-Shabaab leaders entered the agency's major regional hospital in the town of Marere, made an inventory of the drugs and equipment they intended to commandeer, and ordered all staff and patients to leave. Somali medics pleaded for a gradual discharge of critically ill patients, but this was refused and the order stood that the hospital was to be empty by the following afternoon. The only concession made was that patients would be allowed to leave with their oral drugs and nutritional supplies.

'But this did little to soften the anguish of hospital personnel as they were forced to remove patients from oxygen machines and carry comatose patients out the front door,' said an internal report commissioned by MSF into the impact of its withdrawal from Somalia. One staff member was quoted as describing this as 'a horrible and barbaric sight'.

MSF later learned that six children from the hospital's inpatient feeding centre along with two TB patients died over the following days. 'Many more are presumed to have met the same fate,' the internal report said.

The closure of Marere hospital could not have come at a worse time. The region was in the grip of a malaria epidemic and hospital admissions peaked at 900 in July 2013, just before MSF ordered its closure. Marere also served as a referral hospital for much of south-western Somalia and the local Somali Red Crescent reported that 27 children died in its clinics in the weeks following the closure because it had nowhere else to send them.

MSF said that its withdrawal from Somalia was one of the most difficult decisions it had ever taken. With lives lost and an impoverished health system substantially undermined, there were questions over whether such extreme action was justified. It meant leaving parts of Somalia that were relatively secure as well as those that were conflict-ridden and dangerous. Among the other agencies at work in East Africa, MSF's admirers judged the decision to be out of character. A political point may have been made about Somali unreliability, but were things ever likely to change in this enduring fratricidal conflict? In taking this stance, had MSF given in to grandstanding?

There were second thoughts even within the organisation. Just two years on from its withdrawal and as this book went to press, MSF was actively planning a return to Somalia. It would be an international MSF mission that put overseas staff on the ground, going beyond the option of 'remotely' managing Somali colleagues from outside the country. If that happened, it would be another test of nerve for MSF and a test of resolve for the wider humanitarian movement that had been forced into retreat in the war on terror.

CHAPTER 15

RUNNING OUT
OF WORDS

New York

Five thousand miles from the front lines of the Syrian conflict, the only weapons in the United Nations armoury in New York were words. In the course of 2014, the UN deployed tens of thousands of them in its efforts to secure an effective humanitarian response to the suffering. The words it used betrayed frustration and impotence in the face of this enormous crisis.

In February 2014, Security Council resolution 2139 said the UN was 'appalled' by the violence in Syria and expressed its 'grave alarm' at deteriorating humanitarian conditions, including the 'dire situation' in besieged communities. After 'deploring' and 'condemning', it issued a series of 'demands' for humanitarian access and said it wanted monthly progress reports from the Secretary-General.

Ban Ki-moon's June 2014 report, the fourth he had produced since the resolution was passed, said that the humanitarian situation had 'further deteriorated'; that there had been 'no improvement' in 'access to all the people in need'; and that UN assistance had 'only reached two besieged communities'. There had been 'no development'

in the UN's requests to mount cross-border aid operations 'in order
to facilitate greater access to those in need in hard-to-reach areas'.

The barriers to the UN's capacity to work across Syria's international frontiers were political and diplomatic. Every Security
Council resolution on getting aid to the victims of the conflict
began with a 'strong commitment to the sovereignty, independence,
unity and territorial integrity of Syria'. This meant that the Syrian
government had the final say as to where UN aid went. With
Security Council backing from Russia and China, the Syrians
consistently said no to cross-border humanitarian operations into
rebel-held areas.

Independent aid-givers over the border in Turkey were scornful
about the UN's meek response to Syria's veto. One NGO country
director complained to me early in 2014 that the UN was 'hog-
tied' to the Damascus regime, while another observed that Syria
represented a 'dreadful UN failure' because it was forced to ignore a
large part of the humanitarian emergency.

In other crises, the United Nations reckoned to coordinate the
entire international humanitarian response, including the contribution of the major NGOs. Here, the most the UN could offer
was unofficial and 'soft' coordination. 'In some ways, it's back to the
1980s,' said one country director. 'I'm not having to run round in lots
of circles to do my job. I just get on with it.'

Finally the Security Council got something of an act together.
The initiative came not from Western aid-givers – the US, the UK
or France – but from three non-permanent members of the council:
Australia, Luxembourg and Jordan. Security Council resolution 2165,
which was passed in July 2014, still spoke of the UN being 'appalled'
and of its 'grave alarm', but this time added that it was 'deeply
disturbed by the continued, arbitrary and unjustified withholding
of consent to relief operations' and so authorised UN humanitarian

agencies and their partners to use four new crossing points into Syria – one from Jordan, one from Iraq and two from Turkey.

By the grim standards of the Syrian emergency, this was progress. Ban Ki-moon's report to the Security Council in November 2014, his ninth that year, still emphasised that humanitarian conditions had 'continued to deteriorate', but he now said that there had been 'some gains' in terms of UN agencies and their partners 'making deliveries both across borders and within the Syrian Arab Republic'. In the previous month there had been 30 cross-border shipments – 23 from Turkey and seven from Jordan.

As 2014 ended and the fourth anniversary of the Syria conflict approached, one of the UN's top humanitarian officials gave eloquent expression to her frustrations. Valerie Amos – Baroness Amos, a former minister in Tony Blair's government – had by then been head of the UN's humanitarian coordinating agency OCHA for four years, a period spanning the whole course of the Syrian emergency.

Her position as Under-Secretary-General for humanitarian affairs gave her regular access to the Security Council to brief members on the crisis. She told them in December 2014 that, despite the passing of resolution 2139 earlier in the year, the 'parties to the conflict continue to ignore the most basic principles of humanity'. In February, the death toll had been 100,000. It was now closer to 200,000, with around 1 million injured.

'Every time we use a new figure in relation to the Syrian crisis we say that it is unprecedented,' she went on. 'We have run out of words to fully explain the brutality, violence and callous disregard for human life which is a hallmark of this crisis. The international community has become numb to its impact ...'

As the Syrian war entered its fifth year in March 2015, Lady Amos joined other UN humanitarian agency chiefs in asking the question: 'What does it take to end the crisis and end the suffering?'

They offered no answer, but said: 'The credibility of the international community is at stake.'

Valerie Amos was soon to leave her position at the United Nations, but not before she had delivered another briefing to the Security Council. It was now more than a year since they had passed resolution 2139 and still the war raged on, characterised by 'breathtaking levels of savagery', she said. The Secretary-General had 'submitted report after report highlighting the failure of the parties to meet their basic minimum legal obligations'.

She underlined how the UN's authority was being flouted and governments of the world were being ignored. 'The inability of this Council and countries with influence over the different parties at war in Syria to agree on the elements for a political solution in the country means that the humanitarian consequences will continue to be dire for millions of Syrians,' she said.

Access for humanitarian supplies continued to be denied despite the new Security Council resolutions. In the early months of 2015, the UN had sought permission to run aid convoys to 33 locations within Syria. All but three of these requests were turned down by the Syrian authorities, and even from the permitted shipments the security forces stripped out surgical and medical supplies. No such aid was to reach civilians beyond the control of the government.

More than 400,000 Syrians were now living under siege, almost half of them besieged by their own government 'despite their assertions that they have a responsibility to look after their own people', Lady Amos said. 'The authority of this Council is being undermined.'

In a further formal statement on the Syrian crisis – made at a UN funding conference in Kuwait at the end of March 2015 – Valerie Amos returned more sharply to the theme of Syrian culpability. 'What kind of government,' she asked, 'besieges its own people, drops barrel bombs and at the same time speaks of its responsibility to protect its own people?'

Ever since the shocks of the Balkan wars and the Rwanda genocide of the 1990s, the phrase 'responsibility to protect' had come to sum up the UN's doctrine for building a better, more humane international order. At a UN summit in 2005, world governments formally agreed that they had a 'responsibility to protect' their people from genocide, war crimes, ethnic cleansing and crimes against humanity, and that, if they should 'manifestly fail', the international community should act collectively in a 'timely and decisive manner'.

The UN Secretary-General produced a series of reports on the 'responsibility to protect'. He even had his own special adviser on the subject. The Security Council weighed in with resolutions about it and everyone at the UN came to use the neat little mnemonic 'R2P'. But none of this did much to help the people of Syria in their years of torment.

Citing the principle of 'responsibility to protect', UN officials in the Middle East expressed their outrage at the conduct of the Syrian government and their dismay at the inadequacy of the world's response. 'National sovereignty confers obligations as well as privileges,' one senior UN official told me. 'Sovereignty has to be exercised for the well-being of the people and the Syrians are simply not being told that enough.'

This official described the Syrian regime as behaving with 'unspeakable brutality' towards its own citizens and complained that it was not being confronted with sufficient firmness by the humanitarian community – either by the UN's own officials in Damascus or by the international NGOs based there. 'The Syrians are literally getting away with murder,' he said.

Before UN resolution 2165 forced the opening up of a few important crossing points for aid shipments in the fourth year of the conflict, the outside world had shown a 'fearful respect for the border', the UN official said. Even the United Nations 'must cravenly ask for permission to cross it or to work over it in any circumstances. We keep checking and we still have to ask.'

UN paralysis in the field was a reflection of divisions between the five permanent members of the Security Council. For years the Western powers backed the moderate Syrian opposition while Russia and China supported the government of Bashar al-Assad. The result was a selective application of international law and consequent double standards. 'We drag some African warlord before the International Criminal Court,' said the UN official, 'but we let Assad get away with murder.'

At the United Nations in New York, I was told to avoid the 'F' word. F stands for failure, and the UN Secretariat doesn't care to admit to such a thing. The extent of the failure over Syria was impossble to deny, though – failures within Syria allied to international failures to halt, resolve or even ameliorate the conflict. The question was: whose failures were they?

'In the end it's seen as a failure of the United Nations,' a senior official in the UN's humanitarian affairs office in New York told me. 'But what it really is is a failure of some of its member states and in particular of the member states on the UN Security Council. International rules are being violated not only by those who violate them, but also by those who fail to enforce them or to abide by their treaty obligations.'

Within the humanitarian affairs office at the UN, there were debates over how best to respond to the stand-off between East and West in the Security Council. The senior official I spoke to had favoured a bolder approach in the early years of the conflict. 'We should have used our standing and our leverage to make the point that, when access is being arbitrarily withheld and is increasing civilian suffering, it becomes a method of warfare and we need to do more.'

If you seek formal Security Council clearance to cross the border in order to deliver aid, he argued, you are likely to be refused. By invoking the humanitarian imperative and doing it anyway, you stand some chance of success. Inside Syria, you also risk being expelled, as happened to NGOs such as Mercy Corps that tried to operate on both sides of the border. But expelling the United Nations is a far bigger step than removing an NGO and may not have had the support of the Syrian government's allies on the Security Council.

'There is always this fear for a humanitarian organisation and you have to make the calculation,' the senior official said. 'Will I get kicked out? Will I do a disservice to the people by being kicked out? I'm not saying this is not a serious consideration, but in the end you need to take a risk.'

The passing of Security Council resolution 2165, which finally, in the fourth year of the conflict, authorised cross-border aid shipments into Syria, appeared to vindicate the gamble. The resolution was an affront to Damascus and was passed in defiance of Syrian wishes and notions of Syrian sovereignty. Yet the ceiling did not fall in: neither the Russians nor the Chinese used their veto and UN agencies remained in place in Damascus. The question arose: in the light of international failure and paralysis over Syria, should the United Nations have acted more boldly in the cause of humanity?

'Someone once told me that if the United Nations wants to be a world power, it needs to behave like a world power,' said the senior UN official in New York. 'Well, we will never be a world power, but we need to be more cognisant of the standing and the leverage and the power that we do have, and how difficult it is to kick us out. We need to play this card.'

In a world where humanitarian responses are under increasing assault – in safe and prosperous countries as much as in poor and disordered ones – many will support the idea that the United Nations and its agencies should be seen and heard much more from the world's conflict zones. Like the International Committee of the Red Cross, it might care and dare more often to defy diplomatic convention by speaking out. A stand-off within the Security Council and fearfulness among Western powers over direct engagement in the world's troubles have left a humanitarian vacuum that good agencies have an obligation to try to fill.

The Syrian disaster will define the era for humanitarians, just as the Balkan crises and the Rwanda genocide defined the 1990s. 'Syria is one of those existential crises for the international, multilateral, humanitarian and political system around the UN,' the senior official said. 'You will be faced with many of the same questions that were faced over Sarajevo and Srebrenica, only worse. Once this is over, there will be a lot of questions about rules and compliance and willingness. Those who appeal to compliance for international law will be asked about their own willingness to contribute to its enforcement.'

In contrast to the 1990s and the emergence through the United Nations of the 'responsibility to protect', we now live in an era of Western disengagement and defensiveness. A brave new humanitarian doctrine failed the test of time in just two decades. 'Right now I feel there is an environment of global shoulder-shrugging and of apathy,' said the UN official.

'The only outrage I sense these days is over the actions of ISIL [Islamic State of Iraq and the Levant] – of terrorism and counter-terrorism – and I am afraid we are at risk over the next few years of replacing the moral imperative of "you have to help civilians and protect them against mass atrocities" with a far stronger imperative of "you need to defeat terrorism and these barbaric and beastly acts wherever you encounter them".'

The global war on terror has had the effect of fortifying one historically significant as well as contentious concept at the United Nations – that of the 'integrated mission'. In conflict states, the priority for the UN and its paymasters became the provision of military and political support for struggling governments. As well as being accredited to them and giving them aid, the United Nations would help win their wars for them. And the UN's humanitarian agencies would need to play their part.

This put immediate pressure on the key humanitarian principle of neutrality. 'You cannot be neutral between a legitimate side and a reprehensible side,' a UN official told the humanitarian aid expert Fiona Terry in Afghanistan.[1] Such questioning of the classical humanitarian stance caused problems for many aid workers. 'The UN is suspect in Muslim eyes,' I was told flatly by Fadlullah Wilmot, the head of international programmes for Islamic Relief in Australia, 'because they've given up on neutrality.'

It was the war in Afghanistan and the seemingly endless conflict in Somalia that established the pattern of 'integrated missions' in the new war zones. The UN's humanitarian agencies resisted them and were often uncomfortable inside them, but the Security Council's drive on 'fragile' and 'terror' states was unambiguous and humanitarian objections were swept aside. The aid agencies had to rely on the Secretary-General's assurance that integration 'can yield significant benefits for humanitarian operations'.

In a letter reaffirming the policy in 2008, Ban Ki-moon declared that integration arrangements 'should take full account of recognised humanitarian principles, allow for the protection of humanitarian space, and facilitate effective humanitarian coordination with all humanitarian actors'. These reassurances were put to the test, and found wanting, in a report commissioned by the United Nations itself.

In Afghanistan, a country intended as a dazzling advertisement for Western-led reconstruction, the report set out a catalogue of failings and compromises on the humanitarian front.[2] It revealed how international and Afghan NGOs became so anxious to avoid association with the UN's integrated mission that many 'stopped or severely restricted their visits to UN offices' and some pulled out of the UN's coordination arrangements altogether.

As for the UN's own humanitarian operations in Afghanistan, 'some agencies reported having access to only about half the country'. ACBAR, the Afghan body responsible for coordinating non-government relief and development efforts, refused even to discuss a joint strategy to expand access with the United Nations. It declared that its UN counterpart OCHA, the Office for the Coordination of Humanitarian Affairs, was 'not an independent organisation since it is part of the integrated mission'.

The need to make and sustain contact with the Taliban – a 'non-state armed actor', in the jargon – underlined another major difference between independent humanitarianism and the UN's integrated mission. The report spoke of how 'UN mission leaders used their authority in the UN integrated presence to limit humanitarian engagement with non-state armed actors when this was deemed detrimental to political objectives ...', adding that OCHA's early efforts to establish contact with the Taliban 'were effectively curtailed because staff were not able to travel to meet Taliban representatives without security escorts'.

Summing up the way Afghans saw foreign humanitarian aid, the UN-commissioned report quoted the academic commentator

Antonio Donini, a former director of OCHA in Kabul, as observing that, 'in Afghanistan, whether they like it or not, aid agencies are seen as embedded in an externally-driven nation-building process that is being attacked by insurgents and that … is deeply flawed and unpopular'.[3]

In Somalia, I encountered a vivid example of the confusion and danger that can arise from the ignorant assumption that humanitarian aid is just another weapon to be deployed in the global war on terror. The episode left NGO workers exasperated and would further have convinced the jihadists of al-Shabaab that Western humanitarianism was at best suspect, at worst part of the Western military effort.

What happened was that the UN joined forces with the African Union – the organisation with troops on the ground in Somalia – to run a special course for NGOs and others on 'civil–military coordination'. It ran for five days in Nairobi, in neighbouring Kenya, at the end of 2013 and focused 'on the use of foreign military and civil defence assets in support of humanitarian activities in the specific context of Somalia'.

A senior UN humanitarian official described civil–military coordination as 'a critical instrument to advance the humanitarian action in Somalia' and said that the course was 'a unique opportunity bringing the humanitarians and AMISOM [the African Union Mission in Somalia] to understand each other'.

Then, inexplicably, AMISOM issued a press release drawing public attention to the exercise. It was still viewable online a year after the course had finished. 'Why the heck are they doing this?' said one of the very few Western aid workers permanently located in Mogadishu. 'It's a propaganda coup for the enemy! Do the training, but then shut up about it!'

Publicity of this sort risked pushing independent aid workers directly into the line of fire. It may have been no coincidence that in January 2014, a few weeks after the AMISOM press release, al-Shabaab issued a statement that for the first time placed non-UN humanitarian agencies on its list of targets. As I have already noted, the statement insisted that Somalis should neither work for these agencies nor visit their offices, because they were 'invaders' who were 'being fought and struggled against …'

Among independent aid organisers in Nairobi, al-Shabaab's threats were yet more grounds to be worried about aid worker safety. 'They named NGOs as a target and that had never happened before,' I was told by a senior aid coordinator. 'This was the first statement that put us in the same pot as the UN.'

In fact, a key objective for many aid agencies headquartered in Nairobi was to distance themselves as far as possible from United Nations operations over the border in Somalia. For a few of them, that meant formal withdrawal from the UN's official aid coordinating bodies. That came at a price because major Western donors channelled much of their multimillion-dollar relief funding through the UN, and private aid agencies needed to get a share of the money if they were to stay in business in the region.

'I have these donors in here the whole time asking me, "Why are the NGOs not using our stability fund? Why are you not sharing more information with us?",' said the aid coordinator. 'The problem is that we would need substantial independent financial resources to be independent of them, and only a few like Médecins Sans Frontières and the International Committee of the Red Cross can really do that.'

Past experience pointed to the UN's consistent distrust of independent humanitarian activity in Somalia. In the process of UN-led efforts in political reconstruction, aid agencies were warned not to make contact with al-Shabaab and advised to concentrate instead on building up government capacity and legitimacy.[4]

At one point in 2009, the United Nations special representative for Somalia, a senior Mauritanian diplomat called Ahmedou Ould-Abdallah, declared: 'In this kind of tragic situation, those who claim neutrality can also be complicit. The Somali government needs support – moral and financial – and Somalis, both at home and in the diaspora, as well as the international community, have an obligation to provide both.'

This was confirmation, if it was needed, of how partisan aid had become in the war on terror and how suspicious an 'integrated' UN mission could be of the humanitarian principles many of its workers still espoused. It underlined how far the United Nations had travelled from its early, idealistic days, when the independence of its great humanitarian agencies was widely recognised and their impartiality respected. Those who suffered as a result of conflict could, if they were lucky, still rely on the UN for a measure of material support. But they could no longer expect their welfare to be at the heart of the UN's mission.

CONCLUSION

HOW MANY CHEERS FOR NEUTRALITY?

For the West's army of aid workers, the war on terror has confirmed the strategic role they are now expected to play in the world's most dangerous crises. Their task, as governments and official funders see it, is no longer simply to save or improve lives. It is to help stabilise parts of the world that are a danger to their own people and to those living beyond their borders.

In conflicts where the vital interests of Western powers are engaged, this presents a direct challenge to the principles of independence, impartiality and neutrality to which many aid agencies still subscribe. Ever since 9/11, there has been argument and dispute over whether humanitarians should be re-examining, and probably discarding, the articles of faith by which they have tried to live. Times have changed, and humanitarian principles will apparently have to change with them.

Dr Cheryl Benard, an analyst with the RAND Corporation, chose the occasion of the withdrawal from Afghanistan by Médecins

Sans Frontières (Doctors Without Borders in the US) in 2004 to argue that the organisation had 'missed a paradigm change in global conflict'.[1] MSF, which sets its face against armed protection, had just pulled out of the country after the Taliban murdered five of its workers. As it left, MSF complained that by blurring the distinctions between military action and civil assistance the Western powers had fatally compromised the work of independent humanitarians.

'In this deeply regrettable new situation,' wrote Dr Benard, after studying Western reconstruction efforts in Afghanistan, 'security, development and aid are parts of an inseparable whole, and until stability is achieved, humanitarians will have to operate under the cover of arms – or not at all. An objective assessment of the facts would lead organisations like Doctors Without Borders to demand more military presence, not less; closer cooperation with the military, not a separation of spheres.'

In an echo of the Bush administration's view of 'old Europe' and the 'quaint' Geneva Conventions, Dr Benard added that the 'principle championed by Doctors Without Borders – that civilian professionals providing medical help to the suffering will be granted safe passage – is now part of our nostalgic past'.

Two American academics were equally dismissive of the approach of the International Committee of the Red Cross. In their book *Sword and Salve: Confronting New Wars and Humanitarian Crises,*[2] Peter Hoffman and Thomas Weiss describe the ICRC's fundamental principles as 'the protestations of traditionalists', adding that, for the humanitarians, business as usual is 'not an option'.

'While apt in earlier periods and still practical in many interstate wars (as well as natural disasters), neutrality and impartiality are of limited applicability in "stateless" complex emergencies,' they argue. 'Working on all sides and staying clear of politics is not only impossible but may actually make matters worse.'

They wrote their book, they said, 'to build bridges between the wisdom of warriors and the hearts of humanitarians,' but it was the humanitarians who would apparently have to make the adjustments. They had 'seen the future in Afghanistan and Iraq'.

Arguments over the relevance of principle in humanitarian affairs arose in the 1990s after the Wall came down and when the Cold War was succeeded by ugly hot ones. Aid agencies were on the ground at each of these turning points – from the mission in 1991 to protect the Kurds under a no-fly zone in northern Iraq; through US boots on the ground in starving, collapsing Somalia in 1992; to the NATO bombing campaign in Kosovo in 1999.

'I have my doubts, looking at the array of conflicts in which humanitarian relief is called for today,' observed Emma Bonino, Europe's Commissioner for Humanitarian Affairs at a conference in New York in 1998, 'that being neutral is still at all possible, or indeed ethically just.' Should agencies such as the ICRC 'be unable to distinguish right from wrong, the aggressor from the victim, the killers from the dead bodies?' she asked. 'What absurd wisdom could call for this organised ethical confusion?'[3]

A senior official of the ICRC at the conference stoutly defended its principles, specifically that of neutrality. Francis Amar, head of the ICRC's international organisations division, came up with this brisk rejoinder to Ms Bonino. 'The purpose of neutrality,' he said, 'is action.' Those of us who have witnessed first-hand the robustness of some of the ICRC's operations in recent decades can confirm that its principles, notably its neutrality, do indeed act as a spur, not a barrier, to action. There is, frankly, no more effective humanitarian agency in the world.

To be sure, the war on terror threatens the ICRC's capacity in the field. No organisation can carry on regardless of killings and kidnappings. When violence escalates or incidents proliferate or local authorities become too obstructive, the ICRC pulls back, regroups, reduces its profile, reconsiders its work plan and keeps talking. Not once in the present century has it pulled out of a country for reasons of security.

The organisation's principles have everything to do with this. All seven of them are read out – in four languages, including Arabic – at the start of every international conference of the Red Cross and Red Crescent movement.* This ritual has now been repeated at regular intervals for half a century. It has outlived many political generations and several geo-political eras. In the field, it lends the organisation a strong, if understated, sense of its own rectitude and a fervent confidence in its mission.

It is just as well that the ICRC did not heed those siren calls after 9/11 to abandon principle and rely instead on Western military power to build better societies on the world's disordered periphery. All that was deemed positive about the 'humanitarian' military interventions of the 1990s ran into the sands in Afghanistan and Iraq, to be replaced by public and political reluctance to engage on the ground at all. Humanitarian aid workers are still expected to be there on the front line, but they are on their own once again.

More than 40 years on from its foundation, Médecins Sans Frontières remains something of a chip off the old ICRC block. The two agencies regularly collaborate in the field, and each misses the other one when it is absent. They both continue to assert their principles, and despite internal debate along the way, MSF has stuck to its commitment to neutrality.

Far from recasting its relationship with the Western military, as Dr Cheryl Benard had proposed, MSF returned on its own terms

---

* The seven are: Humanity, Impartiality, Neutrality, Independence, Voluntary Service, Unity and Universality.

to Afghanistan in 2009 to open hospitals in some of the country's most violent provinces.

No weapons would be allowed inside any of its facilities – a condition it applied to international troops as well as to the Afghan army and the Taliban – and it would neither seek armed protection for its staff nor travel in armoured vehicles. To keep the MSF flag flying meant building relationships with all sides in a complex war. None of these arrangements would save the lives of the 30 staff, patients and others killed in the US bombing raid on Kunduz hospital in October 2015.

While MSF and the ICRC do their best, in the European tradition, to stand by the original Red Cross commitment to neutrality, there is ambivalence among the Anglophone agencies. For as long as neutrality represented no real challenge to their conduct – as was the case for most of their history – it was an easy enough pledge for NGOs and others to make.

In 2003, the second year of the Afghan war and just as the Iraq war was getting under way, even the US and British governments endorsed a set of 'good humanitarian donorship' principles that included neutrality. Official aid-givers agreed 'that humanitarian action must not favour any side in an armed conflict or other dispute where such action is carried out'. Many actions taken by the US and UK in Iraq and Afghanistan – and elsewhere – have clearly run counter to this undertaking.

The most common formulation I encountered in discussions with American and British NGOs was that humanitarian principles were 'operational tools', not 'biblical texts'. Some make a point of proclaiming their commitment to neutrality in public while arguing in private that Western government funding is a greater priority than scrupulous non-alignment. Save the Children, for instance, underlined its commitment to neutrality when it came under

Pakistani pressure because of spying accusations that linked the agency to the death of Osama bin Laden, but otherwise continued to make the case for getting as much backing as possible from Western governments for its child-focused programmes in Pakistan.

Headquarters staff at Oxfam emphasised to me that notions of neutrality had little or no relevance to its work on rights-based development, even in conflict countries, while closer to the front I was nevertheless assured by some of its field managers that 'we have to be unimpeachable' on the matter of neutrality and independence.

The United Nations finds itself in a similar fix. In its public pronouncements it subscribes to humanitarian principles, but then places its great humanitarian agencies within 'integrated missions' whose overriding task is to win the war on terror. In a single paragraph of the resolution establishing a 'One UN' mission in Somalia in 2013, the Security Council insisted that the UN work alongside African Union soldiers against al-Shabaab 'while ensuring the humanity, impartiality and neutrality and independence of humanitarian assistance'. It is one thing to issue such commands from New York; it is another to manage their fallout in the mayhem of Mogadishu.

UN humanitarians resisted their subordination in Somalia – and were supported by their Secretary-General Ban Ki-moon – but failed to carry the day. The Western powers, no longer with boots on the ground, were content to see others sent to the front. As the UN adjusted to new political realities, some officials argued that it was the humanitarian principles themselves, not the UN's approach to them, which needed adjustment. One idea canvassed with apparent seriousness was that the principles of 'independence and impartiality' be retained, but that the awkward word 'neutrality' should be dropped in favour of the bland, ultimately meaningless, 'integrity'.

What is unknowable is the extent to which the confusion over principles contributed to the rising tide of violence against aid workers. The evidence suggests that extremists know only too well who they are targeting and why, and are quite capable of drawing distinctions between aligned and non-aligned aid agencies. For some jihadists, of course, all Western institutions and Westerners are targets.

The number of aid worker victims tripled in the decade to 2013 and fell back in 2014, mainly because fewer risks were being taken and because it was now national, not international, staff who were more directly in the line of fire. The war on terror had brought about a shift in the mechanics of aid delivery, where the most hazardous work was undertaken by locals, funded and sometimes managed remotely by the international NGOs.

The enormous Syria crisis accelerated these changes. At the heart of the conflict were the courageous Syrians who acted as the eyes and ears as well as the helping hands of the outside world. Some of them worked over the border for the big aid agencies, others for Syrian NGOs founded abroad to respond to the conflict. It was these diaspora organisations that took many of the humanitarian initiatives inside the country. It was their workers who complained that funders were often slow and inflexible in their response to changing needs on the ground and unduly constrained by official anxiety that not a penny of Western money should ever slip into the wrong pocket. New aid from the Arab Gulf offered a more flexible source of funding.

The world's humanitarians were preparing for their own UN global summit as this book went to press. The first World Humanitarian Summit in Istanbul in May 2016 could scarcely have come at a more fateful time. Massive refugee movements – driven by conflict – were the worst in modern times. They had swept into Turkey, crashed onto the shores of southern Europe and lapped around the continent that gave birth to modern humanitarianism.

What would the summit achieve? 'It'll be a cocktail party for the status quo,' offered one senior NGO official. 'A blancmange,' suggested another. It would surely need to acknowledge the extent of the failure of international humanitarian institutions to stand up to barbarity at the national level. It would have at least to respond massively to the human dislocation created by a new world disorder. The gap between emergency appeals and funding commitments would have to be narrowed. Attention would have to be paid to a new aid 'architecture' and proper allowance made for a world no longer run by the West. Local aid workers in the eye of the storm need to be able to influence more, 'subcontract' less. Western nations would have to be pressed on the impact of counter-terror laws on humanitarian efforts in the field.

Lip service would be paid at the summit to fundamental humanitarian principles, but they deserved more than that. Independence, impartiality and neutrality are not just abstract concepts. They provide the best approach to even the worst of contemporary conflicts. They do not in themselves provide access behind the lines, still less any guarantee of safety, but they offer the moral confidence to make the attempt.

All of humanity in all its cultures recognises the humanitarian instinct, but 150 years ago in Geneva, in the middle of Europe, humanitarianism became an institution that grew into a great international movement. Its heart has kept beating while a corporate aid industry has grown up around it. In a new age of turmoil, it remains one of Europe's greatest gifts to the world. If it is to survive and flourish in the twenty-first century, its principles need to be reasserted. Humanitarian aid has to be much more than an adjunct to foreign and security policy.

NOTES

INTRODUCTION

1   Abby Stoddard et al., *Aid Worker Security Report 2014. Unsafe Passage: Road Attacks and their Impact on Humanitarian Operations*. London: Humanitarian Outcomes, 2014. Available at https://aidworkersecurity.org/sites/default/files/Aid%20Worker%20Security%20Report%202014.pdf.
2   'Aid Worker Security Report 2015: Figures at a Glance'. London: Humanitarian Outcomes, 2015.
3   Sean Healy and Sandrine Tiller, *Where Is Everyone? Responding to Emergencies in the Most Difficult Places*. London: MSF, May 2014.

1   END OF THE WHITE SAVIOUR

1   Eva Svoboda and Sara Pantuliano, 'International and Local/Diaspora Actors in the Syria Response'. Working paper. London: Humanitarian Policy Group, Overseas Development Institute (ODI), March 2015.
2   Svoboda and Pantuliano, op. cit.
3   Fabrice Weissman, 'Scaling Up Aid in Syria: The Role of the Diaspora Networks', Humanitarian Practice Network website, 10 July 2013. Available at http://odihpn.org/blog/scaling-up-aid-in-syria-the-role-of-diaspora-networks/.

2   DEVELOPMENT AT GUNPOINT

1   Barbara Stapleton, 'A Means to What End? Why PRTs Are Peripheral to the Bigger Political Challenges in Afghanistan', *Journal of Military and Strategic Studies*, vol. 10, issue 1, 2007.
2   Quoted in Ashley Jackson and Simone Haysom, *The Search for Common Ground: Civil Military Relations in Afghanistan, 2002–13*. London: Overseas Development Institute, 2013.
3   Gerald McHugh and Lola Gostelow, *Provincial Reconstruction Teams and Humanitarian–Military Relations in Afghanistan*. London: Save the Children, 2004.

4   Ashley Jackson, *Nowhere to Turn: The Failure to Protect Civilians in Afghanistan*. Oxford: Oxfam International, November 2010.

5   *Whose Aid Is It Anyway? Politicizing Aid in Conflicts and Crises*. Briefing paper 145. Oxford: Oxfam, 2011.

6   Sippi Azerbaijani-Moghaddam et al., *Afghan Hearts, Afghan Minds: Exploring Afghan Perceptions of Civil–Military Relations*. London: British & Irish Agencies Afghanistan Group and European Network of NGOs in Afghanistan, 2008.

7   Fiona Terry, 'The International Committee of the Red Cross in Afghanistan: Reasserting the Neutrality of Humanitarian Action', *International Review of the Red Cross*, vol. 93, no. 881, 2011.

8   Jackson and Haysom, op. cit.

9   David Rieff, *A Bed for the Night: Humanitarianism in Crisis*. London: Vintage, 2002.

10 Jenny McAvoy and Joel Charny, *Civil–Military Relations and the US Armed Forces*. Humanitarian Exchange 56. London: Overseas Development Institute, 2013.

11 McAvoy and Charny, op. cit.

12 Michiel Hofman (MSF country representative, Afghanistan, 2009–11), 'Dangerous Aid in Afghanistan,' Foreign Policy website, January 2011. Available at http://foreignpolicy.com/2011/01/12/dangerous-aid-in-afghanistan/.

3   MEETINGS WITH REMARKABLE MEN

1   Paul Barker, 'Queries from Afghanistan', *Friends Journal*, September 2003. I have relied on this article for other details of Paul Barker's earlier experiences in Afghanistan.

4   TAKING A BULLET FOR POLIO

1   Declan Walsh, 'Fallout of Bin Laden Raid: Aid Groups in Pakistan Are Suspect', *The New York Times*, 2 May 2012.

5   FRONTIER MANOEUVRES

1   Marc Ambinder and D. B. Grady, 'The Command: Deep inside the President's Secret Army', Kindle Edition, excerpted in *The Atlantic*, Washington DC, 15 February 2012.

2   Mark Mazzetti, *The Way of the Knife: The CIA, a Secret Army and a War at the Ends of the Earth*. New York: Penguin, 2013.

3   Jeremy Scahill, *Dirty Wars: The World is a Battlefield*. London: Serpent's Tail, 2013.
4   Mazzetti, op. cit.
5   Medea Benjamin, *Drone Warfare: Killing by Remote Control*. Noida: HarperCollins India, 2013.

6   *BLUE UN, BLACK UN*
1   Seán D. Naylor, 'Profit and Loss in Somalia,' Foreign Policy website, 22 January 2015. Available at http://foreignpolicy.com/2015/01/22/delta-force-somalia-terror-blackwater-bancroft/.
2   Kyle Westaway, 'Turkey is Poised to Cash in on a Stable Somalia', 17 September 2013. Available at http://kylewestaway.com.

7   *DELAY COSTS LIVES*
1   London School of Hygiene and Tropical Medicine and the Johns Hopkins University Bloomberg School of Public Health, *Mortality among Populations of Southern and Central Somalia Affected by Severe Food Insecurity and Famine during 2010–2012*. Rome and Washington DC: FAO and FEWS NET, 2013.
2   Tracy McVeigh, 'Charity President Says Aid Groups Are Misleading the Public in Somalia', *Guardian*, 3 September 2011.
3   *A Dangerous Delay: The Cost of Late Response to Early Warnings in the 2011 Drought in the Horn of Africa*. Joint Agency Briefing Paper. Oxford: Oxfam and Save the Children, 18 January 2012.
4   Jeremy Konyndyk, 'Will the US Stand by as Famine Looms in Somalia?', *The Huffington Post*, 7 July 2011.
5   Kate Mackintosh and Patrick Duplat, *Study of the Impact of Donor Counter-Terrorism Measures on Principled Humanitarian Action*. New York and Oslo: United Nations Office for the Coordination of Humanitarian Affairs and Norwegian Refugee Council, 2013.

8   *ACTS OF FAITH*
1   'Children of Syria', BBC 2, 28 July 2014.
2   Osman Bahadir Dinçer et al., *Turkey and Syrian Refugees: The Limits of Hospitality*. Washington DC and Ankara: Brookings Institution and USAK, November 2013.
3   Global Humanitarian Assistance, *Global Humanitarian Assistance Report 2015*. Bristol: Development Initiatives, 2015.

4   Global Humanitarian Assistance, 2015, op. cit.
5   *Turkish Review*, Istanbul, 30 June 2010.
6   Marie Juul Petersen, 'Sacralized or Secularized Aid? Positioning Gulf-based Muslim Charities', in Robert Lacey and Jonathan Benthall (eds) *Gulf Charities and Islamic Philanthropy in the 'Age of Terror' and Beyond*. Berlin: Gerlach Press, 2014.
7   Global Humanitarian Assistance, *Global Humanitarian Assistance Report 2014*. Bristol: Development Initiatives, 2014.
8   Khalid Al-Yahya and Nathalie Fustier, 'Saudi Arabia as a Global Humanitarian Donor' in Lacey and Benthall, op. cit.
9   Global Humanitarian Assistance, 2015, op. cit.

9 WITH ALL THOSE WHO SUFFER

1   Henry Dunant, *A Memory of Solferino*. Geneva: ICRC, 1959. Originally published in English by American National Red Cross, 1939.
2   François Bugnion, 'Birth of an Idea: The Founding of the International Committee of the Red Cross and of the International Red Cross and Red Crescent Movement: From Solferino to the Original Geneva Convention (1859–1864)', *International Review of the Red Cross*, vol. 94, no. 888, 2012.
3   James Crossland, *Britain and the International Committee of the Red Cross, 1939–1945*. Basingstoke: Palgrave Macmillan, 2014.
4   David P. Forsythe, *The Humanitarians: The International Committee of the Red Cross*. Cambridge: Cambridge University Press, 2005.
5   Jean Pictet, 'The Fundamental Principles of the Red Cross: Commentary,' ICRC, 1 January 1979. Available at www.icrc.org/eng/resources/documents/misc/fundamental-principles-commentary-010179.htm.
6   Fiona Terry, 'The International Committee of the Red Cross in Afghanistan: Reasserting the Neutrality of Humanitarian Action,' *International Review of the Red Cross*, vol. 93, no. 881, March 2011.
7   Pierre Krähenbühl, 'The Militarization of Aid and its Perils,' ICRC, 22 February 2011. Available at www.icrc.org/eng/resources/documents/article/editorial/humanitarians-danger-article-2011-02-01.htm.
8   Forsythe, op. cit.

10 WHEN AID BECOMES A CRIME

1   Kate Mackintosh and Patrick Duplat, *Study of the Impact of Donor Counter-Terrorism Measures on Principled Humanitarian Action*. New York and Oslo: United Nations Office for the Coordination of Humanitarian Affairs and Norwegian Refugee Council, July 2013.

2   *Deadly Combination: Disaster Conflict and the US Material Support Law.*
    Washington DC: Charity & Security Network, April 2012.
3   Jérémie Labbé, 'Counterterrorism Efforts Bring Unintended Suffering:
    Interview with Jan Egeland›, Global Observatory, International Peace
    Institute, 19 September 2013. Available at http://theglobalobservatory.org/
    2013/09/counterterrorism-laws-bring-unintended-suffering-interview-
    with-humanitarian-jan-egeland/.
4   Elizabeth Brown Pryor, *Clara Barton: Professional Angel.* Philadelphia:
    University of Pennsylvania Press, 1987.
5   *U.S. Muslim Charities and the War on Terror: A Decade in Review.*
    Washington DC: Charity & Security Network, December 2011.

11 DOING WELL BY DOING GOOD

1   Scott Higham et al., 'Doing Well by Doing Good: The High Price of
    Working in War Zones', *The Washington Post,* 14 May 2014.
2   Scott Higham, 'Nonprofit Contractor Sent Government $1.1 Million Bill
    for Parties and Retreats', *The Washington Post,* 13 March 2015.
3   Scott Higham, 'Top USAID Contractor Allegedly Billed Taxpayers for
    Redskins Tickets, Alcohol', *The Washington Post,* 9 February 2015.
4   Rajiv Chandrasekaran, *Little America: The War Within the War for
    Afghanistan.* London: Bloomsbury, 2012.
5   *The First 40: A History of DAI.* Bethesda, MD: DAI, 2010.

12 THE POLICE, NOT THE STASI

1   Tony Blair, 'Rethinking Leadership for Development'. Speech at Overseas
    Development Institute, London, 19 October 2011.
2   Barbara Stapleton, 'A Means to What End? Why PRTs Are Peripheral
    to the Bigger Political Challenges in Afghanistan', *Journal of Military and
    Strategic Studies,* vol. 10, issue 1, 2007.
3   *Assessing the Impact of the Scale-up of DFID's Support to Fragile States.* Report
    40. London: Independent Commission for Aid Impact, February 2015.
4   Richard Kerbaj, 'Charities Chief Goes to War on Islamists', *The Sunday
    Times,* 20 April 2014.
5   Tim Ross et al., 'Charity Commission: British Charities Investigated for
    Terror Risks', *The Sunday Telegraph,* 1 November 2014.
6   Adam Belaon, *Muslim Charities: A Suspect Sector.* London: Claystone,
    November 2014.
7   Victoria Metcalfe-Hough et al., *UK Humanitarian Aid in the Age of
    Counter-terrorism: Perceptions and Reality.* HPG Working Paper. London:
    Humanitarian Policy Group, Overseas Development Institute, March 2015.

13 MAKING POVERTY HISTORY?

1   Clare Mulley, *The Woman Who Saved the Children: A Biography of Eglantyne Jebb, Founder of Save the Children*. London: Oneworld Publications, 2009.
2   Mulley, op. cit.
3   Dorothy F. Buxton and Edward Fuller, *The White Flame: The Story of the Save the Children Fund*. London: Longmans, Green and Co. and Weardale Press, 1931.
4   Quoted in Mulley, op. cit.
5   Maggie Black, *A Cause for Our Times: Oxfam, the First 50 Years*. Oxford: Oxfam, 1992.
6   Black, op. cit.
7   Tony Vaux, *The Selfish Altruist: Relief Work in Famine and War*. London: Earthscan, 2001.
8   Peter Gill, *A Year in the Death of Africa: Politics, Bureaucracy and the Famine*. London: Paladin, 1986.
9   *A Dangerous Delay: The Cost of Late Response to Early Warnings in the 2011 Drought in the Horn of Africa*. Joint Agency Briefing Paper. Oxford: Oxfam and Save the Children, 18 January 2012.
10 Alison Benjamin, 'Exposing the Double Think of Humanitarian Aid', *Guardian*, 14 June 2001.
11 Peter Gill, *Drops in the Ocean: The Work of Oxfam, 1960–1970*. London: Macdonald and Co., 1970.
12 Peter Apps, 'Breaking a Decades-long Trend, the World Gets More Violent,' Reuters, 20 March 2015. Available at http://blogs.reuters.com/great-debate/2015/03/20/breaking-a-decades-long-trend-the-world-gets-more-violent/.
13 'Code of Conduct on Images and Messages Relating to the Third World,' adopted by the General Assembly of the Liaison Committee of Development NGOs to the European Communities, 1989.

14 FRENCH LESSONS

1   Quoted in Rony Brauman, 'Médecins Sans Frontières and the ICRC: Matters of Principle', *International Review of the Red Cross*, vol. 94, no. 888, Winter 2012.
2   Karl Blanchet and Boris Martin (eds), *Many Reasons to Intervene: French and British Approaches to Humanitarian Action*. London: C. Hurst & Co., 2011.
3   Fabrice Weissman, 'Silence heals … From the Cold War to the War on Terror, MSF Speaks Out: A Brief History', in Claire Magone et al. (eds), *Humanitarian Negotiations Revealed: The MSF Experience*. London: MSF and C. Hurst & Co., 2011.

4 Quoted in Weissman, op. cit.

5 David Rieff, *A Bed for the Night: Humanitarianism in Crisis*. London: Vintage, 2002.

6 Jonathan Whittall, 'Pakistan: The Other Side of the COIN', in Magone, op. cit.

7 Jean-Hervé Bradol, 'MSF in the Land of Al-Qaeda and the Islamic State', Crash, Fondation Médecins Sans Frontières, November 2014.

8 Unni Karunakara and Jean-Christophe Dollé, 'The Limits of Humanitarian Aid: MSF and TB in Somalia', MSF, October 2013. Available at http://blogs.plos.org/speakingofmedicine/2013/10/23/the-limits-of-humanitarian-aid-msf-and-tb-in-somalia/.

15 RUNNING OUT OF WORDS

1 Fiona Terry, 'The International Committee of the Red Cross in Afghanistan: Reasserting the Neutrality of Humanitarian Action', *International Review of the Red Cross*, March 2011.

2 Victoria Metcalfe et al., *UN Integration and Humanitarian Space: An Independent Study Commissioned by the UN Integration Steering Group*. London and Washington DC: Humanitarian Policy Group, Overseas Development Institute, and Stimson Center, December 2011.

3 Antonio Donini, *Humanitarian Agenda 2015: Afghanistan Country Study*. Somerville MA: Feinstein International Center, Tufts University, 2006.

4 Metcalfe, op. cit.

CONCLUSION

1 Cheryl Benard, 'Afghanistan Without Doctors,' *Wall Street Journal*, 12 August 2004.

2 Peter J. Hoffman and Thomas G. Weiss, *Sword and Salve: Confronting New Wars and Humanitarian Crises*. Lanham MD: Rowman and Littlefield Inc., 2006.

3 Quoted in Larry Minear, 'The Theory and Practice of Neutrality: Some Thoughts on the Tensions', *International Review of the Red Cross*, no. 833, March 1999.

BIBLIOGRAPHY

Ahmed, Akbar, *The Thistle and the Drone: How America's War on Terror Became a Global War on Tribal Islam*. Noida: HarperCollins India, 2013.

Barnett, Michael, *Empire of Humanity: A History of Humanitarianism*. Ithaca NY: Cornell University Press, 2011.

Benjamin, Medea, *Drone Warfare: Killing by Remote Control*. Noida: HarperCollins India, 2013.

Benthall, Jonathan and Jerome Bellion-Jourdan, *The Charitable Crescent: Politics of Aid in the Muslim World*. London and New York: I. B. Tauris, 2003.

Benthall, Jonathan and Robert Lacey (eds), *Gulf Charities and Islamic Philanthropy in the 'Age of Terror' and Beyond*. Berlin: Gerlach Press, 2014.

Black, Maggie, *A Cause for Our Times: Oxfam, the First 50 Years*. Oxford: Oxfam, 1992.

Blanchet, Karl and Boris Martin (eds), *Many Reasons to Intervene: French and British Approaches to Humanitarian Action*. London: C. Hurst & Co., 2011.

Bowden, Mark, *Black Hawk Down*. London: Bantam Press, 1999.

Braithwaite, Rodric, *Afgantsy: The Russians in Afghanistan, 1979–89*. London: Profile, 2012.

Brown Pryor, Elizabeth, *Clara Barton: Professional Angel*. Philadelphia: University of Pennsylvania Press, 1987.

Buxton, Dorothy F. and Edward Fuller, *The White Flame: The Story of the Save the Children Fund*. London: Longmans, Green and Co. and Weardale Press, 1931.

Chandrasekaran, Rajiv, *Little America: The War Within the War for Afghanistan*. London: Bloomsbury, 2012.

Cowper-Coles, Sherard, *Cables from Kabul: The Inside Story of the West's Afghanistan Campaign*. London: HarperPress, London, 2011.

Dalrymple, William, *Return of a King: The Battle for Afghanistan*. London: Bloomsbury, 2013.

Donini, Antonio (ed.), *The Golden Fleece: Manipulation and Independence in Humanitarian Action*. Sterling VA: Kumarian Press, 2012.

Donini, Antonio, Norah Niland and Karin Wermester (eds), *Nation-building Unraveled? Aid, Peace and Justice in Afghanistan*. Bloomfield CT: Kumarian Press, 2004.

Duffield, Mark, *Global Governance and the New Wars: The Merging of Development and Security*. London: Zed Books, 2014.

Dunant, Henry, *A Memory of Solferino*. Geneva: International Committee of the Red Cross, 1959. Originally published in English by American National Red Cross, 1939.

Durand, Roger, *Henry Dunant, 1828–1910*. Geneva: Henry Dunant Society, 2011.

Foley, Conor, *The Thin Blue Line: How Humanitarianism Went to War*. London and New York: Verso, 2008.

Forsythe, David P., *The Humanitarians: The International Committee of the Red Cross*. Cambridge: Cambridge University Press, 2005.

Gill, Peter, *Drops in the Ocean: The Work of Oxfam, 1960–1970*. London: Macdonald and Co., 1970.

— *A Year in the Death of Africa: Politics, Bureaucracy and the Famine*. London: Paladin, 1986.

Guest, Robert, *The Shackled Continent: Africa's Past, Present and Future*. London: Macmillan, 2004.

Harper, Mary, *Getting Somalia Wrong? Faith, War and Hope in a Shattered State*. London: Zed Books, 2012.

Hoffman, Peter J. and Thomas G. Weiss, *Sword and Salve: Confronting New Wars and Humanitarian Crises*. Lanham MD: Rowman and Littlefield, 2006.

Hussain, Zahid, *The Scorpion's Tail: The Relentless Rise of Islamic Militants in Pakistan – and How it Threatens America*. New York: Free Press, 2010.

Johnston, Philip, *Somalia Diary: The President of CARE Tells One Country's Story of Hope*. Atlanta GA: Longstreet Press, 1994.

Jones, Mervyn, *Two Ears of Corn: Oxfam in Action*. London: Hodder and Stoughton, 1965.

Lamb, Christina, *Farewell Kabul: From Afghanistan to a More Dangerous World*. London: William Collins, 2015.

Ledwidge, Frank, *Losing Small Wars: British Military Failure in Iraq and Afghanistan*. New Haven CT and London: Yale University Press, 2011.

Lewis, Ioan, *Understanding Somalia and Somaliland: Culture, History and Society*. London: C. Hurst & Co., 2008.

Magone, Claire, Michael Neuman and Fabrice Weissman (eds), *Humanitarian Negotiations Revealed: The MSF Experience*. London: C. Hurst & Co. for Médecins Sans Frontières, 2011.

Maren, Michael, *The Road to Hell: The Ravaging Effects of Foreign Aid and International Charity*. New York: Free Press, 1997.

Mazzetti, Mark, *The Way of the Knife: The CIA, a Secret Army, and a War at the Ends of the Earth*. New York: Penguin, 2013.

Médecins Sans Frontières and Fabrice Weissman (ed.), *In the Shadow of 'Just Wars': Violence and Humanitarian Action*. Ithaca NY: Cornell University Press, 2004.

Moorehead, Caroline, *Dunant's Dream: War, Switzerland and the History of the Red Cross*. London: HarperCollins, 1998.

Mulley, Clare, *The Woman Who Saved the Children: A Biography of Eglantyne Jebb, Founder of Save the Children*. London: Oneworld Publications, 2009.

Polman, Linda, *War Games: The Story of Aid and War in Modern Times*. London: Viking, 2010.

Rashid, Ahmed, *Descent into Chaos: How the War Against Islamic Extremism Is Being Lost in Pakistan, Afghanistan and Central Asia*. London: Allen Lane, 2008.

— *Pakistan on the Brink: The Future of Pakistan, Afghanistan and the West*. London: Allen Lane, 2012.

Rieff, David, *A Bed for the Night: Humanitarianism in Crisis*. London: Vintage, 2002.

Scahill, Jeremy, *Dirty Wars: The World is a Battlefield*. London: Serpent's Tail, 2013.

Shawcross, William, *The Quality of Mercy: Cambodia, Holocaust and Modern Conscience*. London: André Deutsch, 1984.

Sireau, Nicolas, *Make Poverty History: Political Communication in Action*. Basingstoke and New York: Palgrave Macmillan, 2009.

Steele, Jonathan, *Ghosts of Afghanistan: The Haunted Battleground*. London: Portobello Books, 2011.

Strada, Gino, *Green Parrots: A War Surgeon's Diary*. Milan: Edizioni Charta, 2004.

Terry, Fiona, *Condemned to Repeat? The Paradox of Humanitarian Action*. Ithaca NY: Cornell University Press, 2002.

Vaux, Tony, *The Selfish Altruist: Relief Work in Famine and War*. London: Earthscan, 2001.

Whitaker, Ben, *A Bridge of People: A Personal View of Oxfam's First Forty Years*. London: Heinemann, 1983.

INDEX

ARTUR WIECZYŃSKI

STOJAK

novaeres
WYDAWNICTWO INNOWACYJNE

Redakcja i korekta: Anna Brynkus-Weber
Projekt okładki: Monika Kodrzycka
Projekt typograficzny i skład: Monika Burakiewicz
Druk i oprawa: Elpil

Wydanie pierwsze

ISBN 978-83-7722-160-0

Novae Res – Wydawnictwo Innowacyjne
al. Zwycięstwa 96/98, 81-451 Gdynia
tel.: 58 735 11 61, e-mail: dialog@novaeres.pl, http://novaeres.pl

Publikacja dostępna jest w księgarni internetowej zaczytani.pl

Wydawnictwo Novae Res jest partnerem
Pomorskiego Parku Naukowo-Technologicznego w Gdyni.

Pomorski Park Naukowo-Technologiczny

ROZDZIAŁ

1

Już nigdy nie zobaczę ich wszystkich w komplecie. Szkoda, przez półtora roku można było niektórych polubić, ale te dojazdy... Te dojazdy mnie wykańczały.

Gdybym mieszkał bliżej centrum Warszawy, może miałoby to jakiś sens. Z Janek na Okęcie, z Okęcia do centrum, a potem jeszcze do Sochaczewa? Taką trasę można pokonywać, jadąc do babci na wakacje.

W Warszawie siedzę od dwóch lat. Przyjechałem tu z kumplem, on szybko wrócił, ja zostałem. Było mi głupio wracać tak bez niczego. Żałuję? Nie wiem, ale kto wie, co bym teraz robił, gdybym wtedy też z nim wyjechał.

Ojciec mój jest strażakiem, a matka całe życie nie pracuje. Jest kurą domową i to tyle o niej.

Kiedyś też chciałem gasić pożary, ale w wieku pięciu lat straciłem słuch. Po tygodniu odzyskałem, ale tylko na jedno ucho i marzenie o byciu strażakiem pozostało marzeniem.

To, że jestem w połowie głuchy, wykrywa tylko audiogram, ludzie są zbyt ułomni. Ja też czasami zapominam, że z moim prawym uchem jest coś nie tak. W przeciwieństwie do audiogramu. Wredne gówno!

*

Dziś ostatni raz byłem na batonach; jak by się to komu nie kojarzyło, do klubów gejowskich nie chadzam. Batony – tak nazywałem fabrykę czekolady w Sochaczewie. Pracowałem tam jako agent ochrony albo cieć – jak kto woli. Wcześniej była jeszcze praca fizyczna przy produkcji plandek. Robiłem tam z tym samym kolesiem, który potem odbił ode mnie i wrócił do domu. To była naprawdę harówa, a my nie bardzo sobie radziliśmy. Szybko to rzuciłem, by już po paru dniach zostać BIZNESMANEM.

Od pierwszej godziny mojej misji czułem się głupio. Potem zrobiło mi się gorąco, zachciało mi się pić, a pasek ciężkiej torby, wypchanej cudownymi zapalniczkami z Chin, zaczął coraz brutalniej wrzynać mi się w ramię. Chciałem choć przez chwilę odpocząć; przycupnąć gdzieś w cieniu, odetchnąć, ale moja opiekunka, gruba, wysoka blondynka z szerokimi jak płetwy stopami, nie pozwalała mi na to. Co chwilę powtarzała wyuczone jak pacierz słowa: „Dziś chodzisz po ulicy, jutro jesteś KIMŚ". Mamrotała te bzdury, kiedy tylko zauważała kolejny atak zrezygnowania rysujący się na mojej spoconej twarzy.

Nie wiem, co mi wtedy do łba strzeliło, że tyle z nią łaziłem. Dlaczego nie uciekłem? Przecież ona mi się nawet nie podobała, była gruba. Badanie opinii publicznej? Dobre sobie. Co ma wspólnego przeprowadzanie ankiet z jakimś nachalnym wciskaniem ludziom chińskiego gówna? Ona mówiła, że to sprzedaż bezpośrednia. Sprzedaż bezpośrednia?... Niech jej będzie.

Po całym dniu łażenia w kółko byłem zły na samego siebie, a jej stopy wydawały mi się jeszcze większe. Nie mogłem się pogodzić z tym, że jestem aż tak ugrzecznionym dupkiem. Zero asertywności.

Na koniec dnia poszedłem z nią zdać jakiś bzdurny raport do ich nawiedzonego, z przyklejonym na stałe uśmiechem, bossa i z głośnym aplauzem zostałem przyjęty do zaczarowanego grona. Ze szczęścia prawie się rozpłakałem. To dziwne, że mnie chcieli, tamtego dnia sprzedałem tylko jedną zapalniczkę. Widać miałem potencjał.

Więcej tam nie poszedłem, dałem sobie spokój. Raz na zawsze straciłem szansę bycia „kimś".

Połowa wielkich karier zaczyna się przez przypadek? Być może, ja też pracy w ochronie nie planowałem. Wcześniej nawet nie śmiałem o tym myśleć. Samo słowo „ochrona" kojarzyło mi się zawsze z mocnymi facetami. Nigdy nie sądziłem, że tak naprawdę agentem ochrony może zostać każdy... no dobra, prawie każdy.

*

To taki historyczny moment. Wielu pamięta początek stanu wojennego i ten słynny plakat z tytułem filmu: *Czas apokalipsy*. Żaden inny tytuł nie przemówiłby wtedy tak bardzo do niepewnych jutra szarych ludzi.

Stan wojenny minął, kino wyburzono, a na jego miejscu powstał imponujących rozmiarów połyskujący w słońcu moloch. Nieraz przejeżdżając obok tramwajem, nie mogłem oderwać od niego oczu. Za każdym razem liczyłem piętra. Trzynaście. Nie wysoki? A jednak robi wrażenie.

*

Krzysiek siedzi przy stole w kuchni. Widząc, jak taszczę swoje nieprane już dwa miesiące ochroniarskie uniformy, robi zdziwioną minę. On często wybałusza tak oczy. Z początku mnie tym irytował, ale przez te sześć miesięcy, od kiedy z nimi tu mieszkam, zdążyłem już przywyknąć do jego tępej gęby.

– Cześć – mówię do niego i wchodzę do pokoju.

Mieszkamy razem: on, ja i jego starszy o dwa lata brat, Wiesiek. W trójkę zasmradzamy jeden nieduży pokój na poddaszu.

To dzięki Wieśkowi tu mieszkam. Wcześniej pracował ze mną na plandekach. Tego samego deszczowego dnia rzuciliśmy robotę i nasze drogi się rozeszły. Nie na długo, bo chociaż Warszawa mała nie jest, spotkaliśmy się na przejściu dla pieszych. Zaproponował mi, bym zamieszkał z nim i jego bratem w jednym pokoju w Jankach. Właścicielka domu, podstarzała piękność, pani Bożena, i tak chciała im kogoś dokooptować. Jej zdaniem piętnastometrowy pokój na poddaszu jest wystarczająco duży, by pomieścić więcej niż dwóch lokatorów. Wprowadziłem się prawie od razu, a oni nie musieli się już dłużej przejmować, że Bożena wpakuje im do pokoju Kubę Rozpruwacza.

– Jebłeś te batony?

Jak on to mówi, jebłem; w końcu od tygodnia o niczym innym nie gadałem. Gdy tylko dowiedziałem się, że jest możliwość przejścia na ten ekskluzywny obiekt, nie wytrzymałem i musiałem się pochwalić.

Oni też pracują w ochronie. Wiesiek, podobnie jak ja, po plandekach wdepnął w to gówno, a potem wciągnął w nie brata. Obaj stoją w hipermarkecie w Jankach i choć też niedużo im płacą, stoją, bo robota jest na miejscu... Szczęściarze.

– Koniec z Sochaczewem! – krzyczę, rzucając uniformy na, jak zawsze niezaścielony, tapczan. – Wystarczy już tych dojazdów; chociaż nie powiem, fajną ekipę miałem.

Krzysiek macha ręką.

– No, ale teraz będziesz miał przynajmniej bliżej, nie? No i kasowo chyba lepiej, co?

– Trochę, ale kokosów, nie będzie.

– Na godzinę ile dostałeś?

Wzruszam ramionami. Co go to kurwa obchodzi?!

– Trochę więcej – odpowiadam bez emocji, a na jego pucułowatej twarzy pojawia się niezadowolenie.

– Tam nie jest lekko – mówi, drapiąc się po czole.

– A na batonach było? Cały czas tylko jakieś bzdurne obchody. Tam chociaż się nie kurzy i łazić tyle nie trzeba.

– Ale się nastoisz, zobaczysz. Kiedyś robił tam taki jeden od nas, miesiąca nie wytrzymał. Narzekał, że było przejebane. Zobaczysz, nastoisz się.

Patrzę na niego i zastanawiam się, czy to jego gadanie teraz to z zazdrości, czy z troski.

– Na batonach też była rotacja; co chwilę to przyjmował się jakiś, to zwalniał, i tak na okrągło. Niektórzy to by chcieli na leżąco pracować. Ten twój koleś to pewnie jakaś miękka faja. Za bardzo się nad sobą rozczulał.

Krzysiek kręci głową.

– W Jankach już trochę robi, a nogi w dupę wchodzą. Tam miesiąca nie wytrzymał – powtarza.

– Chciałem mieć bliżej i wreszcie będę miał. Ty myślisz, że tak łatwo obiekt zmienić? Z początku nie chcieli się zgodzić, ale jak powiedziałem, że całkiem z firmy odejdę, to poszli mi na rękę. Jutro nie muszę wstawać o piątej. Teraz będę wychodził do pracy jak człowiek.

*

W nocy źle śpię, przekręcam się z boku na bok i cały czas myślę o tym nowym miejscu. Już taki jestem, kiedy coś nieznanego przede mną, to w nocy nie mogę spać. Pewnie dlatego rano czuję się jak po hucznej imprezie, chyba nie zrobię dobrego wrażenia. Żałuję, że nie poprosiłem w firmie o parę dni wolnego między dyżurami. Przecież mogłem powiedzieć, że mam do załatwienia jakieś ważne sprawy rodzinne. Może by się zgodzili.

*

Na Puławskiej jestem sporo przed czasem. Za szybko wyszedłem z domu. Za szybko wyszedłem na autobus. Za szybko przesiadłem się w tramwaj. Wszystko zrobiłem za szybko. Tak bardzo nie chciałem się spóźnić, że teraz mam jeszcze pół godziny czasu.

Pierwszy dyżur i od razu doba. Na batonach robiłem dwunastki. Tam był inny system, ale w końcu dwadzieścia cztery na czterdzieści osiem, czemu nie? Godzin więcej, kasy więcej, a po dyżurze dwa dni wolnego. Super! Nie ma się czym przejmować, przywyknę, a cztery pięćdziesiąt na godzinę to o trzydzieści groszy więcej niż miałem na batonach. Godzin też niemało, no i się nie kurzy. Będzie dobrze. Zresztą, ja nie zamierzam tu długo pracować; tu i ogólnie w ochronie. Ta robota niczego nie wnosi, człowiek wyrabia tylko te godziny, a z czasem staje się coraz bardziej pokręconym zwierzątkiem. Niektórzy mówią, że to taka sadza na CV. Ja już półtora roku brudzę sobie tym życiorys, ale kiedyś z tym skończę, będę miał swój sklep spożywczy. Nie chcę do końca życia być nic nieznaczącym cieciem, bo chociaż na identyfikatorze jest napisane: „Agent ochrony", to taki ze mnie agent jak z koziej dupy trąba. Trzeba być kompletnym idiotą, żeby stać dwanaście godzin na linii kas w hipermarkecie i uważać się za agenta; w hipermarkecie, w biurowcu, na parkingu – gdziekolwiek. Agentem był Bond, ale on miał licencję na zabijanie. Ja mam zdarte zelówki swoich niemiłosiernie schodzonych butów i wielką nadzieję, że może tym razem firma nie przekręci mnie na kolejnej wypłacie.

*

Przechodzę przez wielkie obrotowe drzwi. Nieraz już takie widziałem, ale teraz pierwszy raz mam okazję sam przez nie przejść. Nawet nie trzeba ich pchać, są na jakiś czujnik, czy coś takiego.

Ogromna recepcja, zakończone niklowanymi balustradami hole windowe z czterema windami naprzeciwko siebie. Jeden nad drugim, aż do trzynastego piętra. Po prawej stronie, pewnie tylko dla ozdoby, podświetlana sporych rozmiarów marmurowa rzeźba. Wszędzie szkło, nikiel i granitowe błyszczące płyty. Pełen wypas, pópis luksusu, który przytłacza, a zarazem nie pozwala przejść obojętnie. Teraz ja będę tu pracował, pilnował porządku tu będę.

Co miesiąc, kiedy w niemiłosiernie długiej jak linia metra kolejce stoję po wypłatę, w krótkiej rozmowie i po kolejnym wypalonym dla towarzystwa papierosie z przypadkowym agentem jeden pyta drugiego: „Gdzie stoisz?". To takie standardowe pytanie, coś w stylu: „Jak się masz?". Bo jeśli ktoś stoi na marketach, centrach handlowych albo innych biurowych molochach, to wiadomo, że nie ma się najlepiej. Na pierwszym miejscu są hipermarkety. To najgorsze obiekty, nikt nie chce tam stać, dlatego Krzyśka i Wieśka, jak by nie było, zaliczam do twardzieli. Z biurowcami bywa różnie, stać też trzeba, ale marketów nic nie przebije. Najlepiej mają ci z cieciówek; ci z cieciówek mają luz.

Jeszcze przed batonami, na samym początku kariery, miałem okazję zaliczyć dwa dwunastogodzinne dyżury w jednym z takich miejsc. Stała na Żoliborzu, a w niej trzech na zmianie; tak zwany cieć dowódca i dwóch cieci nie dowódców. Cała nasza trójka łaziła pomiędzy samochodami. Pilnowaliśmy, by nikt ich nie ukradł. Na wypadek zagrożenia mieliśmy ze sobą stałą łączność radiową – pełna profeska.

Na stanie były dwie, trochę już zdezelowane krótkofalówki. Jedna była czymś obklejona, bo kiedyś wpadła komuś do talerza z zupą. Druga względnie czysta, ale podobnie jak tamta też jakoś dziwnie do rąk się kleiła. Miał ją przy sobie dowódca – cichutki, wystraszony koleś, którego największą pasją było gotowanie i nocne wycieczki po warszawskich burdelach. Nie krył się z tym, z gotowaniem zresztą też. Palnik miał jeden, ale za to gazowy, podłączony do małej turystycznej butli. Wcześniej mieli dużą, ale zajmowała zbyt wiele miejsca.

Dowódca Jasiek robił dla wszystkich obiady. Jego zgrana drużyna kupowała produkty w oddalonym o kilkadziesiąt metrów sklepie, też chronionym przez agentów z naszej firmy. Pieniądze na jedzenie zarabiali na boku. Dostawali je za pilnowanie lewych aut. To byli stali klienci. Stawiali samochody wzdłuż ogrodzenia i mogli iść spokojnie spać. Niektórzy płacili z góry, niektórzy później, ale płacili. Za takie pilnowanie można było kupić dużo jedzenia. Tamtą cieciówkę wspominam najmilej. Tu na gotowanie nie byłoby szans.

*

Podchodzę do młodego agenta o dziecięcej twarzy; wcześniej myślałem, że to prawdziwy recepcjonista; to przez ten jego galowy uniform. Wygląda w nim, jakby się z wesela urwał. Nawet oczy ma przekrwione, taki pooczepinowy zmęczony gość.

– Tak, słucham pana? – Podnosi się z krzesła, co za kultura. Jest bardzo szczupły i chyba zapomniał dziś użyć dezodorantu.

– Mam zacząć tu pierwszy dyżur – mówię.

– W firmie powiedzieli, że mam zapytać o pana... – Myślę chwilę. – O pana Arka Mojsa.

– Marka! Marka Mojsa – poprawia mnie, z miejsca nabierając pewności siebie. Przed chwilą dowiedział się, że jestem nikim, nikim ważnym.

– Na drugi raz nie właź głównym wejściem. Tędy mogą wchodzić tylko pracownicy centrum i goście.

– A którędy mam wchodzić? – pytam, starając się patrzeć mu prosto w oczy.

Chłopak bierze do ręki długopis.

– Twoje nazwisko?

– Patryk Boszczuk – odpowiadam, a on zapisuje je na jakiejś kartce. – To jakim wejściem mam wchodzić? – pytam znowu.

– Poczekaj. – Łapie za telefon. Zarozumialec.

Stoję i czekam, aż ten ważniak gdzieś zatelefonuje.

– Marek? – jego twarz promienieje. – Słuchaj, Mareczku, jest tu u mnie nowy. Mówi, że ma dziś zacząć u nas dyżur. Wiesz coś o tym? Tak, tak, jasne – śmieje się głośno i kątem oka zerka na mnie. – Jasne, Mareczku, che, che. Nie ma sprawy. Tak, już go do ciebie kieruję. No to na razie, che, che...

Jeszcze chwilę po odłożeniu słuchawki uśmiech nie znika mu z twarzy. On z tym Mareczkiem musi być bardzo zżyty.

– Słuchaj – mówi, podnosząc palec. Zaczyna zataczać nim w powietrzu jakieś dziwne figury. – Pójdziesz tą alejką, o tą, nie?! I dojdziesz do tamtych przeszklonych drzwi, o widzisz. Do tamtych, widzisz je?

Wzrokiem szukam przeszklonych drzwi.

– O tamte chodzi? – Wskazuję na jakieś drzwi znajdujące się najbliżej holu windowego.

– Niee! – Kręci głową. – W tamte drzwi włazisz. O, tamte, widzisz je? W tamte przy tym saloniku prasowym.

Mrużę oczy. Koło jakiego saloniku?

– Gdzie?

– No tee, na wprost koło tych, skarpet – denerwuje się.

O czym on gada? Koło jakich skarpet? Jeszcze bardziej wytężam wzrok. Rzeczywiście, dopiero teraz zauważam. W szybie wystawowej, obok gazet i jakichś powystawianych gęsto pierdół, wiszą takie czarne w foliowym opakowaniu. A więc to jest ten salonik prasowy. Nigdy bym nie zgadł. To normalny mały boks handlowy z mydłem i powidłem, a prasę to oni chyba tylko tak przy okazji sprzedają.

– Aaa, widzę! – odpowiadam, ciesząc się, jakbym znalazł igłę w stogu siana. – A potem, jak dalej?

Chłopak patrzy na mnie groźnie, ale ta jogo szczeniacka twarz nie budzi respektu. Z taką buzią to do piaskownicy.

– Spokojnie, już ci mówię – odpowiada, jakby od niechcenia. – Jak już miniesz te drzwi, nie? To jakieś pięć metrów dalej po prawej stronie będziesz miał kible. Pierwszy damski, drugi męski, a potem to już drzwi na monitoring. Zapukasz i poczekasz, aż ktoś wyjdzie. Tylko pamiętaj, nie właź bez pukania.

Podnoszę z podłogi torbę. Dobrze, że zaczynam w niedzielę, przynajmniej będzie spokojniej.

Podchodzę do białych drzwi z przyklejoną na środku małą tabliczką z napisem: „Monitoring". Tak jak mi tamten mówił, pukam. Pukam trzy razy, nie za mocno, ale zdecydowanie. Nie lubię takich momentów, bo choć nie chcę się denerwować, to i tak czuję w żołądku coraz to większy kamień.

Drzwi się otwierają, a mnie zaczyna piec twarz.

– Wchodź pan. – Przede mną stoi zwalisty, wysoki facet. – No, dawaj tu – niecierpliwi się.

Wchodzę i staję na środku pomieszczenia. Jakoś dziwnie tu śmierdzi.

– Dzień dobry, nazywam się Boszczuk...

– Dobra – przerywa mi. – Wiem, jak masz pan na imię. – Facet spogląda na zegarek. – Lepiej powiedz mi, dlaczego dopiero teraz jesteś pan na obiekcie?

– Dlaczego? – powtarzam za nim, próbując jednocześnie zrozumieć sens tak postawionego pytania.

– Jak ja teraz panu obiekt pokażę? Pierwszy dzień i już pan taki wtop zaliczasz? Aż strach pomyśleć, co będzie potem.

– Przecież jeszcze nie ma ósmej – tłumaczę mu.

– No, nie ma – nerwowo potakuje. – Nie ma, a co byś pan chciał, żeby już była? No pewnie, najlepiej na dziesiątą chciał byś pan do roboty przychodzić, co? Gdzieś pan wcześniej stał, na jakim obiekcie?

– Na fabryce czekolady w Sochaczewie.

– Nie musisz mi pan gadać, gdzie to jest. Wiem, gdzie mamy fabrykę czekolady. Pewnie żeś pan tam tylko batony wpierdalał, co? – Śmieje się teraz, a ja próbuję się śmiać razem z nim. Niech wie, że też, tak jak on, mam poczucie humoru.

– Nie, nie było lekko, trochę trzeba było chodzić.

– Trochę? A trzepałeś pan torby?

Kręcę głową.

– Nie trzepałeś pan toreb? – dziwi się. – Ale chyba pan wiesz, że przy trzepaniu to łap nie możesz pan do środka wkładać?! To niezgodne z prawem. Wkładać łap do toreb nie wolno!

– A jak by trzeba było?

Facet znowu się uśmiecha. Tym razem jednak od razu widać, że ten jego uśmiech to nie z sympatii do mnie.

– Pan normalnie na przepisach się, kurwa, nie znasz. Jak by trzeba było? Co to w ogóle za pytanie jest? Jak pan trzepiesz torby, to nie wolno łap wkładać, i koniec. Tylko zajrzeć, spojrzeć można, nic więcej. Jak byś pan tu taki numer odpierdolił, to firma od razu na pysk z obiektu leci.

Dałby już spokój, przecież ja tylko pytałem. Do tej pory nikt mi o tym trzepaniu nie gadał. Chyba nie polubię go tak, jak ten agent z recepcji.

Na batonach miałem w miarę normalnego inspektora. Wszyscy ci zawracający dupę panowie nazywają się „inspektorzy". Tak samo zresztą na wyrost, jak my – agenci. Inspektor z batonów zachowywał się normalnie i tylko czasem śmiał się ze mnie i mówił, że jestem zakręcony jak baranie rogi. Mówił tak najczęściej wtedy, kiedy kontrolowałem wyjeżdżające przez bramę towarową samochody ciężarowe. Często zdarzało się, że zapominałem zabrać ze sobą długopis. Trzeba było spisać nazwisko i numer przepustki kierowcy, takie tam rutynowe czynności. W pośpiechu wracałem po długopis, a po chwili jeszcze po jakąś kartkę. Właśnie wtedy mówił, że jestem zakręcony jak baranie rogi. Nie tylko do mnie tak gadał, do innych też; nawet na obsługującego wagę towarową dowódcę zmiany. To dodawało mi otuchy.

Dowódca na batonach nie gotował. Pewnie nie potrafił tak, jak tamten z cieciówki na Żoliborzu, ale za to był nie mniej w porządku. Przez półtora roku tylko raz mnie zdenerwował; zaraz pierwszego dnia, kiedy nasza firma przejmowała obiekt. Od razu został mianowany dowódcą naszej zmiany. Nikt nie protestował, nie wnikał, czy to dobrze, czy źle. Ktoś musiał być tym dowódcą, więc inspektor razem z szefem rejonu, obciętym na jeża kurduplem z bałaganem w oczach, zadecydowali, że dowódcą zostanie Wojtek. Przesądził o tym staż w firmie. Wojtek miał trzydzieści parę lat, pracował najdłużej i jak do tej pory, tylko na hipermarketach. Był zahartowanym w staniu agentem, dlatego teraz miał już raczej tylko siedzieć. Od stania i łażenia była cała reszta ludzi, tak różniących się od siebie, jak linie papilarne na opuszkach palców – od studiujących zaocznie luzaków po przewrażliwionych, utrzymujących całe rodziny, zadłużonych w bankach służbistów.

Właśnie tego pierwszego dnia dowódca wydaje mi polecenie. Taki prawie rozkaz, jak w wojsku. Każe mi stanąć w długim tunelu z blachy falowanej. Mam stać u wylotu i pilnować, by żaden z pracowników fabryki nie wynosił batonów. Jest październik, wieje tam jak cholera i zamiast jednej godziny, stoję prawie trzy. Kiedy wreszcie przychodzi zmiennik, jestem skostniały z zimna, a z nerwów ledwo mogę gadać.

Wracam na warownię. Pierwsze, co chcę zrobić, to powiedzieć, co sądzę o takim dowódcy jak on; o dowódcy, co o swoich ludzi nie dba; ale w porę gryzę się w jęzor. Potem Wojtek już nigdy nie zapominał o mnie i zawsze na czas podsyłał mi zmiennika, czy to na tunel, czy na parking, a w nocy pozwalał trochę pokimać na krześle. W porządku był z niego dowódca.

*

Zadymione pomieszczenie, długie, kiszkowate. Rzędy szarych metalowych szafek, w rogu poplamiony stół i dwa wysiedziane biurowe krzesła. Trafiam do przebieralni, palarni, jadalni – do takiego pomieszczenia socjalnego trzy w jednym. Cała masa obcych twarzy przygląda mi się, jakbym miał ze dwie głowy.

Inspektor Marek Mojs mnie tu przyprowadził. Sam nawet z nawigacją satelitarną bym nie trafił, tym bardziej że jesteśmy teraz jak górnicy, głęboko pod powierzchnią. Prowadził mnie jakąś jasną klatką ewakuacyjną. Od parteru schodziliśmy cały czas tylko w dół. Tak, na pewno jesteśmy głęboko pod powierzchnią.

– Cisza! – Na widok pana inspektora prawie wszyscy stają na baczność. – To wasz nowy kolega – mówi. – Zostawiam go tu, a ty Adaś – zwraca się do szczupłego niskiego faceta w okularach – wstaw go gdzie tam trzeba.

Adaś kiwa posłusznie głową, a potem mierzy mnie badawczym wzrokiem – biorąc pod uwagę grubość jego wpadających w fiolet szkieł leczniczych, oceniam, że bardzo słabym wzrokiem.

– Jasne, Mareczku. – Podchodzi do mnie bliżej. – Jak masz na imię? – pyta.

– Patryk – odpowiadam.

– A więc Patryka damy dzisiaj na klateczki – mówi. – A potem, na nockę, to się jeszcze zobaczy. – Uśmiecha się do mnie. – Na rozgrzewkę będą klateczki.

– Ja miałem iść dziś na klateczki! – odzywa się jakiś niski agent z garbatym nosem. Wygląda, jakby od paru nocy nie spał. – Wczoraj mówiłeś. Adaś! Mówiłeś, że dziś będę miał klateczki, pamiętasz?

Adaś z głupkowatą miną drapie się za uchem, a inspektor patrzy teraz na niego bez entuzjazmu.

– Czyś ty zgłupiał? Na minusiku go zostaw – mówi. – Pierwszy dzień i na klateczki nowego chcesz dać? Na klateczki to trzeba sobie zasłużyć – śmieje się. Adaś też dołącza do niego. Zaczynają się śmiać, a właściwie jakoś tak stękać. Jakby czymś się zakrztusili.

– O, właśnie, Mareczku, masz rację. Kolega nowy to na klateczki za szybko. – Patrzy teraz na tego niskiego z nosem jak papuzi dziób. – A ty, kurwa, daj już spokój – zwraca się do tamtego. – Nie przypominam sobie, żebym ci klateczki obiecywał. – Nachyla się do niego. – Po tym, co ostatnio odjebałeś, to w ogóle możesz zapomnieć!

O czym oni mówią? Jakie klateczki? Wyciągam z torby uniformy.

– Masz tylko takie? – pyta inspektor, a dowódca bez aprobaty kręci głową.

– Słucham?

– Nie pobrałeś galówek?

– Nie.

– A nie powiedzieli ci w biurze, jaki to obiekt? Chyba wiedziałeś, gdzie idziesz, nie? – Patrzą na siebie. – No i co ja mam teraz z tobą, chłopie, zrobić? Na hole windowe cię przecież nie dam.

– Mówię ci, zostaw go u Zbycha – radzi inspektor.

– Masz rację, dam go na minusiki. A jak kolega pobierze marynareczkę, to piętérka zwiedzi.

Nie wiem, o czym ten okularnik gada. To jakiś lizus, wazeliniarz; wchodzący w dupę obślizgły typ.

Na szafkę też trzeba tu zasłużyć. Jedyne, co mnie może pocieszyć, to fakt, że nie tylko ja jeżdżę z całą garderobą. Połowa ekipy nie ma tu szafek ubraniowych, ale to się niebawem zmieni – tak mówi inspektor. Jeśli tak mówi, to może tak będzie, zobaczymy.

*

Minusiki? Pewnie jestem za mało bystry, ale nigdy bym na to nie wpadł. Nie domyśliłbym się, że chodzi po prostu o parkingi podziemne. Teraz, jak już wiem, to ta nazwa nawet mi leży. Gorzej jest z przetrwaniem na tym minusiku. Dowódca Adaś, po rozesłaniu wszystkich agentów na posterunki, osobiście mnie tu przyprowadza. Podczas krótkiej drogi chwali się swoim stażem w ochronie. Na tym obiekcie, jak mówi, pracuje najdłużej i zna jego wszystkie zakamarki. Słucham go z „zachwytem". Jeszcze zanim wychodzimy z przebieralnio-jadalnio-palarni, zaczyna wspominać, jak kiedyś w windzie zasłabła młoda kobieta. Z dumą mówi, że osobiście zadzwonił po karetkę. A potem sam zaprowadził lekarza do kobiety potrzebującej dawki świeżego tlenu. Z rozdrażnieniem w głosie opowiada, jak niepotrzebnie ratował jej życie, bo ta – jak ją nazwał – „kurwa" nawet mu nie podziękowała.

– A komu zawdzięcza, że dycha? – Patrzy na mnie. – No właśnie, mnie to zawdzięcza! Kurwa jedna.

– Może nie wiedziała, że to ty.

– Jak nie wiedziała?! – oburza się. – Przecież podałem im swoje nazwisko, tym medykom w karetce. Już ona dobrze wiedziała!

Idziemy przez rozległy parking. Pełno tu głośno szumiących dmuchaw. Pompują powietrze, tylko dlaczego takie ciepłe? Gorąco.

– No, się masz, Zbychu?! – wita się teraz z wysokim, wąsatym facetem.

Jesteśmy w jakimś ponurym, małym pomieszczeniu z dużym oknem wychodzącym na parking.

– O, świeża krew – mówi ten z wąsami. Potem głośno się śmieje i wyciąga do mnie żylastą łapę – Cześć! Zbychu jestem.

– Patryk – odpowiadam.

Podajemy sobie ręce.

– Chłopie, gdzieś ty tu przylazł? – Cały czas się śmieje. – Kolejny żołnierz Marka? – Porozumiewawczo puszczają do siebie oko, ale zaraz mnie pociesza: – Dobrze będzie – mówi. – Damy radę. – Patrzy na mnie. – Patryk, tak?

– Tak – z trudem łapię powietrze.

– Damy radę, Patryk – powtarza.

Tu jest jak w kominie – ciemno i pełno dymu. Pewnie dużo pali; mam nadzieję, że nie będę musiał z nim siedzieć. Kątem oka patrzę na czarnobiałe monitory. Nic się nie dzieje, nic się nie rusza; tylko parking, filary, nawet samochodów nie ma. Pewnie dlatego, że to niedziela.

– Zbychu, zostawię ci tu chłopaka. Powiedz mu, w czym rzecz, a ja idę do siebie, bo ten będzie znowu pierdolił.

– Zmienił już tego rzęcha?

– Nie, ale napalił się na nowego.

– O kurwa, patrz, jaki burżuj, nie?

– A tam, burżuj – krzywi się. – W kredycie bierze, promocja jest. Dwa rowery za darmo dorzucają.

25

– Składaki – śmieje się Zbychu. – Pewnie bez
siodełka, co?
– Dwa górale. Mówi, że mi je sprzeda, bo mu
te rowery koło chuja latają.
– Kupisz?
– Może. – Otwiera drzwi. Znowu słychać szum
dmuchaw. – Dobra, idę, kurwa, pięterka obejść.
Pokaż młodemu, co ma robić. Wpadnę jeszcze
potem.
Wychodzi.
– Na razie – odpowiada leniwie Zbychu i chwyta za leżącą na blacie biurka paczkę papierosów.
– Palisz? – Chce mnie poczęstować.
A co tam, nawet jak nie zapalę, to się na-
wdycham. Lepiej truć się własnym niż biernie
cudzym petem.
– Zapalę – odpowiadam. – Ale tak w ogóle to
nie, nie palę. To znaczy nie palę dużo – tłumaczę i wyciągam rękę po papierosa, starając się
zgrabnie wyciągnąć go z paczki.
– Pewnie, zajaraj sobie. Tu jeszcze możesz,
bo potem, jak już będziesz na obchodach – grozi palcem – to broń cię, kurwa, Panie Boże.
Kiwam posłusznie głową i biorę od niego zapalniczkę. Przypalam sobie papierosa. Ostatni raz paliłem może z tydzień temu. Wiesiek
kupił piwo, to zapaliłem, tak dla towarzystwa.
Sam rzadko kupuję fajki. Następnym razem
kupię i poczęstuję Zbycha. W końcu w porządku z niego facet. Fajki mi nie żałuje.

*

Na batonach miałem paru kolegów, jednym z nich był Agata. Tak na niego mówiliśmy, bo miał długie przerzedzone jasne włosy. Chował je pod służbową czapką i tylko w nocy, kiedy nikt nie widział, pozwalał im trochę pooddychać świeżym powietrzem

Agata był typem wesołka, chociaż jeśli było trzeba, potrafił się nie śmiać. Kiedy na obiekt przyjeżdżali ci z samej góry, trzeba było zachować powagę. Przyjeżdżali na kontrolę i wtedy nie tylko Agata miał poważną minę.

Najgorszy był ten obcięty na jeża kurdupel z bałaganem w oczach. Raz, w napadzie złości, obrzucił jednego z agentów bateriami do krótkofalówek. Kurdupel wpadł w furię, bo tamten próbował reanimować spodnie biurowymi zszywkami, a do tego miał brudne gacie. Szary lampas go zgubił; gdyby nie on, może by mu uszło. Ale niestety, kurdupel dopatrzył się, że lampas zamiast być biały, jest szary, a potem to już poszło. Kazał mu stanąć na środku warowni i obrócić się dookoła. Agent przed chwilą wrócił z obchodu i teraz zamiast przycupnąć na krześle, musiał jak na rozkaz prezentować swoje znoszone wdzianko. Co za pech! Trafiło na jednego z flejtuchów. No i te biurowe zszywki. Im też nie można ufać. Kiedy tak się obracał, może jeszcze jedna trzymała się swojego miejsca. Reszta odpadła albo wisiała ledwo uczepiona jednym końcem za materiał. Spodnie na dupie się rozjechały i wyszło na jaw. Gacie jasne, z tyłu w rdzawe plamy. Te plamy to nie był wzór fabryczny, każdy to widział.

– Srasz pan w galoty?

Trochę chce mi się śmiać i cieszę się, że z moim szwem na tyłku jest wszystko w porządku. Nie wiem, co bym zrobił, gdyby przy wszystkich okazało się, że i ja mam gacie we wzory.

– Obróć się pan! No, obróć się pan! – krzyczy kurdupel.

Agent ma wystraszone oczy, ale próbuje nadrobić miną. Wygląda, jakby chciał wykrzyczeć: „To nie ja, to nie ja je tak osrałem!".

Kurdupel łapie za wsadzoną w ładowarkę baterię do krótkofalówki. Mieliśmy ich trochę, nieustannie musiały się ładować. Nikt się nie spodziewał, że za wyzwiskami w kierunku obsrańca polecą twarde, kanciaste baterie. Nie wiedzieliśmy, co robić. Przecież nie można ot tak rzucać w człowieka. Nie na obiekcie chronionym.

Obsraniec przez moment czuł się pewnie jak kamienowany. W jego kierunku poleciała niejedna bateria. Bałem się, że po bateriach polecą krzesła, a potem – kto wie – może kurdupel porwie się nawet do bicia?

Kiedy przestaje, wszyscy na krótko łapiemy oddech. Ten idiota każe stanąć Agacie obok kulącego się obsrańca.

– Stań pan przy nim – mówi. – Niech wszyscy zobaczą, jak ma wyglądać agent na służbie.

Agata ma czysty kołnierzyk, a kiedy staje przy tamtym, widać, że lampas też.

– Zdejmij pan czapkę.

Agata z głupawym uśmiechem patrzy na kurdupla.

– No, zdejmij pan czapkę! – powtarza, spodziewając się zapewne grzecznie zaczesanej na bok grzywki. A tu coś takiego? Spod czapki wysypują się włosy – długie, potargane, sięgające do ramion splątane blond włosiska. – Co to jest?! – krzyczy kurdupel.

– Co? – Agata próbuje udawać, że nie wie, o co chodzi. Wygląda komicznie z tą miną.

– To! – Podchodzi do niego bliżej, ale zaraz potem odwraca się i patrzy na naszego inspektora. – Widzisz to co ja? – pyta groźnie.

– Widzę, ale...

– Co, kurwa, ale? Przyjąłeś na obiekt hipisa?

– Pojęcia nie miałem...

– Nie miałeś? To on tu cały czas w berecie zapierdala? Nigdy go nie zdejmuje?

Nie odpowiada, robi tylko taką dziwną minę; taką, jakby zaciągnął się mocnym papierosem i nie mógł wypuścić dymu z płuc.

– Ostatni raz jesteś pan dziś w tym kołtunie, ostatni raz – powtarza kurdupel.

– Albo długie włosy, albo robota – mówi inspektor. Potem spogląda na obsrańca. – A ty zszyj spodnie i wypierz gacie.

Obsraniec robi się jeszcze bardziej czerwony, Agata bije się z myślami, a inspektor? A inspektor znowu ma taką minę, jakby dusił się dymem z papierosa.

*

Zbychu wyciągnął spod biurka jakiś gruby zeszyt i z hukiem ciska nim o blat.

– Zobacz... – mówi. Przez chwilę nad czymś się zastanawia. – Cholera... – Pstryka palcami. – No, to jak ty miałeś, kolego, na imię?

– Patryk, Patryk Boszczuk – przypominam mu i uśmiecham się na znak, że to nic takiego zapomnieć w tak krótkim czasie po raz kolejny czyjegoś imienia.

– O! No właśnie. Nie mam pamięci do was wszystkich – tłumaczy się, wertując z wywalonym językiem kartki w zeszycie. – Zobacz, Patryk – podsuwa mi go pod nos – tu się wpiszesz, dobra? – Podwija mankiet niebieskiej służbowej koszuli i mrużąc oczy, zaczyna się wpatrywać w tarczę zegarka. – Mamy ósmą trzydzieści. Dobra, to wpisz godzinę w tej rubryce, o, w tej. – Pokazuje palcem na jakąś tabelę.

– Tu? – pytam, chcąc się upewnić, czy chodzi nam o tę samą rubrykę.

– Tak – odpowiada, wypuszczając w moim kierunku kłęby białego dymu. – Tak, a tu z boku wpisz swoje imię i nazwisko. Od tej godziny objąłeś minusiki – mówi tryumfalnym tonem i za-

czyna się głośno śmiać, z trudem łapiąc oddech.
– Dobra, to teraz zacznij od minus jeden. Wiesz
o co chodzi? Masz cały czas patrolować parking. Łaź tak, by było cię całego widać w kamerach, to bardzo ważne. Wiesz, na wypadek
jakiejś awarii zawsze sprawdzają zapis z kamer;
muszą wtedy widzieć, że wszystko było tak jak
należy.
 Kiwam głową.
– Mam chodzić tak, by mnie widziały kamery?
 Znowu częstuje mnie porcją dymu.
– Nie, kolego, ty nie masz tu chodzić. Ty masz
patrolować parking i dokładnie zwracać na
wszystko uwagę. Wiesz, ja tu, a ty tam. Razem
musimy tworzyć zgrany duet. – Teraz uśmiech
znika mu z twarzy i znowu robi poważną minę. –
Powiedzmy to sobie szczerze: jeśli ty dasz dupy
na minusikach, to ja dostanę po uszach. Tu mam
monitory i muszę dokładnie obserwować twój
posterunek. – Rozkłada bezradnie ręce. – No,
niestety, kolego, tak już jest. Taki podział, nic
na to nie poradzisz. Pamiętaj, zawsze wszystko
zgłaszasz do mnie i pytasz, jak czegoś nie jesteś
pewny. Zrozumiałeś?
 Zastanawiam się, czy dziś też muszę zwracać szczególną uwagę.
– Dziś też?
 Zbychu mruży oczy.
– Jak powiedziałeś?
– No bo jest niedziela i parkingi prawie puste.

Zbychu odpala kolejnego papierosa.

– Słuchaj no, kolego! – Pewnie znowu zapomniał, jak mam na imię. – Prawie? Prawie? – denerwuje się. – Nawet jeśli byłby tu zaparkowany, zdezelowany wózek dziecięcy bez kółek, to masz koło niego łazić i nie spuszczać go z oczu, tak jakby był ze złota. Już ci mówiłem, masz dokładnie patrolować teren i na wszystko zwracać uwagę. Na grilla tu nie przyszedłeś, prawda? Więc proszę cię, nie zadawaj już takich dziwnych pytań, bo przestaniemy się lubić.

Chciałbym, żeby żartował, ale on mówi to jak najbardziej poważnie. Cholera, chyba za szybko go oceniłem. To psychol.

Nie chcę już dłużej drażnić go trudnymi pytaniami. Stoję, wpatruję się w nieruchomy czarnobiały obraz na jego monitorach. Nie wiem, czy już teraz powinienem zacząć łazić po tych pustych parkingach. A może mam tu stać? Nie wiem kompletnie nic prócz tego, że we dwóch mamy dziś tworzyć „zgrany" duet.

Nie jestem przyzwyczajony do takiego łażenia. Nie, żebym spodziewał się adrenaliny, ale nawet dłubanie w nosie niesie z sobą więcej emocji. Patrolowanie pustego parkingu nie ma sensu, ale nie tu. Tu jest inaczej. Obiekt chroniony to obiekt chroniony, więc czy są samochody, czy ich nie ma, trzeba patrolować, dokładnie patrolować teren i zdawać na bieżąco relację.

Jeszcze zanim wychodzę z zadymionej kanciapy Zbycha, dostaję od niego niewielką laminowaną ściągę z kryptonimami.

– Masz i się ucz – mówi. – Najlepiej, jak od razu będziesz jechał kodem, to bardzo ważne.

Pełno nic niemówiących mi słów, najwidoczniej ma to jednak jakiś sens. Skoro samochód to naparstek, a włamanie do tego naparstka to cięcie, to w razie konieczności będę nawijał w zupełnie nieznanym języku. Czemu ma służyć ten wewnętrzny slang? I co będzie, jak zapomnę albo coś mi się pokręci? Bylebym tylko po robocie nie kaleczył polszczyzny.

Najbardziej z tych głupot podoba mi się prośba o przerwę. Jak będę chciał coś zjeść, to mam powiedzieć: „bufet" – brzmi logicznie. Za to prośba o kibel wydaje mi się kompletną bzdurą, no bo jak można, chcąc się wysikać, krzyczeć: „plaża"? Przecież to jeszcze bardziej pognębia. Duszno, nogi bolą, a tu o plażę prosić? To bez sensu.

Jak wrócę na stancję, to pominę ten temat. Bracia będą ciekawi, jak jest na nowym obiekcie, to im powiem. Powiem, że jest fajnie. Zagram im na nerwach, niech mi trochę pozazdroszczą. Nie muszą znać prawdy.

Minus jeden i do interkomu. Minus dwa i też do interkomu, minus jeden, minus dwa, interkom, i tak w kółko. Od tego patrolowania może się w głowie zakręcić. Interkom wisi na minusach w holu windowym. Po każdym

„dokładnym" obchodzie muszę za jego pośrednictwem zgłosić, że wszystko jest w najlepszym porządku. Średnio co dziesięć minut powiadamiam Zbycha, że wszystko jest okej. Podpierając się ściągą, mówię mu, że tajfun na niebiesko. Jakby był, nie daj Boże, na czerwono, to by znaczyło, że coś jest nie tak. Wtedy dopiero, z tego, co zrozumiałem, bezpośrednio przez krótkofalówkę. Wyjaśnić bym musiał kryptonimem, w czym rzecz, ale jak tajfun na niebiesko, to gadać już dalej niczego nie trzeba.

Do siedemnastej nic nie jem. To dziwne, bo już parę razy mówiłem, że „bufet", ale Zbychu powiedział, że „klamka". Jakby powiedział, że „szpula", to mógłbym wziąć od niego klucz.

Każdy agent na posterunku ma prawo odpocząć. Przez kwadrans musi się wyrobić z jedzeniem. Jak to wcześniej przedstawił mi Zbychu, może zjeść posiłek i zregenerować siły. Sielanka. Ja już dreptczę tyle godzin i słyszę tylko „klamka". Inni też nie mają lekko, nie zauważyłem, żeby którykolwiek zjechał do Zbycha po klucz. Zapomnieli o przerwie? Ile można łazić bez jedzenia. Z minusów puszcza Zbychu, z reszty posterunków dowódca.

By trochę odpocząć, zgłaszam „plażę". Co jak co, ale do kibla musi mnie puścić.

– Chciałem zgłosić plażę! – mówię głośno i zastanawiam się, dlaczego dopiero teraz o to proszę. Chociaż na kiblu trochę odpocznę! – Plaża!

Plażę chciałem zgłosić! – powtarzam do interkomu. Zbychu jest niewzruszony, cały czas odpowiada, że „klamka".

Otwieram drzwi od kanciapy Zbycha. Wiem,
że to niedopuszczalne. Niedopuszczalne tak
bez pozwolenia z posterunku schodzić. Chcę
go zapytać, o co tu chodzi i dlaczego cały czas
częstuje mnie tymi „klamkami".

Uśmiecham się. Zupełnie tak, jakbym wcale
nie był na niego wkurwiony. Komu normalne-
mu byłoby teraz do śmiechu? Przecież gdybym
naprawdę musiał na kibel, to już dawno naro-
biłbym w gacie.

– Mam takie pytanie...

– Co ty, kurwa?! – Nie daje mi skończyć. – Czy
ty sobie zdajesz sprawę, co teraz zrobiłeś? Właśnie samowolnie, bez mojej zgody, opuściłeś
swój posterunek! Wracaj, póki jeszcze nie jest
za późno. Wracaj, to udam, że niczego nie widziałem. – Wstaje z krzesła i podchodzi do mnie.
– No, spierdalaj stąd!

– Ale ja...

– Nie ma ale... Jak będzie przerwa, to ci powiem; teraz wracaj na posterunek. No już, kurwa, człowieku nie odpierdalaj maniany!

Wracam. Czuję się tak, jakbym dostał obu-
chem w łeb. Nie mogę uwierzyć, że to się dzieje naprawdę. Skurwysyn, nawet mnie nie wy-
słuchał, tylko kazał wracać na parking. Na posterunek. Jaki, kurwa, posterunek?!

*

Po dziewięciu godzinach patrolowania Zbychu mówi: „Szpula". Mówi to w momencie, kiedy tracę już nadzieję. Jak wariat pędzę po klucz od naszej „jadalni" i gdy proszę o niego, Zbychu mówi, że mam wziąć torbę i zjeść tu. Mówi, że ma do mnie parę ważnych pytań. Moja radość z przerwy pęka jak nakłuty szpilką balon.

Jakby mi kto dupę skopał, wracam z torbą i siadam na drugim wolnym krześle. Wyciągam zrobione wczoraj kanapki. Zawsze przygotowuję je wieczorem, rano by mi się nie chciało. Całe się zagrzały, nic dziwnego – gorąco tu.

Poczęstowałbym go kanapką, czemu nie. Rodzice uczyli, że trzeba się dzielić. Ale jak...? Z nim, z takim chujem? Z takim chujem nie warto się niczym dzielić, nie po tym, co do mnie powiedział.

– Jedz sobie, jedz – mówi cicho. Ten jego spokój nie wróży nic dobrego. To taka cisza przed burzą. – W międzyczasie zrobię ci krótki sprawdzian z wiedzy ogólnej. Wiesz, takie tam wiadomości, które każdy pracownik ochrony powinien mieć w małym paluszku.

– Że co?

– Jedz, jedz, mi to jeszcze chwilę zajmie. – Schyla się po jakiś papierowy skoroszyt. – Jedz, jedz – powtarza. – Spokojnie.

Odechciało mi się jeść; najchętniej to bym sobie teraz zapalił.

– Będziesz mi robił sprawdzian? – pytam. – Jak w szkole?

Nie patrzy na mnie, tylko kiwa głową i uśmiecha się od niechcenie.

– No, nie przesadzajmy – mówi. – W szkole stawiają oceny do dziennika, a ja dziennika nie mam – śmieje się. – Sprawdzę tylko tak z krótka twoją wiedzę. Wiesz, takie tam rzeczy, które powinien wiedzieć każdy agent. – Patrzy teraz na moją nierozwiniętą z papieru kanapkę. – Nie jesz? Przerwa trwa piętnaście minut.

– Nie, nie jestem głodny – odpowiadam, chowając ją z powrotem do torby.

– To nie marnujmy w takim razie czasu. – Wyciąga ze skoroszytu jakieś papierzyska i zaczyna czytać: – „Pracownik ochrony podczas wykonywania zadań w granicach chronionego obiektu ma prawo do…"?

Patrzy na mnie, jakby to, że teraz zadaje mi takie pytania, było czymś normalnym. Przecież ja pojęcia nie mam, jakie ma prawa pracownik ochrony. To znaczy wiem, że powinien przychodzić do pracy trzeźwy i nie powinien się za bardzo spoufalać z pracownikami chronionego obiektu. Nie powinien, bo wtedy różnie może być, szczególnie jak się spoufali z krągłą kucharką z dużymi cyckami.

*

Na batonach pracował taki, co się za bardzo spoufalił. Wszyscy, nie wiem dlaczego, mówiliśmy na niego szwagier. Przyjeżdżał do pracy odpicowany w bordowy garnitur i choć nie musiał, zawsze podpierał się zdobioną drewnianą laską. Śmialiśmy się z niego, bo ta laska pasowała do niego jak siodło do świni, ale facet miał styl i swoje wiedział.

Któregoś razu zaprzyjaźnił się z pewną kucharką. Szczery był i koleżeński. Nie ukrywał, że żonę ma chudą jak drzazga. I w ogóle nie ukrywał, że ma żonę. A Dorota? (Ta kucharka).

– O, Dorota to jest kobieta! – mówił. – Ma na czym usiąść i czym pooddychać.

I tak jego zachwyt szybko przerodził się w płomienny romans. Walił kucharkę Dorotę, a potem wychwalał jej tłustą dupę. Mówił, że całe życie ruchał kościste, i teraz to on dopiero wie, że żyje.

Któregoś razu przyjechał do pracy bez laski i w rozciągniętym wełnianym swetrze. Był zły, bo kucharka Dorota zakochała się w nim na zabój. Głupia, narobiła sobie nadziei, a on już się nabzykał. Wcześniej tego nie przewidział. Zaczął jej unikać. Odwiedziła go w domu; wiedziała, gdzie mieszka. Idiota!

Od tamtego czasu przyjeżdżał na obiekt z dużym turystycznym plecakiem i cały czas w tym wieśniackim wełnianym swetrze. Często się zdarzało, że zostawał na kolejne zmiany. Parę razy spał w szatni, potem się zwolnił.

A Dorota? Dorota nie nakładała nam już tak dużych porcji.

*

– No to jak? Wiesz? – Zbychu przygląda mi się z uwagą. Już się nie zastanawiam, czy on jest całkiem normalny. – Chłopie, to są podstawowe zagadnienia – mówi. – Bez tej wiedzy nie powinieneś progu tego obiektu przekraczać.

Muszę coś powiedzieć; dlaczego nigdy wcześniej nikt mnie o to nie pytał?

– No, chodzi o to, że... – Mrużę oczy. – Chodzi o to, że pracownik ochrony ma z uwagą obserwować chroniony teren i...

Zbychu parska dzikim śmiechem.

– Przecież o tym każdy głupi wie. Powiedz mi, jakie masz prawa, kiedy jesteś w pracy. Co możesz, a czego ci nie wolno. Kurwa!

Znowu udaję, że się zastanawiam.

– To znaczy mam prawo wylegitymować pracownika i...

Wytrzeszcza szeroko oczy.

– A dalej? Słucham, jakie masz jeszcze prawa? – Wnikliwie wpatruje się w leżące na blacie biurka wygniecione papierzysko. Cwaniaczek, tam ma wszystko napisane. Ciekawe, czy bez tego byłby taki mądry. – No dalej, człowieku, nie mamy tyle czasu, przerwa ci się kończy. Czekam, co masz mi do powiedzenia?

Dobrze wie, że już niczego więcej nie wymyślę. Może gdybym tak na spokojnie... to może dałbym radę, ale teraz, przy nim?

– Zapomniałem – mówię. – Wiedziałem, ale zapomniałem.

– Jak zapomniałeś? Ty nawet mi o tym nie gadaj! Agent ochrony i nie zna swoich kompetencji?! Jak ja teraz mogę cię na minusiki puścić? Przecież ty nic nie wiesz! – Myśli chwilę. – Zrobię dla ciebie wyjątek, pozwolę ci jeszcze dokończyć tu służbę. Do dziewiętnastej będziesz patrolował teren, a potem – ciężko wzdycha – potem będę musiał powiedzieć Adasiowi, żeby cię postawił na Chocimską. Przez noc nie ma ruchu, to się nie skompromitujesz. Dopiero nad ranem zaczyna się robić ciasno. Tak, na Chocimską cię postawimy. Zmiataj! – Macha łapą. – O dziewiętnastej dostaniesz zmianę i zgłosisz się do Adasia.

Łapię za klamkę, jak najszybciej chcę stąd wyjść.

– Aha, i jeszcze jedno. – Mierzy mnie wzrokiem. – Masz szczęście, że trafiłeś na mnie. Dam ci szansę, ale następnym razem to już taki dobry nie będę. Chyba się rozumiemy?

Stoję jedną nogą za progiem jego kanciapy.

– Jasne, przeczytam sobie o tych obowiązkach...

– Kompetencjach – przerywa mi i znowu patrzy na kartkę. – To jest: – zaczyna czytać – „O prawach agenta ochrony".

– Dobrze, o prawach agenta ochrony – powtarzam za nim. – Przeczytam.

– Zmiataj! – Teraz lekko się uśmiecha. – O dziewiętnastej przyjdzie człowiek, żeby cię zmienić.

*

Przez kolejne dwie godziny jeszcze dwa razy odwiedzam ponurą norę Zbycha. Nagle nie tak zacząłem chodzić po parkingach. Nie było mnie całego widać w monitorach – zjebał mnie.

O dziewiętnastej mam naprawdę dość. Teraz już jestem na dwieście procent pewny, że Zbychu to psychol. Kto wie, co by się ze mną stało, gdybym miał dreptać tu do rana. Może by mnie pobił, a potem uśmiechnął się i łaskawie poczęstował papierosem? Kto wie.

ROZDZIAŁ

2

Mówi się, że dobro wraca, że spokojem można więcej zdziałać niż krzykiem. Mówi się, że czasy niewolnictwa minęły i każdy decyduje o własnym losie, nikt nie może nikogo do niczego zmuszać. Ale czy to prawda? GÓWNO PRAWDA!

Mojs i cała jego wazeliniarska świta nie mają zasad. Zastanawiam się, czy ci ludzie zawsze byli tacy, czy dopiero później takimi się stali. W obozach koncentracyjnych nazywaliby się kapo. Gnębiliby swoich po to, by uratować od komory gazowej własną dupę.

Tu nie ma komór gazowych, krematoriów, drutów kolczastych pod prądem, a mimo to Mojs i jego mendy to faszyści.

*

Na stancji nie opowiadam za wiele o pracy, zresztą bracia nie pytają. Tylko raz, gdy po którymś dyżurze wróciłem z ciężkimi powiekami, spytali, jak było, tylko raz.

Oni rzadko mają wolne. Każdego ranka zachrzaniają do marketu. Dziś nie poszli do pracy, pewnie dlatego ich widok tak mnie irytuje. Człowiek zmęczony to człowiek drażliwy; idę spać. Nie chcę konfliktów. Wróciłem z dyżuru, jestem zmęczony. Odkąd mieszkamy razem, tylko raz się pokłóciliśmy. Poszło o garnek.

Agata zwolnił się z batonów. Często gadał, że rzuci tę robotę w cholerę. Opowiadał, że wyemigruje do Hiszpanii, bo tam jest ciepło, a Hiszpanki są dużo piękniejsze od Polek. Z początku myślałem, że tylko się tak zgrywa, że wcale nie zamierza zwalniać się z batonów. Uwierzyłem dopiero wtedy, kiedy ogłosił to inspektorowi. Dyżur bez tego pajaca?

Okazja smutna, ale zawsze to okazja. Agata chciał, żebyśmy poszli do knajpy na Ochocie. Można w niej było siedzieć, pić piwo i na żywo oglądać psie wyścigi. Przychodziła tam stała ekipa starych znerwicowanych hazardzistów. Ich widok był nawet ciekawszy od widoku ścigających się wychudzonych hartów. Nie poszliśmy, za drogo.

Agata wrócił ze mną do Janek. Całą drogę gadał o swoich hiszpańskich planach. Mówił, że zatrudni się na budowie, a po robocie będzie używał prawdziwego życia. Chciał, żebym jechał z nim, ale jakoś nie mogłem sobie wyobrazić siebie mocującego się z cegłami.

– Jedź ze mną – namawiał mnie. – Pierdolnij to, tak jak ja. Tu nic dobrego cię nie czeka –

tłumaczył. – Tam to przynajmniej będziesz wiedział, za co robisz. Najważniejsze to pojechać i zaczepić się do pierwszej lepszej roboty.

– Jesteś pewny? A jak nie znajdziesz, to co wtedy?

Nawet nie chciał o tym słyszeć.

– Co ty gadasz? – denerwował się. – Ja nawet gnój mogę wyrzucać, byleby się zaczepić. Jak mam się dawać wykorzystywać, to za sensowne pieniądze. – Brzmiało logicznie.

Po drodze z przystanku na stację kupił dziesięć piw; jak stwierdził, tak na dobry początek. Dwa wypiliśmy po drodze. Nie licząc godziny, podczas której dowódca Wojtek pozwolił mam pokimać trochę na krześle, trzeba przyznać, jakby nie było, że obaj byliśmy zmęczeni. Dwa piwa po nieprzespanej nocy mają moc. Pewnie dlatego wchodząc po schodach, czuję, że porządnie kręci mi się w głowie.

Wrzuciłem na patelnię dwa pęta kiełbasy zwyczajnej. Zawsze kupuję zwyczajną – jest dobra i tania. Usmażyłem ją z cebulą, a potem zjedliśmy ze smakiem do chleba z masłem. Pychota! Wszystko popijaliśmy piwem prosto z butelki, jak prawdziwi twardziele.

– Masz gościa? – To Bożena, właścicielka tego przybytku. Usłyszała obcy głos, to wdrapała się na górę. Jej głowa tkwiąca między futryną a niedomkniętymi drzwiami z miejsca onieśmiela Agatę.

- Dzień dobry, pani Bożenko. Usiądzie pani z nami? - Zawsze tak do niej mówię - pani Bożenko. Nauczyłem się od braci. Piętnastego każdego miesiąca zbiera od nas za czynsz. Lekką ręką zgarnia patola, a do tego jeszcze gdzieś pracuje. Nikt nie wie, gdzie.

W mojej firmie z wypłatami grają na zwłokę. Nigdy nie mogę być pewien, kiedy wypłacą zarobione pieniądze. Jednego miesiąca płacą planowo, a przez trzy następne - jak im się chce. Przez to nie mogę zagwarantować Bożenie, że zapłacę w terminie. Jak się człowiek nagminnie spóźnia z płaceniem czynszu, to trzeba być miłym dla wyrozumiałej pani właścicielki: zapraszać do stołu, a jak się ma, to papierosem albo kieliszkiem wódki poczęstować. Ona nie odmawia, jest kobietą z krwi i kości. Poczeka, czasami nawet tydzień czeka, ale grzecznie trzeba, grzecznie i z wyczuciem.

- Nie będę wam przeszkadzać. - Stoi już w kuchni.

- Ale wcale pani nie przeszkadza, pani Bożeno. Kolega z firmy odchodzi, to przyjechał. Chciał zobaczyć, jak mieszkam, bo potem to już pewnie nie będzie okazji.

Bożena uśmiecha się do Agaty.

- To pan też jest ochraniarzem?

Agata kiwa głową.

- Tak, byłem, byłem ochraniarzem - powtarza za nią i śmieje się do mnie.

„Ochraniarz, ochraniacz" – Bożena zawsze tak gada. Często opowiada, że czuje się bezpiecznie, bo wynajmuje pokój trzem ochraniarzom albo ochraniaczom.

– Zwalnia się pan? No tak, to niebezpieczna praca, niebezpieczna – kwituje, siadając przy stole.

– To prawda, bo my to tacy prawie komandosi jesteśmy.

– No, naprawdę.

Z trudem się opanowuję, by nie parsknąć śmiechem.

– A, usiądę na chwilę – mówi Bożena. Teraz trzeba zaproponować jej piwo. Czemu nie?!

Wstaję od stołu i podchodzę do wiszącej nad zlewem suszarki na naczynia. Chwytam za szklankę.

– Zimnym piwkiem pani nie pogardzi? – Tak jak mówiłem, pełna kultura, a Bożena lubi piwo.

Siedzi z nami dobrą godzinę i opowiada o swoim byłym mężu, co ją dla młodej zdziry zostawił. To jej ulubiony temat – po raz kolejny może nabluzgać na tego, jak to ona mówi, „starego chuja".

Po godzinie Agata poznaje całą historię chuja, a Bożena w końcu schodzi do siebie.

Tego dnia dopijamy się na stancji. Wcześniej chcieliśmy pójść jeszcze do jakiejś knajpy, ale nie wyszło. Zostajemy w Jankach.

Ledwo pamiętam. Wieczorem chyba jeszcze częstowałem braci piwem, jak wrócili z pracy.

Ledwo pamiętam, a Agata został na noc. Położyliśmy się jak dwa geje do jednego łóżka i szybko usnęliśmy twardym snem.

Nad ranem obudził mnie smród. Otwieram oczy, nie widzę końca swojego tapczanu. Spoglądam na twarz Agaty, jego widzę – śpi. Podnoszę się z łóżka i wybiegam do kuchni. Cholera! Teraz sobie przypomniałem. W nocy zachciało mi się jeść. Wstawiłem jajka, miały być takie na twardo.

Potem cały dzień wietrzyłem poddasze. Dobrze, że się nie podusiliśmy. Wtedy ten jeden raz pokłóciłem się z braćmi, spaliłem im prawie nowy garnek.

*

Doba na centrum nie należy do łatwych. Człowiek zaczyna się zastanawiać, czemu to wszystko służy i czy aby nie uczestniczy w jakimś sadystycznym eksperymencie. No bo jak można głodzić ludzi i obserwować to na monitorach? Bez możliwości zjedzenia czegokolwiek trzeba stać w jednym miejscu przez dwanaście godzin albo łazić jak debil w kółko. Snuć się między samochodami na dusznych minusikach.

Po paru godzinach stania dźwięk co chwilę otwieranych wind nie robi na mnie już takiego wrażenia. Wiem, w każdym momencie może tu wjechać Mojs albo jakaś inna świnia. Dlatego jeszcze ani razu do dziewiętnastej nie pozwalam sobie na wpasowanie dupy w ten wygodny fotel, który stoi tuż za mną. Po pięciu godzinach stania na fotelu siada diabeł. Kusi mnie.

– Usiądź – mówi. – Usiądź, Patryk. Kurwa, człowieku, ileż można stać? No, usiądź, usiądź choć na chwilę, frajerze.

Jestem twardym agentem, więc do dziewiętnastej i tym razem jakoś wytrzymam. No, chyba że nie wytrzymam. Nie, nie mogę się złamać. Widzą mnie przecież na monitorach. Cholera, gdyby nie to... Po co oni zamontowali za mną to bezduszne gówno, i jeszcze ten fotel? Dlaczego on tu jest?

– Siadaj, Patryk, siadaj śmiało, przecież ledwo stoisz... – Tylko to słyszę.

Wytrzymam!

Godzę się na propozycję jednego z ociekających wazeliną dowódców. Czuję, że ładuję się w niezły kanał, ale godzę się.

Walnąć pod rząd dwie doby? To przecież szaleństwo, ale ten przydupas Mojsa i jego pieprzony adiutant, te dwie śmierdzące łajzy tak ładnie do mnie mówią. Jak dobrzy znajomi, proszą mnie o pomoc. Mają to opanowane do perfekcji, a ja zbyt długo tu stoję, by nie polecieć na ich nawijkę.

Śmierdziel w popielatej marynarce uśmiecha się. I ten jego adiutant, skurwysyn jeden! Dobrze wiem, że donosi na chłopaków. Dobrze wiem. Lata po kamerach i wszędzie zagląda.

Gdyby mógł, to w dupę by nam wjechał tą kamerą. Potem gada, że tego nie było widać, tamten przycupnął na chwilę, a jeszcze inny zbyt długo wylegiwał się na plaży. Dzięki takim łajzom Mojs wie o wszystkim.

Na każdej zmianie takich złamasów mają. Oni są jeszcze gorsi od selekcyjnych dowódców. Mówimy na nich: „adiutanci".

– Słuchaj, Patryk.

Teraz też próbuję się uśmiechnąć, ale jakoś trudno mi to przychodzi.

– Mam mały problem – mówi dowódca.

Chcę złapać odpowiednią ostrość, dlatego mrużę oczy i patrzę na niego.

– Co się stało? – pytam. Tak naprawdę miałbym to gdzieś, gdyby ten problem był rzeczywiście jego. Jeśli on mówi, że ma problem, to znaczy że tak naprawdę problem będę miał ja.

– Słuchaj. – Adiutant zaczyna potakiwać głową. – Bo widzisz, za dwa dni święta wielkanocne, nie? No i wiesz, chłopak chciałby jechać na święta do domu, a ty i tak masz daleko, to pewnie nie jedziesz, co? To wiesz... Wziąłbyś dobę za chłopaka, a potem, wiesz, jakbyś kiedyś chciał, to wiesz, on weźmie za ciebie, nie?

Myślę chwilę.

– A za kogo?

Macha ręką.

– Patryk, a czy to ważne?

Wzruszam ramionami.

– Za takiego Piotrka, nie znasz go, to przecież inna zmiana. Ale wiesz, jeszcze nie wiadomo, czy rzeczywiście za niego, bo może się okazać, że, wiesz, że może za kogoś innego. Zresztą Marek gadał coś o dodatkowym zasileniu, wiesz jak jest – święta.

Teraz zastanawiam się, czy nie powiedzieć mu, że jednak jadę odwiedzić rodzinę. Dwie doby?

– Ale to przecież aż dwie doby, dwie noce bez spania. Nogi to już wtedy na pewno mi w dupę wejdą.

– A, co ty tam gadasz. W dupę? – denerwuje się. – Jakie dwie noce? Gdzieś cię zamelinujemy, spokojnie, już ty się nie przejmuj. Pokimasz w pierwszą i drugą noc, zobaczysz. Mówię ci, będzie dobrze. A potem, jak po wypłatę staniesz, to od razu ci się miło na sercu zrobi, nie?

Znowu myślę chwilę i patrzę na adiutanta.

– Ale na pewno... Będę mógł się przespać?

– No przecież, inaczej bym cię nie prosił. Pewnie, że tak. A może Marek jeszcze jakąś premię za dyspozycyjność dorzuci. Wiesz, takie rzeczy się liczą, on potrafi docenić.

Fajnie by było, gdyby ktoś wreszcie coś u mnie docenił. Jak na razie, nie miałem okazji pokazać Mojsowi, jaki wartościowy ze mnie pracownik. Dowódca mówi, że będę mógł trochę pospać, pewnie u nich, na monitoringu. Już prędzej wolałbym na gołym cemencie gnaty złożyć, niż być posądzonym o układ z nimi, ale dwie doby to dwie doby. Jak zaproszą, trudno, skorzystam.

– Dobra – zgadzam się.

Adiutant znowu zaczyna potakiwać łbem, a dowódca z szerokim uśmiechem klepie mnie po ramieniu.

– Przerwa dziś będzie? – pytam.

– Ciężko z tym – odpowiada. – Ogólnie dziś jest niezły młyn. Nie ma człowieka na podmianki, każdy obsadza posterunki. – Podwija mankiet u marynarki i patrzy na zegarek. – Wiesz, może tak o siedemnastej będę coś więcej wiedział. Podeślę ci wtedy kogoś...

– A on? – Pokazuję paluchem na adiutanta. – On nie może podmieniać ludzi?

Adiutant robi zdziwione oczy, ale się nie odzywa.

– Nie da rady – mówi dowódca. Patrzy na niego, potem na mnie. – Dobra, zrobimy dla ciebie wyjątek, Patryk. To taka nagroda za to, że się zgodziłeś. Zjedź sobie szybciutko na minusiki do Zbycha po kluczyk i coś zjedz. Tylko pamiętaj, tak na jednej nodze i w razie czego nie chwal się chłopakom, bo zacznie się niepotrzebny pisk. My tu chwilę postoimy za ciebie. Uwijaj się z tym jedzeniem szybciutko, dobra?

Nie czekając dłużej, podbiegam do windy. Złapać wolną o tej porze to nie lada wyczyn. Od czternastej ludzie zaczynają urywać się z pracy i to urywanie trwa średnio do szesnastej. Potem na piętrach robi się luźniej.

*

Boję się tego dnia, kiedy z obładowaną jedzeniem torbą stawię się na obiekcie. Właściwie to wcale nie jestem przekonany, że dobrze zrobiłem. To wstyd pójść na rękę takim łajzom. Piotrek? Może i jest na tamtej zmianie jakiś Piotrek. Może nawet jest tam kilku Piotrków. I co z tego, skoro i tak się zgodziłem.

Nie chcę się zadręczać, ale boję się tych czterdziestu ośmiu godzin na centrum. Im dłużej o tym myślę, tym bardziej jestem pewien – źle zrobiłem.

Wiesiek puka się po czole.

– Padniesz tam, zobaczysz. Oni szukali frajera. Ja olałbym taką zabawę, chrzaniłbym ich.

– Nie będzie tak źle – mówię bez przekonania. – Postawiłem im sztywny warunek. Pierwsze to spanie, bez tego nie byłoby nawet mowy.

– A dalej? – wytrzeszcza oczy. – Może co godzina nowa dupa, co?

– O tym nie pomyślałem, ale co mi po dupie, gdybym miał głodny łazić?

Trochę narzekałem, opowiadałem im, że są problemy z przerwami na jedzenie. Żaliłem się, że nawet jeśli jakimś cudem puszczą mnie na przerwę, to cały czas tylko krzyczą przez radio, żebym już wracał. Zanim zjadę do Zbycha po klucz, mija dobre pięć minut. Powrót zajmuje tyle samo. Na jedzenie zostaje tyle, co nic.

Ostatnio taki jeden z mojej zmiany chciał przemycić kanapkę. Miał to gdzieś, czy go puszczą na przerwę, czy nie. Bystrzak Mojs go prześwietlił. W ostatniej chwili, gdy chłopak wchodził do windy, dostrzegł podejrzaną wypukłość pod olimpijką. Wystarczyło. Chłopak dostał działę i wyszło mu tak, jakby cały dyżur stał za połowę stawki. Na posterunku nie moż na wnosić jedzenia.

Braciom sprzedałem wersję poprawioną. U mnie dobro wygrywa – tamten szczęśliwie wykiwał Mojsa i nażarł się do syta. Do syta? Tak, bo miał skurczony żołądek.

– Jak mi nie zrobią przerwy, to pieprzę tę całą umowę! A ty? Na święta wyjeżdżasz? – Chcę zmienić temat.

– Jasne – odpowiada.

– To przywieź trochę domowego żarcia.

Wiesiek minę ma nietęgą.

– Z tym domowym żarciem to może być problem – mówi. – Mama niedomaga. Lekarze gadają, że to rak – wzdycha ciężko. – To mogą być jej ostatnie święta.

Nie wiem, co powiedzieć. Chcę go pocieszyć, w końcu lekarze to tylko ludzie; moją babkę też już raz pochowali. Od tamtego czasu minęło dziesięć lat, a ona żyje do tej pory i ma się całkiem dobrze.

– A tam rak! – Wzruszam ramionami. – Teraz medycyna coraz lepsza, nawet raka potrafią wyleczyć. Co chwilę się słyszy, że poradzili sobie z jakimś beznadziejnym przypadkiem.

– Dobrze by było – mruczy ponuro. – Ale z nią to może nie być tak różowo. Za późno ją obejrzeli. Zresztą – denerwuje się – jak mieli szybciej cokolwiek u niej wykryć, skoro ona wcale do lekarzy nie chodziła. Nie musiała. Całe życie nie chorowała, a teraz coś takiego...

Macham ręką.

– Nie przejmuj się, trzeba wierzyć. Bez tego to nawet katar ciężko znieść.

Boję się raka, zawsze kojarzy mi się z kostuchą.

*

W małym garnku gotuję pięć jaj na twardo – w końcu jutro święta. Dwa opakowania hermetycznie zapakowanych parówek. Trzy konserwy rybne, jeden pasztet drobiowy. Do tego cztery jabłka, żeby było zdrowo, i dwa bochenki chleba, krojonego.

Mimo że pakuję uniformy, bez problemu mieszczę to wszystko w torbie. Cały czas zastanawiam się, czy nie za mało będę miał tego jedzenia. A jak mi zabraknie? Jak mi zabraknie, to już pewnie pod sam koniec. Nie ma się czym martwić, z głodu nie zdechnę.

*

Bożena informuje nas, że zaraz po świętach wprowadzi się do nas jakiś z Koszalina.

– To bardzo miły chłopak – mówi. – Na pewno się z nim dogadacie.

Wiemy, że jest pazerna. W tych czasach to nic dziwnego. Tylko że w naszym małym pokoju stoją już trzy łóżka. Po cholerę wciskać nam jeszcze czwarte? I pakować nam jakiegoś typa z Koszalina. Koszalin? A gdzie to jest, ten Koszalin?

– Pani Bożenko! – Wiesiek robi cierpiącą minę. – Przecież u nas i tak już ścisk. No niech pani sama zobaczy, pani Bożenko. – Podchodzi do wiszącej, udającej drzwi, zielonej, grubej kotary. Odchyla ją. – No, niechże pani zobaczy, pani Bożenko. Przecież to mała klitka. Gdzie tu jeszcze dodatkowy tapczan wstawiać?

Nie jest zadowolona. Co ona myślała, że będziemy się cieszyć? Zrobi, co będzie chciała, jest właścicielką, a z większej kasy i tak nie zrezygnuje.

– Wiesiek! Co ty, chłopaku, opowiadasz? Zobacz! – Wchodzi do naszego pokoju. – Przede wszystkim powinniście tu dokładnie posprzątać. Jak w ogóle można mieszkać w takim syfie? Kiedy będzie tu posprzątane, to jeszcze dwa tapczany wejdą.

„Jasne! Czemu od razu nie postawić piętrowych pryczy?" – myślę sobie i przez chwilę zastanawiam się, ile lat będę się jeszcze musiał błąkać po takich stancjach. Na własne mieszkanie nie mam szans, a za pieniądze z pensji ledwo udaje mi się związać koniec z końcem.

– Pani Bożenko, posprzątamy – pociesza ją Wiesiek. – Ale po co pakować nam jakiegoś obcego? Jeszcze będą przez niego problemy...

– Problemy? – powtarza za nim nerwowo Bożena. – Co ty gadasz? Gdybym tak myślała, to ciebie też nie powinnam przyjąć pod swój dach. Daj już spokój! – Macha ręką. – Lepiej zróbcie tu porządek.

Wychodzi.

– Świnia jedna – syczy Wiesiek. – Teraz to, kurwa, dopiero będziemy mieli wesoło. Ona nie może się nażreć do syta tą kasą, cały czas jej mało.

– Może tamten się nie wprowadzi – mówię.

– Przecież sam gadałeś, że kiedyś też jakiś już miał się do was wprowadzać. A potem? Zrezygnował.

– Nic dziwnego! – przerywa mi. – Trzy stówy za łóżko płacić? Przecież już za dwie można coś w Jankach znaleźć. Człowiek głupi, że tyle tu siedzi. Kurwa, ona już zbiła na mnie majątek. Świnia jedna!

– Cicho... – uspakajam go.

– Pierdolę to.

Żal mi dupę ściska – święta wielkanocne, a tu do pracy. Cały czas pocieszam się, że przecież, jak wszystko, i te dwie doby w końcu miną.

Czuję niepokój. Wystarczy, że pomyślę o Mojsie, Zbychu z minusików i tej całej uprzywilejowanej grupie obślizgłych wazeliniarzy. Na myśl o nich, bez wkładania palucha, chce mi się rzygać.

Mimo że stoję tu już miesiąc, w dalszym ciągu nie mam szafki. Tak już będzie zawsze. Mojsa znowu o nią pytał nie będę. Ostatnim razem nawet nie chciał ze mną rozmawiać. Powiedział tylko, że mam mu dupy jakąś głupią szafką nie zawracać. Tak mi powiedział. Potem przez chwilę czułem się jak ostatni frajer. Frajer, bo podkuliłem ogon. Bałem się, że mnie zdzieli. On jest bardzo nerwowy i nie rozmawia z byle kim. Nic mu nie odpowiedziałem, tylko spuściłem łeb. Więcej już o szafkę pytał nie będę.

*

U ciecia najważniejsze są wytrzymałe nogi. Ja mam słabe – już po paru godzinach stania na pięterkach zaczynają mnie boleć; najpierw pięty, potem całe stopy, kolana. Wieczorem bolą mnie już nawet pachwiny. Nic fajnego, człowiek czuje się jak chory na reumatyzm staruszek. I tylko świadomość, że tuż obok ktoś inny być może czuje się tak samo, pozwala jakoś to znieść – w grupie zawsze łatwiej.

Ten obiekt to takie piekło. Z zewnątrz nowoczesny, ślicznie błyszczący, wysoki budynek, a w środku ból, głód i ludzkie tragedie. Nie wytrzymam tego długo, nie dam rady. Już pierwszego dnia żałowałem, że przeniosłem się z batonów. Mogłem trafić gorzej? Nie wiem, może gdzie indziej biją? Jeśli tak, to ja mam tu jak u Pana Boga za piecem.

Wcześniej na przywitanie podawałem każdemu rękę, teraz tylko mówię: „Cześć", i to wszystko. Tutaj ciężko jest się dobrze z kimś poznać. Jedyną okazją, by chwilę pogadać, są takie momenty jak ten, kiedy nasz profesjonalny dowódca nie zacznie jeszcze wysyłać na posterunki. Większość nie jest zbyt rozmowna. O wielkich przyjaźniach nie ma tu nawet mowy.

– Minusiki! – krzyczy Adaś. – Pójdziesz na minusiki.

To do mnie?

– Dwie doby – mówię mu. – Dwie doby pod rząd stoję.

Nie oczekuję zachwytu, ale mam nadzieję, że teraz zmieni zdanie. Może by tak klateczki? Klateczki są najlepsze. Można siedzieć na schodach i tylko co jakiś czas łeb trzeba wystawić, by sprawdzić, czy nic się nie dzieje. Byłem, to wiem.

– Jutro zostaję na drugą dobę – powtarzam, ale on tylko wzrusza ramionami.

– Pójdziesz na minusiki, kolego. Nikt mi nie przekazywał, że czterdzieści osiem. A teraz nie będę już niczego zmieniał, bo wszystko się popierdoli.

Co mnie to obchodzi, że nikt mu nie mówił?!

– Mam na minusiki iść?

– A co?

Gówno!

– Nic.

Zostawiam torbę na ziemi i wychodzę. Jestem takim dupkiem, nie walczę o swoje. Przecież on potrafi tylko grzać dupę na monitoringu. Nie ma pojęcia, jakim idiotą jest Zbychu. A może ma, tylko jeden i drugi udaje kolegę.

Witam się ze Zbychem.

– Cześć, cześć. – On tak zawsze: „Cześć, cześć", i przez pierwszą chwilę próbuje być serdeczny. – To co, Patryk? Dziś walczymy razem?

– Tak – odpowiadam i już teraz nie mogę na niego patrzeć.

Chcę wyjść, ale on coś do mnie gada.

– Dziś trzeba zwrócić szczególną uwagę na minus dwa – mówi. – Wiesz, mamy święta; lepiej, żeby nie było problemów. Wiesz, o co chodzi?

– Jasne – odpowiadam, potakując głową. Wychodzę.

*

Zbychu ma u siebie TONFĘ. Raz powiedziałem, że to pałka, to mnie opierdolił i kazał mówić na nią pałka wielofunkcyjna typu TONFA. Od tamtego czasu nawet na nią nie patrzę. Nie patrzę do momentu, kiedy ten idiota zaczyna mi nią znowu machać przed nosem.

– Stań prosto – mówi do mnie. – Stań, nie bój się. – Zaciskam zęby. – No, nie płosz się tak – wywija nią i cały czas mnie uspakaja.

Boję się, że zaraz przywali mi w głowę. Zamykam na chwilę oczy. Na chwilę, bo on uderza w obudowę monitora.

– Dobrze wymiatam? Widzisz? To jest wymiatanie, przeciwnik nie ma żadnych szans!

Jak chce wymiatać, to niech się przyjmie do firmy sprzątającej. Kiwam głową, a on znowu z hukiem uderza w monitor. Dziwne, że jeszcze go nie rozwalił.

Mam nadzieję, że to koniec, ale nieee... Teraz wkłada mi TONFĘ pod pachę, a drugą łapą przytrzymuje mnie za twarz.

– A to jest chwyt transportowy – sapie.

Czuję smród, jakbym wsadził nos do pełnej śmierdzących petów popielniczki.

– Aaaaaa! – krzyczy.

W tym samym momencie przewracam się na ziemię. Może to i jest chwyt transportowy, ale chyba właśnie wyrwał mi ramię ze stawu.

– Ałaaaaa! – Teraz ja krzyczę, a on cały czas trzyma mnie swoją śmierdzącą łapą za twarz.

– To boli! – drę się. – Puszczaj!

– Ma boleć – uspakaja mnie – bo to chwyt transportowy. Tylko ty się, kurwa, źle ustawiłeś. Stań inaczej, to powtórzymy. – Łapie mnie pod pachy i pomaga podnieść się z podłogi.

– Nieee! – protestuję. – Może innym razem.
– Demonstracyjnie masuję ramię. – Ręka mnie
boli – tłumaczę mu. – Już wystarczy.
– Mięczak z ciebie – śmieje się.
– Mięczak? Prawie wyrwałeś mi rękę.
Parska.
– Tak, kurwa! Może jeszcze głowę ci urwa-
łem, co? Idź i się poskarż! Najlepiej od razu
rozpłacz się Mojsowi w klapy, to może cię przy-
tuli.
– Nie będę się skarżył. Mówię tylko, że boli
mnie ramię.
– I co? Może to moja wina? Mówiłem ci, że
się źle ustawiłeś. Jakbyś się dobrze ustawił, to
wszystko by poszło jak trzeba. Przestań się,
człowieku, podniecać, przecież nic ci, kurwa,
nie jest.
Nie pytając go, czy mogę, wychodzę na parking. Co robić? Jak mnie następnym razem zawoła, będę udawał, że nie słyszę, albo powiem,
że mi radio padło. Tak, powiem, że mi padła
krótkofalówka.
Dlaczego nie jestem dwumetrowym osiłkiem
z łapami jak bochny chleba? Wtedy ten idiota
odnosiłby się do mnie z szacunkiem. Jak nie, to
ja bym go naderwał. Metr siedemdziesiąt wzro-
stu w rozchodzonych butach z twarzą zmęczo-
nego chłostą pokutnika – to nie robi na nikim
wrażenia.

*

Wcześniej to mi się zdarzało, kiedy miałem czegoś naprawdę dość. A teraz? Cholera, ja prawie cały czas, jak jakiś psychol, gadam do siebie. Łażąc po minusikach, stojąc na pięterkach, na Chocimskiej, mamroczę pod nosem. Teraz też – snuję się po pustym parkingu i cały czas bluzgam na Zbycha: „Ty chuju, ty gnoju", i takie tam. Cały czas. Wszędzie kamery. Trzeba improwizować. Kiedy łapię się na tym, że gadam do siebie, to udaję, że żuję gumę. Nie chciałbym być wzięty za obłąkańca, nieświadomie memłającego japą.

*

Na samą myśl o jajach na twardo, jak pies na widok kości, dostaję ślinotoku. Nie liczyłem, że zrobią podmiankę na czas, ale dziś chyba zupełnie sobie przerwę odpuścili.

– Bufet!

Cisza. Nie chcę rozdrażniać idioty. On już pewnie podwieczorek wpierdala.

– Bufet!

Idę do niego; nie chcę, ale idę (kurwa mać, ja pierdolę...). Dobrze, że mam gumę.

Zbychu zrywa się na równe nogi. To, że przerwałem mu sen, jest nieważne. Jestem głodny, chce mi się jeść!

– Co się stało? Dlaczego nie zgłaszasz do interkomu obchodów?

Bezczelny, zaspany, przesiąknięty nikotyną chuj.

– Chciałem pójść coś zjeść. Jestem głodny, a przerwy cały czas nie ma. W torbie mam parówki, jeszcze się zepsują.

– A ja się pytam, dlaczego nie zgłaszasz obchodów?

– Zgłaszam, tylko nie słyszałeś. – Spałeś, debilu. – Cały czas zgłaszałem, poważnie.

– Poważnie to się w grobie leży, ale dobra, nie będę tego roztrząsał. Masz tu klucze, tylko szybko.

Chwytam za nie jakby były z porcelany i delikatnie wkładam do kieszeni. Teraz na chwilę zapominam, że to palant, i nawet czuję wobec niego wdzięczność. W końcu pozwala mi jeść bez regulaminowej podmianki. Może jednak nie jest taki zły.

Biegnę do przebieralni. Micha mi się cieszy, jakbym za chwilę kończył dyżur. Z radości jeszcze bardziej chce mi się jeść.

Siadam przy chropowatym od zaschniętych plam stole. Otwieram torbę i pierwsze, co czuję, to zapach tych jaj na twardo. W tym samym momencie uświadamiam sobie, że zapomniałem odsypać sobie trochę soli do papieru. Trudno, zjem bez, ponoć zdrowiej. Majonezu też nie mam; dobrze, że o chlebie nie zapomniałem.

Przerwa trwa kwadrans, ale Zbychu nie powiedział, ile mogę tu siedzieć. Kazał tylko się uwijać, a to znaczy że posiedzę dłużej. W końcu są święta.

Bóg mi świadkiem, chcę wszystko puścić w niepamięć, ale kiedy tu wchodzi i zaczyna mnie szarpać, to jak kostka lodu wrzucona do gotującej się wody, wszystko we mnie topnieje i pęka. Cała ta chwilowa sympatia, zbudowana na jajach na twardo bez majonezu i soli – wszystko to ginie.

W pierwszym momencie nie mogę uwierzyć. To naprawdę on? Przecież jeszcze parę minut temu z przymkniętymi pobłażliwie oczami pozwolił mi zjeść. A teraz? A teraz chyba o tym zapomniał, bo cały czas mną szarpie.

– Co ty, kurwa, sobie myślisz! – krzyczy. – Jesteś jakimś wybrańcem?

Jakim wybrańcem? Ja tylko cieszyłem się, że zjem, a teraz prawie dławię się kęsem jaja na twardo.

(Kurwa, ty chuju!!!)

– O co ci chodzi, Zbyszek?

– Wypierdalaj na parking! Jakbym wiedział, że jesteś taki bezczelny, to mógłbyś zapomnieć o przerwie!

Podnoszę się z krzesła i poprawiam wygnieciony przez jego łapska uniform.

– Ja jestem bezczelny? – Boję się, że zaraz wpadnie w jeszcze większą furię – przecież to wariat. – Mówiłeś, że mogę iść...

– Nie dyskutuj, kurwa, ze mną, tylko wypierdalaj, bo zaraz wpiszę cię w raport. Mojs ci wtedy zajebie taką działę, że spuchniesz. Zobaczysz!

– Za co działę? – Dalej nie mogę zrozumieć całej tej sytuacji. Dlaczego ten idiota tak się pieki? – Za co miałbym dostać tę działę? Za to, że jestem głodny? Czy za to, że ty śpisz i nie słyszysz, jak zgłaszam obchody?

Uśmiecha się szeroko, a jego jeszcze przed chwilą wściekłe, pełne agresji spojrzenie staje się niemal landrynkowe. Kolejna maska? Widać ma ich wiele.

– O czym ty, kolego, mówisz? Kto śpi? – Mruży przekrwione oczy.

– Noo, nie ja – odpowiadam. – Ja cały czas tylko łażę.

– Chyba, kurwa, jesteś niepoważny. Kończ już to żarcie i zacznij robić obchody.

Wychodzi i trzaska drzwiami.

(Wypierdalaj!)

*

Mój ojciec za parę lat pójdzie na, jak to on zwykł mówić, zasłużoną emeryturę. Fajnie, ja w jego wieku będę mógł zapomnieć o zasłużonej emeryturze. Właściwie to cholera wie, kim będę w jego wieku. Jak na razie wszystko przemawia za tym, że nikim. Mówi się, że jeśli ktoś wdepnie w cieciostwo, to już nigdy z niego nie wyjdzie. Bardzo chciałbym wierzyć, że i tu zdarzają się wyjątki. Agata miał wyjechać do Hiszpanii na budowę, ale wcale bym się nie zdziwił, gdybym go tu któregoś dnia zobaczył. Pewnie by powiedział, że nie wyszło, i tym razem to już naprawdę tylko na chwilę. Z tej chwili zrobiłby się rok, potem jeszcze jeden i... No właśnie, można się zasiedzieć, a potem jest już za późno, by cokolwiek zmienić. Zostaje się cieciem na dobre, do śmierci. A szanse, by w tym zawodzie doczekać emerytury, są tak wątłe, jak morale przeciągniętego przez minusiki stojaka.

Na batonach pracował taki jeden. On podzielił wszystkich agentów ochrony na dwie grupy. Pierwsza grupa to tacy jak ja. Z obolałymi nogami drepczą wzdłuż linii kas w marketach. Stoją na piętrach wysokich biurowców, łażą po parkingach. Czasami trzymają w ręku trzeszczące krótkofalowe radio z antenką, ale i tak gówno znaczą.

Tacy jak ja to ciecie classic. Jeśli classic czuje w sercu misję, to ma lepiej. Nic tak nie uskrzydla, jak wiara w to, co się robi. Takich nie brakuje, tacy są wszędzie. Szczycą się tym, że pracują w ochronie. Do domu wracają w swoich przepoconych cieciowskich uniformach – już nieraz takich widziałem. Jadąc tramwajem na dyżur, z dumą prezentują naszywki z logiem firmy: Pantera, Jastrząb, albo jakiś inny drapieżnik. Agencje ochrony lubią „mocne" nazwy. Niejeden trafiający tam od razu czuje awans społeczny i z dumą prezentuje na plecach swej czarnej kurtki gumowany napis: „Ochrona", nawet wtedy, kiedy zbiera porozrzucane na parkingu wózki sklepowe, łączy je w długie rzędy i pcha, pcha pod wiatę. Zimą odśnieża, a latem podlewa i strzyże trawniki. To agent ochrony! Człowiek do zadań specjalnych, za marne grosze wyrabiający dwieście procent normy.

Druga grupa to ciecie exclusive, tak zwana interwencja w samochodach albo konwojenci w pancerkach. Kiedyś myślałem, że to tacy trochę antyterroryści, bo ubrani tak jakoś podobnie. A na firmowych ulotkach reklamowych to nawet i lepiej. Prawdziwi zamaskowani supermeni. Ale to też ciecie; niejednokrotnie są jeszcze gorsi od zwykłych stojaków.

Na mojej zmianie pracuje eksexclusive, ma na imię Jurek. Przenieśli go do Mojsa, jak sam mówił, za karę. Miał za długie czasy dojazdów i nie bardzo potrafił spamiętać te wszystkie obiekty chronione. Na początku chcieli go wywalić, bo pojechał na wezwanie tam, gdzie nie trzeba, a potem z każdym kolejnym dyżurem jeszcze bardziej się gubił. Mieli zamiar go wywalić, ale ostatecznie dali mu szansę – przenieśli go tu, na centrum.

W szatni opowiadał o swoich byłych kolegach z grup interwencyjnych. Mówił, że jeździł kiedyś z takim jednym, jak go nazwał, kurwiarzem. Kurwiarz przez cały czas tylko o bzykaniu gadał. Przez cały dyżur chwalił się, ile to dup w życiu przeleciał. W samochodowym schowku trzymał zawsze świeżą prasę kolorową. Raz w godzinach pracy tak się tą prasą rozochocił, że wzięło go na burdel. Niestety, dostali alarm i z jazdy do burdelu ostatecznie wyszły nici. Potem, kiedy mieli razem nockę, wyszedł na siku i długo nie wracał. Jurek poszedł go szukać, bo znowu wezwanie, nie wiadomo, gdzie jechać, a tu kurwiarza nigdzie nie ma. Znalazł go pod drzewem, jak siedząc w kucki, bawił się małym. Tak się brandzlował, że o bożym świecie zapomniał, a przecież Jurek śpieszył się na alarm.

Innym razem jeździł z facetem, który widział tylko na jedno oko. Na dodatek miał biedak padaczkę i strasznie seplenił. Facet podszedł do sprawy uczciwie. Powiedział, że ma epilepsję, ale Jurek nie zrozumiał. Pomyślał, że to chodzi o to ślepe oko, no i stało się. Traf chciał, że nowy kolega już na pierwszym dyżurze dostał ataku, i wtedy Jurek dowiedział się, że ta epilepsja to nie ślepe oko, że facet najzwyczajniej w świecie ma padaczkę, że nim rzuca i że już nie będą mogli razem jeździć.

Choć z początku obiecał sobie, że tego nie zrobi, to rano podpierdolił faceta do inspektora. Inspektor kazał nie rozpowiadać o tym, co stało się na dyżurze. Następną służbę przejeździł już z innym kolegą, a faceta z padaczką zwolnili.

Jurek miał potem moralniaka, ale nie chciał drugi raz patrzeć, jak facetem telepie. Żeby poprawić sobie humor, powtarzał, że to w końcu jest ochrona, a nie szpital. Tak sobie tłumaczył i tak sobie tłumaczy do dziś. Szpital czy nie – w tej branży grupę inwalidzką dobrze jest mieć. To podnosi kwalifikacje i zwiększa szanse na długą pracę. Dla firm ochroniarskich dobry agent to niepełnosprawny agent. Tamten z padaczką miał pecha – z wodogłowiem i garbem na plecach pewnie pracowałby do dziś.

*

Podchodzę do Zbycha; na jego widok trochę trzęsą mi się kolana. Nie ze strachu. Po prostu nie mogę już patrzeć na tego głupka, denerwuję się cały. On chyba zapomniał, że jeszcze przed momentem szarpał mną jak liną cumowniczą. Zapomniał, bo teraz patrzy na mnie i głupio się uśmiecha.

Kładę klucz na brzegu jego biurka. Staram się na niego nie patrzeć. (Masz, chuju).

– Oddaję – mówię cicho i jak rozgniewana panienka po nieudanej randce odkręcam się na pięcie.

Chcę z stąd wyjść, jak najszybciej opuścić to zadymione, ciemne pomieszczenie, ale on zaczyna teraz do mnie gadać. Nie jestem na tyle silny, by go zignorować. Odwracam się z powrotem do niego i próbuję tak jak on udawać, że nic się nie stało.

– No, jeszcze tylko dwie godzinki, nie? – mówi, patrząc na zegarek.

Kiwam głową i zastanawiam się: „Po cholerę on mi teraz to gada?".

– Będę już szedł – łapię za klamkę.

– Patryk!

Znowu odwracam się do niego.

– Mam nadzieję, że się dobrze zrozumieliśmy?

Znowu zagadka?

– Zrozumieliśmy?

Przeciąga się na krześle.

– Bo coś tam gadałeś, że niby spałem, nie?

Macham ręką.

– Pewnie mi się zdawało.

Wychodzę.

*

W takie dni chciałoby się znowu być małym dzieckiem i w napięciu czekać na prezent. Pamiętam z jaką radością wyczekiwałem świąt, szczególnie tych Bożego Narodzenia. Święta wielkanocne z powodu prezentów zawsze były na drugim miejscu – na Wielkanoc było ich mniej. No i Mikołaj, Mikołaj to był ktoś. Zając nie miał już takiej charyzmy.

*

Cała noc na ulicy? Myślałem, że dadzą mi klateczki! Po dwunastce na minusikach dowalili mi Chocimską. Lepiej być nie mogło! Na Chocimskiej na pewno oka nie zmrużę, a przecież miałem trochę pokimać. Jutro czeka mnie druga doba! Nie, nie mogę tak się dawać – idę do Mojsa, muszę to wyjaśnić. Przypomnę mu, że jutro mam drugą dobę, pewnie o tym zapomniał. Coś musiało im się pokręcić; nie będę przez to całą noc po ulicy łaził. Nie taka była umowa.

Pukam do drzwi. Już słyszę głośny śmiech Mojsa; po co miałby spędzać święta z rodziną?! Drzwi otwiera adiutant. Kiedy mnie widzi, robi duże oczy.

– A czego ty tu chcesz? – pyta, zatrzymując mnie w progu.

– Muszę pogadać z inspektorem. – Przeciskam się między nim a futryną, a dowódca, widząc mnie, wykrzywia usta.

Mojs patrzy raz na mnie, raz na niego. Wygląda, jakby chciał zwymiotować.

– Co kurwa? – Mruga nerwowo powiekami. – Co on tu robi?

– Nie wiem – mówi Adaś. – Powinien być na Chocimskiej. – Wstaje z krzesła. – Co ty tu robisz?

– Jutro mam drugą dobę i chciałem spytać, czy nie da się zmienić mi posterunku. Bo jutro...

– Co, kurwa?! Czego ty, kurwa, chcesz? Co jutro?! – Dowódca wytrzeszcza oczy. – Wiesz, co ty teraz zrobiłeś?!

Przecież wiem, co zrobiłem. Chcę tylko coś powiedzieć, wytłumaczyć, dlaczego tak, ale teraz włącza się Mojs. Nie, żebym bardzo liczył na obronę z jego strony, w końcu zszedłem z posterunku, i takie tam. Są święta, a ja jutro będę stać tu drugą dobę; zgodziłem się.

– Spierdalaj pan na posterunek! No już, nie widzę cię tutaj! – Podchodzi do drzwi. Otwiera je nerwowo, szarpiąc za klamkę. Otwiera je na całą szerokość i wypycha mnie na korytarz. – Na posterunek! – powtarza. Jego krzyk odbija się echem od ścian, a adiutant zamyka z trzaskiem drzwi.

Nie wierzę, to jakiś absurd! Gdzie ta wdzięczność, gdzie?! Zostaję sam, sam z moim problemem. Skurwiele.

Teraz najchętniej zrzuciłbym z siebie te uniformy i poszedł na stancję, nawet na piechotę. Do rana bym doszedł, a potem? Potem położyłbym się do łóżka i spał całą dobę. Jak sobie pomyślę, jaki jestem głupi, to aż chce mi się wyć. Ja tego nie wytrzymam. Dlaczego się zgodziłem na ten drugi dyżur? Już teraz jestem zmęczony i chyba naprawdę zaraz stąd wyjdę, tylko wtedy ten skurwiel mi nie zapłaci. Za samowolne zejście z obiektu wyrzucają i zamiast pieniędzy za przepracowane godziny dostaje się marne ochłapy. Tak robią, już nieraz o tym słyszałem; beznadziejna sprawa. Nikt nie wygra z tą bandą oszustów.

*

Wracam na Chocimską. I pomyśleć, że wczoraj była ciepła noc. „CHOCIMSKA, NIE ŚPIJ! NIE WIDAĆ CIĘ W KAMERACH! NO JUŻ, ŁAZISZ!" – odgrywają się na mnie, cały czas to słyszę. Nie mogę sobie poukładać tego wszystkiego w głowie. Z nerwów aż mnie mdli.

Łażę w tę i z powrotem. I tak do rana? Nie inaczej. Ci z monitoringu pewnie cały czas patrzą na mnie. A może nie patrzą? Kiedy zaczynam się nad tym zastanawiać, na chwilę przystaję. Kucam i odpoczywam, przez moment. Pod pretekstem rozwiązanego sznurowadła. Kucam. Odwiązuję, zawiązuję i znowu wstaję. Jak sobie pomyślę, że jest tyle innych zawodów, a ja wybrałem akurat pracę ciecia, to aż mnie skręca. Który normalny facet dobrowolnie uczestniczyłby w takim cyrku. Na batonach miałem chociaż kumpla, a tu? Tacy, jak to się mówi, anonimowi koledzy z szatni, i na tym koniec. Szkoda, że nie można łazić we dwóch, stać parami na pięterkach. Wtedy byłoby inaczej, można by pogadać, pożalić się do kolegi. A tak, cały czas sam ze sobą, jak jakiś pustelnik na podglądzie. Przesrane.

Po drugiej stronie ulicy chrapliwie szczeka pies. To bernardyn. Jest stary, ledwo łazi i pewnie to szczekanie kosztuje go niemało zdrowia. On pilnuje terenu przychodni lekarskiej, ja pilnuję centrum biznesowego. Cieć z przychodni prawie nie wychodzi ze swej ciepłej budki. Fajnie ma, nie musi łazić. Zresztą, po co ma łazić?! Całą noc śpi jak w domu, od pilnowania ma psa. Na kontrolę też nikt do niego nie przyjeżdża; ale w agencji Comando Plus gorzej płacą, a mnie po opłaceniu wynajmu i tak zostaje ledwo na śmieciowe jedzenie. Inaczej ma taki były trep, żołnierz znaczy, albo gliniarz. Oni mogą pracować w Comando Plus. Jedna czwarta cieci to tacy byli policyjni lub wojskowi, młodzi „zasłużeni" emeryci po czterdziestce. To oni zaniżają nam stawki, im się zawsze opłaca. Mają niemałe emerytury – emerytury, o których styrany robotą sześćdziesięciopięcioletni cywil może sobie tylko pomarzyć. I gdzie tu, kurwa, sprawiedliwość?

– CHOCIMSKA! CHOCIMSKA, ZGŁOŚ SIĘ!

Czego oni chcą? Przecież łażę!

– Zgłaszam się.

– NIE ŚPIJ, CHOCIMSKA!

– Nie śpię.

Już długo ich nie słyszałem, może z godzinę. Przecieram oczy i przyśpieszam kroku. Jest północ, do rana jeszcze daleko. Po jaką cholerę patrzę cały czas na zegarek? Co dyżur obiecuję sobie, że nie będę na niego zerkał, i co dyżur nie mogę wytrwać w tym postanowieniu. Dopiero jutro o tej porze zacznę odliczać, a teraz ponucę coś pod nosem, tak dla otuchy, albo pogwiżdżę, gwizdanie wychodzi mi lepiej. Nucić to można w łazience, przy goleniu.

Ten cholerny pies znowu szczeka. Przecież nikt nie kręci się pod ich bramą – zauważyłbym to.

– Zamknij się – syczę pod zziębniętym nosem. – Zamknij się, kudłaty, stary kundlu. Zdechniesz od tego szczekania. Zobaczysz, zdechniesz jeszcze dziś.

Tamten cieć twardo śpi. Wynieśliby takiego razem z budą, a on by się nawet nie ocknął. Spałby dalej, otoczony parawanem zaparowanych szyb.

*

Idziemy z Wieśkiem po piwo. W Jankach stawiają akurat nowy salon samochodowy. Budowy „pilnuje" jakiś cieć. Traf chce, że przechodzimy blisko jego małej budy. Wiesiek ma ochotę pogadać. Tak zwyczajnie chce zapytać o stawkę i takie tam, jak kolega kolegę po fachu. No i wtedy okazuje się, że kolega po fachu śpi w najlepsze. Wszystko można zrozumieć, w końcu spanie to ludzka rzecz, ale tak w biały dzień, kiedy budowlańcy po placu łażą? Niee, aż tak to nie można.

Wiesiek stuka w małe niedomknięte okienko – nic to nie daje. Tamten cały czas śpi jak zabity, leży na styropianie z wywaloną do góry szeroką dupą i głośno chrapie.

– Zobacz! – Wiesiek pokazuje palcem służbową tandetną latarkę. – Weźmiemy ją?

Uchyla szerzej okienko i sięga po nią bez problemu. Chowa ją pod kurtkę i znowu, tym razem dużo mocniej, zaczyna stukać w okno. Żadnej reakcji. Gdyby nie chrapliwy oddech, można by pomyśleć, że facet nie żyje.

– Po cholerę go budzisz? Niech śpi – szepczę, ale Wiesiek tylko się śmieje.

– Zrobimy mu kawał. – Cały czas się śmieje.

– Powiemy mu, że jesteśmy tymi, no... – Drapie się za uchem. – Inspektorami! Zobaczysz, łyknie.

Krzywię się trochę, no bo jak to tak, żeby cieć cieciowi kawały wykręcał?

– Wstawaj pan, nie ma leżenia. Kontrola!

Facet rusza nogą, potem unosi głowę. Chwilę nasłuchuje, aż w końcu jak polany lodowatą wodą zrywa się na równe nogi.

– No, co się dzieje!? – Wiesiek wczuwa się w rolę. – Co pan się tak patrzysz? Przyjechaliśmy na kontrolę, a tu coś takiego!

Facet ma nietęgą minę.

– Na kontrolę? – powtarza zdławionym głosem za Wieśkiem.

– Tak! Da pan dziennik służb.

Facet podaje mu przez okienko jakiś cienki, wymięty zeszyt w kratkę i długopis, a Wiesiek, opierając się o ścianę budy, zaczyna dokonywać wpisu. Potem oddaje mu go z powrotem i każe otworzyć drzwi.

Ładujemy się do ciasnej cieciówki. Strasznie tu nasmrodzone – pierdy i pot. Wiesiek zaczyna się rozglądać i pyta o latarkę:

– A w nocy tak bez latarki obchody pan robisz? – groźnie, tak jak trzeba.

Facet wodzi wzrokiem po pustym miejscu przy oknie. Dobrze wie, że powinna tam stać.

– Tu w nocy widno – tłumaczy. – Lampy świecą.

– No, ale latarkę to pan chyba masz?

– Mam.

– A gdzie?

Jeszcze raz przebiega wzrokiem po miejscu koło uchylonego okna, potem po podłodze i po swoim legowisku z połamanych płyt styropianowych.

– Zepsuła się, to ją do domu zabrałem. Coś nie łączy, naprawić trzeba.

Taka robota by nam chyba pasowała.

– Aha. – Wiesiek kiwa głową ze zrozumieniem i w tej samej chwili wyciąga spod kurtki latarkę. – A to? – pyta z satysfakcją. – Co to jest?

– Latarka – odpowiada facet i zawstydzony spuszcza wzrok.

Obaj z Wieśkiem ciężko wzdychamy; w tym momencie ważą się losy naszego ciecia.

– Tym razem podarujemy panu – mówi Wiesiek. – Ale jeśli jeszcze raz to się powtórzy, to już tacy dobrzy nie będziemy. Na posterunku trzeba być czujnym!

Wychodzimy bez pożegnania, a potem jeszcze długo śmiejemy się z faceta.

*

Teraz za to pokutuję. Tamten w budzie przy grzejniku śni o gołych babach, a ja na Chocimskiej, i zimno jak cholera. Dobrze, że jeszcze deszcz nie pada.

Łażę i gwiżdżę; jak gwiżdżę, to od razu robi mi się lepiej – jak tej dziewczynce z baśni Andersena. Tylko że ona humor poprawiała sobie zapałkami.

Najważniejsze, by się nie załamać i nie stracić... No właśnie, czego nie stracić? Świeżości? Nie wypalić się? Gówno! Po dwóch dobach ciężko będzie mówić o świeżości. W mordę! Masz za swoje, frajerze.

– CHOCIMSKA, GDZIE JESTEŚ?

Podbiegam do interkomu.

– Tak, słucham?

– CO, KURWA, SŁUCHAM?

To Mojs. Co mu się nie podoba? Przecież łażę, jak kazał, tam i z powrotem. A może na chwilę przysnąłem? Niee, przecież cały czas gwiżdżę. Nie ma mowy, jak mógłbym spać i gwizdać. To niemożliwe.

– Tak?

Boże, jaki jestem potulny, brzydzę się sobą. Normalny facet już dawno przez ten głośniczek posłałby mu parę „chujów", a ja? A ja jestem potulną pipką. No cóż, może kiedyś to zmienię.

– ŁAŹ PAN OD KOŃCA DO KOŃCA BUDYNKU! TAK MOŻESZ PAN SOBIE PO PARKU Z PSEM NA SMYCZY SPACEROWAĆ! ZROZUMIAŁEŚ PAN?

(Ty opasły ryju!)

– Dobrze!

*

Już świta. Od godziny zastanawiałem się, czy tam, za tym grubym pniem, nie czai się Mojs. Od godziny wydaje mi się, że tam ktoś stoi, jakby się przede mną chował. Ale po jaką cholerę miałby się chować? Przecież ja i tak już ledwo stoję. Nie, zwyczajnie mam zwidy, bo ta czająca się za drzewem postać to jakaś narośl albo kikut po ściętym konarze. Sprawdziłem to, w końcu jestem ochroniarzem. A teraz, kiedy zrobiło się już całkiem widno, aż sam się sobie dziwię, jak takie głupoty mogły mi do łba trafiać. Przecież to tylko narośle albo... wiadomo, zwykła ścięta gałąź.

W moją stronę idzie człowiek. To chyba nowy, nigdy wcześniej go nie widziałem. Tak, to na pewno nowy. Im jest bliżej, tym bardziej jestem tego pewien. Szczerzy zęby, jakby przed momentem dowiedział się, że idzie na klateczki. Nic z tego, kolego – teraz ty będziesz tu łaził, i tak do wieczora, calutkie dwanaście godzin, a może dłużej, kto wie?

– Cześć!

Dziwnie jest o tej porze widzieć taki entuzjazm. Chłopak wyciąga do mnie rękę.

– Cześć.

– Zmieniasz mnie? – Nawet nie patrzę, czy kiwa głową. Trę oczy i marzę, żeby gdzieś usiąść, chociaż na kwadrans, na pięć minut, na chwilę.

– Tak – odpowiada. – Dowódca mówił, że powiesz mi, o co chodzi.

– O co chodzi? – powtarzam za nim, łapiąc ostrość. Dać mu do zrozumienia, że to prostacka robota? Na czym miałoby polegać to moje wprowadzenie go na ten posterunek? Co tu tłumaczyć? – Gdzie wcześniej stałeś?

– Nigdzie – odpowiada. – To moja pierwsza robota.

Znowu zaczynam trzeć oczy. Co tu gadać? Przy nim jestem prawdziwym zawodowcem – to zobowiązuje. Przybieram swobodną pozę i na chwilę nawet zapominam o bólu w nogach. Po nieprzespanej nocy spędzonej na ulicy ciężko jest zgrywać luzaka. Nie wiem zatem, dlaczego próbuję na siłę zamazać własne przekonania. Zamiast powiedzieć mu, żeby stąd spierdalał, zaczynam mu wciskać jakieś banały.

– Widzisz, to jest ulica Chocimska – mówię i na moment robię pauzę. – O, widzisz? – Pokazuję palcem boczną elewację budynku. – Od początku do końca w tamtą stronę i z powrotem, tak masz chodzić. Tylko nie łaź, jakbyś przechadzał się po parku z psem na smyczy. Dokładnie obserwuj teren, to bardzo ważne. Różni się tu kręcą. Teraz są święta, więc będziesz miał luz, ale w normalne dni nie jest tu tak spokojnie. Czasami trzeba nawet ruchem pokierować, prawie jak policja.

Chłopak słucha w milczeniu, jakbym mu przekazywał jakąś bezcenną życiową radę. To skupienie rysujące się na jego twarzy jest przerysowane, tak samo jak moje pieprzenie.

– Musisz bardzo uważać – powtarzam.

Na odchodne pytam go jeszcze o imię, potem odwracam się i wchodzę do budynku. Dziwnie się czuję.

*

Cieszę się, że jestem już na półmetku. W sumie, nie licząc dwunastu godzin spędzonych na minusikach, szarpaniny ze Zbychem i zapamiętanej zbyt dokładnie opasłej mordy Mojsa... W sumie, gdyby nie to, to nawet... Chociaż nieee... Ta Chocimska, Chocimska przed kolejną dobą? Kurestwo!

Nie chcę tego rozpamiętywać, po cholerę psuć sobie humor od samego rana?! Muszę teraz gdzieś przycupnąć; nogi wbijają mi się w tyłek, a stopy drętwieją, bolą, pieką i swędzą na przemian. Są jak nie moje. Najbardziej dokuczają mi pięty. Nie wiem, ale mam wrażenie, jakby miała się przez nie przebić kość. To przez te niewygodne, rozchodzone buciory – wyglądam w nich jak łajza. Już dwa razy chciałem wymienić je na nowe, ale za każdym razem okazuje się, że nie ma mojego rozmiaru. Ostatnio magazynier chciał mi wcisnąć jeszcze gorzej zjechane od moich. Mówił, że ktoś je tylko raz założył. Kłamliwa wesz. Jak mu powiedziałem, że jeśli raz, to pewnie długo ich nie zdejmował, to się zdenerwował i zaczął na mnie krzyczeć. Wydzierał się, że to magazyn mundurowy, a nie Lord i Bata.

*

Wchodzę do szatni. Dziś na posterunki wysyła Henio. To on chciał, żebym wziął tę drugą dobę. Zapytam go teraz, dlaczego nie uzgodnił nic z Adasiem. Powiem mu, że jestem zmęczony, bo w ogóle nie spałem – nawet minuty, a mówił, że będzie dobrze.

Podchodzę do niego.

– Cześć! – Podaję mu rękę i witam się z resztą.

Wracam do dowódcy. Czytając z kartki, zaczyna wysyłać na posterunki. Taka kartka dodaje powagi całej sprawie. To znaczy że nie ma odwrotu, będzie tak, jak na kartce, i koniec. Tylko Mojs może zmienić to, co jest tam napisane. On może dokonywać zmian w planach dowódcy, on może wszystko.

– Na piętereko – mówi do mnie niewzruszonym głosem; jakbym mu nigdy żadnej przysługi nie wyświadczył.

– Na pięterko?

– No! – Nawet na mnie nie patrzy.

– Całą noc po Chocimskiej łaziłem – żalę się, jakbym wierzył, że te moje skargi coś zmienią.

– Nie da się na klateczki? – Mrużę do niego porozumiewawczo oczy, jak do sklepowej, która akurat schowała pod ladą rzadki delikates. Chcę dać do zrozumienia temu ważniakowi, że powinien mnie na klateczki wysłać, że to będzie jedyna słuszna decyzja i wtedy od razu o wszystkim zapomnę. Zapomnę, że mnie okłamał, że nie ma za grosz honoru i że w ogóle jest wredną świnią, która nie potrafi dotrzymać słowa.

– Nie mogę – mówi i pokazuje mi te gryzmoły. – O, zobacz, na klateczki idzie Wojtck. Chłopak źle się czuje. Jak się z nim dogadasz, to nie ma sprawy. Możecie się przecież zamienić, ja nie będę wnikał; tylko musicie się jakoś dogadać.

On dobrze wie, że nikt przy zdrowych zmysłach nie zamieni się na żaden inny posterunek. Ja bym się nie zamienił.

– Który poziom?

– Racja. – Henio robi słodką minę. – Na pierwsze – mówi – żebyś nie musiał wysoko wjeżdżać.

– A mogę chociaż coś zjeść? Do przerwy daleko.

Nadyma policzki.

– Paaatryk, teraz? Kurwa, poczekaj godzinkę, jak się wszystko trochę uspokoi. Ludzie jeszcze nie ustawieni, a ty o bufet krzyczysz. Poczekaj, to ci dam podmiankę. Chociaż... Marek mówił, że wczoraj dałeś ciała, z posterunku zszedłeś? Wzruszam ramionami. Nie będę mu teraz o tym opowiadał; i tak pewnie wszystko dokładnie przekazał mu Adaś.

– Godzinka?

– Tak – kiwa głową. – Aaa, bym zapomniał. Powiedziałeś tamtemu, co ma robić? Temu, co cię zmieniał na Chocimskiej. On jest zieloniutki, pierwszy dyżur – śmieje się.

– Tak, wie, o co chodzi.

– To dobrze – odpowiada z troską.

*

Wdrażanie nie zawsze jest łatwe.

Mówiliśmy na niego „Chemik" albo „Chemiczny Ali", jak kto wolał. Facet, jak sam się chwalił, skończył chemię na Uniwersytecie Warszawskim, ale długo w zawodzie nie pracował. Dlaczego? Nie wiadomo, można się było jedynie domyślać. Był, delikatnie rzecz ujmując, inny, i śmierdział jak rozkładająca się latem padlina. Gadał jakoś tak sylabami, kaczym głosem i często nie na temat. Jednak najgorsze były momenty w szatni, kiedy zdejmował buty, podkoszulek, spodnie i zakładał uniform. Facet za każdym razem, kiedy coś z siebie zdejmował, emitował w atmosferę nieprzeciętny fetor, jakby gnił za życia.

Któregoś dnia na batony przyjął się nowy. Tego dnia Chemik miał mu pokazać, jak wygląda praca na posterunkach. Dowódca powierzył mu to zadanie, a on bardzo głęboko wziął sobie polecenie do serca. Na pytania nowego cały czas odpowiadał tak samo. Gęgał, że wszystko w swoim czasie.

W połowie dnia zdarzył się wypadek, Chemik nie zauważył dyndającej blachy. Była ostra, odstawała od ściany jednej z hal produkcyjnych. W sumie dyndała tam zawsze, każdy ją omijał, więc nie było problemu. Nie było do momentu, aż Chemik się rozkojarzył i zawadził o nią głową. Dokończył obchód z rozciętym czołem, a kiedy wrócił, wyglądał, jakby ktoś próbował oskalpować go tępą piłą do drewna. Dowódca od razu go opierdolił, a potem zaczął szperać w apteczce, w której prócz lateksowych rękawic i obcinacza do paznokci nie było nic.

Pod koniec dyżuru w ranę wdało się zakażenie i musieli wezwać karetkę. Lekarz nie mógł się nadziwić, jak można było tyle godzin wytrzymać z rozpłatanym czołem, przykładając do niego tylko szary papier toaletowy. Dwa dni później braki w apteczce zostały uzupełnione, a Chemik przyszedł z fachowo wykonanym szwem.

*

– Piętro pierwsze zgłasza obecność! – Czekam na odpowiedź.

– POWTÓRZ!

– Piętro pierwsze zgłasza obecność!

Znowu cisza. Chyba mój głos nałożył się na głos jakiegoś innego stojaka. Nie czekając, jeszcze raz krzyczę do interkomu:

– Piętro pierwsze zgłasza obecność!

– DOBRA, PIERWSZE PIĘTRO, PRZYJĄŁEM!

Ciekawe, czy Mojs już jest. A może wcale stamtąd nie wyszedł? Dookoła tylu pochlebców.

Staję prosto z krótkofalówką w ręku i staram się już nie rozmyślać o tej tłustej świni. Nie mogę się doczekać, kiedy dostanę podmiankę i zjadę coś zjeść. Od razu rzucę się na ten pasztet drobiowy. Dobrze, że go kupiłem. Parówek ruszał nie będę, pewnie zdążyły się popsuć.

*

Mija już druga godzina, a ja nie mam podmianki, przez co czas ciągnie się niemiłosiernie. Zaraz znowu krzyknę, przypomnę im o swoim istnieniu. Żałuję, że nie próbowałem nic przemycić, może by się udało i teraz nie skręcałoby mnie z głodu.

Na każdym piętrze stoi dystrybutor do wody, taki zwyczajny, z osadzoną u góry dwudziestolitrową przezroczystą butlą. Kiedyś widziało się je tylko na zagranicznych filmach, teraz stoją w każdej firmie i na nikim nie robią wrażenia. Wodę mogę pić do woli; zimną, bo z drugiego

kranu leci gorąca, za gorąca, by ją pić. Żłopię lodowatą. Jak głodny sutka noworodek obejmuję
ustami kranik z niebieskim przyciskiem. To nie
jest higieniczne, ale akurat gówno mnie to obchodzi. Tylko raz jeden z pracowników centrum
zwrócił mi uwagę. Gadał coś o kubku, żebym
najpierw do kubka. Bałem się, że powie o tym
Mojsowi, ale potem, nadstawiając uszu, znowu
śliniłem niebieski kranik. Nie mam kubka.

Można zasnąć na stojąco; nie, żebym wpa-
dał w głęboki sen, ale coś tam pod kopułą zaczyna się tworzyć. Kilka razy łapię się na tym.
Stoję, zasypiam i coś zaczyna mi się śnić. Taki
sen trwa krótką chwilę, zaledwie jej ułamek,
ale wtedy nogi tracą sztywność, kolana miękną
i robię coś w rodzaju półprzysiadu. Potem otwieram oczy i znowu staram się postawić do pionu.
Stoję sztywno, nie chcę zasnąć; już nie pierwszy raz tak mam. Szkoda, że nie mogę jak koń
spać na stojąco bez obawy, że za moment po-
lecę jak decha na granitową twardą posadzkę.
Nie mogę spać – tu za spanie dostaje się działy.
Działy to kara finansowa, Mojs tak je nazwał.
To sposób na ukaranie ciecia; z początku dotkli-
wy, potem już mniej. Można się przyzwyczaić za
połowę stawki robić. Jak ma się pecha, to nawet kilka takich dział w miesiącu można wyła-
pać. Nikt szczególnie się nie wykłóca; po prostu
dostajesz działę, adrenalina skacze i po wszystkim. Z czasem dwie, trzy na miesiąc to już nor-
ma. Ludzi można wytresować, przyzwyczaić do

wszystkiego; mówić, że czarne to białe, i kazać
im powtarzać, aż w to uwierzą.

*

Kurwa mać, coś za często sikam pod wiatr. No bo
jak to możliwe, że kupuję pasztet drobiowy i akurat ten pasztet ma przebite aluminiowe wieczko? Może to był jedyny przebity pasztet w całym
sklepie i akurat mnie się trafił. Połowa jego po-
wierzchni porosła białym mchem. Pewnie przy
nanoszeniu ceny ktoś za mocno nacisnął pisto-
letem metkującym i przebił to cholerne wieczko.
Nie było widać, metka z ceną przykryła dziurę.
Przez chwilę zastanawiam się, czy taki spleśnia-
ły pasztet mocno by mi zaszkodził, i ze złością
ciskam nim do kosza. Potem wyrzucam parówki.
Mam jeszcze niecałe pięć minut, muszę zdążyć
się najeść, napchać, załadować się na ful.
    Gdy kończę jeść trzecią puszkę rybną, za-
czyna mnie mdlić. Nic dziwnego, tak się spie-
szyłem, że prawie połknąłem te szprotki, a czas
i tak przekroczyłem.
    Kiedy wjeżdżam windą na piętro, czuję przy-
gnębienie. Zawsze mnie to dopada – zawsze,
kiedy wracam z przerwy na piętro.

*

Jest siedemnasta. Nogi nie dają o sobie ani
na chwilę zapomnieć. Coraz bardziej dokucza

mi wredny ból pięt. Jestem mięczakiem, przecież inni tak samo stoją... i pewnie też już
nie mogą wytrzymać. Ciekawe, czy czują ból
w nogach i czy mają dość tej roboty tak samo
mocno jak ja.

O dziewiętnastej usiądę, a teraz zgłoszę plażę po raz kolejny, po raz czwarty, a może piąty?
Nie wiem, ile razy już byłem na kiblu, nie liczyłem. Teraz tak szybko nie wrócę, mogę mieć
srakę. Żarcie w pośpiechu i stres? Ja powinienem nie schodzić z kibla.

– Pierwsze piętro zgłasza plażę!

Nikt nikomu nie powinien zakazywać pój-
ścia do kibla, ale tu bywa różnie. Po zgłoszeniu
plaży nie można tak sobie zwyczajnie odejść od
interkomu, trzeba czekać na decyzję. Jeśli jest
odmowna, można skoczyć na lewiznę, ale wtedy w razie wpadki sranie ma swoją cenę. Uda-
nie się na stronę bez zgody władz to „dzika plaża". Dzika plaża jest dla odważnych, ale warto zaryzykować, by chwilę odpocząć. W końcu
zostawić na minutę lub dwie hol windowy bez
opieki to nic takiego. Te barany na dole nie od-
rywają oczu od monitorów, ale jak do tej pory
mnie się udaje.

– Pierwsze piętro zgłasza plażę! – Niektórzy proszą, ja nie proszę – nie ich. Chciałbym te skrawki poczucia własnej wartości
utrzymać do końca, do momentu gdy skończę
z pracą stojaka i otworzę własny sklep spożywczy. Często o tym myślę; wyobrażam sobie,

jak jadę busem dostawczym po towar do hurtowni; jak wchodzę do sklepu, a za ladą stoi... Właśnie, fajnie by było, żeby to był biznes rodzinny, a więc niech za ladą stoi moja świeżo poślubiona żona. Oczywiście ładna. Stoi i nie może nadążyć z obsługiwaniem klientów. Będzie tam główna sklepowa, a moja żona czasami, tylko tak, do pomocy, jak będzie chciała. W końcu będzie szefową. Tak, niech tylko jej pomaga. Ona będzie miała ładne dłonie, zadbane paznokcie i wszyscy będą mi jej zazdrościć.

Dają mi do zrozumienia, że nici z kibla. Mam to głęboko..., zaraz i tak pójdę, muszę tylko trochę odczekać. Pewnie patrzą teraz na mnie – coś takiego się czuje. I mimo że to tylko szklane oko bezdusznej kamery, to normalnie mam takie wrażenie, że ktoś wywierca mi spojrzeniem dziurę w plecach. Coś takiego się czuje.

Stoję prościutko. Patrzcie sobie, głupie gnoje.

*

Prawie nogi połamałem. Z kibla pod kamerę jest kawałek, a interkom aż huczał:

– PIERWSZE PIĘTRO! GDZIE JESTEŚ? KAMERA CIĘ NIE WIDZI!

Przypomnieli sobie o mnie? Dobrze wiedzą, że wylegiwałem się na „dzikiej plaży". Teraz pewnie robię już za połowę stawki. Dowiem się o tym dopiero przy wypłacie. Adiutant wpisał do kapownika, od której do której nie było mnie widać i działa gotowa. (Chuje).

Mogliby chociaż tak normalnie, po ludzku powiedzieć, a tak człowiek mimo wszystko ma jeszcze złudzenia.

*

Co miesiąc chciałbym choć trochę odłożyć. Na początku planowałem odkładać z wypłaty. Otworzyłem w tym celu konto w banku, bo co to za facet bez oszczędności. Oszczędności i konto w banku trzeba mieć. Jednak plany planami, a życie i tak swoje. Jak do tej pory jeszcze nic nie zaoszczędziłem. Przez prawie rok wpłacam niewielkie kwoty, które zaraz potem wypłacam. Takim jak ja nie powinno się otwierać kont, szkoda zachodu. Mając tę świadomość, coraz niżej spuszczam łeb przy okienku kasowym, gdy proszę o kolejne wyczyszczenie konta.

Kwotę, jaką chciałbym zaoszczędzić, młodsza córka właścicielki Bożeny potrafi wydać w parę godzin. Ostatnio chwaliła się, że była z chłopakiem na zakupach i wydali dziesięć tysięcy. Tak lekką ręką, bo jak to powiedziała: „Co to jest, trochę tego, trochę tamtego, i poszło". Jak można jednego dnia dychę na ubrania przepuścić? Ten jej chłopak to frajer. Układa po ludziach płytki, a potem całą zarobioną kasę na nią wydaje. Ma gest, ale dycha to dycha; ja nawet przez rok tysiaka uzbierać nie mogę.

Zmotywowany jego zarobkami postanowiłem, że też nauczę się kłaść płytki. Chciałem tak między dyżurami, a jakby się okazało, że rzeczywiście jest z tego kasa, to walnąłbym ochronę. Któregoś razu zaproponowałem kolesiowi, że mogę mu pomagać, ale on tylko się roześmiał. Nie mogłem tak od razu się poddać. Zacząłem łazić po budowach i pytać. Nigdzie nie potrzebowali pomocnika, każdy patrzył na mnie jak na idiotę.

Zacząłem tracić nadzieję, szanse na wysokie zarobki oddalały się coraz bardziej. Wtedy przeczytałem ogłoszenie: budują kolejny hipermarket, potrzebują całej armii fachowców budowlanych i niewykwalifikowanych pomocników. „Wreszcie los się do mnie uśmiechnął" – pomyślałem i od razu poczułem się bogaty. Prawie, jakbym miał te dziesięć tysiaków w kieszeni.

Bracia stukali się w czoło i cały czas powtarzali, że się wykończę.

– Ty masz pojęcie, co to znaczy budowa?

– Nie wiem, a wy wiecie? – pytałem. – Tam przynajmniej czegoś się nauczę, zdobędę nowy fach – tłumaczyłem im. – Jak chcecie, to też możecie dorobić. Na początku robota będzie prosta, takie tam: przynieś, podaj... Ale z czasem, z czasem to sam zacznę płytki układać. Pomocnikowi piątaka na godzinę płacą; to chyba żadna krzywda, nie?

Wiesiek patrzył podejrzliwie.

– A powiedz mi, kiedy niby mielibyśmy na tę budowę z tobą jeździć? Przecież my zapierdalamy dzień w dzień.

No tak, zupełnie zapomniałem, ale podobnie jak oni – dorywczo to mogę znaczki na koperty przyklejać. Szybko się o tym przekonuję. Tylko dwa razy idę na budowę; po pierwszym dniu nie mogę wydłubać z nosa kleju do płytek. Gówno, wszędzie to mam – w oczach, w uszach, w gardle, najwięcej w nosie. Przez tydzień wydłubuję te skamieniałe gluty, razem z kłakami.

*

Jest mi zimno – to przez zmęczenie, chociaż najgorszy kryzys chyba mam już za sobą.

Siadam na fotelu. Jakbym miesiąc stał w tym holu – wszystko mnie boli. Nie powinienem sadowić tyłka, jeszcze nie ma dziewiętnastej, ale co tam. Te parę minut nie robi różnicy. Na wszelki wypadek popędzam w zegarku wskazówki i mimo że do dziewiętnastej zostało jeszcze osiem minut, to u mnie jest już dwie po. Jakby tu wjechała jakaś obślizgła menda, to powiem, że u mnie jest po dziewiętnastej.

Odwiązuję buty i wysuwam z nich stopy. Przepocone, śmierdzące, wytarte czarne skarpety prawie przyrosły. Odklejam je od skóry, fajne uczucie. Chłód granitowej posadzki przynosi ulgę. Mógłbym tak siedzieć do rana. Nawet za darmo, byleby już nie wstawać z tego najwygodniejszego na świecie fotela. Za godzinę ktoś mnie zmieni, Henio zrobi roszadę. Ciekawe, gdzie mnie wyśle. Może na klateczki? Powinien, przecież to druga doba, powinien dać mi klateczki, a może zostawi mnie tu? W sumie nie byłoby najgorzej, byleby nie na minusiki albo na Chocimską. Drugą noc po Chocimskiej miałbym dreptać? Nigdy w życiu. Zaczynam gadać sam do siebie, aż echo rozchodzi się po holu. Słyszę to i na chwilę się uspakajam. Potem znowu zaczynam się zastanawiać, na jaki posterunek mnie wyślę; myślę tylko o tym. Wszystko zaczyna się od początku. Ruszam gębą i gadam z samym sobą; chyba zwariuję! Muszę przestać się rozczulać. Chrzanić to, gdzie mnie rzucą, tam mnie rzucą, najwyżej. Jutro rano stąd wyjdę, a drugi raz na żadną dodatkową dobę już się nie zgodzę.

*

Heniek okazał miłosierdzie – do rana będę mógł siedzieć na fotelu. Równy z niego gość.

Od dwudziestej zaczynam obchód dwóch skrzydeł. Za każdym razem zgłaszam przez interkom, tak samo jak na minusikach. Tylko tu na szczęście nie ma Zbycha, no i łazić cały czas nie trzeba. Wystarczy raz na pół godziny, tempo dowolne. Można szybko, można wolno, jak się chce, od końca jednego do końca drugiego.

Byleby widziano mnie w zamontowanych na końcach każdego skrzydła kamerach. To proste: szybki obchód, kamera, a potem fotel, i tak w kółko.

*

Przysnąłem? Chyba tak. Aż dziwne, że mnie nie wołali. Przecież zawsze wołają, jak obchodu w porę się nie zgłosi. Adiutant nad tym czuwa. A może zrobiłem obchód, tylko zapomniałem, że go zrobiłem? Otwieram szeroko oczy, patrzę na zegarek. Dochodzi pierwsza; jeśli nawet spałem, to niedługo.

Jestem okropnie zmęczony, a do tego jeszcze ten szum wentylacji. Przez ten szum jeszcze bardziej mnie muli. Pierwszy raz w życiu zarywam drugą noc z kolei. I pierwszy raz tak ciężko mi walczyć ze snem. Gdybym musiał stać, to już na pewno nie raz zaliczyłbym twardą glebę, chociaż i bez tego boli. To taki dziwny ból, właściwie to nie wiadomo czego, ogólny dyskomfort. Walka z opadającymi powiekami, z kiwającą się na wszystkie strony głową, z wyciekającą kącikiem ust śliną. Gęba jak z waty i wszystko jakieś nieswoje.

*

Dzwonek poprzedzający otwarcie drzwi od windy stawia mnie na równe nogi. Może to Mojs?

Na zmiennika za wcześnie, przecież jeszcze nawet siódmej nie ma.

To dowódca; idzie w moją stronę. Jest sam, bez adiutanta. Z daleka widzę, jak kręci głową. Jest z czegoś bardzo niezadowolony. Tak na wszelki wypadek uśmiecham się do niego. Im jest bliżej, tym wyraźniej słyszę, jak coś mamrocze pod nosem.

– Patryk, jestem pod ścianą! – krzyczy. Mam złe przeczucia – on używa tego tekstu, gdy chce kogoś pogrążyć. Chyba źle spał, oczy ma jakieś takie czerwone. – Patryk! Jest, chłopie, problem, jestem pod ścianą – powtarza.

Cholera, przecież już to gadał. O co mu chodzi?

Teraz ja kręcę głową. Nawet nie chcę słyszeć, że miałbym tu stać dłużej, niż muszę.

– Co się stało? – Tak naprawdę guzik mnie obchodzi, co się stało. Mam w dupie to, z czym do mnie przyszedł. W duchu staram się pocieszać, bo w końcu jeszcze żadne słowa, które mogłyby mnie udusić, nie padły. A to, że jest pod ścianą? Niech sobie jest, to nie moja sprawa.

Próbuję zachować niewzruszoną minę. Chyba nie muszę mu przypominać, że zaraz kończę. Wreszcie! Zostawiam innym obiekt chroniony i jadę do Janek. Jadę SPAĆ!

– Słuchaj no, Patryk, dzwonił chłopaczek. – To nie brzmi najlepiej, co tam nie najlepiej, to brzmi zupełnie źle. – Mówił, że ma jakieś niefajne sprawy rodzinne do załatwienia. Wiesz, takie tam problemy w domu czy coś takiego. Nie chciał o tym za wiele gadać przez telefon. Mówił tylko, że nie może przyjechać. Wskoczy dopiero na nockę i wiesz, to nie byłby żaden problem, ale Adaś... On nie będzie miał obsady. Brakuje ludzi; tydzień temu dwóch zrezygnowało, a teraz jeszcze ten zadzwonił. Sam widzisz, jak jest. No, Patryk, przecież nie strzelę sobie, kurwa, w kolano, nie? Mówię ci, jestem normalnie pod ścianą! Zostałbyś na dzionek? Tylko na dzionek.

Nie wierzę w to, co słyszę. Jak on może proponować mi coś takiego?

– Nie da rady – odpowiadam. – Mówię ci, poważnie, nie da rady! – Stukam się w piersi. – Jakbym mógł, to bym został, ale za godzinę kończę drugą dobę. Drugą dobę! – powtarzam.

Patrzę mu prosto w oczy, a raczej w ten pierdzielony fiolet jego pancernych szkieł leczniczych, spod których łypie na świat.

– Dwie doby? – dziwi się. – A co to takiego? Ja raz na obiekcie prawie tydzień przesiedziałem i zobacz – żyję – uśmiecha się. Chyba chce mi powiedzieć, że czterdzieści osiem godzin na stojaka to nic.

– Na jakim to było obiekcie? – Nie powinienem brnąć w tę rozmowę, tylko sobie szkodzę.

– No, jak to na jakim? Na tym. A coś ty myślał?! Ciężko było, ale jak trzeba, to trzeba.

Nie, nie mogę się zgodzić! Przecież on chce, żebym został na kolejną dobę. To niemożliwe. Nie zostanę.

– Nie da rady, Heniek. Mówię ci, ledwo stoję. Co innego siedzieć na fotelu, a co innego stać na nogach.

Znowu się uśmiecha.

– A kto ci każe stać? Damy cię na klateczki, a tam będziesz miał spokój, nikt ci nie będzie dupy zawracał. Przecież byłeś tam już nie raz.

– Raz.

– Raz? Noo, to wiesz, jak jest.

Kiwam głową i chyba rura zaczyna mi mięknąć. Staram się to sobie wszystko szybko poukładać, ale nie potrafię, jestem zbyt odrętwiały. Przecież nie powinienem nawet wysłuchiwać jego propozycji.

– Nie da rady. Zresztą nie mam nawet już nic do żarcia. Dwie doby to dwie doby. Nie dam rady, Heniek.

– Spokooojnie! – Mruży oczy. – Przecież nie będziesz głodował. Potem ktoś cię podmieni i skoczysz sobie do całodobowego. Jest niedaleko, tu za rogiem.

Jestem zmęczony, a on mi nie odpuszcza. Chyba już wie, że ma mnie w garści, ale na wszelki wypadek cały czas jeszcze kręcę głową.

– Na klateczki mnie dasz?

– No, kurwa, przecież już ci mówiłem, nie? Za piętnaście minut ktoś cię tu zmieni i wtedy dajesz od razu na klateczki. To co, gitara?

Głęboko wzdycham.

– Dobra.

Odchodzi. Nienawidzę siebie!

*

Klateczki. Posterunek marzenie. Nie dla wszystkich, ale ja dziś zostałem wyróżniony. Zasłużyłem – to za moje bohaterstwo, za wytrwałość, za oddanie dla firmy. Przez połowę dnia, choć są ku temu warunki, nie mogę zmrużyć oka. Jestem bardzo zmęczony, ale nie mogę spać. Mam za to cały czas wrażenie, że ktoś za mną stoi, dlatego odwracam się co chwilę i zaraz głośno wykpiwam samego siebie.

Po godzinie trzynastej przychodzi Adaś, chce mnie puścić na przerwę. Gdy podnoszę tyłek ze schodów, przygniata mnie ponurą informacją. Gada, że muszę tu zostać aż do rana. Stukam się w czoło, a on zaczyna na mnie drzeć ryja. Krzyczy, że robić mi się nie chce. Też próbuję na niego krzyczeć, ale nie mam tyle siły. W końcu proszę go, by mnie puścili. Język mi się plącze. Proszę go, by puścił mnie do domu, ale on tylko trzaska metalowymi drzwiami i wychodzi. Nie idę na przerwę, za to wyję z wściekłości jak zbity pies. Mam wrażenie, że żywy stąd nie wyjdę, że zostanę tu na zawsze, że tu zdechnę.

Na klateczkach jestem do rana. Przed ósmą przychodzi do mnie zmiennik. Coś do mnie gada, ale nie mogę go dokładnie zrozumieć. Wyłapuję co* któreś słowo. Jestem zmęczony, boli mnie głowa.

ROZDZIAŁ

3

Przyjechał ze swoją grubą babą, jak on to mówi – konkubiną. Tydzień temu w wieku pięćdziesięciu lat wujek Kazik przeszedł w stan spoczynku. Zwyczajnie na „zasłużoną" emeryturę sobie poszedł. Był żołnierzem; aż dziwne, że tyle w wojsku wysiedział. Jak pamiętam, już od lat gadał, że z armii odchodzi; wreszcie dopiął swego.

Od samego progu nic nie umyka uwadze jego nowej kamery cyfrowej. Dostał ją na odchodne – taki zbiorowy prezent od kolegów z wojska.

– No, no, ale chałupa, no, no – mruczy pod nosem. Jedną ręką wita się z nami, z drugiej nie wypuszcza kamery. Cały czas nagrywa.
– No, no, i popatrz, w końcu da się mieszkać, nie? No, no...

On i mama są niepodobnymi do siebie bliźniakami. Mama jest milcząca, a jemu gęba prawie nigdy się nie zamyka. Mama ma ciemne, gęste włosy, on rzadki wianuszek świńskoblond.

Mógłby się obciąć na pałę – wyglądałby lepiej. Cieszę się, że nie odziedziczyłem koloru włosów po nim.

– Cześć, wujek – witam się z nim, na siłę wzbudzając w sobie entuzjazm. Cholera, chyba kulturalniej byłoby najpierw przywitać się z jego konkubiną. – Dzień dobry pani...

Ma spoconą dłoń.

– Cześć – odpowiada kobieta i uśmiecha się do mnie. – Cześć wszystkim, che, che. Jaka tam pani, che, che... – Jest słodka.

Wujek poznał ją całkiem niedawno – jakieś pół roku temu. Podwoził ją na stopa i tak się w sobie zakochali. Był już kiedyś żonaty, ale po długoletnim małżeństwie przestał się z ciotką dogadywać. Szkoda, bo w przeciwieństwie do niego ciotka była normalna i przywoziła mi zawsze czekolady. Nawet wtedy, kiedy od czekolady bardziej zaczęło mi smakować piwo. Zawsze wyciągała z torebki mleczną i dawała mi ją jeszcze w progu.

– No prowadź, prowadź, gospodarzu, prowadź! – mówi wujek. – Jak ostatni raz tu byliśmy, to jeszcze paneli nie było. Grażynko, pamiętasz? Nie było, nie? – Patrzy teraz jednym okiem na kobietę. – O! – Zauważa kominek. – Obudowaliście kamieniem. Suuuper! – Wchodzi do pokoju.

Wcześniej mieszkaliśmy w bloku w dwupokojowym mieszkaniu. Parę lat temu ojcu zaświtał w głowie pomysł. Przeglądając przypadkowo katalog z projektami domów, oświadczył mamie, że chciałby mieć dom. Z początku ani ja, ani ona nie braliśmy tego poważnie. Ale kiedy cztery lata temu w tajemnicy przed matką kupił „okazyjnie" sześcioarową działkę na obrzeżach naszej miejscowości, zdałem sobie sprawę, że coś zaczyna być na rzeczy. Mama jeszcze długo potem miała do niego żal, że niczego z nią nie uzgodnił, bo ta działka wcale jej się nie podobała. Wtedy bałem się, że ich małżeństwo rozleci się tak samo jak wujka.

Gdyby ojciec wiedział, z czym tak naprawdę chce się zmierzyć, gdyby zdawał sobie sprawę, że ten jego dom i tak nigdy nie będzie wyglądał jak ten z kolorowego katalogu, to zamiast szukać ekipy murarzy, zacząłby szukać kupca na działkę.

Dom stoi, bez elewacji, pod papą, ale jest. Dach to właściwie jedna wielka skorupa z lepiku. Gówno pęka, co rusz to w nowych miejscach, a ojciec już raz spadł, jak zalepiał dziury w papie. Gdyby żył jeszcze ze sto lat, to nasz dom byłby pewnie najładniejszy w okolicy; a tak jest, jaki jest. Z pensji strażaka dwustumetrową willę budować? Przecież miał być malutki.

Wujek nie odpuszcza, obchodzi kominek z każdej strony i nagrywa, nagrywa, nagrywa. Nagrywa z taką zawziętością, że aż żal mu przeszkadzać.

– Jak już wszystko skamerujesz, to chcemy, Kaziu, kopię – mówi mama.

- Jasne siostra, spokojna twoja. Będziesz miała, siostra, pamiątkę – Na chwilę odrywa kamerę od oka i trze je wierzchem dłoni. – Pamią-
teczka będzie, a jak. Potem będziecie mogli sobie obejrzeć, jak już wszystko będzie zrobione.
(Będzie?)
– Powolutku, spokojnie wszystko się zrobi –
odzywa się ojciec. On tak zawsze gada: „Powolutku, spokojnie". – Teraz to dach. – Kiwa głową, jakby sam siebie chciał przekonać, że dobrze gada. – Blachodachówkę trzeba kłaść. Potem jeszcze ocieplić, bo węgla zimą dużo idzie.
Tak, jeszcze przed jesienią ocieplę, a potem się
zobaczy.
Wujek odkłada kamerę na stół. Źle się po-
czuł?... W końcu jakby nie było, to już emeryt.
Nieee, postanowił sobie zrobić teraz przerwę,
krótką przerwę. Ciekawe, kiedy pojedzie.

*

Mój przyjazd jakoś tak nieplanowanie zbiegł się
z jego wizytą. On zawsze odwiedza rodziców
bez zapowiedzi. To znaczy zapowiada się dzień
wcześniej i najczęściej późnym wieczorem. Teraz też – zadzwonił i oświadczył, że przyjedzie
nagrać nasz dom. Potem długo gadał jeszcze
o tej kamerze, co ją w prezencie od kolegów
z wojska na odchodne dostał. Aż mama, zmę-
czona przytakiwaniem do słuchawki, udała, że
ktoś puka do drzwi.

Ona zazwyczaj cieszy się z każdych jego od-
wiedzin; z ojcem jest inaczej. Po telefonie przez
dobrą godzinę tłumaczy jej, że mogła powiedzieć Kazikowi, że akurat wyjeżdżają i przez
długi czas nie będzie ich w domu. Jednak teraz
zachowuje się tak, jakby zapomniał, co wczoraj jej gadał. Mogłoby się wydawać, że jest nawet bardziej zadowolony z jego przyjazdu niż
mama.

Ja nie wpadam w euforię, nie lubię przeby-
wać w towarzystwie takich dziwaków, jak on;
nawet jeśli ten dziwak jest bratem mojej mamy.
Dlatego chcąc odpocząć od gadki wujka, snuję
się po tym dużym niewykończonym domu, ale
jakoś nie mogę znaleźć sobie miejsca. Najpierw
siedzę w salonie i wysłuchuję jego przechwa-
łek, potem wstaję, idę na górę – pusto, gołe
tynki. Schodzę. Szuram kapciami po cemento-
wych schodach i znowu słyszę wujka. Wchodzę
do kuchni. Kuchnia jako jedyne pomieszczenie jest zrobiona na tip-top. Siedząc w niej, na
chwilę zapomina się o całej reszcie domu.

– Co tak chodzisz? – pyta mama. Ona wie, że
nie przepadam za wujkiem, ale znowu udaje
zdziwioną.

Wzruszam ramionami.

– Na długo przyjechali?

Przykłada palec do ust.

– Cicho. – Patrzy na mnie w taki sposób, jakbym zrobił coś złego. – Przecież nie pytałam.
Posiedzą trochę i pojadą.

– Dziwna ta jego konkubina – szepczę, prze-
chylając się w jej stronę. – Szkoda, że się roz-
wiódł z ciotką, nie?

Mama znowu przykłada palec do ust. Tym
razem jednak już tak groźnie na mnie nie patrzy. Przymyka tylko lekko powieki.

– Dobra, idź już do nich. Jak to wygląda? Ojciec z nimi, a ty ze mną tu. Idź i spytaj, co ta
pani chce do picia, bo Kazik to wiem. No, idź
spytaj – pogania mnie.

Wstaję i wychodzę z kuchni.

– Czego się pani napije, kawy czy...?

– Herbatkę proszę, che, che – odpowiada.

Wujka nie pytam. Wracam do mamy.

*

Do obiadu ojciec stawia butelkę wódki. Wujek
też nie przyjechał z pustymi rękami. Co prawda, czekolady mi nie dał, ale za to przywiózł,
jak sam mówi, dobry koniak. Taka gorzała
z trudem przechodzi mi przez gardło. Śmierdzi
to jak bimber i smakuje nie lepiej. Dlatego po
spróbowaniu go piję już tylko sok.

– A ty wiesz, siostra, że twój chrześniak mieszkanie ma dostać?

Ten chrześniak to mój o dwa lata starszy kuzyn; syn wujka, niedoszły inżynier i od zawsze
uczulony na słońce grubas. Wydaje się, że jeśli
taka fujara została żołnierzem, to chyba każdy
może.

105

Wujek od godziny tłumaczy rodzicom, że dużo trudniej było zmienić kategorię synowi, niż załatwić szkołę wojskową. No, ale w końcu się udało i teraz Piotruś wydaje szwejom rozkazy, tak mówi.

– Dziewczynę ma, blondynę!

– Eee, to, Kazik, na wesele zbieraj – śmieje się mama. – Zobaczysz, ani się obejrzysz, jak... – znowu się śmieje – jak dziadkiem zostaniesz!

– Ładna dziewucha – wujek z melancholią w oczach potakuje głową. – Wysoka, opalona, na solarium chodzi... O! I studiuje.

– A co? – dopytuje się ojciec.

– Co, co?

– No, co studiuje ta jego dziewczyna?

– Aaa, na biznesmenkę się uczy.

Ojciec robi duże oczy.

– Na co?

– No, na biznesmenkę, marketingu się uczy. Jest najlepsza na studiach! Piotrek wiedział, co bierze.

– No proszę, proszę... – Mama zawsze tak mówi, jak nie wie, co powiedzieć. – To się chłopakowi udało. A to mieszkanie to z wojska dostanie, tak? Służbowe mu przydzielą?

Wujek nie odpowiada. Teraz patrzy na mnie; chyba nie słyszał jej pytania.

– A ty co porabiasz? Cały czas w Warszawie siedzisz?

Kiwam głową.

– Stary do straży nie chce cię wkręcić?

– Ale gdzie? – odzywa się ojciec. – On to nie. Kazik, przecież do straży to zdrówko idealne musi być.

– A co mu jest? Chłop jak dąb, co ty chcesz od niego? Wyższy od ciebie, jak Piotrek.

Dopiero teraz się dowie, że jestem w połowie głuchy? Niee, przecież on wie. Wszyscy w rodzinie wiedzą. A może nie wie?

– Tato, daj już spokój – mówię, a wujek robi zdziwioną minę. Jego konkubinie na chwilę znika z twarzy serdeczny uśmiech. Wygląda teraz dużo starzej. Pewnie wie o tym, dlatego cały czas tak michę jarzy.

– A co ci jest? – pyta wujek, patrząc podejrzliwie.

Co ja mam mu teraz opowiadać? Chrzanię go!

– Nic.

– No to o co chodzi?

Wzruszam ramionami. Na ratunek rusza ojciec. Nie byłby sobą, gdyby im wszystkiego nie wyłożył. Po cholerę jakaś obca baba ma wiedzieć, że gorzej słyszę? Przecież to moje ucho i moja sprawa. Jestem kim jestem, staruszkom na ulicy torebek nie wyrywam. Pracuję, „zarabiam”. Coś jest nie tak? No chyba, bo wujek patrzy teraz na mnie jakoś tak inaczej. Widzę wyraźnie, patrzy inaczej.

– To ty dalej w tej ochronie robisz? – Krzywi się, jakby właśnie zjadł coś niedobrego.

– Tak – odpowiadam. – Ale teraz stawka lepsza, nie mogę narzekać.

– Czyli mówisz, że krzywdy nie ma?

– Nie ma źle – odzywa się ojciec.

Mógłby się już lepiej na ten temat nie wypowiadać. Wystarczy, że robi ze mnie inwalidę. Ani on, ani matka nie mają pojęcia, jaki zaszczuty ze mnie cieć. Nie muszą o tym wiedzieć. Na pytanie: „Jak w pracy?", zawsze odpowiadam tylko jedno: „Wszystko w porządku". Tak im mówię. Co to zmieni, jak zacznę się nad sobą użalać?

– Patryk w wieżowcu pracuje. Mówię ci, Kazik, wielki świat.

Tato chce najwyraźniej udowodnić, że nie tylko Piotrusiowi w życiu się powodzi. Jego syn też jest kimś – pracuje w wieżowcu.

– Ta ochrona to państwówka? – pyta wujek.

Dobrze wie, że nie. Specjalnie tak pyta. Jak go znam, nie przebolałby tego, że mógłbym mieć lepiej niż on i jego Piotruś.

– Nie – odpowiadam.

– Eee, to co to za robota. Prywaciarz to prywaciarz, coś mu się nie spodoba i do widzenia. – Macha ręką. – Ja zawsze powtarzam: państwówka to państwówka, a najlepiej wojsko. Kasa nie jest zła, emerytura szybko.

– Nie ma źle – powtarza ojciec. – Już ty się, Kazik, nie martw. Robotę chłopak ma w stolicy. Radzi sobie, a z czasem to może i jakiś awans mu się trafi. A może też, tak jak twój, jakąś biznesmenkę pozna. Ty myślisz, że mało w tej Warszawie biznesmenek po ulicach łazi?

– A co, kręci się koło ciebie jakaś? Noo, Patryk, pochwal się wujkowi.

– Przyglądam się takiej jednej. – Nie dam się. Zaraz mu opowiem, to mu kieliszek w gardle stanie. Niech sobie nie myśli, że los tylko dla Piotrusia jest łaskawy.

– Masz dziewczynę? – Mama jest zdziwiona.

– I nic nam nie mówiłeś?

– To jeszcze krótka znajomość – tłumaczę jej – ale skoro wujek pyta, to nie będę ukrywał, że coś tam się dzieje.

– No co ty taki tajemniczy jesteś? Opowiadaj! – Wujek aż podskakuje na fotelu. – No, mów, chłopie.

– O czym?

– Chyba jest o czym, co? – śmieje się.

Dzwonek telefonu przerywa nam „rozmowę". Mama wstaje od stołu.

– Tak, słucham. – Jej głośny śmiech przykuwa moją uwagę. – Tak, Piotrusiu, dojechali, tak, szczęśliwie, tak!

– O! – Wujek podnosi tyłek z krzesła i szeroko się uśmiecha. – Powiedz mu, niech przyjeżdża! – krzyczy do mamy. – To Piotrek! – tłumaczy nam, jakbyśmy nie wiedzieli.

Udaję, że też się cieszę.

– Powiedz mu, siostra, że Patryk jest! Niech sobie chłopaki pogadają. Nie widzieli się już kupę czasu! – Kiwa głową. – Nie? Długo już Piotrka nie widziałeś, nie? Patryk?

– Długo – powtarzam za nim.

109

- Poczekaj! - Podbiega do mamy i prawie wyrywa jej słuchawkę z dłoni. - Co, synek? Tak, tak... jest. No, w Warszawie. No, tak! - Na moment odrywa słuchawkę od ucha. - Patryk! - Cholera! Jakbym wiedział, że będę dziś musiał jeszcze rozmawiać z Piotrusiem, to nie poprzestałbym na ojcowskiej flaszce. - Patryk... No, chodź tu!

Kurwa mać, gdyby on tylko zdawał sobie sprawę, jak bardzo nie mam ochoty gadać przez telefon z jego Piotrusiem!

Wstaję od stołu i wolno podchodzę do telefonu. Zanim dostaję słuchawkę, wujek nawija jeszcze przez dobry kwadrans; jakby się z nim sto lat nie widział; a ja stoję koło niego i czekam, aż skończy się cieszyć.

- Cześć, kuzyn!

Piotruś chyba też coś pił.

- Cześć.

Przez ten mój wymuszony entuzjazm ciężko jest mi złapać równy oddech. Powiedziałbym nawet, że mocno się stresuję, bo już po pierwszym pytaniu Piotrusia najchętniej pierdolnąłbym słuchawką o podłogę.

- Gdzie cieciujesz?

- Co...?

Udaję, że nie usłyszałem, że wszystko gra, ale tak naprawdę aż cały się gotuję. Jak ten grubas w ogóle może tak stawiać pytanie? Kurwa mać, komandos z platfusem! Przecież gdyby nie łapówy i znajomości wujka, nigdy nie dostałby się do szkoły wojskowej. Dobrze pamiętam, jak po komisji poborowej, jeszcze zanim poszedł na studia, gadał, że generałów do wojska nie biorą. A teraz tatuś pomógł zmienić kategorię i Piotruś jest żołnierzem. Przecież to jakiś absurd.

– Pytam, kuzyn, gdzie teraz cieciujesz!

– Słabo cię słyszę! – Nie będę z nim gadał. Pierdolę go!

Delikatnie odkładam słuchawkę i wchodzę do salonu.

– Już? – dziwi się mama. – Tak szybko się nagadaliście?

– Zakłócenia były. Przerwało.

– To zadzwoń do niego, pogadajcie sobie.

– Mamę, podobnie jak wujka, nie opuszcza entuzjazm. – Kaziu, jaki jest do was numer, bo nie znam na pamięć?

– Jeszcze sobie pogadamy, ale innym razem. Dzwonek.

– Idź odbierz, to pewnie Piotruś – krzyczy wujek.

Jest coraz bardziej wstawiony, ojciec i mama zresztą też. Tylko ta konkubina jakoś się trzyma, a może tylko tak mi się wydaje. Ona się wcale nie odzywa. To się z wujkiem dobrali. Piękna i bestia.

*

Jeszcze dwa razy udaję, że nie mogę zrozumieć Piotrusia, aż w końcu Piotruś daje sobie spokój. Potem, żeby odreagować, przełamuję się i zmuszam się do strzemiennego. Robię sobie drinka z „dobrego koniaku" wujka, czym wzbudzam jego oburzenie.

– Koniak z oranżadą mieszać? – nie może się nadziwić.

Po tym zbezczeszczeniu idę spać.

ROZDZIAŁ

4

Dziś jest szczególny dzień. Mojs osobiście robi nam odprawę. Jak zawsze jest wściekły i ma spocone czoło.

– Panowie! – krzyczy. – Tylko bez ściemy, bo bez pytania wypierdolę, nawet nie będzie gadania. Nie ma łażenia i zgłaszania jakiegoś szczania. Jak ktoś chce się wysrać, to niech sobie pampersa na dupę założy, i chuj.

(Cooo?)

Henio stoi i kiwa głową. Wygląda, jakby chciał stąd uciec, tylko coś każe mu tu stać i posłusznie kiwać łbem, potakiwać każdemu wykrzyczanemu przez Mojsa słowu.

To całe poruszenie jest spowodowane imprezą, która ma się dziś odbyć w Atrium na piątym piętrze. Atrium to taka oaza, miejsce, gdzie pracownicy centrum mogą coś zjeść, poczytać prasę, pogadać. Dziś odbędzie się tam otwarcie fundacji słynnej polskiej biegaczki, więc niecodzienny dyżur mi się trafia. Wcześniej, gdy jeszcze tu nie stałem, kręcili film.

Taki jeden stojak mi o tym opowiadał. To właśnie on i jeszcze inny koleś zostali zaangażowani do statystowania w jednej scenie. Opowiadał, że główną rolę grała sama Figura, więc sprawa była wielka z każdej strony. Mówił, że ta Figura to naprawdę niezła dupa, tylko myślał, że jest dużo wyższa.

Wtedy, tak jak i teraz, Mojs wprowadził pełne obostrzenia na kibel i tak samo jak dziś krzyczał, że wszystkich wypierdoli z roboty. Tamtego dnia solidną działką ukarał ponad połowę ekipy. Tych dwóch, co statystowało w filmie, też. Po zdjęciach urwali się na papierosa i adiutant ich wypatrzył. Działę jakoś by znieśli – za statystowanie zarobili równowartość dwóch stawek za dyżur, ale kiedy pół roku później jeden z nich z całą rodziną wybrał się do kina, okazało się, że akurat tę scenę z jego udziałem wycięli. Bez pytania? Wycięli go, jak przechodził korytarzem. Dobrze, że kasy nie kazali mu zwrócić.

*

Wiem, że nie mogę podejść do balustrady, ale dziś jakoś szczególnie mnie kusi. Postawili mnie na siódmym piętrze, więc głupio byłoby nie spojrzeć z góry na atrium. Chcę zobaczyć, co tam się dzieje, przez chwilę popatrzeć na zamontowany specjalnie na tę okazję duży ekran.

Podchodzę. Jestem już w zabronionej dla mnie strefie. Idę chyba za wolno. Przyspieszam; widzę już trochę ekranu. Podchodzę jeszcze bliżej. Czuję się tak, jakbym właśnie wszedł na pole minowe. Gdyby to było naprawdę pole minowe, to z moim szczęściem od razu rozerwałoby mnie na drobne kawałki. Muszę uważać. Nie staję blisko balustrady, chociaż chyba mam ją już na wyciągnięcie ręki. Tak mi się wydaje, ale nie będę tego sprawdzał. Na ekranie leci film z jakiejś olimpiady sportowej. Tak! To ta biegaczka, to ona tam biegnie. Szybko zasuwa. Wygląda trochę jak facet, przegania wszystkich. Wygrywa, cieszy się, unosząc ręce w tryumfalnym geście. Następny film – to znowu ona, biegnie, pewnie wygra. Wracam pod kamerę.

„PROSZĘ PAŃSTWA! PROSZĘ PAŃSTWA!" – cały czas to słyszę. Głośna muzyka, jak na jakimś festynie, i to „PROSZĘ PAŃSTWA!". To jakiś znany głos. Pewnie to ta wychudzona prezenterka z telewizji, o której wszyscy mówią, że prawie nic nie je, tylko wodę mineralną żłopie. Widać, czasem też chałturzy. Za to dzisiejsze „PROSZĘ PAŃSTWA" mogłaby pewnie całego spożywczaka towarem zarzucić. Słyszałem, że w telewizji to każdy dobrze zarabia; nawet pani pogodynka przechadzająca się od jednego końca mapy do drugiego, z promiennym uśmiechem zapowiadająca burze – każdy!

Już nie raz mijałem się na ulicy z niejedną taką gwiazdą. Wiadomo, gdzie jak gdzie, ale tu, w stolicy, „gwiazd" jest od zawalenia. Jak się pierwszy raz taką mija, to ma się dziwne wrażenie. Jak do tej pory tylko w telewizji, w pełnym makijażu, a tu... Widzi się taką gwiazdeczkę i porównuje z zapamiętanym obrazem. Potem rozczarowanie. Gwiazda smarka w chusteczkę, idzie jakoś tak niezgrabnie, jest niska albo w ogóle kurdupel i zamiast się uśmiechać, ma wykrzywione usta. A w telewizji? Już sobie wyobrażam, jakim byłbym ciachem, gdyby mnie fachowo upudrowali.

Znowu podchodzę do balustrady; właściwie to przyciąga mnie do niej zapach żarcia. Ci ważniacy nie mogą tak z pustymi żołądkami uśmiechać się do siebie. Stąd wszystko dobrze widzę. Widzę jak wpieprzają, jak wpierdalają, jak żrą niczym wygłodniałe świnie. Szkoda, że nie jestem jedną z nich – wpierdalałbym tak samo, aż by mi do gardła podeszło.

Właśnie zobaczyłem Mojsa. Jakby mi kto palec do oka wsadził. Cofam się szybko, ale nie chcę jeszcze iść pod kamerę. Popatrzę na niego, jak przechadza się między tymi VIP-ami, jak się mizdrzy, jak udaje jednego z nich. Przyjemniaczek.

Podchodzi do szerokiego stołu, pełno na nim jedzenia. Z tej perspektywy to całe żarcie zlewa się w jedną kolorową, pachnącą masę. Nakłada sobie na talerz; wystarczyłoby tego dla kilku. Za bardzo wychylam się przez balustradę. Nie mogę, przecież wystarczy, że przejedzie wzrokiem po balkonach, i już po mnie. Wracam, idę się napić wody.

Nogi mam coraz bardziej zaprawione. Jeszcze miesiąc temu po paru godzinach stania miałem dosyć. A teraz? Teraz jest lepiej, chociaż cały czas zdarzają się kryzysy, czasami już po dwóch godzinach stania. Mam na to sposób. Po prostu kucam, prawie jak w kościele. Kucam minutę, może dwie. To nic, że kolana w spodniach się wypychają, i tak wyglądam jak pierdoła. Jak wszystko boli, to człowiek nie myśli o wizerunku. Byleby się nie wyłożyć w pierwszym pełnym przysiadzie.

Dziś dużo mniejszy ruch na piętrze. Nie wiem, czy na wszystkich, ale pewnie tak. Większość pracowników centrum jest na Atrium i tylko czasami ktoś wjedzie na piętro, jednak zaraz znowu wchodzi do windy i zjeżdża z powrotem.

Zasady są proste. Każdy z tych wychodzących z windy lub wchodzących do windy podchodzi do mnie i okazuje przepustkę. Ile razy by nie zjechali i wjechali, zawsze po powrocie na piętro muszą okazać przepustkę. Ja rzucam spojrzenie i uśmiechając się, mówię „dziękuję". Teraz to już mówię „dziękuję", kiedy jeszcze nie wyciągną przepustki z kieszeni. Ot, taka zawodowa rutyna. Przez dwa miesiące nauczyłem się twarzy na pamięć, więc nie sprawdzam wnikliwie, nie porównuję zdjęcia z facjatą. Po co? Co innego, jeśli na pięterko wjedzie jakiś GOŚĆ. Gość powinien mieć

identyfikator przyczepiony w widocznym miejscu. Może przypiąć go sobie nawet na rozpor-
ku, byleby było widać. Wtedy w skupieniu porównuję identyfikator z dowodem tożsamości
i też grzecznie dziękuję – cała filozofia pracy
na pięterkach. Czasami zdarza się, że gość
niechętnie okazuje dowód, zasłaniając się tym,
że pokazywał już na dole, w recepcji. Wtedy
trzeba zachować zimną krew i nie odpuszczać
– dowód musi pokazać. Kiedy wreszcie pokaże,
grzecznie dziękuję, ale już się nie uśmiecham.
Twardym trzeba być.

*

Jest po godzinie czternastej, kiedy na piętro
wjeżdża Mojs. Idzie w towarzystwie jakiegoś
faceta, coś mu tłumaczy, pokazuje windy, ściany. Tamten tylko potakuje. Pierwszy raz widzę tego typa. Jest wbity w przyciasny popie-
laty garnitur. Może to jakiś VIP z imprezy na
Atrium?
    – Dzień dobry – mówię głośno.
    Choć widziałem Mojsa na odprawie, to kła-
niam się tak, jakbym go dzisiaj pierwszy raz
widział. Nie odpowiada. Tylko tamten pochyla
lekko głowę. To już coś.
    – Stój pan równo – mówi Mojs. – Nie przy
ścianie, tylko tu! – Pokazuje paluchem. – O! Tu
pan stój. – Kręci z niezadowoleniem głową. – To
jest nowy inspektor.

Facet wyciąga świeżo wystawioną lamino-waną przepustkę i przystawia mi ją do oczu. Chcę przeczytać nazwisko, ale zbyt blisko mi ją podsuwa. Cofam się.

– Polecenia tego pana masz wykonywać tak samo, jakbym ja ci je wydawał.

(Ma zastępcę?)

Odchodzą, ale nie są na tyle daleko, bym nie zrozumiał, co Mojs gada do tego nowego.

– To są zwykłe ciecie, na jednego strzała. Mówię ci, krótko z nimi trzeba.

Facet na mnie zerka, potem znowu patrzy na uświadamiającego go Mojsa. Odchodzą dalej, pod drzwi windy. Teraz facet zaczyna coś gadać. Nie mogę nic usłyszeć. Mojs naciska podświetlony przycisk przywołujący windę.

Przez chwilę wyobrażam sobie, jak z pięści uderza mnie w twarz. Łapę to on ma rzeczywiście niemałą; ciekawe, czy już tu kogoś uderzył. A może to on jest na jednego strzała? Pozory często mylą, ale nie będę tego sprawdzał. Nie jestem wyrywny; poza tym moja potyczka zakończyłaby się pewnie ciężkim nokautem dla mnie.

*

Dźwięk aplauzu przeplatany wzmocnionym aparaturą nagłaśniającą głosem pani prowadzącej obijają się o połyskujące ściany. Podchodzę do balustrady. Mogliby już skończyć; ileż można wysłuchiwać tego jcj „PROSZĘ PAŃSTWA!"?!

Dzwonek windy. Leniwie odwracam się do tyłu. Tu naprawdę nie można być niczego pewnym. No bo dlaczego facet, który przed momentem w towarzystwie Mojsa wsiadł do windy, znowu tu jest? Nawet gdyby nie wiedział, że nie mogę tu legalnie stać, to moje płochliwe zachowanie i tak wszystko zdradza. Szybko wracam pod kamerę; mogę się jedynie cieszyć, że tym razem jest sam. Mojs nie byłby taki spokojny, od razu by mnie opierdolił, a nockę na bank spędziłbym na Chocimskiej albo u Zbycha. Miałbym przegwizdane, no i działę. Tak, działa byłaby na pewno.

Patrzę na niego. Próbuję robić dziarską minę, ale na próbach się kończy. On za to zaczyna przechadzać się jak kot, zaraz zacznie ocierać się o moje nogawki. Dziwny jest. Po cholerę znowu tu wjechał? Przecież już mnie poznał, dowiedział się, że jestem na jednego strzała. Po co mi się teraz tak przygląda?

Zaciskam zęby i patrzę na jego starannie wypastowane brązowe buty. Nie mam odwagi wyżej podnieść wzroku, cały czas myślę o tym, że kiedy tu wjechał, ja zamiast pod kamerą stałem tam i gapiłem się na żrących ludzi.

Dzwonek windy. Nie ma go? Wsiadł. Na pewno pomylił piętra. Co za ulga.

– SIÓDME PIĘTRO, ZGŁOŚ SIĘ DO INTERKOMU!

Czego oni chcą? Przecież stoję pod kamerą.

- Zgłasza się siódme piętro!
- DLACZEGO NIE WYLEGITYMOWAŁEŚ PANA?
- Którego pana?

O co im chodzi? Przecież zawsze wszystkich legitymuję.

- DZIESIĘĆ MINUT TEMU NIE WYLEGITY-MOWAŁEŚ CZŁOWIEKA!

Kurwa, przecież przez ostatnie dziesięć minut nikogo nie musiałem legitymować. W co oni chcą mnie wkręcić?

Opieram się o interkom, nie wiem, co powiedzieć. To znaczy może i wiem, ale przez ten cholerny głośnik kiepsko się prowadzi z mojej pozycji jakąkolwiek dyskusję.

- Zawsze wszystkich legitymuję – odpowiadam uparcie, wierząc, że coś im się pochrzaniło. Pewnie nabijają się ze mnie; Mojsowi się nudzi, więc szuka rozrywki.

- NIE WYLEGITYMOWAŁEŚ PANA INSPEKTORA!

Oni robią sobie ze mnie jaja. Odchodzę od interkomu i ustawiam się najładniej, jak potrafię. Nie mogę tak się dawać, nie będę ich pajacem do rozrywki.

- SIÓDME PIĘTRO, ZGŁOŚ SIĘ DO INTERKO-MU! – W tle słyszę tego faceta, jakby opowiadał o mnie.

Można tak dręczyć człowieka? Nie podchodzę... Nie podchodzę od razu.

- Zgłasza się siódme piętro – mówię głośno i wyraźnie, tak jak każą.

Szum. Znowu przedostaje się rozmyta dyskusja z pomieszczenia monitoringu, i tak jest za każdym razem, kiedy któryś z nich naciska przycisk.

– DLACZEGO NIE WYLEGITYMOWAŁEŚ CZŁOWIEKA?

(Kurwa! Człowieka, człowieka).

– Jakiego człowieka?

– INSPEKTORA!

Nie wiem, co odpowiedzieć – jakby mi ktoś knebel do mordy wcisnął.

– SIÓDME PIĘTRO!

– Tak?

– DLACZEGO NIE WYLEGITYMOWAŁEŚ CZŁOWIEKA?

Kurwa mać, nie wiem. Co mam powiedzieć? Że myślałem, że nie muszę? Że do głowy by mi nie przyszło, że ten „człowiek" robi zwyczajną podpuchę? To wszystko to jakieś wielkie gówno, popis prowokacji i faszyzm. Mam im powiedzieć, że nie tylko ja tak myślę? Że w tamtym tygodniu powiedziała to pracująca tu kobieta, widząc, jak stoję od samego rana, jak nogi włażą mi w dupę, a mimo to uśmiecham się do niej? Nawet wtedy, kiedy mija mnie i ciągnie za sobą długi ogon zapachu stołówki. Wraca z przerwy – z przerwy! Nie z wyścigu na czas, z próby napchania się najszybciej jak tylko można, by nie stać do rana z burczącym z głodu bebechem.

Ona, ta miła kobieta, spytała, dlaczego nie usiądę. Wtedy jej powiedziałem... powiedziałem, że nie mogę, że muszę tak stać do dziewiętnastej, pod kamerą. Nie kryła zdziwienia i stwierdziła, że to faszyzm. Na pewno dobra z niej kobieta.

Nie powiem im tego – to by i tak gówno dało. Sam rewolucji nie zrobię, co najwyżej mogę się zwolnić. A zwolnię się, kurwa, stąd na pewno, tylko jeszcze trochę, i odejdę. A na odchodne pokażę Mojsowi środkowy palec. Szkoda że to nie można było już teraz, w tym momencie. Zjechałbym windą i po sprawie, koniec, inny świat.

Jeszcze trochę.

*

Brzuch mnie rozbolał. To ze zdenerwowania. Jestem lżejszy o połowę kasy za dyżur i mam przed sobą mało optymistyczną wizję kolejnego posterunku. Ciekawe, do czyjej kieszeni idą te wszystkie pieniądze z dział. Czy Mojs okrada nas i wszystko zostawia sobie? A może dzieli się ze swoją obślizgłą świtą? Odpala im jakiś procent? Pieniądze przecież i tak są wypłacane za pracę stojaka. Mojs nie informuje tych, którzy płacą firmie za ochronę budynku. Nie leci do nich i nie opowiada, że tego i tego dnia jeden z drugim stoją za połowę. Oficjalnie każdy stoi za pełną stawkę.

Te wszystkie działy to taki wewnętrzny zło-
dziejski twór. Firma nie chwali się nim kontra-
hentom. Mogłoby to zburzyć wizerunek oparty
na humanitaryzmie, który bije z plakatów reklamowych. Chociaż kandydatów do pracy i tak
by nie zabrakło. Tu nie trzeba być fachowcem,
przyjmą wszystkich, jak leci. Najważniejsze
jest to, by szybko zapomnieć o swoim ja. Wtedy proces przystosowawczy przebiegnie bez
zakłóceń. U mnie zamiana w zwierzątko idzie
jak po grudzie. Może to kwestia nieustannego
myślenia o własnym sklepie spożywczym? Pamięć, że nie zawsze tu stałem, w tych zdezelo-
wanych przepoconych buciorach, myśląc tylko
o tym, by ten dyżur jak najszybciej się skończył.

Od samego początku, kiedy tylko zacząłem
tu pracę, tak mam. Zaczynam dyżur i już myślę
o jego końcu. To głupie, ale nic nie mogę z tym
zrobić. Od pierwszej godziny tak jest i potem
zaczyna się już tylko końcowe odliczanie.

– Siódme piętro zgłasza plażę!

Nie czekam, idę. Dostałem już za swoje. Za
cały dyżur kasy wziąć mi nie mogą, chyba nie
mogą. Zresztą sam już, kurwa, nie wiem.

Nie tylko ja mam dziś problemy z żołądkiem.
Z boku jakiś nieszczęśnik naprawdę cierpi. Nie
mam pewności, czy usłyszał, jak wchodziłem
do sąsiedniej kabiny, ale moja obecność nie
przeszkadza mu jęczeć. Mogłoby się wydawać,
że ci krawaciarze nie mają żadnych problemów,

a tu coś takiego. W jego przypadku to już chyba nie jest zwykłe zatrucie. Jak tu srać? Facet jęczy, jakby go na ruszt nabijali. Normalnie powinno się zapytać, czy wszystko u niego w porządku, ale ja zostawię go w spokoju. Niech walczy. Kibel to jedno z niewielu miejsc, gdzie człowiek może być naprawdę sobą.

*

Koniec! Wreszcie! Stoję przy balustradzie. Atrium szybko pustoszeje. Za dwie godziny będę mógł usiąść, a teraz? A teraz widzę, jak jeden ze stojaków ładuje sobie na talerz jedzenie, za nim drugi. Wyglądają, jakby kradli coś bardzo cennego. Są przyczajeni, przygarbieni i w ogóle cały czas rozglądają się dokoła. Patrzę na nich i aż mnie skręca z zazdrości. Plastikowe pojemniki pełne żarcia! Podchodzę do windy. Nie myślę teraz o niczym innym, tylko o tym, by też ukręcić coś dla siebie. Włażę do windy, to tylko dwa piętra – dwa piętra dzielą mnie od tego jedzenia. Nieprzyjemne uczucie strachu równoważy przyjemność spojrzenia z bliska na to wszystko.

Nic dziwnego, że nie dali rady. Tym, co zostało, można by wykarmić połowę Warszawy. I chociaż wszystko jest już zimne, teraz nie mogę powstrzymać radości.

Podchodzę do połyskującego urządzenia. To taka długa lada podgrzewająca wcześniej całe to jadło. Jakaś młoda kobieta, pracownica firmy cateringowej, patrzy na mnie kątem oka.

Chwytam za plastikowy pojemnik; mógłby być głębszy.

– Można? – pytam ją, chociaż tak naprawdę jej odpowiedź jest dla mnie nieistotna.

– Proszę – odpowiada; uśmiecha się do mnie. Nie odwzajemniam jej uśmiechu, nie mam na to czasu. Jestem głodny.

Z pojemnikiem pełnym mięsa w brązowym, stężałym sosie wracam na swoje piętro. Już w windzie zaczynam jeść. Smakuje super.

Do dziewiętnastej zostały jeszcze dwie godziny. Nie będę jadł na stojąco; gdzieś słyszałem, że od tego można dostać wrzodów żołądka. Siadam.

Jeszcze nigdy zimny sos nie smakował mi tak bardzo. Z chlebem byłoby lepsze, ale co tam. Szkoda tylko, że tak szybko to zjadam. O! I już. Koniec. Mówiłem, pojemnik jest za płytki. Mogłem jeść wolniej. Zjadę po dokładkę? A co mi tam, tyle jedzenia ma się zmarnować? Jeszcze tylko podejdę do balustrady, zobaczę, czy teren czysty; może Mojs też wpadł na resztki.

Za późno. Nic dziwnego. Od razu mogłem zjechać po dokładkę; teraz mam za swoje. Całe to zimne żarcie trafia do dużych plastikowych pojemników, aż żal patrzeć. Ciekawe, co potem z nim zrobią. Pewnie wyrzucą, dadzą świniom albo może odgrzeją i podadzą na innej imprezie. Kto wie, może i to dzisiejsze gościło już wcześniej pod innym adresem. Na żarciu to można ludzi w konia robić. Karmę dla psa podać jako wykwintny pasztet i wszyscy będą się zachwycać. Kiedy chce się jeść, wyobraźnia zanika, a żarcie z recyklingu może smakować jak najświeższa cielęcinka.

Recykling czy nie, przydałyby mi się gacie na zmianę. Znowu mam srakę, a na dodatek przed momentem walnąłem bąka z kleksem. Co za wstyd! Teraz jest mi głupio przed samym sobą. Może te pampersy to rzeczywiście nie byłby taki zły pomysł? Założyłbym sobie takiego na dupę i problem z głowy. Potem takie zgrabne zawiniątka dawalibyśmy Mojsowi do przeliczenia. Dowódca albo jego adiutant zapisywałby stan inwentarza. Tak, temu skurwielowi należałaby się taka fucha. Najlepiej, gdyby jeszcze przy wszystkich wnikliwie sprawdzał zawartość. A potem? Żeby tylko to ode mnie zależało. Zafundowałbym mu takiego hard core'a, że już więcej by tu nie przylazł. Płakałby i rzygał na przemian. Łajza jedna.

To na pewno przez to żarcie; ale czym jest sraka w porównaniu z uczuciem sytości – nawet jeśli jest okupione pieczeniem dupy. Jedyne, z czym nie mogę się pogodzić, to ten cholerny kleks. Myślałem, że będzie wszystko w porządku, a tu coś takiego.

Śmierdzę! Jeśli mi nie dadzą Chocimskiej, to sam o nią poproszę. Cała noc na świeżym powietrzu to chyba dla mnie najlcpsza perspek-

tywa. Dobrze mnie przewietrzy, to może rano
w szatni nikt nie poczuje, że prawie narobiłem
w galoty. A może zdejmę i spuszczę je w kiblu?
Niee, dziwnie by było tak po obiekcie chronionym bez gaci łazić.

*

Chciałem, to mam – do rana Chocimska. Nie
będę zacierał rąk ze szczęścia. Dobrze, że nie
spuściłem gaci w kanał – mogłoby mnie prze-
wiać. Póki co, noce są jeszcze chłodne, a dwanaście godzin to dwanaście godzin.

*

Jak można odłożyć poważną kwotę, kiedy zarabia się śmiesznie mało? Coraz mniej we
mnie wiary, z wagą też nie jest najlepiej. Gdy
zacząłem tu pracować, wyglądałem jak człowiek, a teraz? Schudłem, widzę to po ubra-
niach, szczególnie wtedy, kiedy wciągam na
siebie spodnie. Niemożliwe, żcby aż tak się
rozciągnęły. Zawsze byłem chudzielcem, ale
teraz zaczynam przypominać anorektyka, a do
tego przyplątały się problemy z żołądkiem. Nie
wiem, ile jeszcze tu wytrzymam, i chyba nie
chcę tego sprawdzać.

*

Czasami można posłuchać ciekawych rozmów. Ciekawe rozmowy to takie, kiedy ktoś nie daje już psychicznie rady i zaczyna puszczać w eter swoje gorzkie żale. Ze zmęczenia prowadzi jakiś bezsensowny monolog. Chaotyczna plątanina słów, gadka o czymś, ale tak naprawdę nie wiadomo, o co chodzi, bo bohater zamieszania jest u kresu.

Ostatnio taki jeden chyba zwariował. Ni stąd, ni zowąd zaczął krzyczeć przez krótkofalówkę, wyzywać dowódcę Heńka. Bluzgał, ile wlezie, aż w końcu ucichł. Przez chwilę było wesoło, potem jeszcze miałem nadzieję, że go usłyszę, że dalej będzie mieszał Heńka z błotem, ale nic z tego. Zdjęli go z posterunku i wyrzucili. Jednak naprawdę ciekawie robi się dopiero wtedy, kiedy ktoś zaczyna o cokolwiek grzecznie prosić. Kiedy na przykład zaczyna się uskarżać na ból, jakikolwiek ból. Cierpliwie wywołuje przez radio dowódcę, ale zamiast odpowiedzi – cisza. Wtedy naprawdę jest ciekawie. Teraz też. Od dobrej godziny jakiś na piętrze prosi, by go puścili do domu. Jest bardzo szczery – mówi, że zarzygał hol windowy. Relacjonuje nam to wszystko na żywo. Słychać, jak przystraja posadzkę, bo ani na chwilę nie puszcza przycisku krótkofalówki. Jego beczenie słychać na wszystkich posterunkach. Prawdziwy męczennik – rzyga za nas wszystkich, i chwała mu za to.

– Idę do domu! – krzyczy.

– Nie możesz zejść z posterunku.

Wreszcie jakaś odpowiedź.

– Ale źle się czuję!

Znowu słychać beczenie i urwaną odpowiedź dowódcy.

– Do rana już niedaleko...

Patrzę na zegarek. Dowcipni są, przecież do końca zostało jeszcze osiem godzin.

– Źle się czuję! – powtarza.

Cisza. Biorą go na przetrzymanie, ale on jest nieugięty.

– Mam mdłości i...

– Kurwa, zamknij pan ryj!

Mojs? Nie byłem pewny, czy ta świnia jeszcze tu jest. Trudno uwierzyć, że takie rzeczy dzieją się naprawdę.

– Co „zamknij ryj"?!

Chłopak ma jaja.

– Coś powiedział?

– Że źle się czuję!

– Rano pójdziesz do domu, a teraz, kurwa, przestań jęczeć. Tylko radio blokujesz.

– Czyli co?

– Czyli gówno! Nie bądź ciota i przestań wisieć na radiu.

– Idę do domu!

Ma jaja.

– Tylko spróbuj!

– Paweł weź moją torbę – gada do swojego brata ciotecznego. Przyjęli się na ten obiekt razem.

– Jak, kurwa, zejdziesz z posterunku, to możesz już tu nie wracać! Słyszysz?! – krzyczy Mojs.

– Paweł?

– Tak? – Głos mu drży; pewnie wolałby na ten czas nie być jego kuzynem.

– Weź moją torbę, dobra?

– A co?

– Idę do domu. Weź z szatni moją torbę! – powtarza.

– Do domu?

– Do domu.

– Dobra – odpowiada kuzyn cichutko i ze strachem.

Mojs, gdyby mógł, za samowolne zejście z posterunku podcinałby gardła.

*

Parę dni temu rozmawiałem z moim inspektorem z batonów. Aż dziw bierze, że czasami na niego psioczyłem. Nie wiem, po co tu przyszedł; pewnie miał jakąś sprawę do Mojsa. Kiedy mnie zobaczył, od razu zrobił wielkie oczy. Stałem na Chocimskiej, było jeszcze przed południem, i wtedy do mnie podszedł. Zaczął pytać, jak mi się tu pracuje i takie tam bzdury. Chcąc pokazać, jak bardzo sobie polepszyłem sytuację, próbowałem udać zadowolenie, ale już po krótkiej chwili sztuczny entuzjazm zaczął się ulatniać. Kto wie, co by było, gdyby facet jeszcze trochę przy mnie postał. Może zacząłbym go prosić, by zabrał mnie stąd z powrotem na batony. Rozmowa z nim – normalna i tak inna od wściekłego bełkotu Mojsa – przywołała fajne wspomnienia, normalny czas. Tego mi teraz najbardziej brakuje. Tu wszystko zdaje się nienormalne, wynaturzone, zboczone. Tak samo jak polecenia wydawane przez tych popaprańców.

*

– Mam na imię Dominik, ale możecie mówić na mnie Dulian.

Mrużę oczy. To ten nowy, ten, co miał się już jakiś czas temu do nas wprowadzić. Ten z Koszalina.

– Jak? – Wiesiek patrzy na niego podejrzliwie.

– Dulian – powtarza. – Tak na mnie mówią od bachora. Taką mam ksywkę.

Wyciąga z kieszeni mocno wytartej kurtki dżinsowej paczkę papierosów i ostentacyjnie rzuca ją na stół. Po chwili jednak podnosi ją i wyciąga z niej papierosa. Nie częstuje nas, sam sobie odpala, a potem z powrotem rzuca paczkę na blat. Mógł chociaż zapytać, czy chcemy. Jak ma z nami mieszkać, to musi się nauczyć kultury.

– Mogę? – Nie czekając na odpowiedź, wyciągam papierosa. Normalnie bym tak nie zrobił, ale on nas nie poczęstował.

– Słuchaj – zaczyna leniwie – jak leżą, to pal. Nie pytaj, tylko bierz – mówi. Patrzy teraz na Wieśka, potem przeskakuje wzrokiem na Krzyśka. – Proszę, wy też się częstujcie, śmiało.

Twarze braci pogodnieją. Nowy okazuje się ludzkim człowiekiem, ma gest. Jest w porządku. Wiesiek patrzy na brata. Krzysiek kiwa głową i też sięga po papierosa.

– O, proszę, lepsze się pali? – mówi z właściwym sobie przekąsem.

Dulian wypuszcza w jego stronę kłęby dymu, jakby zaciągnął się na raz całym papierosem. Wykrzywia usta.

– Jak już się truć, to lepszymi – odpowiada, rozglądając się z lekko zblazowaną miną po pokoju. – Przydałaby się satka. Zresztą już rozmawiałem z panią Bożeną. Mówiła, że bez problemu mogę zamontować talerz.

– Talerz? – dziwię się.

– Antenę satelitarną. – Patrzy na telewizor. – Ile macie teraz kanałów?

– Cztery, ale trochę śnieżą – odpowiada Krzysiek.

– Jak zamontujemy satkę, to będzie sto cztery albo i lepiej. A obraz to będzie taki, że mucha nie siada, jak na widokówce z wakacji, zobaczycie.

– Gdzie pracujesz? – pytam.

– Mówi wam coś Forum Plaza?

– Forum co? – Wiesiek mruży oczy.

– Fo-rum Pla-za – powtarza powoli.

- Nie.

- Taki nowoczesny wieżowiec na Alejach Jerozolimskich. Biały taki.

Niech on już lepiej nic o nowoczesnych wieżowcach nie gada.

- Aaa, już wiem – mówi Wiesiek.

- No, to właśnie tam instalację elektryczną kładziemy.

- To ty elektryk jesteś – cieszy się Krzysiek.

- My na ochronie robimy. W Jankach na markecie z bratem stoję, a on – pokazuje na mnie paluchem – na centrum biznesowym stoi.

- Wychodzicie na swoje?

- Dobrze jest – odpowiadam. – Ale ja jeszcze tylko trochę i potem coś swojego otworzę.

- Własny biznes ci się marzy? – pyta, a Wiesiek zaczyna chichotać. Zawsze wyśmiewa ten mój sklep spożywczy, Krzysiek zresztą też. Teraz przy tym nowym chcą pokazać, że to mrzonki. – A jaki?

- Spożywczy – odpowiadam, a on od razu kręci głową.

- Hipermarkety cię wykończą, zobaczysz. – Cmoka, jakby mu ość między jedynki weszła.

- Nieee, spożywczy to już nie to, co kiedyś. – Zaczyna opowiadać teraz o jakimś facecie, co go market z torbami puścił, bo musiał sprzedawać po kosztach, aż w końcu plajtę zaliczył.

- Niee, sklep spożywczy to nie – powtarza.

- Pożyjemy, zobaczymy – mówię i przez moment zastanawiam się, czy on aby nie ma racji.

O zgrozo, do końca za ciecia robić? Nie, nigdy! Prędzej czy później będę miał ten sklep, a bracia niech sobie kręcą łbami, razem z nim. – Nie wszyscy zakupy robią w marketach.

– Jak tam uważasz – odpowiada i znowu zaczyna się rozglądać po pokoju. – Ale mieszkacie sobie fajnie. Moje łóżko to które?

– Te. – Wiesiek wskazuje ręką na wniesiony już przed tygodniem zdezelowany wąski tapczan.

Dulian patrzy na niego.

– Chyba ktoś tu nasikał – śmieje się.

– Położysz koc i nie będzie widać – pociesza go Krzysiek.

– To wypłowiałe, sprane gówno? – pokazuje palcem na złożony kraciasty koc.

Czego on się spodziewał? Jeszcze dobrze się nie wprowadził, a już marudzi, ważniak jeden. Nie lubię takich jak on. Koc mu się nie podoba! Spojrzałby lepiej na siebie. Sam wygląda jak łachudra, a do tego, co najgorsze, nie wierzy w mój biznesplan.

ROZDZIAŁ

5

Cały dzień na klateczkach – tak można pracować. Teraz na pewno będzie lepiej. Pierwsza dowódcza doba Arka. Pracuje tu tyle, co ja, ale bez wątpienia dużo lepiej potrafi sobie radzić z Mojsem. Od początku wiedział pod jakim kontem ma wchodzić mu w dupę. Będzie dobrze.

Traktuje mnie ulgowo – od razu wysyła na klateczki, mnie, a nie kogo innego. W porządku jest! Jeszcze taki jeden z mojego przydziału i kto wie, może adiutantem zostanę?

Do tej pory dowódców było dwóch, Adaś i Henio. Dzielili się między sobą dyżurami. Arek wszedł na trzeciego, tak na próbę. Tamci za dużo godzin w miesiącu wyrabiali, to Mojs dorzucił im Arka. Teraz Adaś i Henio mówią, że żaden z nich nie zarobi, bo godzin będzie mało. Chcą się zwolnić, to znaczy tak między sobą gadają. Gdzie będą mieli lepiej? Tu tylko siedzą na dupach i do interkomu krzyczą. Gdzie będą mieli lepiej?

Ciekawe, czy Mojsa kiedyś wywalą. Na razie wydaje się, że nie ma na niego silnych. Ktoś musiałby go porządnie pogrążyć, puścić w obieg jakąś plotkę. Na przykład że jest zbokiem, że widzieli go, jak obciąga fujarę Zbychowi. Dwie pieczenie na jednym ogniu. Anonimowy telefon, szybka ciekawa informacja, i gotowe. Łatwo można zniszczyć opinię „człowieka", wystarczy jeden telefon. Mojs na to zasługuje. Im dłużej o tym myślę, tym bardziej mam ochotę coś takiego wykręcić. Już widzę ten jego opasły czerwony ryj pełen wstydu.

W dzieciństwie należałem do tych, co na kolonii nie pluli wychowawcy do zupy. Bałem się, że wyszłoby to na jaw, że jakimś trafem to właśnie moja ślina będzie pechowa i oberwę za wszystkich. Jestem tchórzem? Jak coś komuś ginie, to od razu dostaję wypieków na gębie i mimo że nic nie zwinąłem, to czuję się jakoś dziwnie. Nie mam predyspozycji do podkładania komuś świni, ale może w słusznej sprawie dałbym radę. Cholera, ja na samą tylko myśl o tym sram w gacie. Co będzie, jak mnie złapią? Za coś takiego można pójść do więzienia. Bawić się w oprawcę? Niee, nie nadaję się do tego, to sport ekstremalny. Tak jest bezpieczniej.

Nocka na minusikach. Nic dziwnego – po takiej labie nie mogło być inaczej. Że też ten palant Zbychu musi być na mojej zmianie! Gdyby nie on, to te minusiki nie byłyby aż takie straszne. Samo łażenie to nie problem. Porażająca charyzma Zbycha – to jest problem. Trochę już odwykłem od niego. W ostatnim czasie najczęściej stałem na piętrach, a teraz z nim do rana.

– MINUS, ZGŁOŚ SIĘ DO INTERKOMU!

Który już raz mnie woła? Po co każą nam taszczyć te krótkofalówki, skoro i tak tylko przez trzeszczący interkom krzyczą? Chociaż on mógłby inaczej. A potem się dziwi, że nie mogę go zrozumieć.

– Tak, zgłasza się minus! – Jestem trochę zasapany, dziś jest wyjątkowo duszno, a na dodatek zaczęła mnie boleć głowa.

– DO MNIE!

(Kurwa, jak do jakiegoś kundla!)

– Słucham?

– DO MNIE!

– Idę!

Czego on chce? Przecież łażę; łażę tak, by mnie całego widział w monitorze. On jest na tym punkcie przewrażliwiony, na wielu innych punktach zresztą też.

Czego tym razem chce? Naciskam klamkę, otwieram drzwi. Wchodzę do jego okopconej nory.

– Jestem.

– Widzę. – Zaciąga się papierosem. Po co wplątywać go w afery? Rak płuc wykończy go szybciej. – Słuchaj. – Przygląda mi się uważnie. – Dzwonił pracownik centrum i mówił, że ma ujebaną antenę. Wiesz coś o tym?

– Antenę?

- Tak, w samochodzie.

Kręcę głową. Nie powinienem tak.

- To znaczy... W jakim samochodzie?

Ładuje zgaszonego peta do wypełnionej po brzegi dużej szklanej popielnicy.

- Kurwa! Ty nie rzucaj mi tu zagadek. To ja ci zadaję pytanie. Przestań pajacować! Jeszcze raz ci mówię, że dzwonił facet i gadał, że ktoś mu ułamał antenę! Tak trudno zrozumieć? Trudno?

Ten dyżur będzie długi.

Nakręca się coraz bardziej, a mnie coraz mocniej boli głowa. W takich momentach naprawdę mam dosyć i wiem jedno: człowiek nie powinien tak się czuć.

Muszę w końcu coś powiedzieć.

- Może już wjechał z taką urwaną?

Zbychu parska nerwowym śmiechem i wyciąga z paczki kolejnego papierosa. Odpala go, ale wcześniej kopie stojące przed sobą krzesło.

- Co ty mi tu, kurwa, pierdolisz?! To ty jesteś na minusach, a ja tu. Ty patrolujesz cały obszar, ja siedzę tu i koordynuję twoje ściemnianie. Tam jest twój ogródek, a tu mój, więc co ty mi teraz takie herezje głosisz? Nie wiesz, po co tu jesteś? Zapomniałeś, co ci mówiłem? Masz dokładnie patrolować teren i wszystkiemu bacznie się przyglądać. Zobaczysz, że z tego będzie gruba afera. Jak chuj afera będzie i to ty dostaniesz po dupie, nie ja. Nie zauważyłeś, nie zgłosiłeś, więc jesteś cipa, a nie ochroniarz! A teraz wypierdalaj, muszę napisać z tego zdarzenia notatkę służbową dla inspektora.

Wychodzę. W środku aż cały się trzęsę. Nie sposób wszystko ogarnąć wzrokiem. Może gdyby ten debil nie wołał mnie co chwilę pod ten cholerny interkom... może wtedy dawałbym radę.

Idę usiąść na moment na schodach ewakuacyjnych.

Czasami tu odpoczywam. Siadam na podłodze i opieram głowę o zimną balustradę. Tą klatką też można przejść na inny poziom, ale Zbychu mówi, że mam się przemieszczać między minusami windą, bo wtedy jestem monitorowany. Jestem bezpieczny, tak mówi.

Nie mogę przestać myśleć o tej antenie. Wjeżdżam na wyższy poziom; wcześniej oczywiście informuję o tym Zbycha. Nie mogłoby być inaczej. Nie odpowiada, pewnie jest zajęty pisaniem tej notatki służbowej. On jest tchórzem. Myślę, że nawet za samochód skradziony na jego oczach odpowiadałby każdy, tylko nie on. Taki fiut zawsze znajdzie kozła ofiarnego. Wtedy, kiedy o mały włos nie zwichnął mi ramienia, też była tylko i wyłącznie moja wina. Nie tak się ustawiłem? Palant.

*

Mojs stoi z założonymi rękoma i patrzy na mnie.

– Nie ma się co przejmować – mówi Zbychu. Wygląda tak, jakby chciał go do siebie

140

przytulić. – Kolega pokryje koszty i będzie, Marek, po sprawie.

– Banda cieci! – krzyczy Mojs. – Kurwa! Zero wyników, tylko żreć i srać cały czas by chcieli. Łażą i gówno widzą. – Podchodzi do Zbycha. – Pokaż to. Kurwa, ten raport pokaż!

Zbychu w pośpiechu podaje mu kartkę formatu A4 z zapisaną do połowy stroną.

– Proszę, tu wszystko jest napisane. Jest tak, jak było.

Mojs, jakby wcale go nie słuchał, bierze w pulchne łapy kartkę i zaczyna czytać. Cały czas z niedowierzaniem kręci głową. Stoję przed nimi i zastanawiam się, ile taka antena może kosztować. Z tego, co mi wiadomo, ten facet poinformował o wszystkim, dopiero jak dotarł do domu. Wcześniej pewnie nic nie zauważył.

Mojs kończy czytać.

– Podpisz – mówi oschle do Zbycha.

– Jasne. Nie podpisywałem, bo chciałem, żebyś wcześniej to przeczytał.

– Przeczytałem. Podpisz.

– Może być? – Najwidoczniej domaga się pochwały, ale Mojs nie odpowiada, robi się za to jeszcze bardziej nerwowy.

Zbychu drugi raz nie ryzykuje. Szybko chwyta za długopis i bez wahania podpisuje się pod własną notatką.

– On też. – Mojs wskazuje na mnie paluchem. – Jego podpis też musi być.

Zbychu podaje mi zapisaną kartkę.

– Masz, podpisz.

Biorę ją do ręki i zaczynam czytać:

Dnia ósmego maja o godzinie 21.12 dyspozytor poziomu minus jeden i minus dwa, Zbigniew Czostak, otrzymał telefon od pracownika centrum z informacją o ułamanej antenie w swoim aucie. Z rozmowy z poszkodowanym dyspozytor poziomu minus jeden i minus dwa dowiedział się, że auto musiało ulec uszkodzeniu w trakcie postoju w godzinach: 20.20– 20.50, ponieważ w tych godzinach auto znajdowało się na strzeżonym parkingu, a jego właściciel przebywał na terenie centrum. Niezwłocznie po telefonie Pana Karola Pażyckiego o zaistniałym zdarzeniu został poinformowany inspektor ochrony, Pan Marek Mojs, który zapoznał się z wyżej wymienionym zdarzeniem.

W międzyczasie został wezwany pracownik ochrony, Patryk Boszczuk, który pełnił służbę na poziomach minusowych. Pracownik przyznał się do niedopełnienia czynności służbowych, jednocześnie tłumacząc, że nie zauważył nic podejrzanego. Pracownik ochrony Patryk Boszczuk został pouczony i sam zobowiązał się do pokrycia wszelkich kosztów związanych z kupnem i zamontowaniem nowej anteny.

Nie podpisywać? Przecież taka antena może kosztować majątek. Chociaż właściwie... to tylko zwykła antena samochodowa, nic więcej.

- Dużo mnie to wyniesie? - pytam, uwieszając się spojrzeniem Mojsa.

- Zależy - odpowiada. - Jak się będziesz tak ociągał, to na pewno więcej.

- Podpisuj - pogania mnie Zbychu i nerwowo stuka palcem w leżącą na biurku kartkę. - Podpisuj i będzie po sprawie.

- A karę też dostanę?

Mojs patrzy na zegarek.

- Masz jeszcze pięć sekund. Jak się wyrobisz, to potraktuję cię ulgowo. - Zaczyna odliczać: - Pięć, cztery, trzy...

(Nie tak szybko).

Nie ma czasu na kalkulację, chwytam za długopis.

- Dwa...

Podpisałem.

- Jeden!... No, masz szczęście, ale mało brakowało. A swoją drogą, co tamten robił o tej porze w pracy? - Patrzy na Zbycha. - Coś mu się z godzinami popierdoliło?

Zbychu uśmiecha się słodko.

- Nie, Mareczku, on po coś tylko na chwilę przyjechał. No i wtedy... - Rozkłada bezradnie ręce. - No i wtedy, widzisz, stało się, ale to może i dobrze. Teraz wezmą się przynajmniej do roboty. Już zaczęło się im wydawać, że wystarczy odbębnić swoje i do domu, a tu proszę. - Wytrzeszcza oczy. - Czasami jednak coś się dzieje. Dobrze, że co gorszego się nie stało, bo do końca życia byś się nie wypłacił, a tak – trochę poboli i przestanie. To cię nauczy czujności.

– Dużo taka antena kosztuje?

W głębi duszy czuję, że nie powinienem niczego podpisywać. Nic dziwnego, że dla nich jestem zwykłym frajerem. Następnym razem nie dam się w nic wrobić. Jak będą chcieli, żebym coś podpisał, wypnę się na nich. Najwyżej mnie zwolnią, żadna strata.

– Zobaczysz na paragonie – odpowiada Zbychu.

Mojs szybko składa notatkę na cztery części i nie żegnając się, wychodzi. Zbycha to mocno dekoncentruje. Po zatrzaśnięciu drzwi jego gęba smutnieje.

– Idź już – mówi cicho i z melancholią w oczach patrzy przez szybę na oddalającą się coraz mniejszą postać Mojsa.

Wychodzę.

Do rana kalkuluję i przeliczam. W pamięci sumuję miesięczne wydatki i dokładam do nich wymyślony, za każdym razem inny, koszt tej cholernej anteny. Im bliżej rana, tym większym jestem optymistą, aż w końcu zmęczony przestaję się tym zadręczać.

*

Dulian jeszcze nie zamontował satki. Od paru dni nie chodzi też do pracy. Mówi, że miał niebezpieczny wypadek, że tramwaj go przeciągnął

przez jedną stację, bo mu się w drugim wago-
niku w ostatnich drzwiach noga nieszczęśliwie
zakleszczyła. Rzeczywiście, wtedy miał rozdar-
te spodnie, nogawki jakby zakrwawione i beł-
kotał coś jak w amoku. Czuć było też od niego
gorzałą. Ani ja, ani bracia nie chcieliśmy go pytać, ale na drugi dzień sam nam powiedział.

W pierwszej chwili zachciało mi się śmiać.
No bo jak tramwaj tak za nogę, i on żyje? Ale
potem aż mnie zmroziło. Teraz już wiem, że to
bzdury. Dulian sprzedał Bożenie inną wersję.
Powiedział jej, że miał wypadek w pracy, że
jakaś wciągarka czy coś takiego nogi mu prawie połamała. Dwie wersje – która prawdziwa?
Pewnie żadna. Jak było naprawdę i dlaczego
Dulian przyszedł wtedy z wyszarpaną dupą?
Prawdy nikt się nie dowie. Pewne jest jedno –
on ma teraz wolne i chociaż, jak sam mówi, nie
był u lekarza, to jest na chorobowym.

*

– Patryk?
– Tak...
– Wybierasz się może do sklepu?
Cały czas mnie tym zadręcza.
– Nie.
– Aha.

Próbuje wziąć mnie na litość. Rozumiem,
że bolą go nogi, ale już od tygodnia chce się
mną wysługiwać. Na początku, kiedy jeszcze

wszyscy wierzyliśmy w ten jego tramwaj, bez słowa sprzeciwu służyliśmy mu pomocą. Ale kiedy po drugim dniu jego rekonwalescencji pani Bożena opowiedziała nam, jakie to nieszczęście przytrafiło się Dominikowi w pracy, nasz humanitaryzm ostygł i teraz on musi się poruszać na własnych, prawie połamanych nogach. No, może jakby jeszcze fajką poczęstował..., ale jego szczodrość trwała krócej niż moja wiara w jego wymyślone historie. Zresztą, jak ze wszystkim, z kasą też jest u niego słabiutko. Nasz burżuj umarłby z głodu, gdyby nie lodówka. Jak na razie jeszcze nikt nie wpadł na to, by zamykać ją na kłódkę. Do tej pory nie kradliśmy sobie nawzajem jedzenia, ale od paru dni jest inaczej.

Już trzeci raz słyszę wyraźnie to łapczywe mlaskanie. Zawsze dochodzi z kuchni, kiedy on jest przekonany, że śpimy. Teraz też. Podnoszę głowę. Bracia chrapią. Obudzić ich? Fajnie by było przyłapać go na gorącym uczynku. W końcu, jak już chce na krzywy ryj, to niech się chociaż zapyta. Wiem, jak to jest, kiedy bebechy skręcają się z głodu, ale tak kraść komuś jedzenie? Idę.

Nie zdaje sobie sprawy, że stoję tuż za nim. Mroczna scena; tylko kuchennego tasaka brakuje.

– Zgłodniałeś?

Kobiecie w ciąży bym tak nie zrobił, ale jemu? Mam nadzieję, że serce ma zdrowe.

– Mógłbyś się tak nie skradać? – Odkłada z powrotem cienki plaster wędliny.

– Nie przesadzaj. Wystraszyłeś się? – Mrużę oczy. – Dlaczego?

– Niee. – Kręci głową.

– Jak chcesz coś szamać, to powiedz. – Patrzę mu prosto w oczy i przez chwilę czuję się jak pozytywny bohater. – Już chyba zjadłeś co twoje. Zjadłeś już parę dni temu, nie?

Dulian robi głupkowatą minę, podobną do tej, którą robią dzieci, kiedy wysłuchują głośnej reprymendy.

– Jutro wracam do pracy. Wezmę od szefa zaliczkę, to załaduję wam całą lodówkę żarciem, zobaczysz.

Jakoś mu nie wierzę.

– Koniec chorobowego?

Podnosi się z klęczek i zaczyna uderzać po wychudzonych udach.

– O, zobacz, Patryk, już wszystko w porządku. – Przechadza się po kuchni. – O! Widzisz, jest okej, nie?

– Całkiem okej – odpowiadam i otwieram lodówkę. Wyjmuję sześć kupionych dziś jaj.

– Masz ochotę na jajecznicę?

Zaciera ręce.

– To ja pokroję chlebek. – Z radością zagląda do plastikowego chlebaka.

Nie mam pojęcia, czyj chlebek zamierza pokroić, ale jajecznica smakuje nawet o pierwszej w nocy. No i to uczucie, że nie jest się aż takim skurwysynem. Może kiedyś on podzieli się ze mną jedzeniem...

*

Następnego dnia Dulian, wbrew wcześniejszym zapowiedziom, nie wstaje do pracy. Choć go o to wcale nie pytam, tłumaczy, że już się podnosił z łóżka, ale kiedy spojrzał na mnie...
– Tak smacznie spałeś – mówi – to się jeszcze na chwilę położyłem, no i masz... Zasnąłem.
To jego tłumaczenie tylko mnie rozbawia. Jeszcze trochę, a gotów będę go karmić za samo to jego pokrętne pieprzenie. Jak w ogóle mogłem widzieć w nim cwaniaczka?! Przecież to łamaga.

*

Coraz bardziej jestem przekonany, że te dwa gnoje mnie wrobiły. Rozmawiałem z takim jednym, co pracuje tu pół roku dłużej ode mnie. Jak mu powiedziałem, że będę musiał zapłacić za urwaną antenę, to się głośno roześmiał i popukał w czoło. Powiedział, że już kiedyś chcieli wrobić kogoś w podobną sprawę, ale nie dali rady. Tamten zaczął się odgrażać, wystraszył ich wujkiem z policji, i Mojs dał sobie spokój.
Mając taką wiedzę, nie cieszy mnie nawet to, że koszty anteny rozłożyli mi na dwie raty. Brałem pod uwagę różne kwoty, ale żeby aż dwie stówki i jeszcze pięć dych za założenie płacić?!

Nerwowo miętolę w palcach paragon.

– Drogo – syczę pod nosem i cały czas myślę o tym, co mi powiedział tamten koleś.

– Drogo? – Mojs wytrzeszcza oczy. – Masz szczęście, że to tańsza podróbka. Za oryginał nawet w pięciu ratach byś się nie wypłacił. Facet jest w porządku, poświęcił swój czas i coś tańszego ci znalazł.

(Mnie?)

– Za taką fatygę to butelka dobrej wódki mu się należy.

– I tak drogo. – Niech sobie nie myśli, że będę skakał z radości. Na drugi raz do niczego się nie przyznam, niczego nie podpiszę. Nie ma auta, nie ma człowieka. Jest tylko jakaś pogrążająca mnie notatka służbowa. Myślałem, że będzie taniej.

– Za takie gapiostwo powinieneś dostać jeszcze działę. Będę ci się teraz, Boszczuk, dokładniej przyglądał, i mówię ci... – Podchodzi bliżej. Czuję jego oddech. – Na twoje miejsce mam dziesiątki lepszych od ciebie.

Wzruszam ramionami i chociaż nie jest to łatwe, patrzę mu teraz prosto w oczy.

– Każdego da się wymienić.

(To do ciebie, debilu!)

– Wracaj na piętro, i zostaw już ten paragon.

– Nie mogę go zabrać?

– Co? Chyba ochujałeś! Widziałeś cenę? Paragon zostaje tu. – Klepie łapą po blacie stołu. – Tu go połóż i wracaj. Nie przyszedłeś tu, kurwa, na kawę. Idź już!

Myślę o tym, jaki z niego chuj. Może rzeczywiście puścić anonim, skompromitować jego i Zbycha. Przecież nie pogrążyłbym dobrych ludzi; dobrych ludzi zostawia się w spokoju. Pomógłbym sobie i innym, to żaden grzech. Ze złem trzeba walczyć, a Mojs to samo zło. Nie będzie mnie męczyć sumienie, a kiedy to zrobię, wreszcie sobie udowodnię, że nie jestem taką strachliwą pipką.

*

On chyba nieszybko przestanie kraść nam żarcie z lodówki. Mówił, że ma spoko szefa, ale trzeba być kompletnym idiotą, by łudzić się, że po tygodniowej samowolce pozwoli mu wrócić do pracy.

Zapowiadało się, że będzie inaczej, ale bracia nie lubią Duliana. Mówią, że to łachudra. Mnie on tylko śmieszy. Pierwszego dnia, kiedy się wprowadził, wydał mi się zupełnie inną osobą. To nie jest zły koleś, tylko trochę się pogubił. Ma problemy z mówieniem prawdy, ale nie bywa nadęty. Krzychu bywa, Wiesiek też. Coraz częściej. Za długo razem mieszkamy. Jak widzą, że gadam z Dulianem, to robią się zazdrośni.

Dulian jest zupełnie inny, no i ma niepewną przyszłość. Choć to nie Etiopia, prawdopodobnie już niebawem padnie z głodu.

*

Można mieszkać z kimś pod jednym dachem i tak mało o tej osobie wiedzieć.

Dziś pierwszy raz wybrałem się z Dulianem do sklepu. Z powodu braku funduszy dla niego wyprawa do spożywczego była wyprawą czysto towarzyską. Właściwie to nie wiem, po cholerę on w ogóle ze mną poszedł.

Ten sklep, w którym zawsze robię zakupy, to taki mały market samoobsługowy. Znają mnie tu już trochę i zdarza się, że przed wypłatą na krechę nic nie pożałują.

– Wziąłbyś mi papierosy? – pyta. Nie owija w bawełnę. Podchodzi do mnie, uśmiechając się głupkowato. Jarać mu się chce? Nic dziwnego, od kiedy stracił płynność finansową, co dłuższym zagaszonym petem nie wzgardzi. – Oddam ci.

– Z czego?

– Będzie dobrze – uspakaja mnie, nie przestając się uśmiechać.

Co go tak cieszy? Wizja śmierci głodowej? Przecież to nic miłego. Już lepiej podciąć sobie żyły. Moje miękkie serducho też ma swój limit. Niech sobie nie myśli, że trafił na sponsora. Fajki kupię, ale dla siebie, no i piwo wezmę... Dwa piwa.

Wychodzimy ze sklepu. Dulian od razu wyciąga łapę po piwo. Zastanawiam się, czy wszystko kupiłem.

– Chodź, Patryk, usiądziemy sobie i wypijemy w spokoju piwko. – Pomlaskuje, jakby już je smakował. – Jak ludzie, na ławeczce.

Patrzę na niego i podaję mu puszkę zimnego piwa.

– A gdzie ty ławeczki tu widzisz?

– No, choćby tu. – Pokazuje jakiś sypiący się, gęsto porośnięty chwastami murek, jakby pozostałość jakiegoś fundamentu czy coś takiego.

– Tu? – pytam z niedowierzaniem. – Na cemencie?

– Noo, usiądziemy sobie i spokojnie wypijemy. Po co w chałupie siedzieć, kiedy taka ładna pogoda, nie?

– Zaraz nas gliny spiszą, że chlejemy w miejscu publicznym.

– To powiesz im, że jesteśmy z ochrony.

– Co?

Robi zdziwione oczy.

– Powiemy, że jesteśmy ochroniarzami, to nic nam nie zrobią.

O czym on gada? To jakieś brednie, ale nie będę wyprowadzał go z błędu – niech sobie tak myśli.

– Lepiej się nie narażać.

– To usiądziemy tyłem do ulicy. Nie będzie widać, że coś pijemy. O zobacz. – Sadowi się na sypiącej się podmurówce, podkładając pod tyłek wyciągnięty z kieszeni foliowy, przeźroczysty worek. – I co? – Otwiera piwo. – Widzisz, dobrze jest, nie? Nic nie widać, no, sam zobacz. – Zaczyna pić, potem głośno beka. – No, siadaj Patryk.

– Tak na cemencie? – powtarzam, krzywiąc się.

– Poczekaj. – Wyciąga drugi taki sam foliowy worek. – Siadaj.
– Więcej ich nie masz? – śmieję się.
– Nie, ale mam co innego. – Rozsuwa zamek kurtki. – Taaraamm! – Zza pazuchy wyciąga paczkę jednorazowych maszynek do golenia. – Taaraamm!
– Skąd to masz?

Bierze łyk piwa.

– Trzeba sobie jakoś radzić, nie?
– Ukradłeś to?... No, nie gadaj, że ukradłeś.

Nie odpowiada.

– O, i jeszcze to. – Wyciąga butelkę wody po goleniu. – Taaraamm!

Nie wiem, co powiedzieć. On chwali się, że ukradł, a ja mogę się jedynie cieszyć, że go nie złapali.

– Ukradłeś? – powtarzam. – Zajebałeś to?!
– Daj spokój! Od razu zajebałeś. Było, to sobie wziąłem. Zresztą to dla ciebie, masz. – Kładzie mi maszynki na kolanach.

– Dla mnie?
– No.
– Daj spokój, nie potrzebuję. Jak będę chciał, to sobie kupię.
– Jak chcesz, ale to dobre maszynki. – Chowa je pod kurtkę. – Zobacz. – Znowu je wyciąga. – Markowy towar.

Przyglądam się im kontem oka.

– Pokaż. – Biorę do rąk szeleszczące foliowe opakowanie. – No dobra, wezmę je. – Nie

153

podejrzewałem się o to, ale sklep przecież przez to nie zbankrutuje. Chowam je głęboko do siatki; na samo dno, pod zakupy. – Wodę zostawiasz dla siebie? – Jakoś nie najlepiej mi z tym, że wziąłem od niego ten gorący towar. Czuję się teraz tak, jakbym sam to ukradł.

– Jak chcesz to pachnidło, to też mogę ci dać.

Patrzę na niego podejrzliwie.

– Wodę po goleniu zostaw dla siebie. I tak nie powinienem brać od ciebie tych maszynek. – Kręcę głową. – Pij szybciej i idziemy.

Robi zdziwioną minę.

– A ty nie pijesz?

– Nie teraz.

– Wyluzuj!

Ma rację. Otwieram swoje. Głośny syk przywraca uśmiech jego twarzy.

– Noo, i prawidłowo.

– Nie piłem jeszcze tak.

– Jak?

– No tak, że prawie pod samym sklepem.

Wykrzywia usta.

– A, daj spokój, zobacz. – Rozgląda się. – Jest ładna pogoda, cieplutko, a ty byś chciał w chałupie się kisić?

Faktycznie, podświadomie tylko odliczam czas do następnego ustawienia się na piętrach, na minusach, na Chocimskiej. Jestem zaprogramowanym sztywniakiem, nie potrafię oddzielić pracy od czasu wolnego. Jak tak dalej pójdzie, to wszystko stanie się jedną niekończącą się udręką. Nie potrafię odpoczywać. On ma rację – fajnie jest żłopać browar pod gołym niebem, nie zaprzątając sobie głowy niczym innym. Potrafię tak? Kiedyś potrafiłem – kiedyś, kiedy jeszcze nie musiałem sam robić sobie jedzenia, a nad wszystkim czuwała mama. To było tak niedawno...

– Pij szybciej, to kupię jeszcze po jednym. Za te maszynki – śmieję się, podnosząc tyłek z foliowej reklamówki.

Dulian też wstaje.

– Skoro nalegasz...

– Nalegam? Dowcipny jesteś. A co, może nie chcesz?

– Nieee! Ja tylko tak. Ale poczekaj! Jeszcze nie wypiłeś. Wypij, to pójdziemy razem.

– Nie potrzebuję adrenaliny.

– Daj spokój. – Krzywi się. – Wypijemy piwko, to pójdziemy.

– Ale maszynek nie weźmiesz?

– Po co nam maszynki? Najpierw trzeba te zużyć, che, che.

Tak jak mówił, maszynek nie bierze... Bierze piwo. Istny magik. Nie wiem, jak mogłem wcześniej nie zauważyć tego wybrzuszenia pod jego badziewną kurtką.

–Taaraamm. – Zza pazuchy wyciąga dwie puszki piwa. – Twoje zdrowie, Patryk.

– Trzecie?!

– No, a coś ty myślał? Jak impreza to impreza, nie?

To dlatego tak szybko wyrwał do lodówki po piwo, kiedy za nie płaciłem. Sklepowe mi tu ufają, a on był ze mną. Do głowy by im nie przyszło, że zamiast dwóch piw mój kolega weźmie cztery.

– Cztery wziąłeś.

Dopina zamek kurtki.

– Wziąłem sześć – mówi ze spokojem w głosie.

– Pojemne masz łapy, ale do spożywczego już ze mną nie wejdziesz. Nigdy.

Podaje mi piwo.

– Twoje zdrowie, Patryk – powtarza. – Chyba się cieszysz, co? Zimny browarek to jest to; ty wziąłeś dwa na łeb, ja wziąłem dwa na łeb. – Kiwa głową. – Jest po równo. – Bierze łyka. – Aha. – Teraz prawie zachłystuje się piwem. – No, i maszynki w prezencie dostałeś, nie? Pachnidła nie chcesz, to nie. Zostawię dla siebie, ale maszynki, pamiętaj, są twoje.

– Kiedyś ci nie pójdzie, zobaczysz. Ktoś wreszcie cię złapie i narobisz sobie kłopotów.

Dulian patrzy na mnie. Pierwszy raz nie widzę w jego oczach emocji. Wygląda z tym dziwnie.

– Spokojnie, już nie raz mi nie poszło.

– Jak?

– Normalnie, nie poszło i już.

– Złapali cię?

– Złapali, potem wypuścili. Różnie bywało.

Dobrze, że wcześniej o tym nie wiedziałem.

– A jak cię złapali, to co? Co się działo?

Rozbawia go to pytanie.

- Co się działo? Chujowo się działo. Ostatnio dostałem wpierdol od ochroniarzy. A wcześniej dwa razy zgarnęła mnie psiarnia.
- Pobili cię ochroniarze?
- Noo, skopali po nogach. Ale psiarnia, jak mnie pierwszy raz zgarnęła, to szybko wypuściła, za mało sobie wziąłem. Dopiero potem, jak mnie drugi raz zwinęli, to się skończyło wyrokiem.
- Poszedłeś siedzieć?
- No coś ty! Od razu siedzieć. Do kryminału za parę stówek? Dostałem zawiasy – i tyle. Teraz muszę tylko trochę bardziej uważać.
- Masz wyrok w zawieszeniu i kradniesz? Jesteś nienormalny.

Kręci głową, jakbym to teraz ja gadał jakieś niedorzeczności.

- Przecież ci mówiłem, że uważam. No i Bóg nade mną czuwa. Takie sklepiki jak ten to sama przyjemność. Spożywczanki miłe, od razu widać, że można brać, ile się chce. Bez ograniczeń! W hipermarketach jest dużo gorzej. Pamiętasz, jak wtedy przyszedłem taki trochę rozbity? Wtedy, co wam powiedziałem, że tramwaj mnie za nogę ciągnął? Wtedy miałem niefart. Zobaczyli, jak biorę. Właściwie to tylko darmową fasolkę po bretońsku szamałem. Lubię fasolkę; już kilka razy tam się stołowałem, no i chuje mnie w końcu upolowali. Dostałem za całokształt.
- Dostałeś za fasolkę?

– Za fasolkę! Pomyślałbyś? Ale i tak co zżar-
łem, to moje. Na tamtej hali spożywczej jest
taki dział garmażeryjny, można sobie zama-
wiać do woli, to zamawiałem. Żarcie nakładali
do plastikowych pojemników, potem w foliowy
worek, a na ten worek naklejali jeszcze kod pa-
skowy. Można było legalnie szamać na miejscu.
Potem pojemnik do kosza i tylko ten worek
z kodem przy kasie babie pokazać. Ja miałem
na to swój sposób. Jak już zjadłem, to pojemnik do śmietnika, a worek z kodem paskowym
przykrywałem w koszyku innymi workami, bez
kodu. Przy kasie kasowali mnie za tanią drob-
nicę, a worek z kodem w koszyku przed kasą
zostawał. I tyle, cała filozofia.
– No, ale w końcu cię dorwali. To chyba nie
był to taki dobry sposób?
– Dorwali? – Denerwuje się. – Dorwali, bo
tam, kurwa, tyle kamer, to mnie dorwali. Ale
na początku, nie mogę powiedzieć, pełna kultura była. Ochroniarz grzecznie poprosił o paragon, a potem zaprowadzili mnie do jakiegoś
pomieszczenia, jakby magazyn czy coś takiego. Tam na palecie stał wysmarowany resztką
sosu z fasoli ten cholerny pojemnik, ten mój.
Wyciągnęli go z kosza! A potem to już poszło.
Przybiegło jeszcze takich dwóch karków i za-
częli mnie kopać. Do teraz nie wiem, czy oni
mnie puścili, czy ja im stamtąd sam spierdoliłem. Jak biegłem, to zahaczyłem o jakieś badziewie i rozprułem spodnie. Co miałem wam

powiedzieć, że dostałem wpierdol od ochroniarzy? Wy też jesteście ochroniarze. Ale trafiłem, co?

– Jak już kłamiesz, to trzymaj się jednej wersji. Bożenie powiedziałeś, że jakaś maszyna w pracy prawie ci nogi połamała, nie?

Dulian rozdziawia gębę.

– Bożena wam tak powiedziała?

– A co, nie powiedziałeś jej tak?

Myśli chwilę.

– Trochę mnie poniosło z tym tramwajem, więc musiałem złagodzić wersję.

– No to złagodziłeś, a ona opowiedziała nam, jak to cudem uszedłeś z życiem.

– A wy jej powiedzieliście?

– Ja nie, ale oni potem mogli przy okazji. Bracia mają z nią lepszy kontakt.

Dulian łapie się za głowę.

– Głupio wyszło, ale co tam. – Prostuje się. – Teraz już nic nie zrobię, nie?

Wiedziałem, że on to pokręcony typ, ale żeby aż tak był wygięty...

– Chyba lepiej, że cię pobili. Jak by wezwali policję, to byś teraz siedział.

– Przecież ci mówiłem, Bóg nade mną czuwa. Nie stresuj się już tak tym tematem.

– Mam nadzieję, że nas nie skojarzą.

Parska śmiechem.

– Co, boisz się, że odpowiesz za współudział? Daj spokój, jak by był jakiś problem, to się nie znamy. Po co miałbym cię w to wpierdalać?

Przecież ty jesteś od pilnowania, żeby nic nie ginęło, nie?

Wykrzywiam usta.

– To ty daj spokój.

Chyba naigrawa się ze mnie.

– Co?

– Dupa by ci spuchła, jakbyś musiał tyle godzin stać w jednym miejscu. – Niech wie, że to piwo to nie za darmochę. – Nie jest lekko.

Patrzy na mnie.

– A ty, gdzie jesteś tym ochroniarzem? W banku czy gdzie? Z braćmi przecież nie robisz, nie?

– Nie.

– No to gdzie robisz?

– W takim tam molochu.

– W molochu gdzie?

– Gdzie i gdzie. Na cholerę ci to wiedzieć? Zresztą bracia ci mówili zaraz na początku, jak się tylko u nas zjawiłeś... Dobrze znasz Warszawę?

– Noo. – Mruży oczy, gibając się na boki. – Było się w paru miejscach.

– No jasne. Wiesz, gdzie kiedyś stało kino Belgrad? To właśnie tam.

– Chujowo jest?

– Chujowo jest – powtarzam za nim. – Szkoda gadać. Nogi w dupę wchodzą. Zresztą bracia nie mają lepiej. Oni też swoje wystać muszą. Niepotrzebnie odchodziłem z batonów.

– Skąd?

- Z batonów – to taka fabryka słodyczy. Źle nie było, tylko daleko. Do Sochaczewa musiałem jeździć. Ale teraz wiem, że źle zrobiłem. Tu, gdzie teraz stoję, jest chujowo, bardzo chujowo. A najgorszy jest ten inspektor.
- Inspektor? Kurwa, jak w policji.

Macham ręką.

- Taki z niego inspektor, jak ze mnie agent. W tych firmach wszystko jest nazywane na wyrost. Szkoda gadać. Niepotrzebnie wdepnąłem w to gówno. To jeden wielki syf.

Nie wiem, czy to odpowiednia osoba na przelewanie swoich żalów. W końcu to lekkoduch, złodziej i cholera wie, kto jeszcze. To piwo za bardzo rozwiązało mi język.

- Przejebane.
- No.
- To pierdolnij to i znajdź sobie coś innego.
- Tak jak ty?
- Spokojnie, rozglądam się, niedługo coś będę miał. W moim zawodzie roboty jest w pizdu. Zobaczysz, już niedługo coś znajdę.
- Ja będę miał sklep spożywczy. Wtedy, jak się do nas wprowadziłeś, mówiłeś, że to kiepski interes, ale ludzie zawsze jeść będą.

Wzrusza ramionami.

- Ja ci życzę, Patryk, jak najlepiej. A kiedy już będziesz mieć ten swój spożywczy, to się u ciebie zatrudnię jako sprzedawca. – Śmieje się głośno.

– Musiałbym do reszty zwariować. Cały towar pod kurtką w godzinę byś wyniósł. Do mojego sklepu nie będziesz miał wstępu.

– No co ty, swoich nie okradam.

– Chyba że z jedzenia, co?

– Jedzenie to co innego.

– Aha.

– Kasy nie ruszam.

Nie bardzo chce mi się wierzyć w tę jego złodziejską szlachetność. Pieniędzy na stole zostawiał nie będę.

ROZDZIAŁ

6

Przecież nie znam się na budowlance, nawet kafli kłaóó się nic nauczyłem, a ten idiota chce, żebym nadzorował pracę fachowców. Jakbym wiedział, o co chodzi, to bym w ochronie nie robił. Mogłem dotrwać, co tam pozlepiane kłaki w nosie; teraz może nie musiałbym tu stać.

– Mam ich pilnować?

Adaś zerka kątem oka na dwuosobową ekipę ubraną w poplamione robocze drelichy.

– Kurwa, zobacz, cwaniaczki jedne, patrzą tylko, żeby co zajebać – mruczy pod nosem. – Masz ich mieć na oku, pilnuj ich i jakby coś, zgłaszaj.

Cały czas nie mam pojęcia, co znaczy to „jakby coś".

– Jakby co?

– Co?

– Że co, że... – Ciężko mi się wysłowić. – No, że oni...

Adaś nerwowo strzela z palców.

– Mojs powiedział, że mam tu wystawić człowieka, który będzie pilnował, by tamci nie walili w chuja. A co to znaczy, to już ty powinieneś najlepiej wiedzieć. Co ty myślisz, że nie wiem? Wszyscy jak jeden walicie w chuja. Jakbym miał to wszystko zgłaszać Markowi, to tylko na same działy musielibyście robić.

– Ja nie walę.

– Niee, tylko co?

Patrzę mu teraz prosto w jego fałszywe szczurze ślepia. Jeśli ja jestem na jednego strzała, to on jest na połowę albo na ćwierć. Nawet po całej dobie stania na Chocimskiej dałbym sobie z nim bez problemu radę. Złamas jeden, uczepił się Mojsa i póki ten go nie pstryknie, to sam się nie odczepi. Wpiął się mocno pazurkami.

– Co oni mają tu robić?

– Demontaż starych i montaż nowych drzwi. W całym prawym skrzydle na piątym piętrze będą wymieniane, bo wcześniej zamontowali złe. Mają robić do szesnastej każdego dnia, aż zrobią. Masz mieć na nich oko i pilnować, żeby te cwaniaczki nie rozlazły się po piętrze. Jak co zajebią, to będzie na ciebie.

– Ale skąd będę wiedział, czy coś zajebali?

Adaś przewraca nerwowo oczami.

– No i, kurwa, właśnie dlatego masz mieć ich na oku. Pół biedy, jak zajebią spinacz biurowy, gorzej dla ciebie, jak zapierdolą co większego. Patrz cały czas na nich i nie spuszczaj ich z oczu.

– A jak będę chciał pójść do kibla?

– Wtedy zgłaszasz plażę i ktoś na chwilę cię podmieni. Może nawet ja przyjdę na ten czas, tylko, kurwa, nie przesadzaj. Dziś na holu windowym cały czas stać nie musisz. W skrzydłach też są zamontowane kamery. Tak że spokojnie, bez szaleństwa – będzie cię widać. A jak ktoś wjedzie na pięterko, to go legitymujesz i biegusiem wracasz do roboli, proste?

Dla kogo proste, dla tego proste.

– Oni są za daleko holu, nie usłyszę dzwonka windy.

Ciągnie wzdycha i podchodzi do „roboli". Teraz nie jest już tak pewny siebie. Robole nawet na niego nie patrzą, jeden z nich siłuje się z drzwiami. Chyba chce je wyciągnąć. Adaś staje obok niego. Uśmiecha się do nich, ale tamci nie odwzajemniają uśmiechu. Mają go w dupie. Podchodzi do mnie.

– Stań w tym miejscu. – Tupie nogą w przezroczystą folię zabezpieczającą wykładzinę przed zabrudzeniem. – Stąd będziesz widział, co się dzieje przy windach. – Patrzy w stronę roboli. – Ich też będziesz widział. Chodź stań tu i zobacz.

Podchodzę do niego. Chcę się ustawić dokładnie w tym miejscu, w którym tupał nogą. Folia szeleści i przykleja się do butów. Ma się wrażenie, że zaraz się przerwie. Delikatnie stawiam kroki, jakbym szedł po cienkim lodzie.

– Tutaj. – Adaś wyciąga szyję. – O, widzisz, nie jest źle, co? Wszystko widać, nie?

– No – odpowiadam. – Coś tam widać.

– Dobra, to stój tu i działaj. Działaj – powtarza, odchodząc.

Patrzę na jego przygarbioną sylwetkę do momentu, aż znika za wyjściem ze skrzydła. Zaraz potem słyszę dzwonek otwieranej windy. Wychodzę na hol, to Adaś. Chcę wrócić. Kolejny dzwonek – z sąsiedniej windy wychodzą dwie osoby. Proszę je o przepustkę, rzut oka na zdjęcia i oddaję je z powrotem. Wracam do skrzydła. Stoję parę sekund, kiedy znowu słyszę dzwonek. To samo. Proszę o przepustki, patrzę na fotografie i wracam do mojego strategicznego punktu obserwacyjnego.

Podchodzę do roboli. Co jak co, ale jakieś dzień dobry by im się należało. Ich jest dwóch, ja jeden.

– Dzień dobry – próbuję przekrzyczeć grające głośno małe radio. Ten, który jeszcze niedawno wyciągał drzwi, teraz uderza dużym młotem w odstające od ramy zawiasy.

– Cześć! – krzyczy, a jego kolega macha do mnie ręką. – Kazali ci tu tak stać? – pyta, nie patrząc na mnie. Cały czas uderza w zawiasy, aż w końcu... udaje się, facet wygrywa. Rama jest uszkodzona; część, w której były zamontowane te nieszczęsne zawiasy, oderwała się od ściany. – Eee! Zobaczcie, jakie teraz, kurwa, ościeżnice tłuką. – Śmieje się i kolejnym mocnym uderzeniem odbija od ściany resztę ramy.

– Kurwa, co to za badziewie? Kiedyś to robili

drzwi, a ościeżnicy za chuja młotkiem bym nie rozpierdolił. Łom się wyginał, a ściany to fleksem trzeba było ciąć.

– Za Gierka wszystko solidniejsze robili – odzywa się drugi.

– Noo, a teraz to, zobacz. – Podnosi z podłogi kawałek połamanej ramy. – Jakaś to, kurwa, sklejka, czy co? – Kręci głową. – Kupiliby porządne, metalowe, to by im na sto lat albo i dłużej starczyło. Dobrze, że chociaż tamte, co je wstawiać będziemy, to z litego, a nie takie gowna. – Z niekrytą pogardą rzuca z powrotem na podłogę ten kawałek ramy. – Metalowe by kupili i mieliby spokój – powtarza, wykrzywiając usta. – Masz tak tu stać? – pyta znowu.

– Tak – odpowiadam.

– Na chuj? – Drugi ścisza radio. – Idź se, kurwa, chłopaku usiądź. Na chuj tu stoisz jak ten kołek?

Zbieram się do odpowiedzi. Prawdy im nie powiem. Nie powiem im, że muszę mieć na nich oko i takie tam bzdury.

– Nie mogę – odpowiadam. – Trochę tu, trochę...

– Co się, kurwa, dziwisz – przerywa mi drugi i śmieje się, świszcząc. – Ochroniarz, to nas chroni, a coś ty, kurwa, myślał?

Patrzy na mnie z wyszczerzonymi zębami.

– Tak. – Kiwam głową i też próbuję udać, że mnie to śmieszy. Ciekaw jestem, czy już widzą we mnie dupka, czy zobaczą go za chwilę.

Jeszcze tyle godzin stania i gapienia się na nich. Przecież nikt nie lubi, jak mu się na ręce patrzy. Idę stąd.

*

Wychodzę na hol, stoję tam chwilę i wracam. Potem znowu na hol i tak w kółko, jest to jakiś sposób.

Dzwonek. Z windy wychodzi Mojs, za nim idzie Adaś. Powinienem być tam, gdzie kazał mi stać, a ja teraz stoję koło balustrady. Nie mam nic na swoją obronę, kompletnie nic. Cholerne parę metrów i byłbym bezpieczny. Powiedziałbym, że usłyszałem dzwonek windy, to szybko wyskoczyłem na hol – i tyle. Tu nie powinienem stać.

Próbuję trzymać głowę prosto, ale wzrok sam opada i wbija się w posadzkę; jakby tu wjechał jakiś faraon z Egiptu, a nie zwyczajny cham z Warszawy.

– Czego tam szukałeś? – pyta Mojs, a Adaś z nerwów zagryza wargi.

– Na chwilę tylko – odpowiadam, dławiąc się własnym głosem.

– Miałeś pilnować tamtych i co, kurwa? Znowu widoki z góry podziwiasz? – Krzywi się. – Mówiłeś, że ich pilnuje, a ten znowu w chuja wali! – Patrzy przez chwilę na Adasia. – Tego, że jesteś lżejszy o połowę kasy, nie muszę ci już chyba tłumaczyć?! – Odwraca się do mnie plecami, a ja zaczynam czuć dziwny zapach, jakby mi się skóra fajczyła. To z nerwów. Nienawidzę go, jak Boga kocham, nienawidzę Mojsa. Jakby tu teraz obok była budka telefoniczna, to na pewno bym zadzwonił. Tak od razu do firmy, bez żadnej krępacji. Zadzwonię, zrobię to na pewno, nie ma innej możliwości. Miarka się przebrała. Zadzwonię, tylko jeszcze nie wiem dokładnie, kiedy. Może jutro? Przecież im szybciej, tym lepiej. Nie będą trzymać w firmie zboka.

Staję w wyznaczonym miejscu. Mojs zaczyna się przechadzać po remontowanym skrzydle, za nim jak cień ciągnie się Adaś.

Dzwonek windy. Wychodzę na hol. Kiedy wracam, Mojs rozmawia już z robolami. Gada do nich jak nie on. Jest miły i w ogóle nawija, jakby ich bardzo lubił. Adaś nie zabiera głosu.

– Stoisz tam? – krzyczy Mojs.

– Stoję – odpowiadam, starając się opanować drżenie głosu.

Głośny śmiech. Obydwaj faceci wychylają głowy z pomieszczenia na korytarz. Patrzą na mnie, jak w jaki obraz wlepiają we mnie gały. Widzę to kątem oka. Tak, teraz już wiedzą, że jestem zwyczajnym dupkiem. Tylko dupek może się godzić na takie traktowanie. Już niedługo, może nawet jutro, ktoś w firmie otrzyma wiadomość. Gdy o tym myślę, zaczynam się czuć lepiej i brnę w imaginacjach dalej. Próbuję ułożyć sobie w głowie cały plan działania i już po chwili odczuwam strach. Zaczynam analizować, a czarne myśli tańczą z tlącym się optymizmem. Czy ja jestem jeszcze normalny? Może już dawno zwariowałem i tylko to, że nie robię głupich min i nie pluję na innych, sprawia, że jeszcze tu pracuję. Ale czy gdybym naprawdę postradał zmysły, gdybym zwariował, to zastanawiałbym się nad tym? Jak to mówi brat mamy, wujek Kazik, pewnie miałbym na to WYJEBANE. Więc jeśli jeszcze zastanawiam się nad swoim stanem, to chyba niezupełnie ze mną źle.

– Stoisz tam?

Ośmiesza mnie. Przecież widzi, że stoję. Jak mim udający posąg prawie się nie ruszam, zaraz oddychać przestanę.

Mojs wychodzi z remontowanego pomieszczenia i idzie w moją stronę. Żeby tak tylko przeszedł koło mnie i bez słowa wsiadł do windy. Zatrzymuje się i z taką miną, jakby o czymś zapomniał, wraca do nich. Słyszę, że znowu coś gada, ale nie mogę zrozumieć, co. Słyszę za to jego głośny śmiech, tamci dwaj też się śmieją. Teraz Adaś wystawia łeb na korytarz. Patrzy na mnie, ja też patrzę na niego. Niech nie myśli, że się go boję. Jak chce, to może się tak gapić na mnie do rana, mam to w dupie.

Przechodzą koło mnie, nic nie mówią, chociaż tyle. Staram się mieć hardą minę, ale cała gęba mnie piecze; jakby ktoś mnie wytrzaskał cienką witką. Dzwonek! Idę, choć wiem, że to ich winda. Kiedy do niej włażą, Mojs ogląda się przez ramię. Przystaję na moment – niech widzi, że czuwam, że się interesuję, że właśnie byłem gotów sprawdzić przepustkę. Znikają za płynnie zamykającymi się stalowymi drzwiami.

Podchodzę do roboli. Obaj siedzą na wyciągniętych drzwiach, jedzą kanapki.

– Smacznego – mówię do nich i zaczynam wpatrywać się badawczo w nierówne krawędzie otworu, który został po odbitej ramie. Palcami dotykam ściany, jakbym coś sprawdzał. Dobrze by było, gdybym wiedział, po co tak tego dotykam, ale ja to robię dla samej czynności, żeby w ogóle coś robić; żeby czymś wypełnić tę chwilę.

– To był twój szef? – pyta jeden.

– Tak – odpowiadam.

– A ten mniejszy, ten cichy, to kto?

Kpiąco macham ręką.

– Dowódca – wyjaśniam przez zaciśnięte zęby.
– Był cichy? – pytam, jakbym chciał się upewnić, czy dobrze usłyszałem. Nie powinienem ich o to pytać; może to podpucha?

Facet kiwa tylko głową i pakuje resztę kanapki do gęby. Miele nią na wszystkie strony, jak krowa przeżuwająca zielsko, i cały czas kiwa głową.

– Przejebane tak stać, co?

Oni też to widzą?

– Co zrobić? Trzeba – gadam, jakbym sam w to wierzył. – Do dziewiętnastej, potem usiądę.

– Kuuurwa! – Patrzy na zegarek. – To jeszcze masz trochę. – Śmieje się i wyciąga z foliowego woreczka drugą kanapkę. – I tak bez żadnej przerwy, cały czas tu stać musisz?

Skoro pyta, to mu powiem. Nawet jeśli to koledzy Mojsa, niech wiedzą, że „ochraniarz" w tym kraju lekko nie ma.

– Muszę – odpowiadam. – A o jedzeniu to lepiej zapomnieć. Jak się myśli o przerwie, to nogi bolą i czas się bardziej dłuży.

Robią duże oczy.

– A chuj z taką robotą, toż to zdechnąć idzie. – Wyciąga do mnie worek z kanapką. – Masz i jedz, bo tu uschniesz. Bierz śmiało, kurwa, tak cały dzień bez jedzenia? Masz i jedz.

Podchodzę do niego.

– Tylko to tak między nami, dobra?

– Co między nami? – Zdziwiony mruży oczy. – Aaa! Kurwa, nie przejmuj się. Pewnie, że między nami. – Patrzy na kolegę. – Nalej mu herbaty, bo się chłopak zadławi.

Staje koło nich, tu nie ma kamery, więc żadna obślizgła menda mnie teraz nie zobaczy. Muszę się uwijać. Mojs, jak zły duch, może się pojawić w każdym momencie; to, że był tu przed chwilą, nie daje żadnej gwarancji, że za chwilę go nie zobaczę.

– Dziękuję wam, panowie. – W jedną rękę biorę kanapkę, w drugą chwytam pomazany kubek od termosu. – Dzięki – powtarzam, wgryzając się zębami w miąższ chleba. Pycha!

Z ciepłą słodką herbatą wszystko smakuje lepiej. Nawet jeśli mają mnie za dupka, nie zmienia to faktu, że są dobrymi ludźmi.

Zjedzona kanapka z czarnym salcesonem i musztardą mocno podnosi mnie na duchu. I jakby tego było mało, o czternastej dostaję zmiennika. Niemożliwe, mogę zjechać na przerwę.

Gdy wracam, przez chwilę czuję się jak naciągacz wyłudzający czyjeś jedzenie, ale kiedy robole robią mi kawę, na nowo czuję się normalnie. Zresztą kiedy wracam z przerwy, od razu im wyjaśniam, że to wyjątkowa sytuacja, że nie spodziewałem się, i takie tam. Mówią, żebym się nie tłumaczył, więc przestaję nawijać o podarowanej mi przerwie.

Teraz obserwuję ich bez skrępowania, a na hol windowy wychodzę od niechcenia. Po kawie pozwalam sobie nawet wziąć od nich papierosa. Palimy, stojąc przy otwartym oknie, inaczej mogłaby się załączyć jakaś czujka przeciwpożarowa albo inne gówno.

*

Przez następny dyżur też pilnuję roboli, a trzy tygodnie później Mojs woła mnie z minusików do siebie. Krzyczy, że w dwóch pomieszczeniach, w których wymieniano drzwi podczas mojego dyżuru, została zniszczona podłoga.

– Jak ich, kurwa, pilnowałeś! – krzyczy mi do ucha. – Zniszczyli podłogę!

- Podłogę – powtarzam za nim.
- Przypalona w paru miejscach i pocięta. Wykładzinę zniszczyli! Oni tam jarali, a ty na to spokojnie patrzyłeś? – Łapie się za głowę, a potem nerwowo chwyta za słuchawkę telefonu. Na klawiaturze wystukuje jakiś numer i rozsiada się wygodnie na wysiedzianym pikowanym fotelu. Patrzę raz na Mojsa, raz na dowódcę Arka, potem jeszcze na zapisującego coś w zeszycie adiutanta. Co on tam pisze? Te gnidy zawsze coś piszą, jakby prowadziły tajne kroniki. Już trzeci raz tu jestem i za każdym razem adiutant bazgra coś w zeszycie.
- Dzień dobry. – Gęba Mojsa robi się czerwona. – Z tej strony Marek Mojs, szef ochrony. Dzwonię, proszę pani, w sprawie tej wypalonej wykładzinki. – Marszczy czoło. – Tak. – Dłuższa cisza. – Tak, tak, zgadza się. Tak, tak. – Potakuje głową, a rumieńce nie znikają mu z ryja.
- Pomieszczenie czterysta pięć i czterysta siedem, tak? – Patrzy na mnie i cały czas potakuje głową. – Dobrze, przyprowadzę go, nie ma problemu... Tak, oczywiście... Do widzenia, kłaniam się, do widzenia pani. – Odkłada słuchawkę i wstaje z fotela. Podchodzi do Arka, nachyla się nad nim. – Idę mu to pokazać.

- Jasne. – Arek zakłada ręce na kark i lekko mruży oczy. – Będzie, szefie, afera...? – pyta przyciszonym głosem.

- Nie mogłem wszystkiego widzieć – tłumaczę, nie czekając, aż Mojs mu odpowie. – Przecież miałem pilnować całego holu windowego i tamtych dwóch...

– Pytał cię kto? – przerywa mi Mojs. – Jeszcze będziesz miał okazję sobie pogadać, a teraz zamknij się i nie próbuj mnie bardziej wkurwiać. Pójdziesz ze mną i zobaczysz, cieciu jeden, efekt swojej pracy!

– Nie jestem cieciem – odpowiadam i podchodzę bliżej drzwi.

Mojs parska śmiechem, podchodzi do adiutanta i wyrywa mu zeszyt.

– Nie, kurwa, a kim jesteś? – Wachluje się nim. (Spocona, zasapana świnia!)

– Nie jestem cieciem – powtarzam. – A pan ludzi nie szanuje – zaciskam zęby. Mogłem tego nie mówić.

– Pierdolisz, Boszczuk, jak połamany. – Uśmiecha się do Arka. – Pierdoli jak połamany, nie? – Arek kiwa głową. – O szacunku będzie mi tu teraz gadał. – Łapie za klamkę i otwiera drzwi. – Idziemy!

Kierujemy się do windy. Prawie biegnie, a ja próbuję za nim nadążyć. Po drodze mijamy ludzi, do większości z nich Mojs się uśmiecha, a do niektórych nawet macha zeszytem. Po co wziął go ze sobą?

Na holu windowym znowu zaczyna krzyczeć. Krzyczy na opierającego się o ścianę stojaka. Naciska na podświetlony na czerwono przycisk przywołujący windę, cały czas drze ryja.

Z windy wysiada parę osób. Twarz Mojsa błyskawicznie łagodnieje. Wjazd z tym gnojem zdaje się trwać dłużej niż normalnie, jakbym wjeżdżał na szczyt wieży Eiffla. Wjechaliśmy, a on od razu zaczyna się czepiać następnego stojaka. Ten tu ma chyba kryzys; wygląda, jakby dopiero otworzył oczy i podniósł się z pełnego przysiadu. Patrzę na niego i słucham, jak Mojs dosadnie udziela mu wskazówek. Poucza, jak ma prawidłowo stać, by było go widać całego w monitorze. Facet jest jeszcze chudszy ode mnie. To nie najlepszy moment na tego typu przemyślenia, ale patrząc na jego wypchane w spodniach kolana, zaczynam się zastanawiać, czy ja kiedykolwiek się ożenię. Moje są tak samo wypchane. Największy przystojniak w tak szpetnym wdzianku nie miałby szans nawet u mało wymagającego pasztetu. Te uniformy chyba specjalnie są tak szyte, żeby wyglądać w nich jak ostatnia cipa. Wygięte sylwetki agentów potęgują jeszcze niekorzystny efekt.

– Idziemy. – Mojs przypomniał sobie, po co tu wjechaliśmy.

Na znak solidarności rzucam krótkie spojrzenie w kierunku stojaka i wchodzę z Mojsem do prawego skrzydła budynku. Nie byłem tu, od czasu kiedy pilnowałem tamtych dwóch. Pracowali tu jeszcze później, ale kto inny miał ich na oku. Idąc korytarzem, patrzę na nowe drzwi. Nie znam się, ale jak dla mnie to profesjonalna robota. I pomyśleć, że jeszcze przed miesiącem były tu inne, stare. Nie widać nawet śladu wymiany, wszystko ładnie, równiutko; naprawdę fachowa robota.

Mojs zatrzymuje się przed drzwiami z numerem czterysta pięć, łapie za klamkę, ale nie otwiera drzwi, jakby nie był pewny, czy chce wejść do środka. A jednak. Drugą ręką złożoną w pięść zaczyna pukać, a potem zdecydowanie naciska klamkę. Zaciemniony korytarz na moment jaśnieje światłem wypuszczonym z pomieszczenia. Mojs wchodzi pierwszy.

– Dzień dobry. – Podchodzi do siedzącej na obrotowym krześle szczupłej, jeszcze młodej kobiety. Podają sobie ręce, a on całuje jej dłoń.

– Dzień dobry – powtarzam za nim.

Kobieta podnosi tyłek z krzesła, a Mojs od razu włazi między jej biurko a okno przysłonięte do połowy zieloną przeciwsłoneczną roletą.

– Aha – mówi, drapiąc się po brodzie. – Tak to wygląda – Z udawanym skupieniem mruczy pod nosem.

– O, tu i tu. Widzi pan, panie Marku, w tych miejscach – mówi kobieta i kuca nad jakimś ciemnym punktem. Dotyka go palcem, drapie paznokciem. Mojs też przypatruje się z zaangażowaniem i tak jak ona, badawczo dotyka podłogi swoim porośniętym jasnymi włosami paluchem.

– Tak, to ewidentnie po niedopałka – mówi Mojs. Odrywa oczy od przypalonej wykładziny i zaczyna się gapić na mnie. Ona też.

- Podejdź tu – mówi Mojs.

– Wystarczy, jak stanie tutaj. – Kobieta odsuwa krzesło od biurka. – O, tutaj! Stąd dobrze widać.

Po jaką cholerę mi to pokazują? Jego to jeszcze rozumiem. Lubi budować niezdrowe napięcie, ale ona? Ona mogłaby sobie darować. Przecież i tak Mojs zrobi to, co będzie chciał. Po co ta cała wizja lokalna? Na co to wszystko?

Patrzę na nią i kiwam głową. Nie muszę jak głupi cały czas gapić się na ten, jak dla mnie prawie niewidoczny, wypalony ślad. Już się napatrzyłem. Na Mojsa gapił się też nie będę. Dłuższe patrzenie w jego kierunku kończy się u mnie mdłościami.

– Widziałem – mówię do niej.

– Czy ci panowie, którzy wymieniali tu drzwi, palili papierosy?

– Nie wiem – odpowiadam. – Nie widziałem, musiałem jeszcze sprawdzać przepustki na holu windowym. Może palili, kiedy byłem tam albo gdy zjechałem na przerwę.

– Taaak, akurat – wtrąca się Mojs. – Najlepiej zwalić całą winę na kogoś. Zostałeś puszczony na przerwę obiadową, a kolega, który cię zmieniał, takiej szansy już nie miał. Dzięki niemu mogłeś zjeść, tak jak inni zresztą. Dzięki niemu – powtarza. – A teraz chcesz całą winą obarczyć... – Zagląda do swoich tajnych zapisków. Otwiera zeszyt, mruży oczy. – Karol cię zmieniał. Tak, to był Karol. – No, kto jak kto, ale on na pewno nie dałby ciała. – Śmieje się pod nosem, patrząc teraz na kobietę. – Ten Karol to zastępca dowódcy – tłumaczy jej. – Wie pani, czasami aż sam mówię, żeby trochę zwolnił tępo. Chłopak jest ambitny, ma wyniki i pewnie daleko zajdzie. – Znowu patrzy na mnie, wkładając zeszyt pod pachę. – Powiedziałbyś, Patryk, jak było, zamiast nas czarować. – Śmieje się, łagodnie zerkając na kobietę.

– Proszę pana – mówi spokojnym głosem kobieta. – Dobrze by było, gdyby pan sobie jednak coś przypomniał. Wiadomo, nie zawsze wszystko da się przewidzieć, nie wszystko da się zauważyć, ale pan w końcu miał dyżur na tym piętrze. Czy nie tak?

– Tak, tak – wtrąca się Mojs i znowu otwiera ten cholerny kapownik. – O! Mam tu. Jest napisane wyraźnie, że w dniu, w którym wymieniano drzwi od pokoju czterysta pięć, to ty pełniłeś tu dyżur. Zresztą tak samo, jak wtedy, kiedy wymiano drzwi w pokoju czterysta siedem. – Macha ręką. – Tam wykładzina wygląda jeszcze gorzej, ale to potem. Teraz skupmy się na tym, co tu widzimy. Na pewno nie czułeś dymu z papierosa? Patryk, chyba nie chcesz nam powiedzieć, że widząc, jak palą, spokojnie na nich patrzyłeś. A może paliłeś razem z nimi, co? – Znowu patrzy do zeszytu. – Tu jest czarno na białym. O, proszę, cały harmonogram, wszystko tu jest. O! Proszę. – Podchodzi do mnie. – Zobacz sobie. Jaki dzień, od której do której, w jakich salach wymieniane były drzwi i który stał na piętrze. Wszystko jest jasno i przejrzyście zapisane, sam widzisz.

Kiwam głową. Tylko to mogę zrobić. Co jak co, ale przecież nie przyznam się, że paliłem tu z nimi papierosy. W tej czy w innej sali być może któryś z nich przypalił tę cholerną wykładzinę. Może to nawet ja ją przypaliłem. Nie wiem.

– Naprawdę nie widziałem. Nie czułem też żadnego dymu – tłumaczę im, wzruszając ramionami.

Kobieta głośno wzdycha.

– Kurczę, to niedobrze – mówi, wykrzywiając wymalowane czerwoną szminką wąskie usta. – Nie będziemy mogli domagać się pokrycia kosztów. – Pokazuje na mnie palcem. – Niczego nie zauważyłeś. Nawet jeśli oskarżymy ich o zniszczenie wykładziny, to i tak nic to nie da.

– A może już wcześniej ktoś ją przypalił? – wyrywam się, mając nadzieję, że ona podzieli moje przypuszczenia.

– Nie. Wcześniej, zanim zaczął się ten nieszczęsny remont, wszystko było w porządku. Tu nie wolno palić, zresztą tak jak w każdym innym pomieszczeniu. Tu obowiązuje całkowity zakaz. Palić można jedynie w wyznaczonych miejscach. Na terenie budynku jest ich kilka. W pomieszczeniach biurowych nikt nie pali. To z całą pewnością ci pracownicy od drzwi, nikt inny nie odważyłby się papierosów tu palić. – Patrzy na

Mojsa. – No to trudno, panie Marku. – Rozkłada bezradnie ręce. – W takim razie nic nie da się zrobić.

Mojs posłusznie kiwa głową.

– Wyjdź i poczekaj na korytarzu – mówi do mnie z fałszywie zatroskaną miną.

Z wielką przyjemnością stąd wyjdę.

– Do widzenia – mówię, kłaniając się grzecznie kobiecie. Wychodzę.

Pogadam ze stojakiem. Opowiem mu, po co wjechałem z tą świnią na jego piętro. W przeciwnym razie pomyśli, że ja tak towarzysko, że Mojs mnie zwerbował. Gdy człowiek stoi sam tyle godzin, różnie kombinuje; nie chciałbym paść ofiarą głupich domysłów.

Facet patrzy na mnie podejrzliwie. To jest właśnie to – jeszcze gęby nie otworzył, a mnie już pieką uszy i czuję się jak pierdolony konfident.

– Daj spokój. – Macham ręką i staję naprzeciw niego. Znam go tyle, co z szatni. To wszystko.
– Mojs chce mnie wpierdolić na minę – żalę się.

– Co?

– Gada, że nie dopilnowałem tych, co wymieniali tu drzwi. Niby mieli przypalić papierosami wykładzinę. Może i przypalili, kto ich tam wie.

– Odejdź.

– Co?

– Odejdź. – Facet macha łapami jak w transie. – Nie możemy gadać. Odejdź od kamery, bo zobaczą.

– Spokojnie – mówię i staję przy interkomie. Nie mam pewności, czy aby na pewno w tym miejscu kamera mnie nie łapie. Sam wymagam pocieszenia.

– Na pewno nie zobaczą?

Czy on nie może się choć trochę wyluzować? Widać, że proces zdziczenia ma już za sobą.

– Na pewno? – pyta w kółko.

– Nie widać – odpowiadam i słyszę dobiegający z prawego skrzydła dźwięk zamykanych drzwi.

Facet jest przerażony, znowu zaczyna machać łapami.

– Odejdź dalej – syczy. – Odejdź.

Już nic mu nie opowiem, za późno. Czekam na Mojsa.

– Za niedopełnienie obowiązków służbowych powinienem cię, Boszczuk, zwolnić! – Wychodzimy z windy. – To cię uderzy po kieszeni – mówi, nie patrząc na mnie.

– Po kieszeni? – powtarzam za nim, ale on nie odpowiada. Szarpie tylko za klamkę i wchodzi z powrotem na monitoring.

Chcę wejść za nim, spytać go jeszcze raz o tę kasę, którą znowu chce mi zabrać, ale on staje w progu, zagradzając mi drogę swoją szeroką dupą.

– A ty, kurwa, gdzie? Z powrotem na minusy zapierdalaj!

Trzaska drzwiami.

Zaczyna mi się kręcić w głowie. Tępo rozglądam się dookoła, zaraz się przewrócę. Parę metrów i byłbym wolny. Wystarczy tylko przejść przez tamte drzwi i zapomnieć. Stoję nieruchomo, w głowie kołacze mi się jedna i ta sama myśl: nie wracać już na poziom minusowy, na minusy, minusiki. Wyjść stąd jak tamten, co zarzygał swoje piętro. Zostawić to wszystko za sobą.

On już chyba nigdy do pracy nie pójdzie. Na co mu praca, skoro ma koleżankę z mięsnego. Dulian poznał ją przed tygodniem. Ma na imię Aniela, ma samochód i już raz była u nas na stancji. Dziś też będzie, przywiezie nam coś dobrego do jedzenia.

– Chabaninę przytaszczy – cieszy się Dulian i z wywalonym jęzorem zaciera ręce. – Szyneczki i takie tam mięsiwa.

– Podzielisz się z kolegami?

– Paaatryk. – Patrzy na mnie spod brwi. – Właduje się do lodówki i finał. Teraz to już nie będziecie się musieli martwić – foczka o nas zadba, zobaczysz.

Dulian tak na nią mówi, bo Aniela jest tłusta jak foka w sezonie zimowym, ale on lubi grube. Powiedział mi to, zanim jeszcze pierwszy raz ją tu przyprowadził. Gadał, że lubi takie szerokie, tłuste dupy i trzęsące się oponki. Ona ma jedno i drugie, a do tłustego zadka i trzęsącej się opony można jeszcze dołożyć podwójny podbródek. Pikanterii dodaje to, że jest starsza od Duliana o sześć lat. Lubi starsze? Tego nie mówił, pewnie zapomniał. Nie zapomniał się za to pochwalić, że już ją trzymał za cycka. Z wypiekami na twarzy opowiadał mi, że lewy cycek Anieli jest sporo mniejszy od prawego. Teraz w niedługim czasie planuje ją bzyknąć. A jak już ją bzyknie raz, dwa, może nawet trzy razy, to ją odstawi na bocznicę. Tak mówił.

– O której przyjedzie? – pytam, patrząc na zegarek.

– O siedemnastej – odpowiada. – Dziś robi na pierwszą zmianę; powinna zaraz tu być. – Podchodzi do okna. – O! I o wilku mowa – krzyczy z nosem przyklejonym do szyby. – Jedzie! – cieszy się jak dziecko. – Chodź, zobacz. Jedzie!

– Wierzę ci – mruczę, zastanawiając się, czy nie powinienem okazać choć odrobiny entuzjazmu. Podnoszę się z krzesła i staję za nim. – Noo. – Nie patrzę nawet w okno. Siadam.

Dzisiaj wydaje mi się jeszcze większa. Może dlatego, że założyła na siebie jakąś ogromną czerwoną narzutę w czarną kratę. Coś podobnego widziałem kiedyś w westernach. Mówią na to poncho czy jakoś tak. Spod tego wystaje jej tylko głowa i muskularne łydki. Przy jej łydkach moje to patyczki, łydki kenijskiego maratończyka.

– Cześć. – Znowu wstaję z krzesła. Witam się z nią, a wzrokiem szukam wieprzowiny.

– Hej – odpowiada Aniela i kładzie na naszym kuchennym stole przezroczystą foliową siatkę. Jedno małe pęto kiełbasy i to wszystko? Przecież to nie jest szyneczka i takie tam mięsiwa. Co to jest?

Trzeba zachować zimną krew, nawet jeśli przyniosła tylko samotne pęto taniej kiełbasy. Chyba na chwilę zapomniałem, że słów Duliana nie można brać poważnie. Ma wybujałą wyobraźnię, po raz kolejny się o tym przekonałem. Ja już to wiem, ona jeszcze nie. Ciekawe, ile czasu zajmie jej przekonanie się o tym.

– Jak było w pracy? – pyta Aniela.

– Dziś miałem wolne – odpowiadam.

To nie do mnie? Patrzy na Duliana i na znak, że usłyszała, od niechcenia kiwa tylko głową.

– A u ciebie, misiaczku? – Cały czas patrzy na niego.

Misiaczek wszystkiego mi nie powiedział.

– Dobrze – odpowiada i z adekwatnie strudzoną miną zaczyna ją głaskać po dużych policzkach. – Muszę wziąć parę dni wolnego i trochę odpocząć – mówi spokojnie, patrząc jej prosto w oczy. – Może ty też wzięłabyś trochę wolnego, co?

Próbuję na nich nie patrzeć, ale uszu zakrywał sobie nie będę. Słucham więc dalej, jak ten idiota gada od rzeczy.

– Wyjechalibyśmy w góry albo nad morze, co?

(Pierdu, pierdu).

– W górach jeszcze nie byłam, ale bardziej wolałabym nad morze. Do Sopotu albo do Gdańska.

Dulian z melancholią w oczach kiwa głową.

– Gdzie tylko, skarbie, sobie życzysz. Może być Sopot – mówi przyciszonym na granicy słyszalności głosem. – Zarezerwuje się tylko wcześniej jakiś hotelik i jedziemy.

– W Sopocie tanio nie jest – wtrącam się, burząc tym samym tę piękną atmosferę. – Osobiście nie byłem, ale słyszałem, że ceny nad morzem są konkretne.

– A w Warszawie to co, tanio jest? – oburza się Aniela. – Wszystko drogie.

– Noo. – Dulian wzdycha ciężko. – I tylko ta robota i robota. Coś od życia też się przecież czasami należy, a nad morzem to można rybkę świeżą zjeść, bursztynów poszukać, jodem pooddychać. Nie ma co porównywać. Morze to morze.

Zastanawiam się, co ten romantyk zrobi, jeśli ona rzeczywiście zechce jechać nad to morze. Jak wybrnie, co jej powie? Że mimo szczerych chęci nie udało mu się wziąć wolnego w pracy? Pewnie jest niezastąpionym fachowcem i bez niego firma od razu padnie. Ciekawe, jakich jeszcze bzdur jej naopowiadał, gdzie pracuje i na jakim stanowisku.

Wychodzę z kuchni. Idę do pokoju, ale oni człapią za mną. Dulian włącza telewizor i rzuca się na tapczan, ona kładzie się przy nim. Nakrywają się kocem. To dziwne, ale mieszczą się pod nim.

*

Nie tylko włosy stają mi na rękach, kiedy kątem oka widzę rytmicznie unoszący się koc. Ciche jęki Anieli powodują, że szczerze zazdroszczę teraz Dulianowi. I mimo że jej szeroka dupa z powodzeniem mogłaby robić za falochron, to jęczy całkiem, całkiem. Z takim pojękiwaniem dałaby radę dubbingować niemieckie hardcore'owe klasyki albo udawać szczupłą lolitkę w sekstelefonie.

*

Ciężkie kroki na schodach i godzina 20.30 oznaczają tylko jedno – bracia po całym dniu stania wracają na stancję; ze zrobionymi po drodze zakupami: chleb, wędlina, jakieś piwo i zawsze chipsy. O tej porze nie chce im się już przyrządzać kolacji, więc piwo i duża paka słonych chipsów na ogół załatwiają sprawę. Ja też zaczynam przejmować od nich te zwyczaje. Może dlatego coraz częściej boli mnie w nocy żołądek i tak jak oni mam niemiłosiernie śmierdzące gazy.

Na jej widok ni to się uśmiechają, ni to się krzywią. W przeciwieństwie do mnie widzą Anielę pierwszy raz. Wiesiek przez chwilę patrzy spode łba, a Krzysiek? Cały czas je chipsy – wyciąga po kilka naraz z szeleszczącej paczki i garściami pakuje je sobie do gęby. Gdy tak łapczywie żre, jego oczy stają się jeszcze bardziej tępe, jak u jakiegoś kudłatego małpoluda.

– Cześć chłopaki. – Dulian udaje, że ich widok go cieszy, ale nawet on nie potrafi teraz ukryć prawdziwych emocji. Co on, do cholery, zapomniał? Przecież oni zawsze o tej porze ściągają na stancję. – Poznajcie się, to jest Aniela.

Wiesiek podchodzi do niej.

– Cześć. – Podaje jej rękę, a ona próbuje się wygramolić spod koca. Jest chyba lekko zawstydzona, bo poncho całkiem jej się podwinęło, odsłaniając dużo za dużo.

Wiesiek robi zdziwione oczy. Mogła już leżeć pod tym kraciastym kocem. Ciekawe, czy te jego duże oczy to z zachwytu. Może on też lubi takie tłuste foki?

Krzysiek nie podchodzi do niej. Rzuca tylko krótkie „cześć" i nie przestając żreć, siada na brzegu swojego tapczanu.

– Z pracy? – pyta Aniela, a Dulian, jakby chcąc ich uwolnić od wyjaśnień, sam odpowiada na jej pytanie.

– Tak, z pracy – mówi półszeptem.

Ma się wrażenie, że chciałby się ukryć za jej wielkimi plecami. Dobrze wie, że mogą jej odsłonić nieco prawdy o nim. Ma tego pełną świadomość, dlatego nie czekając, aż bracia go skompromitują, proponuje jej nocny spacer.

– Przejdziemy się? – pyta, podnosząc się z tapczanu.

Aniela potakuje głową.

– Już późno – mówi. – Jadę.

Kiedy wstaje, słychać, jak brzęczą wszystkie sprężyny.

– Skąd jesteś? – pyta ją Wiesiek.

– Z Raszyna – odpowiada.

– Eee, to blisko.

– No, tylko parę kilometrów.

Dulian coraz bardziej się kuli.

– Gdzie będziesz szła, jeszcze wcześnie. Zobacz. – Pokazuje paluchem wiszący na ścianie zegar. – Dopiero po dwudziestej.

– No tak – śmieje się Aniela. – Za dziesięć dziewiąta, che, che.

Siada z powrotem na tapczanie i znowu słychać te sprężyny.

– A pracujesz gdzie? – pyta Wiesiek.

– Też w Raszynie, w sklepie mięsnym.

Krzysiek parska śmiechem.

Chwila ciszy...

– Co? – pyta Aniela. – W mięsnym – powtarza, patrząc na niego, jakby spodziewała się, że coś do niej powie.

– To na brak jedzenia nie możesz narzekać – odzywa się Wiesiek i chcąc zatrzeć niefortunną reakcję brata, gada, że sam by chciał w mięsnym kiełbasy sprzedawać. – Nie byłoby tam miejsca dla mnie? – śmieje się. – Już ja bym sobie krzywdy nie dał zrobić. Nie ma jak w mięsnym pracować, zawsze do domu coś można wynieść, nie?

– Czasami – odpowiada Aniela.

– Eee – śmieje się Krzysiek. –To teraz on już nie będzie z burczącym bebechem łaził. – Patrzy na Duliana. – Już nie będziesz nam z lodówki wyżerał, nie?

– Bardzo śmieszne... bardzo... – odzywa się Dulian, a potem zaczyna coś szeptać Anieli do ucha.

– Zaraz, zaraz pójdziemy, jeszcze chwila – uspokaja go.

– Jak chcesz – odpowiada cicho.

Jest podenerwowany. Patrzę na niego. Nie chciałbym być teraz na jego miejscu, ale przecież wiedział, o której wracają.

*

– Co ty jej nagadałeś? Jaka praca?

Wychodzimy do kuchni zapalić papierosa. Bracia zostają z Anielą w pokoju.

– Nic jej nie nagadałem.

– Chrzaniłeś, że pracujesz? Przecież nigdzie nie pracujesz.

Patrzy na mnie przez chwilę, a potem zaciąga się głęboko papierosem.

– A skąd wiesz?

Uśmiecha się.

– Pracujesz?

– No, nie, jeszcze nie, ale mam coś na oku. Ona niech myśli, że gdzieś robię – tu chodzi, kurwa, o wizerunek. Przecież nie muszę jej się ze wszystkiego spowiadać. Zresztą ona to takie sekspogotowie. Już ci mówiłem, nic stałego – znowu się śmieje, kątem oka zerkając na przedpokój. – Widziałeś, jak ją Wiesiek z każdej strony obcina?

– Obcina? – powtarzam za nim.

– Nie widziałeś, jak na nią patrzy, jak ją bajeruje?

– Może ją polubił.

– Tak, kurwa, akurat. Ma ochotę ją wyruchać. – Mruży oczy. – Jak chce, to niech ją rucha.

Gaszę papierosa w popielniczce.

– A skąd miałeś kasę na fajki i te browary? Krzysiek, zrobił wielkie oczy, kiedy postawiłeś przed nim te piwa. Od razu przestał ci dopierdalać, a robiło się już naprawdę nieprzyjemnie.

Dulian nerwowo marszczy brwi.

– Ten grubas ma szczęście, że mieszka z bratem. Do Wieśka nic nie mam, nawet do strawienia jest, ale ten to, kurwa, ciężki typ. Od samego początku wiedziałem, że to idiota. – Znowu zerka do przedpokoju. – A teraz też? Sam słyszałeś. Jak chce się przypierdalać, to niech się przypierdala, ale nie przy dupie. Zresztą... – Macha niedbale ręką i też gasi papierosa. – Mam to gdzieś.

– To skąd miałeś tę kasę? – pytam znowu.

Uśmiecha się szelmowsko.

– No, kurwa, jak to skąd? Od niej pożyczyłem, ale oddam. Spokojnie, zobaczysz.

– Znasz ją kilka dni i już kasę od niej wyciągasz?

– No i co? – cieszy się.

– Myślałem, że ją kochasz. – Próbuję mieć poważną minę, ale nie mogę powstrzymać się od śmiechu.

Dulian stuka się w czoło.

– Chyba zwariowałeś. Kochasz? Najpierw trzeba się wyszaleć, a potem, noo, może bliżej trzydziestki, o jakimś tam kochaniu zacząć myśleć. Myślenie nic nie kosztuje, nie? – Znowu rechocze jak żaba. Patrzę na zegarek, wychodzimy z kuchni.

*

Aniela zostaje u nas na noc, a następnego dnia wczesnym rankiem Bożena robi nam wszystkim pobudkę. Nie ma jeszcze szóstej, a ona z krzykiem wbiega do pokoju. Jak głupia drze się na całe gardło i straszy, że wyrzuci nas wszystkich na bruk. Najbardziej wydziera się na Wieśka.

– Co to jest? – Ściąga z niego kołdrę. – Burdelu z domu robić nie pozwolę! – krzyczy i każe Anieli się wynosić.

Dlaczego spod kołdry Wieśka wystają jej pulchne stopy? Wiesiek ma taką zmieszaną minę. Wszyscy jeszcze prawie śpimy. Nie pamiętam, ile wczoraj poszło piw. Wiem tylko, że Dulian przynajmniej dwa razy leciał do sklepu.

Po fajki, bo zabrakło, a potem jeszcze raz, po fajki i piwo, bo też się skończyło. Pewnie wydał wszystkie pożyczone od niej pieniądze. Teraz szybko jej nie odda. Pewnie wcale jej nie odda. Aniela cały czas jest w poncho. Nie zdjęła go do spania? Wiesiek rozkłada bezradnie ręce.

– Pani Bożenko, ja nie mam pojęcia, jak to się stało – tłumaczy, wskazując na Anielę palcem. – To jego znajoma. – Pokazuje teraz na Duliana.

– Ja też nie wiem, ale to moja wina – odzywa się Aniela. – W nocy poszłam do łazienki i chyba pomyliłam łóżka. Było ciemno, nic nie widziałam – tłumaczy, patrząc na Bożenę.

– No widzi pani, pani Bożenko? Mówiłem.

Aniela wybiega z pokoju, Dulian za nią. Jeszcze przez chwilę słychać, że coś do niej gada, coś jej tłumaczy. Potem z zaczerwienioną twarzą wraca do nas i dalej wysłuchuje wrzasków Bożeny. Nie wiem, jak bracia, ale ja to pierwszy raz widzę ją w takim stanie. Szczerze mówiąc, nie mogę zrozumieć, dlaczego się tak wścieka. Czym się przejmuje? Na jej miejscu bardziej bałbym się kontroli skarbowej, tyle kasy na boku z wynajmu bierze. Wystarczy jeden życzliwy i odpokutuje za grzechy. Ja tym życzliwym nie będę. Jedyny anonim, który chodzi mi po głowie, to donos na Mojsa, i niech tak zostanie.

*

Cały czas nie wiem, ile odciągną mi za tę zniszczoną wykładzinę. Otuchy dodaje jedynie to, że nie ja jeden nie dopilnowałem swoich „obowiązków służbowych". Dwóch innych też ma dostać po kieszeni. Dowiaduję się o tym w szatni.

– Przecież oni wcale nie będą wymieniać tej wykładziny – mówi jeden.

– Nie będą – przytakuje drugi.

Kiwam głową.

– Szukają frajerów – mówię.

– Mojs szuka. Odciągnie nam z wypłaty i będzie miał na te swoje dziwki. Jak mi zajebie z wypłaty, to chcę mieć to na piśmie – mówi pierwszy, przecierając brudną szmatą buty.

– Tak, akurat będziesz miał na piśmie – odzywa się drugi. – Te działy to też bezprawnie nam biorą, i co? Ktoś wie w ogóle, co się z tymi pieniędzmi dzieje? To tak samo, jak z tą cholerną wykładziną. Nie byłoby tak, ale ludzie się na to godzą. Robią z nami, co chcą. W innych firmach też tak jest. Za wszystko kasują. Nawet jak masz czysty mundur i wypastowane buty, to i tak znajdą coś, za co kasę zabiorą. Tak już jest, bo ludzie się na to godzą – powtarza.

Chce jeszcze coś powiedzieć, ale do szatni wchodzi Henio. Jak zawsze, i teraz trzyma w ręku listę, zaczyna wyczytywać. Tamten tam, tamten tam... i tak dalej. Stoję i czekam. Czuję ulgę, kiedy obsadza minusiki. Przez chwilę nawet się łudzę, że da mnie na klateczki, ale tylko przez chwilę, bo na klateczki wysyła innego. Cho-cimska?... Nie! A więc zostały już tylko piętorka. Czekam. Nie wyczytał mnie? Jak nie na piętorka, to gdzie? Może puści mnie do domu? Boże, to by była miła niespodzianka. A może mnie wywalili? To też byłaby miła niespodzianka.

– Dziś będziesz mi pomagał. Zabieraj swoją torbę, idziemy – mówi Henio.

Ci, którzy jeszcze nie wyszli z szatni, patrzą teraz na mnie. Dziwnie patrzą, podejrzliwie, może z zazdrością? Dziwnie patrzą.

– Mam pomagać? – pytam głośno, nie kryjąc zaskoczenia. – Jak?

– Normalnie – odpowiada. – Dziś siedzisz ze mną. Karol ma wolne, ty go zastąpisz. – Kieruje się do drzwi wyjściowych. – No chodź, czasu nie ma. A wy, panowie, na co czekacie? Prze-cież wiecie, gdzie macie iść – mówi do pozosta-łych. Cały czas wlepiają we mnie gały.

Ten idiota nawet nie wie, jak mnie „uszczę-śliwił". Przecież niejeden chciałby mu poma-gać, tak na ochotnika. Tu nie brakuje dupow-krętów z ambicjami. Robić za adiutanta? Nie aspiruję do takiej funkcji. To ostatnia rzecz, na jaką miałbym ochotę.

Idąc za Heniem, zastanawiam się, dlacze-go akurat na mnie padło. Przecież niczym się nie wyróżniam, nie słodzę i nie uśmiecham się serdecznie do Mojsa. Jestem zwykłym, niczym niewyróżniającym się stojakiem – i tyle. Więc dlaczego ja?

Zapytam. Co mi tam, muszę wiedzieć, skąd taka głupia decyzja. Może jeszcze coś da się zmienić. Z chęcią pójdę na każdy posterunek, nawet do Zbycha na minusiki łazić, byleby tylko nie siedzieć z Mojsem.

– Całą dobę będę musiał ci pomagać?

– Co?

Podchodzę bliżej Henia.

– Cały dyżur?

– Co cały dyżur?

– Cały dyżur będę ci musiał pomagać?

– A co?

– Pytam tylko – udaję, że to dla mnie nic takiego.

– A co, kurwa, nie cieszysz się?

Przecież nie powiem mu, że się cieszę. Lepiej już o nic nie będę pytał. Niech się dzieje; tylko że już teraz czuję się jak konfident.

Wchodzimy na monitoring. Od progu czuję ten charakterystyczny smród. Mojsa jeszcze nie ma. To dobrze. Jak przyjdzie, śmierdzieć będzie bardziej.

Henio każe mi usiąść przy kilku czarnobiałych monitorach.

– Tu masz konsolę – mówi, przysuwając do mnie jakieś nieduże plastikowe ustrojstwo. – Zobacz, joystick i parę takich tam guzików, nic prostszego. Do dyspozycji masz kilkanaście kamer, wszystko widzisz na ekranach. Na razie nic nie ruszaj. Patrz tylko, a jak któryś wyjdzie z kadru, to od razu zgłaszaj, do mnie zgłaszaj. Zrozumiałeś czy powtórzyć?

– Zrozumiałem. – Kiwam głową. – Nic nie ruszać, tylko patrzeć, tak?

– Dokładnie; patrzeć, czy nie wychodzą z kadru. Potem pokażę ci, jak ta zabaweczka działa, ale na razie to tylko to. – Siada przy drugim stole, otwiera zeszyt formatu A4 i zaczyna w nim coś zapisywać.

Niełatwo ogarnąć wzrokiem wszystkie te okienka. Monitorów jest pięć, plus dwa dodatkowe przy stole Henia. Każdy z ekranów jest podzielony na cztery obrazy. Wtedy robi się tak zwany poczwórny ekran. Dzięki temu na jednym ekranie widzę kilka posterunków na raz. Chocimska, recepcja i piętra – wszystko jak na dłoni. Minusów nie widzę, ale i tak oczy bolą. Minusy widzi tylko Zbychu.

Na dwóch posterunkach nie ma człowieka. Dopiero teraz to zauważam. Zastanawiam się, czy jeszcze trochę nie poczekać ze zgłoszeniem tego Heniowi. Pewnie kolesie urwali się na dziką. Poczekam, pewnie zaraz wrócą. Jest, ale tylko jeden.

– Poziom drugi zgłasza plażę. – To ten, co przed chwilą z niej wrócił. Cwaniaczek. BRAWO!

Henio nachyla się nad cienkim czarnym mikrofonem; ja mam taki sam.

– Możesz! – krzyczy. Potem podchodzi do mnie i zaczyna się wpatrywać w monitory. – Aaa, to ten – mówi, opierając się łokciem o mój bark.

– Jeszcze nawet godziny nie stoi, i widzisz? Już mu się do kibla spieszy.

– Może go pogoniło.

– Taaak, kurwa, akurat. Stać mu się nie chce – i tyle. Miej na niego oko. Ty! A gdzie jest ten z czwórki?

Zauważył.

– No właśnie... Miałem ci powiedzieć.

– Poziom czwarty, nie widać cię w kamerze! – krzyczy, jakby walczył o własne życie. – Poziom czwarty!

Mała ciemna postać (stąd tak nas widać) właśnie wskoczyła na swoje miejsce. Stoi – co za ulga.

– Zgłasza się poziom czwarty!

– Nie było cię widać!

– A teraz?

Chłopak ma poczucie humoru. Henio już mu nie odpowiada. Podaje mi za to swój zmęczony zeszyt.

– Masz – mówi, kładąc zeszyt przede mną. – Trzeba będzie napisać z tego notatkę służbową.

– Notatkę służbową? Z czego?

– No, jak to z czego! – denerwuje się. – To taki dupochron jest – tłumaczy. – Na wypadek, gdyby ktoś z administracji chciał prześledzić nagrania. Jak zobaczą, że nie było człowieka, to ja po dupie dostanę, nikt inny. To taki dupochron jest – powtarza.

Jakbym teraz słyszał Zbycha.

– Z każdego, nawet chwilowego zniknięcia trzeba taką notatkę pisać? – krzywię się, wyrażając swoją dezaprobatę.

Ale Henio to zakuty łeb i prócz nieskończonej liczby przykazań Mojsa nic do niego nie dociera, moja skrzywiona gęba też. Nie próbuję więc z nim dalej dyskutować. Dyżur przed nami – cały dzień i cała noc. Wytrzymam.

*

Po szóstej notatce służbowej przestaję liczyć. Teraz już wiem, dlaczego te mendy nie wypuszczają długopisu z łapy. Oni cały czas, na okrągło, chlastają te debilne notatki. Te wypociny różnią się tylko tym, że na każdej kolejnej jest inne nazwisko i godzina „wykroczenia". To takie pisanie dla pisania, szkoda na to czasu i papieru. Pisząc to, zastanawiam się, ile lewizn już przegapiłem. Co którąś przegapiam celowo. To niemałe ryzyko, ale ta świadomość leczy trochę moje sumienie. Chociaż...? Sam już nie wiem, kto jest większym nieszczęśnikiem. Czy ja, czy ten, na którego te pieprzone notatki piszę? Jedno jest pewne – nawet gdybym miał zarabiać krocie, na adiutanta bym się nie nadawał.

Myślałem, że on, ciągnąc mnie tu, skonsultował to z Mojsem – widać, nie bardzo. Mojs na mój widok robi zdziwioną minę.

– On? – kpiącym tonem pyta Henia. – Jego wziąłeś? – krzywi się i pokazuje na mnie paluchem.

Henio uśmiecha się i chcąc zmienić temat, pyta o Karola, swojego adiutanta.

– Co z Karolem?

Mojs wzrusza ramionami.

– Do wyjebania – odpowiada. – Jak se chciał ulżyć, to mógł strzepać w kiblu gruchę albo na pigalak pójść – śmieje się, nerwowo krążąc wokół mnie wzrokiem. – Tamta go podjebała, ma chłopak pecha. – Rozkłada bezradnie ręce.

Gapię się w monitory, piszę notatki i tak w kółko. Mojs cały czas gada o jakiejś sprzątaczce i o tym adiutancie Karolu. Podobno złapał ją za tyłek, kiedy męską ubikację sprzątała.

– Za dupę ją chwycił – mówi, śmiejąc się do Henia.

Henio też zaczyna się śmiać.

– Za dupę – powtarza za Mojsem. – Za dupę, che, che.

– Tak gadała, że za dupę. Od razu poleciała do ich szefa – wiesz, tego łysego, co dziesięć lat w Stanach przesiedział. On tam sam kąty wymiatał, a tu, cwaniaczek, firmę sprzątającą sobie otworzył. Biznesman, kurwa jego mać. – Macha łapą. – Chuj z nim. W każdym razie ta młoda cipa powiedziała mu o tym, a ten piany dostał i do naszego starego przekręcił. Aaa! I jeszcze do administracji poszedł. Teraz tamci już wiedzą, a nasz stary, wiesz, jaki jest – nie lubi ryzyka. Dzisiaj będę z nim gadał. Powiem mu, że Karol nic nie chciał od tego kocmołucha, ale zobaczymy, jak będzie. Stary się boi, że przez to firma kontrakt straci. – Kiwa głową. – Pogadam z nim, będzie dobrze.

– Karol jest w porządku – odzywa się z przejęciem Henio. Aż trudno uwierzyć, że jeszcze przed momentem się śmiał. – W porządku jest – powtarza.

Mojs wytrzeszcza oczy.

– Spokojnie. Mówiłem, że pogadam? To pogadam, o piętnastej zadzwonię. Przecież trzeba, kurwa, powalczyć o człowieka. A co stary zrobi, nie wiem – mówi, z wysiłkiem wypuszczając z siebie głośnego pierda.

„Świnia w każdym calu" – myślę sobie i znowu patrzę w monitory. Słyszę ich głośny śmiech i czekam, aż powie coś jeszcze – coś o tej seksaferze, co ją adiutant Karol ze sprzątaczką w kiblu rozpętał. Ale Mojs już nic więcej na ten temat nie gada. Pierdzi potem jeszcze kilka razy, czym bardzo rozwesela Henia. Śmierdzi.

Jest czternasta, zgłaszam kolejną lewiznę. Teraz zgłaszam wszystkie, nie odpuszczam nikomu. Od chwili kiedy Mojs dojrzał pusty posterunek, informuję o każdym zniknięciu. Nie zgłosiłem specjalnie. Mojs porządnie mnie opieprzył i dał ostrzeżenie. Gdyby znał moje prawdziwe intencje, pewnie od razu dostałbym działę. Nie będę ginął za innych, co mi po takim bohaterstwie. Nikt z uratowanych nie złoży się potem na mnie. Więc podpierdalam, choć nie chcę. Podpierdalam, bo muszę!

*

Mojs wstaje z fotela. Od godziny nieustannie opowiada Heniowi, że stary, jak nazywa dyrektora naszej firmy, bardzo go lubi. Mówi, że dał mu wolną rękę, bo wyniki jego pracy są co najmniej imponujące.

– Stary nie lubi srania w pieluchy, słuchaj. Pamiętasz? – mówi do Henia. – Musisz pamiętać, w końcu już jakiś czas tu robisz, nie?

– Za miesiąc dwa lata minie – z dumą w głosie odpowiada Henio.

– Ile? – pyta z niedowierzaniem Mojs. – Dwa?

– No, dwa lata już będzie i trzeci rok zacznie lecieć. Adaś przyszedł po mnie, a potem ty, Mareczku, przyszedłeś. Pamiętasz, jak ci obiekt pokazywaliśmy, bo tamten, co miał ci przekazać obowiązki, na chorobowe sobie poszedł? Pamiętasz? Nic ci nie powiedział, a miał cię wprowadzić i wszystko pokazać. Pamiętasz?

– Co? – Mojs wykrzywia usta, jakby to, co Henio teraz gada, było kompletną bzdurą. – Bo tamten chuj... – Marszczy czoło. – Jak on miał?

– Sławek – bez chwili namysłu podpowiada Henio.

– O! No właśnie. Jakoś tak miał – kiwa głową. – Jaki, kurwa, z niego był inspektor? Sam mówiłeś, że prawie wcale go na obiekcie nie było,

a jak już przyszedł, to tylko na chwilę i spierdalał. Sam tak mówiłeś.

Albo te kontrole... Kurwa, jak można udawać, że się nie widzi, jak inni w chuja lecą?
Łazili na zwolnienia! Łazili, bo pozwalał. Sam
w chuja walił, to mu było wszystko jedno. Stary
mówił, że nie był z niego zadowolony.

– Szkoda gadać – kwituje Henio. Gdyby dla
potwierdzenia słów Mojsa kiwał tylko głową,
mogłoby to znaczyć, że może jest innego zda-
nia, że może nie do końca zgadza się z Mojsem
co do oceny jego poprzednika. Więc nie szczę-
dząc krytyki, wypowiada swoją opinię. – Do niczego był – mówi. – Do niczego. Ludzie się go
nie słuchali. Tak, do niczego był. – Nie spuszcza wzroku z Mojsa.

Nie wiem, dlaczego, ale to jego kiwanie łbem
i mnie się udziela. Przez chwilę też tak potakuję,
jakbym się chciał przypodobać tej śmierdzącej
świni.

Mojs chwyta za słuchawkę telefonu. Jest dokładnie godzina piętnasta. Jedną ręką wystukuje numer, a paluch drugiej przykłada do ust.

– Teraz, kurwa, cicho. Dzwonię do starego.
Ciiicho.

Nie mam pojęcia, kogo on ucisza. Ja przecież
siedzę i słowem się nie odzywam. Odpowiadam
tylko wtedy, kiedy naprawdę muszę. A Henio?
Henio jest przerażony. Kto ma być cicho?

– Dzień dobry, dyrektorze, Marek Mojs kłania się z tej strony. Panie dyrektorze, dzwonię,

bo byliśmy umówieni, że do pana zadzwonię
i porozmawiamy na temat tamtego, co chciał tę
sprzątaczkę zgłuszyć. Wie pan, tego ode mnie
z centrum. Tak, tak, dokładnie, panie dyrektorze, właśnie tego. – Mojs, szczerząc się, puszcza oko do Henia. Widać jest z siebie zadowolony. – Panie dyrektorze, to co z nim robimy? –
Kiwa głową. – Tak, tak... Oczywiście. Jeśli chodzi o mnie, to całkowicie się z panem zgadzam.
Tak, panie dyrektorze, jasne, tylko trzeba mu
to wręczyć, zanim zachce mu się pójść na jakieś lewe zwolnienie. No właśnie, panie dyrektorze, pójdzie na L4 i wszystko się pokrzyżuje,
a tak – mamy problem z głowy. – Uśmiecha się
do Henia i znowu puszcza do niego oko. – Tak,
tak, też tak uważam, panie dyrektorze. Pewnie,
że tak, che, che. Oczywiście, zadzwonię do niego, tak. – Marszczy czoło. – Panie dyrektorze,
niech się pan nie martwi, nie będzie problemu.
Na pewno, che, che. Jasne, panie dyrektorze,
kłaniam się, do widzenia. – Odkłada słuchawkę. – No to z głowy! – wzdycha, patrząc na Henia. – Stary jest nieugięty. Mówi, że do wyjebania. – Wykrzywia usta. – Nic nie mogłem zrobić,
sam słyszałeś, uparł się.
   Wolałbym wpaść po szyję do parującej gno-
jowicy, niż siedzieć z nim w jednym pomieszczeniu. Jak można być tak zakłamanym chujem? To miała być walka o człowieka? To była
najbardziej skurwysyńska rozmowa przez telefon, jaką kiedykolwiek słyszałem. Jak taka

świnia może wytrzymać sama ze sobą, patrzeć w lustro?!

– Do zwolnienia? – pyta smutno Henio, ale ja w ten jego smutek wcale nie wierzę. To taka sama menda jak Mojs, tylko menda mendzie we władzy nierówna.

Mojs rozkłada ręce.

– Co mogłem? Nic nie mogłem. Ze starym trzeba jak z dzieckiem. Nie ma co przeginać. Powiedział, że nie, to nie. Mówił, że zostawienie Karola to dla firmy strzał w kolano. Muszę do niego zadzwonić i powiedzieć, że ma iść do biura. Powiem, że nie wiem, o co chodzi. Stary chce mu osobiście wręczyć wypowiedzenie, w przeciwnym razie...

– Pójdzie na L4 i wszystko się pokrzyżuje – przerywa mu Henio, powtarzając wcześniej zapamiętaną formułkę.

– No właśnie, sam widzisz. – Mojs wytrzeszcza oczy. – A tak, krótka piłka i po sprawie. Ale powiem ci, że szkoda Karola. Żeby przez jakąś śmieciarę wymówienie z roboty dostawać. Szkoda chłopaka.

– Na drugim piętrze nie ma człowieka – przerywam im ich pełną smutku rozmowę. Pośpieszyłem się, już jest; chyba tylko na chwilę wyszedł mi z kadru. To na pewno nie była żadna lewizna. – Odwołuję! – krzyczę. – Wszystko w porządku, wrócił.

Mojs podchodzi do mnie.

– Co? – pyta zdziwiony. – Jakie odwołuję? Co odwołujesz? Jak wrócił, to znaczy że go nie było. Zapisz to albo dupy nie zawracaj.

– Co tu opisywać? – Nie powinienem z nim dyskutować. – Przecież to było tylko parę sekund.

– Pisz, i koniec! – włącza się z furią Henio. – Inspektor mówił, że masz napisać z tego notatkę, to pisz i nie dyskutuj!

– Dobra – odpowiadam. – Nie ma problemu. Jeśli inspektor każe... – mówię z przekąsem i biorę do ręki długopis.

– Coś ci się, Boszczuk, nie podoba? – odzywa się Mojs.

Wskazuję palcem na siebie.

– Nie, dlaczego? Tylko wydaje mi się, że...

– Że co? – przerywa mi Henio. – Niech ci się nie wydaje. Ty tu nie jesteś od tego, żeby ci się coś wydawało. Masz robić to, co do ciebie należy; od wydawania są inni.

Unoszę ręce.

– W porządku, już nic nie mówię, ale moim zdaniem, nic takiego się nie stało.

– Weź już się, kurwa, zamknij! – krzyczy Mojs. – Na chuj go tu sadzałeś? – Patrzy na Henia. – Innych nie było? Musiałeś jego na monitoring ciągnąć?

Henio nic nie odpowiada. Spuszcza tylko łeb, jak skarcone dziecko postawione do kąta, w oczekiwaniu, aż ta świnia coś do niego powie. Bardzo przeżywa każdą, nawet najmniejszą uwagę ze strony Mojsa. Pod tym względem jest bardzo wrażliwym człowiekiem.

Guru może zrobić ze swoim wyznawcami wszystko. Ciekawe, czy sympatycy Mojsa potrafiliby powiedzieć „nie". Oni wszyscy chyba pozapominali, że ta świnia to tylko pracownik firmy ochroniarskiej. Tak samo jak ja, w każdej chwili do zwolnienia. Dziś siedzi i wydaje polecenia, a jutro? A jutro, kto wie, życie bywa nieprzewidywalne. Oby jak najszybciej odbił sobie zad przy twardym lądowaniu.

*

Pierwszy raz, od kiedy tu pracuję, żałuję, że robią przerwę obiadową. Żałuję, bo teraz wszyscy zobaczą, że siedzę dziś za adiutanta. Wolałbym już nic nie jeść, byle nie musieć podmieniać wszystkich na piętnaście minut. Zresztą nawet nie jestem głodny, co jakiś czas coś podjadam. Adiutant, podobnie jak dowódca, nie musi czekać na przerwę, torbę z żarciem ma zawsze przy sobie.

*

Połowa patrzy na mnie, jakbym im matkę zabił. Tłumaczą się winni, więc mówię im tylko, żeby się uwijali – i tyle. Muszę tak gadać, bo to ja mam pilnować ich czasu. Mojs powiedział, że to do mnie będą mieli pretensje ci, dla których nie starczy minut. Każdemu przypominam, że ma tylko kwadrans, ale jest, jak jest. Przez piętnaście minut to nawet dobrze wysrać się nie można. Prawie do dziewiętnastej odwiedzam wszystkie posterunki, potem wracam na monitoring.

Mojs właśnie przyszedł. Dziś wieczorem osobiście poprzesuwał ludzi na posterunkach. Nie wiem, do której z nami posiedzi. Gdybym tylko mógł, to bym go spytał; tak normalnie, po ludzku. Spytałbym go, do której z nami będzie czy jakoś tak. Coś w rodzaju pytania, jakie zadaje się podczas niechcianej wizyty krewnych, pojawiających się bez zapowiedzi, z których wyjazdu człowiek cieszy się jak z wyjazdu wrednej teściowej. Właśnie tak bym go zapytał.

Henio wyciąga z szuflady wysłużoną talię kart o zabrudzonych krawędziach.

– Rozegramy partyjkę? – zwraca się do Mojsa. – Chodź, Mareczku, ostatnio karta mi nie szła; może teraz pójdzie mi lepiej.

Kiedyś mówiłem mamie, że największa kara, jaka mogłaby mnie w życiu spotkać, to odsiadka dożywocia w celi z dwoma karciarzami. To, co prawda nie jest cela, a ja jutro rano stąd wyjdę i pojadę do Janek, ale widok tej talii, którą Henio ostukuje blat stołu, wywołuje u mnie strach.

Kiedyś byłem na dwutygodniowej kolonii; teraz już nawet nie pamiętam, jaka to była miejscowość. Dobrze za to pamiętam rozgrywki w pokoju, kiedy grupa chłopaków, począwszy od nieporadnego tasowania, grała godzinami, wciągając mnie w karciane turnieje.

Nie wiem, co bardziej zdecydowało o tym, że wtedy znienawidziłem karty: czy to, że najczęściej przegrywałem, czy to, że ci karciani zapaleńcy nie potrafili przestać grać?

– Nie łudź się, i tak przepierdolisz – odpowiada Mojs, przesuwając krzesło w moją stronę.

– Zobaczymy, Mareczku, zobaczymy – śmieje się Henio i też dostawia do mnie swoje krzesło. – Gramy!

– Ja nie gram – mówię, udając teraz szczególne zaangażowanie w obserwację tego, co dzieje się na monitorach. Nawet przysuwam do siebie konsolę, jakbym miał zaraz wykonać na niej jakąś skomplikowaną operację. Na początek ścieram z niej kurz, zwyczajnie – palcami. Niech widzą, że jestem zajęty, że co jak co, ale na grę w karty to ja teraz pozwolić sobie nie mogę. Wydaje się jednak, że Henio wcale tego nie widzi. Z wywalonym jęzorem co trzecią kartę rzuca w moją stronę. Zaraz skończy rozdawać, a ja znowu będę musiał im powiedzieć, że nie gram.

Skończył.

– Nie gram – powtarzam, nie odrywając wzroku od monitorów. Palce trzymam na guziczkach, jestem skupiony. Nie przeszkadzać!

– Co? – Henio wykrzywia usta.

– Nie gram, nie potrafię – tłumaczę mu.

– W remika nie potrafisz?

– Ani w remika, ani w pokera, ani w nic, nie lubię kart.

– Mówiłem ci – kogoś ty tu przywlókł? – odzywa się Mojs. – A w Piotrusia kiedyś grałeś? – śmieje się i chwyta za moje karty. – Taki komplecik miał, zobacz. – Pokazuje Heniowi. – Masz, jeszcze raz rozdaj. – Rzuca nimi nerwowo o blat. – Zagramy bez niego.

– Co to za gra, tak we dwóch? – Henio spogląda na mnie groźnie. – A w chuja też nie umiesz? Kurwa, w chuja to przecież każdy potrafi! Normalnie zaczynasz od dziewiątki serce i schodzisz po kolei.

– Daj spokój! – krzyczy Mojs. – Jak nie, to nie, w dupie z nim. Rozdawaj, bo czasu nie ma. Zagramy w makao. A ty, kurwa, gap się w te swoje telewizorki i tylko – grozi mi palcem – tylko spróbuj ściemniać, to zobaczysz! Ty mi się, Boszczuk, już od samego początku nie podobałeś. W chuja grać nie potrafisz, ale w niego walisz, a kasę to byś chciał za *free* brać.

– W co walę? – Jak do tej pory tylko słucham tego skurwysyna. Nie mogę dać się do końca spipcić.

– A co, zdziwiony jesteś?

– Noo... tak. Bo przecież robię to, co do mnie należy, nie?

Mojs parska jak koń.

– Robię! Che, che, robię? Dobre sobie. A co ty takiego, kurwa, robisz? Że stoisz albo łazisz tam i z powrotem? Co to za robota jest?

– A jaka miałaby być?

– Zamknij się i już mnie bardziej nie wkurwiaj! Bo ci zaraz... KURWA!

– Spokojnie, Marek, nie denerwuj się – uspakaja go Henio.

– Co spokojnie? Gówniarz jeden będzie mi tu pierdolił... Rozdawaj!

Na rozkaz Mojsa Henio jeszcze raz szybko tasuje karty. Słyszę ich charakterystyczny szelest. Nie patrzę na nich, teraz na szczęście nie siedzą już przy mnie. Mojs złożył dupę przy stanowisku Henia. Niech grają do rana, śmierdziele.

*

Oczy same mi się zamykają. Jest pierwsza w nocy. Mojs wyszedł pół godziny temu. Nie wiem, czy pojechał do domu. Nie wiem, ale niech już tu nie wraca.

Napiłbym się kawy, może wtedy poczułbym się lepiej. Nie mam kawy, Henio też nie ma. On ma chory żołądek i pije tylko rumianek albo samą przegotowaną wodę. Napiłbym się kawy.

*

Mojs pojechał do domu, Henio mi powiedział. Mojs nigdy nie mówi, gdzie idzie albo że jedzie już do domu. Jak kończy pracę, to z nikim się nie żegna, żadne „cześć" ani takie tam. Po prostu podnosi dupę z fotela i z trzaskiem zamyka za sobą drzwi. Zarozumiała świnia. Dlatego nikt nigdy nie wie, czy on tak na chwilę, czy może na dłużej. W ciągu dnia, jak mówi Henio, różnie, raz na pięć minut, a raz to nawet na parę godzin znika z obiektu. Teraz Henio, choć stara się to ukryć, cieszy się nie mniej ode mnie. Mojs od ponad godziny nie wraca! Patrzy na zegarek.

– E! – Macha ręką. – Marek pojechał, pojechał spać – mruczy pod nosem. Pojechał do domu, pojechał spać... na pewno – powtarza potakując głową.

W nocy jest tu zupełnie inaczej. Powieki opadają, spać się chce, ale jak nie ma Mojsa, to czas jakoś leci i nawet notatek tyle pisać nie trzeba.

Trochę się obawiam reakcji chłopaków. Nie, żebym tak bardzo liczył się z ich zdaniem. To przecież żadni koledzy, ale na pewno będą gadać, komentować i pytać o Bóg wie co. Na szczęście Mojs nie był zadowolony, że tu jestem. Z pewnością już nigdy nie dostanę szansy bycia adiutantem. A jeśli jakimś cudem stałoby się inaczej, to się nie zgodzę. Chrzanię to, niech biorą kogoś innego i niech wcześniej sprawdzą, czy potrafi grać przynajmniej w chuja.

*

Jeszcze siódmej nie ma, a ten znowu jest z nami. Pił, wyraźnie czuć od niego alkohol.

Wszystkich poucza, a do pracy na gazie przychodzi?

Może trochę spałem? Jeśli nawet, i tak ledwo na oczy widzę. Henio spał wsparty głową o blat. Zasnął ze dwie godziny przed przybyciem Mojsa. Około czwartej, może trochę wcześniej, jakoś tak.

Nie pamiętam, kiedy i mnie głowa poleciała. Nie wiem, ile spałem i czy w ogóle spałem, może tylko tak mi się wydawało. Chciałbym wierzyć, że złapałem trochę snu.

Ledwo siedzę. Usnąłbym od razu, byleby mi pozwolono kimnąć się na tym krześle. Nawet nie opierałbym głowy o blat. Spałbym na siedząco, udając, że nie śpię.

– Cześć, Mareczku!

To Adaś. Podchodzi do Mojsa i podaje mu rękę na przywitanie. Potem wita się z Heniem. Na końcu podchodzi do mnie i też podaje mi rękę. – A co to się stało? – pyta zdziwiony, patrząc na mnie.

– Nieporozumienie – odpowiada Mojs.

– Aż tak źle było? – śmieje się Adaś, nie mogąc jeszcze wyhamować szybkiego oddechu. Biegł?

Patrzę teraz na Mojsa. Jestem ciekaw, co ma do powiedzenia, ale on tylko macha łapą.

– Rób listę – mówi do Adasia. – Zaraz pójdziemy zrobić odprawę.

Odprawa – to brzmi poważnie. Tu wszystko brzmi poważnie, ma tak brzmieć. Wtedy banał nabiera znaczenia. Donos to notatka służbowa, a chore fanaberie psychola to procedura albo regulamin, jak kto woli. My też – agenci, jak w jakimś filmie akcji. Gdyby jeszcze ta cała terminologia przekładała się na pracę i zarobki... A ja jestem zmęczony, głodny, wykoślawiony. I jak zawsze, tak i teraz nie mogę się doczekać końca tego kurewskiego dyżuru.

– Już robię – odpowiada Adaś.

Adiutanci i dowódcy przebierają się na monitoringu. Pod ścianą stoją trzy podwójne metalowe szafki, takie same jak w naszej szatniojadalnio-palarni.

Patrzę na zegarek, jest za dziesięć siódma.

– Mogę już iść? – pytam, patrząc na Henia.

– Jeszcze nie – odpowiada. – Nie masz podmianki. Pójdziesz z inspektorem i z dowódcą na odprawę; potem będziesz wolny.

– Na odprawę?

– No, chyba że wcześniej dostaniesz podmiankę. – Spogląda na zegarek. – Dobra, to ja się przebieram – mówi, uśmiechając się do Mojsa.

Wstaje z krzesła, a jego miejsce zajmuje ubrany już w służbowe uniformy Adaś. Jest pełen zapału, jak strateg wojenny przed kolejną zwycięską bitwą.

Moje zmęczenie gryzie się z jego nieprzyzwoitą rześkością. Gdyby nie podpuchnięte oczy Henia, można by pomyśleć, że to coś dziwnego.

ROZDZIAŁ

8

Bracia wrócili z pogrzebu. Umarła im matka, rak ją pokonał. Pierwszy raz widzę ich takich. Od godziny siedzą w pokoju i słowem się do siebie nie odezwali. Żal mi braci, chciałbym ich jakoś pocieszyć, podnieść na duchu, ale nie potrafię. Co można powiedzieć? Że wszystko będzie dobrze? Że trzeba żyć dalej? Oni wiedzą, że trzeba.

Jest mi głupio, bo teraz bardziej martwię się tym, że za zniszczoną wykładzinę Mojs ma mi zabrać równowartość trzech dobówek. Nie powinienem w takiej chwili myśleć o tak prozaicznych rzeczach, nie teraz. Oni nie mają już mamy, a ja czymś takim się przejmuję. Może dlatego, że dla mnie to była nieznana kobieta. Kiedy przed świętami wielkanocnymi pocieszałem Wieśka, tylko wtedy, w tamtej chwili, pomyślałem o niej. Pomyślałem, że gdzieś tam jest, że się męczy. Potem już nigdy, ani przez chwilę. I co? Umarła. Jak wyglądała? Nie wiem. Co powiedzieć? Jak ich pocieszyć? Też nie wiem, i cały czas tylko o tej cholernej wykładzinie myślę.

Wychodzę do kuchni zapalić papierosa. Jak się wczoraj dowiedziałem, że ta świnia tyle kasy mi zabierze, to po pracy spaliłem trzy na raz, aż mnie gardło rozbolało. A jak przyjechałem rano do Janek, to po drodze na stancję kupiłem sobie jeszcze cztery piwa i do tych piw wyjarałem z pół paczki. Pierwszy raz za jednym razem tyle spaliłem.

Wczoraj jeszcze nie wiedziałem, dlaczego braci nie ma od trzech dni. Myślałem, że tak po prostu pojechali do domu – i tyle. Dziś już wiem... Nieee, nie mogę przestać myśleć o tej wykładzinie!

Powiedziałem Dulianowi, co zamierzam zrobić. Nigdy nie podejrzewałbym siebie o taką szczerość w stosunku do tego idioty, ale wczoraj rano byłem okropnie wściekły. Wstał z łóżka, gdy kończyłem to czwarte piwo, no i jęzor mi się rozwiązał. Teraz żałuję, żałuję, że mu to powiedziałem. On stwierdził, że na moim miejscu już dawno by Mojsa załatwił. Akurat!

Nikt nie powinien wiedzieć. Powiem mu, że to gadanie to był tylko taki zgryw, że tak naprawdę to nigdzie nie zamierzam dzwonić, bo i po co.

Jego od wczoraj nie ma. Mówił, że jedzie do foki, że zostanie u niej na noc, bo ona ma wolną chatę, a on musi ją „porządnie wyruchać" – tak mówił. Ciekawe, kiedy wróci.

Wchodzę do pokoju, w ustach czuję smak dymu z papierosa. Siadam na swoim tapczanie i próbuję przybrać jak najbardziej odpowiednią pozę. Staram się, podobnie jak bracia, tępo patrzeć w podłogę. Niestety, coraz częściej podnoszę wzrok, by spojrzeć we włączony telewizor. Oni go włączyli. Przerywam swoją żałobę, kładę się na tapczanie i już ani na chwilę nie spuszczam wzroku z telewizora. Robię nawet trochę głośniej; a co tam, przecież nie będę przez cały dzień smucił się i zamartwiał z powodu czyjejś śmierci. Nie znałem tej kobiety.

Jutro idę na dyżur, już teraz o tym myślę. Zawsze tak mam. Jak sobie uświadomię, że w tym miesiącu wezmę dużo niższą wypłatę, to znowu chce mi się palić. Wychodzę z pokoju, za mną wychodzi Krzysiek.

– Masz fajki? – pyta, wyprzedzając mnie przed wejściem do kuchni.

– Mam – odpowiadam spokojnie, wskazując palcem stół. – Leżą, pal – mówię do niego i czekam, aż chwyci za paczkę.

Wyciąga, tylko dla siebie, i rzuca ją z powrotem na blat stołu. Burak jeden, przecież ja też chcę.

Z papierosem w ustach czeka, aż mu przypalę. Przypalam, a co tam, w końcu wrócił dziś z pogrzebu.

Siedzimy i nic. Jak by nie było, grobowa atmosfera. Przez to wydaje się, że papieros jakoś

dłużej się pali. Szkoda, że nie ma Duliana, może
by coś powiedział. Zrobiłoby się wtedy choć na
chwilę inaczej.

*

Wraca wieczorem. Zalega z czynszem już trzeci miesiąc; pewnie dlatego zaraz za nim do pokoju wkracza rozwścieczona Bożena.
– Masz pieniądze? – pyta oschle.
  Chyba tylko dlatego jeszcze go nie wyrzu-
ciła, że za duzo jest jej winien. Cały czas ma
nadzieję, że on ureguluje swoje zobowiązania
finansowe. Trzy czynsze to w końcu niema-
ła suma, a jak go wywali, to gówno dostanie.
Ona i tak już tych pieniędzy nie zobaczy. On
jej nie zapłaci, to pewne. W dalszym ciągu nie
ma pracy, a to, że jeszcze nie zdechł z głodu,
to tylko zasługa foki. Jest w nim zakochana.
Od tamtego czasu, kiedy obudziła się pod koł-
drą Wieśka, już do nas nie przychodzi. Czasami tylko Dulian coś o niej gada, najczęściej
opowiada, jak ją posuwa. Lubi o tym gadać.
Mówił, że robił to z nią nawet w magazynie,
na skrzynkach z kiełbasą. Ja mu nie wierzę.
W biały dzień na tyłach mięsnego? Nieee, nie
wierzę, to bzdury.
  – Pani Bożenko – Dulian ma taką minę, jakby go porządnie bolała głowa. – Poczeka pani,
pani Bożenko, jeszcze parę dni. Wszystko ure-
guluję i kwiatka kupię, zobaczy pani, pani Bo-

żenko. Ładną czerwoną różę, zobaczy pani. Pani Bożenko.

Ona nie wie, że bracia wrócili z pogrzebu, pewnie dlatego nie okazuje współczucia. Wydaje się, że nawet ich nie zauważa, mnie też. Za to Duliana ani na moment nie spuszcza z celownika.

– Już od dwóch miesięcy tak gadasz! – krzyczy. – Jak tak można? Czekam do końca tygodnia, a potem porozmawiamy inaczej.

Wychodzi.

– Ssspierdalaj – syczy pod nosem Dulian.

Patrzę na niego.

– Wyrzuci cię, zobaczysz – szepczę, spoglądając na Wieśka.

– To niech mnie wypierdoli.

– Wcześniej jeszcze ci da – odzywa się Krzysiek. – Mordę ci obije, i dobrze zrobi – dodaje, patrząc na niego pogardliwie.

– Sam masz mordę – oburza się. – Ja cię, Krzychu, nie obrażam – dodaje, chcąc tym samym załagodzić sytuację. Boi się Krzyśka, Wieśka zresztą też. – Nic do ciebie nie mam, ale mordę to ma pies.

– Świnia – wtrąca Wiesiek. – Świnia ma mordę – mówi, leżąc na boku.

– Świnia? – dziwi się Krzysiek. – Świnia to ma ryj. Zresztą, kurwa, nieważne. – Teraz znowu patrzy na Duliana. – Na pewno tak łatwo ci nie podaruje. Tyle kasy jej wisisz i myślisz, że co?

Dulian wzrusza ramionami.

– No co? Teraz nie mam. Jak zarobię, to już jej mówiłem. Zapłacę! Ale to moja sprawa, nie?

Wiesiek kiwa głową.

– Mieszkał tu kiedyś taki jeden, co Bożenę ostro wkurwił... Pamiętasz, Krzysiek? – Patrzy na brata. – No, ten, co te chińskie zupki tak na okrągło żarł? Cały czas tylko to wpierdalał, aż zajadów dostał.

– Aaa! Ten. No, pamiętam. Z Bożeną się nie rozliczył i spierdolił, nie?

– Noo. Nie zapłacił jej, a potem, pamiętasz? Spotkaliśmy go, jak w Jankach z obitą gębą nowego lokum szukał, nie? Pamiętasz?

Dulian mruży oczy.

– Nie mów, że to ona go tak obiła.

Wiesiek cmoka, wykrzywiając usta.

– Ona nie – cmoka. – Ktoś jej pomógł – szepcze cicho, pochylając się w stronę Duliana. – Co ty, kurwa, myślisz, że Bożena karków nie zna. Kiedyś swój prywatny biznes miała. Już ona zna, kogo trzeba. Obić ryj jednemu czy drugiemu – jaki to problem? Jak zna kogo trzeba, to żaden problem, a z tobą to by sobie sama poradziła. To krewka babka jest. Lepiej nie spierdalaj tak jak tamten.

Dulian znowu wzrusza ramionami.

– Ja tam pierdolę. Gęba nie szklanka – śmieje się, trąc ręką po chudym policzku.

Jeśli to prawda, to mieszkam u bandziora, ale nie chce mi się wierzyć w te kryminalne opowiastki. Jeśli chcieli wystraszyć tym

Duliana, to niech im będzie. On już nieraz po gębie dostał; jak dostanie znowu, to nic takiego. Dla niego bardziej bolesne niż złamany nos byłoby zapłacenie Bożenie za te trzy miesiące.

*

– Braciom umarła mama – szepczę.
Siedzimy w kuchni i jemy kanapki z białym salcesonem od Anieli.
– Poważnie?
– No przecież bym sobie tego nie wymyślił. Miała raka i umarła. Dziś wrócili z pogrzebu.
– Raka? – kręci głową. – To przejebane. A czego raka miała?
– Co?
– Czego raka miała? – pyta z gębą pełną chleba.
– Nie wiem. Jakiego by nie miała, przecież i tak umarła.
– Teraz to każdy na raka umiera – mówi Dulian. – Ja też kiedyś na raka pierdolnę, na pewno pierdolnę na raka. Moja babka miała raka, dwóch wujków od strony ojca też na raka umarło. Na pewno na raka pierdolnę.
– Nie kracz.
– Dobra – krzywi się. – Nie gadajmy już o tym.
Chwila ciszy.
– Pamiętasz, jak ci wczoraj rano powiedziałem, że chcę pogrążyć mojego szefa?

– Pamiętam. Mówiłeś, że rozsiejesz w firmie informację, że to pedał.

– Niee – śmieję się nerwowo. – Wczoraj byłem w dziwnym nastroju. To przez to, że dowiedziałem się, ile mi potrąci z pensji za tę wykładzinę. Trochę się wkurwiłem – i tyle.

Dulian jest zdziwiony.

– Popuścisz?

– Niedługo się zwolnię, muszę tylko znaleźć coś innego, niekoniecznie w ochronie. Na budowę pójdę, za pomocnika. Może przynajmniej czegoś się nauczę.

– Wczoraj gadałeś co innego. Zresztą ja na twoim miejscu już dawno bym go ujebał. Trzeba go upierdolić, takie szmaty nie powinny się panoszyć. Ma szczęście, że na mnie nie trafił.

Parskam śmiechem.

– A co byś mu niby zrobił? Teraz tak gadasz. Zobaczyłbyś, jak to jest, jakbyś tam stał. Normalnie od razu fujara ci mięknie, to nie takie proste. Ten chuj wysysa energię z każdego.

– No, kurwa, nie dziwota. Mówiłeś, że wam tam jeść nie pozwalają, to jak możesz mieć energię? – Pokazuje palcem ostatnie dwie kanapki leżące na białym staroświeckim talerzu w kwieciste wzorki. – Zobacz, ja teraz jem jak król, Aniela o mnie dba. Popatrz tylko – klepie się po brzuchu. – Jak tak dalej pójdzie, to zacznę szelki nosić, paskiem się nie dopnę. Tak będzie, zobaczysz.

– Zobaczę? – śmieję się. – Przecież Bożena wcześniej cię wywali... Wywali cię, zanim na szelki uzbierasz.

Dulian próbuje zrobić groźną minę.

– Przestań już gadać o tej pazernej małpie. Sram na nią i na tę jej obskurną stancję – denerwuje się. – Czynsz czynszem, ale dziś to już, kurwa, mogła dać sobie spokój. Tu takie nieszczęście, a ta za mną do pokoju wlatuje i o kasę krzyczy. Widziałeś jakiej piany dostała? Zachłanna stara picz.

– Nie taka znowu stara – mówię, zerkając na drzwi od kuchni.

– Niee... A co, może młoda?

– Ciszej, bo cię usłyszy i za tę starą picz jeszcze dziś wylecisz. Wisisz jej kasę – i tyle. Na jej miejscu siedziałbyś cicho?

– Bronisz jej?

– Nie.

– Chrzanię ją – ciężko wzdycha. – Nie gadajmy już o niej. Kurwa, jak nie rak, to ona. – Przeciąga się leniwie, aż krzesło skrzypi. – Wypiłbym piwko, a najlepiej dwa. Dwa piwka bym wypił.

Patrzy na mnie. Dobrze wiem, o co mu chodzi, ale nic z tego, jutro mam dyżur... Chociaż... Też bym wypił piwo.

– Stawiasz? – pytam, choć wiem, że gówno z tego wyjdzie.

Znowu się przeciąga.

– A może na flaszkę się zrzucimy, co?

– Jutro mam dyżur.

Smutnieje.

– Dyżur – powtarza za mną. – Ale co to jest jedna flaszka na dwóch? – Zaczyna liczyć na palcach. – Jak teraz pójdziemy do sklepu, to w godzinkę ją rozpracujemy. O której musisz jutro wstać?

– O wpół do siódmej.

– Eee! No to czym ty się przejmujesz? Jak za pół godzinki zaczniemy, to... – mruży oczy – godzina, może dwie, i będziesz mógł pójść spać. Raz, dwa, trzy... – znowu liczy. – Człowieku, prawie siedem godzin snu będziesz miał. Mało? Bracia są dziś smutni, to pewnie się nie dorzucą. Kupimy pół litra i wypijemy tu, w kuchni. Przynajmniej nie będziemy nikomu przeszkadzać.

– A pieniądze masz?

Wyciąga z kieszeni wygnieciony banknot dziesięciozłotowy i ostentacyjnie rzuca go na stół.

– Dorzuć dyszkę i będzie dobrze – mówi, wyciągając z paczki ostatniego papierosa.

– Na napój nie starczy – chwytam w palce tę wymiętoloną dychę, a on wybałusza oczy.

– Nie bądź sknera. Przecież nic się nie stanie, jak dołożysz złotówkę więcej. Ja mam tylko tyle, ale to już ostatnie puste dni. Od następnego tygodnia, jak dobrze pójdzie, zaczynam robotę u Anieli w sklepie.

– Jak dobrze pójdzie?

– Tak, muszę tylko sobie wyrobić książeczkę sanepidowską i tyle.

– Będziesz kiełbasę sprzedawał? – Próbuję go sobie wyobrazić w rzeźniczym fartuchu.

– A co?

– Mówiłeś, że jesteś elektrykiem.

– Bo jestem – oburza się.

– I wolisz kiełbasę sprzedawać?

– Już ty się nie martw. Przy żarciu najlepiej robić, chłopie! Aniela na wędliny grosza nie wydaje, a coś ty myślał.

– To ty teraz burżujem zostaniesz. Wędliny za friko, tylko chleb będziesz musiał kupować. No, chyba że chleb też sobie weźmiesz... Szybko dla Bożeny uzbierasz.

Przez mój sarkazm niejeden straciłby ochotę na wódkę. On nie traci, coraz bardziej mnie naciska... Ulegam.

*

Po paru kieliszkach wraca temat Mojsa. Znowu zaczynam tłumaczyć Dulianowi, że nie mam zamiaru nigdzie dzwonić. Jak nakręcony w kółko o tym gadam.

– Jeszcze tylko trochę, może miesiąc, góra dwa. – Zaciągam się papierosem. Kupiłem nową paczkę, przy wódce chce się palić. – Chrzanię to... Gdybym planował tam dłuższą karierę, to wtedy tak, ale... nieee. – Kręcę głową. – Nie planuję. Nigdzie nie będę dzwonił. Ruszysz gówno, to zacznie śmierdzieć.

Mówiąc mu o tym, naprawdę odchodzi mi ochota na ten telefon. Co prawda, mógłbym jeszcze wysłać anonim, jak w filmach sensacyjnych – treść ułożona z wyciętych z gazety liter; ale i w tym przypadku pewnie zesrałbym się w gacie.

*

Flaszka na dwóch i taki ból głowy? To wszystko wina fajck. Bardziej niż głowa bolą mnie oczy, bolą i pieką jednocześnie

Bezlitosna prawda dociera do mnie z chwilą, w której patrzę na zegarek. Zwlekam się z łóżka. Jest prawie siódma, dziś pierwszy raz spóźnię się do pracy. Szybko zaczynam pocieszać samego siebie, że to pierwszy raz. Pierwszy raz to żadna recydywa. Każdy kiedyś się spóźni, ja spóźnię się dziś.

Dulian śpi, bracia też. Nie wstali do pracy? Pewnie mają wolne. Biegnę do łazienki. W pośpiechu przemywam twarz zimną wodą, na mycie zębów nie ma już czasu. Guma miętowa załatwi wszystko, a jak nie, to dwie gumy, chociaż na jakiś czas.

Wczoraj stanęło na tym, że to Dulian wykona ten kompromitujący telefon. Tyle pamiętam. Teraz znowu jestem przekonany, że to bardzo zły pomysł. Kiedy on chce dzwonić? Dziś? Gadał coś, że dziś. Idiota ze mnie, trochę wódy i proszę, godzę się na wszystko. Obudzę go i powiem, że ma nigdzie nie dzwonić. Po cholerę w ogóle wczoraj z nim piłem?!

Wchodzę do pokoju, przez ramię mam przewieszoną torbę z uniformem.

Niee, jednak nie będę nic mu gadał, niech śpi. Kurwa, jestem chwiejny jak rozpieszczona panienka. Ale teraz tak sobie myślę, że jeśli on dziś zadzwoni, to nikt nie będzie mnie podejrzewał. Będę na dyżurze, będę stał na piętrze, może łaził po Chocimskiej albo po minusikach, i z pokorą znosił Zbycha. Gdziekolwiek mnie rzucą, będę miał alibi. Nie ma się czym przejmować. Mojs ma tylu wrogów; do głowy mu nie przyjdzie, że maczałem w tym palce. A wiadomość pójdzie. Nawet jeśli taka informacja go nie zniszczy, to na pewno na długo złamie tej świni karierę. Mnie to wystarczy.

Wychodzę. Spokojnie, wszystko ułożyłem sobie w głowie, będzie dobrze. Gdybym nie musiał się jeszcze spieszyć na ten cholerny przystanek...

*

Przyspieszam kroku. Pukam. Nie czekam, aż adiutant otworzy mi drzwi – jestem porządnie spóźniony. Wchodzę. Znowu ten smród.

– Cześć – mówię, kiwając do Henia. Nie ma Mojsa? – Trochę się spóźniłem, autobus mi uciekł – tłumaczę mu, starając się, by zabrzmiało to jak najbardziej wiarygodnie. – Uciekł – powtarzam, czekając, co powie.

– Marek cię zajebie – mówi przyciszonym głosem. – Zapierdalaj szybko do szatni i przebieraj się. Idź zmienić tego na minusach, on już tam ledwo drepcze.

Nie mówi tego z troski o tamtego. Ta gadka jest tylko po to, żebym miał wyrzuty sumienia. To co, że tamten łazi dłużej? Co z tego? Ja tu trzy doby pod rząd waliłem... I co? Trzy doby! Więc co z tego, że jakiś wymięty stojak godzinę dłużej między samochodami się poszwenda?

Biegnę do windy. Zastanawiam się, czy Mojsa jeszcze nie ma na obiekcie, czy może jest, tylko teraz ta świnia gdzieś łazi w wiadomym tylko sobie celu. Wolałbym się na niego nie natknąć. Cały czas kołacze mi się po głowie ta myśl. Dziś Dulian zadzwoni do biura... Zadzwoni? Mówił, że zadzwoni, ale z nim nigdy nic nie wiadomo. Pewnie tylko tak gadał. Chociaż... już sam nie wiem. On jest nieprzewidywalny, on może zadzwonić.

Znowu czuję strach. Inaczej się o tym myśli, kiedy jest się z dala od tego całego syfu. Chciałbym mieć to za sobą. Chciałbym tu przyjść i nie spotkać już nigdy Mojsa. Dowiedzieć się, że go wyrzucili, udać zdziwienie. Zapytać, za co, i takie tam.

Zbliżam się do klatki Zbycha. Wzrokiem szukam tego, którego mam zmienić. Nigdzie go nie widzę, i dobrze.

Zbychu patrzy na mnie spode łba. Dym. Ledwo łapię powietrze; i do tego ta jego wredna, ponura gęba

– Możesz mi dać klucz? – pytam i wyciągam do niego łapę.

Leniwie podciąga mankiet koszuli i patrzy na zegarek.

– A tobie się coś nie popierdoliło? O której to się na posterunek przychodzi? Zobacz. – Przekręca nadgarstek w taki sposób, żebym widział tarczę jego zegarka.

Mrużę oczy, ale godziny i tak nie mogę odczytać. Stoję za daleko.

– Która? – Jak na jego wrażliwość to chyba zbyt bezczelne pytanie.

Rzuca we mnie kluczem.

– Masz, kurwa, i się przebierz, a potem biegiem do mnie.

– Nie musisz we mnie, kurwa, rzucać! – syczę pod nosem.

– Co? – Ze zdziwienia aż mruży oczy. – Ja w ciebie rzucam?

Nie odpowiadam, tak jest lepiej. Schylam się tylko po leżący na podłodze klucz i wychodzę. Niech sobie nie myśli, że będę się śpieszył. Jest duży, o ponad głowę wyższy, ale tak łatwo się nie dam. To taki chojrak na pół gwizdka. Zgrywa ważniaka, bo chce, by ci, co tu łażą, czuli do niego respekt. Mojsa wyrzucą, ale on zostanie. On i jeszcze paru innych. Ciężko mi o tym teraz myśleć. Jednym telefonem nie załatwi się tych wszystkich mętów, a podkładać każdemu świnię? Tak się nie da.

Wchodzę do szatni. Po cholerę tak się spieszę? Muszę być twardy, nie mogę się przejmować tym, co jest teraz. Jutro będzie lepiej, tylko niech to jutro szybciej nadejdzie, bo inaczej naprawdę zwariuję. Totalna przeplatanka postanowień, huśtawka nastrojów. Stawiać czoła wyzwaniom? Czemu nie?! Gorzej, kiedy życie staje się jednym ponurym wyzwaniem – wyzwaniem, któremu nie można sprostać.

*

Będzie szkolenie, przed chwilą się dowiedziałem. Jutro muszę zostać dłużej, bo jakiś facet będzie nam pokazywał, jak się bronić przed niebezpiecznym narzędziem – przed nożem, siekierą i kijem bejsbolowym. Zbychu mi to powiedział, on też jest tym szkoleniem zaskoczony. Człowiek, który tak świetnie włada pałką wielofunkcyjną typu TONFA, nie powinien być zaskoczony.

– Chyba oszaleli – mówi, kręcąc głową.

Udławiłby się tą końcówką tlącego się peta i byłoby o jednego idiotę mniej. Ten pet wydaje się prawie wrastać w jego dolną wargę. On ma tam, na tej wardze, taki ciemny wklęsły ślad. Takie zagłębienie jak w popielniczce. Taką rynienkę, w którą na chwilę można odłożyć papierosa.

– Jak chcą robić szkolenia, to niech wynajmą porządną salę gimnastyczną. Siadaj! – Podsuwa mi krzesło.

Od momentu kiedy rzucił we mnie kluczem, minęła zaledwie godzina, a on jakby o tym zupełnie zapomniał. Proponuje mi, żebym usiadł?

– Postoję. – To się nazywa asertywność.

– Jak chcesz. – Przysuwa krzesło z powrotem do siebie.

Ciekaw jestem, czy zawołał mnie tylko po to, by mi powiedzieć o tym szkoleniu, czy ma dla mnie jeszcze jakieś wiadomości. Skoro tamten facet będzie nas szkolił z samoobrony, to może teraz on, tak na rozgrzewkę, zrobi mi krótki sprawdzian z branżowych tematów.

– Słuchaj, Patryk. – Już jest sympatycznie. – Nie chciałbyś sobie trochę dorobić?

A jednak – moja radość była przedwczesna. Jeśli coś takiego proponuje taki idiota, to trzeba jak najszybciej się ewakuować.

– Dorobić? – Jak najszybciej, ale nie od razu. Niech się wypowie; dam mu trochę czasu.

Wysuwa szufladę i wyjmuje z niej jakiś kolorowy katalog ze zdjęciami sportowych aut. Potem delikatnie kładzie go przed sobą na blacie. Zaczyna wertować połyskujące kartki.

– O! – Zatrzymuje się na zakreślonej stronie. – Zobacz – mówi, podając mi ten katalog. – Fajna zabawka, co?

Biorę katalog do rąk i patrzę na kilka zdjęć jakiegoś sportowego auta. Nawet nie wiem, jaki to model.

– Fajny – odpowiadam. W dalszym ciągu nie wiem, o co chodzi. Co to ma wspólnego z dodatkowym zarobkiem?

– To maserati – wyjaśnia z dumą, zabierając mi katalog. – Maserati, najnowszy rocznik, ponad dwieście koni pod maską. Człowieku, takim diabłem to można każdy asfalt zwijać.

– Na pewno! – Jakoś nie wzbudza we mnie entuzjazmu. Co z tego?

– Spójrz tutaj. – Pokazuje mi napisane pod zdjęciem czarnym flamastrem cyfry.

To jakaś data, ale nie dzisiejsza, wczorajsza też nie. Dziś mamy 10 maja 1996 roku, a tu? To maj 1997 roku. W dalszym ciągu nic z tego nie łapię.

– Nie rozumiem – mówię, ale on tylko się uśmiecha. – Tysiąc dziewięćset dziewięćdziesiąty siódmy rok?

– Tak, zgadza się. Do maja następnego roku będę taką zabaweczką jeździł – klepie łapą po zdjęciu. – To mój cel.

Wiedziałem, że z nim nie jest wszystko w porządku.

– Dostaniesz spadek? – pytam, próbując się nie śmiać.

– Jaki spadek, spokojnie. Zarobię na to cacko.

Z całą pewnością jest nienormalny.

– Ciężko będzie ci uzbierać przez rok tyle kasy. Taki samochód dużo kosztuje, a w ochronie aż tyle nie płacą.

Moja, jak mogłoby się wydawać, logiczna argumentacja wcale go nie przekonuje.

– Spokojnie. W życiu trzeba spełniać marzenia. Tutaj to nawet jak bym całe życie odkładał wypłatę do wypłaty, to o czymś takim mógłbym tylko marzyć. A ja już ci powiedziałem, zamierzam spełniać swoje marzenia. – Chowa katalog z powrotem do szuflady i wyciąga coś innego. Tym razem nie jest to gazeta z drogimi sportowymi autami. To jakaś kolorowa duża ulotka z wizerunkiem uśmiechniętych twarzy na tle banknotów. – Zobacz! – Unosi ją. – To są prawdziwie szczęśliwi ludzie. Chcesz być jednym z nich?

– Pewnie – odpowiadam, nie mogąc się doczekać, co ten debil dalej powie.

– Nic prostszego – mówi, machając tą kolorową kartką papieru jak wachlarzem. – Zarabianie pieniędzy, dużych pieniędzy, nie jest takie trudne. Powiem więcej, zarabianie pieniędzy jest banalnie prostą sprawą. Ale do rzeczy – gada jak na szkoleniu dla akwizytorów. W akwizycję nie dam się wciągnąć. – Zarabianie zaczyna się tu. – Kładzie ulotkę na blat i podobnie jak wcześniej w katalog, teraz w nią wali łapą. – Witaj w Big Rainbow – mówi rozanielonym, jakby nie swoim głosem. Pierwszy raz go takim widzę.

– W Big co?

– W Big Rainbow – powtarza.

– To jakaś firma?

– To nie firma, Patryk, to grupa ludzi, która postanowiła wreszcie spełniać swoje marzenia. Coś jak jedna wielka rodzina, do której ty też możesz niedługo należeć. Ja już należę, teraz tobie daję taką szansę. Nie myśl, że to jakaś sekta. Nic z tych rzeczy – śmieje się. – Big Rainbow to nie sekta.

Ostatnia rzecz, na jaką miałbym ochotę, to mieć takiego durnia w rodzinie. A ja już kiedyś słyszałem podobne gadki, tylko wtedy miałem sprzedawać na ulicy chiński szajs.

– Akwizycja?

– No coś ty – oburza się. – Żadna akwizycja. Na początku trzeba tylko trochę popracować. To znaczy ludzi musisz znaleźć do współpracy – i tyle. Chodzi o to, by utworzyć silne podstawy, a potem to już tylko pieniążki liczysz. Wiesz, dom też musi mieć mocny fundament, żeby stał, a drzewo mocne korzenie.

(Psychol, jak Boga kocham).

– Ja jestem dopiero na początku tej drogi, a ty, jak wejdziesz, też od samych dołów startujesz.

Już więcej nie musi nic mówić. Ten jego złoty interes to nic innego, jak zwykła piramidka. Frajerzy na dole robią dla tych u góry, werbują kolejnych, którzy mają werbować następnych. To żaden cud, tylko zwykły wyzysk. Parę lat temu w Święto Zmarłych ojciec spotkał na cmentarzu dawnego kumpla ze szkoły. Facet nalegał na szybkie spotkanie, mówił, że tyle ma mu do opowiedzenia. Rodzice wymienili się adresami, a ten już następnego dnia przyjechał z pełnymi kartonami jakichś magicznych detergentów. Od progu zachwalał ich cudowne właściwości. Szampon do włosów miał równie dobrze radzić sobie z zabrudzonym dywanem, a w ostateczności mógł służyć jako najskuteczniejszy na świecie środek na kaca. Wszystko ekologiczne i w ogóle super najlepsze. On sam, jak się chwalił, już niedługo miał się stać milionerem. Jako dobroczyńca potrafiący się dzielić swoim szczęściem nie mógł nie dać szansy innym. Pół nocy namawiał i roztaczał czarodziejskie wizje, aż w końcu pojechał, na drugi dzień rano, obrażony jak dziecko, że ani ojciec, ani matka nie mają ochoty zostać jego partnerami w biznesie. Rodzice nie byli zainteresowani sprzedażą na jego konto, a w naszej małej mieścinie ciężko byłoby im znaleźć kolejnych frajerów.

Facet, który chciał usłać różami życie moich rodziców, niedługo potem na prostej drodze uderzył w drzewo. Zginął na miejscu. Rodzice mówili, że to było samobójstwo. Ja tam nie wiem, ale o podobnych piramidkach słyszałem później jeszcze kilka razy. Wchodzić w takie układy z kimkolwiek to nie dla mnie, a już na pewno nie ze Zbychem.

Nie miałem pojęcia, że ludzie nadal dają się w coś takiego wciągać. Ja się nie dam, ale czy powiedzieć mu o tym teraz? Przecież go nie lubię. Niech się staje milionerem, a niedługo sam skończy na drzewie.

– Na razie nie mam czasu – mówię. – Ale potem może skorzystam.

Zbychu marszczy brwi.

– Może? Chłopie, nie ma na co czekać. Im szybciej w to wejdziesz, tym lepiej dla ciebie.

– Na pewno.

Sprzedam mu teraz odwrotną historyjkę, niech mu będzie.

– Wiem, ale na razie mam parę innych spraw do załatwienia, nie mógłbym się w pełni poświęcić. A to by się odbiło na wynikach. Na razie nie mogę, ale na tym rzeczywiście da się zarobić. Moi rodzice do dziś żałują, że nie weszli w podobny układ. Teraz byłbym synem bogaczy.

Zbychowi aż błyszczą oczy

– A co, mieli okazję?

– Tak, ale ją zmarnowali. Zamiast nich inni zarabiają teraz grubą kasę.

– No widzisz! – Podnosi się z krzesła. – Mówiłem ci, nie ma na co czekać. Chcesz tak jak oni zmarnować życiową okazję?

– No co ty?! Ale teraz nie mogę. Już ci mówiłem, mam sporo spraw do załatwienia. Jak się z nimi uporam, to się do ciebie zgłoszę.

Zbychu mruży podejrzliwie oczy.

– Ale nie zapomnij – mówi. – Ja już zaczynam konstruować siatkę. To znaczy strukturę własnej piramidy buduję.

– A masz już kogoś?

– Nie, ale to tylko kwestia czasu. Zresztą ten chłopaczek, co go dziś zmieniłeś – jemu też o tym mówiłem. Widziałem, że się napalił, więc chyba coś z tego będzie. W tamtym tygodniu byłem na specjalnym szkoleniu. Był tam taki facet – przyjechał jaguarem, zaczynał w Big Rainbow rok temu i proszę, jaguarem przyjechał. On to szkolenie prowadził. Kurwa, jak opowiadał, ludzie normalnie płakali. Mówił, że w życiu trzeba sobie wyznaczyć cel. On sobie wyznaczył. Jego marzeniem był właśnie ten jaguar. Wyciął sobie z podobnego katalogu zdjęcie i zawiesił nad łóżkiem. No i data, do kiedy – data musi być. Pokazywał nam wszystkim ten obrazek z tą datą. Przyjechał identycznym. Kurwa, co za gość! – Na chwilę jakby z powrotem przeniósł się na to spotkanie z facetem z jaguara. Minę ma taką, jakby opalił się zielskiem. – Dobra, Patryk – Koniec wspomnień? – Weź się teraz trochę przejdź, a potem, jak będziesz chciał, to przyjdź, opowiem ci jeszcze, jak było na spotkaniu.

Wychodzę bez słowa. Jak będzie chciał mieć słuchacza, to wystarczy, że mnie zawoła. Będę musiał przyjść. Kurwa, niech już da mi spokój

Ciekawe, jak długo ujadę na tych obiecankach. Jedno jest pewne, dziś już się na mnie

nie wydrze; dziś i pewnie przez najbliższe parę dyżurów. Tylko co potem? A może on faktycznie dorobi się majątku? Mówią, że głupi ma zawsze szczęście, ale to tylko takie powiedzonko, jak wiele innych zresztą, niosących w sobie tyle prawdy, co nieprawdy. Pięćdziesiąt na pięćdziesiąt procent – jak z szansą na bufet.

*

Przez chwilę mieliśmy nawet nadzieję, że zorganizują je w innym terminie. Nie było dokładnie wiadomo, czy facet przyjedzie. Jednak pojawił się parę minut po dziewiątej. Taki mały z dużą turystyczną kolorową torbą, pełną „niebezpiecznych narzędzi".

Henio mówi, że to były antyterrorysta, więc sprawa jest poważna. Jak zawsze, po Chocimskiej ledwo stoję na nogach. Całą noc rozmyślałem, czy zobaczę rano Mojsa. Szczególnie nad ranem. Nad ranem zmęczony mózg resztką rezerw dostaje kopa i w odrętwiałej głowie tworzą się obrazy. Widziałem, jak z zawstydzoną gębą ostatni raz wchodzi do pomieszczenia monitoringu. Przecież musi zabrać resztę swoich rzeczy. Tylko dlatego tam wchodzi. Z nikim nie rozmawia. Jest wściekły i jak najszybciej chce wyjść, oddalić się od jeszcze do wczoraj swojego obiektu. Tak, właśnie to widziałem oczyma wyobraźni, dlatego trudno jest mi ukryć zdziwienie, kiedy widzę go teraz. Jak mało kiedy, jest w dobrym humorze, i jak nigdy dotąd – w dresie. Wygląda w nim jak kulomiot.

Kiedy wita się serdecznie z facetem, moja gęba płonie. Momentami wydaje mi się, że patrzy na mnie kątem oka. On już wszystko wie? Nie... Nic nie wie, jestem panikarzem. Jeśli on tu jest, to znaczy że Dulian nigdzie nie zadzwonił. Będę zachowywał się normalnie, a jak wrócę na stancję, od razu zapytam Duliana. Jeśli jeszcze nie zadzwonił, to dobrze, niech nigdzie nie dzwoni. Nie chcę. Wolę sam się stąd zwolnić, niż czuć taką niepewność.

Mojs zauważa, że nie wszyscy zostali po dyżurze. Faktycznie, ze zmianą, która wczoraj rano skończyła pracę, jakoś nas mało.

– Trochę brakuje – mówi do Henia. – Kilku twoich i chyba paru ze zmiany Arka. Nie?

Henio kiwa głową. Jak zawsze, ma „profesjonalnie" sporządzoną listę. Daje ją Mojsowi, a on zaczyna głośno wyczytywać nazwiska. Zatrzymuje się na chwilę przy moim. Potem leci dalej, aż do ostatniego. Tłumaczę sobie, że przecież nie tylko przy moim nazwisku pauzował, przy innych też przystawał; a może on tak przy wszystkich? Ale nie, przy moim zrobił dłuższą przerwę i chyba jakoś tak spojrzał dziwnie; jak to się mówi, spod byka. Nieee, tylko mi się wydawało. On często patrzy w ten sposób, co w tym dziwnego?

Wszyscy wchodzimy do obszernego pomieszczenia. To chyba jakaś sala konferencyjna czy coś takiego. W rogu pod sufitem wisi duży telewizor. Jest zamontowany na specjalnym metalowym ramieniu, tuż nad magnetowidem.

– Siadajcie – mówi Mojs. – Pan instruktor puści wam film instruktażowy.

Facet stawia tę wielką torbę na podłodze. Z jej bocznej kieszeni wyciąga kasetę wideo.

– Dzień dobry – kłania się jak japoński samuraj. – Dziś pokażę wam materiał nagrany do celów szkoloniowych. Jest to film zrealizowany w ośrodku szkolenia policji. To będzie zaledwie mała próbka tego, co może was czekać podczas wykonywania swoich obowiązków na obiektach, na których pracujecie bądź będziecie w przyszłości pracować. Ja nazywam się Krzysztof Łobczyński i jestem instruktorem technik samoobrony. Czy ktoś już teraz ma do mnie jakieś pytania?

Facet obrzuca salę wzrokiem. Cisza. Jakiś z nie mojej zmiany podnosi palec.

– Czego! – pyta Mojs. – Masz jakieś bolączki? To słuchamy. – Zerka na faceta. – Pytaj, pytaj – powtarza już nieco łagodniej.

– Proszę pana. – Chłopak wstaje z krzesła. – Pan będzie nam tylko pokazywał ten film czy...

– Pokazywać to ty możesz – przerywa mu Mojs. – Pan instruktor wyświetli wam wszystkim materiał instruktażowy, a potem z każdym z was przeprowadzi indywidualne szkolenia.

Chłopak siada na krześle.

- Jeszcze ktoś ma jakiś problem?

Cisza, nikt nie podnosi ręki. Mojs wyjaśnił wszystko dokładnie.

- Proszę, panie Krzysztofie. – Uśmiecha się do faceta jak wdzięcząca się lolitka. – Niech pan kontynuuje.

Facet powoli spuszcza wzrok z Mojsa.

- Dobrze, panowie – mówi. Jego głos przy ryku Mojsa wydaje się wyjątkowo spokojny. Zaraz usnę. – Proszę uważnie oglądać film i na bieżąco pytać, jeśli są jakieś wątpliwości. Taśmę zawsze można zatrzymać, a wątpliwości wyjaśnić. Tak że pytać, nie bać się. Wszystko wytłumaczę.

Wkłada kasetę w kieszeń magnetowidu i pilotem włącza telewizor. Przez pierwszą minutę nic się nie dzieje. W chwilę potem okazuje się, że magnetowid nie jest podłączony do telewizora.

Mojs głośno się śmieje, wraz z nim Zbychu, Henio i Adaś. Potem wszyscy zaczynamy się śmiać, nawet w pełni opanowany pan instruktor samoobrony rechocze.

- No to byśmy sobie pooglądali – mówi, podłączając wiszący z tyłu telewizora czarny kabel. Nie spieszy się. – Łowcę szumów, che, che – dodaje, patrząc na Mojsa.

- No! – Mojs kiwa łbem i rozpina zamek od bluzy dresowej. – Łowca szumów, część pierwsza – dodaje i znowu wszyscy zaczynają się śmiać.

Ja też się śmieję, ale ten śmiech to bardziej owczy pęd niż reakcja na „zabawną puentę". Tak już jest – jak Mojs żartuje, to trzeba się śmiać.

– Kurczę! – Facet mruży z niedowierzaniem oczy. – A co to?

Na ekranie pojawia się obraz, ale coś jest nie tak, bo pan instruktor wpatruje się w ekran telewizora.

– Niee, to nie ta kaseta – ciężko wzdycha. – Dali mi nie tę kasetę, co trzeba. To jest szkolenie dla konwojentów – wyjaśnia nerwowo.

– Panie Krzysztofie, mówi się trudno – uspokaja go Mojs niczym wyrozumiały ojciec. – Niech sobie zobaczą, na czym polega praca konwojenta.

Widać, że słowa Mojsa wyraźnie poprawiły instruktorowi humor. Znowu jest spokojny – prawdziwy mnich klasztoru Shaolin. Ciekawe, czy rzeczywiście był tym antyterrorystą.

*

Już pół godziny uczymy się, na czym polega niebezpieczna praca konwojenta. Facet co chwilę zatrzymuje taśmę i komentuje, choć nikt o nic nie pyta. Teraz opowiada, jak w trakcie drogi jeden z kolegów chciał się wysikać.

– Nie ma zmiłuj się – mówi. – Zatrzymasz się i kulka w łeb. Pierwszy zawsze obrywa kierowca. Pamiętajcie, w trakcie konwojowania nie można się pod żadnym pozorem zatrzymywać.

Jak chcesz sikać, sikaj do słoika, a jak srać... – Rozkłada bezradnie ręce. – Sraj też do słoika. Nie ma zmiłuj się – powtarza. – Parę lat jeździłem pancerką, to wiem. A różnie bywało – mówi z dumą. – Ile to ja się z ludźmi naużerałem, aż w końcu wszystko zaczęło grać. Hełmy nie na czachach, kamizelki odpięte, luźne. Jeden pali peta, drugi w nochalu paluchem dłubie. Kurwa! – mówię. Ludzie! Przecież to nie dożynki!

Ktoś zgłasza pytanie.

– Proszę pana, naprawdę sikali do słoików?

Mojs nie przerywa, widać sam jest ciekaw, a facet, nadymając policzki, zbiera się do odpowiedzi.

– Oczywiście – mówi. – Większość czasu przejeździłem w konwojach jako dowódca. Nawet bratu, kiedy jeździł w mojej sekcji, kazałem sikać do słoika. Konwój to konwój, sikanie w przydrożnym rowie może się skończyć kulką w łeb. Pamiętajcie o tym.

– A co wyście myśleli?! – odzywa się Mojs. Patrzy teraz na mnie. – To nie to, co tu, tylko po kiblach skaczecie. Jak u Pana Boga za piecem macie, ale to się zmieni. Czas wziąć się do roboty! – krzyczy, a pan instruktor puszcza dalej film szkoleniowy.

Konwój to konwój. Ale sikanie do słoika? Z tym to chyba przesadził. Widziałem kiedyś taki amerykański film. Pamiętam, facet też nie mógł się zatrzymać. Sikał do butelki po piwie, a w bagażniku wiózł zmasakrowane zwłoki.

Może instruktor oglądał ten sam film? Jeśli oni faktycznie do słoików sikali, to albo on ma wielką charyzmę, albo ci jego koledzy są nienormalni. Dobrze, że w hełmy srać im nie kazał.

Znowu zatrzymuje film. Tym razem problem leży gdzie indziej. Facet omawia pozycje konwojentów podczas przenoszenia pakietów z pieniędzmi. Gada o jakimś trezorze i o obserwacji terenu zgodnie z ruchem wskazówek zegara. Może to i ciekawe, ale moje wskazówki pokazują już dziesiątą i coraz bardziej chce mi się spać. Cały czas ziewam i już nawet o telofonie Duliana nie myślę.

Nie wiem, ale chyba na moment przysnąłem, przy samej końcówce. Nie moja wina, że instruktor siedział cicho. Nic nie gadał, nie komentował. Nie opowiadał o swoich przeżyciach w „pancerce". Poszło mi oko, ale chyba nikt tego nie zauważył.

Po seansie mamy krótką przerwę. Pięć minut na papierosa. Nawet nie wychodzę z sali. Wolę siedzieć na krześle, bolą mnie nogi i mam otartą piętę. Powieki ciążą mi coraz bardziej i naprawdę, gdyby mi pozwolono, zasnąłbym szybciej niż trwa pierdnięcie, krótkie pierdnięcie. Jestem jak te zwłoki przewożone w bagażniku. Urządzać szkolenia zwłokom? Co innego tamci z drugiej zmiany, oni są wyspani. Kurwa! Jak ja im tego zazdroszczę.

*

– Panowie! – Facet stoi w szerokim rozkroku. – Teraz przejdziemy do części praktycznej. Wiem, że to, co dziś będę wam chciał zaprezentować, to trochę za mało, ale lepiej mało niż nic. Prawda?

Wszyscy kiwają głowami, ja też. Mógłbym tak kiwać do końca tego szkolenia, bylebym nie musiał już nic więcej robić.

Facet ma zastrzeżenia co do naszego ubioru. Dopiero teraz to zauważył?

– Lepiej by było, gdybyście wszyscy byli, tak jak wasz szef, w dresach – mówi, pokazując palcem Mojsa.

– Może i tak, ale ja dopiero wczoraj dowiedziałem się, że mam to szkolenie z samoobrony. Jakbym wiedział wcześniej, to bym zabrał dres – tłumaczy Zbychu. Już niedługo będzie mógł olać Mojsa. Szczęściarz, siła Big Rainbow bije od niego.

Instruktor wyciąga z torby siekierę. Widać żarty się skończyły – to nie jest plastikowa atrapa, to prawdziwa stalowa siekiera na drewnianym trzonku. Na dodatek niezabezpieczona żadną osłonką, niczym. Zbychu podchodzi do faceta.

– Prawdziwa? – pyta, delikatnie dotykając kciukiem jej połyskującego ostrza.

– Prawdziwa – odpowiada facet.

– Jak się bawić – to się bawić! – mówi Zbychu. – Pewnie, prawdziwy napastnik gumową siekierą nie będzie w łeb walił.

Instruktor bierze siekierę do ręki.

– Panowie, co to za narzędzie, to chyba nikomu nie muszę tłumaczyć – mówi, podrzucając ją w ręku. – To jest siekiera, bardzo niebezpieczne narzędzie; szczególnie w rękach agresywnego napastnika. Nie będę wam opowiadał, co takie niebezpieczne narzędzie potrafi zrobić z człowieka, ale jestem pewien, że każdy się domyśla. W starciu z ciosem praktycznie nie mamy żadnych szans, zwłaszcza jeśli chodzi o głowę. Głowa jest bardzo wrażliwa na cios takim żelastwem; pół biedy, kiedy trafi nas w rękę. Wtedy jeszcze jest możliwość ucieczki. Pokażę teraz parę technik, które pozwolą wam obezwładnić napastnika, a następnie odebrać mu to niebezpieczne narzędzie. Kto na ochotnika?

Chowam się za plecami „kolegi".

– Nikt? – śmieje się.

– To może ty. – Mojs wyznacza jednego pozoranta, ale ten ma opory. Nie podchodzi. – No, dawaj tu, co się tak kulisz?

– Niech się pan nie obawia – uspokaja go instruktor. – A zresztą, to nie ja będę atakował, tylko pan. No, niech pan podejdzie.

Dobrze, że nie wskazał na mnie.

Wyznaczony niepewnie podchodzi do instruktora.

– Bierz siekierę – mówi Mojs. – No co ty, siekiery się boisz? Przecież cię nie ugryzie. Bierz ją!

Chłopak chwyta trzonek w obie dłonie. Ciężar siekiery przegina go do przodu.

– Niech pan zrobi lekki rozkrok. – Facet demonstruje, jak pozorant ma stanąć. – Nogi szeroko. O, właśnie tak.

Wszyscy na nich patrzą. Chłopak unosi siekierę, a instruktor przybiera odpowiednią pozycję. Mocno, prawie jakby chciał przykucnąć, ugina nogi w kolanach.

Chłopak zadaje cios. Cholera! Jeszcze nie teraz? No, chyba nie. Instruktor przewraca się na podłogę. Nikt się tego nie spodziewał.

Cichy jęk i jego ciężkie sapanie „budzą" mnie. Chyba trafił go prosto w czoło. Podchodzę bliżej. Wszyscy otaczają siedzącego na podłodze instruktora. Teraz przypomina mi się, jak jeszcze przed chwilą tłumaczył, że człowiek trafiony siekierą w głowę nie ma szans. Teraz będzie musiał zmienić swoje myślenie. Przecież cały czas stęka, jeszcze nie umarł. Podnosi się z podłogi. Leci mu krew, dużo krwi, ale żyje.

Mojs szybko otwiera drzwi i razem z nim wychodzi z sali. Potem wybiega Henio z Adasiem i Arkiem. To dziwne, ale chłopak cały czas stoi z siekierą w rękach. Nikt nie waży mu się jej odebrać – nie po tym, co się stało.

Podchodzę do niego bliżej.

– Co on nie widział, że siekiera leci? – dziwi się, odkładając ją na podłogę.

– W twoich rękach to naprawdę niebezpieczne narzędzie – krzyczy do niego Zbychu. – Nie powinieneś go jeszcze atakować. Nie wydał komendy!

Chłopakowi trzęsą się ręce.

– Nie wydał? – powtarza za Zbychem.

– A co, kurwa, wydał? Słyszałeś coś? Słyszał który, żeby padła jakaś komenda?

Ktoś mówi, że nie, pozostali kręcą głową, ja też.

– Żeś mu zajebał! – krzyczy ktoś inny.

Wraca Mojs, przychodzi tylko na chwilę. Zabiera dużą torbę instruktora; ogłaszając koniec szkolenia, wychodzi z sali.

ROZDZIAŁ

9

Dulian uciekł, spieprzył przed Bożeną. Od tygodnia już z nami nie mieszka, nawet się nie pożegnał. Wiedziałem, że weźmie dupę w troki.

Najbardziej tęskni za nim Bożena. Już zapowiedziała, że teraz to taka głupia nie będzie. Mówiła, że od każdego nowego lokatora będzie pobierać kaucję za jeden miesiąc do przodu. Ja tam nie wiem, ale wydaje mi się, że mało kto przystanie na takie warunki.

Cały czas zastanawiam się, czy on zadzwonił wtedy do firmy i puścił w obieg tę kompromitującą Mojsa informację. Nie zdążyłem się zapytać. Sukinsyn mógł chociaż zostawić kartkę. Napisać, czy zadzwonił, czy nie. Jakoś tak, nic więcej. Wiadomość powinien zostawić.

*

Ktoś rozniósł plotkę, że instruktor od samoobrony nie żyje. Potem mówiono, że żyje, tylko leży w szpitalu. Jak to możliwe? Przecież dostał tylko siekierą w głowę.

Wszystko z nim w porządku, a jednak... Zbychu mi to powiedział. On zawsze ma najświeższe informacje; chociaż o kursie samoobrony dowiedział się jak każdy – w ostatniej chwili.

Dziś znowu mam minusiki. Od kiedy zaoferowałem swój udział w budowaniu jego piramidki, zmienił do mnie stosunek. Teraz każdy może liczyć na jego łaskę, pod jednym tylko warunkiem – musi wejść do szczęśliwej rodziny Big Rainbow.

– Wiesz co, Patryk? – mówi. – Ja tam pierdolę to maserati.

Zmienił zdanie?

– Drogie? – O co ja pytam?! Przecież wiadomo, że nie tanio. By kupić taki samochód, musiałby zbudować piramidkę równą piramidzie Cheopsa. A on, jak na razie, tylko obmyśla strategię działania.

– Nie – śmieje się. – Tu nie o pieniądze chodzi.

No tak, przecież sam powiedział, że zarabianie to banalnie prosta sprawa. Słucham go dalej.

– Tak sobie pomyślałem, że takie autko to nie na nasze polskie drogi. Nawet nie mógłbym się nim dobrze rozpędzić, no i serwisów brak. Widziałeś gdzieś serwis maserati?

– Nie.

– No, sam widzisz! – Rozkłada bezradnie ręce.

Naprawdę ma problem.

– Ja takiego samochodu nawet na oczy nie widziałem.

– No widzisz. Kupię, a potem dupa! Ani się rozpędzić takim, ani naprawić, a ja tam pierdolę po fachowcach od młota łazić – denerwuje się. – Tylko autoryzowany warsztat. Taki samochód wymaga fachowej obsługi, nie?

– Jasne – odpowiadam i zastanawiam się, czy aby nie powinienem chodzić teraz po parkingu.

– Pójdę już – mówię, otwierając drzwi, ale Zbychu macha łapą.

– Daj spokój, gdzie będziesz szedł? Jeszcze się nałazisz, daj spokój. Masz. – Częstuje mnie kolejnym papierosem. – Zajaraj sobie. Jak spalisz, to się przejdziesz.

Szczerze mówiąc, już wolę łazić, niż wysłuchiwać tych dyrdymał. On cały czas tylko o tym Big Rainbow gada i o tym, jacy będziemy niebawem bogaci. Nie myślę mu w tym przeszkadzać. Rozmowa z nim to jak dialog z pijanym, więc słucham tych jego bredni i przytakuję. Przytakuję, kiedy tylko trzeba, ale udawanie entuzjazmu to męcząca robota. Powoli zaczynam żałować, że nie postawiłem sprawy jasno. Mogłem od razu powiedzieć, że w nic nie wchodzę, przynajmniej byłoby po staremu. A tak, mam w Zbychu „przyjaciela". Nawet nie chcę myśleć, co będzie później.

*

Od początku zarabiam psie pieniądze, ale w tym miesiącu to już naprawdę gówno wziąłem. Przez tę cholerną wykładzinę stać mnie będzie tylko na chleb z margaryną, no, chyba że Bożena rozbije mi czynsz na raty. Wtedy może jakoś uciągnę ten wózek. Przecież wie, że jestem uczciwy, zawsze płacę. Często grubo po terminie, ale płacę. To nie moja wina, że firma nie wypłaca pieniędzy na czas, a od braci pożyczał nie będę. Oni sami ciągle narzekają, że kasy im brakuje, zawsze narzekają. Pójdę do Bożeny i powiem, jak jest; ona zna życie, zrozumie.

*

To mi musi smakować, innego wyjścia nie mam. Gdybym tak jadł od początku, na pewno bym coś zaoszczędził. Na jedzenie wydaje się najwięcej, a cebula droga nie jest. Ma dużo witamin i można ją przyrządzać na wiele sposobów. Da się z niej zrobić sos, zupę albo tak zwyczajnie, na surowo do pomidora, tylko trzeba mieć pomidora. Mnie najlepiej smakuje smażona, trochę przypalona, z chlebem. Jak dotąd, zawsze w zestawie z kiełbasą... Teraz będzie bez kiełbasy, i już.

Nie wiem, czy to duma, czy po prostu straciłem wiarę w to, że Bożena mi pomoże. Wczoraj wieczorem przyszła do nas i przez dobrą godzinę gadała o Dulianie. Bracia ją pocieszali, a ja słuchałem, jak klnie i wyzywa go od oszustów.

253

Potem zaczęła się czepiać mnie. Nie wiem, może gdybym, tak jak bracia, połączył się z nią w bólu, może wtedy nie snułaby podejrzeń.

Spytała, czy nie wiem, gdzie on się teraz podziewa. Kiedy jej powiedziałem, że nie mam pojęcia, zaczęła się na mnie wydzierać. Gadała, że na pewno wiem, tylko nie chcę jej powiedzieć, że go kryję, bo – jak się sama wyraziła – trzymaliśmy się razem.

Nie zamierzałem zaprzeczać. Przeciwnie – powiedziałem jej, że pod koniec to faktycznie Dulian już tylko ze mną rozmawiał. Przypomniałem jej też, jak go na początku zachwalała. Jak mówiła, że to miły chłopak, i takie tam. Teraz jest na mnie obrażona, ale mam to w dupie. Powiedziałem tylko, jak było – widać niepotrzebnie. Jeszcze jej nie zapłaciłem. Może też się po cichu ulotnię – jak Dulian? Tylko że nie mam gdzie się podziać, muszę jej zapłacić. A cebuli przecież całe życie żarł nie będę. Dam radę?

*

Wiem, że to nieprzyzwoite, ale teraz i mnie zdarza się podbierać braciom z lodówki. Cebulą, choć zdrowa, jakoś nie mogę się najeść. Przydałaby się osobista foczka z mięsnego. Mogłaby być brzydka i gruba jak Aniela, byleby karmiła do syta. Jak tak dalej pójdzie, bracia mnie zdemaskują; wtedy im powiem, że już od tygodnia jem tylko smażoną cebulę z chlebem. Może zmięknie im serce i pozwolą mi podłączyć się na chwilę do ich koryta.

Przez tę perwersję kulinarną czuję się jak ostatni frajer; szczególnie kiedy cały dzień obiecuję sobie, że nic już im z lodówki nie zakoszę. A wieczorem? Wieczorem przegrywam z wcześniejszymi mocnymi postanowieniami. Dulian nic sobie z tego nie robił, ale mnie to rozwala. Żebrak musi mieć mocną psychikę.

Zadzwoniłem do rodziców, nie było innego wyjścia. Poprosiłem ich o dwieście złotych pożyczki. Nie robili problemów, zresztą nawet nie brałem tego pod uwagę. Pewnie gdyby wiedzieli, że od jakiegoś czasu zapycham się tylko cebulą, wysłaliby mi więcej.

Od dnia, kiedy przyjechałem do Warszawy, to moja druga prośba o pieniądze. Za pierwszym razem nie miałem oporów, ale teraz było inaczej. Gdyby nie to, że na cebulę nie mogę już patrzeć, o pożyczkę pewnie bym drugi raz nie poprosił. W takich chwilach docenia się najbliższych. Muszę częściej ich odwiedzać.

*

Źle się czuję, a pieniądze jeszcze nie przyszły. Pewnie przyjdą dziś, tylko że dziś jestem w pracy. Szkoda, że zlikwidowałem to konto w banku, ale po cholerę miałem płacić za jego prowadzenie? Nigdy nie mogłem nic na nim uzbierać; teraz by się przydało. Na konto byłoby szybciej.

Gęba mi się śmieje, jak tylko pomyślę, że jutro zjem normalny posiłek. Gdyby jeszcze nie ten ból głowy, który trzyma mnie od rana, i to, że Mojs chce ze mną gadać. Dzisiaj na odprawie dziwnie mi się przyglądał, a potem powiedział, że jutro musi ze mną porozmawiać. Nie tylko ze mną. To samo powiedział jeszcze paru innym stojakom. Dlaczego dopiero jutro? Nie chcę się na tym skupiać, ale tylko o tym myślę. Szkoda, że nie mam minusików. Zapytałbym Zbycha, może coś więcej by mi powiedział.

Mogłem odnaleźć Duliana, teraz miałbym jasną sytuację, a tak, Mojs cały czas kołacze mi się po głowie. Już nawet o jedzeniu nie myślę, tylko o tej tłustej świni. Co jakiś czas pocieszam się, że nawet jeśli Dulian zadzwonił, dlaczego podejrzenie miałoby paść na mnie? Ja? To on dzwonił.

*

Dwa lata w firmie bez umowy. Na zlecenie to można truskawki zbierać. Nawet urlop mi nie przysługuje, a ja potrzebuję urlopu, tak od zaraz. Muszę odpocząć, nabrać sił, świeżości.

Czuję się coraz bardziej samotny. Przydałoby się jakieś normalne towarzystwo, nie tylko wyciągająca łapę po pieniądze Bożena, zgorzkniali

256

bracia i koledzy z szatni, których tak naprawdę nie ma. Kiedy łapię głębszy dołek, wyobrażam sobie siebie za te dziesięć, dwadzieścia lat. Widzę, jak wsiadam do tramwaju z torbą na ramieniu. Nie wiem, dlaczego, ale ta torba cały czas jest ciemnogranatowa, jak ta, w której teraz wszystko wożę. Dlaczego nie jest kolorowa? Nie wiem. Jadę na kolejny dyżur. Nie mam już żadnych marzeń, nie mam uśmiechu na twarzy. Mam tylko ciemną torbę, a w niej w pośpiechu przyrządzone kanapki. Gdzie mieszkam? Pewnie na jakiejś stacji, tylko teraz jej właścicielka patrzy na mnie, jak na człowieka, któremu nie wyszło w życiu; jak na podstarzałego nieudacznika, niemającego żony, dzieci, niemającego nic, tylko tę cholerną granatową torbę z kanapkami. Muszę zmienić torbę.

Kiedy stoję tu, na piętrze, słyszę szczątkowe rozmowy przechodzących obok ludzi. Widzę ich szerokie uśmiechy i entuzjazm. Nie znam ich i nic o nich nie wiem. Oni też mają pewnie swoje problemy, ale z każdą z tych osób mógłbym się zamienić na życie. Tak w ciemno, bo moje, jak dla mnie, jest coraz trudniejsze do wyprostowania. Nie powinienem tak myśleć...

*

Mojs, mimo wcześniejszych zapowiedzi, nie przeprowadził z nikim rozmowy. Nie mam pojęcia, co on kombinuje. Po dyżurze poszedłem na monitoring, ja i jeszcze paru innych, ale nie chciał z nami gadać. Powiedział tylko, że nie ma dla nas czasu i że mamy spierdalać do domu. Dobrze, że pieniądze od rodziców doszły.

Muszę skontaktować się z Dulianem. Jednak. Niech powie, czy zadzwonił – chcę to wiedzieć. Cały dyżur o tym myślałem. Wydawało mi się, że Mojs jest bardziej wkurwiony niż zwykle; wtedy, kiedy kazał nam „iść" do domu. Coś musi być na rzeczy.

*

Jak do tej pory, nie łaziłem po Raszynie, nie musiałem; i chociaż za każdym razem, jadąc do Janek, przejeżdżałem przez tę dużą wiochę, nawet do głowy by mi nie przyszło, że będę tu dreptał w poszukiwaniu grubej foki z mięsnego. Jak jakiś detektyw, zamiast kupować kiełbasę, rozglądam się za foką Duliana.

Na moje szczęście, choć wiocha duża, to mięsnych jak na lekarstwo. A co tam mięsnych. Właściwie to tu tylko jeden taki typowy jest, a reszta to małe działy mięsne w zwyczajnych spożywczakach. Aniela mi to powiedziała – ona pracuje właśnie w tym jedynym prawdziwym. Dobrze, że od razu się na niego natknąłem. Może dlatego, że stoi przy głównej ulicy, tuż obok przystanku autobusowego i biegnącej nad ulicą tak zwanej kładki dla pieszych.

Udaje, że mnie nie widzi. Od początku czułem, że za mną nie przepada. Teraz nie ma wyjścia, na nic jej się zda to udawanie. To nie hipermarket w Jankach, musi mnie w końcu dostrzec.

– Cześć – mówię, podchodząc do lady.

Uśmiecha się od niechcenia. Tak, nie lubi mnie, to widać.

– Cześć – odpowiada. – Ty tu?

– Szukam Duliana.

– Kogo? – Mruży oczy.

Zapomniałem, dla niej to Dominik albo Misiu. Pamiętam – tak na niego mówiła.

– Dominika szukam – poprawiam się. – Nie wiesz, gdzie się teraz podziewa? Już u nas nie mieszka...

– Wiem – przerywa mi. – Mówił, że nie mógł się dogadać z braćmi.

– No. – Kiwam głową. Niech sobie tak myśli.

– Nie wiesz, gdzie teraz jest?

– A co on mnie? – oburza się.

Zastanawiam się, jak jej to powiedzieć.

– Chodzicie ze sobą czy jakoś tak, nie?

– Jakoś tak? – powtarza za mną. – Już nie.

– Aha. – Myślę chwilę. – To szkoda.

– Jak dla kogo, ja nie żałuję – odpowiada. – Poczekaj, zaraz przyjdę – zwraca się teraz do obsługującej klientów stojącej obok niej starszej kobiety.

Wychodzi przed sklep. Idę za nią.

– Pokłóciliście się? – Nie jestem przekonany, czy ona chce o tym gadać.

- Oszukał mnie - mówi, poprawiając przekrzywiony, brudny od resztek mięsa fartuch.
- Zrobił cię na kasę?
- Niee, tylko zabawił się na boku z moją znajomą, byłą znajomą. Tydzień temu małą imprezę urządziłam, no i... - Widać, że jeszcze to przeżywa. - Trochę wypiliśmy... - Macha ręką. - Nieważne, już się nie spotykamy; ale jak chcesz, mam do niego adres. Chyba mam, o ile go nie wywaliłam. Poczekaj tu. - Wchodzi do sklepu.

Tak szybko? Nawet nie musiałem jej tłumaczyć. Jakby czytała w moich myślach. Nie mogę się już doczekać jej powrotu.

- Masz - mówi głośno, wręczając mi wygniecioną kartkę.
- Jednak nie wyrzuciłaś - cieszę się.
- Nie. Dziwię się, że nie próbował się z tobą skontaktować. Z takim kumplem?
- Kumplem? - powtarzam za nią.
- No, kumplem. On cię chwalił i mówił, że jesteś w porządku, nie to, co bracia. Chociaż Wiesiek, moim zdaniem, jest okej. Ten drugi... No... - Pstryka palcami.
- Krzysiek!
- O, tak! Ten to jakiś dziwny jest, no i z tą waszą właścicielką też jakoś tak głupio wyszło. Naprawdę nie wiem, jak ja się wtedy u niego w łóżku znalazłam. W nocy poszłam do łazienki, a potem? Pewnie się pomyliłam. Tak, musiałam się pomylić, było ciemno. Kurwa, obciach był

jak nie wiem, nie? Ale... – Macha ręką. – Było, minęło, a swoją drogą, możesz pozdrowić tego Wieśka – uśmiecha się.

– Dzięki, pozdrowię; na pewno się ucieszy.

Nie jestem przekonany, czy Aniela rzeczywiście pomyliła te tapczany. On się nie chwalił, a ja twardo spałem, ale ona od razu polubiła Wieśka.

*

Na Ursynów warszawiacy mówią „sypialnia stolicy". To z pewnością największe blokowisko, jakie w życiu widziałem. Nie podoba mi się tu, zbyt ponuro, jak w holu windowym. Blok podobny do bloku, z prefabrykowanych płyt. Betonowe mrowisko. Pierwszy raz tu jestem, zresztą w ogóle jeszcze słabo znam Warszawę. Pałac Kultury, centrum – to co każdy. Ale na Ursynowie jeszcze nie byłem.

Aniela powiedziała, że on remontuje komuś mieszkanie i na czas remontu w nim mieszka. Czy tak jest? Ona mówiła szczerze, ale czy Dulian powiedział jej prawdę?

W przeciwieństwie do szukania mięsnego w Raszynie tutaj odnaleźć zapisany na kartce adres to niełatwa sprawa. Niby wszystko mam zapisane: ulicę, numer bloku, mieszkania, ale okazuje się, że z adresem jest coś nie tak. Obłęd! Po godzinie łażenia spotykam miejscowego, który sugeruje, że może ulice w adresie są pozamieniane. Ma rację, mieszkanie znajduje się na ulicy, na której miał być przystanek. A dzielnica? Dzielnica się zgadza.

*

Mieszkanie jest na parterze. Trzy dzwonki do drzwi. Nikt nie otwiera. Jeszcze raz patrzę na wygniecioną kartkę, mam już dość jej widoku. Znowu naciskam guzik dzwonka. Tym razem jeden, ale bardzo długi, nachalnie długi sygnał. Cisza. Jakiś starszy facet z psem na smyczy schodzi po schodach. Przygląda mi się uważnie – widzę to kątem oka. Pies obwąchuje mi nogawkę; nie wiem, czy głośniej sapie pies, czy facet.

– Chodź, chodź – szepcze do kundla i mija mnie, udając, że to moje natarczywe dzwonienie wcale go nie obchodzi.

Chcę już odejść, kiedy drzwi się otwierają; w progu stoi Dulian. To dziwne, ale przez chwilę czuję się tak, jakbym odwiedził kogoś z rodziny. Jego zdziwiona gęba i potargana matowa czupryna błyskawicznie poprawiają mi nastrój.

– Ja pierdolę! – mówi na przywitanie. – Jak mnie znalazłeś?

– Mam swoje sposoby – odpowiadam i nie czekając, aż mnie zaprosi, wchodzę do środka.

Faktycznie, on coś tu remontuje. Bajzel jak nie wiem co i pełno porozrzucanych papierowych worków.

– Foczka ci dała namiary? Byłeś u niej?

Kiwam głową.

– Znalazłem jej sklep. Skąd mógłbym wiedzieć, że tu siedzisz? Remontujesz coś, tak? – Rozglądam się. – Dawno zacząłeś?

Macha ręką.

– Daj spokój. – Wpatruje się w podłogę. – Wjebałem się po uszy. Myślałem, że pójdzie szybciej, a tu... Kurwa, jeszcze tyle roboty!

Jeszcze raz rozglądam się po mieszkaniu.

– To po co to zaczynałeś?

– Po co, po co. No, kuuurwa, dla kasy.

– Wiesz co? – Że też gadam z nim o tym, zamiast od razu przechodzić do konkretów. – Pamiętasz naszą ostatnią rozmowę? Wtedy, kiedy piliśmy wódkę w kuchni.

Mruży oczy.

– Pamiętam, piliśmy bez braci, nie? Bo oni byli mocno śnięci. A ty na drugi dzień zapierdalałeś do pracy.

– No właśnie. Wtedy ostatni raz gadaliśmy. Jak przyszedłem z dyżuru, to ciebie już nie było, uciekłeś.

Jeszcze bardziej mruży oczy.

– No, nie mów, że będziesz mi teraz, kurwa, kazania prawił. Spierdoliłem! Mówiłem ci, że jej nie zapłacę. Ta suka i tak finansowo dobrze stoi. Spierdoliłem, i już. A co ci do tego? Tobie kasy nie wiszę, nie?

– Mam to gdzieś, że spierdoliłeś! Przyjechałem tu, bo chciałem się dowiedzieć, czy zadzwoniłeś.

263

Wtedy, jak piliśmy, mówiłeś, że zadzwonisz i powiesz, że ten mój szef to zbok. Pamiętasz? Mówiłeś, że zadzwonisz. Potem już nie było okazji o tym pogadać.

Wykrzywia usta.

– Eee, to dlatego tu przyjechałeś? – śmieje się. – No tak, coś tam było, że cię wkurwia, i takie tam, że ogólnie chuj z niego, nie? Tak, teraz sobie przypominam, ale coś ty, nigdzie nie dzwoniłem. Daj spokój, Patryk. Ważniejsze sprawy były...

Mam ochotę go teraz uściskać.

– To dobrze. Już jest wszystko w porządku. Jest okej i nigdzie nie trzeba dzwonić.

– Znowu strach cię obleciał, co? Człowieku, ja o tym twoim palancie to na śmierć zapomniałem. Ale jak chcesz, to...

– Nie, nie – przerywam mu. – Nic nie chcę. Lepiej mi pokaż, z czym się tak zmagasz.

– No jak to z czym? Zobacz.

Prowadzi mnie do łazienki, a w zasadzie do pomieszczenia po łazience. Poznaję po muszli klozetowej ubrudzonej szarym pyłem.

– Kułem stare tynki i posadzkę.

Mało co z tego rozumiem. Jak dla mnie, to po prostu zniszczone pomieszczenie – i tyle. Nie mam pojęcia o takiej robocie. A on?

– Potrafisz takie rzeczy robić?

Dulian wzrusza ramionami.

– A czemu nie? – Wyciąga z kieszeni paczkę papierosów. – Pal! – Częstuje mnie. – Dziś frajer ma przyjść z zaliczką. – Zaciera ręce. – Kaska będzie. – Cieszy się.

– Długo już tu siedzisz? – Przypalam sobie papierosa.

– Siedzisz? – obrusza się. – Patryk! Ja tu sobie żyły wypruwam! Człowieku, ty nie masz nawet pojęcia, ile tu jeszcze roboty zostało. W pojedynkę nie dam rady. Już ci mówiłem – za mało czasu.

– Masz termin? – Gówno mnie obchodzi, czy ma, czy nie. Dla mnie liczy się to, że nigdzie nie zadzwonił. Wreszcie spojrzę na Mojsa bez strachu.

Dulian spluwa na pokrytą gruzem podłogę.

– A tam, termin. Nie mam żadnego terminu. Facet jest w porządku, zaliczkę już jedną dał; na samym początku, jak zacząłem skuwać to gówno. Tylko tak zapytał, ile będę robił.

– I co powiedziałeś?

– Powiedziałem, że tak dokładnie nie da się wyliczyć, bo roboty jest sporo. Samo skuwanie zajmie parę dni, a gdzie tu jeszcze ściany równać i nowe płytki kłaść? Powiedziałem mu tylko, że postaram się jak najszybciej z tym uwinąć.

– To czym się martwisz, skoro on taki do rany przyłożyć? Skończysz, jak zrobisz.

Gasi papierosa o ścianę.

– Wcale się nie martwię. Zobaczy się, jak będzie. – Patrzy na zegarek. – Masz jakąś kasę?

– Coś tam mam.

– Tu między blokami jest taki mały sklepik. Wziąłbyś dwa browarki, jeden dla siebie, drugi dla mnie. O szesnastej przyjdzie frajer z kasą, to ci odstawię. Spokojnie. Nie martw się, kasa będzie, na bank.

*

Facet jest punktualny i – jak da się zauważyć – nawet bardziej naiwny niż ja. Do szesnastej wypijamy z Dulianem po dwa browarki. Wiadomo było, że po pierwszym przyjdzie ochota na kolejnego.

Teraz, kiedy zaliczka w garści, Dulian żegna pana właściciela optymistycznymi wizjami. Facet, co prawda, od razu zauważył, że robota idzie wolno, ale swoje „niesprawiedliwe" sądy szybko studzi. Mówi, że on to właściwie na takiej pracy się nie zna, dlatego wynajął fachowca. Fachowca? Dobre sobie.

– W porządku jest, nie? – pyta mnie Dulian zaraz po jego wyjściu. – Zobacz – mówi, trzymając w dłoni kilka banknotów. Jeszcze raz je przelicza. – No, i trochę grosza wpadło.

– Dziwny gość – mówię. – Tak lekką ręką kasę rozdaje?

– Mówiłem ci, że to frajer.

– Może myślał, że ci pomagam.

– Swoją drogą, mógłbyś – śmieje się i chowa pieniądze do kieszeni.

– Ja? – dziwię się. – Lepiej zasuwaj po piwo! – Pokazuję palcem drzwi od pokoju. – No, dawaj! – popędzam go. – Jak chcesz, mogę pójść z tobą.

– Marne pocieszenie – śmieje się Dulian.

*

Siedzimy do późnej nocy i pijemy piwo. Z każdą kolejną godziną Dulian jest coraz bardziej pewny, że uda mu się szybko uporać z remontem. Dlatego, kiedy budzę się następnego dnia w południe, jestem, delikatnie mówiąc, zdziwiony. Nie z tego powodu, że tak długo spałem. Jak tu nie przespać połowy dnia, kiedy prawie całą noc się piło? Jestem zdziwiony, bo on mówi, że ma w dupie ten cały remont i dalej już nie robi.

– Pierdolę to! – syczy pod nosem. Chyba jeszcze całkiem nie wytrzeźwiał, ja też.

– Coś się stało? – Podnoszę się z rozłożonej wersalki.

Spaliśmy razem. Nie pamiętam dokładnie, która była godzina, kiedy skończyliśmy pić. Wiem tyle, że było późno, bardzo późno.

– Zwijam się stąd. Dziś!

– Co? Przecież jeszcze wczoraj byłeś takim optymistą. Nawet mówiłeś, że to całe mieszkanie mógłbyś odszykować bez większego wysiłku. Pamiętasz?

– Nie. – Tak, z całą pewnością jest jeszcze pijany.

– No, jak? – dziwię się. – Gadałeś, że wystarczy tydzień i łazienka będzie nie do poznania. Tak gadałeś, a teraz chcesz spierdolić? No co ty?!

– Daj spokój.

– Co?

– Co z tego, że gadałem?

– Powiesz mu, że nie dokończysz roboty?

Śmieje się nerwowo.

– Powiem? Nic mu nie powiem. Zresztą trochę mu nabiłem na telefon. Jak się zorientuje, to odciągnie mi za remont. Jest już prawie koniec miesiąca, niedługo może przyjść rachunek. Kiedy przychodzą rachunki?

– Nie wiem.

– Nie wiesz?

– Nie wiem.

– Nie wyrobię się. Przyjdzie rachunek, i dupa blada.

– Chuj z ciebie.

Ziewa. Widać moje słowa robią na nim tyle wrażenia, co rozgnieciony komar na ścianie.

– Co ty powiesz? Moja wina, że frajer zostawił czynny telefon? Przecież mógł na ten czas schować aparat albo zabrać go ze sobą. Co on, kurwa, myślał – że ja z budki będę dzwonił? Z budki, kiedy telefon pod nosem? – Macha ręką. – Jeszcze jak bym tylko po znajomych dzwonił... – Patrzy na mnie chwilę, potem podnosi się i podchodzi do komody. Otwiera ją i wyciąga jakieś kolorowe pisemko pornograficzne. – Zobacz – mówi, rzucając je na stół. – Aż się roi od spragnionych rozmowy gorących panienek. – Podnosi świerszczyka i zaczyna wertować kartki. – O! Z tą gadałem. Suka ma fantazję, a jakie cycki ma. Zobacz, Patryk. – Przystawia mi gazetkę do oczu.

Zaczyna mi rosnąć w gaciach. Nie powiem, fajna dupa, ale czy warta aż takich poświęceń? Dla niego warta.

– Ciekawe, czy te cycki to prawdziwe, co? – zastanawia się. – Niee! – Wpatruje się w zdjęcie nagiej seksbomby. – Na pewno nie są prawdziwe.

– Idioto! – Stukam się w czoło. – Pewnie gadałeś z jakąś szkaradą.

Teraz przypomina mi się foka. Ona też wtedy, pod jego spranym kocem, miała fajny jęk, a do dziewczyny ze zdjęcia to jej tak daleko, jak stąd do księżyca i z powrotem. Kiedyś oglądałem program o takich „ślicznych" panienkach. To był amerykański sekstelefon. Gruba Murzynka z gęstym afro podawała się za filigranową blondynkę.

– Chyba nie myślałeś, że naprawdę gadałeś z tą ze zdjęcia?

Myśli chwilę.

– Nawet jeśli to nie była ta ze zdjęcia, to skąd możesz wiedzieć, że to jakiś pasztet?

– Nie wiem, ale i tak jesteś idiota! – Śmieję się. – Długo z nią gadałeś?

– Kilka razy po parę minut.

– To ty krótkodystansowiec jesteś! – Śmieję się jeszcze głośniej, a on robi się czerwony na gębie. – Parę minut i już? – Nie mogę się przestać śmiać. Pierwszy raz widzę na jego gębie cień zmieszania.

*

Nie naciągnąłby faceta wystarczająco, gdyby nie zadzwonił jeszcze ten ostatni raz. Mówi, że do rodziców, do Koszalina, ale na rozmowę z rodzicami mi to nie wygląda.

Gada prawie pół godziny, potem spokojnie odkłada słuchawkę.

– Masz okazję – dzwoń, nic nie płacisz.

Myślę teraz o mamie. Cieszyłaby się z mojego telefonu. Pewnie by spytała, czy doszły pieniądze. Gdybym miał pewność, że facet potem do nich nie zadzwoni, to... Tak, chyba bym przekręcił. Przecież w porównaniu z rozmowami Duliana to by był znikomy występek.

– Nie. On ma pewnie założony biling. Potem zacznie drążyć temat. Wolałbym, żeby nie wydzwaniał do moich starych.

– Co ty gadasz? – denerwuje się. – Miałby jakieś dochodzenie robić? Daj spokój, nie pękaj. Zadzwoń.

– Niee. – Kręcę głową.

– Jak chcesz. – Patrzy na telefon. – Niee, on nie będzie po obcych ludziach wydzwaniał.

Wystraszył się? Nie pomyślał o bilingu?

– Jutro jadę do domu – mówi. – Muszę odpocząć.

– Od czego? Aż tak się narobiłeś?

Zaczyna się śmiać, a potem podchodzi do telefonu.

– Teraz to już naprawdę ostatni raz – mówi, chwytając za słuchawkę.

– Pożegnaj się z koleżanką; powiedz jej, że połączenia do niej drogie – może oddzwoni.

Jakby tego nie słyszał, szybko wystukuje numer. Tym razem rozmawia jeszcze dłużej, jest bezlitosny. Chciałbym już opuścić to zdemolowane mieszkanie.

✳

Wychodzimy. Zostawia klucze u sąsiadów z naprzeciwka. Mówi im, że właściciel prosił go, by tak zrobił. Sąsiedzi, jacyś starsi ludzie, są zaskoczeni. Mimo to bez słowa sprzeciwu przyjmują klucze.

– Pan budowlaniec, od remontu. – Przygarbiona kobieta uśmiecha się serdecznie. Chyba jest chora, bo policzki ma mocno zapadnięte. Może ma, bidulka, raka i umrze, jak matka braci.

Dulian też się do niej uśmiecha.

– Tak, wczoraj skończyłem. Właściciel miał osobiście odebrać klucze, ale nie może przyjechać; ma jakieś ważne sprawy – tłumaczy.

Zza mikrej postury kobiety wyłania się jakiś dziadek, to pewnie jej mąż. Jest równie miły jak ona, od razu uśmiecha się szeroko, prezentując perfekcyjną biel swojej protezy dentystycznej.

– Tak, przechowamy kluczyki – gada, jakby nie słyszał, że chwilę wcześniej kobieta mówiła dokładnie to samo.

Dulian jeszcze raz dziękuje. Ja, choć nie wiem, po co, też. Potem jeszcze przez moment słyszę, jak przy otwartych drzwiach kłócą się, gdzie mają leżeć te klucze. Solidni starzy ludzie.

*

Za taką łajzę nie powinno się ryzykować. Teraz już nie potrafię o nim inaczej myśleć. Kiedy spierdolił przed Bożeną, miałem jeszcze złudzenia, ale nie... On już się nie zmieni. Zawsze będzie drobnym złodziejaszkiem uciekającym przed odpowiedzialnością. Zawsze, aż do momentu kiedy w końcu ktoś powiesi go za jaja na gałęzi. Jeśli nie umrze powieszony za jaja, to zgnije w kryminale. Skoro mam tę świadomość, to po cholerę godzę się, by przenocować go na dziko u nas w pokoju? Dlatego że jeszcze tak niedawno z nami mieszkał? Nie wiem.

Nie obchodzi mnie, co zrobi, gdzie pójdzie. Mam to gdzieś. Zresztą, z tego, co słyszałem, wybiera się do domu. Niech jedzie, ja wracam na stancję.

– Przekimam u was tylko jedną noc.

– Chyba zwariowałeś! Nie ma mowy – odpowiadam. – Masz kasę dla Bożeny? Jak tak, to w porządku. Może pozwoli ci zostać tę jedną noc.

272

– Przestań! Co ty się tak tej Bożeny boisz? Wejdę cichaczem, przekimam nockę, a rano już mnie nie będzie. Mówiłem ci, wracam jutro do Koszalina.

– Wracaj dzisiaj.

– Dziś! Dziś już nie da rady, połączenia nie mam.

– To wracaj po klucze.

– Po klucze?

– Przed chwilą oddałeś klucze tym dziadkom. Po co? Skoro chciałeś spierdolić, to mogłeś z tym poczekać do jutra!

– Do jutra nie.

– Dlaczego?

– Bo nie! – powtarza. – Nie mogłem już patrzeć na tę rozpierduchę. Przecież mówiłem ci, że wjebałem się z tym remontem. – Ciężko wzdycha. – No dobra, przyznam się. Nie potrafię kłaść płytek. To znaczy potrafię, ale słabo, no... nie za dobrze. Lepiej idzie mi skuwanie. Warszawa jest duża, facet szybko kogoś znajdzie. Wystarczy, że gazetę kupi albo ogłoszenie na słupie przyklei. Nie ma problemu, od razu znajdzie dobrego fachowca.

– Takiego jak ty?

– No, nie mów. Łazieneczkę ładnie mu skułem. Teraz tylko płytki położyć, i finał.

– Nie da rady – odpowiadam, przyspieszając kroku.

Gdybym tak mógł mu uciec. Nie musiałem zostawać na noc, mogłem wypić piwo i wrócić do Janek. Mogłem, ale tego nie zrobiłem, a teraz mam za swoje. Nie uwolnię się od niego.

*

Dulian leży na „swoim" tapczanie, usnął od razu. On nie ma z tym problemu, a ja chyba za bardzo się wszystkim przejmuję. Cały czas tylko nasłuchuję, czy nie skrzypią schody. Boję się, że Bożena tu przyjdzie i wyrzuci nas wszystkich. Bracia tak mówili. Na początku, jak go zobaczyli, zrobili wielkie oczy, a kiedy im powiedział, że chce się u nas jedną noc przekimać, to Krzysiek od razu chciał lecieć do Bożeny. Nie poszedł – Wiesiek powiedział, żeby dał sobie spokój. Jakby co, to oni o niczym nie wiedzą – na tym stanęło; a potem poszli spać. Teraz pewnie nie będą się do mnie odzywać – w końcu ze mną tu przyszedł. Nasłuchuję. Boję się, że Bożena przyjdzie.

*

Nie przygotuję sobie kanapek, teraz nie ma na to czasu. Ze zmęczenia czuję piasek w oczach, ale cieszę się, że ta noc już minęła. Bracia wstali i pałętają się po kuchni, Dulian jeszcze śpi. Muszę go obudzić, niech stąd idzie jak najszybciej. Niech jedzie do Koszalina i niech już nigdy nie zawraca mi dupy. Ta noc kosztowała mnie zbyt wiele stresu.

– Wstawaj – szepczę do niego. – No, wstawaj.

Leży na brzuchu.

– Już – odpowiada i leniwie podnosi się z tapczanu. – I było tyle gadać?

– Zamknij się! – Nie mogę znieść jego widoku. – Ubieraj się i spadaj stąd.

– Wyjdę razem z tobą.

Szybko podrywam się z łóżka. Wolałbym już nie konfrontować się dziś z braćmi. Jeszcze będzie ku temu okazja.

– Ja już jestem gotowy. Idziemy – mówię, wciągając na siebie spodnie.

– Nie ujmmy nin?

Zaciskam zęby.

– Idziemy – powtarzam nerwowo. – Nie przeciągaj struny.

– W porządku, przecież nic nie mówię.

Wychodzę z pokoju; nie mogę przestać nasłuchiwać. Mam wrażenie, że dziś bracia wyjątkowo głośno gadają. Teraz tylko muszę zejść z nim na dół niezauważony. To nie jest proste – Bożena często wychyla łeb, by zobaczyć, który z nas złazi. Wtedy albo coś do nas gada, albo tylko się chwilę gapi, czekając, aż usłyszy serdeczne „dzień dobry".

Stopień po stopniu powoli mijam pokój na półpiętrze. Jeszcze trochę i będziemy na dole. Kątem oka patrzę na Duliana. Nie mam pojęcia, z czego ten idiota się teraz śmieje; nie będę się pytał. Mam to gdzieś. Chcę się jak najszybciej z nim pożegnać i już nigdy więcej go nie spotkać.

Serce wali mi jak głupie. Łapię za klamkę, otwieram drzwi, wychodzimy. Puszczam go przed siebie i wypycham na zewnątrz. Podchodzimy do furtki. Szkoda, że nie ma na głowie czarnego worka na śmieci. W takim worku wyglądałby lepiej, byłby nie do rozpoznania. Chcę wierzyć, że Bożena nie stoi teraz przy oknie. Niech stanie za chwilę, tylko jeszcze nie teraz. Zamknę furtkę najciszej, jak potrafię. O, właśnie tak.

– Nie oglądaj się! – mówię do niego. – Idź, nie oglądaj się.

Chyba się udało. Tak, na pewno się udało.

Mam jeszcze trochę czasu. Po drodze na przystanek wejdę do sklepu – muszę kupić jakieś jedzenie. Zrobią przerwę? Nie wiem; to osobna i jak zwykle, niepewna sprawa, ale jedzenie muszę kupić.

Dulian coś do mnie mamrocze. Nie mam ochoty z nim gadać. Nie słucham go, chcę tylko zrobić te zakupy i jechać na ten cholerny dyżur. Resztki sympatii, którymi go darzyłem, uleciały jak powietrze z dziurawego materaca. Gdyby miał w sobie choć trochę moralności, a nie był tylko żywym organizmem, bez zasad i charakteru, wtedy próba powiedzenia mu, jakim jest dupkiem, miałaby jakiś sens. Może by się zawstydził? Może...

*

Świadomość, że nie muszę się już obawiać gniewu Mojsa, przynosi ulgę; podobnie jak to, że nie jadę tym samym autobusem, co Dulian. Chciał, ale „szlachetnie" ustąpiłem mu miejsca. Poczekałem na następny, a on odjechał. Nawet się nie pożegnaliśmy. Po prostu wsiadł, przez szybę kiwnął do mnie głową i pojechał, a ja wreszcie poczułem się lepiej.

Muszę sobie wynająć jakąś inną stancję; niekoniecznie w Jankach, a już na pewno bez braci. Oni chyba mają mnie dość – ile można mieszkać razem? Lubimy się coraz mniej, a po tym? Kto wie? Może nie lubią mnie już wcale?

*

Pewnie zobaczył mnie w tej kamerze nad wejściem. Tak przypadkiem na pewno się na mnie nie natknął. Nad drzwiami, tymi, którymi możemy wchodzić na obiekt, wisi jedna kamera i jak każda, przekazuje obraz na monitoring.

– Patryk!

Stoję już w holu i czekam na windę.

– Poczekaj. – To Adaś. Jest coraz bliżej. Widzę wyraźnie, jak kręci łbem. Jakby był z czegoś bardzo niezadowolony. Pewnie znowu coś mu nie pasuje.

– Co? – pytam, opierając się ramieniem o granitową płytę. Jej chłód czuję przez materiał.

– Nie mam dla ciebie najlepszych wieści.

Dobrze, że odnalazłem Duliana.

– Co się stało?

Podchodzi do mnie całkiem blisko.

– Słuchaj, ja tam do ciebie nic nie mam, ale Marek już od jakiegoś czasu ci się przyglądał...

– No i? – przerywam mu, nie mogąc się już doczekać, co powie dalej. – No, i co?

– Chodzi o to, że Mojs cię nie chce. To znaczy ty i jeszcze paru innych już tu nie stoicie.

Patrzę na niego chwilę.

– Nie stoimy?

– No. – Szybko potakuje głową. – Nie stoicie. Na twoje miejsce przyjął już nowego. Sprawdził go, nadaje się. Tamten przedwczoraj walnął dobę. Marek kazał mu przyjść, bo na zmianie Arka brakuje ludzi. Facet cały następny miesiąc będzie jechał doba na dobę, ale się cieszył. Marek nawet nie musiał go namawiać. On jest zajebany w bankach, ma kredyty, dwójkę dzieciaków i niepracującą babę. Od razu się zapytał, czy można będzie dorabiać. Takich teraz potrzeba, bo rotacja jak chuj. Cały czas kogoś brakuje, więc zapchajdziur potrzeba jak najwięcej. Jak pierwszy raz po minusikach łaził, to nawet na przerwę nie polazł. Cały czas tylko kółka napierdalał, Zbychu mi mówił. O kibel to tylko raz krzyczał. Marek dał mu już ksywkę Terminator, che, che – śmieje się, ale momentalnie znowu staje się poważny. – Masz iść do biura – mówi. – Tam coś ci znajdą. Tylko pamiętaj, nie daj się wpierdolić w jakieś gówno.

- A jest jeszcze większe gówno? – Teraz ja się śmieję. Pierwszy raz w tym miejscu szczerze, bez obawy. Patrzę mu prosto w oczy. Lepszej wiadomości nie mógł mi dziś sprzedać. – Mogę iść, tak?

- Tak... To powodzenia, stary.

Nie wyciągam do niego ręki na pożegnanie, w dupie mam jego błogosławieństwo. Odchodzę. Idę wolno, nie spieszę się. Mojs chyba nie myślał, że będę go prosił o szansę. Tłusta świnia! Nawet nie wie, ile dla mnie zrobił.

Mijam drzwi od monitoringu, kątem oka je łapię. Z oddali dobiega do mnie dźwięk dzwonka otwieranych wind. Potem następny niewyraźny dzwonek, ledwo słyszalny. Jestem coraz dalej. Nie będę się oglądał, nie ma za czym. Uśmiecham się cały czas sam do siebie. Jakbym z powodzeniem przeprowadził jakąś tajną akcję, niewykonalną dla innych. Jeszcze tylko parę metrów. Wyszedłem z tego syfu i już się nie cofnę!

Podchodzę do kolesia łażącego po Chocimskiej. To jeszcze stara zmiana. Znam go tyle, co z szatni.

- Już tu nie pracuję! – krzyczę. – Mojs ze mnie zrezygnował.

Chłopak jest blady z niewyspania i ledwo łazi. Znam to. Patrzy na mnie, próbując okazać resztki hardości. Minę ma niewzruszoną, tak jakby to, że już tu nie pracuję, nie było czymś wspaniałym. Witam się z nim. Ma zimną rękę.

Po całej nocy na Chocimskiej każdemu jest zimno.

– Co, końcówka?

Patrzy na zegarek.

– No – odpowiada. Na jego twarzy dalej nie widzę entuzjazmu.

– Spokój miałeś?

– Spokój...

– Ja już mam luz! – Moja radość kontrastuje z jego... smutkiem?

– Wyrzucili cię?

Kiwam głową.

– Mojs przyjął na moje miejsce nowego... lepszego.

– Lepszego?

– Noo. Adam powiedział, że mam iść do biura, zapytać o nowy obiekt.

– Aha. – Patrzy na mnie tępo.

– Coś dla mnie znajdą... – Po co ja w ogóle mu to gadam? – No dobra, to spokojnej końcówki. – Znowu wyciągam do niego rękę. – Trzymaj się! – mówię i czekam chwilę, aż coś do mnie powie. Nie odpowiada.

Mojs pewnie już wtedy chciał nam to powiedzieć. Zabrakło mu odwagi? W końcu wysłał do mnie posłańca. Niee, pewnie jeszcze nie ma go na obiekcie. On nie miałby skrupułów; gdyby mógł, sam powiedziałby mi to prosto w oczy. Na pewno by powiedział.

*

Podchodzę do czegoś w rodzaju wysokiej drewnianej lady. Po drugiej stronie stoi trzech facetów. Pewnie inspektorzy. Jeden, ten najwyższy, ma kręcone włosy. Dwaj pozostali mniej rzucają się w oczy. Reszta krawaciarzy siedzi przy biurkach. Gwar jak cholera, telefony dzwonią, ciężko cokolwiek usłyszeć. Kolejka jedna, długa, przy samej ladzie rozproszona. Faceci zza lady przyjmują do pracy. Każdego jak leci. Niektórzy będą mieli szczęście, trafią na cieciówki. Inni już po pierwszym dyżurze będą psioczyć na robotę. Tylko mała cząstka zawiedzionych wypnie się na ochronę i znajdzie sobie normalną pracę. Reszta spróbuje szczęścia w innych agencjach, za mniejszą lub większą stawkę. Połowa z tej kolejki to tacy poszukiwacze. Ja też? Nie chciałbym tak myśleć, ale jest, jak jest. Idę na łatwiznę? Przecież obcowanie ze Zbychem, z Mojsem i całą resztą fałszywych debili do łatwych nie należało.

Jestem coraz bliżej lady. Stąd słyszę, jak jeden z siedzących przy biurku inspektorów krzyczy do słuchawki. Facet wygląda jak zabiedzony wymoczek. Pasowałby idealnie na pięterka albo na minusiki. Ciekawe, czy do Zbycha też by tak pyszczył. Na pewno tę robotę to po znajomości dostał i teraz opierdala jakiegoś biedaka. W takich agencjach taka gnida staje się jeszcze większą gnidą, a każdy, kto pod nim, to śmieć. Normalni też są, jednak ci normalni nie mają łatwo, bo jak tu być człowiekiem, kiedy dokoła tylu popaprańców z przerośniętym ego. Inspektor z batonów był normalny.

– Dzień dobry. – Jestem już przy ladzie.

– W czym mogę pomóc?

Trafiam do tego z lokami. Jest naprawdę wysoki i ma kręcone jak pudel jasne włosy. Obciachowo w nich wygląda, jakby sobie trwałą zrobił. Takie loki można mieć na jajach, ale nie na głowie.

– Pan Mojs mnie przysłał – tłumaczę mu. – Wcześniej stałem na fabryce czekolady w Sochaczewie, a teraz zakończyłem pracę na centrum u pana Mojsa.

– Gdzie? – Krzywi się.

– U pana Mojsa – powtarzam. – Na centrum biznesowym.

– Aaa, u Marka pan stałeś.

Nie wiem, dlaczego oni wszyscy, ci inspektorzy, mówią do nas w taki dziwny sposób. Muszą tak mówić? Może każą im tak bezosobowo nawijać. To pewnie jakiś sprawdzony psychologiczny trik. Mojs też tak gadał: „WEŹ PAN, IDŹ PAN". Sami między sobą tak nie gadają, to na pewno celowe. Taka gadka ma pokazać, kto tu rządzi, a ten, co tego słucha, od razu ma się poczuć jak nic nieznaczący cieć.

– Tak. Powiedział, że mam przyjść do biura i zapytać o jakiś nowy dla mnie obiekt.

– A coś pan zbroił, że Marek się na pana wypiął? – śmieje się, przyglądając mi się z uwagą.

– Nic – odpowiadam. – Znaleźli na moje miejsce nowego, a ja miałem przyjść i zapytać o jakiś inny obiekt – powtarzam.

Kiedyś bym nie pomyślał, ale słowo „OBIEKT" już zawsze będzie mi się kojarzyć z „ochroną 24 h".

– Poczekaj pan. – Facet odchodzi. Jest teraz w głębi sali. Podchodzi do jakiegoś pustego biurka. Podnosi słuchawkę i wystukuje numer. Chwilę czeka, wsparty lewą ręką o blat, aż w końcu zaczyna ruszać ustami. Próbuję odczytać coś z ruchu jego warg, ale szybko daję sobie z tym spokój. Zresztą on, potakując głową, co chwilę spogląda w moją stronę. Czekam, aż skończy gadać. Skończył. Podchodzi do lady.

– Popytałem trochę o pana, no i Marek – krzywi się – nie potwierdza pana wersji. Mówi, żeś pan się do pracy nie nadawał, to pana wymienił. A do biura to miałeś pan tylko umundurowanie przynieść, zdać znaczy.

– Zdać?...

– Tak – przerywa mi. – Coś żeś pan pokręcił.

Kiwam głową, jakbym się teraz z nim zgadzał, ale nie zgadzam się, nie zgadzam się z nim wcale.

– Właściwie to dowódca mi powiedział, że mam zapytać w biurze o jakiś nowy obiekt. Mówił, że przekazuje informację od inspektora.

Facet ciężko wzdycha.

– No i co ja mam teraz z panem zrobić? – Zadziera głowę do góry i drapie się długopisem po gładko ogolonym podbródku. – Dobra, zrobimy tak: pojedziesz pan ze mną na lakiery.

(Lakiery?)

Patrzy na zegarek.

– Pojedziemy za jakieś piętnaście minut. Jutro ma być tam człowiek na zastępstwie. Zamiast niego byś pan wskoczył. A z Markiem... pogadam. – Uśmiecha się do mnie. – Ludziom trzeba dawać szansę.

*

To jakaś przemysłowa ulica. Pełno tu hurtowni, firm i co drugi budynek oklejony logiem naszej firmy. Widzę to, siedząc w samochodzie.

– Jest tu trochę naszych obiektów – mówię bez zachwytu, niby sam do siebie, niby do niego.

Facet rozgląda się na boki, jakby miał gdzieś koncentrowanie się na drodze.

– No – odpowiada. – Przybywa, z każdym dniem przybywa.

Chyba jest z tego bardzo dumny. Szkoda, że ja nie czuję tego tak, jak on. Zastanawiam się, czy ten entuzjazm to nie kolejna wyuczona sztuczka.

Przejeżdżamy obok postawionego na sztorc paskowanego, pomarańczowo-białego szlabanu.

– To tu? – pytam, patrząc na przybliżający się coraz bardziej kremowy, jednopiętrowy budynek z czerwonymi filarami. W porównaniu z centrum to karmnik dla sikorek, ale jakoś mnie to nie martwi.

– Tak, jesteśmy na miejscu – odpowiada z zadowoleniem facet.

Parkujemy bokiem do frontu budynku. Nie wjechał na ułożony z szarej kostki brukowej parking, znajdujący się po mojej stronie. Widać pewnie zawsze tak staje.

Jeszcze dobrze nie wysiadłem z samochodu, kiedy podchodzi do nas otyły, podstarzały agent. Spod ciemnogranatowej służbowej olimpijki wystaje mu błękitna wygnieciona koszula. Nie wciągnął jej dobrze do spodni, wygląda niechlujnie.

– Witam, panie Maćku! – krzyczy jak do przygłuchego.

– Witam, witam! – Inspektor, nie zwracając uwagi na wyciągniętą koszulę, podaje mu rękę. – Przywiozłem wam człowieka. Zacznie od jutra.

Agent nieufnie mierzy mnie wzrokiem.

– Za kogo?

– Za Piotrka.

Wykrzywia usta.

– Za Piotrka? – dziwi się i jeszcze bardziej wykrzywia usta. – A co z nim?

– On coś miesza – mówi inspektor. – Nieważne. – Macha ręką.

Agent znowu na mnie patrzy. Mógłby dać sobie spokój, i tak mnie nie przestraszy. Co on sobie myśli?

– Pracowałeś już w ochronie? – pyta mnie.

Teraz ja na niego patrzę, patrzę mu prosto w oczy. Zupełnie bez entuzjazmu – to go peszy... Nie powiedział mu nic o koszuli?

Stajemy przy wejściu do budynku. Przez przeszklone białe drzwi widzę zatopioną w mroku ladę, podobną do tej, jaką mają w biurze. To chyba jakaś recepcja, ale nie widzę dokładnie. Stoję za daleko.

Prawie na całej długości frontowej elewacji znajdują się duże okna; coś jak witryny sklepowe. Wszystko dobrze przez nie widać. Ludzie ubrani w białe ogrodniczki, kobiety i mężczyźni, chodzą po obszernym pomieszczeniu. Jakieś urządzenie potrząsa dużą puszką farby. To pewnie specjalistyczny mieszalnik albo coś takiego. Patrzę chwilę na tę dziwną maszynę.

– I co, zadowolony pan jesteś? Obiekt się podoba? – pyta inspektor.

– Tak, jest w porządku. – Co mogę powiedzieć innego?

Mógłbym stać na nocki nawet w prosektorium, byleby nie wracać na centrum.

– Tak, podoba mi się – powtarzam, jakby z obawy, że mój entuzjazm jest zbyt mało widoczny.

– Wejdźmy do środka – mówi, a agent, wyprzedzając go, otwiera na oścież drzwi.

Tak, nie myliłem się. Teraz widzę wyraźniej. Vis-à-vis drzwi jest jakaś taka recepcja z wysoką ladą. Zza niej wystaje tylko czubek głowy z jasnoblond włosami.

– Dzień dobry, pani Agnieszko – mówi inspektor w kierunku blond włosów.

Po prawej stronie wyłożone siwą wykładziną prowadzące do góry schody. Na półpiętrze zawracają. Inspektor od razu wyjaśnia, że te schody prowadzą do biura:

– Na górze masz pan część biurową, a tutaj rządzi pani Agnieszka.

Teraz widzę twarz – to jakaś młoda dziewczyna. Uśmiecha się do inspektora. Potem patrzy na mnie i też się uśmiecha.

– Tu, za panią Agnieszką – pokazuje palcem przeszklone matową szybą drzwi – tu ciodni kuię gowość – tłumaczy. – A tam... – Odkręca się tyłem do kobiety i pokazuje jakieś wejście. – Tam będziesz miał pan swoje miejsce, o tam.

Wchodzimy w trzech do pomieszczenia, gdzie mam mieć swoje miejsce. To taki łącznik między częścią biurową a częścią, w której mieszają i sprzedają te wszystkie kolorowe chemikalia. Pomieszczenie mierzy nie więcej niż dziesięć metrów kwadratowych. Okno wychodzi na parking, na zielone prefabrykowane ogrodzenie i dalej, na główną ulicę. Przy jedynej ścianie czarne biurko, na biurku czajnik. Po obu stronach biurka dwa krzesła, jakoś tak nietypowo. Przez pomieszczenie co jakiś czas ktoś przechodzi, z biura do sklepu i na odwrót. Inspektor podchodzi do okna i ścisza małe radio stojące na białym parapecie.

– I jak? – pyta znowu. – Nie jest źle, co?

– Nie, nie, w porządku jest.

– Dobra – zwraca się teraz do agenta. – Jeszcze jutro zapoznasz pan dokładnie nowego kolegę. Powiesz pan, o co chodzi, i w ogóle, nie?

Agent uśmiecha się szeroko.

– Jasne, panie Maćku. – Patrzy na mnie. – Zmieniamy się o ósmej, ale dobrze by było, żebyś tak za dziesięć albo jeszcze wcześniej był.

– Dobra – odpowiadam i jeszcze przez chwilę patrzę na czajnik.

*

W drodze powrotnej mój nowy inspektor wreszcie przechodzi do konkretów.

– Ile pan miałeś na centrum? – Pyta o stawkę.

– Cztery pięćdziesiąt na godzinę.

– Na biznesowym cztery i pół płacą?

Nie wiedział?

– Tak, cztery i pół na godzinę.

– No tak! – Kiwa głową. – To wszystko zależy od zleceniodawcy, ale cztery i pół? – szepcze sam do siebie. – To teraz będziesz pan miał o pięćdziesiąt groszy więcej.

– Więcej?!

– No, mówię, że więcej! A co, mało?

Zaciskam usta, z trudem opanowując radość. Jakby mnie kto po stopach łaskotał, a ja nie mógłbym się śmiać. Nie chcę, żeby mój nowy inspektor, tak inny od Mojsa, bardzo inny, zupełnie inny – nie chcę, żeby zauważył, że się cieszę, bo jeszcze mi stawkę zmniejszy. Niee... Przecież sam wyraźnie powiedział: „Wszystko zależy od zleceniodawcy", ale i tak nie będę się przy nim cieszył. W końcu pewności nie ma, różnie może być. Pewne jest to, że kiedyś każdy umrze. Tak samo jak to, że Bożena za parę dni wyciągnie łapę po kolejny czynsz; całą w pierścionkach. Który to już czynsz? Nie wiem, nie liczę, bo i po co. Pewne jest to, że bracia i tym razem kupią po drodze z pracy paczkę chipsów, a Krzysiek zje większość, zanim dojdzie na stancję. Pewne jest to, że rodzice mnie kochają Jeszcze dziś do nich zadzwonię i podziękuję za pieniądze. Że też od razu tego nie zrobiłem.

*

„Coś pan pokręciłeś" – powiedziałby inspektor. Tak, już prawie ósma, a ja jeszcze na miejsce nie doszedłem. Tamten wczoraj powiedział, żebym był trochę wcześniej. Za szybko wysiadłem, chyba dwa albo trzy przystanki za szybko. Źle zapamiętałem.

Biegnę, torba podskakuje mi na ramieniu. Jeszcze pięć, może osiem minut i powinienem być na miejscu. Pierwszy dzień i od razu spóźnienie. Pocieszam się, że to w końcu będzie tylko parę minut, ale i tak głupio mi z tym.

Na parkingu stoją już jakieś samochody. Czuję zdenerwowanie. Przyznam się, a co tam

– powiem, dlaczego się spóźniłem, powiem, jak było.

To nie ten agent. Ten, co tu stał wczoraj, był gruby i stary, a ten jest chudy i gdzieś tak w moim wieku. Patrzy na mnie, twarz ma pogodną, nawet się uśmiecha.

– Dzień dobry – mówi do mnie. – W czym pomóc?

– Dzień dobry – odpowiadam. – Sorry za spóźnienie. – Nie wnikam, dlaczego zamiast tamtego zmieniam tego. Dla mnie to bez różnicy; niech mi tylko powie, co ma powiedzieć, i może iść do domu. – Trochę się spóźniłem – powtarzam, wchodząc do już mojego pomieszczenia.

– A, to ty – kwituje. – Janusz mówił, że Maćkowi coś się pochrzaniło. On cię wczoraj tu przywiózł i powiedział, że będziesz tu stał? – Macha ręką. – Bałagan mają w tym biurze. Weź, lepiej jedź tam do nich i powiedz Maćkowi, że przecież tu jest komplet. – Siada na krześle, tuż przy elektrycznym czajniku. Włącza go.

Patrzę na niego chwilę. Kurwa, najlepiej bym zrobił, gdybym już nie pytał o żaden obiekt. Może rzeczywiście rozliczyć się z uniformów i spróbować inaczej?

– Można stąd zadzwonić do biura?

Agent kręci głową. Szum czajnika staje się teraz nie do zniesienia.

– Mówię ci, przejedź się do biura i powiedz, że na lakierach jest komplet. Spokojnie, Maciek coś ci znajdzie.

Cały czas do mnie gada, ale przez ten szum nie słyszę. Wychodzę, bez pożegnania, nie ma miejsca na serdeczności. Jestem wkurwiony, niepotrzebnie się cieszyłem.

Jadę do biura. Po drodze podejmuję decyzję, jestem już całkowicie pewien – zwalniam się! Nie ma tego złego, co by na dobre nie wyszło. Może tak miało być – miałem się wkurwić i wreszcie odejść z ochrony. Odchodzę na dobre, czas najwyższy! Ileż można! Zaniosę im tylko uniformy – jak się nie rozliczę, odciągną mi z wypłaty.

W drzwiach mijam się z inspektorem.

– A co pan tu robisz? Dlaczego pan nie jesteś na obiekcie?

Teraz muszę mu tylko powiedzieć, że się zwalniam i że już nie potrzebuję do szczęścia żadnego obiektu.

– Co się stało?

– Tam jest komplet – odpowiadam. – Jakiś facet stamtąd powiedział, że na lakierach jest komplet.

Dlaczego ja mu to mówię? Przecież nie po to tu przyszedłem. Dobra. Spytał, to powiedziałem. Teraz dowie się, że nie chcę już tu pracować – tu i w żadnej innej pieprzonej agencji ochrony.

– Nie było Janusza? – Myśli chwilę, zadzierając głowę. – Spokojnie – pociesza mnie. – Dobrze, że pan przyszedłeś. Zaraz zawiozę pana z powrotem, on już tam nie stoi.

– Nie stoi?

– Nie.

Niełatwo tak od razu znaleźć coś innego. Rzucę robotę i z czego będę żył? Poprawiam torbę na ramieniu. Przecież zawsze można odejść. A nowy inspektor? Widać normalny człowiek, nie to co Mojs.

Podczas drogi dowiaduję się, że ten, co miało go dziś nie być, już od roku stoi na lakierach. Stoi, a teraz, jak zechce, postoi gdzie indziej; a jak nie, to do widzenia. Prawdopodobnie za bardzo spoufalił się z pracownikami hurtowni, a teraz jeszcze chorować zaczął.

– Piotrek da się lubić – tłumaczy mi inspektor. – Chłopak komunikatywny jest. Nawet do biura na dyspozytora chcieliśmy go wziąć, ale ostatnio to już przegiął. Za towarzyski się zrobił, na grille zaczął z nimi łazić. Ci z lakierów zrobili imprezę, a on z nimi.

Tam na tyłach budynku mają taką ogrodową altanę. Będziesz pan widział. I parę krzaków. Czasami integrują się przy sobocie. Wszystko rozumiem, oni to oni – mają wolne; ale nie on, i to jeszcze na służbie? Jak chciał, mógł zjeść kiełbasę, ale piwo pić?

– Piwo pił?

– Oni mówili, że nie, ale czuć było od niego piwskiem. A teraz jeszcze te lewe zwolnienia zaczął przynosić. – Uderza ręką w kierownicę. – Jak udaje chorego, to niech po Marszałkowskiej w nocy nie paraduje. Widziałem go, ale mnie nie poznał. Pijany jak świnia z kumplami szedł. Za dobrze tu miał. – Potakuje nerwowo głową. – Za dobrze, to teraz wysypiska śmieci popilnuje. Jak będzie chciał; a jak nie, to wypad.

Nie komentuję jego decyzji; nie wiem, co odpowiedzieć. Zastanawiam się tylko, czy to wysypisko śmieci to naprawdę taka tragedia. Do Mojsa na centrum by go dał. To by była kara.

Na mój widok robi posępną minę.

– Dzień dobry, panie Maćku – mówi, gasząc papierosa w wystawionej przed budynek wysokiej metalowej popielnicy.

– Przebieraj się pan!

– Dlaczego?

– Nie będę teraz tłumaczył, dlaczego. Przeniesiony pan będziesz na inny obiekt.

– Na inny obiekt? Dlaczego?

– Już mówiłem, nie będę teraz tłumaczył.

Z budynku wychodzi jakiś facet w popielatym garniturze, a za nim następny, też w garniturze. Stają przy popielnicy. Jeden wyciąga paczkę papierosów i częstuje kolegę; chce poczęstować też agenta, ale tamten kręci głową i wchodzi do budynku. Idziemy za nim. Guzik mnie obchodzi jego dalsza kariera, ale... No właśnie, dziwnie jakoś.

– Miało dziś pana tu nie być. Dzwoniłeś pan do biura, że jesteś chory.

– Już się lepiej czuję – odpowiada ponuro.

– No, ja myślę. Inaczej byś pan po mieście nocą pijany nie łaził. Tydzień temu widziałem. Szedłeś pan w towarzystwie. Widziałem, aż przystanąłem, ale żeś pan mnie nie widział. A zwolnienie? Na chorobowym pan byłeś, nie? Jakiegoś zaprzyjaźnionego lekarza pan masz? No dobra, przebieraj się pan, bo czasu nie ma.

– A na jakim obiekcie mam stać?

– Zaraz stać. Tam to chodzić trzeba i tych, no... szperaczy przeganiać. Na wysypisku komunalnym. Dobra stawka będzie i system taki jak tu, dwadzieścia cztery na czterdzieści osiem. Przebieraj się pan, czasu nie ma. Koledze szafkę zwolnić trzeba, niech się zainstaluje.

– Na wysypisko? Przecież tam śmierdzi! – W pośpiechu rozpina służbową koszulę.

– A tu nie śmierdzi? Śmierdzi, tylko żeś się pan już do tego smrodu przyzwyczaił. – Inspektor patrzy teraz na mnie. – Śmierdzi, nie?

Kiwam głową.

– Noo, cały czas mówię, żeś się pan przyzwyczaił. Tam też pan przywykniesz, nie będzie źle.

– Nie będę tam stał, nie na wysypisku. Czego innego pan nie ma?

Inspektor mruży oczy.

– Mam, ale wszędzie komplet.

– To ja rezygnuję – mówi. – Nie będę za szperaczami się uganiał! Jeszcze mnie jakiś czymś zarazi.

Inspektor rozkłada bezradnie ręce.

– Jak pan chcesz. Czyli zdajesz pan dziś mundurek i się rozstajemy, tak?

– Jeśli nic innego nie może mi pan zaproponować, to...

Czeka chwilę, jakby liczył, że inspektor coś powie, ale on znowu tylko rozkłada ręce. Żadna inna propozycja z jego ust nie pada.

*

Szatnia mała, ale własną szafkę mam, jak na batonach. Na centrum nie było szans, a tu, proszę, od razu pierwszego dnia dostałem.

Inspektor pojechał parę minut temu, agent zabrał się razem z nim. Wcześniej pokazał mi jeszcze taką plastikową tablicę z telefonami alarmowymi. Wisi przybita pinezkami do boku biurka. Machnął ręką na gaśnicę i powiedział, że od godziny dwudziestej trzeba robić obchody wkoło budynku. Potem wyciągnął jeszcze zeszyt z szuflady biurka i wpisał zakończenie służby. Ja wpisałem rozpoczęcie. Pojechali.

Dziwnie się czuję; nikogo tu nie znam, ale mam wrażenie, że każdy mi się przygląda.

Staję przy parapecie, podkręcam głośniej radio. Jakaś zagraniczna piosenka, za głośno. Ściszam z powrotem do granicy słyszalności, patrzę przez okno. Przez chwilę myślę jeszcze o tym agencie. Ciekawe, jak ja postąpiłbym na jego miejscu. Nie jest mi go żal. Przez cały długi rok dobrze się tu bawił, pił piwo w pracy. Idiota.

Obejdę budynek. Nie wiem, jak często mam go obchodzić w ciągu dnia i czy w ogóle mam, tamten nic o tym nie wspominał. Mówił, że od dwudziestej co jakiś czas. Co jakiś czas? Co ile? Rzucam okiem na wpisy z poprzednich służb. Nic. Rozpoczęcie, zakończenie dyżuru, rozpoczęcie, zakończenie dyżuru. Wertuję jeszcze parę kartek wstecz. To samo: rozpoczęcie i zakończenie. Po cholerę taki gruby zeszyt? Tu wystarczyłaby kartka i wpis pod wpisem kratka pod kratką. Po co marnować tyle papieru? Oni tak piszą, inspektor się nie czepia – w porządku. Wychodzę.

Staję przy popielnicy. Pamiętam, że tamten palił papierosa. Gdy przyjechałem z inspektorem, akurat gasił peta. Też bym zapalił, ale... On pracował tu trochę, to sobie pozwalał. Palił, grillował, pił piwo. Z góry lał na robotę. Zapaliłbym, ale nie, nie będę ryzykował; jeszcze mnie ktoś tu podpierdoli. Mijam pomalowane na czerwono stalowe filary, które podtrzymują część budynku. Dyskretnie patrzę przez duże okna – pełno ludzi. Większość z tych twarzy już dzisiaj widziałem. Kłaniałem się im, mówiłem „dzień dobry". Odpowiadali; przyglądali mi się z uwagą, ale odpowiadali. Jeden nawet powiedział cześć i podał mi rękę, jakby mnie znał od dawna. Pełna kultura.

Teraz widzę tę altankę, o której mówił inspektor. Faktycznie, stoi za budynkiem. Tu jest zupełnie inaczej niż od strony ulicy – równiutko skoszona, soczyście zielona trawa, spokój, a za ogrodzeniem jakaś prywatna posesja. Przy ogrodzeniu od strony posesji duży kojec ogrodzony aluminiową siatką. W środku na cementowanej posadce dwa psy.

Podchodzę bliżej. To owczarki niemieckie. Bardzo wychudzone, wyliniałe i poranione. Leżą. Zmierzwiona sierść poobklejana zaschniętymi odchodami. Jak oni mogą tu grillować? Obok utytłane gównem, ledwo żywe psy, a tu ogrodowa altana, wypielęgnowana trawa i alejka z czerwonej kostki brukowej, prowadząca do dużego okopconego, murowanego grilla.

Ci od tych psów najwyraźniej nie mają serca. Ale jak pracownicy lakierów mogą to akceptować? Nie widzą tego, co się tuż obok nich dzieje? Pies próbujący zjeść własne gówno! Pierwszy raz widzę coś takiego. Następnym razem wezmę więcej jedzenia.

Mając cały czas w pamięci to, co widziałem przed chwilą, podchodzę do blondynki, do miłej pani Agnieszki, i choć wcale nie jest mi wesoło, próbuję się do niej uśmiechać. Chcę pogadać z nią o tych psach.

– Pan za Piotrka?

– Tak – odpowiadam, uśmiechając się do niej.
– Byłem się rozejrzeć... Tamte psy, za budynkiem...

– Stare – przerywa mi.

– Zabiedzone...

– Stare – powtarza. – Nie chcą jeść.

Zastanawiam się, jak jej to powiedzieć.

– Nie chcą jeść? – dziwię się.

Nie będę jej opowiadał, co próbowały zjeść. Albo nie integruje się tam na tyłach, albo udaje głupią.

– Ci właściciele to chyba nie bardzo dbają o te psy. W kojcu nieposprzątane i...

Nie, nie będę jej już więcej o tym gadał. Odchodzę, a ona się uśmiecha, nie odrywając wzroku od rozjaśniającego jej twarz monitora. Miła pani z sekretariatu, taka jaka powinna być.

*

Jest po dwunastej, kiedy przyjeżdża inspektor. Stoję przy parapecie, słucham radia.

Od czasu kiedy karmiłem psy, minęły ze dwie godziny, a ja jeszcze ze cztery razy tam byłem. Dobrze, że wtedy nie przyjechał. Mógłby mieć pretensje, że nie pilnuję wejścia. Ciekawe, czy on wie o tych psach.

Nie wchodzi. Staje tylko na krawędzi chodnika i jakby czegoś wypatrywał, gapi się na ulicę. Patrzy na przejeżdżające nią samochody. Wychodzę z budynku i podchodzę do niego. Staję obok, prawie ramię w ramię. Czuję od niego mocny zapach perfum. Pewnie nosi w kieszeni flakon jakiejś markowej podróbki.